Principles of Finance

Parrino • Kidwell • Bates

Principles of Finance FIN 311
Northern Arizona University

Wiley Custom Learning Solutions

ISBN 978-1-118-94349-6
Printed and bound by Strategic Content Imaging.

10 9 8 7 6 5 4 3

Contents

Selected Abbreviations and Notation

$\beta =$	beta (a measure of systematic risk)
$\Delta =$	change (e.g., ΔP = change in price level, ΔS = change in sales level)
$\rho =$	correlation
$\sigma^2\,(\sigma) =$	variance (standard deviation)
$x =$	fractional weight of investment or component of capital
Add WC $=$	addition to working capital
APR $=$	annual percentage rate
ARR $=$	accounting rate of return
$b =$	dividend payout ratio
C $=$	coupon payment (bond), call option value
Cap Exp $=$	capital expenditures
CF $=$	cash flow
CF Opns $=$	cash flow from operations
CFI $=$	cash flow to investors
CFLTA $=$	cash flow invested in long-term assets
CFNWC $=$	cash flow invested in net working capital
CFOA $=$	cash flow from operating activity
CIP $=$	call interest premium
CO $=$	crossover level of unit sales
COGS $=$	cost of goods sold
CV $=$	coefficient of variation
D $=$	dividend (stock)
D&A $=$	depreciation and amortization
DOL $=$	degree of operating leverage
DPO $=$	days' payables outstanding
DRP $=$	default risk premium
DSI $=$	days' sales in inventory
DSO $=$	days' sales outstanding
E($\bullet$) $=$	expected value (E(R) = expected return, etc.)
EAC $=$	equivalent annual cost
EAR $=$ EAY $=$	effective annual rate (yield)
EBIT $=$	earnings before interest and taxes
EBITDA $=$	earnings before interest, taxes, depreciation, and amortization
EBT $=$	earnings before taxes
EFN $=$	external funding needed
EOQ $=$	economic order quantity
EROA $=$	EBIT return on assets
F $=$	face value (bond)
FC $=$	fixed costs
FCF $=$	free cash flows
FV $=$	future value
$FVA_n =$	future value of an n period annuity

FXR =	foreign exchange or currency risk premium
g =	growth rate
i =	nominal rate of interest
IGR =	internal growth rate
IRR =	internal rate of return
k =	cost of capital (debt or equity)
m =	number of payments per year
MAT =	maturity adjustment to cost of a loan
MRP =	marketability risk premium
MV =	market value
n =	number of periods
NCF =	net cash flow
NCFOA =	net cash flow from operating activities
NOPAT =	net operating profits after tax
NPV =	net present value
NWC =	net working capital
OC =	operating cycle
Op Ex =	cash operating expenses
p =	probability
P =	price (P_0 = price at time zero, etc.), put option value
P/E ratio =	price/earnings ratio
PB =	payback period
PI =	profitability index
PR =	prime rate
PV =	present value
PV annuity factor =	present value of annuity factor
PVA_n =	present value of an n period annuity
PVP =	present value of a perpetuity
r =	real rate of interest
R =	return (R_{rf} = risk free, R_i, $R_{Portfolio}$, etc.)
ROA =	return on assets
ROE =	return on equity
S =	Sharpe Ratio
SGR =	sustainable growth rate
t =	tax rate
TV =	terminal value
V =	value (e.g., $V_{Firm} = V_{Assets} = V_{Debt} + V_{Equity}$)
VC =	variable costs
WACC =	weighted average cost of capital

WileyPLUS

WileyPLUS is a research-based online environment for effective teaching and learning.

WileyPLUS builds students' confidence because it takes the guesswork out of studying by providing students with a clear roadmap:

- what to do
- how to do it
- if they did it right

It offers interactive resources along with a complete digital textbook that help students learn more. With *WileyPLUS*, students take more initiative so you'll have greater impact on their achievement in the classroom and beyond.

For more information, visit www.wileyplus.com

WileyPLUS

ALL THE HELP, **RESOURCES**, AND PERSONAL **SUPPORT** YOU AND YOUR STUDENTS NEED!

www.wileyplus.com/resources

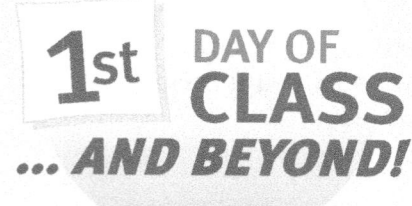

1st DAY OF **CLASS** *...AND BEYOND!*

2-Minute Tutorials and all of the resources you and your students need to get started

WileyPLUS

Student Partner Program

Student support from an experienced student user

Wiley Faculty Network

Collaborate with your colleagues, find a mentor, attend virtual and live events, and view resources
www.WhereFacultyConnect.com

WileyPLUS

Quick Start

Pre-loaded, ready-to-use assignments and presentations created by subject matter experts

Technical Support 24/7 FAQs, online chat, and phone support
www.wileyplus.com/support

Your *WileyPLUS* Account Manager, providing personal training and support

ESSENTIALS OF
CORPORATE
FINANCE

Robert Parrino

Lamar Savings Centennial Professor of Finance
University of Texas at Austin

David S. Kidwell

Professor of Finance and Dean Emeritus
University of Minnesota

Thomas W. Bates

Department Chair and Associate Professor of Finance
Arizona State University

WILEY

VICE PRESIDENT & EXECUTIVE PUBLISHER	George Hoffman
EXECUTIVE EDITOR	Joel Hollenbeck
EDITORIAL OPERATIONS MANAGER	Yana Mermel
CONTENT EDITOR	Jennifer Manias
ASSISTANT EDITOR	Courtney Luzzi
SENIOR EDITORIAL ASSISTANT	Erica Horowitz
DIRECTOR OF MARKETING	Amy Scholz
SENIOR MARKETING MANAGER	Karolina Zarychta
MARKETING ASSISTANT	Mia Brady
SENIOR PRODUCT DESIGNER	Allison Morris
PRODUCT DESIGNER	Greg Chaput
MEDIA SPECIALIST	Elena Santa Maria
SENIOR CONTENT MANAGER	Dorothy Sinclair
SENIOR PRODUCTION EDITOR	Valerie Vargas
SENIOR PHOTO EDITOR	Jennifer MacMillan
SENIOR DESIGNER	Maureen Eide

The CFA Institute Materials used in this book are reproduced and republished from the CFA Program Materials with permission from the CFA Institute. The authors and publisher are grateful for permission to use this material.

This book was set in Minion Pro by Aptara, Inc. and printed and bound by Courier/Kendallville. The cover printed by Courier/Kendallville.

This book is printed on acid free paper. ∞

Founded in 1807, John Wiley & Sons, Inc. has been a valued source of knowledge and understanding for more than 200 years, helping people around the world meet their needs and fulfill their aspirations. Our company is built on a foundation of principles that include responsibility to the communities we serve and where we live and work. In 2008, we launched a Corporate Citizenship Initiative, a global effort to address the environmental, social, economic, and ethical challenges we face in our business. Among the issues we are addressing are carbon impact, paper specifications and procurement, ethical conduct within our business and among our vendors, and community and charitable support. For more information, please visit our website: www.wiley.com/go/citizenship.

Evaluation copies are provided to qualified academics and professionals for review purposes only, for use in their courses during the next academic year. These copies are licensed and may not be sold or transferred to a third party. Upon completion of the review period, please return the evaluation copy to Wiley. Return instructions and a free-of-charge return mailing label are available at www.wiley.com/go/returnlabel. If you have chosen to adopt this textbook for use in your course, please accept this book as your complimentary desk copy. Outside of the United States, please contact your local sales representative.

ISBN: 978-0-470-44465-8
BRV ISBN: 978-1-118-21810-5

Printed in the United States of America

10 9 8 7 6 5 4 3 2 1

Dedication

ROBERT PARRINO

To my parents, whose life-long support and commitment to education inspired me to become an educator, and to my wife, Emily, for her unending support.

DAVID KIDWELL

To my parents, Dr. William and Margaret Kidwell, for their endless support of my endeavors, to my son, David Jr., of whom I am very proud, and to my wife, Jillinda, who is the joy of my life.

THOMAS BATES

To my wife, Emi, and our daughters, Abigail and Lillian. Your support, patience, fun, and friendship make me a better educator, scholar, and person.

ROBERT PARRINO

Lamar Savings Centennial Professor of Finance
McCombs School of Business, University of Texas at Austin

A member of the faculty at University of Texas since 1992, Dr. Parrino teaches courses in regular degree and executive education programs at the University of Texas, as well as in customized executive education courses for industrial, financial, and professional firms. He has also taught at the University of Chicago, University of Rochester, and IMADEC University in Vienna. Dr. Parrino has received numerous awards for teaching excellence at University of Texas from students, faculty, and the Texas Ex's (alumni association).

Dr. Parrino has been involved in advancing financial education outside of the classroom in a variety of ways. As a Chartered Financial Analyst (CFA) charterholder he has been very active with the CFA Institute, having been a member of the candidate curriculum committee, served as a regular speaker at the annual Financial Analysts Seminar, spoken at over 20 Financial Analyst Society meetings, and as a past member of the planning committee for the CFA Institute's Annual Meeting. In addition, Dr. Parrino is the founding director of the Hicks, Muse, Tate & Furst Center for Private Equity Finance at the University of Texas. Dr. Parrino was Vice President for Financial Education of the Financial Management Association (FMA) from 2008 to 2010 and is serving as an academic director of the FMA from 2011 to 2013. Since 2009 Dr. Parrino has served as a member of the Scientific Panel for the Center for Corporate Investor Responsibility in the Sim Kee Boon Institute of Financial Economics at Singapore Management University.

Dr. Parrino is also co-founder of the Financial Research Association and is Associate Editor of the *Journal of Corporate Finance*. Dr. Parrino's research includes work on corporate governance, financial policies, restructuring, and mergers and acquisitions, as well as research on private equity markets. He has published his research in a number of journals, including the *Journal of Finance, Journal of Financial Economics, Journal of Financial and Quantitative Analysis, Journal of Law and Economics, Journal of Portfolio Management*, and *Financial Management*. Dr. Parrino has won a number of awards for his research.

Dr. Parrino has experience in the application of corporate finance concepts in a variety of business situations. Since entering the academic profession he has been retained as an advisor on valuation issues concerning businesses with enterprise values ranging to more than $1 billion and has consulted in areas such as corporate financing, compensation, and corporate governance. Dr. Parrino is currently on the advisory council of Virgo Capital, a private equity firm, and was previously President of Sprigg Lane Financial, Inc., a financial consulting firm with offices in Charlottesville, Virginia, and New York City. While at Sprigg Lane, he was on the executive, banking, and portfolio committees of the holding company that owns Sprigg Lane. Before joining Sprigg Lane, Dr. Parrino was on the Corporate Business Planning and Development staff at Marriott Corporation. At Marriott, he conducted fundamental business analyses and preliminary financial valuations of new business development opportunities and potential acquisitions. Dr. Parrino holds a B.S. in chemical engineering from Lehigh University, an MBA degree from The College of William and Mary, and M.S. and Ph.D. degrees in applied economics and finance, respectively, from University of Rochester.

DAVID S. KIDWELL

Professor of Finance and Dean Emeritus Curtis L. Carlson School of Management, University of Minnesota

Dr. Kidwell has over 30 years experience in financial education, as a teacher, researcher, and administrator. He has served as Dean of the Carlson School at the University of Minnesota and of the School of Business Administration at the University of Connecticut. Prior to joining the University of Connecticut, Dr. Kidwell held endowed chairs in banking and finance at Tulane University, the University of Tennessee, and Texas Tech University. He was also on the faculty at the Krannert Graduate School of Management, Purdue University, where he was twice voted the outstanding undergraduate teacher of the year.

An expert on the U.S. financial system, Dr. Kidwell is the author of more than 80 articles dealing with the U.S. financial system and capital markets. He has published his research in the leading journals, including *Journal of Finance, Journal of Financial Economics, Journal of Financial and Quantitative Analysis, Financial Management,* and *Journal of Money, Credit, and Banking.* Dr. Kidwell has also participated in a number of research grants funded by the National Science Foundation to study the efficiency of U.S. capital markets, and to study the impact of government regulations upon the delivery of consumer financial services.

Dr. Kidwell has been a management consultant for Coopers & Lybrand and a sales engineer for Bethlehem Steel Corporation. He currently serves on the Board of Directors and is the Chairman of the Audit and Risk Committee of the Schwan Food Company. Dr. Kidwell is the past Secretary-Treasurer of the Board of Directors of AACSB, the International Association for Management Education, and is a past member of the Boards of the Minnesota Council for Quality, Stonier Graduate School of Banking, and Minnesota Center for Corporate Responsibility. Dr. Kidwell has also served as an Examiner for the 1995 Malcolm Baldrige National Quality Award, on the Board of Directors of the Juran Center for Leadership in Quality, and on the Board of the Minnesota Life Insurance Company.

Dr. Kidwell holds an undergraduate degree in mechanical engineering from California State University at San Diego, an MBA with a concentration in finance from California State University at San Francisco, and a Ph.D. in finance from the University of Oregon.

THOMAS W. BATES

Department Chair and Associate Professor of Finance W. P. Carey School of Business, Arizona State University

Dr. Bates is the Chair of the Department of Finance and Dean's Council of 100 Distinguished Scholars at the W. P. Carey School of Business, Arizona State University. He has also taught courses in finance at the University of Delaware, the Ivey School of Business at the University of Western Ontario, and the University of Arizona where he received the Scrivener teaching award. During his career as an educator, Professor Bates has taught corporate finance to students in undergraduate, MBA, executive MBA, and Ph.D. programs, as well as in custom corporate educational courses.

Professor Bates is a regular contributor to the academic finance literature in such journals as *Journal of Finance, Journal of Financial Economics*, and *Financial Management*. His research addresses a variety of issues in corporate finance including the contracting environment in mergers and acquisitions, corporate liquidity decisions and cash holdings, and the governance of corporations. In practice, Dr. Bates has worked with companies and legal firms as an advisor on issues related to the valuation of companies and corporate governance. Dr. Bates received a B.A. in Economics from Guilford College and his doctorate in finance from the University of Pittsburgh.

Preface

We have written *Essentials of Corporate Finance* for use in an introductory course in corporate finance at the undergraduate level. It is also suitable for advanced undergraduate, executive development, and traditional or executive MBA courses when supplemented with cases and outside readings. The main chapters in the book assume that students are well versed in algebra and that they have taken courses in principles of economics and financial accounting. Optional chapters covering important economic and financial accounting concepts are included for students and instructors seeking such coverage.

Balance Between Conceptual Understanding and Computational Skills

We wrote this corporate finance text for one very important reason. We want to provide students and instructors with a book that strikes the best possible balance between helping students develop an intuitive understanding of key financial concepts and providing them with problem-solving and decision-making skills. In our experience, teaching students at all levels and across a range of business schools, we have found that students who understand the intuition underlying the basic concepts of finance are better able to develop the critical judgment necessary to apply financial tools to a broad range of real-world situations. An introductory corporate finance course should provide students with the concepts and tools that will help them in their subsequent business studies and their personal and professional lives.

Market research supports our view. Many faculty members who teach the introductory corporate finance course to undergraduates express a desire for a book that bridges the gap between conceptually and computationally focused books. This text is designed to bridge this gap: it develops the fundamental concepts underlying corporate finance in an intuitive manner while maintaining a strong emphasis on developing computational skills.

Our goal has also been to write a book and develop associated learning tools that help our colleagues succeed in the classroom—materials that are genuinely helpful in the learning process. Our book offers a level of rigor that is appropriate for finance majors and yet presents the content in a manner that both finance and non-finance students find accessible and want to read. Writing a book that is both *rigorous* and *accessible* has been one of our key objectives, and both faculty and student reviews of the content in this book suggest that we have achieved this objective.

We also provide solutions to many of the challenges facing faculty in an environment where they are asked to teach ever-increasing numbers of students with limited resources. Faculty need a book with learning tools that help them leverage their time. The organization of this book and the supplemental materials, along with the innovative *WileyPLUS* Web-based interface, which offers extensive problem-solving opportunities and other resources for students, provide such leverage to an extent not found with other textbooks.

A Focus on Value Creation

This book is more than a collection of ideas, equations, and chapters. It has an important integrating theme—that of value creation. This theme, which is carried throughout the book, provides a framework that helps students understand the relations between the various concepts covered in the book and makes it easier for them to learn these concepts.

The concept of value creation is the most fundamental notion in corporate finance. It is in stockholders' best interests for value maximization to be at the heart of the financial decisions made within the firm. Thus, it is critical that students be able to analyze and make business decisions with a focus on value creation. The concept of value creation is introduced in the first chapter of the book and is further developed and applied throughout the remaining chapters.

The theme of value creation is operationalized through the net present value (NPV) concept. Once students grasp the fundamental idea that financial decision makers should only choose courses of action whose benefits exceed their costs, analysis and decision making using the NPV concept become second nature. By helping students better understand the economic rationale for a decision from the outset, rather than initially focusing on computational skills, our text keeps students focused on the true purpose of the calculations and the decision at hand.

Integrated Approach: Intuition, Analysis, and Decision Making

To support the focus on value creation, we have emphasized three things: (1) providing an intuitive framework for understanding fundamental finance concepts, (2) teaching students how to analyze and solve finance problems, and (3) helping students develop the ability to use the results from their analyses to make good financial decisions.

1. **An Intuitive Approach:** We believe that explaining finance concepts in an intuitive context helps students develop a richer understanding of those concepts and gain better insights into how finance problems can be approached. It is our experience that students who have a strong conceptual understanding of financial theory are better problem solvers and decision makers than students who focus primarily on computational skills.

2. **Analysis and Problem Solving:** With a strong understanding of the basic principles of finance, students are equipped to tackle a wide range of financial problems. In addition to the many numerical examples that are solved in the text of each chapter, this book has 950 end-of-chapter homework and review problems that have been written with Bloom's Taxonomy in mind. Solutions for these problems are provided in the Instructor's Manual. We strive to help students acquire the ability to analyze and solve finance problems.

3. **Decision Making:** In the end, we want to prepare students to make sound financial decisions. To help students develop these skills, throughout the text we illustrate how the results from financial analyses are used in decision making.

Organization and Coverage

To help students develop the skills necessary to tackle investment and financing decisions, we have arranged the book's 17 chapters into five major building blocks, that collectively comprise the seven parts of the book, as illustrated in the accompanying exhibit and described below.

Introduction

Part 1, which consists of Chapter 1, provides an introduction to corporate finance. It describes the role of the financial manager, the types of fundamental decisions that financial mangers make, alternative forms of business organization, the goal of the firm, agency conflicts and how they arise, and the importance of ethics in financial decision making. These discussions set the stage and provide a framework that students can use to think about key concepts as the course progresses.

Foundations

Part 2 of the text consists of Chapters 2 through 4. These chapters present the basic institutional, economic, and accounting knowledge and tools that students should understand before they begin the study of financial concepts. Most of the material in these chapters is typically taught in other courses. Since students come to the corporate finance course with varying academic backgrounds, and because the time that has elapsed since students have taken particular prerequisite courses also varies, the chapters in Part 2 can help the instructor ensure that all students have the same base level of knowledge early in the course. Depending on the educational background of the students, the instructor might not find it necessary to cover all or any of the material in these chapters. Some or all of these chapters might, instead, be assigned as supplemental readings.

Chapter 2 describes the services financial institutions provide to businesses, how domestic and international financial markets work, the concept of market efficiency, how firms use financial markets, and how interest rates are determined in the economy. Chapter 3 describes the key financial statements and how they are related, as well as how these statements are related to cash flows to investors. Chapter 4

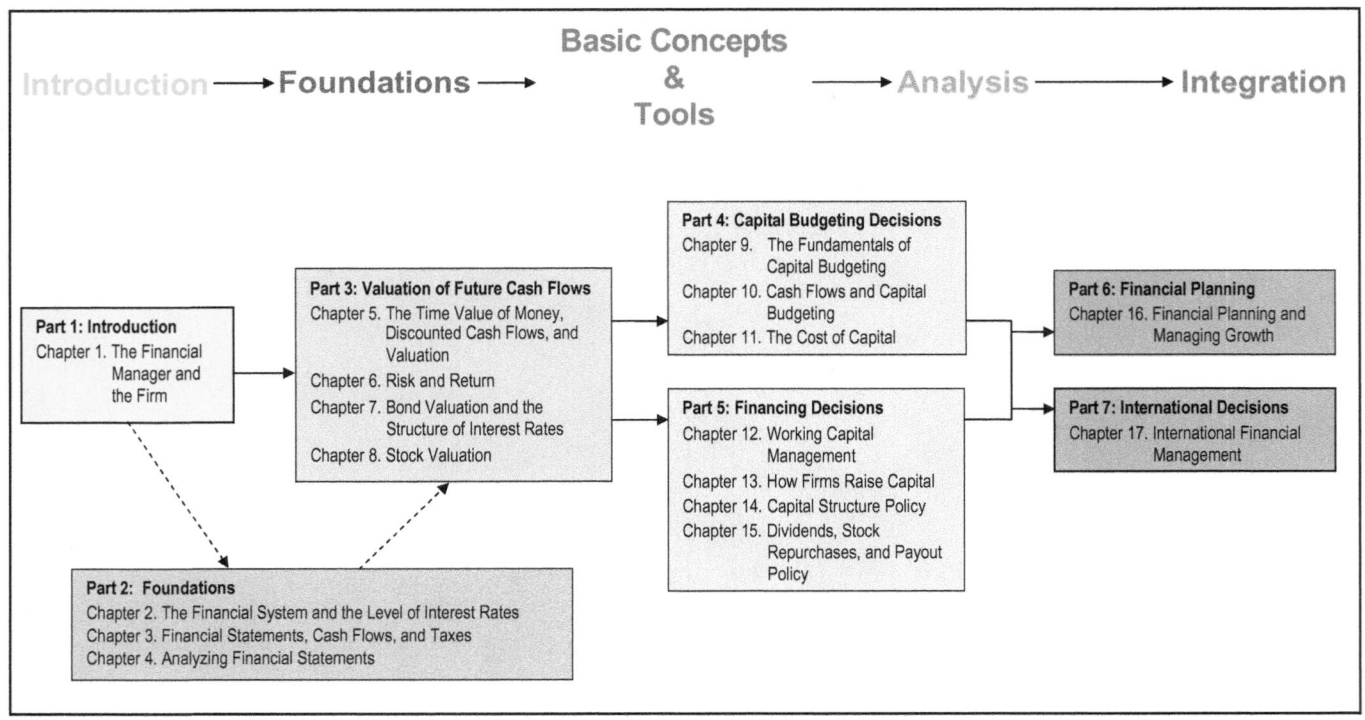

x

discusses ratio analysis and other tools used to evaluate financial statements. Throughout Part 2, we emphasize the importance of cash flows to get students thinking about cash flows as a critical component of all valuation calculations and financial decisions.

Basic Concepts and Tools

Part 3 presents basic financial concepts and tools and illustrates their application. This part of the text, which consists of Chapters 5 through 8, introduces time value of money and risk and return concepts and then applies present value concepts to bond and stock valuation. These chapters provide students with basic financial intuitions and computational tools that will serve as the building blocks for analyzing investment and financing decisions in subsequent chapters.

Analysis

Parts 4 and 5 of the text focus on investment and financing decisions. Part 4 covers capital budgeting. Chapter 9 introduces the concept of net present value and illustrates its application as the principle tool for evaluating capital projects. It also discusses alternative capital budgeting decision rules, such as internal rate of return, payback period, and accounting rate of return, and compares them with the net present value criterion. This discussion provides a framework that will help students in the rest of Part 4 as they learn the nuances of capital budgeting analysis in realistic settings.

Chapter 10 follows with an in-depth discussions of how cash flows are calculated and forecast. The cash flow calculations are presented in Chapter 10 using a valuation framework that will help students think about valuation concepts in an intuitive way and will prepare them for the application of these concepts throughout the remainder of this text.

Chapter 11 explains how the discount rates used in capital budgeting are estimated. This chapter uses an innovative concept—that of the finance balance sheet—to help students develop an intuitive understanding of the relations between the costs of the individual components of capital and the firm's overall weighted average cost of capital. It also provides a detailed discussion of methods used to estimate the costs of the individual components of capital that are used to finance a firm's investments and how these estimates are used in capital budgeting.

Part 5 covers financing decisions. It begins, in Chapter 12, with an introduction to how firms manage their working capital and the implications of working capital management decisions for financing decisions and firm value. This material is followed, in Chapters 13 and 14, with discussions of how firms raise capital to fund their real activities and the factors that affect how firms choose among the various sources of capital available to them. Chapter 14 also includes an appendix on leasing concepts and buy vs. lease analysis. Chapter 15 rounds out the discussion of financing decisions with an introduction to dividends, stock repurchases, stock dividends and splits, and payout policy decisions.

Integration

Part 6, which consists of Chapter 16, covers concepts related to financial planning and forecasting. This discussion helps students understand the relation between growth and financing requirements and how to forecast the funding required to finance the firm's strategy.

Part 7, which consists of Chapter 17, introduces students to important issues that managers must deal with in applying the concepts covered in the text to problems in a multinational context. The globalization of finance makes it critical that students understand how to do this.

Proven Pedagogical Framework

We have developed several distinctive features throughout the book to aid student learning. The pedagogical features included in our text are as follows:

CHAPTER OPENER VIGNETTES ····

Each chapter begins with a vignette that describes a real company or personal application. The vignettes illustrate concepts that will be presented in the chapter and are meant to heighten student interest, motivate learning, and demonstrate the real-life relevance of the material in the chapter.

LEARNING OBJECTIVES ··············

The opening vignette is accompanied by learning objectives that identify the most important material for students to understand while reading the chapter. At the end of the chapter, the Summary of Learning Objectives summarizes the chapter content in the context of the learning objectives.

David Paul Morris/Bloomberg via Getty Images

W hen Blockbuster Inc. filed for bankruptcy protection in September 2010, it looked like Netflix was unstoppable. With the demise of its major competitor in the video rental market, Netflix had become the most successful company in that market through its strategy of renting videos exclusively online and avoiding the high costs associated with operating video rental stores. On the day of the Blockbuster filing, Netflix's stock price closed at $160.47 per share, up from $40.85 just a year earlier. By early July of the following year, its shares were trading for as much as $304.79.

Then Netflix managers made a decision that did not turn out as expected. On July 12, 2011, they announced a new pricing strategy that would raise prices by as much as 60 percent for millions of Netflix subscribers who wanted to both rent DVDs by mail and watch video on the internet. Those two services would be un-bundled and, instead of paying $10 per month for both, customers would have to buy them separately at a cost of at least $16 per month. Customers and investors reacted swiftly and negatively to this announcement. During the fiscal quarter from July to September 2011, Netflix lost 800,000 U.S. subscribers and its stock price dropped to $113.27.

While Netflix managers did announce on October 10, 2011, that they were reversing their decision to unbundle the DVD rentals and video streaming, the damage had been done. The company's stock price continued to drift down, finishing the year at $70 per share. Perhaps sensing that Netflix was especially vulnerable after the events of 2011, Verizon Communications and Coinstar Inc. announced plans to work together to bundle streaming video and DVD

Learning Objectives

1. Explain the relation between risk and return.

2. Describe the two components of a total holding period return, and calculate this return for an asset.

3. Explain what an expected return is and calculate the expected return for an asset.

4. Explain what the standard deviation of returns is and why it is very useful in finance, and calculate it for an asset.

5. Explain the concept of diversification.

6. Discuss which type of risk matters to investors and why.

7. Describe what the Capital Asset Pricing Model (CAPM) tells us and how to use it to evaluate whether the expected return of an asset is sufficient to compensate an investor for the risks associated with that asset.

CHAPTER SIX

183

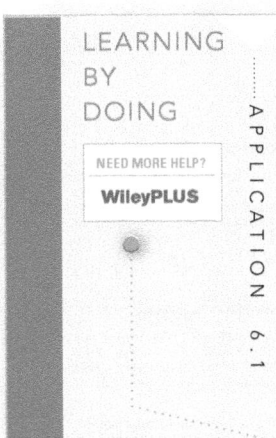

LEARNING BY DOING

APPLICATION 6.1

NEED MORE HELP?
WileyPLUS

Calculating the Return on an Investment

PROBLEM: You purchased a beat-up 1974 Datsun 240Z sports car a year ago for $1,500. Datsun is what Nissan, the Japanese car company, was called in the 1970s. The 240Z was the first in a series of cars that led to the Nissan 370Z that is being sold today. Recognizing that a mint-condition 240Z is a much sought-after car, you invested $7,000 and a lot of your time fixing up the car. Last week, you sold it to a collector for $18,000. Not counting the value of the time you spent restoring the car, what is the total return you earned on this investment over the one-year holding period?

APPROACH: Use Equation 6.1 to calculate the total holding period return. To calculate R_T using Equation 6.1, you must know P_0, P_1, and CF_1. In this problem, you can assume that the $7,000 was spent at the time you bought the car to purchase parts and materials. Therefore, your initial investment, P_0, was $1,500 + $7,000 = $8,500. Since there were no other cash inflows or outflows between the time that you bought the car and the time that you sold it, CF_1 equals $0.

SOLUTION: The total holding period return is:

$$R_T = R_{CA} + R_I = \frac{P_1 - P_0 + CF_1}{P_0} = \frac{\$18,000 - \$8,500 + \$0}{\$8,500} = 1.118, \text{ or } 111.8\%$$

LEARNING BY DOING APPLICATIONS

Along with a generous number of in-text examples, most chapters include several Learning by Doing Applications. These applications contain quantitative problems with step-by-step solutions to help students better understand how to apply their intuition and analytical skills to solve important problems. By including these exercises, we provide students with additional practice in the application of the concepts, tools, and methods that are discussed in the text.

BUILDING INTUITION

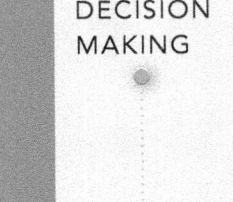

MORE RISK MEANS A HIGHER EXPECTED RETURN

BUILDING INTUITION

The greater the risk associated with an investment, the greater the return investors expect from it. A corollary to this idea is that investors want the highest return for a given level of risk or the lowest risk for a given level of return. When choosing between two investments that have the same level of risk, investors prefer the investment with the higher return. Alternatively, if two investments have the same expected return, investors prefer the less risky alternative.

Students must have an intuitive understanding of a number of important principles and concepts to successfully master the finance curriculum. Throughout the book, we emphasize these important concepts by presenting them in Building Intuition boxes. These boxes provide a statement of an important finance concept, such as the relation between risk and expected return, along with an intuitive example or explanation to help the student "get" the concept. These boxes help the students develop finance intuition. Collectively the Building Intuition boxes cover the most important concepts in corporate finance.

DECISION MAKING

EXAMPLE 6.2

Choosing between Two Investments

SITUATION: You are trying to decide whether to invest in one or both of two different stocks. Stock 1 has a beta of 0.8 and an expected return of 7.0 percent. Stock 2 has a beta of 1.2 and an expected return of 9.5 percent. You remember learning about the CAPM in school and believe that it does a good job of telling you what the appropriate expected return should be for a given level of risk. Since the risk-free rate is 4 percent and the market risk premium is 6 percent, the CAPM tells you that the appropriate expected rate of return for an asset with a beta of 0.8 is 8.8 percent. The corresponding value for an asset with a beta of 1.2 is 11.2 percent. Should you invest in either or both of these stocks?

DECISION: You should not invest in either stock. The expected returns for both of them are below the values predicted by the CAPM for investments with the same level of risk. In other words, both would plot below the line in Exhibit 6.11. This implies that they are both overpriced.

DECISION-MAKING EXAMPLES

Throughout the book, we emphasize the role of the financial manager as a decision maker. To that end, 16 chapters include Decision-Making Examples. These examples, which emphasize the decision-making process rather than computation, provide students with experience in financial decision making. Each Decision-Making Example outlines a scenario and asks the student to make a decision based on the information presented.

END-OF-CHAPTER PEDAGOGY

SUMMARIES OF LEARNING OBJECTIVES AND KEY EQUATIONS

At the end of the chapter, you will find a summary of the key chapter content related to each of the learning objectives listed at the beginning of the chapter, as well as an exhibit listing the key equations in the chapter.

SUMMARY OF Learning Objectives

1 Explain the relation between risk and return.

Investors require greater returns for taking greater risk. They prefer the investment with the highest possible return for a given level of risk or the investment with the lowest risk for a given level of return.

2 Describe the two components of a total holding period return, and calculate this return for an asset.

The total holding period return on an investment consists of a capital appreciation component and an income component. This return is calculated using Equation 6.1. It is important to recognize that investors do not care whether they receive a dollar of return through capital appreciation or as a cash dividend. Investors value both sources of return equally.

3 Explain what an expected return is and calculate the expected return for an asset.

The expected return is a weighted average of the possible returns from an investment, where each of these returns is

5 Explain the concept of diversification.

Diversification is reducing risk by investing in two or more assets whose values do not always move in the same direction at the same time. Investing in a portfolio containing assets whose prices do not always move together reduces risk because some of the changes in the prices of individual assets offset each other. This can cause the overall volatility in the value of an investor's portfolio to be lower than if it consisted of only a single asset.

6 Discuss which type of risk matters to investors and why.

Investors care about only systematic risk. This is because they can eliminate unsystematic risk by holding a diversified portfolio. Diversified investors will bid up prices for assets to the point at which they are just being compensated for the systematic risks they must bear.

7 Describe what the Capital Asset Pricing Model (CAPM) tells us and how to use it to evaluate whether the ex-

SUMMARY OF Key Equations

Equation	Description	Formula
6.1	Total holding period return	$R_T = R_{CA} + R_I = \dfrac{P_1 - P_0}{P_0} + \dfrac{CF_1}{P_0} = \dfrac{\Delta P + CF_1}{P_0}$
6.2	Expected return on an asset	$E(R_{Asset}) = \sum_{i=1}^{n} (P_i \times R_i)$

Self-Study Problems

6.1 Kaaran made a friendly wager with a colleague that involves the result from flipping a coin. If heads comes up, Kaaran must pay her colleague $15; otherwise, her colleague will pay Kaaran $15. What is Kaaran's expected cash flow, and what is the variance of that cash flow if the coin has an equal probability of coming up heads or tails? Suppose Kaaran's colleague is willing to handicap the bet by paying her $20 if the coin toss results in tails. If everything else remains the same, what are Kaaran's expected cash flow and the variance of that cash flow?

6.2 You know that the price of CFI, Inc., stock will be $12 exactly one year from today. Today the price of the stock is $11. Describe what must happen to the price of CFI, Inc., today in order for an investor to generate a 20 percent return over the next year. Assume that CFI does not pay dividends.

6.3 The expected value of a normal distribution of prices for a stock is $50. If you are 90 percent sure that the price of the stock will be between $40 and $60, then what is the variance of the stock price?

6.4 You must choose between investing in stock A or stock B. You have already used CAPM to calculate the rate of return you should expect to receive for each stock given each one's systematic risk and decided that the expected return for both exceeds that predicted by CAPM by the same amount. In other words, both are equally attractive investments for a diversified investor. However, since you

SELF-STUDY PROBLEMS WITH SOLUTIONS

Five problems similar to the in-text Learning by Doing Applications follow the summary and provide additional examples with step-by-step solutions to help students further develop their problem-solving and computational skills.

Solutions to Self-Study Problems

6.1 Part 1: $E(\text{cash flow}) = (0.5 \times -\$15) + (0.5 \times \$15) = 0$
$$\sigma^2_{\text{Cash flow}} = [0.5 \times (-\$15 - \$0)^2] + [0.5 \times (\$15 - \$0)^2] = 225$$
Part 2: $E(\text{cash flow}) = (0.5 \times -\$15) + (0.5 \times \$20) = \$2.50$
$$\sigma^2_{\text{Cash flow}} = [0.5 \times (-\$15 - \$2.50)^2] + [0.5 \times (\$20 - \$2.50)^2] = \$306.25$$

6.2 The expected return for CFI based on today's stock price is ($12 − $11)/$11 = 9.09 percent, which is lower than 20 percent. Since the stock price one year from today is fixed, the only way that you will generate a 20 percent return is if the price of the stock drops today. Consequently, the price of the stock today must drop to $10. It is found by solving the following: $0.2 = (\$12 − x)/x$, or $x = \$10$.

6.3 Since you know that 1.645 standard deviations around the expected return captures 90 percent of the distribution, you can set up either of the following equations:

$$\$40 = \$50 - 1.645\sigma \quad \text{or} \quad \$60 = \$50 + 1.645\sigma$$

and solve for σ Doing this with either equation yields:

$$\sigma = \$6.079 \text{ and } \sigma^2 = 36.954$$

6.4 A comparison of the Sharpe Ratios for the two stocks will tell you which has the highest expected return per unit of total risk.

$$S_A = \frac{E(R_A) - R_{rf}}{\sigma_{R_A}} = \frac{0.10 - 0.05}{0.25} = 0.20$$

$$S_B = \frac{E(R_B) - R_{rf}}{\sigma_{R_B}} = \frac{0.15 - 0.05}{0.40} = 0.25$$

Stock B has the highest expected return per unit of risk.

CRITICAL THINKING QUESTIONS

At least ten qualitative questions, called Critical Thinking Questions, require students to think through their understanding of key concepts and apply those concepts to a problem.

Critical Thinking Questions

6.1 Given that you know the risk as well as the expected return for two stocks, discuss what process you might utilize to determine which of the two stocks is a better buy. You may assume that the two stocks will be the only assets held in your portfolio.

6.2 What is the difference between the expected rate of return and the required rate of return? What does it mean if they are different for a particular asset at a particular point in time?

6.3 Suppose that the standard deviation of the returns on the shares of stock at two different companies is exactly the same. Does this mean that the required rate of return will be the same for these two stocks? How might the required rate of return on the stock of a third company be greater than the required rates of return on the stocks of the first two companies even if the standard deviation of the returns of the third company's stock is lower?

6.4 The correlation between stocks A and B is 0.50, while the correlation between stocks A and C is −0.5. You already own stock A and are thinking of buying either stock B or stock C. If you want your portfolio to have the lowest possible risk, would you buy stock B or C? Would you expect the stock you choose to affect the return that you earn on your portfolio?

QUESTIONS AND PROBLEMS

The Questions and Problems, numbering 26 to 48 per chapter, are primarily quantitative and are classified as Basic, Intermediate, or Advanced.

Questions and Problems

BASIC ▷ **6.1 Returns:** Describe the difference between a total holding period return and an expected return.

6.2 Expected returns: John is watching an old game show rerun on television called *Let's Make a Deal* in which the contestant chooses a prize behind one of two curtains. Behind one of the curtains is a gag prize worth $150, and behind the other is a round-the-world trip worth $7,200. The game show has placed a subliminal message on the curtain containing the gag prize, which makes the probability of choosing the gag prize equal to 75 percent. What is the expected value of the selection, and what is the standard deviation of that selection?

6.3 Expected returns: You have chosen biology as your college major because you would like to be a medical doctor. However, you find that the probability of being accepted to medical school is about 10 percent. If you are accepted to medical school, then your starting salary when you graduate will be $300,000 per year. However, if you are not accepted, then you would choose to work in

INTERMEDIATE ▷ **6.13 Expected returns:** José is thinking about purchasing a soft drink machine and placing it in a business office. He knows that there is a 5 percent probability that someone who walks by the machine will make a purchase from the machine, and he knows that the profit on each soft drink sold is $0.10. If José expects a thousand people per day to pass by the machine and requires a complete return of his investment in one year, then what is the maximum price that he should be willing to pay for the soft drink machine? Assume 250 working days in a year, and ignore taxes and the time value of money.

6.14 Interpreting the variance and standard deviation: The distribution of grades in an introductory finance class is normally distributed, with an expected grade of 75. If the standard deviation of grades is 7, in what range would you expect 95 percent of the grades to fall?

6.27 David is going to purchase two stocks to form the initial holdings in his portfolio. Iron stock has ◁ ADVANCED an expected return of 15 percent, while Copper stock has an expected return of 20 percent. If David plans to invest 30 percent of his funds in Iron and the remainder in Copper, what will be the expected return from his portfolio? What if David invests 70 percent of his funds in Iron stock?

10.29 FITCO is considering the purchase of new equipment. The equipment costs $350,000, and an ◁ CFA PROBLEMS additional $110,000 is needed to install it. The equipment will be depreciated straight-line to zero over a five-year life. The equipment will generate additional annual revenues of $265,000, and it will have annual cash operating expenses of $83,000. The equipment will be sold for $85,000 after five years. An inventory investment of $73,000 is required during the life of the investment. FITCO is in the 40 percent tax bracket, and its cost of capital is 10 percent. What is the project NPV?
a. $47,818.
b. $63,658.
c. $80,189.
d. $97,449.

CFA PROBLEMS

Problems from CFA readings are included in the Question and Problem section in appropriate chapters.

9.4 Net present value: Management of Franklin Mints, a confectioner, is considering purchasing a new jelly bean-making machine at a cost of $312,500. They project that the cash flows from this investment will be $121,450 for the next seven years. If the appropriate discount rate is 14 percent, what is the NPV for the project?

EXCEL PROBLEMS

Nearly all problems can be solved using Excel templates at the student Web site and within *WileyPLUS*.

SAMPLE TEST PROBLEMS

Finally, five Sample Test Problems call for straightforward applications of the chapter concepts. These problems are intended to be representative of the kind of problems that may be used in a test, and instructors can encourage students to solve them as if they were taking a quiz. Solutions are provided in the Instructor's Manual.

Sample Test Problems

6.1 Friendly Airlines stock is selling at a current price of $37.50 per share. If the stock does not pay a dividend and has a 12 percent expected return, what is the expected price of the stock one year from today?

6.2 Stefan's parents are about to invest their nest egg in a stock that he has estimated to have an expected return of 9 percent over the next year. If the return on the stock is normally distributed with a 3 percent standard deviation, in what range will the stock return fall 95 percent of the time?

6.3 Elaine has narrowed her investment alternatives to two stocks (at this time she is not worried about diversifying): Stock M, which has a 23 percent expected return, and Stock Y, which has an 8 percent expected return. If Elaine requires a 16 percent return on her total investment, then what proportion of her portfolio will she invest in each stock?

6.4 You have just prepared a graph similar to Exhibit 6.9, comparing historical data for Pear Computer Corp. and the general market. When you plot the line of best fit for these data, you find that the slope of that line is 2.5. If you know that the market generated a return of 12 percent and that the risk-free rate is 5 percent, then what would your best estimate be for the return of Pear Computer during that same time period?

6.5 The CAPM predicts that the return of MoonBucks Tea Corp. is 23.6 percent. If the risk-free rate of return is 8 percent and the expected return on the market is 20 percent, then what is MoonBucks's beta?

● END-OF-CHAPTER ETHICS CASES

Ethics is an important topic in finance and this text addresses ethical issues in several ways. In Chapter 1, we introduce a framework for consideration of ethical issues in corporate finance. Many ethical issues can be analyzed in the context of informational asymmetry between parties to a transaction, conflicts of interest, breaches of confidentiality, and breaches of fiduciary duty (principal-agent relationships); we highlight examples of such analyses throughout the text. In addition, six ethics cases are included throughout this book in order to help students better understand how to analyze ethical dilemmas in the context of the framework. Real company examples are presented, including timeless cases about Arthur Anderson and Martha Stewart's scandal involving ImClone, and more timely topics such as the subprime mortgage crisis and the advent of sustainable living plans by corporations. Each case includes questions for follow-up discussion in class or as an assignment.

Instructor and Student Resources

Essentials of Corporate Finance features a full line of teaching and learning resources that were developed under the close review of the authors. Driven by the same basic beliefs as the textbook, these supplements provide a consistent and well-integrated learning system. This hands-on package guides *instructors* through the process of active learning and provides them with the tools to create an interactive learning environment. With its emphasis on activities, exercises, and the Internet, the package encourages *students* to take an active role in the course and prepares them for decision making in a real-world context.

WileyPLUS *WileyPLUS* is a research-based online environment for effective teaching and learning. *WileyPLUS* builds students' confidence because it takes the guesswork out of studying by providing students with a clear roadmap: **what to do, how to do it, if they did it right**. This interactive approach focuses on the following:

Confidence: Research shows that students experience a great deal of anxiety over studying. That's why we provide a structured learning environment that helps students focus on **what to do**, along with the support of immediate resources.

Motivation: To increase and sustain motivation throughout the semester, *WileyPLUS* helps students learn **how to do it** at a pace that's right for them. Our integrated resources—available 24/7—function like a personal tutor, directly addressing each student's demonstrated needs with specific problem-solving techniques.

Success: *WileyPLUS* helps to ensure that each study session has a positive outcome by putting students in control. Through instant feedback and study objective reports, students know **if they did it right**, and where to focus next, so they achieve the strongest results.

With *WileyPLUS*, our efficacy research shows that students improve their outcomes by as much as one letter grade. *WileyPLUS* helps students take more initiative, so you'll have greater impact on their achievement in the classroom and beyond.

What do students receive with *WileyPLUS*?

- The complete digital textbook, saving students up to 60% off the cost of a printed text.

- Question assistance, including links to relevant sections in the online digital textbook.
- Immediate feedback and proof of progress, 24/7.
- Integrated, multi-media resources—including Narrated PowerPoint Review, Animated Learning by Doing Applications, Pre-requisite Course Reviews, Concept Review Videos, Excel Templates, and much more—that provide multiple study paths and encourage more active learning.

What do instructors receive with *WileyPLUS*?

- Reliable resources that reinforce course goals inside and outside of the classroom.
- The ability to easily identify those students who are falling behind.
- Media-rich course materials and assessment content including Instructor's Manual, Solutions Manual, Test Bank, PowerPoint Slides, Computerized Test Bank, Pre- and Post-Lecture Quizzes, Video Teaching Guide and much more.
- **www.wileyplus.com**

For Instructors.

Companion Web Site. www.wiley.com/college/parrino houses an extensive support package to help you maximize your teaching effectiveness. We offer useful resources for instructors with varying levels of experience and different instructional circumstances.

Instructor's Manual. Included for each chapter are lecture outlines, a summary of learning objectives and key equations, and alternative approaches to the material. The *Solutions Manual* includes detailed solutions to the Before You Go On questions, Self-Study Problems, Critical Thinking Questions, and all of the Questions and Problems at the end of each chapter.

Test Bank. With over 1,500 questions, the Test Bank includes multiple choice, true/false, and short answer problems. All of these questions and problems are classified by the level of difficulty and the learning outcome. The *Computerized Test Bank* allows instructors to create and print multiple versions of the same test and also allows users to modify and add questions and customize exams.

PowerPoint Presentations. The PowerPoint presentations contain a combination of key concepts, figures and tables, and problems and examples from the textbook as well as lecture notes and illustrations.

For Students.

The *Essentials of Corporate Finance* student Web site provides a wealth of support materials that will help students develop their conceptual understanding of class material and increase their ability to solve problems. On this Web site students will find Excel templates, study tools, Web quizzing, and many other useful resources: www.wiley.com/college/parrino.

ACKNOWLEDGMENTS

The colleagues listed below provided valuable feedback during the development process and added greatly to the content and pedagogy of the book. Their commitment to teaching and willingness to become involved in such a project was a source of inspiration to the authors. We would like to acknowledge the contribution made by the following professors whose thoughtful comments contributed to the quality, relevancy, and accuracy of this text:

Reviewers

Anastasios Moysidis, Florida International University
Andrew Head, Western Kentucky University
Anne Marie Whyte, University of Central Florida
Antonio Rodriguez, Texas A&M International University
Beverly Hadaway, University of Texas at Austin
Camelia Ferrua Rotaru, St. Edwards University
Christopher Pope, University of Georgia
Dalton Bigbee, Northeastern State University
Dave Bourff, Boise State University
Deanne Butchey, Florida International University
Denis Boudreaux, University of Louisiana
Devrim Yaman, Western Michigan University
Dong Nyonna, Austin Peay State University
Emy Tice, Northern Arizona University
Giles Bootheway, St. Bonaventure University
Greg Richey, California State University, San Bernardino
Heidi Toprac, University of Texas at Austin
Helen Saar, Dixie State College of Utah
Hendrik Devos, University of Texas at El Paso
Ivelina Pavlova, Universithy of Houston, Clear Lake
James DeMello, Western Michigan University
Jennifer Foo, Stetson University
Jim Keys, Florida International University
Juan Cabrera, Ramapo College of New Jersey
Ladd Kochman, Kennesaw State Universitiy
Lan Liu, California State University, Sacramento

Lawrence Schrenk, American University
Ling Lo, Western Kentucky University
Lyle Cadey, Averett University
Maria Ramjerdi, Monclair University
Michael Slates, Bowling Green State University
Michael Williams, University of Denver
Morgan Bridge, Colorado Mesa University
Nancy Jay, Mercer University
Narayanan Jayaraman, Georgia Tech
Nick Panepinto, Flagler College
Paul Weinstock, Ohio State University
Philip Romero, University of Oregon
Praveen Das, University of Louisiana, Lafayette
Qi Sun, California State University, San Marcos
Qin Lian, Louisiana Tech University
Richard Gregory, Eastern Tennessee State University
Richard Marcus, University of Wisconsin, Milwaukee
Steve Beach, Pont Radford University
Steve Ciccone, University of New Hampshire
Susan White, University of Maryland
Suzan Murphy, University of Tennessee, Knoxville
Tavey Ronen, Rutgers University
Thomas Krueger, Texas A&M University, Kingsville
Thomas Secrest, Coastal Carolina University
Timothy Haight, Chapman University
Tom Geurts, George Washington University
Wesley Wang, University of Scranton
Ying Ying Shao, Towson University
Yixin Liu, University of New Hampshire

Advisory Board

Anita Pennathur, Florida Atlantic University
Beverly Hadaway, University of Texas at Austin
Christopher Pope, University of Georgia
G. Michael Phillips, California State University, Northridge
Heidi Dybevik, University of Iowa
Helen Saar, Dixie State College of Utah
Hendrik Devos, University of Texas at El Paso
Jim Estes, California State University, San Bernardino
Lan Liu, California State University, Sacramento
Praveen Das, University of Louisiana, Lafayette
Shady Kholdy-Sabety, California State University, Pomona
Susan Crain, Missouri State University
Suzan Murphy, University of Tennessee, Knoxville
Thomas Secrest, Coastal Carolina University
Tom Geurts, George Washington University

Class Testers

Amadeu DaSilva, California State University, Fullerton
Curtis Nicholls, Bucknell University
Deborah Giarusso, University of Northern Iowa
Duong Le, University of Arkansas
Ed Graham, University of North Carolina, Wilmington
George Kutner, Marquette University

Helen Simon, Florida International University
Javad Gorjidooz, Embry Aeronautical University
John Kallianiotis, University of Scranton
Kathleen McNichol, LaSalle University
Michael Donovan, Cedarcrest College
Michael Sullivan, University of Nevada, Las Vegas
Mike Toyne, Northeastern State University
Murray Sabrin, Ramapo College of New Jersey
Onur Arugaslan, Western Michigan University
Patrick Simanjuntak, Hampton University
Paulette Schwerdt, Baker University
Peppi Kenny, Western Illinois University
Peter Del Piano, Johnson & Wales University
Rahul Verma, University of Houston
Robert Balik, Western Michigan University
Ronald Filante, Pace University
Shawn Tysiak, University of Toledo
Sundaram Srinivasan, Ball State University
Tammie Simmons-Mosley, California State University, Eastbay
Thomas Tallerico, Dowling College
Vance Lesseig, Texas State University
Zane Dennick-Ream, Robert Morris University

The following people developed valuable student and instructor resources available on the book companion site and *WileyPLUS:*

Babu Baradwaj, Towson University
Heidi Toprac, University of Texas at Austin
James Dow, G. Michael Phillips, and Kenneth Leslie, California State University, Northridge
Karen Hamilton, Georgia Southern University
Mary Lou Poloskey, The University of Texas at Austin
Pamela LaBorde, Western Washington University
Patrick Lach, Eastern Illinois University
Shawn Tysiak, University of Toledo
Steven Lifland, Highpoint University
Wendell Licon, Arizona State University

Publishing Team

We also thank the Wiley publishing team who were always calm, supportive, and gracious under fire as we suffered the travail of college textbook writing, where deadlines are always yesterday. Those showing extraordinary patience and support include Joseph Heider, Senior Vice President and General Manager; Tim Stookesberry, Vice President, Product and eBusiness Development; George Hoffman, Vice President and Publisher; and Susan Elbe, Vice President, Market Development and Marketing. Those warranting special praise are Jennifer Manias, Content Editor, who coordinated the complex scheduling of the book and all of its resources; Joel Hollenbeck, Executive Editor; Karolina Zarychta, Senior Marketing Manager; Amy Scholz, Director of Marketing; and the Wiley sales force for their creativity in selling our book. Other Wiley staff who contributed to the text and media include Erica Horowitz, Senior Editorial Assistant; Courtney Luzzi, Assistant Editor; Allie Morris, Senior Product Designer; Greg Chaput, Product Designer; Elena Santa Maria, Media Specialist; Valerie Vargas, Senior Production Editor; Maureen Eide, Senior Designer; Kathleen Pepper, Photo Editor; our meticulous copyeditor, Heath Lynn Silberfeld; and, of course, Jackie Henry, Senior Project Manager at Aptara.

Colleagues

Robert Parrino would also like to thank some of his colleagues for their inspiration and helpful discussions. Among those who have significantly influenced this book are Robert Bruner of University of Virginia, Jay Hartzell of University of Texas at Austin, and Mark Huson of University of Alberta. Special thanks are owed to Clifford Smith, of University of Rochester, whose classes really helped Dr. Parrino make sense of finance. In addition, recognition should go to Michael J. Barclay, who inspired generations of students through his selfless support and example and who was both a great researcher and teacher.

David Kidwell would like to thank some of his former professors and colleagues for their inspiration and willingness to share their intellectual capital. George Kaufman and Michael Hopewell who contributed to Dr. Kidwell's knowledge of economics and finance and were critical professors during his doctoral program at the University of Oregon. Richard West, former dean and professor at the University of Oregon, who unlocked the secrets of research and inspired Dr. Kidwell's love of teaching and scholarship. Robert Johnson of Purdue University whose dignity and academic bearing served as an academic role model and whose love of teaching and research inspired Dr. Kidwell to follow in his footsteps and to write this book. David Blackwell of Texas A&M University who helped conceptualize the idea for the book and contributed numerous insights to various chapters during the book's writing. Finally, to John Harbell and Jonas Mittelman, of San Francisco State University who started Dr. Kidwell on his academic journey.

Thomas Bates would like to thank the professors, co-authors, and colleagues who have made him a better scholar and educator, including Robert Williams, who first introduced him to the analytical elegance of economics, and Kenneth Lehn who inspired him to pursue excellence in research and teaching in the field of finance.

Brief Contents

Contents

PART 3 VALUATION OF FUTURE CASH FLOWS

PART 4 CAPITAL BUDGETING DECISIONS

PART 5 FINANCING DECISIONS

PART 6 FINANCIAL PLANNING

PART 7 INTERNATIONAL DECISIONS

The Financial Manager and the Firm

George Hunter/Superstock

On May 24, 2012, Apollo Global Management, LLC, announced the completion of a $7.15 billion purchase of El Paso Corporation's oil and gas exploration and production business. This business, which would become an independent company named EP Energy, had drilling rights on almost 3.3 million acres of land with oil and gas reserves at varying levels of development. EP Energy had been acquired by Apollo and several other investors through a leveraged buyout—a transaction in which the purchaser uses a lot of debt to help pay for the acquisition.

Why did the investors decide to purchase El Paso Corporation's exploration and production business, and how did the El Paso managers and the investment group arrive at the $7.15 billion price tag? Surely the investors did not plan to lose money. Apollo, a very successful investor in the energy sector, believed that EP Energy was an excellent investment even at a cost of $7.15 billion. Sam Oh, a partner at Apollo, stated, "We are delighted to partner with one of North America's leading exploration and production franchises led by a world-class team of managers." By taking advantage of the operational experience of the management team and by using a great deal of debt financing, EP Energy was expected to earn high returns for its investors.

Investors in leveraged buyouts like the EP Energy transaction use many of the concepts covered in this chapter and elsewhere in this book to create the most value possible. Managers of leveraged buyout firms like Apollo are paid in a way that provides them with strong incentives to focus on value creation. They create value by investing in companies only when the benefits exceed the cost, managing the assets of the companies they buy as efficiently as

Learning Objectives

1. Identify the key financial decisions facing the financial manager of any business.

2. Identify common forms of business organization in the United States and their respective strengths and weaknesses.

3. Describe the typical organization of the financial function in a large corporation.

4. Explain why maximizing the current value of the firm's stock is the appropriate goal for management.

5. Discuss how agency conflicts affect the goal of maximizing stockholder value.

6. Explain why ethics is an appropriate topic in the study of corporate finance.

possible, and financing those companies with the least expensive combination of debt and equity. This chapter introduces you to the key financial aspects of these activities, and the remainder of the book fills in many of the details.

CHAPTER PREVIEW

This book provides an introduction to corporate finance. In it we focus on the responsibilities of the financial manager, who oversees the accounting and treasury functions and sets the overall financial strategy for the firm. We pay special attention to the financial manager's role as a decision maker. To that end, we emphasize the mastery of fundamental financial concepts and tools which are used to make sound financial decisions that create value for stockholders. These financial concepts and tools apply not only to business organizations but also to other venues, such as government entities, not-for-profit organizations, and sometimes even your own personal finances.

We open this chapter by discussing the three major types of decisions that a financial manager makes. We then describe common forms of business organization. After next discussing the major responsibilities of the financial manager, we explain why maximizing the value of the firm's stock is an appropriate goal for a financial manager. We go on to describe the conflicts of interest that can arise between stockholders and managers and the mechanisms that help align the interests of these two groups. Finally, we discuss the importance of ethical conduct in business.

1.1 THE ROLE OF THE FINANCIAL MANAGER

1 LEARNING OBJECTIVE

wealth
the economic value of the assets someone possesses

The financial manager is responsible for making decisions that are in the best interests of the firm's owners, whether the firm is a start-up business with a single owner or a billion-dollar corporation owned by thousands of stockholders. The decisions made by the financial manager or owner should be one and the same. In most situations this means that the financial manager should make decisions that maximize the value of the owners' stock. This helps maximize the owners' **wealth**. Our underlying assumption in this book is that most people who invest in businesses do so because they want to increase their wealth. In the following discussion, we describe the responsibilities of the financial manager in a new business in order to illustrate the types of decisions that such a manager makes.

Stakeholders

stakeholder
anyone other than an owner (stockholder) with a claim on the cash flows of a firm, including employees, suppliers, creditors, and the government

Before we discuss the new business, you may want to look at Exhibit 1.1, which shows the cash flows between a firm and its owners (in a corporation, the stockholders) and various stakeholders. A **stakeholder** is someone other than an owner who has a claim on the cash flows of the firm: *managers,* who want to be paid salaries and performance bonuses; *other employees,* who want to be paid wages; *suppliers,* who want to be paid for goods or services they provide; the *government,* which wants the firm to pay taxes; and *creditors,* who want to be paid interest and principal. Stakeholders may have interests that differ from those of the owners. When this is the case, they may exert pressure on management to make decisions that benefit them. We will return to these types of conflicts of interest later in the book. For now, though, we are primarily concerned with the overall flow of cash between the firm and its stockholders and stakeholders.

It's All About Cash Flows

productive assets
the tangible and intangible assets a firm uses to generate cash flows

To produce its products or services, a new firm needs to acquire a variety of assets. Most will be long-term assets, which are also known as **productive assets**. Productive assets can be tangible assets, such as equipment, machinery, or a manufacturing facility, or intangible assets, such

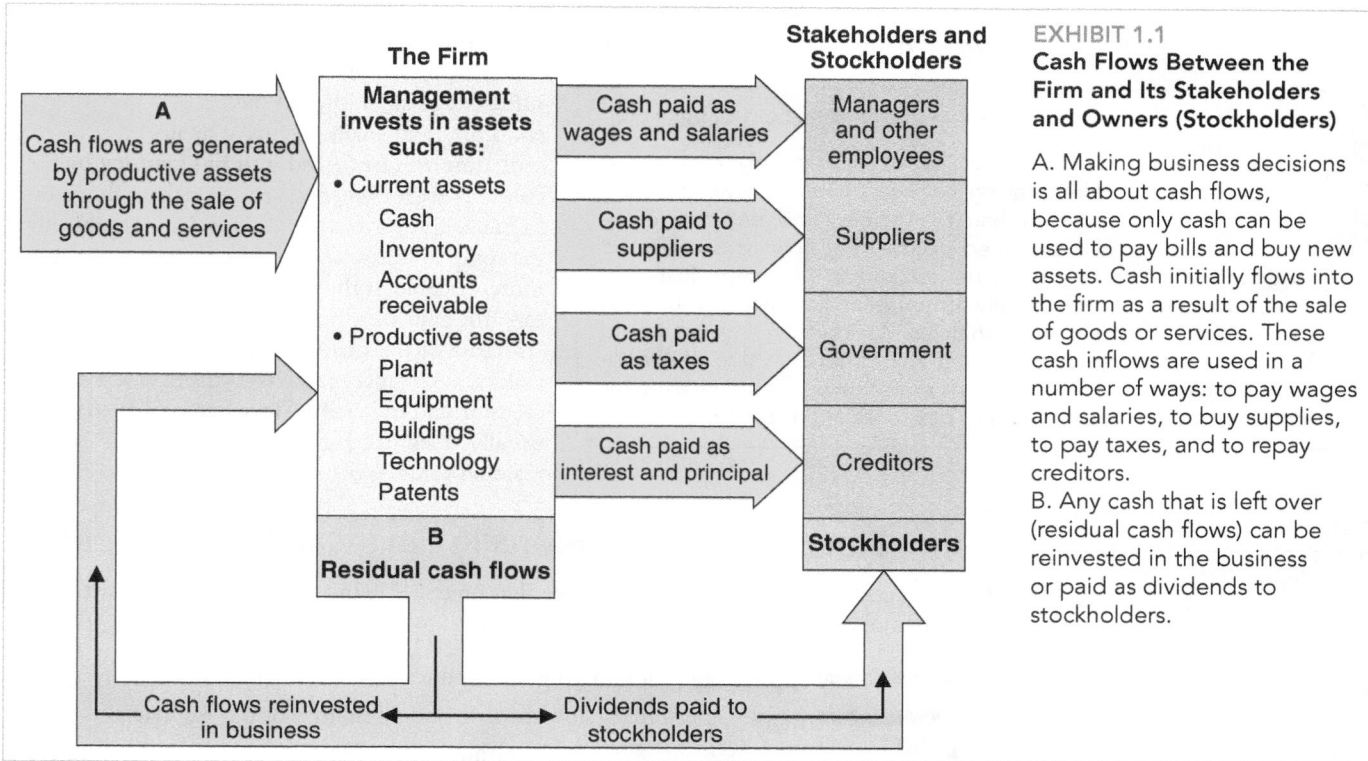

EXHIBIT 1.1

Cash Flows Between the Firm and Its Stakeholders and Owners (Stockholders)

A. Making business decisions is all about cash flows, because only cash can be used to pay bills and buy new assets. Cash initially flows into the firm as a result of the sale of goods or services. These cash inflows are used in a number of ways: to pay wages and salaries, to buy supplies, to pay taxes, and to repay creditors.

B. Any cash that is left over (residual cash flows) can be reinvested in the business or paid as dividends to stockholders.

as patents, trademarks, technical expertise, or other types of intellectual capital. Regardless of the type of asset, the firm tries to select assets that will generate the greatest cash flows for the firm's owners. The decision-making process through which the firm purchases long-term productive assets is called *capital budgeting,* and it is one of the most important decision processes in a firm.

Once the managers of a firm have selected the firm's productive assets, they must raise money to pay for them. *Financing decisions* determine the ways in which firms obtain and manage long-term financing to acquire and support their productive assets. There are two basic sources of funds: debt and equity. Every firm has some equity because equity represents ownership in the firm. It consists of capital contributions by the owners plus cash flows that have been reinvested in the firm. In addition, most firms borrow from a bank or issue some type of long-term debt to finance productive assets.

After the productive assets have been purchased and the business is operating, the managers of the firm will try to produce products at the lowest possible cost while maintaining quality. This means buying raw materials at the lowest possible cost, holding production and labor costs down, keeping management and administrative costs to a minimum, and seeing that shipping and delivery costs are competitive. In addition, day-to-day finances must be managed so that the firm will have sufficient cash on hand to pay salaries, purchase supplies, maintain inventories, pay taxes, and cover the myriad of other expenses necessary to run a business. The management of current assets, such as money owed by customers who purchase on credit, inventory, and current liabilities, such as money owed to suppliers, is called *working capital management.*[1]

A firm generates cash flows by selling the goods and services it produces. A firm is successful when these cash inflows exceed the cash outflows needed to pay operating expenses, creditors, and taxes. After meeting these obligations, managers of the firm can pay the remaining cash, called **residual cash flows,** to the owners as a cash dividend, or reinvest the cash in the business. The reinvestment of residual cash flows in the business to buy more productive assets is a very important concept. If these funds are invested wisely, they provide the foundation for the firm to grow and provide larger residual cash flows in the future for the owners. The reinvestment of cash

residual cash flows
the cash remaining after a firm has paid operating expenses and what it owes creditors and in taxes; can be paid to the owners as a cash dividend or reinvested in the business

---

[1]From accounting, *current assets* are assets that will be converted into cash within one year, and *current liabilities* are liabilities that must be paid within one year.

flows (earnings) is the most fundamental way that businesses grow in size. Exhibit 1.1 illustrates how the revenue generated by productive assets ultimately becomes residual cash flows.

> ### BUILDING INTUITION
>
> **CASH FLOWS MATTER MOST TO INVESTORS**
>
> Cash is what investors ultimately care about when making an investment. The value of any asset—a share of stock, a bond, or a business—is determined by the cash flows it is expected to generate in the future. To understand this concept, just consider how much you would pay for an asset from which you could never expect to obtain any cash flows. Buying such an asset would be like giving your money away. It would have a value of exactly zero. Conversely, as the expected cash flows from an investment increase, you would be willing to pay more and more for it.

A firm is unprofitable when it fails to generate sufficient cash inflows to pay operating expenses, creditors, and taxes. Firms that are unprofitable over time will be forced into **bankruptcy** by their creditors if the owners do not shut them down first. In bankruptcy the company will be reorganized or the company's assets will be liquidated, whichever is more valuable. If the company is liquidated, creditors are paid in a priority order according to the structure of the firm's financial contracts and prevailing bankruptcy law. If anything is left after all creditor and tax claims have been satisfied, which usually does not happen, the remaining cash, or residual value, is distributed to the owners.

bankruptcy
legally declared inability of an individual or a company to pay its creditors

Three Fundamental Decisions in Financial Management

Based on our discussion so far, we can see that financial managers are concerned with three fundamental decisions when running a business:

1. *Capital budgeting decisions:* Identifying the productive assets the firm should buy.
2. *Financing decisions:* Determining how the firm should finance or pay for assets.
3. *Working capital management decisions:* Determining how day-to-day financial matters should be managed so that the firm can pay its bills, and how surplus cash should be invested.

Exhibit 1.2 shows the impact of each decision on the firm's balance sheet. We briefly introduce each decision here and discuss them in greater detail in later chapters.

Capital Budgeting Decisions

A firm's capital budget is simply a list of the productive (capital) assets that management wants to purchase over a budget cycle, typically one year. The capital budgeting decision process addresses which productive assets the firm should purchase and how much money the firm can afford to spend. As shown in Exhibit 1.2, capital budgeting decisions affect the asset side of the balance sheet and are concerned with a firm's long-term investments. Capital budgeting decisions, as we mentioned earlier, are among management's most important decisions. Over the long run, they have a large impact on the firm's success or failure. The reason is twofold. First, capital (productive) assets generate most of the cash flows for the firm. Second, capital assets are long term in nature. Once they are purchased, the firm owns them for a long time, and they may be hard to sell without taking a financial loss.

The fundamental question in capital budgeting is this: Which productive assets should the firm purchase? A capital budgeting decision may be as simple as a movie theater's decision to buy a popcorn machine or as complicated as Boeing's decision to invest more than $6 billion to design and build the 787 *Dreamliner* passenger jet. Capital investments may also involve the purchase of an entire business, such as IBM's purchase of PricewaterhouseCoopers' (PwC) management consulting practice.

Regardless of the project, a good capital budgeting decision is one in which the benefits are worth more to the firm than the cost of the asset. For example, in August 2012 Verizon Communications received government approval to purchase wireless spectrum (the right to use radio frequencies over which voice and data signals are sent) from a group of cable companies for $3.9 billion. Presumably, Verizon expects that the investment will produce a stream of cash flows worth more than that. Suppose Verizon estimates that in terms of the current market value, the future cash flows from the wireless spectrum purchase are worth $5 billion. Is the purchase a good deal for Verizon? The answer is yes because the value of the expected cash flow benefits from the purchase exceeds the cost by $1.1 billion ($5.0 billion − $3.9 billion = $1.1 billion). If the purchase of the wireless spectrum works out as planned, the value of Verizon will be increased by $1.1 billion!

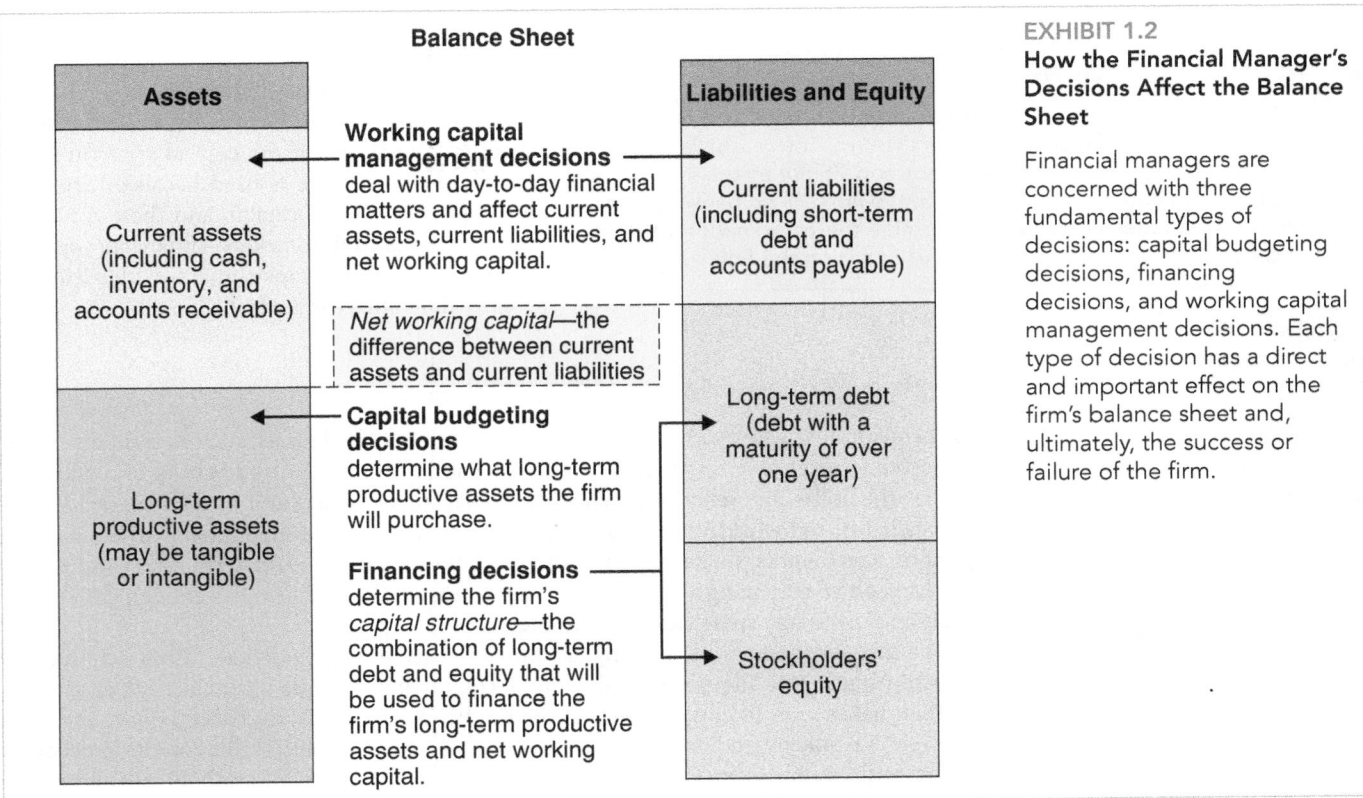

EXHIBIT 1.2

How the Financial Manager's Decisions Affect the Balance Sheet

Financial managers are concerned with three fundamental types of decisions: capital budgeting decisions, financing decisions, and working capital management decisions. Each type of decision has a direct and important effect on the firm's balance sheet and, ultimately, the success or failure of the firm.

Not all investment decisions are successful. Just open the business section of any newspaper on any day, and you will find stories of bad decisions. For example, Universal Picture's 2009 comedy *Land of the Lost* reportedly cost over $140 million in production and advertising expenses, but made only $69.5 million in worldwide box office receipts. Even with U.S. DVD sales of approximately $18 million, the overall cash flows from sales of the movie did not come close to covering its up-front costs. When, as in this case, the cost exceeds the value of the future cash flows, the project will decrease the value of the firm by that amount.

> **SOUND INVESTMENTS ARE THOSE WHERE THE VALUE OF THE BENEFITS EXCEEDS THEIR COST**
>
> **BUILDING INTUITION**
>
> Financial managers should invest in a capital project only if the value of its future cash flows exceeds the cost of the project (benefits > cost). Such investments increase the value of the firm and thus increase stockholders' (owners') wealth. This rule holds whether you're making the decision to purchase new machinery, build a new plant, or buy an entire business.

Financing Decisions

Financing decisions determine how firms raise cash to pay for their investments, as shown in Exhibit 1.2. Productive assets, which are long term in nature, are financed by long-term borrowing, equity investment, or both. Financing decisions involve trade-offs between the advantages and disadvantages of these financing alternatives for the firm.

A major advantage of debt financing is that debt payments are tax deductible for many corporations. However, debt financing increases a firm's risk because it creates a contractual obligation to make periodic interest payments and, at maturity, to repay the amount that is borrowed. Contractual obligations must be paid regardless of the firm's operating cash flow, even if the firm suffers a financial loss. If the firm fails to make payments as promised, it defaults on its debt obligation and could be forced into bankruptcy.

In contrast, equity has no maturity, and there are no guaranteed payments to equity investors. In a corporation, the board of directors has the right to decide whether dividends should be paid to stockholders. This means that if a dividend payment is reduced or omitted

> **BUILDING INTUITION**
>
> **FINANCING DECISIONS AFFECT THE VALUE OF THE FIRM**
>
> How a firm is financed with debt and equity affects the value of the firm. The reason is that the mix between debt and equity affects the taxes the firm pays and the probability that the firm will go bankrupt. The financial manager's goal is to determine the combination of debt and equity that minimizes the cost of financing the firm.

altogether, the firm will not be in default. Unlike interest payments, however, dividend payments to stockholders are not tax deductible.

The mix of debt and equity on the balance sheet is known as a firm's **capital structure**. The term capital structure is used because long-term funds are considered capital, and these funds are raised in **capital markets**—financial markets where equity and debt instruments with maturities greater than one year are traded.

capital structure
the mix of debt and equity that is used to finance a firm

capital markets
financial markets where equity and debt instruments with maturities greater than one year are traded

net working capital
the dollar difference between total current assets and total current liabilities

Working Capital Management Decisions

Management must also decide how to manage the firm's current assets, such as cash, inventory, and accounts receivable, as well as its current liabilities, such as trade credit and accounts payable. The dollar difference between a firm's total current assets and its total current liabilities is called its **net working capital**, as shown in Exhibit 1.2. As mentioned earlier, working capital management is the day-to-day management of the firm's short-term assets and liabilities. The goals of managing working capital are to ensure that the firm has enough cash to pay its bills and invest any spare cash to earn interest.

The mismanagement of working capital can cause a firm to default on its debt and go into bankruptcy, even though, over the long term, the firm may be profitable. For example, a firm that makes sales to customers on credit but is not diligent about collecting the accounts receivable can quickly find itself without enough cash to pay its bills. If this condition becomes chronic, trade creditors can force the firm into bankruptcy if the firm cannot obtain alternative financing.

A firm's profitability can also be affected by its inventory level. If the firm has more inventory than it needs to meet customer demands, it has too much cash tied up in nonearning assets. Conversely, if the firm holds too little inventory, it can lose sales because it does not have products to sell when customers want them. Management must therefore determine the optimal inventory level.

> **BEFORE YOU GO ON**
>
> 1. What are the three most basic types of financial decisions managers must make?
> 2. Explain why you would make an investment if the value of the expected cash flows exceeds the cost of the project.
> 3. Why are capital budgeting decisions among the most important decisions in the life of a firm?

1.2 FORMS OF BUSINESS ORGANIZATION

② LEARNING OBJECTIVE

Firms are organized in a number of different ways in the United States. In this section we discuss some of the more common forms of organization and the factors that business owners consider when they choose which to use. Exhibit 1.3 summarizes key characteristics of common forms of business organization.

Sole Proprietorships

sole proprietorship
a business owned by a single person

A **sole proprietorship** is a business that is owned by a single person. Its life is limited to the period that the owner (proprietor) is associated with the business because there is no ownership interest that can be transferred to someone else—there is no stock or other such interest

EXHIBIT 1.3   **Characteristics of Different Forms of Business Organization**

Choosing the appropriate form of business organization is an important step in starting a business. This exhibit compares key characteristics of the most popular forms of business organization in the United States.

	Sole Proprietorship	Partnership		Corporation		Limited Liability Partnership (LLP) or Company (LLC)
		General	Limited	S-Corp.	C-Corp.	
Cost to establish	Inexpensive	More costly	More costly	More costly	More costly	More costly
Life of entity	Limited	Flexible	Flexible	Indefinite	Indefinite	Flexible
Control by founder over business decisions	Complete	Shared	Shared	Depends on ownership	Depends on ownership	Shared
Access to capital	Very limited	Limited	Less limited	Less limited	Excellent	Less limited
Cost to transfer ownership	High	High	High	High	Can be low	High
Separation of management and investment	No	No	Yes	Yes	Yes	Yes
Potential owner/ manager conflicts	No	No	Some	Potentially high	Potentially high	Some
Ability to provide incentives to attract and retain high-quality employees	Limited	Good	Good	Good	Good	Good
Liability of owners	Unlimited	Unlimited	Unlimited for general partner	Limited	Limited	Limited
Tax treatment of income	Flow-through	Flow-through	Flow-through	Flow-through	Double tax	As elected
Tax deductibility of owner benefits	Limited	Limited	Limited	Limited	Less limited	Limited

that can be sold. A sole proprietorship ceases to exist when the proprietor stops being involved with the business. Many small businesses in the United States are organized this way.

A sole proprietorship is the simplest and least expensive form of business to set up and is the least regulated. To start a sole proprietorship, all you have to do is obtain the business licenses required by your local and state governments.

The ownership structure of a sole proprietorship has both advantages and disadvantages. Among the advantages is the fact that the proprietor does not have to share decision-making authority with anyone and can run the business as he or she chooses.

There are several disadvantages related to the fact that there is no stock or other ownership interest to sell. First, the amount of equity capital that can be raised to finance the business is limited to the owner's personal wealth. This can restrict growth opportunities for the business unless the proprietor is very wealthy. Second, because the proprietor provides all of the equity capital and manages the business, there is no separation of the management and investment roles. This limits the ability of good managers to form a business if they do not also have capital to invest. Third, it can be more costly to transfer ownership. The proprietor must sell the assets of the business directly, rather than indirectly through the sale of an ownership interest in an operating business. The business must essentially be re-established every time it is sold. Fourth, it is not possible to provide employees with compensation in the form of ownership interests, such as stock or stock options, which can help motivate them to work harder.

Another disadvantage of a sole proprietorship is that proprietor faces *unlimited liability*. If someone is harmed by the business, the proprietor's liability extends beyond the money invested in the business. The proprietor can lose some or all of his or her personal wealth.

Finally, profits from a sole proprietorship *flow through* to the sole proprietor's personal tax return, meaning that the business does not pay taxes before profits are distributed to the owner.

Because the business is not subject to income taxes, profits are not subject to double-taxation as is a C-corporation (described later). There are limitations on tax deductions for personal expenses, such as those associated with health insurance, but the costs of these limitations are often outweighed by the benefits from the flow-through of profits in a sole proprietorship.

Partnerships

partnership
two or more owners who have joined together legally to manage a business and share its profits

A **partnership** consists of two or more owners who have joined together legally to manage a business. To form a partnership, the owners (partners) enter into an agreement that details how much capital each partner will invest in the partnership, what their management roles will be, how key management decisions will be made, how the profits will be divided, and how ownership will be transferred in case of specified events, such as the retirement or death of a partner. A *general partnership* is a partnership in which all of the partners are owners of (investors in) the business and active in managing it. In contrast, a *limited partnership* has both *general partners*, who are owners and managers, and *limited partners*, who are owners, but not managers.

Partnerships are more costly to form than sole proprietorships because the partners must hire an attorney to draw up and maintain the *partnership agreement*, which specifies the nature of the relationships between or among the partners. On the other hand, partnership agreements can be amended to allow for the business to continue when a partner leaves. The ability to make the life of a business independent of that of the partners increases the liquidity of the ownership interests, making it easier to raise capital and less costly for the partners to sell their interests at an attractive price.

Many of the other advantages and disadvantages of a general partnership are similar to those of a sole proprietorship. A key disadvantage of a *general partnership* is that, like the proprietor in a sole proprietorship, all partners have unlimited liability. This liability can be even worse than in a sole proprietorship because a general partner can be held liable for all of the partnership's debts and other obligations, regardless of what proportion of the business he or she owns or how the debt or other obligations were incurred.

limited liability
the legal liability of an investor is limited to the amount of capital invested in the business

The problem of unlimited liability is avoided for some partners in a *limited partnership* because limited partners can generally only lose the amount of money that they have invested in the business. In a limited partnership one or more general partners have unlimited liability and actively manage the business, while each limited partner is liable for business obligations only up to the amount of capital he or she invested in the partnership. In other words, the limited partners have **limited liability**. To qualify for limited partner status, a partner cannot be actively engaged in managing the business.

Corporations

corporation
a legal entity formed and authorized under a state charter; in a legal sense, a corporation is a "person" distinct from its owners

Most large businesses are organized as corporations. A **corporation** is a legal entity authorized under a state charter. In a legal sense, it is a "person" distinct from its owners. For example, corporations can sue and be sued, enter into contracts, borrow money, and own assets. They can also be general or limited partners in partnerships, and they can own stock in certain types of other corporations. Because a corporation is an entity that is distinct from its owners, it can have an indefinite life. Corporations hold the majority of all business assets and generate the majority of business revenues and profits in the United States. The owners of a corporation are its stockholders.

Starting a corporation is more costly than starting a sole proprietorship. For example, it requires writing articles of incorporation and by-laws that conform to the laws of the state of incorporation. These documents spell out the name of the corporation, its business purpose, its intended life span (unless explicitly stated otherwise, the life is indefinite), the amount of stock to be issued, and the number of directors and their responsibilities. Over the life of a successful business, these costs are not very important. However, to a cash-strapped entrepreneur, they can seem substantial.

On the other hand, the corporate form of organization has several advantages. For example, shares in a corporation can be sold to raise capital from investors who are not involved in the business. This can greatly increase the amount of capital that can be raised to fund the business.

Another major advantage of a corporation is that stockholders have limited liability for debts and other obligations. Owners of corporations have limited liability because corporations are *legal persons* that take actions in their own names, not in the names of individual owners.

An *S-corporation* is a form of corporation that can be used by private businesses that meet certain requirements. An S-corporation can have only one class of stock and cannot have more than one hundred stockholders or any stockholders that are corporations or nonresident alien investors. In contrast, a *C-corporation*, which is the form used by public corporations, does not face such limits.

While there are more restrictions on S-corporations, there are also advantages. Specifically, all profits earned by an S-corporation pass directly to the stockholders, just as they pass to a sole proprietor or the partners in a partnership. This means that no taxes are paid at the corporate level.

In contrast, a major disadvantage of a C-corporation is that it must pay taxes on the income it earns. If the corporation pays a cash dividend, the stockholders must also pay taxes on the dividends they receive. Thus, the owners of C-corporations are subject to double taxation—first at the corporate level and then at the personal level when they receive dividends.

Corporations can be classified as public or private. Most large companies prefer to operate as public corporations because large amounts of capital can be raised in public markets at a relatively low cost. **Public markets**, such as the New York Stock Exchange (NYSE) and NASDAQ, are regulated by the Securities and Exchange Commission (SEC).[2]

In contrast, **privately held,** or **closely held, corporations** are owned by a small number of investors, and their shares are not traded publicly. When a corporation is first formed, the common stock is often held by a few investors, typically the founder, a small number of key managers, and financial backers. Over time, as the company grows in size and needs larger amounts of capital, management may decide that the company should "go public" in order to gain access to the public markets. Not all privately held corporations go public, however.

 Visit the Web sites of the NYSE and NASDAQ at http://www.nyse.com and http://www.nasdaq .com to get more information about market activity.

public markets
markets regulated by the Securities and Exchange Commission in which securities such as stocks and bonds are publicly traded

privately held, or **closely held, corporations**
corporations whose stock is not traded in the public markets

Limited Liability Partnerships and Companies

Historically, law firms, accounting firms, investment banks, and other professional groups were organized as sole proprietorships or partnerships. For partners in these firms, all income was taxed as personal income, and general partners had unlimited liability for all debts and other obligations of the firm. It was widely believed that in professional partnerships, such as those of attorneys, accountants, or physicians, the partners should be liable individually and collectively for the professional conduct of each partner. This structure gave the partners an incentive to monitor each other's professional conduct and discipline poorly performing partners, resulting in a higher quality of service and greater professional integrity. Financially, however, misconduct by one partner could result in disaster for the entire firm. For example, a physician found guilty of malpractice exposes every partner in the medical practice to financial liability, even if the others never treated the patient in question.

In the 1980s, because of sharp increases in the number of professional malpractice cases and large damages awards in the courts, professional groups began lobbying state legislators to create hybrid forms of business organization. One such hybrid, known as a **limited liability partnership (LLP)**, is now permitted in most states. An LLP combines some of the limited liability characteristics of a corporation with the tax advantage of a partnership. While liability varies from state to state, LLP partners in general have more limited liability than general partners in regular partnerships. Typically, they are not personally liable for any other partner's malpractice or professional misconduct. Like regular partnerships, income to the partners of an LLP is taxed as personal income.

A **limited liability company (LLC)** is another hybrid form of organization that is becoming increasingly common. Like LLPs, LLCs have benefited founders of many businesses that would otherwise have been organized as limited partnerships. They also provide limited liability to the people who make the business decisions in the firm while enabling all investors to retain the flow-through tax advantages of a limited partnership.

You will notice that Exhibit 1.3 indicates that the lives of partnerships, LLPs, and LLCs are flexible. This is because, while partnership and LLC agreements can be written so that their lives are indefinite, they can also be written with a fixed life in mind. For example, private equity and venture capital limited partnerships and LLCs are typically structured so that they last only 10 years.

limited liability partnership (LLP) and limited liability company (LLC)
Hybrid business organizations that combine some of the advantages of corporations and partnerships; in general, income to the partners is taxed only as personal income, but the partners have limited liability

---

[2]We examine the public and private markets in more detail in Chapters 2 and 13.

> **BEFORE YOU GO ON**

1. Why are many businesses operated as sole proprietorships or partnerships?

2. What are some advantages and disadvantages of operating as a public corporation?

3. Explain why professional partnerships such as physicians' groups organize as limited liability partnerships.

1.3 MANAGING THE FINANCIAL FUNCTION

 LEARNING OBJECTIVE

chief financial officer or CFO
the most senior financial manager in a company

As we discussed earlier, financial managers are concerned with a firm's investment, financing, and working capital management decisions. The senior financial manager holds one of the top executive positions in the firm. In a large corporation, the senior financial manager usually has the rank of vice president or senior vice president and goes by the title of **chief financial officer** or **CFO**. In smaller firms, the job tends to focus more on the accounting function, and the top financial officer may be called the controller or chief accountant. In this section we focus on the financial function in a large corporation.

Organizational Structure

Exhibit 1.4 shows a typical organizational structure for a large corporation, with special attention to the financial function. As shown, the top management position in the firm is the chief executive officer (CEO), who has the final decision-making authority among all the firm's executives. The CEO's most important responsibilities are to set the strategic direction of the firm and see that the management team executes the strategic plan. The CEO reports directly to the board of directors, which is accountable to the company's stockholders. The board's responsibility is to see that the top management makes decisions that are in the best interest of the stockholders.

The CFO reports directly to the CEO and focuses on managing all aspects of the firm's financial side, as well as working closely with the CEO on strategic issues. A number of positions report directly to the CFO. In addition, the CFO often interacts with people in other functional areas on a regular basis because all senior executives are involved in financial decisions that affect the firm and their areas of responsibility.

Positions Reporting to the CFO

Exhibit 1.4 also shows the positions that typically report to the CFO in a large corporation and the activities managed in each area.

- The *treasurer* looks after the collection and disbursement of cash, investing excess cash so that it earns interest, raising new capital, handling foreign exchange transactions, and overseeing the firm's pension fund managers. The treasurer also assists the CFO in handling important Wall Street relationships, such as those with investment bankers and credit rating agencies.

- The *risk manager* monitors and manages the firm's risk exposure in financial and commodity markets and the firm's relationships with insurance providers.

- The *controller* is really the firm's chief accounting officer. The controller's staff prepares the financial statements, maintains the firm's financial and cost accounting systems, prepares the taxes, and works closely with the firm's external auditors.

- The *internal auditor* is responsible for identifying and assessing major risks facing the firm and performing audits in areas where the firm might incur substantial losses. The internal auditor reports to the board of directors as well as the CFO.

EXHIBIT 1.4
Simplified Corporate Organization Chart

The firm's top finance and accounting executive is the CFO, who reports directly to the CEO. Positions that report directly to the CFO include the treasurer, risk manager, and controller. The internal auditor reports both to the CFO and to the audit committee of the board of directors. The external auditor and the ethics director also are ultimately responsible to the audit committee.

External Auditors

Nearly every business hires a licensed certified public accounting (CPA) firm to provide an independent annual audit of the firm's financial statements. Through this audit the CPA comes to a conclusion as to whether the firm's financial statements present fairly, in all material respects, the financial position of the firm and results of its activities. In other words, whether the financial numbers are reasonably accurate, accounting principles have been consistently applied year to year and do not significantly distort the firm's performance, and the accounting principles used conform to those generally accepted by the accounting profession. Creditors and investors require independent audits, and the SEC requires publicly traded firms to supply audited financial statements.

 Go to the Web site of CFO magazine at http://www.cfo.com to get a better idea of the responsibilities of a CFO.

The Audit Committee

The audit committee, a powerful subcommittee of the board of directors, has the responsibility of overseeing the accounting function and the preparation of the firm's financial statements. In addition, the audit committee oversees or, if necessary, conducts investigations of significant fraud, theft, or malfeasance in the firm, especially if it is suspected that senior managers in the firm may be involved.

External auditors report directly to the audit committee to help ensure their independence from management. On a day-to-day basis, however, they work closely with the CFO staff. The internal auditor also reports to the audit committee to help ensure his or her independence from management. On a day-to-day basis, however, the internal auditor, like the external auditors, works closely with the CFO staff.

The Compliance and Ethics Director

The SEC requires that all publicly traded companies have a compliance and ethics director who oversees three mandated programs: (1) a compliance program that ensures that the firm complies with federal and state laws and regulations, (2) an ethics program that promotes ethical conduct among executives and employees, and (3) a compliance hotline, which must include a whistleblower program. Like the internal auditor, the compliance director reports to the audit committee to ensure independence from management, though on a day-to-day basis the director typically reports to the firm's legal counsel.

> **BEFORE YOU GO ON**

1. What are the major responsibilities of the CFO?

2. Identify three financial officers who typically report to the CFO and describe their duties.

3. Why does the internal auditor report to both the CFO and the board of directors?

1.4 THE GOAL OF THE FIRM

LEARNING OBJECTIVE

For business owners, it is important to determine the appropriate goal for management decisions. Should the goal be to try to keep costs as low as possible? Or to maximize sales or market share? Or to achieve steady growth and earnings? Let's look at this fundamental question more closely.

What Should Management Maximize?

Suppose you own and manage a pizza parlor. Depending on your preferences and tolerance for risk, you can set any goal for the business that you want. For example, you might have a fear of bankruptcy and losing money. To avoid the risk of bankruptcy, you could focus on keeping your costs as low as possible, paying low wages, avoiding borrowing, advertising minimally, and remaining reluctant to expand the business. In short, you will avoid any action that increases your firm's risk. You will sleep well at night, but you may eat poorly because of meager profits.

Conversely, you could focus on maximizing market share and becoming the largest pizza business in town. Your strategy might include cutting prices to increase sales, borrowing heavily to open new pizza parlors, spending lavishly on advertising, and developing exotic menu items such as *pizza de foie gras*. In the short run, your high-risk, high-growth strategy will have you both eating poorly and sleeping poorly as you push the firm to the edge. In the long run, you will either become very rich or go bankrupt! There must be a better operational goal than either of these extremes.

Why Not Maximize Profits?

One goal for decision making that seems reasonable is *profit maximization*. After all, don't stockholders and business owners want their companies to be profitable? Although profit maximization seems a logical goal for a business, it has some serious drawbacks.

A problem with profit maximization is that it is hard to pin down what is meant by "profit." To the average businessperson, profits are just revenues minus expenses. To an accountant, however, a decision that increases profits under one set of accounting rules can reduce it under another. A second problem is that accounting profits are not necessarily the same as cash flows. For example, many firms recognize revenues at the time a sale is made, which is typically before the cash payment for the sale is received. Ultimately, the owners of a business want cash because only cash can be used to make investments or to buy goods and services.

Yet another problem with profit maximization as a goal is that it does not distinguish between getting a dollar today and getting a dollar some time in the future. In finance, the timing of cash flows is extremely important. For example, the longer you go without paying your credit card balance, the more interest you must pay the bank for the use of the money. The interest accrues because of the *time value of money;* the longer you have access to money, the more you have to pay for it. The time value of money is one of the most important concepts in finance and is the focus of Chapter 5.

Finally, profit maximization ignores the uncertainty, or risk, associated with cash flows. A basic principle of finance is that there is a trade-off between expected return and risk. When given a choice between two investments that have the same expected returns but different risk, most people choose the less risky one. This makes sense because most people do not like bearing risk and, as a result, must be compensated for taking it. The profit maximization goal ignores differences in value caused by differences in risk. We return to the important topics of risk, its measurement, and the trade-off between risk and return in Chapter 6. What is important at this time is that you understand that investors do not like risk and must be compensated for bearing it.

In sum, it appears that profit maximization is not an appropriate goal for a firm because the concept is difficult to define and does not directly account for the firm's cash flows. What we need is a goal that looks at a firm's cash flows and considers both their timing and their riskiness. Fortunately, we have just such a measure: the market value of the firm's stock.

THE TIMING OF CASH FLOWS AFFECTS THEIR VALUE

BUILDING INTUITION

A dollar today is worth more than a dollar in the future because if you have a dollar today, you can invest it and earn interest. For businesses, cash flows can involve large sums of money, and receiving money one day late can cost a great deal. For example, if a bank has $100 billion of consumer loans outstanding and the average annual interest payment is 5 percent, it would cost the bank $13.7 million if every consumer decided to make an interest payment one day later.

THE RISKINESS OF CASH FLOWS AFFECTS THEIR VALUE

BUILDING INTUITION

A risky dollar is worth less than a safe dollar. The reason is that investors do not like risk and must be compensated for bearing it. For example, if two investments have the same return—say 5 percent—most people will prefer the investment with the lower risk. Thus, the more risky an investment's cash flows, the less it is worth.

Maximize the Value of the Firm's Stock

The underlying value of any asset is determined by the cash flows it is expected to generate in the future. This principle holds whether we are buying a bank certificate of deposit, a corporate bond, or an office building. Furthermore, as we will discuss in Chapter 8, when security analysts and investors on Wall Street determine the value of a firm's stock, they consider (1) the size of the expected cash flows, (2) the timing of the cash flows, and (3) the riskiness of the cash flows. Notice that the mechanism for determining stock values overcomes all the cash flow objections we raised with regard to profit maximization as a goal.

Thus, an appropriate goal for management is to maximize the current value of the firm's stock. Maximizing the value of the firm's stock is an unambiguous objective that is easy to measure for a firm whose stock is traded in a public market. We simply look at the market value of the stock in the newspaper or on the Web on a given day to determine the value of the stockholders' shares and whether it went up or down. Publicly traded securities are ideally suited for this task because public markets are wholesale markets with large numbers of buyers and sellers where securities trade near their true value.

What about firms whose stock is not publicly traded, such as private corporations and partnerships? The total value of the stockholder or partner interests in such a business is equal to the value of the owner's equity. *Thus, our goal can be restated for these firms as this: maximize the current value of owner's equity.* The only other restriction is that the entities must be for-profit businesses.

It is important to recognize that maximizing the value of stock, or owner's equity, is not necessarily inconsistent with maximizing the value of claims to the firm's other stakeholders. For example, suppose the managers of a firm decide to delay paying suppliers in an effort to increase the cash flows to the firm's owners. An action such as this is likely to

THE FINANCIAL MANAGER'S GOAL IS TO MAXIMIZE THE VALUE OF THE FIRM'S STOCK

The goal for financial managers is to make decisions that maximize the firm's stock price. By maximizing stock price, management will help maximize stockholders' wealth. To do this, managers must make investment and financing decisions so that the total value of cash inflows exceeds the total value of cash outflows by the greatest possible amount (benefits > costs). Notice that the focus is on maximizing the value of cash flows, not profits.

be met by resistance from suppliers who might increase the prices they charge the firm in order to offset the cost of this policy to them. In the extreme, the suppliers might stop selling their products to the firm, and then both the firm's owners and the suppliers can end up worse off. Consequently, in maximizing the value of the owner's equity, managers make decisions that account for the interests all stakeholders. Quite often, what is best for the firm's owners also benefits other stakeholders.

Can Management Decisions Affect Stock Prices?

An important question is whether management decisions actually affect the firm's stock price. Fortunately, the answer is yes. As noted earlier, a basic principle in finance is that the value of an asset is determined by the future cash flows it is expected to generate. As shown in Exhibit 1.5, a firm's management makes numerous decisions that affect its cash flows. For example, management decides what type of products or services to produce and what productive assets to purchase. Managers also make decisions concerning the mix of debt and equity financing the firm uses, debt collection policies, and policies for paying suppliers, to mention a few examples. In addition, cash flows are affected by how efficient management is in making products, the quality of the products, management's sales and marketing skills, and the firm's investment in research and development for new products. Some of these decisions affect cash flows over the long term, such as the decision to build a new plant, and other decisions have a short-term impact on cash flows, such as launching an advertising campaign.

The firm's managers also must deal with a number of external factors over which they have little or no control, such as economic conditions (recession or expansion), war or peace, and new government regulations. External factors are constantly changing, and management must weigh the impact of these changes and adjust its strategy and decisions accordingly.

EXHIBIT 1.5

Major Factors Affecting Stock Prices

The firm's stock price is affected by a number of factors, and management can control only some of them. Managers exercise little control over external conditions (blue boxes), such as the general economy, although they can closely observe these conditions and make appropriate changes in strategy. Also, managers make many other decisions that directly affect the firm's expected cash flows (green boxes)—and hence the price of the firm's stock.

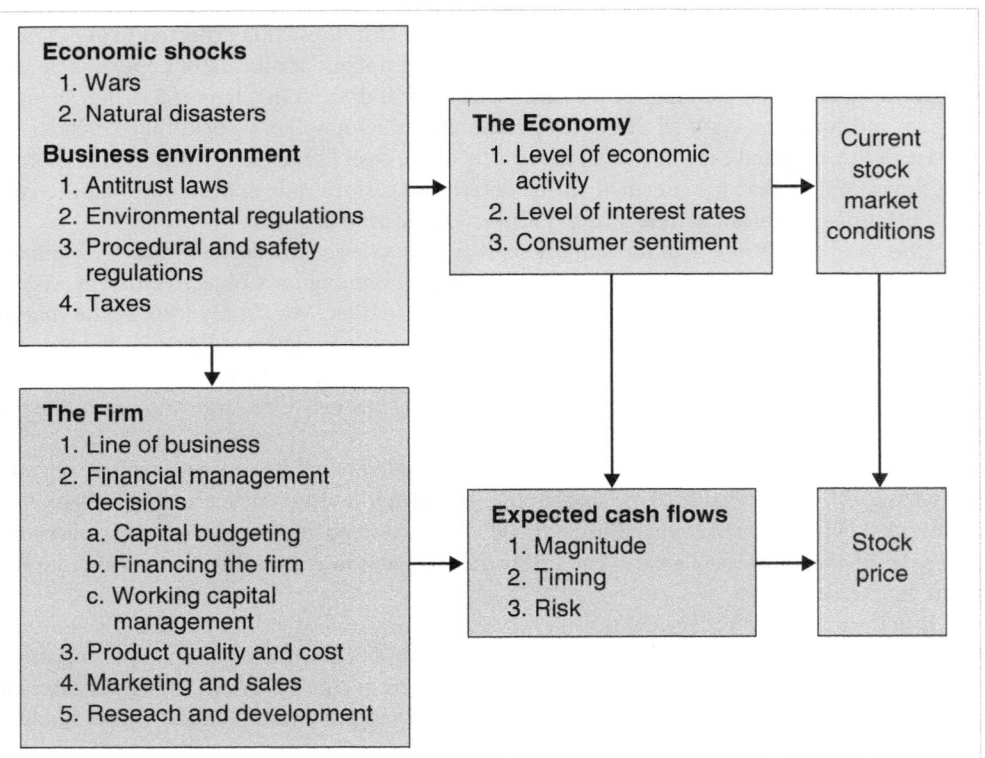

The important point here is that, over time, management makes a series of decisions when executing the firm's strategy that affect the firm's cash flows and, hence, the price of the firm's stock. Firms that have a better business strategy, are more nimble, make better business decisions, and can execute their plans well will have a higher stock price than similar firms that just can't get it right.

> **BEFORE YOU GO ON**

1. Why is profit maximization an unsatisfactory goal for managing a firm?

2. Explain why maximizing the current market price of a firm's stock is an appropriate goal for the firm's management.

3. What is the fundamental determinant of an asset's value?

1.5 AGENCY CONFLICTS: SEPARATION OF OWNERSHIP AND CONTROL

We turn next to an important issue facing stockholders of large corporations: the separation of ownership and control of the firm. In a large corporation, ownership is often spread over a large number of small stockholders who may have little control over management. Managers may therefore make decisions that benefit their own interests rather than those of the stockholders. In contrast, in smaller firms owners and managers are usually one and the same, and there is no conflict of interest between them. As you will see, this self-interested behavior may affect the value of the firm.

LEARNING OBJECTIVE (5)

Ownership and Control

To illustrate, let's continue with our pizza parlor example. As the owner of a pizza parlor, you have decided your goal is to maximize the value of the business, and thereby your ownership interest. There is no conflict of interest in your dual roles as owner and manager because your personal and economic self-interest is tied to the success of the pizza parlor. The restaurant has succeeded because you have worked hard and have focused on customer satisfaction.

Now suppose you decide to hire a college student to manage the restaurant. Will the new manager always act in your interest? Or could the new manager be tempted to give free pizza to friends now and then or, after an exhausting day, leave early rather than spend time cleaning and preparing for the next day? From this example, you can see that once ownership and management are separated, managers may be tempted to pursue goals that are in their own self-interest rather than the interests of the owners.

Agency Relationships

The relationship we have just described between the pizza parlor owner and the student manager is an example of an agency relationship. An agency relationship arises whenever one party, called the *principal*, hires another party, called the *agent*, to perform some service on behalf of the principal. The relationship between stockholders and management is an agency relationship. Legally, managers (who are the agents) have a fiduciary duty to the stockholders (the principals), which means managers are obligated to put the interests of the stockholders above their own. However, in these and all other agency relationships, the potential exists for a conflict of interest between the principal and the agent. These conflicts are called **agency conflicts**.

agency conflicts
conflicts of interest between a principal and an agent

Do Managers Really Want to Maximize Stock Price?

It is not difficult to see how conflicts of interest between managers and stockholders can arise in the corporate setting. In most large corporations, especially those that are publicly traded, there is a significant degree of separation between ownership and management. The largest corporations can have more than one million stockholders. As a practical matter, it is not possible for all of the stockholders to be active in the management of the firm or to individually bear the high cost of monitoring management. The bottom line is that stockholders own the corporation, but managers control the money and have the opportunity to use it for their own benefit.

How might management be tempted to indulge itself and pursue its self-interest? We need not look far for an answer to this question. Corporate excesses are common. High on the list are palatial office buildings, corporate hunting and fishing lodges in exotic places, expensive corporate jets, extravagant expense-account dinners kicked off with bottles of Dom Perignon and washed down with 1953 Margaux—and, of course, a king's compensation package.[3] Besides economic nest feathering, corporate managers may focus on maximizing market share and their industry prestige, job security, and so forth.

Needless to say, these types of activities and spending conflict with the goal of maximizing a firm's stock price. The costs of these activities are called **agency costs**. Agency costs are the costs incurred because of conflicts of interest between a principal and an agent. Examples are the cost of the lavish dinner mentioned earlier and the cost of a corporate jet for executives. However, not all agency costs are frivolous. The cost of hiring an external auditor to certify financial statements is also an agency cost.

agency costs
the costs arising from conflicts of interest between a principal and an agent—for example, between a firm's owners and its management

Aligning the Interests of Management and Stockholders

If the linkage between stockholder and management goals is weak, a number of mechanisms can help to better align the behavior of managers with the goals of stockholders. These include (1) board of directors, (2) management compensation, (3) managerial labor market, (4) other managers, (5) large stockholders, (6) the takeover market, and (7) the legal and regulatory environment.

Board of Directors

A corporation's board of directors has a legal responsibility to represent stockholders' interests. The board's duties include hiring and firing the CEO, setting his or her compensation, and monitoring his or her performance. The board also approves major decisions concerning the firm, such as the firm's annual capital budget or the acquisition of another business. These responsibilities make the board a key mechanism for ensuring that managers' decisions are aligned with those of stockholders.

How well boards actually perform in this role has been questioned in recent years. As an example, critics point out that some boards are unwilling to make hard decisions such as firing the CEO when a firm performs poorly. Other people believe that a lack of independence from management is a reason that boards are not as effective as they might be. For example, the CEO often chairs the board of directors. This dual position can give the CEO undue influence over the board, as the chairperson sets the agenda for and chairs board meetings, appoints committees, and controls the flow of information to the board.

Management Compensation

The most effective means of aligning the interests of managers with those of stockholders is a well-designed compensation (pay) package that rewards managers when they do what stockholders want them to do and penalizes them when they do not. This type of plan is effective because a manager will quickly internalize the benefits and costs of making good and bad decisions and, thus, will be more likely to make the decisions that stockholders want. Therefore, there is no need for some outside monitor, such as the board of directors, to try to figure out whether the managers are making the right decisions. The information that outside monitors have is not as good as the managers' information, so these outside monitors are always at a disadvantage in trying to determine whether a manager is acting in the interest of stockholders.

---

[3] A favorite premeal "quaffing" champagne of young investment bankers on Wall Street is Dom Perignon, known as the "Domer," which is priced in the range of $250 a bottle. Senior partners who are more genteel are reported to favor a 1953 Margaux, a French Bordeaux wine from Château Margaux; 1953 is considered a stellar vintage year, and Margaux 1953 is an excellent but very pricey (about $1,600 per bottle in 2012) choice.

Most corporations have management compensation plans that tie compensation to the performance of the firm. The idea behind these plans is that if compensation is sensitive to the performance of the firm, managers will have greater incentives to make decisions that increase the stockholders' wealth. Although these incentive plans vary widely, they usually include (1) a base salary, (2) a bonus based on accounting performance, and (3) some compensation that is tied to the firm's stock price.[4] The base salary ensures the executive of receiving some minimum compensation as long as he or she remains with the firm, and the bonus and stock price–based compensation are designed to align the manager's incentives with those of the stockholders. The trick in designing such a program is to choose the right mix of these three components so that the manager has the right incentives and the overall package is sufficiently appealing to attract and retain high-quality managers at the lowest possible cost.

Managerial Labor Market

The managerial labor market also provides managers with incentives to act in the interests of stockholders. Firms that have a history of poor performance or a reputation for "shady operations" or unethical behavior have difficulty hiring top managerial talent. Individuals who are top performers have better alternatives than to work for such firms. Therefore, to the extent that managers want to attract high-quality people, the labor market provides incentives to run a good company.

Furthermore, studies show that executives who "manage" firms into bankruptcy or are convicted of white-collar crimes can rarely secure equivalent positions after being fired for poor performance or convicted for criminal behavior. Thus, the penalty for extremely poor performance or a criminal conviction is a significant reduction in the manager's lifetime earnings potential. Managers know this, and the fear of such consequences helps keep them working hard and honestly.[5]

Other Managers

Competition among managers within firms also helps provide incentives for management to act in the interests of stockholders. Managers compete to attain the CEO position and in doing so try to attract the board of directors' attention by acting in the stockholders' interests. Furthermore, even when a manager becomes CEO, he or she is always looking over his or her shoulder because other managers covet that job.

Large Stockholders

All stockholders have an interest in providing managers with incentives to maximize stockholder value. However, as we noted earlier, most stockholders own too few shares to make it worthwhile for them to actively monitor managers. Only large stockholders, those with a significant investment in the firm, have enough money at stake and enough power to make it worthwhile for them to actively monitor managers and to try to influence their decisions. For firms that are publicly traded, many of the large stockholders are institutional investors, such as mutual funds or large commercial banks.

The Takeover Market

The market for takeovers provides incentives for managers to act in the interests of stockholders. When a firm performs poorly because management is doing a poor job, an opportunity arises for astute investors, so-called corporate raiders, to make money by buying the company at a price that reflects its poor performance and replacing the current managers with a top-flight management team. If the investors have evaluated the situation correctly, the firm will soon be transformed into a strong performer, its stock price will increase, and investors can sell their stock for a significant profit. The possibility that a firm might be discovered by corporate raiders provides incentives for management to perform well.

---

[4]This component, which may include stock options, will increase and decrease with the stock price.

[5]Nonquantifiable costs of convictions for crimes are the perpetrators' personal embarrassment and the embarrassment of their families and the effect it may have on their lives. On average, the overall cost of such convictions is higher than even that suggested by the labor market argument.

The Legal and Regulatory Environment

Finally, the laws and regulations that firms must adhere to limit the ability of managers to make decisions that harm the interests of stockholders. An example is federal and state statutes that make it illegal for managers to steal corporate assets. Similarly, regulatory reforms such as the Sarbanes-Oxley Act, discussed next, limit the ability of managers to mislead stockholders.

Sarbanes-Oxley and Other Regulatory Reforms

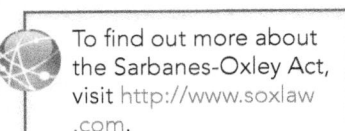

To find out more about the Sarbanes-Oxley Act, visit http://www.soxlaw .com.

Managers of public firms in the United States have long been required to make audited financial statements available to investors that show how their firms have been performing, what their assets are, and how those assets have been financed. Prior to 1933, these disclosure requirements were specified by the individual states in which firms were incorporated. Since the passage of the Securities Act of 1933, also known as the *Truth in Securities Act*, these requirements have been standardized throughout the country. They have evolved to the point at which financial reports must adhere to the Generally Accepted Accounting Principles (GAAP), which are discussed in Chapter 3.

With the longstanding disclosure requirements for public firms, many investors during the latter part of the 1900s were comfortable with the quality of corporate financial statements. However, a series of accounting scandals and ethical lapses by corporate officers shocked the nation in the early years of the twenty-first century. A case in point was WorldCom's bankruptcy filing in 2002 and the admission that its officers had "cooked the books" by misstating $7.2 billion of expenses, which allowed WorldCom to report profits when the firm had actually lost money. The accounting fraud at WorldCom followed similar scandals at Enron, Global Crossing, Tyco, and elsewhere. These scandals—and the resulting losses to stockholders—led to a set of far-reaching regulatory reforms passed by Congress in 2002.[6] The most significant reform measure to date is the Sarbanes-Oxley Act of 2002, which focuses on (1) reducing agency costs in corporations, (2) restoring ethical conduct within the business sector, and (3) improving the integrity of accounting reporting system within firms.

Overall, the new regulations require all public corporations to implement five overarching strategies. (Private corporations and partnerships are not required to implement these measures.)

1. **Ensure greater board independence.** Firms must restructure their boards so that the majority of the members are outside directors. Furthermore, it is recommended that the positions of chair and CEO be separated. Finally, Sarbanes-Oxley makes it clear that board members have a fiduciary responsibility to represent and act in the interest of stockholders, and board members who fail to meet their fiduciary duty can be fined and receive jail sentences.

2. **Establish internal accounting controls.** Firms must establish internal accounting control systems to protect the integrity of the accounting systems and safeguard the firms' assets. The internal controls are intended to improve the reliability of accounting data and the quality of financial reports and to reduce the likelihood that individuals within the firm engage in accounting fraud.

3. **Establish compliance programs.** Firms must establish corporate compliance programs that ensure that they|comply with important federal and state regulations. For example, a compliance program would document whether a firm's truck drivers complied with all federal and state truck and driver safety regulations, such as the number of hours one can drive during the day and the gross highway weight of the truck.

4. **Establish an ethics program.** Firms must establish ethics programs that monitor the ethical conduct of employees and executives through a compliance hotline, which must include a whistleblower protection provision. The intent is to create an ethical work environment so that employees will know what is expected of them and their relationships with customers, suppliers, and other stakeholders.

5. **Expand the audit committee's oversight powers.** The external auditor, the internal auditor, and the compliance/ethics officer owe their ultimate legal responsibilities to the audit committee, not to the firm. In addition, the audit committee has the unconditional power

---

[6]The major laws passed by Congress in this area in 2002 were the Public Accounting Reform and Investor Protection Act and the Sarbanes-Oxley Act.

EXHIBIT 1.6 **Corporate Governance Regulations Designed to Reduce Agency Costs**

Recent regulatory changes that are designed to reduce agency costs. The most important changes resulted from the Sarbanes-Oxley Act, passed by Congress in 2002. The act was aimed at reducing agency costs, promoting ethical conduct, and improving the integrity of accounting reporting systems.

Board of Directors
- Board has a fiduciary responsibility to represent the best interest of the firm's owners.
- Majority of the board must be outside independent directors.
- Firm is required to have a code of ethics, which has to be approved by the board.
- Firm must establish an ethics program that has a complaint hotline and a whistleblower protection provision that is approved by the board.
- Separation of chairman and CEO positions is recommended.
- Board memebers can be fined or receive jail sentences if they fail to fulfill their fiduciary responsibilities.

Audit Committee
- External auditor, internal auditor, and compliance officer's fiduciary (legal) responsibilities are to the audit committee.
- Audit committee approves the hiring, firing, and fees paid to external auditors.
- CEO and CFO must certify financial statements.
- All audit committee members must be outside independent directors.
- One member must be a financial expert.

External Auditor
- Lead partner must change every five years.
- There are limits on consulting (nonaudit) services that external auditors can provide.

Sources: Sarbanes-Oxley Act, Public Accounting Reform and Investor Protection Act, and NYSE and NASDAQ new listing requirements.

to probe and question any person in the firm, including the CEO, regarding any matter that might materially impact the firm or its financial statements.

Exhibit 1.6 summarizes some of the recent regulatory changes that are designed to reduce agency costs.

A noticeable shift has occurred in the behavior of board members and management since the Sarbanes-Oxley Act was passed. Boards appear much more serious about monitoring firms' performance and ratifying important decisions by management. Audit committees, with their new independence and investigative powers, are providing greater oversight over the preparation of financial statements. Stronger internal accounting control systems, compliance programs, and ethics programs are improving the integrity of accounting systems and reducing the likelihood of fraud and other illegal activities. Thus, the Sarbanes-Oxley Act does appear to be having an effect. The major complaint from business has been the cost of compliance.

> **BEFORE YOU GO ON**

1. What are agency conflicts?

2. What are corporate raiders?

3. List the three main objectives of the Sarbanes-Oxley Act.

1.6 THE IMPORTANCE OF ETHICS IN BUSINESS

We have just seen that Congress included ethics program requirements in the Sarbanes-Oxley Act. Why are ethics important to business?

LEARNING OBJECTIVE 6

Business Ethics

The term *ethics* describes a society's ideas about what actions are right and wrong. Ethical values are not moral absolutes, and they can and do vary across societies. Regardless of cultural differences, however, if we think about it, all of us would probably prefer to live in a world where people behave ethically—where people try to do what is right.

In our society, ethical rules include considering the impact of our actions on others, being willing to sometimes put the interests of others ahead of our own interests, and realizing that we must follow the same rules we expect others to follow. The golden rule—"Do unto others as you would have done unto you"—is an example of a widely accepted ethical norm.[7]

Are Business Ethics Different from Everyday Ethics?

The site http://www.web-miner.com/busethics.htm offers a wide range of articles on the role of ethics in business today.

Perhaps business is a dog-eat-dog world where ethics do not matter. People who take this point of view link business ethics to the "ethics of the poker game" and not to the ethics of everyday morality. Poker players, they suggest, must practice cunning deception and must conceal their strengths and their intentions. After all, they are playing the game to win. How far does one go to win?

In 2002, investors learned the hard way about a number of firms that had been behaving according to the ethics of the poker game: cunning deception and concealment of information were the order of the day at WorldCom, Enron, Global Crossing, Tyco, and a host of other firms. The market's reaction to the behavior of these firms was to wipe out $2.3 trillion of stockholder value.

We believe that those who argue that ethics do not matter in business are mistaken. Indeed, most academic studies on the topic suggest that traditions of morality are very relevant to business and to financial markets in particular. The reasons are practical as well as ethical. Corruption in business creates inefficiencies in an economy, inhibits the growth of capital markets, and slows a country's rate of economic growth.

For example, as Russia made the transition to a market economy, it had a difficult time establishing a stock market and attracting foreign investment. The reason was a simple one. Corruption was rampant in local government and in business. Contractual agreements were not enforceable, and there was no reliable financial information about Russian companies. Not until the mid-1990s did some Russian companies begin to display enough financial transparency to attract investment capital.[8]

Types of Ethical Conflicts in Business

We turn next to a consideration of the ethical problems that arise in business dealings. Most problems involve three related areas: agency costs, conflicts of interest, and informational asymmetry.

Agency Costs

As we discussed earlier in this chapter, many relationships in business are agency relationships. Agents can be bound both legally and ethically to act in the interest of the principal. Financial managers have agency obligations to act honestly and to see that subordinates act honestly with respect to financial transactions. Financial managers, when they are guilty of misconduct, present a serious danger to stockholder wealth. A product recall or environmental offense may cause temporary declines in stock prices. However, revelations of dishonesty, deception, and fraud in financial matters can have a huge and longer-lasting impact on the stock price. If the dishonesty is flagrant, the firm may go bankrupt, as we saw with the bankruptcies of Enron and WorldCom.

Conflicts of Interest

Conflicts of interest often arise in agency relationships. A conflict of interest in such a situation can arise when the agent's interests are different from those of the principal. For example, suppose you're interested in buying a house and a local real estate agent is helping you find the home of your dreams. As it turns out, the dream house is one for which your agent is also the listing agent. Your agent has a conflict of interest because her professional obligation to help you find the right house at a fair price conflicts with her professional obligation to get the highest price possible for the client whose house she has listed.

---

[7]The golden rule can be stated in a number of ways. One version, in the Gospel of Matthew, states, "In everything do to others as you would have them do to you." A less noble version you occasionally hear in business is "He who has the gold makes the rules."

[8]In economics, *transparency* refers to openness and access to information.

Organizations can be either principals or agents and, hence, can be parties to conflicts of interest. In the past, for example, many large accounting firms provided both consulting services and audits for corporations. This dual function may compromise the independence and objectivity of the audit opinion, even though the work is done by different parts of the firm. For example, if consulting fees from an audit client become a large source of income, is the auditing firm less likely to render an adverse audit opinion and thereby risk losing the consulting business?

Conflicts of interest are typically resolved in one of two ways. Sometimes complete disclosure is sufficient. Thus, in real estate transactions, it is not unusual for the same lawyer or realtor to represent both the buyer and the seller. This practice is not considered unethical as long as both sides are aware of the fact and give their consent. Alternatively, the conflicted party can withdraw from serving the interests of one of the parties. Sometimes the law mandates this solution. For example, public accounting firms are not permitted to provide certain types of consulting services to their audit clients.

Information Asymmetry

Information asymmetry occurs when one party in a business transaction has information that is unavailable to the other parties in the transaction. The existence of information asymmetry in business relationships is commonplace. For example, suppose you decide to sell your 10-year-old car. You know much more about the real condition of the car than does the prospective buyer. The ethical issue is this: How much should you tell the prospective buyer? In other words, to what extent is the party with the information advantage obligated to reduce the amount of information asymmetry?

Society imposes both market-based and legal solutions for transactional information asymmetries. Consider the prospective car buyer in the previous example. You can be reasonably sure that the buyer understands that he or she has less information about the car's condition than the seller and, as a result, will pay a lower price for the vehicle. Conversely, sellers who certify or provide a warranty with respect to the condition of the vehicle reduce the concerns that buyers have about information asymmetries and therefore tend to receive higher prices.

Legal solutions often require sellers to disclose material facts to buyers or prohibit trading on information that is not widely available. For example, when you sell a car, you are required to disclose to the seller whether it has been in an accident and whether the odometer has been altered. Similarly, in many states home sellers must disclose if they are aware of any major defects in their home. In the investment world, the trading of stocks based on material inside information (e.g., which is not available to the public) has been made illegal in an effort to create a "level playing field" for all investors.

information asymmetry
the situation in which one party in a business transaction has information that is unavailable to the other parties in the transaction

The Importance of an Ethical Business Culture

Some economists have noted that the legal system and market forces impose substantial costs on individuals and institutions that engage in unethical behavior. As a result, these forces provide important incentives that foster ethical behavior in the business community. The incentives include financial losses, legal fines, jail time, and bankruptcy. Ethicists argue, however, that laws and market forces are not enough. For example, the financial sector is one of the most heavily regulated areas of the U.S. economy. Yet despite heavy regulation, the sector has a long and rich history of financial scandals.

In addition to laws and market forces, then, it is important to create an ethical culture in the firm. Why is this important? An ethical business culture means that people have a set of principles—a moral compass, so to speak—that help them identify moral issues and make ethical judgments without being told what to do. The culture has a powerful influence on the way people behave and the way they make decisions.

The people at the top of a company determine whether or not the culture of that company is ethical. At Enron, for example, top officers promoted a culture of aggressive risk taking and willingness, at times, to cross over ethical and even legal lines. The motto "do no evil" was adopted by Google's founders before they took the firm public in 2004.

More than likely, you will be confronted with ethical issues during your professional career. Knowing how to identify and deal with ethical issues is an important part of your professional "survival kit." Exhibit 1.7 presents a framework for making ethical judgments.

EXHIBIT 1.7   **A Framework for the Analysis of Ethical Conflicts**

Dealing with ethical conflicts is an inescapable part of professional life for most people. An analytical framework can be helpful in understanding and resolving such conflicts.

The first step toward ethical behavior is to recognize that you face a moral issue. In general, if your actions or decisions will cause harm to others, you are facing a moral issue. When you find yourself in this position, you might ask yourself the following questions:

1. What does the law require? When in doubt, consult the legal department.

2. What do your role-related obligations require? What is your station, and what are its duties? If you are a member of a profession, what does the code of conduct of your profession say you should do in these circumstances?

3. Are you an agent employed on behalf of another in these circumstances? If so, what are the interests and desires of the employing party?

4. Are the interests of the stockholders materially affected? Your obligation is to represent the best interests of the firm's owners.

5. Do you have a conflict of interest? Will full diclosure of the conflict be sufficient? If not, you must determine what interest has priority.

6. Are you abusing an information asymmetry? Is your use of the information asymmetry fair? It probably is fair if you would make the same decision if the roles of the parties were reversed or if you would publicly advocate the principle behind your decision.

7. Would you be willing to have your action and all the reasons that motivated it reported in the *Wall Street Journal*?

Serious Consequences

In recent years the "rules" have changed, and the cost of ethical mistakes can be extremely high. In the past, the business community and legal authorities often dismissed corporate scandals as a "few rotten apples" in an otherwise sound barrel. This is no longer true today. In 2005, for instance, Bernard J. Ebbers, the 63-year-old CEO of WorldCom, was found guilty of fraud and theft and was sentenced to 25 years in prison. Judge Barbara S. Jones, acknowledging that Ebbers would probably serve the rest of his days in jail, said, "I find a sentence of anything less would not reflect the seriousness of the crime." In the past, sentences for white-collar crimes were minimal; even for serious crimes, there often was no jail time at all. Clearly, business ethics is a topic of high interest and increasing importance in the business community, and it is a topic that will be discussed throughout this book.

> **BEFORE YOU GO ON**

1. What is a conflict of interest in a business setting?

2. How would you define an ethical business culture?

SUMMARY OF **Learning Objectives**

1 Identify the key financial decisions facing the financial manager of any business.

The financial manager faces three basic decisions: (1) which productive assets the firm should buy (capital budgeting decisions), (2) how the firm should finance the productive assets purchased (financing decisions), and (3) how the firm should manage its day-to-day financial activities (working capital decisions). The financial manager should make these decisions in a way that maximizes the current value of the firm's stock.

2 Identify common forms of business organization in the United States and their respective strengths and weaknesses.

Businesses in the United States are commonly organized as a sole proprietorship, a general or limited partnership, a corporation, or a limited liability partnership or company. Most large firms elect to organize as C-corporations because of the ease of raising money; the major disadvantage is double taxation. Smaller companies tend to organize as sole proprietorships or partnerships. The advantages of these forms of organization include ease of formation and taxation at the personal income tax rate. The major disadvantage is the owners' unlimited personal liability. Limited liability partnerships and companies provide owners who makes the business decisions with limited personal liability.

3 Describe the typical organization of the financial function in a large corporation.

In a large corporation, the financial manager generally has the rank of vice president and goes by the title of chief financial officer. The CFO reports directly to the firm's CEO. Positions reporting directly to the CFO generally include the treasurer, the risk manager, the controller, and the internal auditor. The audit committee of the board of directors is also important in the financial function. The committee hires the external auditor for the firm, and the internal auditor, external auditor, and compliance officer all report to the audit committee.

4 **Explain why maximizing the current value of the firm's stock is the appropriate goal for management.**

Maximizing stock value is an appropriate goal because it forces management to focus on decisions that will generate the greatest amount of wealth for stockholders. Since the value of a share of stock (or any asset) is determined by its cash flows, management's decisions must consider the size of the cash flow (larger is better), the timing of the cash flow (sooner is better), and the riskiness of the cash flow (given equal returns, lower risk is better).

5 **Discuss how agency conflicts affect the goal of maximizing stockholder value.**

In most large corporations, there is a significant degree of separation between management and ownership. As a result, stockholders have little control over corporate managers, and management may thus be tempted to pursue its own self-interest rather than maximizing the value of the owners' stock. The resulting conflicts give rise to agency costs. Ways of reducing agency costs include developing compensation agreements that link employee compensation to the firm's performance and having independent boards of directors monitor management.

6 **Explain why ethics is an appropriate topic in the study of corporate finance.**

If we lived in a world without ethical norms, we would soon discover that it would be difficult to do business. As a practical matter, the law and market forces provide important incentives that foster ethical behavior in the business community, but they are not enough to ensure ethical behavior. An ethical culture is also needed. In an ethical culture, people have a set of moral principles—a moral compass—that helps them identify ethical issues and make ethical judgments without being told what to do.

Self-Study Problems

1.1 Give an example of a financing decision and a capital budgeting decision.

1.2 What is the appropriate decision criterion for financial managers to use when selecting a capital project?

1.3 What are some of the things that managers do to manage a firm's working capital?

1.4 Which one of the following characteristics does not pertain to corporations?
   a. Can enter into contracts.
   b. Can borrow money.
   c. Are the easiest type of business to form.
   d. Can be sued.
   e. Can own stock in other companies.

1.5 What are typically the main components of an executive compensation package?

Solutions to Self-Study Problems

1.1 Financing decisions determine how a firm will raise capital. Examples of financing decisions include the decision to borrow from a bank or issue debt in the public capital markets. Capital budgeting involves deciding which productive assets the firm invests in, such as buying a new plant or investing in the renovation of an existing facility.

1.2 Financial managers should select a capital project only if the value of the project's expected future cash flows exceeds the cost of the project. In other words, managers should only make investments that will increase firm value, and thus increase the stockholders' wealth.

1.3 Working capital management is the day-to-day management of a firm's short-term assets and liabilities. Working capital can be managed by maintaining the optimal level of inventory, managing receivables and payables, deciding to whom the firm should extend credit, and making appropriate investments with excess cash.

1.4 The answer that does *not* pertain to corporations is: c. Are the easiest type of business to form.

1.5 The three main components of an executive compensation package are: base salary, bonus based on accounting performance, and compensation tied to the firm's stock price.

Critical Thinking Questions

1.1 Describe the cash flows between a firm and its stakeholders.

1.2 What are the three fundamental decisions the finance team is concerned with, and how do they affect the firm's balance sheet?

1.3 What is the difference between stockholders and stakeholders?

1.4 Suppose that a group of accountants wants to start an accounting business. What organizational form would they most likely choose, and why?

1.5 Why would the owners of a business choose to form a corporation even though they will face double taxation?

1.6 Explain why profit maximization is not the best goal for a company. What is a better goal?

1.7 What are some of the external and internal factors that affect a firm's stock price? What is the difference between these two types of factors?

1.8 Identify the sources of agency costs. What are some ways these costs can be controlled in a company?

1.9 What is the Sarbanes-Oxley Act, and what does it focus on? Why does it focus in these areas?

1.10 Give an example of a conflict of interest in a business setting, other than the one involving the real estate agent discussed in the chapter text.

Questions and Problems

BASIC ▶ **1.1** **Capital:** What are the two basic sources of funds for all businesses?

1.2 **Management role:** What is net working capital?

1.3 **Cash flows:** Explain the difference between profitable and unprofitable firms.

1.4 **Management role:** What three major decisions are of most concern to financial managers?

1.5 **Cash flows:** What is the appropriate decision rule for a firm considering undertaking a project? Give a real-life example.

1.6 **Management role:** What is a firm's capital structure, and why is it important?

1.7 **Management role:** What are some of the working capital decisions that a financial manager faces?

1.8 **Organizational form:** What are the common forms of business organization discussed in this chapter?

1.9 **Organizational form:** What are the advantages and disadvantages of a sole proprietorship?

1.10 **Organizational form:** What is a partnership, and what is the biggest disadvantage of this form of business organization? How can this disadvantage be avoided?

1.11 **Organizational form:** Who are the owners of a corporation, and how is their ownership represented?

1.12 **Organizational form:** Explain what is meant by stockholders' limited liability.

1.13 **Organizational form:** What is double taxation?

1.14 **Organizational form:** What is the form of business organization taken by most large companies and why?

1.15 **Finance function:** What is the primary responsibility of the board of directors in a corporation?

1.16 **Finance function:** All public companies must hire a certified public accounting firm to perform an independent audit of their financial statements. What exactly does the term *audit* mean?

1.17 **Firm's goal:** What are some of the drawbacks to setting profit maximization as the main goal of a company?

1.18 **Firm's goal:** What is the appropriate goal of financial managers? How do managers' decisions affect how successful the firm is in achieving this goal?

1.19 **Firm's goal:** What are the major factors that affect a firm's stock price?

1.20 **Agency conflicts:** What is an agency relationship, and what is an agency conflict? How can agency conflicts be reduced in a corporation?

1.21 **Firm's goal:** What can happen if a firm is poorly managed and its stock price falls substantially below its maximum?

1.22 **Agency conflicts:** What are some of the regulations that pertain to boards of directors that were put in place to reduce agency conflicts?

1.23 **Business ethics:** How can a lack of business ethics negatively affect the performance of an economy? Give an example.

1.24 **Agency conflicts:** What are some ways to resolve a conflict of interest?

1.25 Information asymmetry: Describe what an information asymmetry is in a business transaction. Explain how the inequity associated with an information asymmetry might be, at least partially, solved through the market for goods or services.

1.26 Business ethics: What ethical conflict does insider trading present?

Sample Test Problems

1.1 Why is value maximization superior to profit maximization as a goal for management?

1.2 The major advantage of debt financing is:
   a. It allows a firm to use creditors' money.
   b. Interest payments are more predictable than dividend payments.
   c. Interest payments are not required when a firm is not doing well.
   d. Interest payments are tax deductible.

1.3 Identify three fundamental decisions that a financial manager makes.

1.4 What are agency costs? Explain.

1.5 Identify four of the seven mechanisms that can help better align the goals of managers with those of stockholders.

2

The Financial System and the Level of Interest Rates

Alex Wong/Getty Images, Inc.

HON. BEN S. BERNANKE

CHAPTER TWO

Learning Objectives

1. Describe the role of the financial system in the economy and the two basic ways in which money flows through the system.

2. Discuss direct financing and the important role that investment banks play in this process.

3. Describe the primary, secondary, and money markets, explaining the special importance of secondary and money markets to business organizations.

4. Explain what an efficient market is and why market efficiency is important to financial managers.

5. Explain how financial institutions serve the needs of consumers and small businesses.

6. Compute the nominal and the real rates of interest, differentiating between them.

One of the most important institutional players in the financial system is the Federal Reserve System (called the Fed). In fact, it is sometimes said that the chairman of the Federal Reserve Board is the second most powerful person in the United States—second only to the president. Where does all of this power come from?

It comes from the Fed's role as the nation's central bank—the institution that controls the money supply. The Fed "manages" the nation's economy by conducting monetary policy, which affects how much money is available in the economy. One way it does this is by setting a target short-term interest rate at which large money center banks lend to each other (called the federal funds rate) and by buying and selling Treasury and federal agency securities to achieve this rate. Increases in the money supply put downward pressure on short-term interest rates. Over time, this can lead to increases in the level of economic activity, along with higher inflation. Conversely, decreases in the money supply put upward pressure on short-term interest rates. This can lead to a lower level of economic activity and lower inflation.

Small wonder that when the Fed speaks, everyone stops and listens. Ben Bernanke, the current Fed chairman, described the effects of Fed announcements on the stock market as follows:

> Normally, the [Federal Open Market Committee, or] FOMC, the monetary policymaking arm of the Federal Reserve, announces its interest rate decisions at around 2:15 P.M. following each of its eight regularly scheduled meetings each year. An air of expectation reigns in financial markets in the few

minutes before the announcement. If you happen to have access to a monitor that tracks key market indexes, at 2:15 P.M. on an announcement day you can watch those indexes quiver as if trying to digest the information in the rate decision and the FOMC's accompanying statement of explanation. Then the black line representing each market index moves quickly up or down, and the markets have priced the FOMC action into the aggregate values of U.S. equities, bonds, and other assets.[1]

As you can see, the Fed's policy actions are transmitted quickly through the financial system and ultimately affect the economic well-being of nearly all consumers and businesses. This chapter provides a basic explanation of how the financial system works and discusses interest rates and their movements.

CHAPTER PREVIEW

Chapter 1 identified three kinds of decisions that financial managers make: *capital budgeting decisions*, which concern the purchase of productive assets; *financing decisions*, which concern how assets will be paid for; and *working capital management decisions*, which concern day-to-day financial matters. In making capital budgeting decisions, financial managers should select projects whose cash flows increase the value of the firm. The financial models used to evaluate these projects require an understanding of the concepts covered in this chapter. In making financing decisions, financial managers want to obtain capital at the lowest possible cost, which means that they need to understand how financial markets work and what financing alternatives are available. Finally, working capital management is concerned with whether a firm has enough money to pay its bills and how it invests its spare cash to earn interest. Making decisions in these areas requires knowledge of

the financial system and what determines the level of *interest* rates.

This chapter provides an overview of key concepts, many of which we will revisit in later chapters. We begin the chapter by looking at how the financial system facilitates the transfer of money from those who have it to those who need it. Then we describe direct financing, through which businesses finance themselves by issuing debt and equity, and the important role that investment banks play in the process. Next we describe different types of financial markets that are in the financial system and discuss the concept of market efficiency. We then examine indirect financing and the services that financial institutions provide large and small businesses. Finally, we discuss the factors that determine the general level of interest rates in the economy and explain how interest rates vary over the business cycle.

2.1 THE FINANCIAL SYSTEM

LEARNING OBJECTIVE ①

The financial system consists of financial markets and financial institutions. *Financial market* is a general term that includes a number of different types of markets for the creation and exchange of financial assets, such as stocks and bonds. *Financial institutions* are firms such as commercial banks, credit unions, insurance companies, pension funds, and finance companies that provide financial services to the economy. The distinguishing feature of financial institutions is that they invest their funds in **financial assets**, such as business loans, stocks, and bonds, rather than **real assets**, such as plant and equipment.

The critical role of the financial system in the economy is to gather money from people, businesses, and governments with surplus funds to invest and channel that money to those who need it. Businesses need money to invest in new productive assets to expand their operations

financial assets
assets that are claims on the cash flows from other assets; business loans, stocks, and bonds are financial assets

real assets
nonfinancial assets such as plant and equipment; productive assets are real assets; many financial assets are claims on cash flows from real assets

[1] Ben S. Bernanke, "Remarks at the Fall 2003 Banking and Finance Lecture," Widener University, Chester, Pennsylvania, October 2, 2003.

and increase the firm's cash flow, which should increase the value of the firm. Consumers, too, need money, which they use to purchase things such as homes, cars, and boats—or to pay college tuition bills. Some of the players in the financial system are household names such as the New York Stock Exchange, Bank of America, Goldman Sachs, and State Farm Insurance. Others are lesser-known but important firms, such as the multinational giant AIG.

A well-developed financial system is critical for the operation of a complex industrial economy such as that of the United States. Highly industrialized countries cannot function without a competitive and sound financial system that efficiently gathers money and channels it into the best investment opportunities. Let's look at a simple example to illustrate how the financial system channels money to businesses.

The Financial System at Work

Suppose that, at the beginning of the school year, you receive a $10,000 student loan to help pay your expenses for the year, but you need only $5,000 for the first semester. You wisely decide to invest the remaining $5,000 to earn some interest income. After shopping at several banks near campus, you decide that the best deal is a $5,000 consumer certificate of deposit (CD) that matures in three months and pays 2 percent interest. (CDs are debt instruments issued by a bank that pay interest and are insured by the federal government.)

The bank pools your money with funds from other CDs and uses this money to make business and consumer loans. In this case, the bank makes a loan to the pizza parlor near campus: $30,000 for five years at a 7 percent interest rate. The bank decides to make the loan because of the pizza parlor's sound credit rating and because it expects the pizza parlor to generate enough cash flows to repay the loan with interest. The pizza parlor owner wants the money to invest in additional real (productive) assets to earn greater profits (cash flows) and thereby increase the value of her business. During the same week, the bank makes loans to other businesses and also rejects a number of loan requests because the borrowers have poor credit ratings or the proposed projects have low rates of return.

From this example, we can draw some important inferences about financial systems:

- If the financial system is *competitive*, the interest rate the bank pays on CDs will be at or near the highest rate that you can earn on a CD of similar maturity and risk. At the same time, the pizza parlor and other businesses will have borrowed at or near the lowest possible interest cost, given their risk class. Competition among banks will drive CD rates up and loan rates down.
- The bank gathers money from you and other consumers in small dollar amounts, aggregates it, and then makes loans in much larger dollar amounts. Saving by consumers in small dollar amounts is the origin of much of the money that funds business loans.
- An important function of the financial system is to direct money to the best investment opportunities in the economy. If the financial system works properly, only business projects with high rates of return and good credit will be financed. Those with low rates of return or poor credit will be rejected. Thus, financial systems contribute to higher production and efficiency in the overall economy.
- Finally, note that the bank has earned a tidy profit from the deal. The bank has borrowed money at 2 percent by selling CDs to consumers and has lent money to the pizza parlor and other businesses at 7 percent. Thus, the bank's gross profit is 5 percent (7 percent − 2 percent = 5 percent), which is the difference between the bank's lending and borrowing rates. Banks earn much of their profits from this *spread* between the lending and borrowing rates.

How Funds Flow through the Financial System

We have seen that the financial system plays a critical role in the economy. The system moves money from *lender-savers* (whose income exceeds their spending) to *borrower-spenders* (whose spending exceeds their income), as shown schematically in Exhibit 2.1. The most important group of lender-savers in the economy are households, but some businesses and many state and local governments at times have excess funds to lend to those who need money. As a group, businesses are the borrower-spenders who borrow the most in the economy, followed by the federal government.

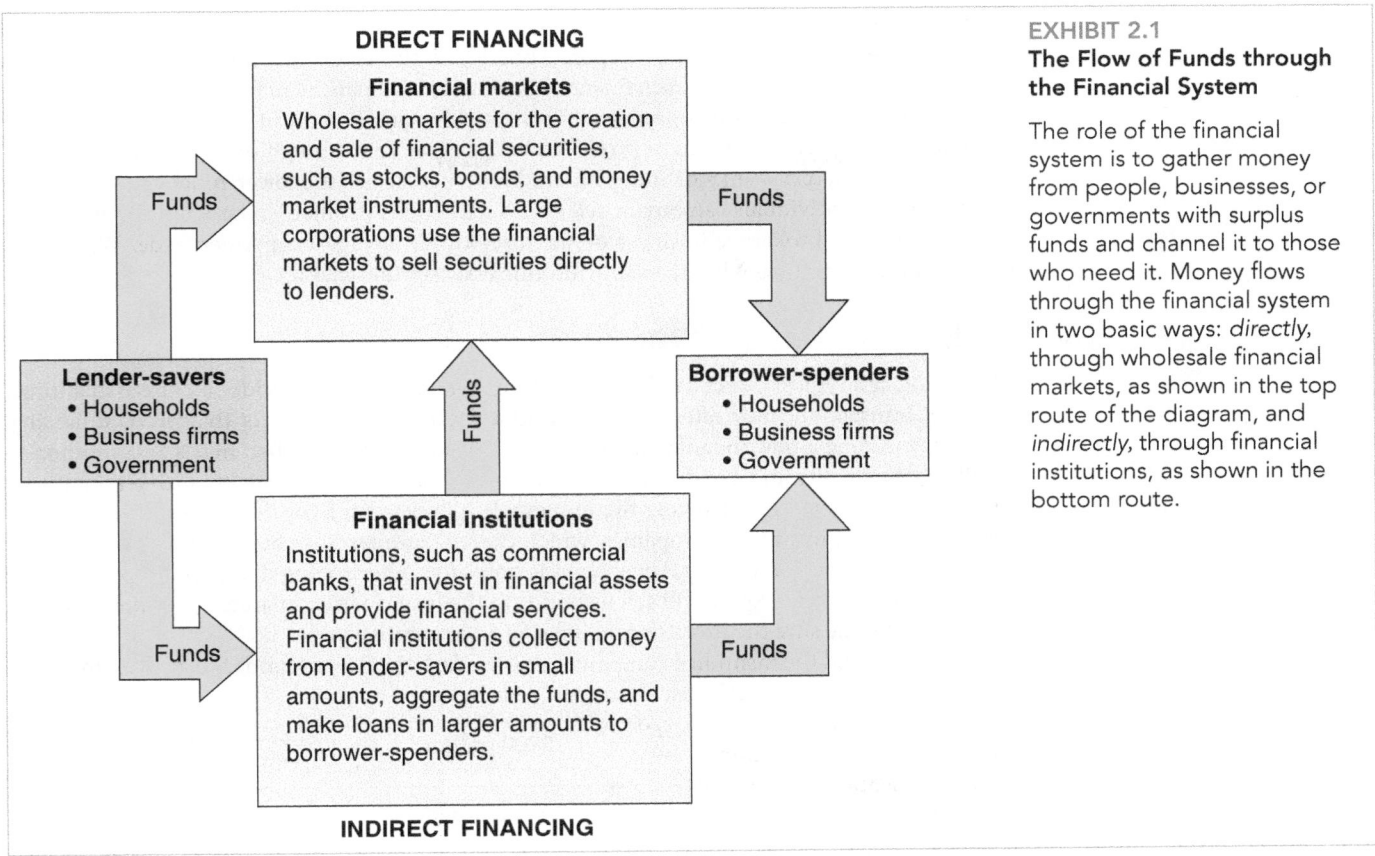

DIRECT FINANCING

Financial markets
Wholesale markets for the creation and sale of financial securities, such as stocks, bonds, and money market instruments. Large corporations use the financial markets to sell securities directly to lenders.

Funds

Funds

Lender-savers
• Households
• Business firms
• Government

Funds

Borrower-spenders
• Households
• Business firms
• Government

Funds

Financial institutions
Institutions, such as commercial banks, that invest in financial assets and provide financial services. Financial institutions collect money from lender-savers in small amounts, aggregate the funds, and make loans in larger amounts to borrower-spenders.

Funds

Funds

INDIRECT FINANCING

EXHIBIT 2.1

The Flow of Funds through the Financial System

The role of the financial system is to gather money from people, businesses, or governments with surplus funds and channel it to those who need it. Money flows through the financial system in two basic ways: *directly*, through wholesale financial markets, as shown in the top route of the diagram, and *indirectly*, through financial institutions, as shown in the bottom route.

The arrows in Exhibit 2.1 show that there are two basic mechanisms by which funds flow through the financial system: (1) funds can flow *directly* through financial markets (the route at the top of the diagram) and (2) funds can flow *indirectly* through financial institutions (the route at the bottom of the diagram). In the following three sections, we look more closely at the direct flow of funds and at the financial markets. After that, we discuss financial institutions and the indirect flow of funds.

> **BEFORE YOU GO ON**

1. What critical economic role does the financial system play in the economy?

2. What are the two basic ways in which funds flow through the financial system from lender-savers to borrower-spenders?

2.2 DIRECT FINANCING

In this section we turn our attention to direct financing, in which funds flow directly through the financial system. In direct transactions, the lender-savers and the borrower-spenders deal directly with one another; borrower-spenders sell securities, such as stocks and bonds, to lender-savers in exchange for money. These securities represent claims on the borrowers' future income or assets. A number of different interchangeable terms are used to refer to securities, including *financial securities*, *financial instruments*, and *financial claims*.

The financial markets in which direct transactions take place are wholesale markets with a typical minimum transaction size of $1 million. For most business firms, these markets provide funds at the lowest possible cost. The major buyers and sellers of securities in the direct financial markets are commercial banks; other financial institutions, such as insurance companies and business finance companies; large corporations; federal, state, and local governments; hedge funds; and some wealthy individuals. It is important to note that financial institutions are

LEARNING OBJECTIVE ❷

major buyers of securities in the direct financial markets. For example, life and casualty insurance companies buy large quantities of corporate bonds and stocks for their investment portfolios. In Exhibit 2.1 the arrow leading from financial institutions to financial markets depicts this flow.

Although few individuals participate in direct financial markets, individuals can gain access to many of the financial products produced in these markets through retail channels at investment or commercial banks or independent brokerage firms (the lower route in Exhibit 2.1). For example, individuals can buy or sell stocks and bonds in small dollar amounts at Bank of America's retail brokerage business or the discount brokerage firm Ameritrade. We discuss indirect financing through financial institutions later in this chapter.

A Direct Market Transaction

Let's look at a typical direct market transaction. When managers decide to engage in a direct market transaction, they often have in mind a specific capital project that needs financing, such as building a new manufacturing facility. Suppose that Apple Inc. needs $200 million to build a new facility and decides to fund it by selling long-term bonds with a 15-year maturity (Apple is planning on borrowing the money). While searching for the financing, Apple contacts a group of insurance companies, which express an interest in buying Apple's bonds. The insurance companies will buy Apple's bonds only after determining that they are priced fairly for their level of risk. Apple will sell its bonds to the insurance companies only after shopping the market to be sure the investors are offering a competitive price.

If Apple and the insurance companies strike a deal, the flow of funds between them will be as shown below:

Apple sells its bonds to the insurance group for $200 million and gets the use of the money for 15 years. For Apple, the bonds are a liability, and it pays the insurance companies (bondholders) interest for use of the money. For the insurance companies, the bonds are an asset that earns interest.

Investment Banks and Direct Financing

Two important participants in the direct financial markets are investment banks and money center banks. **Investment banks** specialize in helping companies sell new debt or equity, although they can also provide other services, such as the broker and dealer services discussed later in this chapter and traditional banking services. **Money center banks** are large commercial banks that provide both traditional and investment banking services throughout the world.

Historically, there was a clear distinction between the activities of investment and money center banks. After the Great Depression (1929–1933) commercial banks were prohibited from engaging in investment banking activities because it was believed that these activities encouraged them to take too many risks. However, this prohibition ended in 1999 with passage of the Financial Services Modernization Act, and then the major money center banks, such as Bank of America, JPMorgan Chase, and Citigroup, started providing investment banking services. Furthermore, after the financial meltdown in 2008, the remaining major independent investment banks, specifically Goldman Sachs and Morgan Stanley, converted themselves into traditional bank holding companies to qualify for government assistance. While there are still small investment banks that focus only on investment banking activities, the large investment and commercial banks are becoming increasingly alike.

Origination

Origination is the process of preparing a security issue for sale. During the origination phase, the investment banker may help the client company determine the feasibility of the project being funded and the amount of capital that needs to be raised. Once this is done, the investment banker helps secure a credit rating, if needed, determines the sale date, obtains legal clearances to sell the securities, and gets the securities printed. If securities are to be sold in the public markets, the issuer must also file a registration statement with the SEC. Issuers that sell securities in the private markets are not required to file a registration statement with the SEC.

investment banks
firms that underwrite new security issues

money center banks
large commercial banks that provide both traditional and investment banking services throughout the world

To get a better idea of all the lines of business in which large investment banking firms engage, go to Goldman Sachs's home page at http://www.goldmansachs.com.

Underwriting

Underwriting is the process by which the investment banker helps the company sell its new security issue. In the most common type of underwriting arrangement, called *firm-commitment underwriting*, the investment banker buys the new securities from the issuing company and resells them to investors. Because the investment banker buys the entire security issue from the company at a fixed price, the issuing company is guaranteed that price. On the other hand, the investment banker takes the risk that the actual price at which the shares are sold is less than the price that is paid to the company. Since issuing companies typically need a certain amount of money to pay for a particular project or to fund operations, and getting anything less than this amount can pose a serious problem, financial managers almost always prefer to have their new security issues underwritten on a firm-commitment basis.[2]

Once the investment bankers buy the securities from the issuer, they immediately offer to resell individual securities to institutional investors and the public at a specified offering price. The underwriters hope to be able to sell the offering at the market-clearing price, which is the price that will allow the entire security issue to be sold during the first day of sale. Underwriting involves considerable risk because it is difficult to estimate the price that will clear the market. If the investment bank has to sell the securities at a price below the price that it paid to the issuing company, the investment bank suffers a financial loss.

The investment banker's compensation is called the *underwriting spread*. It is the difference between the offering price and the price the investment banker pays for the security issue. The underwriting spread is one of the costs to the firm of selling new securities.

Distribution

Distribution is the process of marketing and reselling the securities to investors. Because security prices can take large, unexpected swings, a quick resale of all the securities is important. To that end, the underwriters often form sales syndicates, consisting of a number of different investment banking firms, to sell the securities. If the securities are not sold within a few days, the syndicate is disbanded, and the individual syndicate members sell the unsold securities at whatever price they can get.

Underwriter's Compensation

PROBLEM: Dairy Queen needs to raise $5 million to build three new restaurants and its financial manager decides to issue long-term bonds. The financial manager hires an investment banking firm to help design the bond issue and underwrite it. The issue consists of 5,000 bonds, and the investment banker agrees to purchase the entire issue for $4.8 million. The investment banker then resells the bonds to individual investors at the offering price. The sale totals $5.0 million. What is the underwriter's compensation?

APPROACH: The underwriter's compensation is the underwriting spread, which is the difference between the price at which the bonds were resold to individual investors and the price the underwriter paid for the issue. The underwriting spread per bond is then calculated by dividing the total spread by the number of bonds that are issued.

SOLUTION:

Underwriting spread: $5,000,000 − $4,800,000 = $200,000

Underwriting spread per bond: $200,000/5,000 bonds = $40

Since the bonds are sold for $1,000 each ($5,000,000/5,000 bonds = $1,000 per bond), the underwriting spread is 4 percent of the bond price. Notice that because of the guarantee Dairy Queen gets a check from the underwriter for $4.8 million regardless of the price at which the bonds are resold.

LEARNING BY DOING

APPLICATION 2.1

NEED MORE HELP?

WileyPLUS

---

[2]If the risk of underwriting a new security issue is high, investment bankers may refuse to underwrite the securities for a guaranteed price. Instead, they will underwrite the new issue on a *best-effort basis,* which means that they will sell the securities for the highest price that investors are willing to pay. These issues are discussed in more detail in Chapter 13.

> **BEFORE YOU GO ON**

1. Why is it difficult for individuals to participate in direct financial markets?
2. Why might a firm prefer to have a security issue underwritten by an investment banking firm?

2.3 TYPES OF FINANCIAL MARKETS

3 LEARNING OBJECTIVE

We have seen that direct flows of funds occur in financial markets. However, as already mentioned, *financial market* is a very general term. A complex industrial economy such as ours includes many different types of financial markets, and not all of them are involved in direct financing. Next, we examine some of the more important ways to classify financial markets. Note that these classifications overlap to a large extent. Thus, for example, the New York Stock Exchange fits into several different categories.

Primary and Secondary Markets

primary market
a financial market in which new security issues are sold by companies directly to investors

A **primary market** is any market where companies sell new security issues (debt or equity). For example, suppose Hewlett-Packard (HP) needs to raise $100 million for business expansion and decides to raise the money through the sale of common stock. The company will sell the new equity issue in the primary market for corporate stock—probably with the help of an underwriter, as discussed in Section 2.2. The primary markets are not well known to the general public because they are wholesale markets and the sales take place outside of the public view. A key characteristic of a primary market is that the transaction results in new money going into the firm.

secondary market
a financial market in which the owners of outstanding securities can sell them to other investors

A **secondary market** is any market where owners of outstanding securities can sell them to other investors. Secondary markets are like used-car markets in that they allow investors to buy or sell previously owned securities for cash. These markets are important because they enable investors to buy and sell securities as frequently as they want. As you might expect, investors are willing to pay higher prices for securities that have active secondary markets. Secondary markets are important to corporations as well because investors are willing to pay higher prices for securities in primary markets if the securities have active secondary markets. Thus, companies whose securities have active secondary markets enjoy lower funding costs than similar firms whose securities do not have active secondary markets. In contrast to primary markets, no new money goes into the firm when a secondary market transaction takes place.

Marketability versus Liquidity

marketability
the ease with which a security can be sold and converted into cash

An important characteristic of a security to investors is its marketability. **Marketability** is the ease with which a security can be sold and converted into cash. A security's marketability depends in part on the costs of trading and searching for information, so-called *transaction costs*. The lower the transaction costs, the greater a security's marketability. Because secondary markets make it easier to trade securities, their presence increases a security's marketability.

liquidity
the ability to convert an asset into cash quickly without loss of value

A term closely related to marketability is **liquidity**. Liquidity is the ability to convert an asset into cash quickly without loss of value. In common use, the terms *marketability* and *liquidity* are often used interchangeably, but they are different. Liquidity implies that when the security is sold, its value will be preserved; marketability does not carry this implication.

Brokers versus Dealers

brokers
market specialists who bring buyers and sellers together, usually for a commission

Two types of market specialists facilitate transactions in secondary markets. **Brokers** are market specialists who bring buyers and sellers together when a sale takes place. They execute the transaction for their client and are compensated for their services with a commission fee. They bear no risk of ownership of the securities during the transactions; their only service is that of matchmaker.

Dealers, in contrast, make markets for securities and do bear risk. They make a market for a security by buying and selling from an inventory of securities they own. Dealers make their profit, just as retail merchants do, by selling securities at prices above what they paid for them. The risk that dealers bear is *price risk*, which is the risk that they will sell a security for less than they paid for it.

dealers
market specialists who make markets for securities by buying and selling from their own inventories

Exchanges and Over-the-Counter Markets

Financial markets can be classified as either organized markets (more commonly called exchanges) or over-the-counter markets. Traditional exchanges, such as the New York Stock Exchange (NYSE), provide a physical meeting place and communication facilities for members to buy and sell securities or other assets (such as commodities like oil or wheat) under a specific set of rules and regulations. Members are individuals who represent securities firms as well as people who trade for their own accounts. Only members can use the exchange.

Securities not listed on an exchange are bought and sold in the over-the-counter (OTC) market. The OTC market differs from organized exchanges in that the OTC market has no central trading location. Instead, investors can execute OTC transactions by visiting or telephoning an OTC dealer or by using a computer-based electronic trading system linked to the OTC dealer. Traditionally, stocks traded over the counter have been those of small and relatively unknown firms, most of which would not qualify to be listed on a major exchange. However, electronic trading has become much more important in recent years. Many large well-known firms, such as Google and Microsoft, now trade on electronic exchanges such as NASDAQ. In fact, even in organized markets like the NYSE, most trades are now completed electronically.

Money and Capital Markets

Money markets are global markets where short-term debt instruments, which have maturities of less than one year, are traded. Money markets are wholesale markets in which the minimum transaction is $1 million and transactions of $10 million or $100 million are not uncommon. Money market instruments are lower in risk than other securities because of their high liquidity and low default risk. In fact, the term *money market* is used because these instruments are close substitutes for cash. The most important and largest money markets are in New York City, London, and Tokyo. Exhibit 2.2 lists the most common money market instruments and the dollar amounts outstanding as of June 2012.

money markets
markets where short-term debt instruments are traded

Large companies use money markets to adjust their liquidity positions. Liquidity, as mentioned, is the ability to convert an asset into cash quickly without loss of value. Liquidity problems arise because companies' cash receipts and expenditures are rarely perfectly synchronized. To manage liquidity, a firm can invest idle cash in money market instruments; then, if the firm has a temporary cash shortfall, it can raise cash overnight by selling money market instruments.

Recall from Chapter 1 that capital markets are markets where equity and debt instruments with maturities of greater than one year are traded. In these markets, large firms finance capital assets such as plants and equipment. The NYSE, as well as the London and Tokyo stock exchanges, are capital markets. Exhibit 2.2 also lists the major U.S. capital market instruments and the dollar amounts outstanding. Compared with money market instruments, capital market instruments are less marketable, have higher default risk, and have longer maturities.

Public and Private Markets

Public markets are organized financial markets where the general public buys and sells securities through their stockbrokers. The NYSE, for example, is a public market. The SEC regulates public securities markets in the United States. This agency is responsible for overseeing the securities industry and regulating all primary and secondary markets in which securities are traded. Many corporations want access to the public markets because they are wholesale markets where issuers can sell their securities at the lowest possible funding cost. The downside for corporations selling in the public markets is the cost of complying with the various SEC regulations.

| EXHIBIT 2.2 | **Selected Money Market and Capital Market Instruments, June 2012 ($ billions)** |

The exhibit shows the size of the U.S. market for each of the most important money market and capital market instruments. Notice that the largest security market is the market for corporate stock, followed by those for mortgage debt, corporate bonds, and at a distant fourth, Treasury notes. Compared with money market instruments, capital market instruments are less marketable, have higher default risk, and have longer maturities.

Money market instruments

Treasury bills		$ 1,596
Commercial paper		969
	Total	$ 2,565

Capital market instruments

Treasury notes		$ 6,963
Treasury bonds*		1,961
State and local government bonds		2,939
Corporate bonds		9,845
Corporate stock (at market value)		18,660
Mortgages		13,477
	Total	$53,845

*Includes Treasury inflation-protected securities and Federal Financing Bank securities.

Sources: Board of Governors, Federal Reserve System, Flow of Funds Accounts (June 7, 2012) and Bureau of Public Debt, Monthly Statement of the Public Debt of the United States (June 30, 2012).

private placement
the sale of an unregistered security directly to an investor, such as an insurance company or a wealthy individual

In contrast to public markets, *private markets* involve direct transactions between two parties. Transactions in private markets are often called **private placements**. In private markets, a company contacts investors directly and negotiates a deal to sell them all or part of a security issue. Larger firms may be equipped to handle these transactions themselves. Smaller firms are more likely to use the services of an investment bank, which will help locate investors, help negotiate the deal, and handle the legal aspects of the transaction. Major advantages of a private placement are the speed at which funds can be raised and low transaction costs. Downsides are that privately placed securities cannot legally be sold in the public markets because they lack SEC registration and the dollar amounts that can be raised tend to be smaller.

Futures and Options Markets

Markets also exist for trading in futures and options. Perhaps the best-known futures markets are the New York Board of Trade and the Chicago Board of Trade. The Chicago Board Options Exchange is a major options market.

Futures and options are often called *derivative securities* because they derive their value from some underlying asset. Futures contracts are contracts for the future delivery of such assets as securities, foreign currencies, interest cash flows, or commodities. Corporations use these contracts to reduce (hedge) risk exposure caused by fluctuation in things such as foreign exchange rates or commodity prices. We illustrate the use of futures contracts further in Chapter 17.

Options contracts call for one party (the option writer) to perform a specific act if called upon to do so by the option buyer or owner. Options contracts, like futures contracts, can be used to hedge risk in situations where the firm faces risk from price fluctuations.

> **BEFORE YOU GO ON**

1. What is the difference between primary and secondary markets?

2. How and why do large business firms use money markets?

3. What are capital markets, and why are they important to corporations?

2.4 MARKET EFFICIENCY

Financial markets, such as the bond and stock markets, help bring together buyers and sellers of securities. They reduce the cost of buying and selling securities by providing a physical location or computer trading system where investors can trade securities. The supply and demand for securities are better reflected in organized markets because much of the total supply and demand for securities flows through these centralized locations or trading systems. Any price that balances the overall supply and demand for a security is a market equilibrium price.

Ideally, economists would like financial markets to price securities at their **true (intrinsic) value**. A security's true value is the present value (the value in today's dollars) of the cash flows an investor who owns that security can expect to receive in the future. This present value, in turn, reflects all available information about the size, timing, and riskiness of the cash flows at the time the price was set.[3] As new information becomes available, investors adjust their cash flow estimates and, through buying and selling, the price of a security adjusts to reflect this information.

Markets such as those just described are called efficient markets. More formally, in an **efficient market**, security prices fully reflect the knowledge and expectations of all investors at a particular point in time. If markets are efficient, investors and financial managers have no reason to believe the securities are not priced at or near their true value. The more efficient a market is, the more likely securities are to be priced at or near their true value.

The overall efficiency of a market depends on its *operational efficiency* and its *informational efficiency*. **Market operational efficiency** concerns the cost of bringing together buyers and sellers. The costs of bringing together buyers and sellers are called *transaction costs* and include such things as broker commissions and other fees and expenses. The lower these costs, the more operationally efficient markets are. Why is operational efficiency important? If transaction costs are high, market prices will be more volatile, fewer financial transactions will take place, and prices will not reflect the knowledge and expectations of investors as accurately.

Market informational efficiency is exhibited if market prices reflect all relevant information about securities at a particular point in time. As suggested above, informational efficiency is influenced by operational efficiency, but it also depends on the availability of information and the ability of investors to buy and sell securities based on that information. In an informationally efficient market, market prices adjust quickly to new information as it becomes available. Prices adjust quickly because many security analysts and investors are gathering and trading on information about securities in a quest to make a profit. Note that competition among investors is an important driver of informational efficiency.

Efficient Market Hypotheses

Public financial markets are efficient in part because regulators such as the SEC require issuers of publicly traded securities to disclose a great deal of information about those securities to investors. Investors are constantly evaluating the prospects for these securities and acting on the conclusions from their analyses by trading them. If the price of a security is out of line with what investors think it should be, then investors will buy or sell that security, causing its price to adjust to reflect their assessment of its value. The ability of investors to easily observe transaction prices and trade volumes and to inexpensively trade securities in public markets contributes to the efficiency of this process. This buying and selling by investors is the mechanism through which prices adjust to reflect the market's consensus. The theory about how well this mechanism works is known as the **efficient market hypothesis**. We next discuss the three forms of the efficient market hypothesis, which describe different degrees of market efficiency.

Strong-Form Efficiency. The market for a security is perfectly informationally efficient if the security's price always reflects all information. The idea that all information about a security is reflected in its price is known as the **strong-form of the efficient market hypothesis**. Few people really believe that market prices of public securities reflect all available information, however. It is widely accepted that insiders have information that is not reflected in the security prices. Thus, the concept of strong-form market efficiency represents the ideal case rather than the real world.

---

[3]We discuss how to calculate the present value of future cash flows in Chapter 5.

true (intrinsic) value
for a security, the value of the cash flows an investor who owns that security can expect to receive in the future

efficient market
market where prices reflect the knowledge and expectations of all investors

market operational efficiency
the degree to which the transaction costs of bringing buyers and sellers together are minimized

market informational efficiency
the degree to which current market prices reflect relevant information and, therefore, the true value of the security

 The concept of market efficiency originated with the Ph.D. dissertation that Eugene Fama wrote at the University of Chicago. You can see a video of an interview with Dr. Fama that relates to market efficiency and other concepts discussed in this chapter at http://www.dfaus.com/philosophy/markets-work.html.

efficient market hypothesis
a theory concerning the extent to which information is reflected in security prices and how information gets incorporated into security prices

strong-form of the efficient market hypothesis
the theory that security prices reflect all information

private information
information that is not available to all investors

If a security market were strong-form efficient, then it would not be possible to earn abnormally high returns (returns greater than those justified by the risks) by trading on **private information**—information unavailable to other investors—because there would be no such information. In addition, since all information would already be reflected in security prices, the price of a share of a particular security would change only when new information about its prospects became available.

semistrong-form of the efficient market hypothesis
the theory that security prices reflect all public information but not all private information

public information
information that is available to all investors

Semistrong-Form Efficiency. A weaker form of the efficient market hypothesis, known as the **semistrong-form of the efficient market hypothesis**, holds only that all **public information**—information that is available to all investors—is reflected in security prices. Investors who have private information are able to profit by trading on this information before it becomes public. For example, suppose that conversations with the customers of a firm indicate to an investor that the firm's sales, and thereby its cash flows, are increasing more rapidly than other investors expect. To profit from this information, the investor buys the firm's stock. By buying the stock, the investor helps drive up the price to the point where it accurately reflects the higher level of cash flows.

The concept of semistrong-form efficiency is a reasonable representation of the public stock markets in developed countries such as the United States. In a market characterized by this sort of efficiency, as soon as information becomes public, it is quickly reflected in stock prices through trading activity. Studies of the speed at which new information is reflected in stock prices indicate that by the time you read a hot tip in the *Wall Street Journal* or a business magazine, it is too late to benefit by trading on it.

weak-form of the efficient market hypothesis
the theory that security prices reflect all information in past prices but do not reflect all private or all public information

Weak-Form Efficiency. The weakest form of the efficient market hypothesis is known, aptly enough, as the **weak-form of the efficient market hypothesis**. This hypothesis holds that all information contained in past prices of a security is reflected in current prices but that there is both public and private information that is not. In a weak-form efficient market, it would not be possible to earn abnormally high returns by looking for patterns in security prices, but it would be possible to do so by trading on public or private information.

An important conclusion of the efficient market hypothesis is that at any point in time, all securities of the same risk class should be priced to offer the same expected return. The more efficient the market, the more likely this is to happen. Since both the bond and stock markets are relatively efficient, this means that securities of similar risk will offer the same expected return. This conclusion is important because it provides the basis for identifying the proper discount rate to use in applying the bond and stock valuation models developed in Chapters 7 and 8.

 For an in-depth discussion of market efficiency, visit http://www.investorhome.com/emh.htm.

> **BEFORE YOU GO ON**

1. How does information about a firm's prospects get reflected in its share price?

2. What is strong-form market efficiency? semistrong-form market efficiency? weak-form market efficiency?

2.5 FINANCIAL INSTITUTIONS AND INDIRECT FINANCING

 LEARNING OBJECTIVE

financial intermediation
conversion of securities with one set of characteristics into securities with another set of characteristics

As we mentioned earlier, many business firms are too small to sell their debt or equity directly to investors. They have neither the expert knowledge nor the financing requirements to make transacting in wholesale markets cost effective. When these companies need funds for capital investments or for liquidity adjustments, their only feasible choice is to borrow in the *indirect* market from a financial institution. These financial institutions act as intermediaries, converting financial securities with one set of characteristics into securities with another set of characteristics. This process is called **financial intermediation**. The hallmark of indirect financing is that a financial institution—an intermediary—stands between the lender-saver and the borrower-spender. This route is shown at the bottom of Exhibit 2.1.

Indirect Market Transactions

We worked through an example of indirect financing at the beginning of the chapter. In that situation, a college student had $5,000 to invest for three months. A bank sold the student a three-month consumer CD for $5,000, pooled this $5,000 with the proceeds from other CDs, and used the money to make small-business loans, one of which was a $30,000 loan to a pizza parlor owner. Following is a schematic diagram of that transaction:

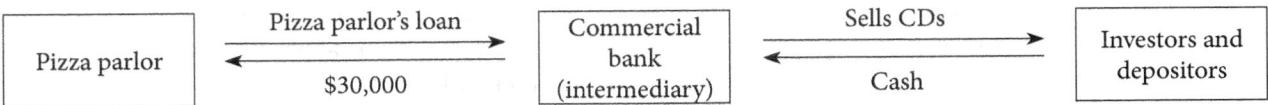

The bank raises money by selling services such as checking accounts, savings accounts, and consumer CDs and then uses the money to make loans to businesses or consumers.

On a larger scale, insurance companies provide much of the long-term financing in the economy through the indirect credit market. These companies invest heavily in corporate bonds and equity securities using funds they receive when they sell insurance policies to individuals and businesses. The schematic diagram for intermediation by an insurance company is as follows:

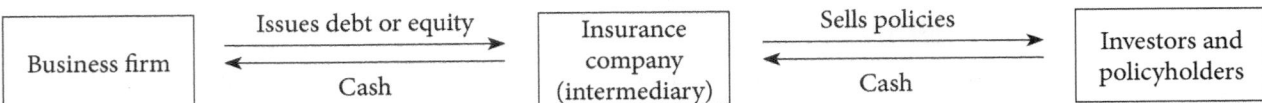

Notice an important difference between indirect and direct financial markets. In the direct market, as securities flow between lender-savers and borrower-spenders, the form of the securities remains unchanged. In indirect markets, however, as securities flow between lender-savers and borrower-spenders, they are repackaged, and their form is changed. In the example above, money from the sale of insurance policies becomes investments in corporate debt or equity. By repackaging securities, financial intermediaries tailor-make a wide range of financial products and services that meet the needs of consumers, small businesses, and large corporations. Their products and services are particularly important for smaller businesses that do not have access to direct financial markets.

Somewhat surprisingly, indirect markets are a much larger and more important source of financing to businesses than the more newsworthy direct financial markets. This is true not only in the United States, but in all industrial countries.

Financial Institutions and Their Services

We have briefly discussed the role of financial institutions as intermediaries in the indirect financial market. Next, we look at various types of financial institutions and the services they provide to small businesses as well as large corporations. We discuss only financial institutions that provide a significant amount of services to businesses.

Commercial Banks

Commercial banks are the most prominent and largest financial intermediaries in the economy and offer the widest range of financial services to businesses. Nearly every business, small or large, has a significant relationship with a commercial bank—usually a checking or transaction account and some type of credit or loan arrangement. For businesses, the most common type of bank loan is a line of credit (often called revolving credit), which works much like a credit card. A line of credit is a commitment by the bank to lend a firm an amount up to a predetermined limit, which can be used as needed. Banks also make term loans, which are fixed-rate loans with a maturity of one year to 10 years. In addition, banks do a significant amount of equipment lease financing. A lease is a contract that gives a business the right to use an asset, such as office space, a truck, or a computer mainframe, for a period of time in exchange for periodic payments. Leases are discussed in the Appendix to Chapter 14.

 For an example of the range of services provided by commercial banks to businesses, visit the small-business section of http://www.pncbank.com.

Life and Casualty Insurance Companies

Two types of insurance companies are important in the financial markets: (1) life insurance companies and (2) casualty insurance companies, which sell protection against loss of property from fire, theft, accidents, and other predictable causes. The cash flows for both types of companies are fairly predictable. As a result, they are able to provide funding to corporations through the purchase of stocks and bonds in the direct credit markets as well as funding for both public and private corporations through private placement financing. Businesses of all sizes purchase life insurance programs as part of their employee benefit packages and purchase casualty insurance policies to protect physical assets such as automobiles, truck fleets, equipment, and entire plants.

Pension Funds

Pension funds invest retirement funds on behalf of businesses or government agencies that provide retirement programs for their employees. Pension funds obtain money from employee and employer contributions during the employee's working years, and they provide monthly cash payments upon retirement. Because of the predictability of these cash flows, pension fund managers invest in corporate bonds and equity securities purchased in the direct financial markets and participate in the private placement market.

Investment Funds

Investment funds, such as mutual funds, sell shares to investors and use the funds to purchase securities. As a result, they are an important source of business funding. For example, mutual funds may focus on purchasing (1) equity or debt securities; (2) securities of small or medium-size corporations; (3) securities of companies in a particular industry, such as energy, computer, or information technology; or (4) foreign investments.

Business Finance Companies

Business finance companies obtain the majority of their funds by selling short-term debt, called commercial paper, to investors in direct credit markets. These funds are used to make a variety of short- and intermediate-term loans and leases to small and large businesses. The loans are often secured by accounts receivable or inventory. Business finance companies are typically more willing than commercial banks to make loans and leases to firms with higher levels of default risk.

Corporations and the Financial System

We began this chapter by saying that financial managers need to understand the financial system in order to make sound decisions. We now follow up on that statement by briefly describing how corporations operate within the financial system. The interaction between the financial system and a large public corporation is shown in Exhibit 2.3. The arrows show the major cash flows for a firm over a typical operating cycle. These cash flows relate to some of the key decisions that the financial manager must make. As you know, those decisions involve three major areas: capital budgeting, financing, and working capital management.

Let's work through an example using Exhibit 2.3 to illustrate how corporate businesses use the financial system. Suppose you are the CFO of a new high-tech firm with business ties to 3M Corporation. The new firm has a well-thought-out business plan, owns some valuable technology, and has one manufacturing facility. The company is large enough to have access to public markets. The company plans to use its core technology to develop and sell a number of new products that the marketing department believes will generate a strong market demand.

To start the new company, management's first task is to sell equity and debt to finance the expansion of the firm. The senior management team and 3M will provide 40 percent of the equity, and the balance will come from an **initial public offering (IPO)** of common stock.

initial public offering (IPO)
the first offering of a corporation's stock to the public

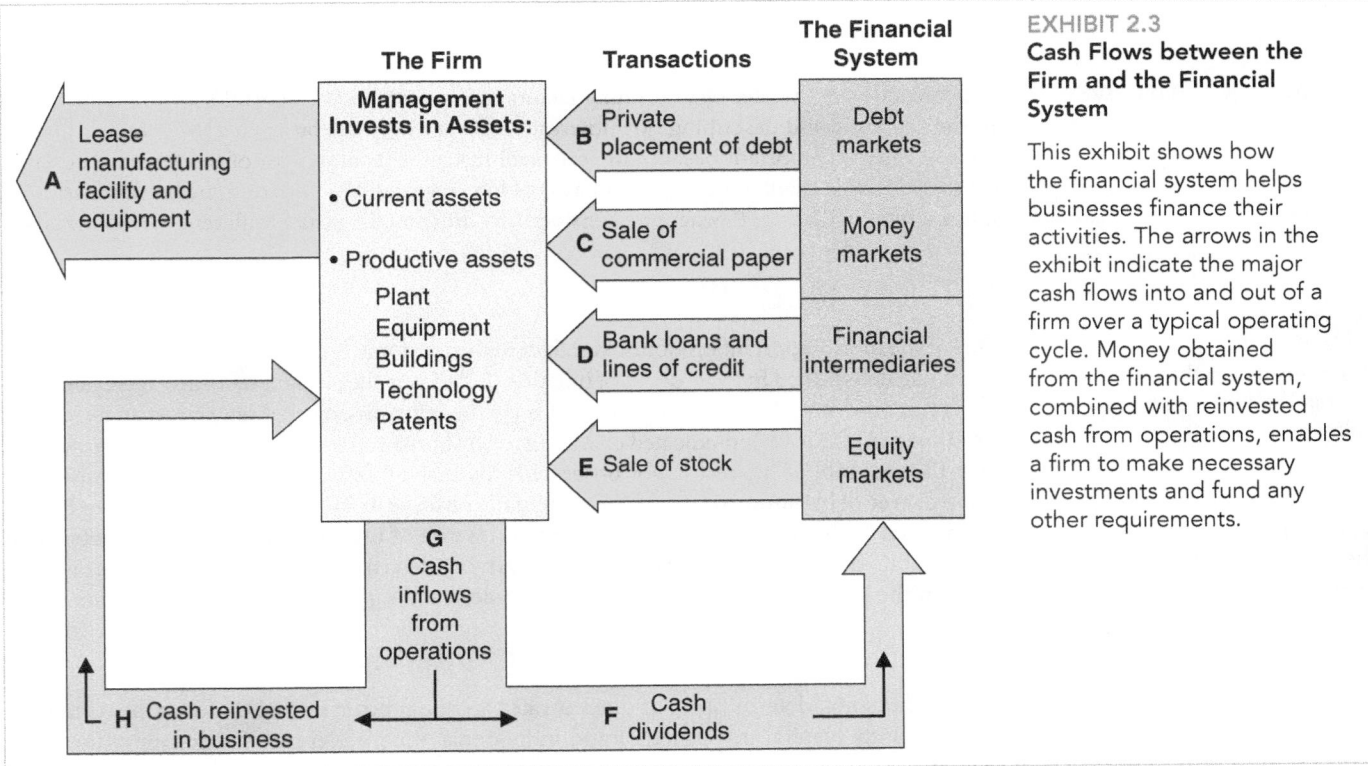

EXHIBIT 2.3

Cash Flows between the Firm and the Financial System

This exhibit shows how the financial system helps businesses finance their activities. The arrows in the exhibit indicate the major cash flows into and out of a firm over a typical operating cycle. Money obtained from the financial system, combined with reinvested cash from operations, enables a firm to make necessary investments and fund any other requirements.

An IPO is a corporation's first offering of its stock to the public. For example, management hires Morgan Stanley as its investment bank to underwrite the new securities. After the deal is underwritten, the new venture receives the proceeds from the stock sale, less Morgan Stanley's underwriting fees (see arrow E in the exhibit).[4]

In addition to the equity financing, 30 percent of the firm's total funding will come from the sale of long-term debt through a private placement deal with a large insurance company (see arrow B). Management decided to use a private placement because the lender is willing to commit to lend the firm additional money in the future if the firm meets certain performance goals. Since management has ambitious growth plans, locking in a future source of funds is important.

Once the funds from the debt and equity sales are in hand, they are deposited in the firm's checking account at a commercial bank. Management then decides to lease an existing manufacturing facility and the equipment necessary to manufacture the new high-technology products; the cash outflow is represented by arrow A.

To begin manufacturing, the firm needs to raise working capital and does this by (1) selling commercial paper in the money markets (arrow C) and (2) obtaining a line of credit from a bank (arrow D). As the firm becomes operational, it generates cash inflows from its productive assets (arrow G). Some of these cash inflows are reinvested in the business (arrow H), and the remainder are used to pay cash dividends to stockholders (arrow F).

> **BEFORE YOU GO ON**

1. What is financial intermediation, and why is it important?

2. What are some services that commercial banks provide to businesses?

3. What is an IPO, and what role does an investment banker play in the process?

---

[4]Chapter 13 contains a detailed discussion of the IPO process.

2.6 THE DETERMINANTS OF INTEREST RATE LEVELS

6 LEARNING OBJECTIVE

We conclude this chapter by examining factors that determine the general level of interest rates in the economy and describing how interest rates vary over the business cycle. Understanding interest rates is important because the financial instruments and most of the financial services discussed in this chapter are priced in terms of interest rates. We will continue our discussion of interest rates in Chapter 7, where we consider why different firms have different borrowing costs.

The Real Rate of Interest

real rate of interest
the interest rate that would exist in the absence of inflation

One of the most important economic variables in the economy is the **real rate of interest**—an interest rate determined in the absence of inflation. *Inflation* is the amount by which aggregate price levels rise over time. The real rate of interest is (1) the inflation-adjusted return earned by lender-savers and (2) the inflation-adjusted cost incurred by borrower-spenders when they borrow.

nominal rate of interest
the rate of interest that is unadjusted for inflation

The real rate of interest is not observable because all industrial economies operate with some degree of inflation. The rate that we actually observe in the marketplace at a given time is unadjusted for inflation and is called the **nominal rate of interest**. The factors that determine the real rate of interest, however, are the underlying determinants of all interest rates we observe in the marketplace. For this reason, an understanding of the real rate is important.

Determinants of the Real Rate of Interest

The fundamental determinants of interest rates are the returns earned on investments in productive assets (capital investments) and individuals' time preference for consumption. Let's examine how these two factors interact to determine the real rate of interest.

Returns on Investments. Recall from Chapter 1 that businesses invest in capital projects that are expected to generate positive cash flows by producing additional real output, such as cars, machinery, computers, and video games. The output generated by a capital project constitutes its return on investment, which is usually measured as a percentage. For example, if a capital project costs $1,000 and produces $180 in cash flows each year, the project's return on investment is 18 percent ($180/$1,000 = 0.18, or 18 percent).

For a capital project to be attractive, its return on investment must exceed the cost of the funds (debt and equity) used to finance it. Intuitively, this makes sense because if an investment earns a return greater than the cost of funding, it should be profitable and thus should increase the value of the firm. For example, if the cost of funding—often called the *cost of capital*—is 15 percent, the capital project mentioned above would be attractive (18 percent > 15 percent) and would therefore be undertaken. If the capital project was expected to earn only 13 percent, though, the project would be rejected (13 percent < 15 percent). The cost of capital is the minimum acceptable rate of return on a capital project.

DECISION MAKING

EXAMPLE 2.2

Capital Budgeting Preview

SITUATION: Sonic Manufacturing Company's capital budget includes six projects that management has identified as having merit. The CFO's staff computed the return on investment for each project. The average cost of funding each project is 10 percent. The projects are as follows:

Project	Return on Investment
A	13.0%
B	12.0
C	10.9
D	10.5
E	9.8
F	8.9

Which capital projects should the firm undertake?

DECISION: The firm should accept all projects with a return on investment greater than the average cost of funding, which is 10 percent in all cases. These projects are A, B, C, and D. As noted in the text, this decision-making principle makes intuitive sense because all projects with a return on investment greater than the cost of funds will increase the value of the firm. In Chapters 9 through 11, we will delve much more deeply into capital budgeting, and you will find out a great deal more about how these decisions are made.

Time Preference for Consumption. All other things being equal, most people prefer to consume goods today rather than tomorrow. This is called a positive time preference for consumption. For example, most people who want to buy a new car prefer to have it now rather than wait until they have earned enough cash to make the purchase. When people consume today, however, they realize that their future consumption may be less because they have forgone the opportunity to save and earn interest on their savings.

Given people's positive time preference for consumption, the interest rate offered on financial instruments determines how much people will save. At low rates of interest, it hardly makes sense to save, so most people will continue to spend money rather than put money aside in savings. To coax people to postpone current spending, interest rates must be raised. At higher rates people save more and spend less.

Equilibrium Condition. We have seen that people spend less when interest rates are higher and that higher interest rates choke off business investment (or spending) because fewer capital projects can earn a high enough return on investment to cover the added interest cost. At the same time, lender-savers want to lend more money when interest rates are high. The real rate of interest depends on the interaction between these two opposing factors. Using a supply-and-demand framework, Exhibit 2.4 shows that the equilibrium market rate of interest (r) is the point where the desired level of borrowing (B) by borrower-spenders equals the desired level of lending (L) by lender-savers.[5]

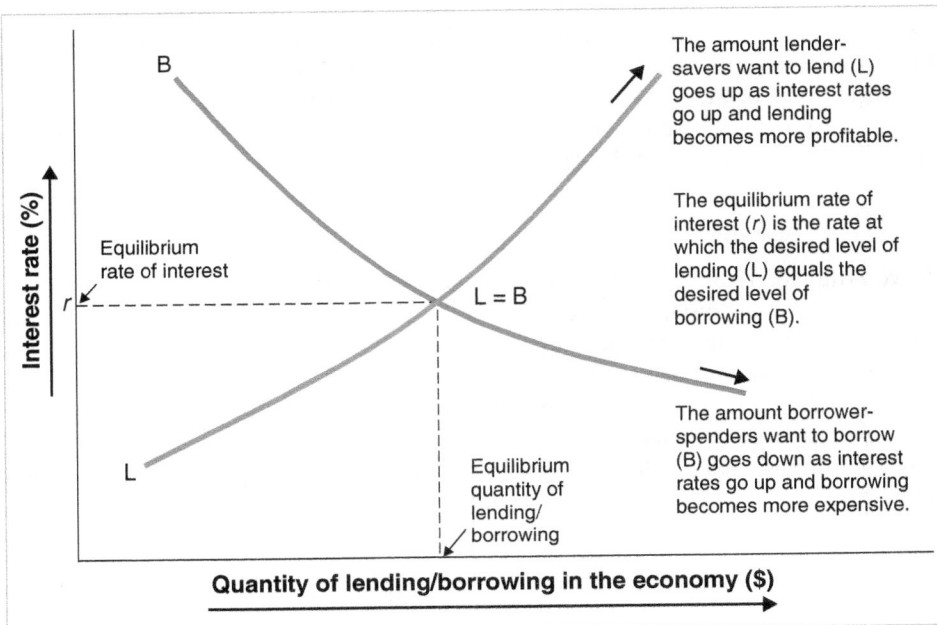

The amount lender-savers want to lend (L) goes up as interest rates go up and lending becomes more profitable.

The equilibrium rate of interest (r) is the rate at which the desired level of lending (L) equals the desired level of borrowing (B).

The amount borrower-spenders want to borrow (B) goes down as interest rates go up and borrowing becomes more expensive.

EXHIBIT 2.4

The Determinants of the Equilibrium Rate of Interest

The equilibrium rate of interest is a function of supply and demand. Lender-savers are willing to supply more funds as interest rates go up, but borrower-spenders demand fewer funds at higher interest rates. The interest rate at which the supply of funds equals the demand for those funds is the equilibrium rate.

---

[5]The model presented here is based on the loanable funds theory of market equilibrium. Saving (or giving up current consumption) is the source of loanable funds, and personal and business spending (or investment) is the use of funds.

Fluctuations in the Real Rate

In the supply-and-demand framework discussed previously, any economic factor that causes a shift in desired lending or desired borrowing will cause a change in the equilibrium rate of interest. For example, a major breakthrough in technology should cause a shift to the right in the desired level of borrowing schedule, thus increasing the real rate of interest. This makes intuitive sense because the new technology should spawn an increase in investment opportunities, increasing the desired level of borrowing. Similarly, a reduction in the corporate tax rate should provide businesses with more money to spend on investments, which should increase the desired level of borrowing schedule, causing the real rate of interest to increase.

One factor that would shift the desired level of lending to the right, and hence lead to a decrease in the real rate of interest, would be a decrease in the tax rates for individuals. Lower individual tax rates would leave saver-lenders with more money to lend. Also, with lower individual tax rates, saver–lenders could receive a lower interest rate and earn the same after-tax return. Another factor would be monetary policy action by the Federal Reserve Bank to increase the money supply. A larger money supply would increase the amount of money available for lending.

Other forces that could affect the real rate of interest include growth in population, demographic variables such as the age of the population, and cultural differences. In sum, the real rate of interest reflects a complex set of forces that control the desired level of lending and borrowing in the economy. The real rate of interest has historically been around 3 percent for the U.S. economy, but has varied between 2 and 4 percent because of changes in economic conditions.

Loan Contracts and Inflation

The real rate of interest does not account for inflation, but price-level changes in the real world are a fact of life, and these changes affect the value of a loan contract or, for that matter, any financial contract. For example, if prices rise due to inflation during the life of a loan contract, the purchasing power of the dollar decreases because the borrower repays the lender with inflated dollars—dollars with less buying power.[6]

To see the impact of inflation on a loan, let's look at an example. Suppose that you lend a friend $1,000 for one year at a 4 percent interest rate. Furthermore, you plan to buy a new surfboard for $1,040 in one year when you graduate from college. With the $40 of interest you earn ($1,000 × 0.04 = $40), you will have just enough money to buy the surfboard. At the end of the year, you graduate, and your friend pays off the loan, giving you $1,040. Unfortunately, the rate of inflation during the year was an unexpected 10 percent, and your surfboard now will cost 10 percent more, or $1,144 ($1,040 × 1.10 = $1,144). You have experienced a 10 percent decrease in your purchasing power due to the unanticipated inflation. The loss of purchasing power is $104 ($1,144 − $1,040 = $104).

The Fisher Equation and Inflation

How do we write a loan contract that provides protection against loss of purchasing power due to inflation? We have no crystal ball to tell us what the actual rate of inflation will be when the loan contract is written. However, market participants collectively (often called "the market") have expectations about how prices will change during the contract period.

To incorporate these inflation expectations into a loan contract, we need to adjust the real rate of interest by the amount of inflation that is expected during the contract period. The mathematical formula used to adjust the real rate of interest for the expected rate of inflation is as follows:

$$1 + i = (1 + r) \times (1 + \Delta P_e) \quad\quad\quad (2.1)$$
$$1 + i = 1 + r + \Delta P_e + r\Delta P_e$$
$$i = r + \Delta P_e + r\Delta P_e$$

---

[6]Recall from economics two important relations: (1) the value of money is its purchasing power—what you can buy with it and (2) there is a negative relation between changes in price level and the value of money. As the price level increases (inflation), the value of money decreases, and as the price level decreases (deflation), the value of money increases. This makes sense because when we have rising prices (inflation), our dollars will buy less.

where:

i = nominal (or market) rate of interest

r = real rate of interest

ΔP_e = expected annualized price-level change

$r\Delta P_e$ = adjustment of the interest rate for expected price-level change

Equation 2.1 is called the Fisher equation. It is named after Irving Fisher, who first developed the concept and is considered by many to be one of America's greatest economists.

Applying Equation 2.1 to our surfboard example, we can find out what the nominal rate of interest should be if the expected inflation rate is 10 percent and the real rate of interest is 4 percent:

$$i = r + \Delta P_e + r\Delta P_e$$
$$= 0.04 + 0.10 + (0.04 \times 0.10)$$
$$= 0.1440, \text{ or } 14.40\%$$

Looking at Equation 2.1, notice that ΔP_e is the *expected* price-level change and not the *realized* (actual) rate of inflation (ΔP_a). Thus, to properly determine the nominal rate of interest, it is necessary to predict prices over the life of the loan contract. Also, recall that the nominal rate of interest is the market rate of interest—the rate actually observed in financial markets. The real and nominal rates of interest are equal only when the expected rate of inflation over the contract period is zero ($\Delta P_e = 0$).[7]

When either r or ΔP_e is a small number, or when both are small, then $r\Delta P_e$ is very small and is approximately equal to zero. In these situations, it is common practice to write the Fisher equation as a simple additive function, where the nominal rate of interest is divided into two parts: (1) the real rate of interest and (2) the anticipated percent change in the price level over the life of the loan contract. The simplified Fisher equation can be written as follows:

$$i = r + \Delta P_e \tag{2.2}$$

Thus, for our one-year loan example:

$$i = 0.04 + 0.10 = 0.1400, \text{ or } 14.00\%$$

The difference in the contract loan rates between the two variations of the Fisher equation is 0.40 percent ($14.40 - 14.00 = 0.40$), a difference of less than 3 percent ($0.40/14.40 = 0.0278$, or 2.78 percent). Thus, dropping $r\Delta P_e$ from the equation makes the equation easier to understand without creating a significant computational error.

Calculating a New Inflation Premium

PROBLEM: The current one-year Treasury bill rate is 2.0 percent. On the evening news, several economists at leading investment and commercial banks predict that the annual inflation rate is going to be 0.25 percent higher than originally expected. The higher inflation forecasts reflect unexpectedly strong employment figures released by the government that afternoon. What is the current inflation premium if the real rate of interest is 0.5 percent? When the market opens tomorrow, what should happen to the one-year Treasury bill rate?

APPROACH: You must first estimate the current inflation premium using Equation 2.2. You should then adjust this premium to reflect the economists' revised beliefs. Finally, this revised inflation premium can be used in the simplified Fisher equation to estimate what the Treasury rate will be tomorrow morning.

(continued)

---

[7]In economics the terms *nominal* and *real* are frequently used as modifiers, as in *nominal GNP* and *real GNP*. *Nominal* means that the data are from the marketplace; thus, the values may contain price-level changes due to inflation. *Real* means the data are corrected for changes in purchasing power.

SOLUTION:

Current inflation premium:

$$i = r + \Delta P_e$$
$$\Delta P_e = i - r$$
$$= 2.0\% - 0.5\%$$
$$= 1.5\%$$

New inflation premium:

$$\Delta P_e = 1.5\% + 0.25\% = 1.75\%$$

The opening Treasury rate in the morning:

$$i = r + \Delta P_e = 0.5\% + 1.75\% = 2.25\%$$

LEARNING
BY
DOING

APPLICATION 2.3

International Loan Rate

PROBLEM: You are a financial manager at a manufacturing company that is going to make a one-year loan to a key supplier in another country. The loan will be made in the supplier's local currency. The supplier's government controls the banking system, and there are no reliable market data available. For this reason, you have spoken with five economists who have some knowledge about the economy. Their predictions for inflation next year are 30, 40, 45, 50, and 60 percent.

What rate should your firm charge for the one-year business loan if you are not concerned about the possibility that your supplier will default? You recall from your corporate finance course that the real rate of interest is, on average, 3 percent over the long run.

APPROACH: Although the sample of economists is small, an average of the economists' estimates should provide a reasonable estimate of the expected rate of inflation (ΔP_e). This value can be used in Equation 2.2 to calculate the nominal rate of interest.

SOLUTION:

$$\Delta P_e = (30\% + 40\% + 45\% + 50\% + 60\%)/5$$
$$= 225\%/5$$
$$= 45\%$$

Nominal rate of interest:

$$i = r + \Delta P_e$$
$$= 3\% + 45\%$$
$$= 48\%$$

This number is a reasonable estimate, given that you have no market data.

Cyclical and Long-Term Trends in Interest Rates

Now let's look at some market data to see how interest rates have actually fluctuated over the past five decades in the United States. Exhibit 2.5 plots the interest rate yield on 10-year government bonds since 1960 to represent interest rate movements. In addition, the exhibit plots the annual rate of inflation, represented by the annual percent change in the consumer price index (CPI). The CPI is a price index that measures the change in prices of a market basket of goods and services that a typical consumer purchases. Finally, the shaded areas on the chart indicate periods of recession. Recession occurs when real output from the economy is decreasing and unemployment is increasing. Each shaded area begins at the peak of the business cycle

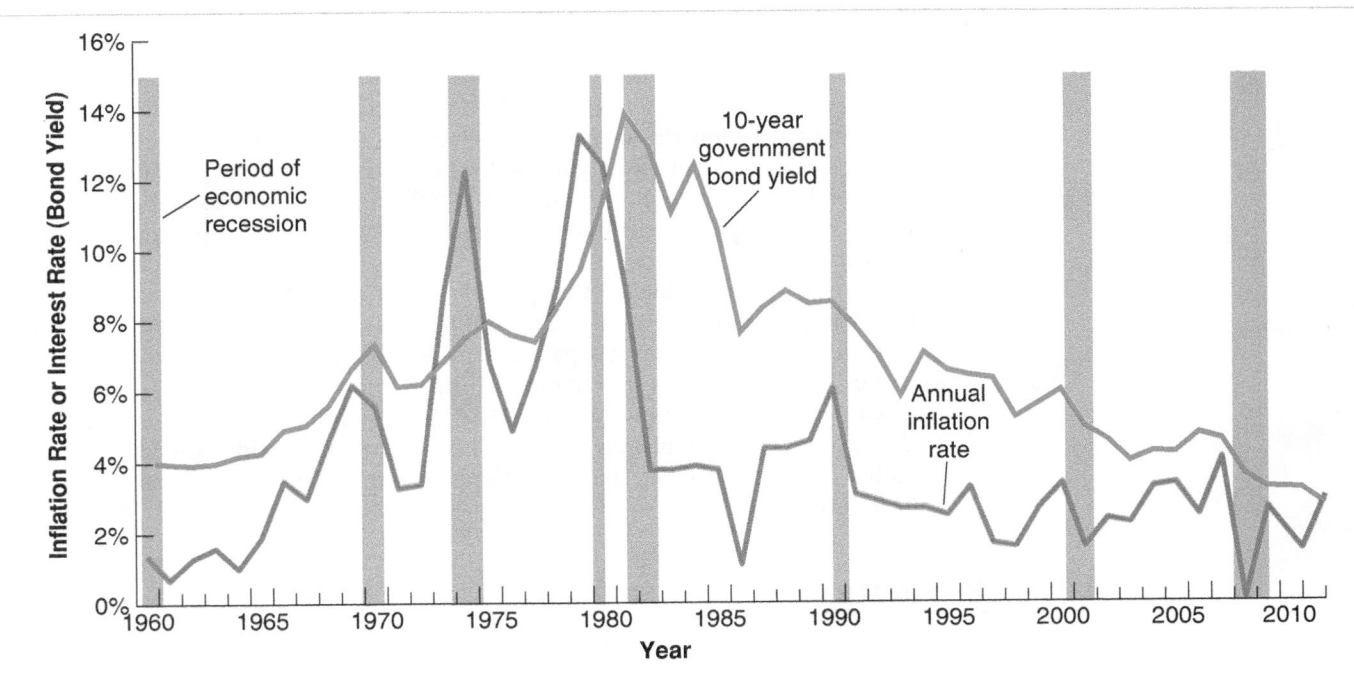

EXHIBIT 2.5

Relation between Annual Inflation Rate and Long-Term Interest Rate (1960–2011)

Based on the graph shown in the exhibit, we can draw two important conclusions about interest rate movements. First, the level of interest rates tends to rise and fall with the actual rate of inflation—a conclusion also supported by the Fisher Equation, which suggests that interest rates rise and fall with the *expected* rate of inflation. Second, the level of interest rates tends to rise during periods of economic expansion and decline during periods of economic contraction.

Sources: Bureau of Labor Statistics, U.S. Department of Labor (http://www.bls.gov/cpi), U.S. Department of the Treasury (http://www.treasury .gov), and Wikipedia (http://en.wikipedia.org).

and ends at the bottom (or trough) of the recession. From our discussion of interest rates and an examination of Exhibit 2.5, we can draw two general conclusions:

1. *The level of interest rates tends to rise and fall with changes in the actual rate of inflation.* The positive relation between the rate of inflation and the level of interest rates is what we should expect given Equation 2.1. Thus, we feel comfortable concluding that inflationary expectations have a major impact on interest rates.

    Our findings also explain in part why interest rates can vary substantially between countries. For example, in 2011 the rate of inflation in the United States was 3.0 percent; during the same period, the rate of inflation in Russia was 9.6 percent. If the real rate of interest is 3.0 percent, the short-term interest rate in the United States should have been around 6.0 percent (3.0 percent + 3.0 percent = 6.0 percent) and the Russian interest rate should have been around 12.6 percent (3.0 percent + 9.6 percent = 12.6 percent). In fact, during January 2011 the U.S. short-term interest rate was about 0.1 percent and the Russian rate was 8.0 percent. Though hardly scientific, this analysis illustrates the point that countries with higher rates of inflation or expected rates of inflation will have higher interest rates than countries with lower inflation rates. The fact that both of these interest rates are below the rates of inflation reflects the weak economic conditions in 2011.

2. *The level of interest rates tends to rise during periods of economic expansion and decline during periods of economic contraction.* It makes sense that interest rates should increase during years of economic expansion. The reasoning is that as the economy expands, businesses begin to borrow money to build up inventories and to invest in more production capacity in anticipation of increased sales. As unemployment begins to decrease, the economic future looks bright, and consumers begin to buy more homes, cars, and other durable items on credit. As a result, the demand for funds by both businesses and consumers increases, driving interest rates up. Also, near the end of expansion, the rate of inflation

begins to accelerate, which puts upward pressure on interest rates. At some point, the Fed becomes concerned over the increasing inflation in the economy and begins to tighten credit, which further raises interest rates, slowing down the economy. The higher interest rates in the economy choke off spending by both businesses and consumers.

During a recession, the opposite takes place; businesses and consumers rein in their spending and their use of credit, putting downward pressure on interest rates. To stimulate demand for goods and services, the Fed will typically begin to make more credit available. The result is to lower interest rates in the economy and encourage business and consumer spending.

Also notice in Exhibit 2.5 that periods of business expansion tend to be much longer than periods of contraction (recessions). Since the end of the Great Depression, the average period of economic expansion has lasted three to four years, and the average period of contraction about nine months. Keep in mind that the numbers given are averages and that actual periods of economic expansion and contraction can vary widely from averages. For example, the last period of business expansion lasted about 6 years (October 2001 to December 2007), and the last recession lasted 18 months (December 2007 to June 2009).

> **BEFORE YOU GO ON**

1. Explain how the real rate of interest is determined.

2. How are inflationary expectations accounted for in the nominal rate of interest?

3. Explain why interest rates follow the business cycle.

SUMMARY OF Learning Objectives

1 **Describe the role of the financial system in the economy and the two basic ways in which money flows through the system.**

The role of the financial system is to gather money from people, businesses, and governments with surplus funds to invest (lender-savers) and channel that money to businesses and consumers who need to borrow money (borrower-spenders). If the financial system works properly, only investment projects with high rates of return and good credit are financed and all other projects are rejected. Money flows through the financial system in two basic ways: (1) directly, through financial markets, or (2) indirectly, through financial institutions.

2 **Discuss direct financing and the important role that investment banks play in this process.**

Direct markets are wholesale markets where lender-savers and borrower-spenders deal directly with one another. For example, corporations sell securities, such as stocks and bonds, directly to investors in exchange for money, which they use to invest in their businesses. Investment banks are important in the direct markets because they help borrower-spenders sell their new security issues. The services provided by investment bankers include origination, underwriting, and distribution.

3 **Describe the primary, secondary, and money markets, explaining the special importance of secondary and money markets to business organizations.**

Primary markets are markets in which new securities are sold for the first time. Secondary markets are markets for securities that

were previously issued. Not all securities have secondary markets. Secondary markets are important because they enable investors to convert securities easily to cash. Business firms whose securities are traded in secondary markets are able to issue new securities at a lower cost than they otherwise could because investors are willing to pay a higher price for securities that have secondary markets.

Large corporations use money markets to adjust their liquidity because cash inflows and outflows are rarely perfectly synchronized. Thus, on the one hand, if cash expenditures exceed cash receipts, a firm can borrow short-term in the money markets. If that firm holds a portfolio of money market instruments, it can sell some of these securities for cash. On the other hand, if cash receipts exceed expenditures, the firm can temporarily invest the funds in short-term money market instruments. Businesses are willing to invest large amounts of idle cash in money market instruments because of their high liquidity and their low default risk.

4 **Explain what an efficient market is and why market efficiency is important to financial managers.**

An efficient market is a market where security prices reflect the knowledge and expectations of all investors. Public markets, for example, are more efficient than private markets because issuers of public securities are required to disclose a great deal of information about these securities to investors and investors are constantly evaluating the prospects for these securities and acting on the conclusions from their analyses by trading them. Market efficiency is important to investors because it assures them that the securities they buy are priced close to their true value.

Explain how financial institutions serve the needs of consumers and small businesses.

One problem with direct financing is that it takes place in a wholesale market. Most consumers and small businesses do not have the skills, financing requirements, or money to transact in this market. In contrast, a large portion of the indirect market focuses on providing financial services to consumers and small businesses. For example, commercial banks collect money from consumers in small dollar amounts by selling them checking accounts, savings accounts, and consumer CDs. They then aggregate the funds and make loans in larger amounts to consumers and businesses. The financial services bought or sold by financial institutions are tailor-made to fit the needs of the markets they serve. Exhibit 2.3 illustrates how businesses use the financial system.

Compute the nominal and the real rates of interest, differentiating between them.

Equations 2.1 and 2.2 are used to compute the nominal (real) rate of interest when you have the real (nominal) rate and the inflation rate. The real rate of interest is the interest rate that would exist in the absence of inflation. It is determined by the interaction of (1) the rate of return that businesses can expect to earn on capital projects and (2) individuals' time preference for consumption. The interest rate we observe in the marketplace is called the nominal rate of interest. The nominal rate of interest is composed of two parts: (1) the real rate of interest and (2) the expected rate of inflation.

SUMMARY OF Key Equations

Equation	Description	Formula
2.1	Fisher equation	$i = r + \Delta P_e + r\,\Delta P_e$
2.2	Fisher equation simplified	$i = r + \Delta P_e$

Self-Study Problems

2.1 Economic units that need to borrow money are said to be:
   a. Lender-savers.
   b. Borrower-spenders.
   c. Balanced budget keepers.
   d. None of the above.

2.2 Explain what the marketability of a security is and how it is determined.

2.3 What are over-the-counter markets (OTCs), and how do they differ from organized exchanges?

2.4 What effect does an increase in demand for business goods and services have on the real interest rate? What other factors can affect the real interest rate?

2.5 How does the business cycle affect the nominal interest rate and inflation rate?

Solutions to Self-Study Problems

2.1 Such units are said to be: b. Borrower-spenders.

2.2 Marketability refers to the ease with which a security can be sold and converted into cash. The level of marketability depends on the cost of trading the security and the cost of searching for information. The lower these costs are, the greater the security's marketability.

2.3 Securities that are not listed on an organized exchange are sold OTC. An OTC market differs from an organized exchange in that there is no central trading location. OTC security transactions are made via phone or computer as opposed to on the floor of an exchange.

2.4 An increase in the demand for business goods and services will cause the borrowing schedule in Exhibit 2.4 to shift to the right, thus increasing the real rate of interest. Other factors that can affect the real interest rate include increases in productivity, changes in technology, or changes in the corporate tax rate. Demographic factors, such as growth or age of the population, and cultural differences can also affect the real rate of interest.

2.5 Both the nominal interest and inflation rates tend to follow the business cycle; that is, they rise with economic expansion and fall during a recession.

Critical Thinking Questions

2.1 Explain why total financial assets in the economy must equal total financial liabilities.

2.2 Why don't small businesses make greater use of the direct credit markets since these markets enable firms to finance their activities at a very low cost?

2.3 Explain the economic role of brokers and dealers. How does each make a profit?

2.4 Why were commercial banks prohibited from engaging in investment banking activities until 1999?

2.5 What are two basic services that investment banks provide in the economy?

2.6 How do large corporations adjust their liquidity in the money markets?

2.7 The CFO of a certain company always wears his green suit on a day that the firm is about to release positive information about his company. You believe that you can profit from this information by buying the firm's shares at the beginning of every day that the CFO shows up wearing this green suit. Describe which form of market efficiency is consistent with your belief.

2.8 Shouldn't the nominal rate of interest (Equation 2.1) be determined by the actual rate of inflation (ΔP_a), which can be easily measured, rather than by the expected rate of inflation (ΔP_e)?

2.9 How does Exhibit 2.5 help explain why interest rates were so high during the early 1980s as compared to the relatively low interest rates in the early 1960s?

2.10 When determining the real interest rate, what happens to businesses that find themselves with unfunded capital projects whose rate of return exceeds the cost of capital?

Questions and Problems

BASIC **2.1** **Financial system:** What is the role of the financial system, and what are the two major components of the financial system?

2.2 **Financial system:** What does a competitive financial system imply about interest rates?

2.3 **Financial system:** What is the difference between saver-lenders and borrower-spenders, and who are the major representatives of each group?

2.4 **Financial markets:** List the two ways in which a transfer of funds takes place in an economy. What is the main difference between these two?

2.5 **Financial markets:** Suppose you own a security that you know can be easily sold in the secondary market, but the security will sell at a lower price than you paid for it. What would this mean for the security's marketability and liquidity?

2.6 **Financial markets:** Why are direct financial markets also called wholesale markets?

2.7 **Financial markets:** Trader Inc. is a $300 million company, as measured by asset value, and Horst Corp. is a $35 million company. Both are privately held corporations. Explain which firm is more likely to go public and register with the SEC, and why.

2.8 **Primary markets:** What is a primary market? What does IPO stand for?

2.9 **Primary market:** Identify whether the following transactions are primary market or secondary market transactions.
   a. Jim Hendry bought 300 shares of IBM through his brokerage account.
   b. Peggy Jones bought $5,000 of IBM bonds from the firm.
   c. Hathaway Insurance Company bought 500,000 shares of Trigen Corp. when the company issued stock.

2.10 **Investment banking:** What does it mean to "underwrite" a new security issue? What compensation does an investment banker get from underwriting a security issue?

2.11 **Investment banking:** Cranjet Inc. is issuing 10,000 bonds, and its investment banker has guaranteed a price of $985 per bond. The investment banker sells the entire issue to investors for $10,150,000.
   a. What is the underwriting spread for this issue?
   b. What is the percentage underwriting cost?
   c. How much did Cranjet raise?

2.12 **Financial institutions:** What are some of the ways in which a financial institution or intermediary can raise money?

2.13 Financial institutions: How do financial institutions act as intermediaries to provide services to small businesses?

2.14 Financial institutions: Which financial institution is usually the most important to businesses?

2.15 Financial markets: What is the main difference between money markets and capital markets?

2.16 Money markets: What is the primary role of money markets? Explain how the money markets work.

2.17 Money markets: What are the main types of securities in the money markets?

2.18 Capital markets: How do capital market instruments differ from money market instruments?

2.19 Market efficiency: Describe the informational differences that separate the three forms of market efficiency.

2.20 Market efficiency: Zippy Computers announced strong fourth quarter results. Sales and earnings were both above analysts' expectations. You notice in the newspaper that Zippy's stock price went up sharply on the day of the announcement. If no other information about Zippy became public on the day of the announcement and the overall market was down, is this evidence of market efficiency?

2.21 Market efficiency: In Problem 2.20, if the market is efficient, would it have been possible for Zippy's stock price to go down in the day that the firm announced the strong fourth quarter results?

2.22 Market efficiency: If the market is strong-form efficient, then trading on tips you hear from Jim Cramer (the host of *Mad Money* on CNBC) will generate no excess returns (i.e., returns in excess of fair compensation for the risk you are bearing). True or false?

2.23 Financial markets: What are the major differences between public and private markets?

2.24 Financial instruments: What are the two risk-hedging instruments discussed in this chapter?

2.25 Interest rates: What is the real rate of interest, and how is it determined?

2.26 Interest rates: How does the nominal rate of interest vary over time?

2.27 Interest rates: What is the Fisher equation, and how is it used?

2.28 Interest rates: Imagine you borrow $500 from your roommate, agreeing to pay her back $500 plus 7 percent nominal interest in one year. Assume inflation over the life of the contract is expected to be 4.25 percent. What is the total dollar amount you will have to pay her back in a year? What percentage of the interest payment is the result of the real rate of interest?

2.29 Interest rates: Your parents have given you $1,000 a year before your graduation so that you can take a trip when you graduate. You wisely decide to invest the money in a bank CD that pays 6.75 percent interest. You know that the trip costs $1,025 right now and that inflation for the year is predicted to be 4 percent. Will you have enough money in a year to purchase the trip?

2.30 Interest rates: When are the nominal and real interest rates equal?

Sample Test Problems

2.1 How are brokers different from dealers?

2.2 What is an investment fund?

2.3 Identify what type of transactions (direct or indirect) the following are:
  a. You buy 200 shares of Fidelity Growth Mutual Fund.
  b. Roger buys a bank CD for $5,000.
  c. Bank of America makes a $25,000 loan to Leila's Coffee Shop.
  d. Nora buys $3,000 of Xerox bonds from a new issue.

2.4 If the nominal rate of interest is 7.5 percent and the real rate is 4 percent, what is the expected inflation premium?

2.5 What is the relation between business cycles and the general level of interest rates?

3 Financial Statements, Cash Flows, and Taxes

CHAPTER THREE

Learning Objectives

1. Discuss generally accepted accounting principles (GAAP) and their importance to the economy.

2. Explain the balance sheet identity and why a balance sheet must balance.

3. Describe how market-value balance sheets differ from book-value balance sheets.

4. Identify the basic equation for the income statement and the information it provides.

5. Understand the calculation of cash flows from operating, investing, and financing activities required in the statement of cash flows.

6. Explain how the four major financial statements discussed in this chapter are related.

7. Identify the cash flow to a firm's investors using its financial statements.

8. Discuss the difference between average and marginal tax rates.

Luay Bahoora/Alamy

On July 24, 2012, after the close of U.S. financial markets, Apple Inc. announced that its corporate earnings for the quarter ended June 30, 2012, were $8.8 billion, or $9.32 per common share outstanding. This represented an increase of 19.6 percent from 2011 and a 164 percent increase from 2010. Even though iPhone sales were up 28 percent and iPad sales were up 84 percent, stock market analysts and investors were disappointed. They had expected even more. As a result, Apple's stock price dropped following the announcement, trading from a high of $609.68 per share on July 24 to a low of $570.00 the next day.

This example illustrates the relation between the information contained in a firm's accounting statements and its stock performance. Public corporations in the U.S. communicate their financial performance to their investors through their financial statements, leading to Wall Street's virtual obsession with accounting earnings. Analysts estimate how much firms should earn in a particular reporting period, and firms that fail to meet these estimates can be punished by falling stock prices. If a firm consistently fails to meet these estimates, its CEO can be out of a job. Pressure to meet analyst expectations has occasionally led managers to misstate accounting results in efforts to mislead analysts and investors. In the wake of several especially large-scale accounting frauds, involving firms such as Enron and WorldCom, Congress and federal regulators tightened accounting standards and oversight of the accounting profession in the early 2000s. Passage of the Sarbanes-Oxley Act, discussed in Chapter 1, is an example of these steps.

Clearly, the correct preparation of financial statements is crucial for investors. In this chapter and the next, we focus on the preparation, interpretation, and limitations of financial statements. The concepts that we discuss in these chapters provide an important foundation for the material discussed in the rest of this book.

CHAPTER PREVIEW

In Chapter 1 we noted that all businesses have owners and stakeholders—managers, creditors, suppliers, and the government, among others—who have claims on the firms' cash flows. The owners and stakeholders in a firm need to monitor the firm's progress and evaluate its performance. Financial statements enable them to do this. The accounting system is the framework that gathers information about the firm's business activities and translates the information into objective numerical financial reports.

Most firms prepare financial statements on a regular basis and have independent auditors certify that the financial statements have been prepared in accordance with generally accepted accounting principles and contain no material misstatements. The audit increases the confidence of the owners and stakeholders that the financial statements prepared by management present a "fair and accurate" picture of the firm's financial condition at a particular point in time.

In fact, it is difficult to get any type of legitimate business loan without audited financial statements.

This chapter reviews the basic structure of a firm's financial statements and explains how the various statements fit together. It also explains the relation between accounting income and cash flow to investors. We examine the preparation of the balance sheet, the income statement, the statement of retained earnings, and the statement of cash flows. As you read through this part of the chapter, pay particular attention to the differences between (1) book value and market value and (2) accounting income and cash flow to investors. Understanding the differences between these concepts is necessary to avoid serious analytical and decision-making errors. The last part of the chapter discusses essential features of the federal tax code for corporations. In finance we make most decisions on an after-tax basis, so understanding the tax code is very important.

3.1 FINANCIAL STATEMENTS AND ACCOUNTING PRINCIPLES

Before we can meaningfully interpret and analyze financial statements, we need to understand some accounting principles that guide their preparation. Thus, we begin the chapter with a discussion of generally accepted accounting principles, which guide firms in the preparation of financial statements. First, however, we briefly describe the annual report.

LEARNING OBJECTIVE ①

The Annual Report

The *annual report* is the most important report that firms issue to their stockholders and make available to the general public. Historically, annual reports were dull, black-and-white publications that presented audited financial statements for firms. Today some annual reports, especially those of large public companies, are slick, picture-laden, glossy "magazines" in full color with orchestrated media messages.

Annual reports typically are divided into three distinct sections. First are the financial tables, which contain financial information about the firm and its operations for the year, and an accompanying summary explaining the firm's performance over the past year. For example, the summary might explain that sales and profits were down because of continuing economic weakness related to the European crisis. Often, there is a letter from the chairman or CEO that provides some insights into the reasons for the firm's performance, a discussion of new developments, and a high-level view of the firm's strategy and future direction. It is important to note that the financial tables are historical records reflecting past performance of the firm and do not necessarily indicate what the firm will do in the future.

 To find annual reports and other corporate filings for U.S. corporations, visit the EDGAR search page maintained by the U.S. Securities and Exchange Commission (SEC) at http://www.sec.gov/edgar.shtml.

The second part of the report is often a corporate public relations piece discussing the firm's product lines, its services to its customers, and its contributions to the communities in which it operates.

The third part of the annual report presents the audited financial statements: the balance sheet, the income statement, the statement of retained earnings, and the statement of cash flows. Overall, the annual report provides a good overview of the firm's operating and financial performance and states why, in management's judgment, things turned out the way they did.

Generally Accepted Accounting Principles

generally accepted accounting principles (GAAP)
a set of rules that defines how companies are to prepare financial statements

In the United States, accounting statements are prepared in accordance with **generally accepted accounting principles (GAAP)**, a set of widely agreed-upon rules and procedures that define how companies are to maintain financial records and prepare financial reports. These principles are important because without them, financial statements would be less standardized. Accounting standards such as GAAP make it easier for analysts and management to make meaningful comparisons of a company's performance against that of other companies.

Accounting principles and reporting practices for U.S. firms are promulgated by the Financial Accounting Standards Board (FASB), a not-for-profit body that operates in the public interest. FASB derives its authority from the Securities and Exchange Commission (SEC). GAAP and reporting practices are published in the form of FASB statements, and certified public accountants are required to follow these statements in their auditing and accounting practices.

You can find more information about FASB at http://www.fasb.org.

Fundamental Accounting Principles

To better understand financial statements, it is helpful to look at some fundamental accounting principles embodied in GAAP. These principles determine the manner of recording, measuring, and reporting company transactions. As you will see, the practical application of these principles requires professional judgment, which can result in considerable differences in financial statements.

The Assumption of Arm's-Length Transactions

Accounting is based on the recording of economic transactions that can be quantified in dollar amounts. It assumes that the parties to a transaction are economically rational and are free to act *independently* of each other. In other words, all transactions are assumed to be "arm's-length transactions." The price you pay for something or the price for which you sell something is what gets recorded on the financial statements. To illustrate, let's assume that you are preparing a personal balance sheet for a bank loan on which you must list all your assets. You are including your BMW 325 as an asset. You bought the car a few months ago from your father for $3,000 when the retail price of the car was $15,000. You got a good deal. However, the price you paid, which would be the number recorded on your balance sheet, was not the market price. Since you did not purchase the BMW in an arm's-length transaction, your balance sheet would not reflect the true value of the asset.

The Cost Principle

book value
the net value of an asset or liability recorded on the financial statements—normally reflects historical cost

Generally, the value of an asset that is recorded on a company's "books" reflects its historical cost. The historical cost is assumed to represent the fair market value of the item at the time it was acquired and is recorded as the **book value**. Over time, it is unlikely that an asset's book value will be equal to its market value because market values tend to change over time. The major exception to this principle is marketable securities, such as the stock of another company, which are recorded at their current market value.

It is important to note that accounting statements are records of past performance; they are based on historical costs, not on current market prices or values. Accounting statements translate the business's past performance into dollars and cents, which helps management and investors better understand how the business has performed in the past.

The Realization Principle

Under the realization principle, revenue is recognized only when the sale is virtually completed and the exchange value for the goods or services can be reliably determined. As a practical matter, this means that most revenues are recognized at the time of sale whether or not cash is actually received. At this time, if a firm sells to its customers on credit, an account receivable is recorded. The firm receives the cash only when the customer actually makes the payment. Although the realization principle seems straightforward, there can be considerable ambiguity in its interpretation. For example, should revenues be recognized when goods are ordered, when they are shipped, or when payment is received from the customer?

The Matching Principle

Accountants try to match revenue on the income statement with the expenses incurred to generate the revenue. In practice, this matching principle means that revenue is first recognized (according to the realization principle) and then is matched with the costs associated with producing the revenue. For example, if we manufacture a product and sell it on credit (accounts receivable), the revenue is recognized at the time of sale. The expenses associated with manufacturing the product—expenditures for raw materials, labor, equipment, and facilities—are recognized at the same time. Notice that the actual cash outflows for expenses may not occur at the same time the expenses are recognized. The figures on the income statement more than likely will not correspond to the actual cash inflows and outflows during the period.

The Going Concern Assumption

The going concern assumption is the assumption that a business will remain in operation for the foreseeable future. This assumption underlies much of what is done in accounting. For example, suppose that Sears has $4.6 billion of inventory on its balance sheet, representing what the firm actually paid for the inventory in arm's-length transactions. If we assume that Sears is a going concern, the balance sheet figure is a reasonable number because in the normal course of business we expect Sears to be able to sell the goods for their cost plus some reasonable markup.

However, suppose Sears declares bankruptcy and is forced by its creditors to liquidate its assets. If this happens, Sears is no longer a going concern. What will the inventory be worth then? We cannot be certain, but 50 cents on the dollar might be a high figure. The going concern assumption allows the accountant to record assets at cost rather than their value in a liquidation sale, which is usually much less.

You can see that the fundamental accounting principles just discussed leave considerable professional discretion to accountants in the preparation of financial statements. As a result, financial statements can and do differ because of honest differences in professional judgments. Of course, there are limits on honest professional differences, and at some point an accountant's choices can cross a line and result in "cooking the books."

International GAAP

Accounting is often called the language of business. Just as there are different dialects within languages, there are different international "dialects" in accounting. For example, the set of generally accepted accounting principles in the United Kingdom is called U.K. GAAP. Given the variation in accounting standards, accountants must adjust financial statements so that meaningful comparisons can be made between firms that utilize different sets of accounting principles. The cost of making these adjustments represents an economic inefficiency that adds to the overall cost of international business transactions.

By the end of the 1990s, the two predominant international reporting standards were the U.S. GAAP and the International Financial Reporting Standards, also known as IFRS. Both FASB and the *International Accounting Standards Board (IASB)* have been working toward a convergence of these rules in an effort to provide a truly global accounting standard. Today most international jurisdictions already utilize IFRS or some close variant of those standards. Consistent with these practices, the U.S. SEC is reviewing proposals for U.S. corporations to adopt IFRS for financial reporting as early as 2015.

You can read more about IFRS at http://www.ifrs.com.

Illustrative Company: Diaz Manufacturing

In the next part of this chapter, we turn to a discussion of four fundamental financial statements: the balance sheet, the income statement, the statement of retained earnings, and the statement of cash flows. To more clearly illustrate these financial statements, we use data from Diaz Manufacturing Company, a fictional Houston-based provider of petroleum and industrial equipment and services worldwide.[1] Diaz Manufacturing was formed in 2003 as a spin-off of several divisions of Cooper Industries. The firm specializes in the design and manufacturing of systems used in petroleum production and has two divisions: (1) Diaz Energy Services, which sells oil and gas compression equipment, and (2) Diaz Manufacturing, which makes valves and related parts for energy production.

In 2013 Diaz Manufacturing's sales increased to $1.56 billion, an increase of 12.8 percent from the previous year. A letter to stockholders in the 2013 annual report stated that management did not expect earnings in 2014 to exceed the 2013 earnings. The reason for caution was that Diaz's earnings are very susceptible to changes in the political and economic environment in the world's energy-producing regions, and in 2013 the environment in the Middle East was highly unstable. Management reassured investors, however, that Diaz had the financial strength and the management team needed to weather any economic adversity.

> **BEFORE YOU GO ON**

1. What types of information does a firm's annual report contain?

2. What is the realization principle, and why may it lead to a difference in the timing of when revenues are recognized on the books and cash is collected?

3.2 THE BALANCE SHEET

 LEARNING OBJECTIVE

balance sheet
a financial statement that shows a firm's financial position (assets, liabilities, and equity) at a point in time

The **balance sheet** reports the firm's financial position at a particular point in time. Exhibit 3.1 shows the balance sheets for Diaz Manufacturing on December 31, 2012 and December 31, 2013. The left-hand side of the balance sheet identifies the firm's assets, which are listed at book value. These assets are owned by the firm and are used to generate income. The right-hand side of the balance sheet includes liabilities and stockholders' equity, which tell us how the firm has financed its assets. Liabilities are obligations of the firm that represent claims against its assets. These claims arise from debts and other obligations to pay creditors, employees, or the government. In contrast, stockholders' equity represents the residual claim of the owners on the remaining assets of the firm after all liabilities have been paid.[2] The basic balance sheet identity can thus be stated as follows:[3]

$$\text{Total assets} = \text{Total liabilities} + \text{Total stockholders' equity} \qquad (3.1)$$

Since stockholders' equity is the residual claim, stockholders would receive any remaining value if the firm decided to sell off all of its assets and use the money to pay its creditors. That is why the balance sheet always balances. Simply put, if you total what the firm owns and what it owes, then the difference between the two is the total stockholders' equity:

$$\text{Total stockholders' equity} = \text{Total assets} - \text{Total liabilities}$$

Notice that total stockholders' equity can be positive, negative, or equal to zero.

It is important to note that balance sheet items are listed in a specific order. Assets are listed in order of their liquidity, with the most liquid assets, cash and marketable securities, at the top. The liquidity of an asset is defined by how quickly it can be converted into cash without loss of value. Thus, an asset's liquidity has two dimensions: (1) the speed and ease with which the asset can be sold and (2) whether the asset can be sold without loss of value. Of course, any asset can be sold easily and quickly if the price is low enough. Liabilities on the balance sheet are listed based on their maturity, with the liabilities having the shortest maturities listed at the top. Maturity refers to the length of time remaining before the obligation must be paid.

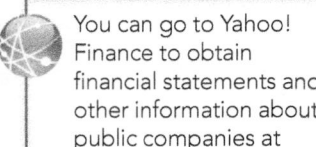 You can go to Yahoo! Finance to obtain financial statements and other information about public companies at http://finance.yahoo.com.

---

[1] Although Diaz Manufacturing Company is not a real firm, the financial statements and situations presented are based on a composite of actual firms.

[2] The terms *owners' equity, stockholders' equity, shareholders' equity, net worth,* and *equity* are used interchangeably to refer to the ownership of a corporation's stock.

[3] An *identity* is an equation that is true by definition; thus, a balance sheet must balance.

EXHIBIT 3.1 Diaz Manufacturing Balance Sheets as of December 31 ($ millions)

The left-hand side of the balance sheet lists the assets that the firm has at a particular point in time, while the right-hand side shows how the firm has financed those assets.

Assets	2013	2012	Liabilities and Stockholders' Equity	2013	2012
Cash[a]	$ 288.5	$ 16.6	Accounts payable and accruals	$ 349.3	$ 325.0
Accounts receivable	306.2	268.8	Notes payable	10.5	4.2
Inventories	423.8	372.7	Accrued taxes	18.0	16.8
Other current assets	21.3	29.9	Total current liabilities	$ 377.8	$ 346.0
Total current assets	$1,039.8	$ 688.0	Long-term debt	574.0	305.6
			Total liabilities	$ 951.8	$ 651.6
Plant and equipment	911.6	823.3	Preferred stock[b]	—	—
Less: Accumulated depreciation	512.2	429.1	Common stock (54,566,054 shares)[c]	50.0	50.0
Net plant and equipment	$ 399.4	$ 394.2	Additional paid-in capital	842.9	842.9
			Retained earnings	67.8	(50.7)
Goodwill and other assets	450.0	411.6	Treasury stock (571,320 shares)	(23.3)	—
			Total stockholders' equity	$ 937.4	$ 842.2
Total assets	$1,889.2	$1,493.8	Total liabilities and equity	$1,889.2	$1,493.8

[a]Cash includes investments in marketable securities.
[b]10,000,000 preferred stock shares authorized.
[c]150,000,000 common stock shares authorized.

Next, we examine some important balance sheet accounts of Diaz Manufacturing as of December 31, 2013 (see Exhibit 3.1). As a matter of convention, accountants divide assets and liabilities into short-term (or current) and long-term parts. We will start by looking at current assets and liabilities.

Current Assets and Liabilities

Current assets are assets that can reasonably be expected to be converted into cash within one year. Besides cash, which includes investments in marketable securities such as money market instruments, other current assets are accounts receivable, which are typically due within 30 to 45 days, and inventory, which is money invested in raw materials, work-in-process inventory, and finished goods. Diaz's current assets total $1,039.8 million.

Current liabilities are obligations payable within one year. Typical current liabilities are accounts payable, which arise in the purchases of goods and services from vendors and are normally paid within 30 to 60 days; notes payable, which are formal borrowing agreements with a bank or some other lender that have a stated maturity; and accrued taxes from federal, state, and local governments, which are taxes Diaz owes but has not yet paid. Diaz's total current liabilities equal $377.8 million.

Net Working Capital

Recall from Chapter 1 that the dollar difference between total current assets and total current liabilities is the firm's net working capital:

$$\text{Net working capital} = \text{Total current assets} - \text{Total current liabilities} \qquad (3.2)$$

Net working capital is a measure of a firm's ability to meet its short-term obligations as they come due. One way that firms maintain their liquidity is by holding more current assets than current liabilities.

For Diaz Manufacturing, total current assets at the end of 2013 were $1,039.8 million, and total current liabilities were $377.8 million. The firm's net working capital was thus:

$$\begin{aligned} \text{Net working capital} &= \text{Total current assets} - \text{Total current liabilities} \\ &= \$1,039.8 \text{ million} - \$377.8 \text{ million} \\ &= \$662.0 \text{ million} \end{aligned}$$

To interpret this number, if Diaz Manufacturing took its current stock of cash and liquidated its marketable securities, accounts receivables, and inventory at book value, it would have $1,039.8 million with which to pay off its short-term liabilities of $377.8 million, leaving $662.0 million of "cushion." As a short-term creditor, such as a bank, you would view the net working capital position as positive because Diaz's current assets exceed current liabilities by almost three times ($1,039.8/$377.8 = 2.75).

Accounting for Inventory

Inventory, as noted earlier, is a current asset on the balance sheet, but it is usually the least liquid of the current assets. The reason is that it can take a long time for a firm to convert inventory into cash. For a manufacturing firm, the inventory cycle begins with raw materials, continues with goods in process, proceeds with finished goods, and finally concludes with selling the asset for cash or an account receivable. For a firm such as The Boeing Company, for example, the inventory cycle in manufacturing an aircraft can be nearly a year.

An important decision for management is the selection of an inventory valuation method. The most common methods are FIFO (first in, first out) and LIFO (last in, first out). During periods of changing price levels, how a firm values its inventory affects both its balance sheet and its income statement. For example, suppose that prices have been rising (inflation). If a company values its inventory using the FIFO method, when the firm makes a sale, it assumes the sale is from the oldest, lowest-cost inventory—first in, first out. Thus, during rising prices, firms using FIFO will have the lowest cost of goods sold, the highest net income, and the highest inventory value. In contrast, a company using the LIFO method assumes the sale is from the newest, highest-cost inventory—last in, first out. During a period of inflation, firms using LIFO will have the highest cost of goods sold, the lowest net income, and the lowest inventory value.

Because inventory valuation methods can have a significant impact on both the income statement and the balance sheet, when financial analysts compare different companies, they make adjustments to the financial statements for differences in inventory valuation methods. Although firms can switch from one inventory valuation method to another, this type of change is an extraordinary event and cannot be done frequently.

Diaz Manufacturing reports inventory values in the United States using the LIFO method. The remaining inventories, which are located outside the United States and Canada, are calculated using the FIFO method. Diaz's total inventory is $423.8 million.

Long-Term Assets and Liabilities

The remaining assets on the balance sheet are classified as long-term assets. Typically, these assets are financed by long-term liabilities and stockholders' equity.

Long-Term Assets

Long-term productive assets are the assets that the firm uses to generate most of its income. Long-term assets may be tangible or intangible. Tangible assets are balance sheet items such as land, mineral resources, buildings, equipment, machinery, and vehicles that are used over an extended period of time. In addition, tangible assets can include other businesses that a firm wholly or partially owns, such as foreign subsidiaries. Intangible assets are items such as patents, copyrights, licensing agreements, technology, and other intellectual capital the firm owns.

Goodwill is an intangible asset that arises only when a firm purchases another firm. Conceptually, goodwill is a measure of how much the price paid for the acquired firm exceeds the sum of the values of the acquired firm's individual assets. There are a variety of reasons why the purchase price of an asset might exceed its value to the seller. Goodwill may arise from improvements in efficiency, the reputation or brands associated with products or trademarks, or even a valuable client base for a particular service. For example, if Diaz Manufacturing paid $2.0 million for a company that had individual assets with a total fair market value of $1.9 million, the goodwill premium paid would be $100,000 ($2.0 million − $1.9 million = $0.1 million).

Diaz Manufacturing's long-term assets comprise net plant and equipment of $399.4 million and intangible and other assets of $450.0 million, as shown in Exhibit 3.1. The term *net plant and equipment* indicates that accumulated depreciation has been subtracted to arrive at the net value. That is, net plant and equipment equals total plant and equipment less accumulated depreciation; accumulated depreciation is the total amount of depreciation expense taken on plant and equipment up to the balance sheet date. For Diaz Manufacturing, the previous method yields the following result:

$$\begin{aligned} \text{Net plant and equipment} &= \text{Total plant and equipment} - \text{Accumulated depreciation} \\ &= \$911.6 \text{ million} - \$512.2 \text{ million} \\ &= \$399.4 \text{ million} \end{aligned}$$

Accumulated Depreciation

When a firm acquires a tangible asset that deteriorates with use and wears out, accountants try to allocate the asset's cost over its estimated useful life. The matching principle requires that the cost be expensed during the period in which the firm benefited from use of the asset. Thus, **depreciation** allocates the cost of a limited-life asset to the periods in which the firm is assumed to benefit from the asset. Tangible assets with an unlimited life, such as land, are not depreciated. Depreciation affects the balance sheet through the accumulated depreciation account; we discuss its effect on the income statement in Section 3.4.

depreciation
allocation of the cost of an asset over its estimated useful life to reflect the wear and tear on the asset as it is used to produce the firm's goods and services

A company can elect whether to depreciate its assets using straight-line depreciation or one of the approved accelerated depreciation methods. All of these methods allow the same amount of total depreciation over an asset's life. However, accelerated depreciation methods allow for more depreciation expense in the early years of an asset's life than straight-line depreciation.

Diaz Manufacturing uses the straight-line method of depreciation. Had Diaz elected to use accelerated depreciation, the value of its depreciable assets would have been written off to the income statement more quickly as a higher depreciation expense, which results in a lower net plant and equipment account on its balance sheet and a lower net income for the period.

Long-Term Liabilities

Long-term liabilities include debt instruments due and payable beyond one year as well as other long-term obligations of the firm. They include bonds, bank term loans, mortgages, and other types of liabilities, such as pension obligations and deferred compensation. Typically, firms finance long-term assets with long-term liabilities. Diaz Manufacturing has a single long-term liability of $574.0 million, which is a long-term debt.

Equity

We have summarized the types of assets and liabilities that appear on the balance sheet. Now we look at the equity accounts. Diaz Manufacturing's total stockholders' equity at the end of 2013 is $937.4 million and is made up of four accounts—common stock, additional paid-in capital, retained earnings, and treasury stock—which we discuss next. We conclude with a discussion of preferred stock. Although a line item for preferred stock appears on Diaz Manufacturing's balance sheets, the company has no shares of preferred stock outstanding.

The Common Stock Accounts

The most important equity accounts are those related to common stock, which represent the true ownership of the firm. Certain basic rights of ownership typically come with common stock; those rights are as follows:

1. The right to vote on corporate matters, such as the election of the board of directors or important actions such as the purchase of another company.
2. The preemptive right, which allows stockholders to purchase any additional shares of stock issued by the corporation in proportion to the number of shares they currently own. This allows common stockholders to retain the same percentage of ownership in the firm, if they choose to do so.
3. The right to receive cash dividends if they are paid.
4. If the firm is liquidated, the right to all remaining corporate assets after all creditors and preferred stockholders have been paid.

A common source of confusion is the number of different common stock accounts on the balance sheet, each of which identifies a source of the firm's equity. The *common stock account* identifies the funding from equity investors that was used to start and maintain the business and is priced at a par value. The par value is an arbitrary number set by management, usually a nominal amount such as $1.

Clearly, par value has little to do with the market value of the stock when it is sold to investors. The *additional paid-in capital* is the amount of capital received from the sale of common stock in excess of par value. Thus, for example, if a new business is started with $40,000 from the sale of 1,000 shares of common stock with a par value of $1, the owners' equity account looks as follows:

Common stock (1,000 shares @ $1 par value)	$ 1,000
Additional paid-in capital	39,000
Total paid-in capital	$40,000

Note the money put up by the initial investors: $1,000 in total par value (1,000 shares of common stock with a par value of $1) and $39,000 additional paid-in capital, for a total of $40,000.

As you can see in Exhibit 3.1, Diaz manufacturing has 54,566,054 shares of common stock with a par value of 91.63 cents, for a total value of $50.0 million (54,566,054 shares × 91.63 cents = $50 million). The additional paid-in capital is $842.9 million. Thus, Diaz's total paid-in capital is $892.9 million ($50.0 million + $842.9 million = $892.9 million).

Retained Earnings

The retained earnings account represents earnings that have been retained and reinvested in the business over time rather than being paid out as cash dividends. The change in retained earnings from one period to the next can be computed as the difference between net income and dividends paid. Diaz Manufacturing's retained earnings account is only $67.8 million. Reading the annual report, we learn that in the recent past the company "wrote down" the value of a substantial amount of assets. This transaction, which will be discussed later in this chapter, also reduced the size of the retained earnings account by reducing net income.

Note that retained earnings are not the same as cash. In fact, as we discuss in Section 3.7 of this chapter, a company can have a very large retained earnings account and no cash. Conversely, it can have a lot of cash and a very small retained earnings account. Because retained earnings appear on the liability side of the balance sheet, they do not represent an asset, as do cash and marketable securities.

Treasury Stock

treasury stock
stock that the firm has repurchased from investors

The **treasury stock** account represents stock that the firm has repurchased from investors. Publicly traded companies can simply buy shares of stock from stockholders on the market at the prevailing price. Typically, repurchased stock is held as "treasury stock," and the firm can reissue it in the future if it desires. Diaz Manufacturing has spent a total of $23.3 million to repurchase the 571,320 shares of common stock it currently holds as treasury stock. The company has had a policy of repurchasing common stock, which has been subsequently reissued to senior executives under the firm's stock-option plan.

You may wonder why a firm's management would repurchase its own stock. This is a classic finance question, and it has no simple answer. One reason is that when a company has excess cash and management believes its stock price is undervalued, it makes sense to purchase stock with the cash. We discuss this in more detail in Chapter 15.

Preferred Stock

Preferred stock is a cross between common stock and long-term debt. Preferred stock pays dividends at a specified fixed rate, which means that the firm cannot increase or decrease the dividend rate, regardless of whether the firm's earnings increase or decrease. However, like common stock dividends, preferred stock dividends are declared by the board of directors, and in the event of financial distress, the board can elect not to pay a preferred stock dividend. If preferred stock dividends are not paid, the firm is typically required to pay dividends that have been skipped in the past before they can pay dividends to common stockholders. In the event of bankruptcy, preferred stockholders are paid before common stockholders but after bondholders and other creditors. As shown in Exhibit 3.1, Diaz Manufacturing has no preferred stock outstanding, but the company is authorized to issue up to 10 million shares of preferred stock.

> **BEFORE YOU GO ON**

1. What is net working capital? Why might a low value for this number be considered undesirable?

2. Explain the accounting concept behind depreciation.

3. What is treasury stock?

3.3 MARKET VALUE VERSUS BOOK VALUE

Although accounting statements are helpful to analysts and managers, they have a number of limitations. One of these limitations, mentioned earlier, is that accounting statements are historical—they are based on data such as the cost of a building that was built years ago. Thus, the value of assets on the balance sheet is what the firm paid for them and not their current **market value**—the amount they are worth today.

Investors and management, however, care about how the company will do in the future. The best information concerning how much a company's assets can earn in the future, as well as how much of a burden its liabilities are, comes from the current market value of those assets and liabilities. Accounting statements would therefore be more valuable if they measured current value. The process of recording assets at their current market value is often called *marking to market*.

In theory, everyone agrees that it is better to base financial statements on current information. Marking to market provides decision makers with financial statements that more closely reflect a company's true financial condition; thus, they have a better chance of making the correct economic decision, given the information available. For example, providing current market values means that managers can no longer conceal a failing business or hide unrealized gains on assets.

On the downside, it can be difficult to identify the market value of an asset, particularly if there are few transactions involving comparable assets. Critics also point out that estimating market value can require complex financial modeling, and the resulting numbers can be open to manipulation and abuse. Finally, mark-to-market accounting can become inaccurate if market prices deviate from the "fundamental" values of assets and liabilities. This might occur because buyers and sellers have either incorrect information, or have either over-optimistic or over-pessimistic expectations about the future.

LEARNING OBJECTIVE 3

market value
the price at which an item can be sold

 For some perspective on mark-to-market accounting, go to http://www.fool.com/investing/dividends-income/2008/10/02/mark-to-market-accounting-what-you-should-know.aspx?source=isesitlnk0000001&mrr=0.50.

A More Informative Balance Sheet

To illustrate why market value provides better economic information than book value, let's revisit the balance sheet components discussed earlier. Our discussion will also help you understand why there can be such large differences between some book-value and market-value balance sheet accounts.

Assets

For current assets, market value and book value may be reasonably close. The reason is that current assets have a short life cycle and typically are converted into cash quickly. Then, as new current assets are added to the balance sheet, they are entered at their current market price.

In contrast, long-term assets, which are also referred to as fixed assets, have a long life cycle and their market value and book value are not likely to be equal. In addition, if an asset is depreciable, the amount of depreciation shown on the balance sheet does not necessarily reflect the actual loss of economic value. As a general rule, the longer the time that has passed since an asset was acquired, the more likely it is that the current market value will differ from the book value.

For example, suppose a firm purchased land for a trucking depot in Atlanta, Georgia, 30 years ago for $100,000. Today the land is nestled in an expensive suburban area and is worth around $5.5 million. The difference between the book value of $100,000 and the market value is $5.4 million. In another example, say an airline company decided to replace its aging fleet of aircraft with new fuel-efficient jets in the late 1990s. Following the September 11, 2001, terrorist attack, airline travel declined dramatically; and during 2003 nearly one-third of all commercial jets were "mothballed." In 2003 the current market value of the replacement commercial jets was about two-thirds their original cost. Why the decline? Because the expected cash flows from owning a commercial aircraft had declined a great deal.

Liabilities

The market value of liabilities can also differ from their book value, though typically by smaller amounts than is the case with assets. For liabilities, the balance sheet shows the amount of money that the company has promised to pay. This figure is generally close to the actual market value for short-term liabilities because of their relatively short maturities.

For long-term debt, however, book value and market value can differ substantially. The market value of debt with fixed interest payments is affected by the level of interest rates in the economy. More specifically, after long-term debt is issued, if the market rate of interest increases, the market value of the debt will decline. Conversely, if interest rates decline, the value of the debt will increase. For example, assume that a firm has $1 million of 20-year bonds outstanding. If the market rate of interest increases from 5 to 8 percent, the price of the bonds will decline to around $700,000.[4] Thus, changes in interest rates can have an important effect on the market values of long-term liabilities, such as corporate bonds. Even if interest rates do not change, the market value of long-term liabilities can change if the performance of the firm declines and the probability of default increases.

Stockholders' Equity

The book value of the firm's equity is one of the least informative items on the balance sheet. The book value of equity, as suggested earlier, is simply a historical record. As a result, it says very little about the current market value of the stockholders' stake in the firm.

In contrast, on a balance sheet where both assets and liabilities are marked-to-market, the firm's equity is more informative to management and investors. *The difference between the market values of the assets and liabilities provides a better estimate of the market value of stockholders' equity than the difference in the book values.* Intuitively, this makes sense because if you know the true market values of the firm's assets and liabilities, the difference must equal the market value of the stockholders' equity.

You should be aware, however, that the difference between the sum of the market values of the individual assets and total liabilities will not give us an exact estimate of the market value of stockholders' equity. The reason is that the total value of a firm's assets depends on how these assets are utilized. By utilizing the assets efficiently, management can make the total value greater than the simple sum of the individual asset values.

Finally, if you know the market value of the stockholders' equity and the number of shares of stock outstanding, it is easy to compute the stock price. Specifically, the price of a share of stock is the market value of the firm's stockholders' equity divided by the number of shares outstanding.

A Market-Value Balance Sheet

Let's look at an example of how a market-value balance sheet can differ from a book-value balance sheet. Marvel Airline is a small regional carrier that has been serving the Northeast for five years. The airline has a fleet of short-haul jet aircraft, most of which were purchased over the past two years. The fleet has a book value of $600 million. Recently, the airline industry has suffered substantial losses in revenue due to price competition, and most carriers are projecting operating losses for the foreseeable future. As a result, the market value of Marvel's aircraft fleet is only $400 million. The book value of Marvel's long-term debt is $300 million, which is

---

[4]We will discuss how changes in interest rates affect the market price of debt in Chapter 7, so for now don't worry about the numerical calculation.

near its current market value. The firm has 100 million shares outstanding. Using these data, we can construct two balance sheets, one based on historical book values and the other based on market values:

Marvel Airlines
Market-Value versus Book-Value Balance Sheets ($ millions)

Assets	Book	Market	Liabilities and Stockholders' Equity	Book	Market
Aircraft	$600	$400	Long-term debt	$300	$300
			Stockholders' equity	300	100
Total	$600	$400		$600	$400

Based on the book-value balance sheet, the firm's financial condition looks fine; the book value of Marvel's aircraft at $600 million is near what the firm paid, and the stockholders' equity account is $300 million. But when we look at the market-value balance sheet, a different story emerges. We immediately see that the value of the aircraft has declined by $200 million and the stockholders' equity has declined by $200 million!

Why the decline in stockholders' equity? Recall that in Chapter 1 we argued that the value of any asset—stocks, bonds, or a firm—is determined by the future cash flows the asset will generate. At the time the aircrafts were purchased, it was expected that they would generate a certain amount of cash flows over time. Now that hard times plague the industry, the cash flow expectations have been lowered, and hence the decline in the value of stockholders' equity.

The Market-Value Balance Sheet

LEARNING BY DOING

PROBLEM: Grady Means and his four partners in Menlo Park Consulting (MPC) have developed a revolutionary new continuous audit program that can monitor high-risk areas within a firm and identify abnormalities so that corrective actions can be taken. The partners have spent about $300,000 developing the program. The firm's book-keeper records the audit program on the firm's balance sheet as an asset valued at cost, which is $300,000. To launch the product, the four partners recently invested an additional $1 million, and the money is currently in the firm's bank account. At a recent trade show, a number of accounting and financial consulting firms tried to buy the new continuous product—the highest offer being $15 million. Assuming these are MPC's only assets and liabilities, prepare the firm's book-value and market-value balance sheets and explain the difference between the two.

APPLICATION 3.1

APPROACH: The main differences between the two balance sheets will be the treatment of the $300,000 already spent to develop the program and the $15 million offer. The book-value balance sheet is a historical document, which means all assets are valued at what it cost to put them in service, while the market-value balance sheet reflects the value of the assets if they were sold under current market conditions. The differences between the two approaches can be considerable.

SOLUTION: The two balance sheets are as follows:

Menlo Park Consulting
Market-Value versus Book-Value Balance Sheets ($ thousands)

Assets	Book	Market	Liabilities and Stockholder's Equity	Book	Market
Cash in bank	$1,000	$ 1,000	Long-term debt	$ —	$ —
Intangible assets	300	15,000	Stockholders' equity	1,300	16,000
Total	$1,300	$16,000		$1,300	$16,000

(continued)

The book-value balance sheet provides little useful information. The book value of the firm's total assets is $1.3 million, which consists of cash in the bank and the cost of developing the audit program. Since the firm has no debt, total assets must equal the book value of stockholders' equity. The market value tells a dramatically different story. The market value of the audit program is estimated to be $15.0 million; thus, the market value of stockholders' equity is $16.0 million and not $1.3 million as reported in the book-value balance sheet.

> **BEFORE YOU GO ON**

1. What is the difference between book value and market value?

2. What are some objections to the preparation of marked-to-market balance sheets?

3.4 THE INCOME STATEMENT AND THE STATEMENT OF RETAINED EARNINGS

 LEARNING OBJECTIVE

In the previous sections, we examined a firm's balance sheet, which is like a financial snapshot of the firm at a point in time. In contrast, the income statement illustrates the flow of operating activity and tells us how profitable a firm was between two points in time.

The Income Statement

income statement
a financial statement that reports a firm's revenues, expenses, and profits or losses over a period of time

The **income statement** summarizes the revenues, expenses, and profitability (or losses) of the firm over some period of time, usually a month, a quarter, or a year. The basic equation for the income statement can be expressed as follows:

$$\text{Net income} = \text{Revenues} - \text{Expenses} \tag{3.3}$$

Let's look more closely at each element in this equation.

Revenues

A firm's revenues (sales) arise from the products and services it creates through its business operations. For manufacturing and merchandising companies, revenues come from the sale of merchandise. Service companies, such as consulting firms, generate fees for the services they perform. Other kinds of businesses earn revenues by charging interest or collecting rent. Regardless of how they earn revenues, most firms either receive cash or create an account receivable for each transaction, which increases their total assets.

Expenses

Expenses are the various costs that the firm incurs to generate revenues. Broadly speaking, expenses are (1) the value of long-term assets consumed through business operations, such as depreciation expense, and (2) the costs incurred in conducting business, such as labor, utilities, materials, and taxes.

Net Income

earnings per share (EPS)
net income divided by the number of common shares outstanding

The firm's net income reflects its accomplishments (revenues) relative to its efforts (expenses) during a time period. If revenues exceed expenses, the firm generates net income for the period. If expenses exceed revenues, the firm has a net loss. Net income is often referred to as profits, as income, or simply as the "bottom line," since it is the last item on the income statement. Net income is often reported on a per-share basis and is then called **earnings per share (EPS)**, where

EXHIBIT 3.2	Diaz Manufacturing Income Statements for the Fiscal Year Ending December 31 ($ millions)

The income statement shows the sales, expenses, and profit earned by the firm over a specific period of time.

	2013	2012
Net sales[a]	$1,563.7	$1,386.7
Cost of goods sold	1,081.1	974.8
Selling and administrative expenses	231.1	197.4
Earnings before interest, taxes, depreciation, and amortization (EBITDA)	$ 251.5	$ 214.5
Depreciation and amortization	83.1	75.3
Earnings before interest and taxes (EBIT)	$ 168.4	$ 139.2
Interest expense	5.6	18.0
Earnings before taxes (EBT)	$ 162.8	$ 121.2
Taxes	44.3	16.1
Net income	$ 118.5	$ 105.1
Common stock dividend	—	—
Addition to retained earnings	$ 118.5	$ 105.1
Per-share data:		
Common stock price		
Earnings per share (EPS)	$ 2.17	$ 1.93
Dividends per share (DPS)	—	—
Book value per share (BVPS)	—	—
Cash flow per share (CFPS)	$ 3.69	$ 3.31

[a]Net sales is defined as total sales less all sales discounts and sales returns and allowances.

EPS equals net income divided by the number of common shares outstanding. A firm's earnings per share tell a stockholder how much the firm has earned (or lost) for each share of stock outstanding.

Income statements for Diaz Manufacturing for 2012 and 2013 are shown in Exhibit 3.2. You can see that in 2013 total revenues from all sources (net sales) were $1,563.7 million. Total expenses for producing and selling those goods were $1,445.2 million—the total of the amounts for cost of goods sold, selling and administrative expenses, depreciation, interest expense, and taxes.[5]

Using Equation 3.3, we can use these numbers to calculate Diaz Manufacturing's net income for the year:

$$\text{Net income} = \text{Revenues} - \text{Expenses}$$
$$= \$1,563.7 \text{ million} - \$1,445.2 \text{ million}$$
$$= \$118.5 \text{ million}$$

Since Diaz Manufacturing had 54,566,054 common shares outstanding at year's end, its EPS was $2.17 per share ($118.5 million/54,566,054 shares = $2.17 per share).

A Closer Look at Some Expense Categories

Next, we take a closer look at some of the expense items on the income statement. We discussed depreciation earlier in relation to the balance sheet, and we now look at the role of depreciation in the income statement.

Depreciation Expense. An interesting feature of financial reporting is that companies are allowed to prepare two sets of financial statements: one for tax purposes and one for managing the company and for financial reporting to the SEC and investors. For tax purposes, most firms elect to accelerate depreciation as quickly as is permitted under the tax code. The reason is that accelerated depreciation results in a higher depreciation expense to the income statement, which in turn results in a lower earnings before taxes (EBT) and a lower tax liability in the first few years after the asset is acquired. The good news about accelerating depreciation for tax purposes is that the firm pays lower taxes but the depreciation expense does not represent a cash flow. The depreciation method does not affect the cost of the asset. In contrast, straight-line depreciation

---

[5]Looking at Exhibit 3.2, we find that the total expenses (in millions) are as follows: $1,081.1 + $231.1 + $83.1 + $5.6 + $44.3 = $1,445.2.

results in lower depreciation expenses to the income statement, which results in higher EBT and higher tax payments. Firms generally use straight-line depreciation in the financial statements they report to the SEC and investors because it makes their earnings look better. The higher a firm's EBT, the higher its net income.

It is important to understand that, as we noted earlier, the company does not take more total depreciation under accelerated depreciation methods than under the straight-line method; the total amount of depreciation expensed to the income statement over the life of an asset is the same. Total depreciation cannot exceed the price paid for the asset. Accelerating depreciation only alters the timing of when the depreciation is expensed.

Amortization Expense.   Amortization is the process of writing off expenses for intangible assets—such as patents, licenses, copyrights, and trademarks—over their useful life. Since depreciation and amortization are very similar, they are often lumped together on the income statement. Both are noncash expenses, which means that an expense is recorded on the income statement, but the associated cash does not necessarily leave the firm in that period. For Diaz Manufacturing, the depreciation and amortization expense for 2013 was $83.1 million.

At one time, goodwill was one of the intangible assets subject to amortization. As of June 2001, however, goodwill could no longer be amortized. The value of the goodwill on a firm's balance sheet is now subject to an annual *impairment test*. This test requires that the company annually value the businesses that were acquired in the past to see if the value of the goodwill associated with those businesses has declined below the value at which it is being carried on the balance sheet. If the value of the goodwill has declined (been impaired), management must expense the amount of the impairment. This expense reduces the firm's reported net income.

Extraordinary Items.   Other items reported separately in the income statement are extraordinary items, which are reserved for nonoperating gains or losses. Extraordinary items are unusual and infrequent occurrences, such as gains or losses from floods, fires, earthquakes, or accidents. For example, in February 2011 BP plc, the large oil company, reported a loss of $4.9 billion for 2010. This was the company's first loss since 1992 and was a direct result of a $40.9 billion extraordinary expense associated with the large 2010 oil spill in the Gulf of Mexico. Diaz Manufacturing has no extraordinary expense item during 2013.

Step by Step to the Bottom Line

You probably noticed in Exhibit 3.2 that Diaz Manufacturing's income statement showed income at several intermediate steps before reaching net income, the so-called bottom line. These intermediate income figures, which are typically included on a firm's income statement, provide important information about the firm's performance and help identify what factors are driving the firm's income or losses.

EBITDA.   The first intermediate income figure is EBITDA, or earnings before interest, taxes, depreciation, and amortization. The importance of EBITDA is that it shows what is earned purely from operations and reflects how efficiently the firm can manufacture and sell its products without taking into account the cost of the productive asset base (plant and equipment and intangible assets). For Diaz Manufacturing, EBITDA was $251.5 million in 2013.

EBIT.   Subtracting depreciation and amortization from EBITDA yields the next intermediate figure, EBIT, or earnings before interest and taxes. EBIT for Diaz Manufacturing was $168.4 million.

EBT.   When interest expense is subtracted from EBIT, the result is EBT, or earnings before taxes. Diaz Manufacturing had EBT of $162.8 million in 2013.

Net Income.   Finally, taxes are subtracted from EBT to arrive at net income. For Diaz Manufacturing, as we have already seen, net income in 2013 was $118.5 million.

In Chapter 4 you will see how to use these intermediate income figures to evaluate the firm's financial condition. Next, we look at the statement of retained earnings, which provides detailed information about how management allocated the $118.5 million of net income earned during the period.

EXHIBIT 3.3 Diaz Manufacturing Statement of Retained Earnings for the Fiscal Year Ending December 31, 2013 ($ millions)

The statement of retained earnings accompanies the balance sheet and shows the beginning balance of retained earnings, the adjustments made to retained earnings during the year, and the ending balance.

Balance of retained earnings, December 31, 2012	$ (50.7)
Add: Net income, 2013	118.5
Less: Dividends to common stockholders, 2013	—
Balance of retained earnings, December 31, 2013	$ 67.8

The Statement of Retained Earnings

Corporations often prepare a statement of retained earnings, which identifies the changes in the retained earnings account from one accounting period to the next. During any accounting period, two events can affect the retained earnings account balance:

1. When the firm reports net income or loss.
2. When the board of directors declares and pays a cash dividend.

Exhibit 3.3 shows the activity in the retained earnings account for 2013 for Diaz Manufacturing. The beginning balance is a negative $50.7 million. The firm's annual report explains that the retained earnings deficit resulted from a $441 million write-down of assets that occurred when Diaz Manufacturing became a stand-alone business in June 2003. As reported in the 2013 income statement (Exhibit 3.2), the firm earned $118.5 million that year, and the board of directors elected not to declare any dividends. Retained earnings consequently went from a negative $50.7 million to a positive balance of $67.8 million, an increase of $118.5 million.

> **BEFORE YOU GO ON**

1. How is net income computed?
2. What is EBITDA, and what does it measure?
3. What accounting events trigger changes to the retained earnings account?

3.5 THE STATEMENT OF CASH FLOWS

LEARNING OBJECTIVE 5

There are times when the financial manager wants to know the details of all the cash inflows and outflows that have taken place during the year and to reconcile the beginning-of-year and end-of-year cash balances. The reason for the focus on cash flows is very practical. Managers must have a complete understanding of the uses of cash and the sources of cash in the firm. Firms must have the cash to pay wages, suppliers, and other creditors, and they often elect to defer cash receipts from sales by providing credit to customers. Managers may also decide to issue new securities to raise cash, or may retire existing liabilities or repurchase equity to use cash. Finally, the purchase and sale of long-term productive assets can have a measurable impact on a firm's cash position. In sum, managers are responsible for a wide variety of transactions that involve sources and uses of cash over an accounting period. The statement of cash flows provides them with what amounts to an inventory of these transactions, and helps them understand why the cash balance changed as it did from the beginning to the end of the period.

Sources and Uses of Cash

The **statement of cash flows** shows the company's cash inflows (receipts) and cash outflows (payments and investments) for a period of time. We derive these cash flows by looking at the firm's net income during the period and at changes in balance sheet accounts from the beginning of the period (end of the previous period) to the end of the period. In analyzing the statement of cash flows, it is important to understand that changes in the balance sheet

statement of cash flows
a financial statement that shows a firm's cash receipts and cash payments and investments for a period of time

accounts reflect cash flows. More specifically, increases in assets or decreases in liabilities and equity are uses of cash, while decreases in assets or increases in liabilities and equity are sources of cash. These changes in balance sheet items can be summarized by the following:

- *Working capital.* An increase in current assets (such as accounts receivable and inventory) is a use of cash. For example, if a firm increases its inventory, it must use cash to purchase the additional inventory. Conversely, the sale of inventory increases a firm's cash position. An increase in current liabilities (such as accounts or notes payable) is a source of cash. For example, if during the year a firm increases its accounts payable, it has effectively borrowed money from suppliers and increased its cash position.
- *Fixed assets.* An increase in long-term fixed assets is a use of cash. If a company purchases fixed assets during the year, it decreases cash because it must use cash to pay for the purchase. If the firm sells a fixed asset during the year, the firm's cash position will increase.
- *Long-term liabilities and equity.* An increase in long-term debt (bonds and private placement debt) or equity (common and preferred stock) is a source of cash. The retirement of debt or the purchase of treasury stock requires the firm to pay out cash, reducing cash balances.
- *Dividends.* Any cash dividend payment decreases a firm's cash balance.

Organization of the Statement of Cash Flows

The statement of cash flows is organized around three business activities—operating activities, long-term investing activities, and financing activities—and the reconciliation of the cash account. We discuss each element next and illustrate them with reference to the statement of cash flows for Diaz Manufacturing, which is shown in Exhibit 3.4.

Operating Activities.   Cash flows from operating activities in the statement of cash flows are the net cash flows that are related to a firm's principal business activities. The most important items are the firm's net income, depreciation and amortization expense, and working capital accounts (other than cash and short-term debt obligations, which are classified elsewhere).

EXHIBIT 3.4	Diaz Manufacturing Statement of Cash Flows for the Fiscal Year Ending December 31, 2013 ($ millions)

The statement of cash flows shows the sources of the cash that has come into the firm during a period of time and the ways in which this cash has been used.

Operating Activities	
Net income	$ 118.5
Additions (sources of cash)	
Depreciation and amortization	83.1
Increase in accounts payable	24.3
Decrease in other current assets	8.6
Increase in accrued income taxes	1.2
Subtractions (uses of cash)	
Increase in accounts receivable	(37.4)
Increase in inventories	(51.1)
Net cash provided by operating activities	$ 147.2
Long-Term Investing Activities	
Property, equipment, and other assets	$ (88.3)
Increase in goodwill and other assets	(38.4)
Net cash used in investing activities	$(126.7)
Financing Activities	
Increase in long-term debt	$ 268.4
Purchase of treasury stock	(23.3)
Increase in notes payable	6.3
Net cash provided by financing activities	$ 251.4
Cash Reconciliation[a]	
Net increase in cash and marketable securities	$ 271.9
Cash and securities at beginning of year	16.6
Cash and securities at end of year	$ 288.5

[a]Cash includes investments in marketable securities.

In Exhibit 3.4, the first section of the statement of cash flows for Diaz Manufacturing shows the cash flow from operations. The section starts with the firm's net income of $118.5 million for the year ending December 31, 2013. Depreciation expense ($83.1 million) is added because it is a noncash expense on the income statement.

Next come changes in the firm's working capital accounts that affect operating activities. Note that working capital accounts that involve financing (bank loans and notes payable) and cash reconciliation (cash and marketable securities) will be classified separately. For Diaz, the working capital accounts that are *sources* of cash are (1) increase in accounts payable of $24.3 million ($349.3 − $325.0 = $24.3), (2) decrease in other current assets of $8.6 million ($29.9 − $21.3 = $8.6), and (3) increase in accrued income taxes of $1.2 million ($18.0 − $16.8 = $1.2). Changes in working capital items that are *uses* of cash are (1) increase in accounts receivable of $37.4 million ($306.2 − $268.8 = $37.4) and (2) increase in inventory of $51.1 million ($423.8 − $372.7 = $51.1). The total cash provided to the firm from operations is $147.2 million.

To clarify why changes in working capital accounts affect the statement of cash flows, let's look at some of the changes. Diaz had a $37.4 million increase in accounts receivable, which is subtracted from net income as a use of cash because the number represents sales that were included in the income statement but for which no cash has been collected. Diaz provided financing for these sales to its customers. Similarly, the $24.3 million increase in accounts payable represents a source of cash because goods and services the company purchased have been received but no cash has been paid out.

Long-Term Investing Activities.   Cash flows from long-term investing activities relate to the buying and selling of long-term assets. In Exhibit 3.4, the second section shows the cash flows from long-term investing activities. Diaz Manufacturing made long-term investments in two areas, which resulted in a cash outflow of $126.7 million. They were as follows: (1) the purchase of plant and equipment, totaling $88.3 million ($911.6 − $823.3 = $88.3) and (2) an increase in goodwill and other assets of $38.4 million ($450.0 − $411.6 = $38.4). Diaz's investments in property, equipment, and other assets resulted in a cash outflow of $126.7 million.

Financing Activities.   Cash flows from financing occur when cash is obtained from or repaid to creditors or owners (stockholders). Typical financing activities involve cash received from the issuance of common or preferred stock, as well as cash from bank loans, notes payable, and long-term debt. Cash payments of dividends to stockholders and cash purchases of treasury stock reduce a company's cash position.

Diaz Manufacturing's financing activities include the sale of bonds for $268.4 million ($574.0 − $305.6 = $268.4), which is a source of cash, and the purchase of treasury stock for $23.3 million, which is a use of cash. The firm's notes payable position was also increased by $6.3 million ($10.5 − $4.2 = $6.3). Overall, Diaz had a net cash inflow from financing activities of $251.4 million.

Cash Reconciliation.   The final part of the statement of cash flows is a reconciliation of the firm's beginning and ending cash positions. For Diaz Manufacturing, these cash positions are shown on the 2012 and 2013 balance sheets. The first step in reconciling the company's beginning and ending cash positions is to add together the amounts from the first three sections of the statement of cash flows: (1) the net cash inflows from operations of $147.2 million, (2) the net cash outflow from long-term investment activities of −$126.7 million, (3) and the net cash inflow from financing activities of $251.4 million. Together, these three items represent a total net increase in cash to the firm of $271.9 million ($147.2 − $126.7 + $251.4 = $271.9). Finally, we add this amount ($271.9 million) to the beginning cash balance of $16.6 million to obtain the ending cash balance for 2013 of $288.5 million ($271.9 + $16.6 = $288.5).

> **BEFORE YOU GO ON**

1. How do increases in fixed assets from one period to the next affect cash holdings for the firm?

2. Name two working capital accounts that represent sources of cash for the firm.

3. Explain the difference between cash flows from financing and investment activities.

3.6 TYING TOGETHER THE FINANCIAL STATEMENTS

LEARNING OBJECTIVE

Up to this point, we have treated a firm's financial statements as if they were independent of one another. As you might suspect, though, the four financial statements presented in this chapter are related. Let's see how.

Recall that the balance sheet summarizes what assets the firm has at a particular point in time and how the firm has financed those assets with debt and equity. From one year to the next, the firm's balance sheet will change because the firm will buy or sell assets and the dollar value of the debt and equity financing will change. These changes are exactly the ones presented in the statement of cash flows. In other words, the statement of cash flows presents a summary of the changes in a firm's balance sheet from the beginning of a period to the end of that period.

This concept is illustrated in Exhibit 3.5, which presents summaries of the four financial statements for Diaz Manufacturing for the year 2013. The exhibit also presents the balance sheet for the beginning of that year, which is dated December 31, 2012. If you compare the changes in the balance sheet numbers from the beginning of the year to the end of the year, you can see that these changes are in fact summarized in the statement of cash flows. For example, the change in the cash balance of $271.9 million ($288.5 − $16.6 = $271.9) appears at the bottom of the statement of cash flows. Similarly, excluding cash and notes payable, the change in net working capital from the beginning to the end of 2013 is $54.4 million, which is calculated as follows: [($751.3 − $367.3) − ($671.4 − $341.8)] = ($384.0 − $329.6) = $54.4.[6] This number is equal to the net working capital investment reflected in the statement of cash flows. Note, too, that the net working capital investment in Diaz's statement of cash flows is just the total change in the firm's investment in the following working capital accounts: accounts payable, other current assets, accrued income taxes, accounts receivable, and inventories. You can also see in Exhibit 3.5 that

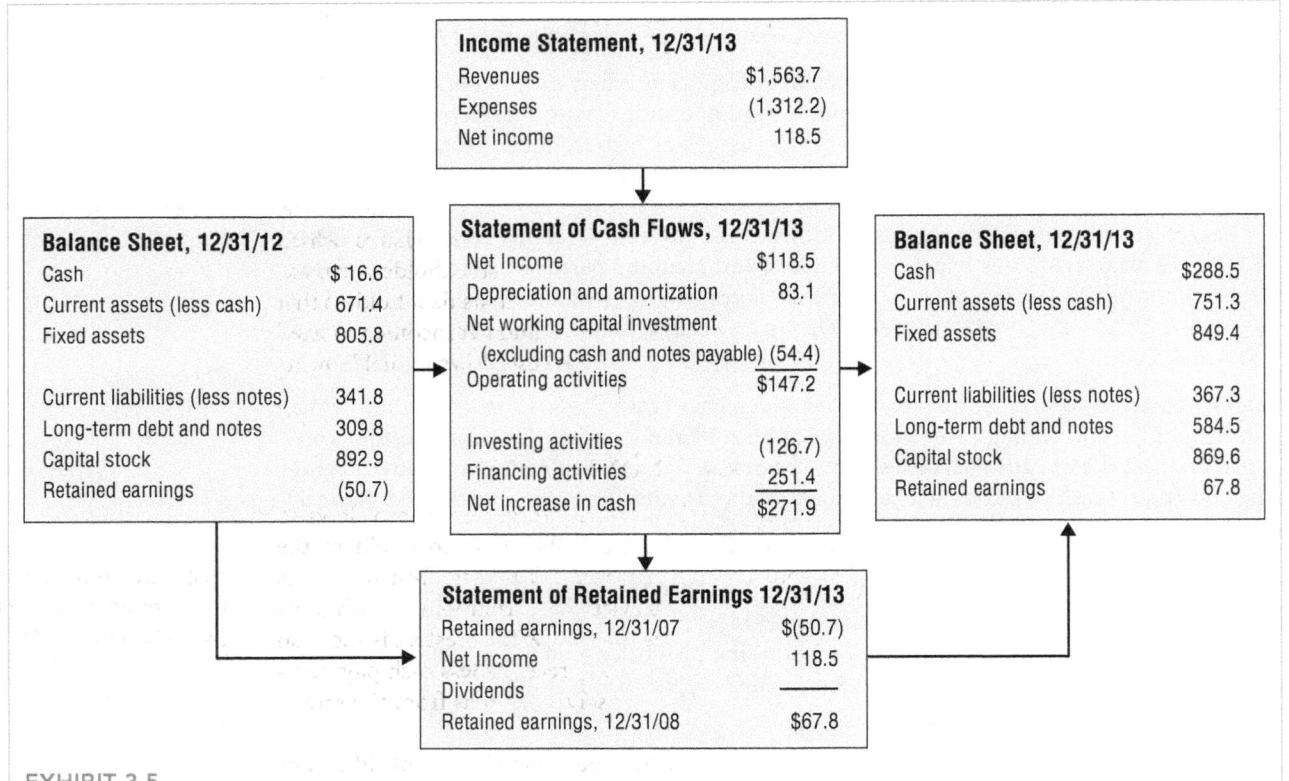

EXHIBIT 3.5

The Interrelations among the Financial Statements: Illustrated Using Diaz Manufacturing Financial Results ($ millions)

The statement of cash flows ties together the income statement with the balance sheets from the beginning and the end of the period. The statement of retained earnings shows how the retained earnings account has changed from the beginning to the end of the period.

---

[6]From the 2013 balance sheet ($ millions): (1) current assets − cash = $1,039.8 − $288.5 = $751.3, and (2) current liabilities − notes payable = $377.8 − $10.5 = $367.3. The calculations are similar for the 2012 balance sheet.

the change in fixed assets, which includes net property plant and equipment, goodwill, and other long-term assets, is $43.6 million ($849.4 − $805.8 = $43.6). This number is equal to the sum of the cash flows from investing activities and depreciation and amortization, −$126.7 + $83.1 = −$43.6, in the statement of cash flows. We add depreciation to investing activities in the latter calculation because the fixed asset accounts in the balance sheet are net of depreciation.

Turning to the liability and equity side of the balance sheet, notice the change in the amount of debt plus equity that the firm has sold in 2013, which is represented by the sum of the long-term liabilities and notes and capital stock in the balance sheet. This sum equals the value of the financing activities in the statement of cash flows. The change in the balance sheet values is calculated as follows: [($584.5 + $869.6) − ($309.8 + $892.9)] = ($1,454.1 − $1,202.7) = $251.4 million.[7] Finally, since Diaz did not pay a dividend in 2013, the change in retained earnings of $118.5 million [$67.8 − (−$50.7) = $118.5] exactly equals the company's net income, which appears on the top line of the statement of cash flows.

Again, the important point here is that the statement of cash flows summarizes the changes in the balance sheet. How do the other financial statements fit into the picture? Well, the income statement calculates the firm's net income, which is used to calculate the retained earnings at the end of the year and is included as the first line in the statement of cash flows. The income statement provides an input that is used in the balance sheet and the statement of cash flows. The statement of retained earnings just summarizes the changes to the retained earnings account a little differently than the statement of cash flows. This different format makes it simpler for managers and investors to see why retained earnings changed as it did.

> **BEFORE YOU GO ON**

1. Explain how the four financial statements are related.

3.7 CASH FLOWS TO INVESTORS

LEARNING OBJECTIVE 7

As we discussed in Chapter 1, the concept of cash flow is very important in corporate finance. Financial managers are concerned with maximizing the value of stockholders' shares, which means making decisions that maximize the value of the cash flows that stockholders can expect to receive. Similarly, the firm has interest and principal obligations to its debt holders that must be met. It is important to recognize that the revenues, expenses, and net income reported in a firm's income statement provide an incomplete picture of the cash flows available to its investors.

Net Income versus the Cash Flow to Investors

Managers and investors are primarily interested in a firm's ability to generate cash flows to meet the firm's obligations to its debt holders and that can be distributed to stockholders; the **cash flow to investors.** These cash obligations and distributions include interest payments and the repayment of principal to the firm's debt holders, as well as distributions of cash to its stockholders in the form of dividends or stock repurchases. Cash flow to investors is the cash flow that a firm generates for its investors in a given period (cash receipts less cash payments and investments), excluding cash inflows from investors themselves, such as from the sale of new equity or long-term interest-bearing debt.

So how is cash flow to investors different from net income? One significant difference arises because accountants do not necessarily count the cash coming into the firm and the cash going out when they prepare financial statements. Under GAAP, accountants recognize revenue at the time a sale is substantially completed, not when the customer actually pays the

cash flow to investors
the cash flow that a firm generates for its investors in a given period, excluding cash inflows from the sale of securities to investors

---

[7]From the 2013 balance sheet, note the following ($ millions): debt = $574.0 (long-term debt) + $10.5 (notes payable) = $584.5 and equity = $50.0 (common stock) + $842.9 (additional paid-in capital) − $23.3 (treasury stock) = $869.6. The calculations for 2012 are made in a similar manner.

firm. In addition, because of the matching principle, accountants match revenues with the costs of producing those revenues regardless of whether these are cash costs to the firm during that period.[8] Finally, cash flows for capital expenditures occur at the time that an asset is purchased, not when it is expensed through depreciation and amortization. As a result of these accounting rules, there can be a substantial difference between the time when revenues and expenses are recorded and when cash is actually collected (in the case of revenue) or paid (in the case of expenses).

Cash flow to investors is one of the most important concepts in finance as it identifies the cash flow in a given period that is available to meet the firm's obligations to its debt holders and that can be distributed to its stockholders. This, in turn, defines the value of their investments in the firm. The cash flow to investors is calculated as the cash flow to investors from operating activity, minus the cash flow invested in net working capital, minus the cash flow invested in long-term assets.

Cash Flow to Investors from Operating Activity

Accounting profits can be converted into cash flow to investors from operating activity by subtracting the taxes that the firm paid during the period from earnings before interest and taxes (EBIT) and adding back all of the firm's noncash expenses. This calculation results in a number that is different from the net cash provided by operating activities that is reported in the statement of cash flows because it does not include cash flows associated with working capital accounts. Unlike the statement of cash flows, when we calculate cash flow to investors, we compute cash flows associated with net working capital separately. We also start from EBIT since interest paid to debt holders has been deducted in the net income calculation and we want to include it in cash flow to investors. Cash flow to investors from operating activity (CFOA) can be formally written as:

$$\text{CFOA} = \text{EBIT} - \text{Current taxes} + \text{Noncash expenses} \tag{3.4}$$

For most businesses, the largest noncash expenses are depreciation and amortization of long-term assets. These are noncash expenses because they are deducted from revenues on the income statement during the years after a long-term asset was purchased, even though no cash is actually being paid out. The cash outflow took place when the asset was purchased. Other noncash items include the following:

- Depletion charges, which are like depreciation but apply to extractive natural resources, such as crude oil, natural gas, timber, and mineral deposits (noncash expense).
- Deferred taxes, which are the portion of a firm's income tax expense that is postponed because of differences in the accounting policies adopted for financial reporting and for tax reporting (noncash expense).
- Expenses that were paid in cash in a previous period (prepaid expenses), such as for rent and insurance (noncash expense).
- Revenues previously received as cash but not yet earned (deferred revenues). An example of deferred revenue would be prepaid magazine subscriptions to a publishing company that are recorded as revenue in a period after the cash has been paid (noncash revenue).

We can use the data from Diaz Manufacturing's 2013 income statement in Exhibit 3.2 to illustrate the calculation of CFOA. If the company had no deferred taxes and the taxes reported in the income statement equal the taxes actually paid by the firm, Diaz's CFOA in 2013 was:

$$\text{CFOA}_{2013} = \$168.4 \text{ million} - \$44.3 \text{ million} + \$83.1 \text{ million} = \$207.2 \text{ million}$$

Cash Flow Invested in Net Working Capital

As we discussed in Section 3.5, changes in current assets and liabilities from one period to the next represent uses and sources of cash. When we calculate the cash flow to investors we

---

[8]The accounting practice of recognizing revenues and expenses as they are earned and incurred, and not when cash is received or paid, is called accrual accounting.

account for these sources and uses by computing the change in net working capital during the period. This change takes into account all the money that has been invested in current assets, including cash and marketable securities, accounts receivable and inventories, and all of the financing that has been received from current liabilities, such as accounts payable and notes payable, during the period. These sources and uses all directly affect the cash flow that is available to investors during the period.

Recall from Equation 3.2 that a firm's investment in net working capital (NWC) at any point in time can be computed as the difference between its total current assets and total current liabilities:

$$\text{Net working capital (NWC)} = \text{Total current assets} - \text{Total current liabilities}$$

We saw earlier that Diaz Manufacturing's investment in NWC at the end of 2013 was:

$$NWC_{2013} = \$1,039.8 \text{ million} - \$377.8 \text{ million} = \$662.0 \text{ million}$$

The corresponding value at the end of 2012 was:

$$NWC_{2012} = \$688.0 \text{ million} - \$346.0 \text{ million} = \$342.0 \text{ million}$$

As is the case with all balance sheet items, the investment in NWC is a snapshot at a point in time. To determine the flow of cash into, or out of, working capital we compute the cash flow invested in net working capital (CFNWC). This equals the difference between NWC at the end of the current period and NWC at the end of the previous period:

$$CFNWC = NWC_{\text{current period}} - NWC_{\text{previous period}} \tag{3.5}$$

For Diaz Manufacturing, CFNWC is:

$$CFNWC_{2013} = NWC_{2013} - NWC_{2012} = \$662.0 \text{ million} - \$342.0 \text{ million} = \$320.0 \text{ million}$$

The positive difference between Diaz Manufacturing's net working capital in 2013 and 2012 indicates that current assets increased by \$320.0 million more than current liabilities during 2013. This net investment in NWC reduced the amount of cash that might otherwise have been available for distribution to the Diaz investors in 2013. Of course, investments in NWC are likely to yield positive cash flows in the future. For example, accounts receivable can be collected, and inventories will eventually be sold. Also, selling items on credit, or having a greater stock of finished inventories can help the company attract new customers. For Diaz Manufacturing, the single largest investment in working capital is the addition of \$271.9 million to cash and marketable securities. We will discuss reasons why firms make investments in cash in Chapter 12.

Cash Flow Invested in Long-Term Assets

Long-term assets, such as land, buildings, and plant and equipment, represent a large portion of the total assets of many firms. Because the purchases and sales of such assets can have a substantial impact on the cash flow to investors, it is very important that we account for them in our cash flow calculations. If a firm is a net investor (buys more than it sells) in long-term assets during a given year, its cash flow to investors will be reduced by the amount of the net purchases. If the firm is a net seller of long-term assets, its cash flow to investors will increase by the value of the net sales.

As we discussed earlier, Diaz Manufacturing had \$911.6 million invested in plant and equipment and \$450.0 million invested in goodwill and other assets at the end of 2013 (Exhibit 3.1). The company's total investment in long-term assets at the end of 2013 was therefore \$911.6 million + \$450.0 million = \$1,361.6 million. The corresponding value at the end of 2012 was \$823.3 million + \$411.6 million = \$1,234.9 million. As with investments in net working capital, we use the change in the value of the long-term assets to compute the amount that a firm invested in long-term investments during a period. Specifically, the cash flow invested in long-term assets (CFLTA) is computed as:

$$CFLTA = \text{Long-term assets}_{\text{current period}} - \text{Long-term assets}_{\text{previous period}} \tag{3.6}$$

It is very important to remember that since depreciation is a noncash charge, we ignore accumulated depreciation when we compute the effects of investment in long-term assets on cash flow to investors. For Diaz Manufacturing, CFLTA in 2013 was:

$$CFLTA_{2013} = \$1,361.6 \text{ million} - \$1,234.9 \text{ million} = \$126.7 \text{ million}$$

where the $1,361.6 million and $1,234.9 million values represent the long-term asset values before accumulated depreciation. This calculation indicates that Diaz Manufacturing invested a total of $126.7 million in long-term assets during 2013. Of this total, $88.3 million ($911.6 − $823.3 = $88.3) was invested in plant and equipment and $38.4 million ($450 − $411.6 = $38.4) was invested in goodwill and other assets. As with investment in net working capital, investments in long-term assets are likely to generate positive cash flows in the future, but reduce the cash flow to investors in the current period.

Cash Flow to Investors: Putting It All Together

Having calculated the cash flow from operating activity, cash flow invested in net working capital, and cash flow invested in long-term assets, we are now ready to compute cash flow to investors (CFI). We use Equation 3.7 to do this:

$$CFI = CFOA - CFNWC - CFLTA \tag{3.7}$$

Note that in this calculation, CFNWC and CFLTA are subtracted from CFOA because investments in both net working capital and long-term assets reduce the cash flow available to investors. Of course, it is possible for either or both of these figures to be negative in a given period. For example, CFLTA will be negative if proceeds for the sale of long-term assets exceed total investments in these assets.

Putting this all together for Diaz Manufacturing, we can see that the company's CFI in 2013 was:

$$CFI_{2013} = \$207.2 \text{ million} - \$320.0 \text{ million} - \$126.7 \text{ million} = -\$239.5 \text{ million}$$

The negative value indicates that Diaz invested more cash than was produced by its operating activity during 2013. This is not uncommon for a rapidly growing company like Diaz, which experienced a net sales increase of almost 13 percent from 2012 to 2013. Fast-growing firms often must invest more cash than they generate. The difference is financed by selling stock to investors or by borrowing money. In such situations, both the old and new investors are counting on the firm to produce cash flows in the future that will compensate them for the investment that they are making now. A brief look at the liability side of the Diaz balance sheet suggests that the negative cash flow to investors was funded largely by issuing new long-term debt.

DECISION MAKING

E X A M P L E   3 . 1

Cash Flow to Investors from Operating Activity

SITUATION: You are a financial manager at Bonivo Corporation and are preparing a report for senior management. You have asked two analysts who work for you to compute cash flow to investors from operating activity during the year that just ended. A short while later they come to your office and report that they cannot agree on how to do the calculation.

The first analyst thinks it should be computed as:

      Net income
    + Depreciation and amortization
    + Increase in accounts payable
    + Increase in accrued income taxes
    − Increase in accounts receivables
    − Increase in inventories
    − Increase in other current assets
    ─────────────────────────────────────
    = Cash flow to investors from operating activity

The second analyst proposes that the calculation is:

$$
\begin{aligned}
&\text{EBIT}\\
&+ \text{ Depreciation and amortization}\\
&- \text{ Taxes paid}\\
\hline
&= \text{Cash flow to investors from operating activity}
\end{aligned}
$$

Which calculation should you use for your report to senior management?

DECISION: You should use the calculation proposed by the second analyst. This is the correct calculation. The calculation proposed by the first analyst is incorrect. The first analyst has computed the net cash provided by operating activities as it is calculated in a statement of cash flows. This calculation does account for the firm's noncash depreciation and amortization expenses, but unlike the calculation of cash flow to investors from operating activity, it incorporates changes in the firm's working capital accounts other than cash and marketable securities. The first analyst also started from net income rather than EBIT. It is important to start from EBIT rather than net income when calculating cash flows for investors because the interest payments to debt holders are not deducted when EBIT is calculated.

Additional Cash Flow Calculations

This section has introduced calculations of the cash distributed to a firm's investors. We will return to the topic of cash flows in Chapter 10. In that chapter we will develop a measure of cash flow that will allow us to determine the incremental cash flows necessary to estimate the value of a capital project.

> **BEFORE YOU GO ON**

1. How does the calculation of net income differ from the calculation of cash flow to investors from operating activity?

2. All else being equal, if a firm increases its accounts payable, what effect will this have on cash flow to investors?

3. What does it mean when a firm's cash flow to investors is negative?

3.8 FEDERAL INCOME TAX

We conclude this chapter with a discussion of corporate income taxes. Taxes take a big bite out of the income of most businesses and represent one of their largest cash outflows. For example, as shown in the income statement for Diaz Manufacturing (Exhibit 3.2), the firm's earnings before interest and taxes (EBIT) in 2013 amounted to $168.4 million, and its tax bill was $44.3 million, or 26.3 percent of EBIT ($44.3/$168.4 = 0.263, or 26.3 percent)—not a trivial amount by any standard. Because of their magnitude, taxes play a critical role in most business financial decisions.

As you might suspect, corporations spend a considerable amount of effort and money deploying tax specialists to find legal ways to minimize their tax burdens. The tax laws are complicated, continually changing, and at times seemingly bizarre—in part because the tax code is not an economically rational document; rather, it reflects the changing and sometimes conflicting political and social values of Congress and the president over time.

LEARNING OBJECTIVE 8

EXHIBIT 3.6   Corporate Tax Rates for 2012

The federal corporate marginal tax rate varies from 15 to 39 percent. Generally speaking, smaller companies with lower taxable income have lower tax rates than larger companies with higher taxable incomes. Smaller businesses are given preferential treatment to encourage new business formation.

(1) Corporations' Taxable Income	(2) Pay This Amount on the Base of the Bracket	(3) Marginal Tax Rate: Tax Rate on the Excess Over the Base	(4) Average Tax Rate at Top of Bracket
$0–$50,000	$ 0	15%	15.0%
50,001–75,000	7,500	25	18.3
75,001–100,000	13,750	34	22.3
100,001–335,000	22,250	39	34.0
335,001–10,000,000	113,900	34	34.0
10,000,001–15,000,000	3,400,000	35	34.3
15,000,001–18,333,333	5,150,000	38	35.0
More than 18,333,333	6,416,667	35	35.0

If you work in the finance or accounting area, a tax specialist will advise you on the tax implications of most decisions in which you will be involved as a businessperson. Consequently, we will not try here to make you a tax expert, but we will present a high-level view of the major portions of the federal tax code that have a significant impact on business decision making.

Corporate Income Tax Rates

Exhibit 3.6 shows the 2012 federal income tax schedule for corporations. As you can see, the marginal tax rate varies from 15 percent to 39 percent (column 3). In general, companies with lower taxable incomes have lower tax rates than larger companies with higher taxable incomes. Historically, the federal income tax code has given preferential treatment to small businesses and start-up companies as a means of stimulating new business formation. In addition, the federal system is a progressive income tax system; that is, as the level of income rises, the tax rate rises. Under the current tax code, which has its origins in the Tax Reform Act of 1986, marginal tax rates do not increase continuously through the income brackets, however. As you can see in Exhibit 3.6, marginal tax rates rise from 15 percent to 39 percent for incomes up to $335,000; they decrease to 34 percent, then increase to 38 percent for incomes up to $18.3 million; and they ultimately rest at 35 percent for all taxable income above $18.3 million.

> The U.S. Department of the Treasury provides a comprehensive tax information site at http://www.irs.gov.

Average versus Marginal Tax Rates

average tax rate
total taxes paid divided by taxable income

marginal tax rate
the tax rate paid on the last dollar of income earned

The difference between the average tax rate and the marginal tax rate is an important consideration in financial decision making. The **average tax rate** is simply the total taxes paid divided by taxable income. In contrast, the **marginal tax rate** is the tax rate that is paid on the last dollar of income earned. Exhibit 3.6 shows both the marginal tax rates and average tax rates for corporations.

A simple example will clarify the difference between the average and marginal tax rates. Suppose a corporation has a taxable income of $150,000. Using the data in Exhibit 3.6, we can determine the firm's federal income tax bill, its marginal tax rate, and its average tax rate. The firm's total tax bill is computed as follows:

$$
\begin{array}{lcr}
0.15 \times \$50,000 & = & \$\ 7,500 \\
0.25 \times (\$75,000 - \$50,000) & = & 6,250 \\
0.34 \times (\$100,000 - \$75,000) & = & 8,500 \\
0.39 \times (\$150,000 - \$100,000) & = & \underline{19,500} \\
& & \$41,750
\end{array}
$$

The firm's average tax rate is equal to the total taxes divided by the firm's total taxable income; thus, the average tax rate is $41,750/$150,000 = 0.278$, or 27.8 percent. The firm's marginal tax rate is the rate paid on the last dollar earned, which is 39 percent.

When you are making investment decisions for a firm, the relevant tax rate to use is usually the marginal tax rate. The reason is that new investments (projects) are expected to generate new cash flows, which will be taxed at the firm's marginal tax rate.

To simplify calculations throughout the book, we will generally specify a single tax rate for a corporation, such as 40 percent. The rate may include some payment for state and local taxes, which will make the total tax rate the firm pays greater than the federal rate.

The Difference between Average and Marginal Tax Rates

PROBLEM: Taxland Corporation has taxable income of $90,000. What is the firm's federal corporate income tax liability? What are the firm's average and marginal tax rates?

APPROACH: Use Exhibit 3.6 to calculate the firm's tax bill. To calculate the average tax rate, divide the total amount of taxes paid by the $90,000 of taxable income. The marginal tax rate is the tax rate paid on the last dollar of taxable income.

SOLUTION:

$$\text{Tax bill} = (0.15 \times \$50,000) + [0.25 \times (\$75,000 - \$50,000)] \\ + [0.34 \times (\$90,000 - \$75,000)]$$
$$= \$7,500 + \$6,250 + \$5,100$$
$$= \$18,850$$

Average tax rate = $18,850/$90,000 = 0.209$, or 20.9%
Marginal tax rate = 34%

Unequal Treatment of Dividends and Interest Payments

An interesting anomaly in the tax code is the unequal treatment of interest and dividend payments. For the most common type of corporation, interest paid on debt obligations is a tax-deductible business expense. Dividends paid to common or preferred stockholders are not deductible, however.

The unequal treatment of interest and dividend payments is not without consequences. In effect, it lowers the cost of debt financing compared with the cost of an equal amount of common or preferred stock financing. Thus, there is a tax-induced bias toward the use of debt financing, which we discuss more thoroughly in later chapters.

> **BEFORE YOU GO ON**

1. Why is it important to consider the consequences of taxes when financing a new project?

2. Which type of tax rate, marginal or average, should be used in analyzing the expansion of a product line, and why?

3. What are the tax implications of a decision to finance a project using debt rather than new equity?

SUMMARY OF Learning Objectives

1 Discuss generally accepted accounting principles (GAAP) and their importance to the economy.

GAAP are a set of authoritative guidelines that define accounting practices at a particular point in time. The principles determine the rules for how a company maintains its accounting system and how it prepares financial statements. Accounting standards are important because without them each firm could develop its own unique accounting practices. This would make it difficult for anyone to monitor the firm's true performance or compare the performance of different firms. The result would be a loss of confidence in the accounting system and the financial reports it produces. Fundamental accounting principles include that transactions are arm's-length, the cost principle, the realization principle, the matching principle, and the going concern assumption.

2 Explain the balance sheet identity and why a balance sheet must balance.

A balance sheet provides a summary of a firm's financial position at a particular point in time. It identifies the productive resources (assets) that a firm uses to generate income, as well as the sources of funding from creditors (liabilities) and owners (stockholders' equity) that were used to buy the assets. The balance sheet identity is Total assets = Total liabilities + Total stockholders' equity. Stockholders' equity represents ownership in the firm and is the residual claim of the owners after all other obligations to creditors, employees, and vendors have been paid. The balance sheet must always balance because the owners get what is left over after all creditors have been paid—that is, Total stockholders' equity = Total assets − Total liabilities.

3 Describe how market-value balance sheets differ from book-value balance sheets.

Book value is the amount a firm paid for its assets at the time of purchase. The current market value of an asset is the amount that a firm would receive for the asset if it were sold on the open market (not in a forced liquidation). Most managers and investors are more concerned about what a firm's assets can earn in the future than about what the assets cost in the past. Thus, marked-to-market balance sheets are more helpful in showing a company's true financial condition than balance sheets based on historical costs. Of course, the reason that marked-to-market balance sheets are not commonly used is that it is difficult to estimate market values for some assets and liabilities.

4 Identify the basic equation for the income statement and the information it provides.

An income statement presents a firm's profit or loss for a period of time, usually a month, quarter, or year. The income statement identifies the major sources of revenues generated by the firm and the corresponding expenses needed to generate those revenues. The equation for the income statement is Net income = Revenues − Expenses. If revenues exceed expenses, the firm generates a net profit for the period. If expenses exceed revenues, the firm generates a net loss. Net profit or net income is the most comprehensive accounting measure of a firm's performance.

5 Understand the calculation of cash flows from operating, investing, and financing activities required in the statement of cash flows.

Cash flows from operating activities in the statement of cash flows are the net cash flows that are related to a firm's principal business activities. The most important items are the firm's net income, depreciation and amortization expense, and working capital accounts (other than cash and short-term debt obligations, which are classified elsewhere). Cash flows from long-term investing activities relate to the buying and selling of long-term assets. Cash flows from financing occur when cash is obtained from or repaid to creditors or owners (stockholders). Typical financing activities involve cash received from the issuance of common or preferred stock, as well as cash from bank loans, notes payable, and long-term debt. Cash payments of dividends to stockholders and cash purchases of treasury stock reduce a company's cash position.

6 Explain how the four major financial statements discussed in this chapter are related.

The four financial statements discussed in the chapter are the balance sheet, the income statement, the statement of cash flows, and the statement of retained earnings. The key financial statement that ties together the other three statements is the statement of cash flows, which summarizes changes in the balance sheet from the beginning of the year to the end. These changes reflect the information in the income statement and in the statement of retained earnings.

7 Identify the cash flow to a firm's investors using its financial statements.

Cash flow to investors is the cash flow that a firm generates in a given period (cash receipts less cash payments and investments), excluding cash inflows from new equity sales or long-term debt issues. Cash flow to investors is the cash flow in a given period that is used to meet the firm's obligations to its debt holders and that is distributed to its equity investors, which in turn defines the value of their investments in the firm over time. The cash flow to investors is calculated as the cash flow to investors from operating activity, minus the cash flow invested in net working capital, minus the cash flow invested in long-term assets.

8 Discuss the difference between average and marginal tax rates.

The average tax rate is computed by dividing the total taxes by taxable income. It takes into account the taxes paid at all levels of income and will normally be lower than the marginal tax rate, which is the rate that is paid on the last dollar of income earned. However, for very high income earners, these two rates can be equal. When companies are making financial investment decisions, they use the marginal tax rate because new projects are expected to generate additional cash flows, which will be taxed at the firm's marginal tax rate.

SUMMARY OF Key Equations

Equation	Description	Formula
3.1	Balance sheet identity	Total assets = Total liabilities + Total stockholders' equity
3.2	Net working capital	Net working capital = Total current assets − Total current liabilities
3.3	Income statement identity	Net income = Revenues − Expenses
3.4	Cash flow from operating activity	$\text{CFOA} = \text{EBIT} - \text{Current taxes} + \text{Noncash expenses}$
3.5	Cash flow invested in net working capital	$\text{CFNWC} = \text{NWC}_{\text{current period}} - \text{NWC}_{\text{previous period}}$
3.6	Cash flow invested in long-term assets	$\text{CFLTA} = \text{Long-term assets}_{\text{current period}} - \text{Long-term assets}_{\text{previous period}}$
3.7	Cash flow to investors	$\text{CFI} = \text{CFOA} - \text{CFNWC} - \text{CFLTA}$

Self-Study Problems

3.1 The *going concern assumption* of GAAP implies that the firm:
  a. Is going under and needs to be liquidated at historical cost.
  b. Will continue to operate and its assets should be recorded at historical cost.
  c. Will continue to operate and that all assets should be recorded at their cost rather than at their liquidation value.
  d. Is going under and needs to be liquidated at liquidation value.

3.2 The Ellicott City Ice Cream Company management has just completed an assessment of the company's assets and liabilities and has obtained the following information. The firm has total current assets worth $625,000 at book value and $519,000 at market value. In addition, its long-term assets include plant and equipment valued at market for $695,000, while their book value is $940,000. The company's total current liabilities are valued at market for $543,000, while their book value is $495,000. Both the book value and the market value of long-term debt is $350,000. If the company's total assets are equal to a market value of $1,214,000 (book value of $1,565,000), what are the book value and market value of its stockholders' equity?

3.3 Depreciation and amortization expenses are:
  a. Part of current assets on the balance sheet.
  b. After-tax expenses that reduce a firm's cash flows.
  c. Long-term liabilities that reduce a firm's net worth.
  d. Noncash expenses that cause a firm's after-tax cash flows to exceed its net income.

3.4 You are given the following information about Clarkesville Plumbing Company. Revenues last year totaled $896, depreciation expenses $75, costs of goods sold $365, and interest expenses $54. At the end of the year, current assets were $121 and current liabilities were $107. The company has an average tax rate of 34 percent. Calculate its net income by setting up an income statement.

3.5 The Huntington Rain Gear Company had $633,125 in taxable income in the year ending September 30, 2012. Calculate the company's tax using the tax schedule in Exhibit 3.6.

Solutions to Self-Study Problems

3.1 One of the key assumptions under GAAP is the *going concern assumption,* which states that the firm:
  c. Will continue to operate and that all assets should be recorded at their cost rather than at their liquidation value.

3.2 The book value and market value of stockholders' equity are shown below (in $ thousands):

Assets			Liabilities and Equity		
	Book	**Market**		**Book**	**Market**
Total current assets	$ 625	$ 519	Total current liabilities	$ 495	$ 543
Fixed assets	940	695	Long-term debt	350	350
			Stockholders' equity	720	321
			Total liabilities		
Total assets	$1,565	$1,214	and equity	$1,565	$1,214

3.3 Depreciation and amortization expenses are: **d.** Noncash expenses that cause a firm's after-tax cash flows to exceed its net income.

3.4 Clarkesville's income statement and net income are as follows:

Clarkesville Plumbing Company
Income Statement for the Fiscal Year Ending
December 31, 2013

	Amount
Revenues	$896.00
Costs	365.00
EBITDA	$531.00
Depreciation	75.00
EBIT	$456.00
Interest	54.00
EBT	$402.00
Taxes (34%)	136.68
Net income	$265.32

3.5 Huntington's tax bill is calculated as follows:

Tax rate	Income Taxed at Indicated Rate	Tax
15%	$50,000	$ 7,500
25	75,000 − 50,000	6,250
34	100,000 − 75,000	8,500
39	335,000 − 100,000	91,650
34	633,125 − 335,000	101,363
Total taxes payable		$215,263

Critical Thinking Questions

3.1 What is a major reason for the accounting scandals in recent years? How do firms sometimes attempt to meet Wall Street analysts' earnings projections?

3.2 Why are taxes and the tax code important for managerial decision making?

3.3 Identify the five fundamental principles of GAAP, and explain briefly their importance.

3.4 Explain why firms prefer to use accelerated depreciation methods over the straight-line method for tax purposes.

3.5 What is treasury stock? Why do firms have treasury stock?

3.6 Define book-value accounting and market-value accounting.

3.7 Compare and contrast depreciation expense and amortization expense.

3.8 Why are retained earnings not considered an asset of the firm?

3.9 How does a firm's cash flow to investors from operating activity differ from net income, and why?

3.10 What is the statement of cash flows, and what is its role?

Questions and Problems

3.1 Balance sheet: Given the following information about Elkridge Sporting Goods, Inc., construct a balance sheet for June 30, 2013. On that date the firm had cash and marketable securities of $25,135, accounts receivable of $43,758, inventory of $167,112, net fixed assets of $325,422, and other assets of $13,125. It had accounts payables of $67,855, notes payables of $36,454, long-term debt of $223,125, and common stock of $150,000. How much retained earnings did the firm have?

3.2 Inventory accounting: Differentiate between FIFO and LIFO accounting.

3.3 Inventory accounting: Explain how the choice of FIFO versus LIFO can affect a firm's balance sheet and income statement.

3.4 Market-value accounting: How does the use of market-value accounting help managers?

3.5 Working capital: Laurel Electronics reported the following information at its annual meeting: The company had cash and marketable securities worth $1,235,455, accounts payables worth $4,159,357, inventory of $7,121,599, accounts receivables of $3,488,121, short-term notes payable worth $1,151,663, and other current assets of $121,455. What is the company's net working capital?

3.6 Working capital: The financial information for Laurel Electronics referred to in Problem 3.5 is all at book value. Suppose marking to market reveals that the market value of the firm's inventory is 20 percent below its book value, its receivables are 25 percent below their book value, and the market value of its current liabilities is identical to the book value. What is the firm's net working capital using market values? What is the percentage change in net working capital?

3.7 Income statement: The Oakland Mills Company has disclosed the following financial information in its annual reports for the period ending March 31, 2013: sales of $1.45 million, cost of goods sold of $812,500, depreciation expenses of $175,000, and interest expenses of $89,575. Assume that the firm has a tax rate of 35 percent. What is the company's net income? Set up an income statement to answer the question.

3.8 Cash flows: Describe the organization of the statement of cash flows.

3.9 Cash flows: During 2013 Towson Recording Company increased its investment in marketable securities by $36,845, funded fixed-assets acquisitions of $109,455, and had marketable securities of $14,215 mature. What is the net cash used in investing activities?

3.10 Cash flows: Caustic Chemicals management identified the following cash flows as significant in its year-end meeting with analysts: During the year Caustic repaid existing debt of $312,080 and raised additional debt capital of $650,000. It also repurchased stock in the open market for a total of $45,250. What is the net cash provided by financing activities?

3.11 Cash flows: Identify and describe the noncash expenses that a firm may incur.

3.12 Cash flows: Given the data for Oakland Mills Company in Problem 3.7, compute the cash flows to investors from operating activity.

3.13 Cash flows: Hillman Corporation reported current assets of $3,495,055 on December 31, 2013, and current assets of $3,103,839 on December 31, 2012. Current liabilities for the firm were $2,867,225 and $2,760,124 at the end of 2013 and 2012, respectively. Compute the cash flow invested in net working capital at Hillman Corporation during 2013.

3.14 Cash flows: Del Bridge Construction had long-term assets before depreciation of $990,560 on December 31, 2012, and $1,211,105 on December 31, 2013. How much cash flow was invested in long-term assets by Del Bridge during 2013?

3.15 Tax: Define average tax rate and marginal tax rate.

3.16 Tax: What is the relevant tax rate to use when making financial decisions? Explain why.

3.17 Tax: Manz Property Management Company announced that in the year ended June 30, 2013, its earnings before taxes amounted to $1,478,936. Calculate its taxes using Exhibit 3.6.

< BASIC

EXCEL®
More interactive Excel® exercises available in

WileyPLUS

INTERMEDIATE >| **3.18** **Balance sheet:** Tim Dye, the CFO of Blackwell Automotive, Inc., is putting together this year's financial statements. He has gathered the following balance sheet information: The firm had a cash balance of $23,015, accounts payable of $163,257, common stock of $313,299, retained earnings of $512,159, inventory of $212,444, goodwill and other assets equal to $78,656, net plant and equipment of $711,256, and short-term notes payable of $21,115. It also had accounts receivable of $141,258 and other current assets of $11,223. How much long-term debt does Blackwell Automotive have?

3.19 **Working capital:** Mukhopadhya Network Associates has a current ratio of 1.60, where the current ratio is defined as follows: Current ratio = Current assets/Current liabilities. The firm's current assets are equal to $1,233,265, its accounts payables are $419,357, and its notes payables are $351,663. Its inventory is currently at $721,599. The company plans to raise funds in the short-term debt market and invest the entire amount in additional inventory. How much can notes payable increase without the current ratio falling below 1.50?

3.20 **Market value:** Reservoir Bottling Company reported the following information at the end of the year. Total current assets are worth $237,513 at book value and $219,344 at market value. In addition, plant and equipment have a market value of $343,222 and a book value of $362,145. The company's total current liabilities are valued at market for $134,889 and have a book value of $129,175. Both the book value and the market value of long-term debt are $144,000. If the company's total assets have a market value of $562,566 and a book value of $599,658, what is the difference between the book value and market value of its stockholders' equity?

3.21 **Income statement:** Nimitz Rental Company provided the following information to its auditors. For the year ended March 31, 2013, the company had revenues of $878,412, general and administrative expenses of $352,666, depreciation expenses of $131,455, leasing expenses of $108,195, and interest expenses equal to $78,122. If the company's tax rate is 34 percent, what is its net income after taxes?

3.22 **Income statement:** Sosa Corporation recently reported an EBITDA of $31.3 million and net income of $9.7 million. The company had $6.8 million in interest expense, and its corporate tax rate was 35 percent. What was its depreciation and amortization expense?

3.23 **Income statement:** Fraser Corporation has announced that its net income for the year ended June 30, 2013, was $1,353,412. The company had EBITDA of $4,967,855, and its depreciation and amortization expense was equal to $1,112,685. The company's tax rate is 34 percent. What was its interest expense?

3.24 **Income Statement:** For its most recent fiscal year, Carmichael Hobby Shop recorded EBITDA of $512,725.20, EBIT of $362,450.20, zero interest expense, and cash flow to investors from operating activity of $348,461.25. Assuming there are no non-cash revenues recorded on the income statement, what is the firm's net income after taxes?

3.25 **Retained earnings:** Columbia Construction Company earned $451,888 during the year ended June 30, 2013. After paying out $225,794 in dividends, the balance went into retained earnings. If the firm's total retained earnings were $846,972, what were the retained earnings on its balance sheet on July 1, 2012?

3.26 **Cash flows:** Refer to the information given in Problem 3.21. What is the cash flow for Nimitz Rental?

3.27 **Tax:** Mount Hebron Electrical Company's financial statements indicated that the company had earnings before interest and taxes of $718,323. The interest rate on its $850,000 debt was 8.95 percent. Calculate the taxes the company is likely to owe. What are the marginal and average tax rates for this company?

ADVANCED >| **3.28** The Centennial Chemical Corporation announced that, for the period ending March 31, 2013, it had earned income after taxes worth $2,768,028.25 on revenues of $13,144,680. The company's costs (excluding depreciation and amortization) amounted to 61 percent of sales, and it had interest expenses of $392,168. What is the firm's depreciation and amortization expense if its tax rate is 34 percent?

3.29 Eau Claire Paper Mill, Inc., had, at the beginning of the current fiscal year, April 1, 2012, retained earnings of $323,325. During the year ended March 31, 2013, the company produced net income after taxes of $713,445 and paid out 45 percent of its net income as dividends. Construct a statement of retained earnings and compute the year-end balance of retained earnings.

3.30 Menomonie Casino Company earned $23,458,933 before interest and taxes for the fiscal year ending March 31, 2013. If the casino had interest expenses of $1,645,123, calculate its tax obligation using Exhibit 3.6. What are the marginal and the average tax rates for this company?

3.31 Vanderheiden Hog Products Corp. provided the following financial information for the quarter ending June 30, 2013:

> Net income: $189,425
> Depreciation and amortization: $63,114
> Increase in receivables: $62,154
> Increase in inventory: $57,338
> Increase in accounts payable: $37,655
> Decrease in other current assets: $27,450

What is this firm's cash flow from operating activities during this quarter?

3.32 Cash flows: Analysts following the Tomkovick Golf Company were given the following balance sheet information for the years ended June 30, 2013, and June 30, 2012:

Assets	2013	2012
Cash and marketable securities	$ 33,411	$ 16,566
Accounts receivable	260,205	318,768
Inventory	423,819	352,740
Other current assets	41,251	29,912
Total current assets	$ 758,686	$ 717,986
Plant and equipment	1,931,719	1,609,898
Less: Accumulated depreciation	(419,044)	(206,678)
Net plant and equipment	$1,512,675	$1,403,220
Goodwill and other assets	382,145	412,565
Total assets	$2,653,506	$2,533,771

Liabilities and Equity	2013	2012
Accounts payable and accruals	$ 378,236	$ 332,004
Notes payable	14,487	7,862
Accrued income taxes	21,125	16,815
Total current liabilities	$ 413,848	$ 356,681
Long-term debt	679,981	793,515
Total liabilities	$1,093,829	$1,150,196
Preferred stock	—	—
Common stock (10,000 shares)	10,000	10,000
Additional paid-in capital	975,465	975,465
Retained earnings	587,546	398,110
Less: Treasury stock	(13,334)	—
Total common equity	$1,559,677	$1,383,575
Total liabilities and equity	$2,653,506	$2,533,771

In addition, it was reported that the company had a net income of $3,155,848 and that depreciation expenses were equal to $212,366 during 2013.

a. Construct a 2013 cash flow statement for this firm.

b. Calculate the net cash provided by operating activities for the statement of cash flows.

c. What is the net cash used in investing activities?

d. Compute the net cash provided by financing activities.

3.33 Cash flows: Based on the financial statements for Tomkovick Golf Company in Problem 3.32, compute the cash flow invested in net working capital and the cash flow invested in long-term assets that you would use in a calculation of the cash flow to investors for 2013.

Sample Test Problems

3.1 The Drayton, Inc., balance sheet shows current assets of $256,312 and total assets of $861,889. It also shows current liabilities of $141,097, common equity of $200,000, and retained earnings of $133,667. How much long-term debt does the firm have?

3.2 Ellicott Testing Company produced revenues of $745,000 in 2013. It had expenses (excluding depreciation) of $312,640, depreciation of $65,000, and interest expense of $41,823. It has an average tax rate of 34 percent. What was the firm's net income after taxes in 2013?

3.3 Tejada Enterprises reported EBITDA of $7,300,125 and net income of $3,328,950 for the fiscal year ended December 31, 2013. During the same period, the company had $1,155,378 in interest expense, $1,023,285 in depreciation and amortization expense, and an average corporate tax rate of 35 percent. What was the cash flow to investors from operating activity during 2013?

3.4 In the year ended June 30, 2013, Tri King Company increased its investment in marketable securities by $234,375, made fixed-assets acquisitions totaling $1,324,766, and sold $77,215 of long-term debt. In addition, the firm had a net inflow of $365,778 from selling assets. What is the net cash used in long-term investing activities?

3.5 Triumph Soccer Club had the following cash flows during the past year: It repaid existing debt of $875,430 while raising new debt capital of $1,213,455. It also repurchased stock in the open market for a total of $71,112. What is the net cash provided by financing activities?

Analyzing Financial Statements 4

© B.O'Kane/Alamy

The last three decades witnessed a major shift in the U.S. retailing marketplace. By taking advantage of logistic and purchasing advantages, large-scale discount chains have been able to reduce their costs and lower prices for consumers, fueling the explosive expansion of retailers such as the Target and Wal-Mart Stores. Competition for customers between these two firms is intense, with Target pursuing a strategy reliant on consumer discretionary purchases, and Wal-Mart focused on very low prices for consumer basics.

Just how do analysts compare the performance of companies like Target and Wal-Mart? One approach is to compare accounting data from the financial statements that companies file with the SEC. Below are data for total sales and net income for Target (TGT) and Wal-Mart (WMT) for their fiscal years ending January 2012:

	TGT ($ millions)	WMT ($ millions)
Total sales	$69,865	$446,950
Net income	$2,929	$15,699

Learning Objectives

1. Explain the three perspectives from which financial statements can be viewed.

2. Describe common-size financial statements, explain why they are used, and be able to prepare and use them to analyze the historical performance of a firm.

3. Discuss how financial ratios facilitate financial analysis and be able to compute and use them to analyze a firm's performance.

4. Describe the DuPont system of analysis and be able to use it to evaluate a firm's performance and identify corrective actions that may be necessary.

5. Explain what benchmarks are, describe how they are prepared, and discuss why they are important in financial statement analysis.

6. Identify the major limitations in using financial statement analysis.

The accounting numbers by themselves are not very revealing. Wal-Mart is a much larger firm than Target, with greater sales and net income. This difference in size makes it difficult to assess the actual performance differences between the two firms. However, if we compute the net profit margin, one of the profitability ratios discussed in this chapter, we can identify more clearly the performance difference between the two retailers. The net profit margins (net income/total sales) for Target and Wal-Mart are 4.19 percent and 3.51 percent, respectively. This means that for every $100 in revenues, TGT is able to generate $4.19 in profit, whereas WMT generates only $3.51. As this example illustrates, one advantage of using ratios is that they make direct comparisons of companies possible by adjusting for size differences.

This chapter discusses financial ratio analysis (or financial statement analysis), which involves the calculation and comparison of ratios derived from financial statements. These ratios can be used to draw useful conclusions about a company's financial condition, its operating efficiency, and the attractiveness of its securities as investments.

CHAPTER PREVIEW

In Chapter 3 we reviewed the basic structure of financial statements. This chapter explains how financial statements are used to evaluate a company's overall performance and assess its strengths and shortcomings. The basic tool used to do this is financial ratio analysis. Financial ratios are computed by dividing one number from a firm's financial statements by another such number in order to allow for meaningful comparisons between firms or areas within a firm.

Management can use the information from this type of analysis to help maximize the firm's value by identifying areas where performance improvements are needed. For example, the analysis of data from financial statements can help determine why a firm's cash flows are increasing or decreasing,

why a firm's profitability is changing, and whether a firm will be able to pay its bills next month.

We begin the chapter by discussing some general guidelines for financial statement analysis, along with three different perspectives on financial analysis: those of the stockholder, manager, and creditor. Next, we describe how to prepare common-size financial statements, which allow us to compare firms that differ in size and to analyze a firm's financial performance over time. We then explain how to calculate and interpret key financial ratios and discuss the DuPont system, a diagnostic tool that uses financial ratios. After a discussion of benchmarks, we conclude with a description of the limitations of financial statement analysis.

4.1 BACKGROUND FOR FINANCIAL STATEMENT ANALYSIS

 LEARNING OBJECTIVE

financial statement analysis
the use of financial statements to evaluate a company's overall performance and assess its strengths and shortcomings

This chapter will guide you through a typical **financial statement analysis**, which involves the use of financial ratios to analyze a firm's performance. First, we look at the different perspectives we can take when analyzing financial statements; then we present some helpful guidelines for financial statement analysis.

Perspectives on Financial Statement Analysis

Stockholders and stakeholders may differ in the information they want to gain when analyzing financial statements. In this section, we discuss three perspectives from which we can view financial statement analysis: those of (1) stockholders, (2) managers, and (3) creditors.

Stockholders' Perspective

Stockholders are primarily concerned with the value of their stock and with how much cash they can expect to receive from dividends and capital appreciation over time. Therefore, stockholders want financial statements to tell them how profitable the firm is, what the return on their investment is, and how much cash is available for stockholders, both in total and on a per-share basis. Ultimately, stockholders are interested in how much a share of stock is worth. We address pricing issues in detail in Chapter 8, but financial analysis is a key step in valuing a company's stock.

Managers' Perspective

Broadly speaking, management's perspective of financial statement analysis is similar to that of stockholders. The reason is that stockholders own the firm and managers have a fiduciary responsibility to make decisions that are in the owners' best interests. Thus, managers are interested in the same performance measures as stockholders: profitability, how much cash is available for stockholders, capital appreciation, return on investment, and the like.

Managers, however, are also responsible for running the business on a daily basis and must make decisions that will maximize stockholder wealth in the long run. Maximizing stockholder wealth does not involve a single big decision, but rather a series of smaller day-to-day decisions. Thus, managers need feedback on the short-term impact these day-to-day decisions have on the firm's financial statements and its current stock price. For example, managers can track trends in sales and can determine how well they are controlling expenses and how much of each sales dollar goes to the bottom line. In addition, managers can see the impact of their investment, financing, and working capital decisions reflected in the financial statements. Keep in mind that managers, as insiders, have access to much more detailed financial information than those outside the firm. Generally, outsiders only have access to published financial statements for publicly traded firms.

Creditors' Perspective

The primary concern of creditors is whether and when they will receive the interest payments they are entitled to and when they will be repaid the money they loaned to the firm. Thus, a firm's creditors, including long-term bondholders, closely monitor how much debt the firm is currently using, whether the firm is generating enough cash to pay its day-to-day bills, and whether the firm will have sufficient cash in the future to make interest and principal payments on long-term debt *after* satisfying obligations that have a higher legal priority, such as paying employees' wages. Of course, the firm's ability to pay interest and principal ultimately depends on cash flows and profitability; hence, creditors—like stockholders and managers—are interested in those aspects of the firm's financial performance.

Guidelines for Financial Statement Analysis

We turn now to some general guidelines that will help you when analyzing a firm's financial statements. First, make sure you understand which perspective you are adopting to conduct your analysis: stockholder, manager, or creditor. The perspective will dictate the type of information you need for the analysis and may affect the actions you take based on the results.

Second, always use audited financial statements if they are available. As we discussed in Chapter 1, an audit means that an independent accountant has attested that the financial statements were correctly prepared and fairly represent the firm's financial condition at a point in time. If the statements are unaudited, your analysis will require extra effort. For example, if you are a creditor considering making a loan, you will need to undertake an especially diligent examination of the company's books before closing the deal. It would also be a good idea to make sure you know the company's management team and accountant very well. This will provide additional insight into the creditworthiness of the firm.

Third, use financial statements that cover three to five years, or more, to conduct your analysis. This enables you to perform a **trend analysis**, which involves looking at historical financial statements to see how various ratios are increasing, decreasing, or staying constant over time.

trend analysis
analysis of trends in financial data over time

Fourth, when possible, it is always best to compare a firm's financial statements with those of competitors that are roughly the same size and that offer similar products and services. If you compare firms of disparate size, the results may be meaningless because the two firms may have very different infrastructures, sources of financing, production capabilities, product mixes, and distribution channels. For example, comparing The Boeing Company's financial statements with those of Piper Aircraft, a firm that manufactures small aircraft, makes no sense whatsoever, although both firms manufacture aircraft. You will have to use your judgment as to whether relevant comparisons can be made between firms with large size differences.

In business it is common to **benchmark** a firm's performance, as discussed in the previous paragraph. The most common type of benchmarking involves comparing a firm's performance with the performance of similar firms that are relevant competitors. For example, Ford

benchmark
a standard against which performance is measured

Motor Company management may want to benchmark the firm against General Motors and Toyota, Ford's major competitors in the world market. Firms can also be benchmarked against themselves. For example, they can compare this year's performance with last year's performance or with a specific goal, such as a 10 percent growth in sales. We discuss benchmarking in more detail later in this chapter.

> **BEFORE YOU GO ON**

1. Why is it important to look at a firm's historical financial statements?

2. What is the primary concern of a firm's creditors?

4.2 COMMON-SIZE FINANCIAL STATEMENTS

 LEARNING OBJECTIVE

common-size financial statement
a financial statement in which each number is expressed as a percentage of a base number, such as total assets or net revenues (net sales)

A **common-size financial statement** is one in which each number is expressed as a percentage of some base number, such as total assets or net revenues (net sales). For example, each number on a balance sheet may be divided by total assets. Dividing numbers by a common base to form a ratio is called *scaling*. It is an important concept, and you will read more about it later in this chapter, in the discussion of financial ratios. Financial statements scaled in this manner are also called *standardized financial statements*.

Common-size financial statements make it easier to evaluate changes in a firm's performance and financial condition over time. They also allow you to make more meaningful comparisons between the financial statements of two firms that are different in size. For example, in the oil and gas field equipment market, Schlumberger Limited is the major competitor of Diaz Manufacturing, the illustrative firm introduced in Chapter 3. However, Schlumberger has over $55 billion in total assets while Diaz Manufacturing's assets total only $1.9 billion. Without common-size financial statements, comparisons of these two firms would be difficult to interpret. Common-size financial statements are also useful for analyzing trends within a single firm over time, as you will see.

Common-Size Balance Sheets

FINANCIAL STATEMENTS & RATIOS: AN ANIMATED TUTORIAL

To create a *common-size balance sheet*, we divide each of the asset accounts by total assets. We also divide each of the liability and equity accounts by total assets since Total assets = Total liabilities + Total equity. You can see the common-size balance sheet for Diaz Manufacturing in Exhibit 4.1. Assets are shown in the top portion of the exhibit, and liabilities and equity in the lower portion. The calculations are simple. For example, on the asset side in 2013, cash and marketable securities were 15.3 percent of total assets ($288.5/$1,889.2 = 0.153), and inventory was 22.4 percent of total assets ($423.8/$1,889.2 = 0.224). Notice that the percentages of total assets add up to 100 percent. On the liability side, accounts payable are 18.5 percent of total assets ($349.3/$1,889.2 = 0.185), and long-term debt is 30.4 percent ($574.0/$1,889.2 = 0.304). To test yourself, see if you can re-create the percentages in Exhibit 4.1 using your calculator. Make sure the percentages add up to 100, but realize that you may obtain slight variations from 100 because of rounding.

What kind of information can Exhibit 4.1 tell us about Diaz Manufacturing's operations? Here are some examples. Notice that in 2013, inventories accounted for 22.4 percent of total assets, down from 24.9 percent in 2012 and 28.6 percent in 2011. In other words, Diaz Manufacturing has been steadily reducing the proportion of its money tied up in inventory. This is probably good news because it is usually a sign of more efficient inventory management.

Now look at liabilities and equity, and notice that in 2013 total liabilities represent 50.4 percent of Diaz Manufacturing's total liabilities and equity. This means that common stockholders have provided 49.6 percent of the firm's total financing and that creditors have provided 50.4 percent of the financing. In addition, you can see that from 2011 to 2013, Diaz Manufacturing substantially increased the proportion of financing from long-term debt holders. Long-term debt provided 21.1 percent ($295.6/$1,398.0 = 0.211) of the financing in 2011 and 30.4 percent ($574.0/$1,889.2 = 0.304) in 2013.

Overall, we can identify the following trends in Diaz Manufacturing's common-size balance sheet. First, Diaz Manufacturing is a growing company. Its assets increased from $1,398.0 million in 2011 to $1,889.2 million in 2013. Second, the percentage of total assets held in

A good source for financial statements is http://finance.yahoo.com.

EXHIBIT 4.1   Common-Size Balance Sheets for Diaz Manufacturing on December 31 ($ millions)

In common-size balance sheets, such as those in this exhibit, each asset account and each liability and equity account is expressed as a percentage of total assets. Common-size statements allow financial analysts to compare firms that are different in size and to identify trends within a single firm over time.

	2013	% of Assets	2012	% of Assets	2011	% of Assets
Assets:						
Cash and marketable securities	$ 288.5	15.3	$ 16.6	1.1	$ 8.2	0.6
Accounts receivable	306.2	16.2	268.8	18.0	271.5	19.4
Inventories	423.8	22.4	372.7	24.9	400.0	28.6
Other current assets	21.3	1.1	29.9	2.0	24.8	1.8
Total current assets	$1,039.8	55.0	$ 688.0	46.1	$ 704.5	50.4
Plant and equipment (net)	399.4	21.1	394.2	26.4	419.6	30.0
Goodwill and other assets	450.0	23.8	411.6	27.6	273.9	19.6
Total assets	$1,889.2	100.0	$1,493.8	100.0	$1,398.0	100.0
Liabilities and Stockholders' Equity:						
Accounts payable and accruals	$ 349.3	18.5	$ 325.0	21.8	$ 395.0	28.3
Notes payable	10.5	0.6	4.2	0.3	14.5	1.0
Accrued income taxes	18.0	1.0	16.8	1.1	12.4	0.9
Total current liabilities	$ 377.8	20.0	$ 346.0	23.2	$ 421.9	30.2
Long-term debt	574.0	30.4	305.6	20.5	295.6	21.1
Total liabilities	$ 951.8	50.4	$ 651.6	43.6	$ 717.5	51.3
Common stock (54,566,054 shares)	0.5	0.0	0.5	0.0	0.5	0.0
Additional paid in capital	892.4	47.2	892.4	59.7	892.4	63.8
Retained earnings	67.8	3.6	(50.7)	(3.4)	(155.8)	(11.1)
Less: Treasury stock	(23.3)	(1.2)	—	—	(56.6)	(4.0)
Total stockholders' equity	$ 937.4	49.6	$ 842.2	56.4	$ 680.5	48.7
Total liabilities and equity	$1,889.2	100.0	$1,493.8	100.0	$1,398.0	100.0

current assets grew from 2011 to 2013, a sign of increasing liquidity. Recall from Chapter 2 that assets are liquid if they can be sold easily and quickly for cash without a loss of value. Third, the percentage of total assets in plant and equipment declined from 2011 to 2013, a sign that Diaz Manufacturing is becoming more efficient because it is using fewer long-term assets in producing sales (below you will see that net sales have increased over the same period). Finally, as mentioned, Diaz Manufacturing has significantly increased the percentage of its financing from long-term debt. Generally, these are considered signs of a solidly performing company, but we have a long way to go before we can confidently reach that conclusion. We will now turn to Diaz Manufacturing's common-size income statement.

Common-Size Income Statements

The most useful way to prepare a *common-size income statement* is to express each account as a percentage of net sales, as shown for Diaz Manufacturing in Exhibit 4.2. *Net sales* are defined as total sales less all sales discounts and sales returns and allowances. You should note that when looking at accounting information and sales numbers as reported, they almost always mean net sales, unless otherwise stated. We will follow this convention in the book. Again, the percent calculations are simple. For example, in 2013 selling and administrative expenses are 14.8 percent of sales ($231.1/$1,563.7 = 0.148), and net income is 7.6 percent of sales ($118.5/$1,563.7 = 0.076). Before proceeding, make sure that you can verify each percentage in Exhibit 4.2 with your calculator.

Interpreting the common-size income statement is also straightforward. As you move down the income statement, you will find out exactly what happens to each dollar of sales that the firm generates. For example, in 2013 it cost Diaz Manufacturing 69.1 cents in cost of goods sold to generate one dollar of sales. Similarly, it cost 14.8 cents in selling and administrative expenses to generate a dollar of sales. The government takes 2.8 percent of sales in the form of taxes.

EXHIBIT 4.2 Common-Size Income Statements for Diaz Manufacturing for Fiscal Years Ending December 31 ($ millions)

Common-size income statements express each account as a percentage of net sales. These statements allow financial analysts to better compare firms of different sizes and to analyze trends in a single firm's income statement accounts over time.

	2013	% of Net Sales	2012	% of Net Sales	2011	% of Net Sales
Net sales	$1,563.7	100.0	$1,386.7	100.0	$1,475.1	100.0
Cost of goods sold	1,081.1	69.1	974.8	70.3	1,076.3	73.0
Selling and administrative expenses	231.1	14.8	197.4	14.2	205.7	13.9
Earnings before interest, taxes, depreciation, and amortization (EBITDA)	$ 251.5	16.1	$ 214.5	15.5	$ 193.1	13.1
Depreciation	83.1	5.3	75.3	5.4	71.2	4.8
Earnings before interest and taxes (EBIT)	$ 168.4	10.8	$ 139.2	10.0	$ 121.9	8.3
Interest expense	5.6	0.4	18.0	1.3	27.8	1.9
Earnings before taxes (EBT)	$ 162.8	10.4	$ 121.2	8.7	$ 94.1	6.4
Taxes	44.3	2.8	16.1	1.2	27.9	1.9
Net income	$ 118.5	7.6	$ 105.1	7.6	$ 66.2	4.5
Dividends	—		—		—	
Addition to retained earnings	$ 118.5		$ 105.1		$ 66.2	

This MSN Web site offers lots of financial information, including ratios for firms of your choice: http://money.msn.com/investing/.

The common-size income statement can tell us a lot about a firm's efficiency and profitability. For example, in 2011, Diaz Manufacturing's cost of goods sold and selling and administrative expenses totaled 86.9 percent of sales (73.0 + 13.9 = 86.9). By 2013, these expenses declined to 83.9 percent of sales (69.1 + 14.8 = 83.9). This might mean that Diaz Manufacturing is negotiating lower prices from its suppliers or is more efficient in its use of materials and labor. Or it could mean that the company is getting higher prices for its products, perhaps by offering fewer discounts or rebates. The important point, however, is that more of each sales dollar is contributing to net income.

The trends in the income statement and balance sheet suggest that Diaz Manufacturing is improving along a number of dimensions. The real question, however, is whether Diaz Manufacturing is performing as well as other firms in the same industry. For example, the fact that 7.6 cents of every sales dollar reaches the bottom line may not be a good sign if we find out that Diaz Manufacturing's competitors average 10 cents of net income for every sales dollar.

> **BEFORE YOU GO ON**

1. Why does it make sense to standardize financial statements?

2. What are common-size, or standardized, financial statements, and how are they prepared?

4.3 FINANCIAL RATIOS AND FIRM PERFORMANCE

 3 LEARNING OBJECTIVE

In addition to the common-size ratios we have just discussed, other specialized financial ratios help analysts interpret the myriad of numbers in financial statements. In this section we examine financial ratios that measure a firm's liquidity, efficiency, leverage, profitability, and market value, using Diaz Manufacturing as an example. Keep in mind that for ratio analysis to be most useful, it should also include trend and benchmark analyses, which we discuss in more detail later in this chapter.

financial ratio
a number from a financial statement that has been scaled by dividing by another financial number

Why Ratios Are Better Measures

A **financial ratio** is simply one number from a financial statement that has been divided by another financial number. Like the percentages in common-size financial statements, ratios eliminate problems arising from differences in size because the denominator of the ratio adjusts, or scales, the numerator to a common base.

Here's an example. Suppose you want to assess the profitability of two firms. Firm A's net income is $5, and firm B's is $50. Which firm had the best performance? You really cannot tell because you have no idea what asset base was used to generate the income. In this case, a relevant measure of financial performance for a stockholder might be net income scaled by the firm's stockholders' equity—that is, the return on equity (ROE):

$$ROE = \frac{\text{Net income}}{\text{Stockholders' equity}}$$

If firm A's total stockholders' equity is $25 and firm B's stockholders' equity is $5,000, the ROE for each firm is as follows:

Firm	ROE Calculation	ROE
A	$5/$25	0.20, or 20%
B	$50/$5,000	0.01, or 1%

As you can see, the ROE for firm A is 20 percent—much larger than the ROE for firm B at 1 percent. Even though firm B had the higher net income in absolute terms ($50 versus $5), its stockholders had invested more money in the firm ($5,000 versus $25), and it generated less income per dollar of invested equity than firm A. Clearly, firm A's performance is better than firm B's, given its smaller equity investment. The bottom line is that accounting numbers are more easily compared and interpreted when they are scaled.

Choice of Scale Is Important

An important decision is your choice of the "size factor" for scaling. The size factor you select must be relevant and make economic sense. For example, suppose you want a measure that will enable you to compare the productivity of employees at a particular plant with the productivity of employees at other plants that make similar products. Your assistant makes a suggestion: divide net income by the number of parking spaces available at the plant. Will this ratio tell you how productive labor is at a plant? Clearly, the answer is no.

Your assistant comes up with another idea: divide net income by the number of employees. This ratio makes sense as a measure of employee productivity. A higher ratio indicates that employees are more productive because, on average, each employee is generating more income. In business, the type of variable most commonly used for scaling is a measure of size, such as total assets or total net sales. Other scaling variables are used in specific industries where they are especially informative. For example, in the airline industry, a key measure of performance is revenue per available seat mile; in the steel industry, it is sales or cost per ton; and in the automobile industry, it is cost per car.

Other Comments on Ratios

The ratios we present in this chapter are widely accepted and are almost always included in any financial workup. However, you will find that different analysts will compute many of these standard ratios slightly differently. Modest variation in how ratios are computed are not a problem as long as the analyst carefully documents the work done and discloses the ratio formula. These differences are particularly important when you are comparing data from different sources.

Short-Term Liquidity Ratios

Liquid assets have active secondary markets and can be sold quickly for cash without a loss of value. Some assets are more liquid than others. For example, short-term marketable securities are very liquid because they can be easily sold in the secondary market at or near the original purchase price. In contrast, plant and equipment can take months or years to sell and often must be sold substantially below the cost of building or acquiring them.

When we examine a company's *liquidity position*, we want to know whether the firm can pay its bills when cash from operations is insufficient to pay short-term obligations, such as payroll, invoices from vendors, and maturing bank loans. As the name implies, *short-term*

insolvency
the inability to pay debts when
they are due

liquidity ratios focus on whether the firm has the ability to convert current assets into cash quickly without loss of value. As we have noted before, even a profitable business can fail if it cannot pay its current bills on time. The inability to pay debts when they are due is known as **insolvency**. Thus, liquidity ratios are also known as *short-term solvency ratios*. The two most important liquidity ratios are the current ratio and the quick ratio.

The Current Ratio

To calculate the current ratio, we divide current assets by current liabilities.[1] The formula is presented below, along with a calculation of the current ratio for Diaz Manufacturing for 2013 based on balance sheet account data from Exhibit 4.1:

$$\text{Current ratio} = \frac{\text{Current assets}}{\text{Current liabilities}} \qquad (4.1)$$
$$= \frac{\$1,039.8}{\$377.8}$$
$$= 2.75$$

Diaz Manufacturing's current ratio is 2.75, which should be read as "2.75 times." What does this number mean? If Diaz Manufacturing were to take its current supply of cash and add to it the proceeds of liquidating its other current assets—such as marketable securities, accounts receivable, and inventory—it would have $1,039.8 million. This $1,039.8 million would cover the firm's short-term obligations of $377.8 million approximately 2.75 times, leaving a cushion of $662.0 million ($1,039.8 − $377.8 = $662.0).

Now turn to Exhibit 4.3, which shows the ratios discussed in this chapter for Diaz Manufacturing for the three-year period 2011 to 2013. The exhibit will allow us to identify important trends in the company's financial statements. Note that Diaz Manufacturing's current ratio has been steadily increasing over time. What does this trend mean? From the perspective of a potential creditor, it is a positive sign. To a potential creditor, more liquidity is better because it means that the firm has a greater ability, at least in the short term, to make payments. From a stockholder's perspective, however, too much liquidity is not necessarily a good thing. If we were to discover that Diaz Manufacturing has a much higher current ratio than its competitors, it could mean that management is being too conservative by keeping too much money tied up in current assets, leaving less cash flow for investors. Generally, more liquidity is better and is a sign of a healthy firm. Only a benchmark analysis can tell us the complete story, however.

The Quick Ratio

The quick ratio is similar to the current ratio except that *inventory* is subtracted from current assets in the numerator. This change reflects the fact that inventory is often much less liquid than other current assets. Inventory is the most difficult current asset to convert to cash without loss of value. Of course, the liquidity of inventory varies with the industry. For example, inventory of a raw material commodity, such as gold or crude oil, is more likely to be sold with little loss in value than inventory consisting of perishables, such as fruit, or fashion items, such as basketball shoes. Another reason for excluding inventory in the quick ratio calculation is that the book value of inventory may be significantly more than its market value because it may be obsolete, partially completed, spoiled, out of fashion, or out of season.

To calculate the quick ratio—or *acid-test ratio,* as it is sometimes called—we divide current assets, less inventory, by current liabilities. The calculation for Diaz Manufacturing for 2013 is as follows, based on balance sheet data from Exhibit 4.1:

$$\text{Quick ratio} = \frac{\text{Current assets} - \text{Inventory}}{\text{Current liabilities}} \qquad (4.2)$$
$$= \frac{\$1,039.8 - \$423.8}{\$377.8}$$
$$= 1.63$$

---

[1] This calculation involves dividing total current assets by total current liabilities. We drop the word *total* in the interest of brevity.

EXHIBIT 4.3	Ratios for Time-Trend Analysis for Diaz Manufacturing for Fiscal Years Ending December 31

Comparing how financial ratios, such as these ratios for Diaz Manufacturing, change over time enables financial analysts to identify trends in company performance.

Financial Ratio	2013	2012	2011
Liquidity Ratios:			
Current ratio	2.75	1.99	1.67
Quick ratio	1.63	0.91	0.72
Efficiency Ratios:			
Inventory turnover	2.55	2.62	2.69
Day's sales in inventory	143.14	139.31	135.69
Accounts receivable turnover	5.11	5.16	5.43
Day's sales outstanding	71.43	70.74	67.22
Total asset turnover	0.83	0.93	1.06
Fixed asset turnover	3.92	3.52	3.52
Leverage Ratios:			
Total debt ratio	0.50	0.44	0.51
Debt-to-equity ratio	1.02	0.77	1.05
Equity multiplier	2.02	1.77	2.05
Times interest earned	30.07	7.73	4.38
Cash coverage	44.91	11.92	6.95
Profitability Ratios:			
Gross profit margin	30.86%	29.70%	27.04%
Operating profit margin	10.77%	10.04%	8.26%
Net profit margin	7.58%	7.58%	4.49%
EBIT return on assets	8.91%	9.32%	8.72%
Return on assets	6.27%	7.04%	4.74%
Return on equity	12.64%	12.48%	9.73%
Market-Value Indicators:			
Price-earnings ratio	22.40	18.43	14.29
Earnings per share	$ 2.17	$ 1.93	$ 1.21
Market-to-book ratio	2.83	1.63	1.39

Note: Numbers may not add up because of rounding.

The quick ratio of 1.63 times means that if we exclude inventory, Diaz Manufacturing had $1.63 of current assets for each dollar of current liabilities. You can see from Exhibit 4.3 that Diaz Manufacturing's liquidity position, as measured by its quick ratio, has been increasing over time.

Note that the quick ratio is usually less than the current ratio, as it was for Diaz Manufacturing in 2013.[2] The quick ratio is a very conservative measure of liquidity because the calculation assumes that the inventory is valued at zero, which in most cases is not a realistic assumption. Even in a bankruptcy "fire sale," the inventory can be sold for some small percentage of its book value, generating at least some cash.

Efficiency Ratios

We now turn to a group of ratios called *efficiency ratios* or *asset turnover ratios*, which measure how efficiently a firm uses it assets. These ratios are quite useful for managers and financial analysts in identifying the inefficient use of current and long-term assets. They are also valuable for a firm's investors who use the ratios to find out how quickly a firm is selling its inventory and converting receivables into cash flow for investors.

Inventory Turnover and Days' Sales in Inventory

We measure inventory turnover by dividing the cost of goods sold from the income statement by inventory from the balance sheet (see Exhibits 4.1 and 4.2). The cost of goods sold is used

---

[2]The quick ratio will always be less than the current ratio for any firm that has inventory.

DECISION MAKING

EXAMPLE 4.1

The Liquidity Paradox

SITUATION: You are asked by your boss whether Wal-Mart or H&R Block is more liquid. You have the following information:

	Wal-Mart	H&R Block
Current ratio	0.88	0.99
Quick ratio	0.23	0.99

You also know that Wal-Mart carries a large inventory and that H&R Block is a service firm that specializes in income-tax preparation. Which firm is the most liquid? Your boss asks you to explain the reasons for your answers, and also to explain why H&R Block's current and quick ratios are the same.

DECISION: H&R Block is much more liquid than Wal-Mart. The difference between the quick ratios—0.23 versus 0.99—pretty much tells the story. Inventory is the least liquid of all the current assets. Because H&R Block does not manufacture or sell goods, it has no inventory; hence, the current and quick ratios are equal. Wal-Mart has a lot of inventory relative to the rest of its current assets, and that explains the large numerical difference between the current and quick ratios.

because it reflects the book value of the inventory that is sold by a firm. The formula for inventory turnover and its value for Diaz Manufacturing in 2013 are:

$$\text{Inventory turnover} = \frac{\text{Cost of goods sold}}{\text{Inventory}} \qquad (4.3)$$

$$= \frac{\$1,081.1}{\$423.8}$$

$$= 2.55$$

The firm "turned over" its inventory 2.55 times during the year. Looking back at Exhibit 4.3, you can see that this ratio remained about the same over the period covered.

What exactly does "turning over" inventory mean? Consider a simple example. Assume that a firm starts the year with inventory worth $100 and replaces the inventory when it is all sold; that is, the inventory goes to zero. If, over the course of the year, the firm sells the inventory and replaces it three times, the firm is said to have an inventory turnover of three times.

As a general rule, turning over inventory faster is a good thing because it means that the firm is doing a good job of minimizing its investment in inventory. Nevertheless, like all ratios, inventory turnover can be either too high or too low. Too high of an inventory turnover ratio may signal that the firm has too little inventory for its customers and could be losing sales as a result. If the firm's inventory turnover level is too low, it could mean that management is not managing the firm's inventory efficiently or that an unusually large portion of the inventory is obsolete or out of date. In sum, inventory turnover that is significantly lower or significantly higher than that of competitors calls for further investigation.

Based on the inventory turnover figure, and using a 365-day year, we can also calculate the *days' sales in inventory*, which tells us how long it takes a firm to turn over its inventory on average. The formula for days' sales in inventory, along with the 2013 calculation for Diaz Manufacturing, is as follows:

$$\text{Days' sales in inventory} = \frac{365 \text{ days}}{\text{Inventory turnover}} \qquad (4.4)$$

$$= \frac{365 \text{ days}}{2.55}$$

$$= 143.14 \text{ days}$$

Note that inventory turnover in the formula is computed using Equation 4.3. On average, Diaz Manufacturing takes about 140 days to turn over its inventory. Generally speaking, the smaller the number, the more efficient the firm is at moving its inventory.

Alternative Calculation for Inventory Turnover

Normally, we determine inventory turnover by dividing cost of goods sold by the inventory level at the end of the period. However, if a firm's inventory fluctuates widely or is growing (or decreasing) over time, some analysts prefer to compute inventory turnover using the average inventory value for the time period. In this case, the inventory turnover is calculated in two steps:

1. We first calculate average inventory by adding beginning and ending inventory and dividing by 2:

$$\text{Average inventory} = \frac{\text{Beginning inventory} + \text{Ending inventory}}{2}$$

2. We then divide the cost of goods sold by average inventory to find inventory turnover:

$$\text{Inventory turnover} = \frac{\text{Cost of goods sold}}{\text{Average inventory}}$$

Note that all six efficiency ratios presented in the chapter (Equations 4.3 through 4.8) can be computed using an average asset value. For simplicity, we will generally use the end of the period asset value in our calculations.

LEARNING BY DOING

APPLICATION 4.1

Alternative Calculations for Efficiency Ratios

PROBLEM: For Diaz Manufacturing, compute inventory turnover during 2013 using the average inventory. Then compare that value with 2.55, the turnover ratio computed using Equation 4.3. Why do the two values differ?

APPROACH: Use the alternative calculation described above. In comparing the two values, you should consider fluctuations in inventory over time.

SOLUTION:

1. $\text{Average inventory} = \dfrac{\text{Beginning inventory} + \text{Ending inventory}}{2}$

$$= \frac{\$372.7 + \$423.8}{2}$$

$$= \$398.3$$

2. $\text{Inventory turnover} = \dfrac{\text{Cost of goods sold}}{\text{Average inventory}}$

$$= \frac{\$1,081.1}{\$398.3}$$

$$= 2.71$$

The 2013 inventory turnover computed with average inventory, 2.71 times, is slightly higher than 2.55 because the inventory increased during the year.

Accounts Receivable Turnover and Days' Sales Outstanding

Many firms make sales to their customers on credit, which creates an account receivable on the balance sheet. It does not do the firm much good to ship products or provide the services on credit if it cannot ultimately collect the cash from its customers. A firm that collects its receivables faster is generating cash faster. We can measure the speed at which a firm converts its receivables into cash with a ratio called accounts receivable turnover; the formula and calculated values for Diaz Manufacturing in 2013 are as follows:

$$\text{Accounts receivable turnover} = \frac{\text{Net sales}}{\text{Accounts receivable}} \qquad (4.5)$$
$$= \frac{\$1,563.7}{\$306.2}$$
$$= 5.11$$

The data to compute this ratio is from Diaz's balance sheet and income statement (Exhibits 4.1 and 4.2). Roughly, this ratio means that Diaz Manufacturing loans out and collects an amount equal to its outstanding accounts receivable 5.11 times over the course of a year.

In most circumstances, higher accounts receivable turnover is a good thing—it means that the firm is making fewer sales on credit and collecting cash payments from its credit customers faster. Such credit is a customer incentive that is used to promote sales, but it can be expensive. As shown in Exhibit 4.3, Diaz's collection speed slowed down slightly from 2011 to 2013. This may be a cause for management concern for at least three reasons. First, Diaz's system for collecting accounts receivable may be inefficient. Second, the firm's customers may not be paying on time because their businesses are slowing down due to industry or general economic conditions. Finally, Diaz may be extending credit to customers that are poor credit risks. Making a determination of the cause would require us to compare Diaz's accounts receivable turnover with corresponding figures from its competitors.

You may find it easier to evaluate a firm's credit and collection policies by using days' sales outstanding, often referred to as DSO, which is calculated as follows:

$$\text{Days' sales outstanding} = \frac{365 \text{ days}}{\text{Accounts receivable turnover}} \qquad (4.6)$$
$$= \frac{365 \text{ days}}{5.11}$$
$$= 71.43 \text{ days}$$

Note that accounts receivable turnover is computed using Equation 4.5. The DSO for Diaz Manufacturing means that, on average, the company converts its credit sales into cash in 71.43 days. DSO is commonly called the *average collection period*.

Generally, faster collection is better. Whether 71.43 days is fast enough really depends on industry norms and on the credit terms Diaz Manufacturing extends to its customers. For example, if the industry average DSO is 77 days and Diaz Manufacturing gives customers 90 days to pay, then a DSO of 71.43 days is an indication of good management. If, in contrast, Diaz gives customers 60 days to pay, the company has a problem, and management needs to determine why customers are not paying on time.

Asset Turnover Ratios

We turn next to a discussion of some broader efficiency ratios. In this section we discuss two ratios that measure how efficiently management is using the firm's assets to generate sales.

Total asset turnover measures the dollar amount of sales generated with each dollar of total assets. Generally, the higher the total asset turnover, the more efficiently management is using total assets. Thus, if a firm increases its asset turnover, management is squeezing more sales out of a constant asset base. When a firm's asset turnover ratio is high for its industry, the firm may be approaching full capacity. In such a situation, if management wants to increase sales, it will need to make an investment in additional fixed assets. Total asset turnover should be interpreted with care when examining trends for a given firm or when benchmarking against competitors. Younger firms and firms with more recent purchases of fixed assets will have a higher book value of assets and therefore lower total asset turnover for a given level of net sales.

The formula for total asset turnover and the calculation for Diaz Manufacturing's turnover value in 2013 (based on data from Exhibits 4.1 and 4.2) are as follows:

$$\text{Total asset turnover} = \frac{\text{Net sales}}{\text{Total assets}} \qquad (4.7)$$
$$= \frac{\$1,563.7}{\$1,889.2}$$
$$= 0.83$$

Total asset turnover for Diaz Manufacturing is 0.83 times. In other words, in 2013, Diaz Manufacturing generated $0.83 in sales for every dollar in assets. In Exhibit 4.3 you can see that Diaz Manufacturing's total asset turnover has declined since 2011. This does not necessarily mean that the company's management team is performing poorly. The decline could be part of a typical industry sales cycle, or it could be due to a slowdown in the business of Diaz Manufacturing's customers. As always, getting a better fix on potential problems requires comparing Diaz Manufacturing's total asset turnover with comparable figures for its close competitors.

The turnover of total assets is a "big picture" measure. In addition, management may want to see how particular types of assets are being put to use. A common asset turnover ratio measures sales per dollar invested in fixed assets (plant and equipment). The fixed asset turnover formula and the 2013 calculation for Diaz are:

$$\text{Fixed asset turnover} = \frac{\text{Net sales}}{\text{Net fixed assets}} \qquad (4.8)$$
$$= \frac{\$1,563.7}{\$399.4}$$
$$= 3.92$$

Diaz Manufacturing generated $3.92 of sales for each dollar of net fixed assets in 2013, which is an increase over the 2012 value of $3.52. This means that the firm is generating more sales for every dollar in fixed assets. In a manufacturing firm that relies heavily on plant and equipment to generate output, the fixed asset turnover number is an important ratio. In contrast, in a service-industry firm with little plant and equipment, *total* asset turnover is more relevant.

Ranking Firms by Fixed Asset Turnover

DECISION MAKING

EXAMPLE 4.2

SITUATION: Different industries use different amounts of fixed assets to generate their revenues. For example, the airline industry is capital intensive, with large investments in airplanes, whereas firms in service industries use more human capital (people) and have very little invested in fixed assets. As a financial analyst, you are given the following fixed asset turnover ratios: 1.74, 3.80, and 11.04. You must decide which ratios match up with three firms: Delta Air Lines, H&R Block, and Wal-Mart. Make this decision, and explain your reasoning.

DECISION: At the extremes, Delta is a capital-intensive firm, and H&R Block is a service firm. We would expect firms with large investments in fixed assets (Delta) to have lower asset turnover than service-industry firms, which have few fixed assets. Wal-Mart is the middle-ground firm, with fixed asset holdings primarily in stores and land. Thus, the firms and their respective fixed asset turnovers are Delta = 1.74, Wal-Mart = 3.80, and H&R Block = 11.04.

Leverage Ratios

Leverage ratios measure the extent to which a firm uses debt rather than equity financing and indicate the firm's ability to meet its long-term financial obligations, such as interest payments on debt and lease payments. The ratios are also called *long-term solvency ratios.* They are of interest to the firm's creditors, stockholders, and managers. Many different leverage ratios are used in industry; in this chapter we present some of the most widely used.

Financial Leverage

The term **financial leverage** refers to the use of debt in a firm's capital structure. When a firm uses debt financing, rather than only equity financing, the returns to stockholders may be magnified. This so-called leveraging effect occurs because the interest payments associated with debt are fixed, regardless of the level of the firm's operating profits. On the one hand, if the firm's operating profits increase from one year to the next, debt holders continue to receive only their fixed-interest payments, and all of the increase goes to the stockholders. On the other hand, if the firm falls on hard times and suffers an operating loss, debt holders receive the same fixed-interest payment (assuming that the firm does not become insolvent and default on

financial leverage
the use of debt in a firm's capital structure; the more debt, the higher the financial leverage

its obligations to debt holders), and the loss is charged against the stockholders' equity. Thus, debt increases the returns to stockholders during good times and reduces the returns during bad times. In Chapter 14 we discuss financial leverage in greater depth and present a detailed example of how debt financing creates the leveraging effect.

The use of debt in a company's capital structure increases the firm's **default risk**—the risk that it will not be able to pay its debt as it comes due. The explanation is, of course, that debt payments are a fixed obligation and debt holders must be paid the interest and principal payments they are owed, regardless of whether the company earns a profit or suffers a loss. If a company fails to make an interest payment on the prescribed date, the company defaults on its debt and could be forced into bankruptcy by creditors.

default risk
the risk that a firm will not be able to pay its debt obligations as they come due

Debt Ratios

We next look at three leverage ratios that focus on how much debt, rather than equity, the firm employs in its capital structure. The more debt a firm uses, the higher its financial leverage, the more volatile its earnings, and the greater its risk of default.

Total Debt Ratio.   The total debt ratio measures the extent to which the firm finances its assets from sources other than the stockholders. The higher the total debt ratio, the more debt the firm has in its capital structure. The total debt ratio and a calculation for Diaz Manufacturing for 2013 based on data from Exhibit 4.1 appear as follows:

$$\text{Total debt ratio} = \frac{\text{Total debt}}{\text{Total assets}} \qquad (4.9)$$
$$= \frac{\$951.8}{\$1,889.2}$$
$$= 0.50$$

How do we determine the figure to use for total debt? Many variations are used, but perhaps the easiest is to subtract total equity from total assets. In other words, total debt is equal to total liabilities. A common alternative measure of debt is the sum of all the firm's interest-bearing liabilities, such as notes payable and long-term debt. Using data from Exhibit 4.1, we can calculate total debt for Diaz Manufacturing in 2013 as follows:

$$\text{Total debt} = \text{Total assets} - \text{Total equity} = \$1,889.2 - \$937.4 = \$951.8$$

As you can see from Equation 4.9, the total debt ratio for Diaz Manufacturing is 0.50, which means that 50 percent of the company's assets are financed with debt. Looking back at Exhibit 4.3, we find that Diaz Manufacturing increased its use of debt from 2012 to 2013. The 2013 total debt ratio of 50 percent appears high, raising questions about the company's financing strategy. Whether a high or low value for the total debt ratio is good or bad, however, depends on how the firm's capital structure affects the value of the firm. We explore this topic in greater detail in Chapter 14.

We turn next to two common variations of the total debt ratio: the debt-to-equity ratio and the equity multiplier.

Debt-to-Equity Ratio.   The *total debt ratio* tells us the amount of debt for each dollar of total assets. The *debt-to-equity ratio* tells us the amount of debt for each dollar of equity. Based on data from Exhibit 4.1, Diaz Manufacturing's debt-to-equity ratio for 2013 is 1.02:

$$\text{Debt-to-equity ratio} = \frac{\text{Total debt}}{\text{Total equity}} \qquad (4.10)$$
$$= \frac{\$951.8}{\$937.4}$$
$$= 1.02$$

The total debt ratio and the debt-to-equity ratio are directly related by the following formula, shown with a calculation for Diaz Manufacturing:

$$\text{Total debt ratio} = \frac{\text{Debt-to-equity ratio}}{1 + \text{Debt-to-equity ratio}}$$
$$= \frac{1.02}{1 + 1.02}$$
$$= 0.50$$

As you can see, once you know one of these ratios, you can compute the other. Which of the two ratios you use is really a matter of personal preference.

Finding a Total Debt Ratio

PROBLEM: A firm's debt-to-equity ratio is 0.5. What is the firm's total debt ratio?

APPROACH: Use the equation that relates the total debt ratio to the debt-to-equity ratio.

SOLUTION:

$$\text{Total debt ratio} = \frac{\text{Debt-to-equity ratio}}{1 + \text{Debt-to-equity ratio}}$$
$$= \frac{0.5}{1 + 0.5}$$
$$= 0.33$$

Solving for an Unknown Using the Debt-to-Equity Ratio

PROBLEM: You are given the follow information about H&R Block's year-end balance sheet for 2012. The firm's debt-to-equity ratio is 2.51, and its total equity is $1.33 billion. Determine the book (accounting) values for H&R Block's total debt and total assets.

APPROACH: We know that the debt-to-equity ratio is 2.51 and that total equity is $1.33 billion. We also know that the debt-to-equity ratio (Equation 4.10) is equal to total debt divided by total equity, and we can use this information to solve for total debt. Once we have a figure for total debt, we can use the balance sheet identity to solve for total assets.

SOLUTION:

$$\text{Total debt} = \text{Debt-to-equity ratio} \times \text{Total equity}$$
$$= 2.51 \times \$1.33 \text{ billion}$$
$$= \$3.34 \text{ billion}$$
$$\text{Total assets} = \text{Total debt} + \text{Total equity}$$
$$= \$3.34 \text{ billion} + \$1.33 \text{ billion}$$
$$= \$4.67 \text{ billion}$$

Equity Multiplier.   The equity multiplier tells us the amount of assets that the firm has for every dollar of equity. Diaz Manufacturing's equity multiplier ratio is 2.02, as shown here:

$$\text{Equity multiplier} = \frac{\text{Total assets}}{\text{Total equity}} \tag{4.11}$$
$$= \frac{\$1,889.2}{\$937.4}$$
$$= 2.02$$

Notice that the equity multiplier is directly related to the debt-to-equity ratio:

$$\text{Equity multiplier} = 1 + \text{Debt-to-equity ratio}$$

This is no accident. Recall the balance sheet identity: Total assets = Total liabilities (debt) + Total stockholders' equity. This identity can be substituted into the numerator of the equity multiplier formula (Equation 4.11):

$$\begin{aligned} \text{Equity multiplier} &= \frac{\text{Total assets}}{\text{Total equity}} \\ &= \frac{\text{Total equity} + \text{Total debt}}{\text{Total equity}} \\ &= \frac{\text{Total equity}}{\text{Total equity}} + \frac{\text{Total debt}}{\text{Total equity}} \\ &= 1 + \frac{\text{Total debt}}{\text{Total equity}} \\ &= 1 + \frac{\$951.8}{937.4} \\ &= 1 + 1.02 \\ &= 2.02 \end{aligned}$$

Therefore, all three of these leverage ratios (Equations 4.9–4.11) are related by the balance sheet identity, and once you know one of the three ratios, you can compute the other two ratios.

Coverage Ratios

A second type of leverage ratio measures the firm's ability to service its debt, or how easily the firm can "cover" its debt payments out of earnings or cash flow. We assess this using coverage ratios. For example, if your monthly take-home pay from your part-time job is $400 and the rent on your apartment is $450, your monthly coverage ratio with respect to rent is $400/$450 = 0.89 times. Because this ratio is less than 1 you will be in some financial distress. Your income does not cover your $450 fixed obligation to pay the rent. If, on the other hand, your take-home pay is $900, your monthly coverage ratio with respect to rent is $900/$450 = 2 times. This means that for every dollar of rent you must pay, you earn two dollars of revenue. The higher your coverage ratio, the less likely you are to default on your rent payments.

Times Interest Earned. Our first coverage ratio is times interest earned, which measures the extent to which operating profits (earnings before interest and taxes, or EBIT) cover the firm's interest expenses. Creditors prefer to lend to firms whose EBIT is far in excess of their interest payments. The equation for the times-interest-earned ratio and a calculation for Diaz Manufacturing from its income statement (Exhibit 4.2) for 2013 are:

$$\begin{aligned} \text{Times interest earned} &= \frac{\text{EBIT}}{\text{Interest expense}} \\ &= \frac{\$168.4}{\$5.6} \\ &= 30.07 \end{aligned} \quad (4.12)$$

Diaz Manufacturing can cover its interest charges about 30 times with its operating income. This figure appears to point to a good margin of safety for creditors. In general, the larger the times interest earned, the more likely the firm is to make its interest payments.

Cash Coverage. As we have discussed before, depreciation is a noncash expense, and as a result, no cash goes out the door when depreciation is deducted on the income statement. Thus, rather than asking whether operating profits (EBIT) are sufficient to cover interest payments, we might ask how much cash is available to cover interest payments. The cash a firm has available from operations to meet interest payments is better measured by EBIT plus depreciation and amortization (EBITDA).[3] Thus, the cash coverage ratio for Diaz Manufacturing in 2013 is:

$$\begin{aligned} \text{Cash coverage} &= \frac{\text{EBITDA}}{\text{Interest expense}} \\ &= \frac{\$251.5}{\$5.6} \\ &= 44.91 \end{aligned} \quad (4.13)$$

---

[3]EBITDA can differ from actual cash flows because of the accounting accruals and the investment in net working capital and fixed assets that we discussed in Chapter 3.

For a firm with depreciation or amortization expenses, which includes virtually all firms, EBITDA coverage will be larger than times interest earned coverage.

Profitability Ratios

Profitability ratios measure management's ability to efficiently use the firm's assets to generate sales and manage the firm's operations. These measurements are of interest to stockholders, creditors, and managers because they focus on the firm's earnings. The profitability ratios presented in this chapter are among a handful of such ratios commonly used by stockholders, managers, and creditors when analyzing a firm's performance. In general, the higher the profitability ratios, the better the firm is performing.

Gross Profit Margin

The gross profit margin measures the percentage of net sales remaining after the cost of goods sold is paid. It captures the firm's ability to manage the expenses directly associated with producing the firm's products or services. Next we show the gross profit margin formula, along with a calculation for Diaz Manufacturing in 2013, using data from Exhibit 4.2:

$$\text{Gross profit margin} = \frac{\text{Net sales} - \text{Cost of goods sold}}{\text{Net sales}} \tag{4.14}$$

$$= \frac{\$1,563.7 - \$1,081.1}{\$1,563.7}$$

$$= 0.3086, \text{ or } 30.86\%$$

Thus, after paying the cost of goods sold, Diaz Manufacturing has 30.86 percent of the sales amount remaining to pay other expenses. From Exhibit 4.3, you can see that Diaz Manufacturing's gross profit margin has been increasing over the past several years, which is good news.

Operating Profit Margin and EBITDA Margin

Moving farther down the income statement, you can measure the percentage of sales that remains after payment of cost of goods sold and all other expenses, except for interest and taxes. Operating profit is typically measured as EBIT. The operating profit margin, therefore, gives an indication of the profitability of the firm's operations, independent of its financing policies or tax management strategies. The operating profit margin formula, along with Diaz Manufacturing's 2013 operating profit margin calculated using data from Exhibit 4.2, is as follows:

$$\text{Operating profit margin} = \frac{\text{EBIT}}{\text{Net sales}} \tag{4.15}$$

$$= \frac{\$168.4}{\$1,563.7}$$

$$= 0.1077, \text{ or } 10.77\%$$

Many analysts and investors are concerned with cash flows generated by operations rather than operating earnings and will use EBITDA in the numerator instead of EBIT. Calculated in this way, the operating profit margin is known as the EBITDA margin.

Net Profit Margin

The net profit margin is the percentage of sales remaining after all of the firm's expenses, including interest and taxes, have been paid. The net profit margin formula is shown here, along with the calculated value for Diaz Manufacturing in 2013, using data from the firm's income statement (Exhibit 4.2):

$$\text{Net profit margin} = \frac{\text{Net income}}{\text{Net sales}} \tag{4.16}$$

$$= \frac{\$118.5}{\$1,563.7}$$

$$= 0.0758, \text{ or } 7.58\%$$

As you can see from Exhibit 4.3, Diaz Manufacturing's net profit margin improved dramatically from 2011 to 2013. This is good news. The question remains, however, whether 7.58 percent is a good profit margin in an absolute sense. Answering this question requires that we compare Diaz Manufacturing's performance to the performance of its competitors, which we will do later in this chapter. What qualifies as a good profit margin varies significantly across industries. Generally speaking, the higher a company's profit margin, the better the company's performance.

Return on Assets

So far, we have examined profitability as a percentage of sales. It is also important that we analyze profitability as a percentage of investment, either in assets or in equity. First, let's look at return on assets. In practice, return on assets is calculated in two different ways.

One approach provides a measure of operating profit (EBIT) per dollar of assets. This is a powerful measure of return because it tells us how efficiently management utilized the assets under their command, independent of financing decisions and taxes. It can be thought of as a measure of the pre-tax return on the total net investment in the firm from operations. The formula for this version of return on assets, which we call EBIT return on assets (EROA), is shown next, together with the calculated value for Diaz Manufacturing in 2013, using data from Exhibits 4.1 and 4.2:

$$\text{EBIT return on assets (EROA)} = \frac{\text{EBIT}}{\text{Total assets}} \qquad (4.17)$$
$$= \frac{\$168.4}{\$1,889.2}$$
$$= 0.0891, \text{ or } 8.91\%$$

Exhibit 4.3 shows us that, unlike the other profitability ratios, Diaz Manufacturing's EROA did not really improve from 2011 to 2013. The very similar EROA values for 2011 and 2013 indicate that assets increased at approximately the same rate as operating profits.

Some analysts calculate return on assets (ROA) as:

$$\text{Return on assets (ROA)} = \frac{\text{Net income}}{\text{Total assets}} \qquad (4.18)$$
$$= \frac{\$118.5}{\$1,889.2}$$
$$= 0.0627, \text{ or } 6.27\%$$

Although it is a common calculation, we advise against using the calculation in Equation 4.18 unless you are using the DuPont system, which we discuss shortly. The ROA calculation divides a measure of earnings available to stockholders (net income) by total assets (debt plus equity), which is a measure of the investment in the firm by both stockholders and creditors. Constructing a ratio of those two numbers is like mixing apples and oranges. The information that this ratio provides about the efficiency of asset utilization is obscured by the financing decisions the firm has made and the taxes it pays. You can see this in Exhibit 4.3, which shows that, in contrast to the very small change in EROA, ROA increases substantially from 2011 to 2013. This increase in ROA is not due to improved efficiency but rather to a large decrease in interest expense (see Exhibit 4.2).

The key point is that EROA surpasses ROA as a measure of how efficiently assets are utilized in operations. Dividing a measure of earnings to both debt holders and stockholders by a measure of how much both debt holders and stockholders have invested gives us a clearer view of what we are trying to measure.

In general, when you calculate a financial ratio, if you have a measure of income to stockholders in the numerator, you want to make sure that you have only investments by stockholders in the denominator. Similarly, if you have a measure of total profits from operations in the numerator, you want to divide it by a measure of total investments by both debt holders and stockholders.

Return on Equity

Return on equity (ROE) measures net income as a percentage of the stockholders' investment in the firm. The return on equity formula and the calculation for Diaz Manufacturing in 2013 based on data from Exhibits 4.1 and 4.2 are as follows:

$$\text{Return on equity (ROE)} = \frac{\text{Net income}}{\text{Total equity}} \qquad (4.19)$$

$$= \frac{\$118.5}{\$937.4}$$

$$= 0.1264, \text{ or } 12.64\%$$

Alternative Calculation of ROA and ROE

As with efficiency ratios, the calculation of ROA and ROE involves dividing an income statement value, which relates to a period of time, by a balance sheet value from the end of the time period. Some analysts prefer to calculate ROA and ROE using the average asset value or equity value, where the average value is determined as follows:

$$\text{Average asset or equity value} = \frac{\text{Beginning value } + \text{ Ending value}}{2}$$

Using the average asset or equity value makes sense because the earnings over a period are generated with the average value of assets or equity.

Alternative Calculations for EROA and ROE Ratios

PROBLEM: Calculate the EROA and ROE for Diaz Manufacturing in 2013 using average balance sheet values and compare the results with the calculations based on Equations 4.17 and 4.19.

APPROACH: First find average values for the asset and equity accounts using data from Exhibit 4.1. Then use these values to calculate the EROA and ROE. In explaining why some analysts might prefer the alternative calculation, consider possible fluctuations of assets or equity over time.

SOLUTION:

$$\text{Average asset or equity value} = \frac{\text{Beginning value } + \text{ Ending value}}{2}$$

$$\text{Average asset value} = \frac{\$1,493.8 + \$1,889.2}{2}$$

$$= \$1,691.5$$

$$\text{Average equity value} = \frac{\$842.2 + \$937.4}{2}$$

$$= \$889.8$$

$$\text{EROA} = \frac{\text{EBIT}}{\text{Total assets}} = \frac{\$168.4}{\$1,691.5}$$

$$= 0.0996, \text{ or } 9.96\%$$

$$\text{ROE} = \frac{\text{Net income}}{\text{Total equity}} = \frac{\$118.5}{\$889.8}$$

$$= 0.1332, \text{ or } 13.32\%$$

Both EROA (9.96 percent versus 8.91 percent) and ROE (13.32 percent versus 12.64 percent) are higher when the average values are used. The reason is that Diaz's total assets grew from $1,493.8 million in 2012 to $1,889.2 million in 2013 and its equity grew from $842.2 million to $937.4 million during the same period.

LEARNING
BY
DOING

APPLICATION 4.4

NEED MORE HELP?

WileyPLUS

Market-Value Indicators

The ratios we have discussed so far rely solely on the firm's financial statements, and we know that much of the data in those statements are historical and do not represent current market value. Also, as we discussed in Chapter 1, the appropriate objective for the firm's management is to maximize stockholder value, and the market value of the stockholders' claims is the value of the *cash flows* that they are entitled to receive, which is not necessarily the same as accounting income. To find out how the stock market evaluates a firm's liquidity, efficiency, leverage, and profitability, we need ratios based on market values.

Over the years, financial analysts have developed a number of ratios, called *market-value ratios*, which combine market-value data with data from a firm's financial statements. Here we examine the most commonly used market-value ratios: earnings per share, the price-earnings ratio, and the market-to-book ratio.

Earnings per Share

Dividing a firm's net income by the number of shares outstanding yields earnings per share (EPS). At the end of 2013, Diaz Manufacturing had 54,566,054 shares outstanding (see Exhibit 3.1 in Chapter 3) and net income of $118.5 million (Exhibit 4.2). Its EPS at that point is calculated as follows:

$$\text{Earning per share} = \frac{\text{Net income}}{\text{Shares outstanding}} \tag{4.20}$$

$$= \frac{\$118,500,000}{54,566,054} = \$2.17 \text{ per share}$$

Price-Earnings Ratio

The price-earnings (P/E) ratio relates earnings per share to price per share. The formula, with a calculation for Diaz Manufacturing for the end of 2013, is as follows:

$$\text{Price-earnings ratio} = \frac{\text{Price per share}}{\text{Earnings per share}} \tag{4.21}$$

$$= \frac{\$48.61}{\$2.17} = 22.4$$

Price per share on a given date can be obtained from listings in the *Wall Street Journal* or from an online source, such as Yahoo! Finance.

What does it mean for a firm to have a price-earnings ratio of 22.4? It means that the stock market places a value of $22.40 on every $1 of net income. Why are investors willing to pay $22.40 for a claim on $1 of earnings? The answer is that the stock price does not only reflect the earnings this year. It reflects all future cash flows from earnings. An especially high P/E ratio can indicate that investors expect the firm's earnings to grow rapidly in the future. Alternatively, a high P/E ratio might be due to unusually low earnings in a particular year and investors might expect earnings to recover to a normal level soon. We will discuss how expected growth affects P/E ratios in detail in later chapters. As with other measures, to understand whether the P/E ratio is too high or too low, we must compare the firm's P/E ratio with those of competitors and also look at movements in the firm's P/E ratio relative to market trends.

Market-to-Book Ratio

The market-to-book ratio compares the market value of the firm's investments to its book value. The formula, with a calculation for Diaz at the end of 2013, is:

$$\text{Market-to-book ratio} = \frac{\text{Market value or equity per share}}{\text{Book value of equity per share}} \tag{4.22}$$

$$= \frac{\$48.61}{\$937.4/54.566}$$

$$= \frac{\$48.61}{\$17.18} = 2.83$$

Book value per share is an accounting number that reflects the cumulative historical investment into the firm's equity account on a per share basis. Market value of equity per share is simply the price per share. A higher market-to-book ratio suggests that the firm has been more effective at investing in projects that add value for its stockholders. A value of less than one could mean that the firm has not created any value for its stockholders.

Concluding Comments on Ratios

We could have covered many more ratios. However, the group of ratios presented in this chapter is a fair representation of the ratios needed to analyze the performance of a business. When using ratios, it is important that you ask yourself, "What does this ratio mean, and what is it measuring?" rather than trying to memorize a definition. Good ratios should make good economic sense when you look at them.

> **BEFORE YOU GO ON**

1. What are the efficiency ratios, and what do they measure? Why, for some firms, is the total asset turnover more important than the fixed asset turnover?

2. List the leverage ratios discussed in this section, and explain how they are related.

3. List the profitability ratios discussed in this section, and explain how they differ from each other.

4.4 THE DUPONT SYSTEM: A DIAGNOSTIC TOOL

By now, your mind may be swimming with ratios. Fortunately, some enterprising financial managers at the DuPont Company developed a system in the 1960s that ties together some of the most important financial ratios and provides a systematic approach to financial ratio analysis.

LEARNING OBJECTIVE 4

An Overview of the DuPont System

The DuPont system of analysis is a diagnostic tool that uses financial ratios to evaluate a company's financial health. The process has three steps. First, management assesses the company's financial health using the DuPont ratios. Second, if any problems are identified, management corrects them. Finally, management monitors the firm's financial performance over time, looking for differences from ratios established as benchmarks by management.

Under the DuPont system, management is charged with making decisions that maximize the firm's return on equity as opposed to maximizing the value of the stockholders' shares. The system is primarily designed to be used by management as a diagnostic and corrective tool, though investors and other stakeholders have found its diagnostic powers of interest.

The DuPont system is derived from two equations that link the firm's return on assets (ROA) and return on equity (ROE). The system identifies three areas where management should focus its efforts in order to maximize the firm's ROE: (1) how much profit management can earn on sales, (2) how efficient management is in using the firm's assets, and (3) how much financial leverage management is using. Each of these areas is monitored by a single ratio, and together the ratios comprise the *DuPont equation*.

The ROA Equation

The ROA equation links the firm's return on assets with its total asset turnover and net profit margin. We derive this relation from the ROA equation as follows:

$$\text{ROA} = \frac{\text{Net income}}{\text{Total assets}}$$

$$= \frac{\text{Net income}}{\text{Total assets}} \times \frac{\text{Net sales}}{\text{Net sales}}$$

$$= \frac{\text{Net income}}{\text{Net sales}} \times \frac{\text{Net sales}}{\text{Total assets}}$$

$$= \text{Net profit margin} \times \text{Total asset turnover}$$

As you can see, we start with the ROA formula presented earlier as Equation 4.18. Then we multiply ROA by net sales divided by net sales. In the third line, we rearrange the terms, coming up with the expression ROA = (Net income/Net sales) × (Net sales/Total assets). You may recognize the first ratio in the third line as the firm's net profit margin (Equation 4.16) and the second ratio as the firm's total asset turnover (Equation 4.7). Thus, we end up with the final equation for ROA, which is restated as Equation 4.23:

$$\text{ROA} = \text{Net profit margin} \times \text{Total asset turnover} \qquad (4.23)$$

Equation 4.23 says that a firm's ROA is determined by two factors: (1) the firm's net profit margin and (2) the firm's total asset turnover. Let's look at the managerial implications of each of these terms.

Net Profit Margin.   The net profit margin ratio can be written as follows:

$$\text{Net profit margin} = \frac{\text{Net income}}{\text{Net sales}} = \frac{\text{EBIT}}{\text{Net sales}} \times \frac{\text{EBT}}{\text{EBIT}} \times \frac{\text{Net income}}{\text{EBT}}$$

As you can see, the net profit margin can be viewed as the product of three ratios: (1) the operating profit margin (EBIT/Net sales), which is Equation 4.15, (2) a ratio that measures the impact of interest expenses on profits (EBT/EBIT), and (3) a ratio that measures the impact of taxes on profits (Net income/EBT). Thus, the net profit margin focuses on management's ability to generate profits from sales by efficiently managing the firm's (1) operating expenses, (2) interest expenses, and (3) tax expenses.

Total Asset Turnover.   Total asset turnover, which is defined as Net sales/Total assets, measures how efficiently management uses the assets under its command—that is, how much output management can generate with a given asset base.

Net Profit Margin versus Total Asset Turnover

The ROA equation provides some very interesting managerial insights. It says that if management wants to increase the firm's ROA, it can increase the net profit margin, total asset turnover, or both. Of course, every firm would like to make both terms as large as possible so as to earn the highest possible ROA. Though every industry is different, competition, marketing considerations, technology, and manufacturing capabilities, to name a few, place upper limits on asset turnover and net profit margins and, thus, ROA. Equation 4.23 suggests that management can follow two distinct strategies to maximize ROA. Deciding between the strategies involves a trade-off between total asset turnover and net profit margin.

The first management strategy emphasizes high profit margin and low asset turnover. Examples of companies that use this strategy are luxury stores, such as jewelry stores, high-end department stores, and upscale specialty boutiques. Such stores carry expensive merchandise that has a high profit margin but tends to sell slowly. The second management strategy depends on low profit margins and high turnover. Typical examples of firms that use this strategy are discount stores and grocery stores, which have very low profit margins but make up for it by turning over their inventory very quickly. A typical chain grocery store, for example, turns over its inventory more than 12 times per year.

Exhibit 4.4 illustrates both strategies. The exhibit shows asset turnover, profit margin, and ROA for four retailing firms for the fiscal year ending closest to December 2011. Tiffany & Co. is a nationwide retailer of high-end jewelry, and Ralph Lauren stores are upscale boutiques that carry expensive casual wear for men and women. At the other end of the spectrum are Wal-Mart, which is famous for its low-price, high-volume strategy, and Whole Foods Markets, a grocery chain based in Austin, Texas.

Notice that the two luxury-item stores (Tiffany & Co. and Ralph Lauren) have lower asset turnover and higher profit margins, while the discount and grocery stores have lower profit margins and much higher asset turnover. Whole Foods and Wal-Mart are strong financial

EXHIBIT 4.4 **Two Basic Strategies to Earn a Higher ROA[a]**

To maximize a firm's ROA, management can focus more on achieving high profit margins or on achieving high asset turnover. High-end retailers like Ralph Lauren and Tiffany & Co. focus more on achieving high profit margins. In contrast, grocery and discount stores like Whole Foods Market and Wal-Mart tend to focus more on achieving high asset turnover because competition limits their ability to achieve very high profit margins.

Company	Asset Turnover	×	Profit Margin (%)	=	ROA (%)
High Profit Margin:					
Ralph Lauren	1.27		9.93		12.61
Tiffany & Co.	0.88		12.05		10.60
High Turnover:					
Whole Foods Market	2.36		3.39		8.00
Wal-Mart Stores	2.31		3.51		8.11

[a]Ratios are calculated using financial results for the fiscal year ending closest to December 2011.

performers in their industry sectors. Their relatively low ROAs of 8.00 and 8.11 percent, respectively, reflect the high degree of competition in the grocery and discount store businesses.

The ROE Equation

To derive the ROE equation, we start with the formula from Equation 4.19:

$$\text{ROE} = \frac{\text{Net income}}{\text{Total equity}}$$

$$= \frac{\text{Net income}}{\text{Total equity}} \times \frac{\text{Total assets}}{\text{Total assets}}$$

$$= \frac{\text{Net income}}{\text{Total assets}} \times \frac{\text{Total assets}}{\text{Total equity}}$$

$$= \text{ROA} \times \text{Equity multiplier}$$

Next, we multiply by total assets divided by total assets, and then we rearrange the terms so that ROE = (Net income/Total assets) × (Total assets/Total equity), as shown in the third line. By this definition, ROE is the product of two ratios already familiar to us: ROA (Equation 4.18) and the equity multiplier (Equation 4.11). The equation for ROE is shown as Equation 4.24:

$$\text{ROE} = \text{ROA} \times \text{Equity multiplier} \qquad (4.24)$$

Interesting here is the fact that ROE is determined by the firm's ROA and its use of leverage. The greater the use of debt in the firm's capital structure, the greater the ROE. Thus, increasing the use of leverage is one way management can increase the firm's ROE—but at a price. That is, the greater the use of financial leverage, the more risky the firm. How aggressively a company uses this strategy depends on management's preference for risk and the willingness of creditors to lend money and bear the risk.

The DuPont Equation

Now we can combine our two equations into a single equation. From Equation 4.24, we know that ROE = ROA × Equity multiplier; and from Equation 4.23, we know that ROA = Net profit margin × Total asset turnover. Substituting Equation 4.23 into Equation 4.24 yields an expression formally called the DuPont equation, as follows:

$$\text{ROE} = \text{Net profit margin} \times \text{Total asset turnover} \times \text{Equity multiplier} \qquad (4.25)$$

We can also express the DuPont equation in ratio form:

$$\text{ROE} = \frac{\text{Net income}}{\text{Net sales}} \times \frac{\text{Net sales}}{\text{Total assets}} \times \frac{\text{Total assets}}{\text{Total equity}} \qquad (4.26)$$

To check the DuPont relation, we will use some values from Exhibit 4.3, which lists financial ratios for Diaz Manufacturing. For 2013, Diaz's net profit margin is 7.58 percent, total asset turnover is 0.83, and the equity multiplier is 2.02. Substituting these values into Equation 4.25 yields:

$$\text{ROE} = \text{Net profit margin} \times \text{Total asset turnover} \times \text{Equity multiplier}$$
$$= 7.58 \times 0.83 \times 2.02$$
$$= 12.71\%$$

With rounding error, this agrees with the value computed for ROE using Equation 4.19.

Applying the DuPont System

In summary, the DuPont equation tells us that a firm's ROE is determined by three factors: (1) net profit margin, which measures the firm's operating efficiency and how it manages its interest expense and taxes; (2) total asset turnover, which measures the efficiency with which the firm's assets are utilized; and (3) the equity multiplier, which measures the firm's use of financial leverage. The schematic diagram in Exhibit 4.5 shows how the three key DuPont ratios are linked together and how they relate to the balance sheet and income statement for Diaz Manufacturing.

The DuPont system of analysis is a useful tool to help identify problem areas within a firm. For example, suppose that North Sails Group, a sailboat manufacturer located in San Diego, California, is having financial difficulty. The firm hires you to find out why the ship is financially sinking. The firm's CFO has you calculate the DuPont ratio values for the firm and obtain some industry averages to use as benchmarks, as shown.

DuPont Ratios	Firm	Industry
ROE	8%	16%
ROA	4%	8%
Equity multiplier	2	2
Net profit margin	8%	16%
Asset turnover	0.5	0.5

Clearly, the firm's ROE is quite low compared to its industry (8 percent versus 16 percent), so without question the firm has problems. Next, you examine the values for the firm's ROA and equity multiplier. The firm's use of financial leverage is equal to the industry standard of 2 times, but its ROA is half that of the industry (4 percent versus 8 percent). Because ROA is the product of net profit margin and total asset turnover, you next examine these two ratios. Asset turnover does not appear to be a problem because the firm's ratio is equal to the industry standard of 0.5 times. However, the firm's net profit margin is substantially below the benchmark standard (8 percent versus 16 percent). Thus, the firm's performance problem stems from a low profit margin.

Identifying the low profit margin as an area of concern is only a first step. Further investigation is necessary to determine the underlying problem and its causes. The point to remember is that financial analysis identifies areas of concern within the firm, but rarely does it tell us all we need to know.

Is Maximizing ROE an Appropriate Goal?

Throughout this book we have stressed the notion that management should make decisions that maximize the current value of the company stock. An important question is whether maximizing the value of ROE, as suggested by the DuPont system, is equivalent to wealth maximization. The short answer is that the two goals are not equivalent, but some discussion is warranted.

A major shortcoming of ROE is that it does not directly consider cash flow. ROE considers earnings, but earnings are not the same as future cash flows. Second, ROE does not consider risk. As discussed in Chapter 1, management and stockholders are very concerned about the degree of risk they face. Third, ROE does not consider the size of the initial investment or the size of future cash payments. As we stressed in Chapter 1, the essence of any business or investment decision is this: What is the size of the cash flows to be received, when do you expect to receive the cash flows, and how likely are you to receive them?

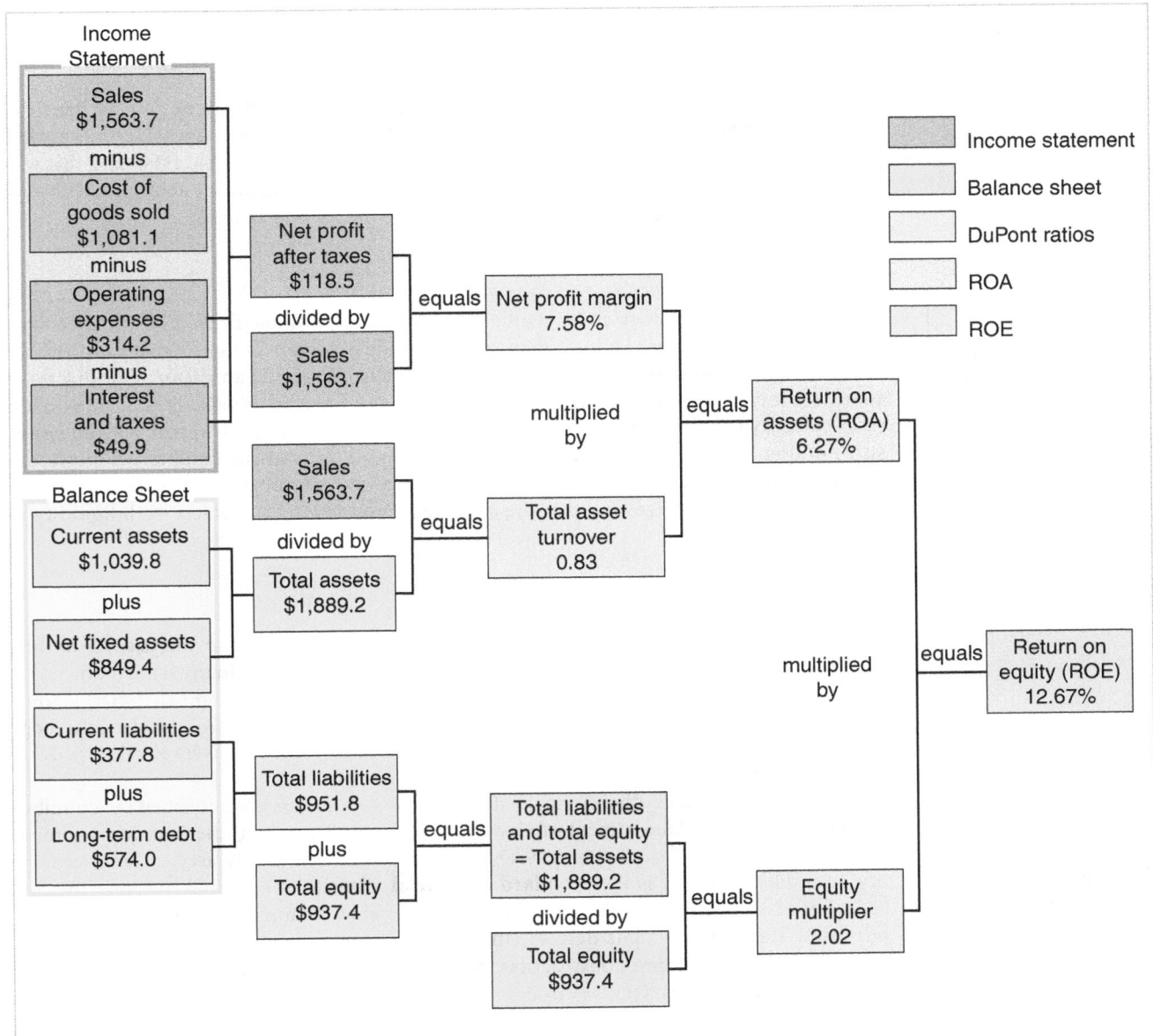

EXHIBIT 4.5
Relations in the DuPont System of Analysis for Diaz Manufacturing in 2013 ($ millions)

The diagram shows how the three key DuPont ratios are linked together and to the firm's balance sheet and income statement. Numbers in the exhibit are in millions of dollars and represent 2013 data from Diaz Manufacturing. The ROE of 12.67 percent differs from the 12.64 percent in Exhibit 4.3 due to rounding.

In spite of these shortcomings, ROE analysis is widely used in business as a measure of operating performance. Proponents of ROE analysis argue that it provides a systematic way for management to work through the income statement and balance sheet and to identify problem areas within the firm. Furthermore, they note that ROE and stockholder value are often highly correlated.

> **BEFORE YOU GO ON**

  1. What is the purpose of the DuPont system of analysis?

  2. What is the equation for ROA in the DuPont system, and how do the factors in that equation influence the ratio?

  3. What are the three major shortcomings of ROE?

4.5 SELECTING A BENCHMARK

5 LEARNING OBJECTIVE

How do you judge whether a ratio value is too high or too low? Is the value good or bad? We touched on these questions several times earlier in this chapter. As we suggested, the starting point for making these judgments is selecting an appropriate benchmark—a standard that will be the basis for meaningful comparisons. Financial managers can gather appropriate benchmark data in three ways: through trend, industry, and peer group analysis.

Trend Analysis

Trend analysis uses history as its standard by evaluating a single firm's performance over time. This sort of analysis allows management to determine whether a given ratio value has increased or decreased over time and whether there has been an abrupt shift in a ratio value. An increase or decrease in a ratio value is in itself neither good nor bad. However, a ratio value that is changing typically prompts the financial manager to sort out the issues surrounding the change and to take any action that is warranted. Exhibit 4.3 shows the trends in Diaz Manufacturing's ratios. For example, the exhibit shows that Diaz's current ratio has improved, suggesting that the company is not having a problem with liquidity at the present time.

> Visit the Web site of the Risk Management Association for a variety of ratio definitions and sample financial ratio benchmarks across different industries: http://www.rmahq.org/ tools-publications/ publications/annual- statement-studies.

Industry Analysis

A second way to establish a benchmark is to conduct an industry group analysis. To do that, we identify a group of firms that have the same product line, compete in the same market, and are about the same size. The average ratio values for these firms will be our benchmarks. Since no two firms are identical, deciding which firms to include in the analysis is always a judgment call. If we can construct a sample of reasonable size, however, the average values provide defensible benchmarks.

Financial ratios and other financial data for industry groups are published by a number of sources—the U.S. Department of Commerce, Dun & Bradstreet, the Risk Management Association, and Standard & Poor's (S&P), to name a few. One widely used system for identifying industry groups is the **Standard Industrial Classification (SIC) System**. The SIC codes are four-digit numbers established by the federal government for statistical reporting purposes. The first two digits describe the type of business in a broad sense (for example, firms engaged in building construction, mining of metals, manufacturing of machinery, food stores, or banking). Diaz's two-digit code is 35: "Industrial and commercial machinery and computer equipment."

Standard Industrial Classification (SIC) System
a numerical system developed by the U.S. government to classify businesses according to the type of activity they perform

More than 400 companies fall into the "Industrial and commercial machinery and computer equipment" code category. To narrow the group, we use more digits. Diaz Manufacturing's four-digit code is 3533 ("oil and gas field machinery and equipment"), and there are only 35 firms in this category. Among firm's within an SIC code, financial ratio data can be further categorized by asset size or by sales, which allows for more meaningful comparisons.

North American Industry Classification System (NAICS)
a classification system for businesses introduced to refine and replace the older SIC system

In 1977, the **North American Industry Classification System (NAICS)** was introduced as a new classification system. It was intended to refine and replace the older SIC codes, but it has been slow to catch on. Industry databases still allow you to sort data by either SIC or NAICS classifications.

Although industry databases are readily available and easy to use, they are far from perfect. When trying to find a sample of firms that are similar to your company, you may find the classifications too broad. For example, Wal-Mart and Nordstrom have the same four-digit SIC code (5311), but they are very different retailing firms. Another problem is that different databases may compute ratios differently. Thus, when making benchmark comparisons, you must be careful that your calculations match those in the database, or there could be some distortions in your findings.

> You can find information about the SIC and NAICS systems at http://www.census.gov/ eos/www/naics/.

Peer Group Analysis

The third way to establish benchmark information is to identify a group of firms that compete with the company we are analyzing. Ideally, the firms are in similar lines of business, are about

EXHIBIT 4.6   Peer Group Ratios for Diaz Manufacturing

Peer group analysis is one way to establish benchmarks for a firm. Ideally, a firm's peer group is made up of firms that are its direct competitors and are of about the same size. The exhibit shows the average financial ratios for public companies that make up the peer group for Diaz Manufacturing for 2011, 2012, and 2013.

	2013	2012	2011
Liquidity Ratios:			
Current ratio	2.10	2.20	2.10
Quick ratio	1.50	1.60	1.50
Efficiency Ratios:			
Inventory turnover	5.40	5.30	5.20
Day's sales in inventory	67.59	68.87	70.19
Accounts receivable turnover	4.90	4.20	4.10
Days' sales outstanding	76.70	89.80	90.00
Total asset turnover	0.87	0.90	0.80
Fixed asset turnover	3.50	3.30	2.40
Leverage Ratios:			
Total debt ratio	0.18	0.11	0.21
Debt-to-equity ratio	0.40	0.20	0.50
Equity multiplier	2.02	1.77	2.05
Times interest earned	7.00	5.60	1.60
Cash coverage	7.50	8.20	1.30
Profitability Ratios:			
Gross profit margin	26.80%	24.10%	19.20%
Operating profit margin	12.00%	6.90%	2.70%
Net profit margin	10.74%	3.30%	0.10%
Return on assets	9.34%	3.30%	0.80%
Return on equity	13.07%	7.00%	1.00%
Market-Value Indicators:			
Price-to-earnings ratio	18.10	38.40	44.60
Earnings per share	$1.65	$3.85	$3.78
Market-to-book ratio	2.84	1.82	1.64

the same size, and are direct competitors of the target firm. These firms form a *peer group*. Once a peer group has been identified, management can obtain the associated financial information and compute average ratio values against which the firm can compare its performance.

How do we determine which firms should be in the peer group? The senior management team within a company will know its competitors. If you're working outside the firm, you can look at the firm's annual report and at financial analysts' reports. Both of these sources usually identify key competitors. Exhibit 4.6 shows ratios for a five-firm peer group constructed for Diaz Manufacturing for 2011 through 2013.

We consider the peer group methodology the best way to establish a benchmark if financial data for peer firms are publicly available. We should note, however, that comparison against a single firm is acceptable when there is a clear market leader and we want to compare a firm's performance and other characteristics against those of a firm considered the best. For example, Ford Motor Company may want to compare itself directly against the automobile manufacturer that is the most productive. It is worthwhile to compare a firm with the market leader to identify areas of weakness as well as of possible strength.

> **BEFORE YOU GO ON**

1. In what three ways can a financial manager choose a benchmark?

2. Explain what the SIC codes are, and discuss the pros and cons of using them in financial analysis.

4.6 USING FINANCIAL RATIOS

So far, our focus has been on the calculation of financial ratios. As you may already have concluded, however, the most important tasks are to *correctly interpret* the ratio values and to *make appropriate decisions* based on this interpretation. In this section we discuss using financial ratios in performance analysis.

Performance Analysis of Diaz Manufacturing

Let's examine Diaz Manufacturing's performance during 2013 using the DuPont system of analysis as our diagnostic tool and the peer group sample in Exhibit 4.6 as our benchmark. For ease of discussion, Diaz's financial ratios and the peer group data are assembled in Exhibit 4.7.

We start our analysis by looking at the big picture—the three key DuPont ratios for the firm and a peer group of firms (see Exhibit 4.7). We see that Diaz Manufacturing's ROE of 12.64 percent is below the benchmark value of 13.07 percent, a difference of 0.43 percent, which is not good news. More dramatically, Diaz's ROA is 3.07 percent below the peer group benchmark, which is a serious difference. Clearly, Diaz Manufacturing has some performance problems that need to be investigated.

To determine the problems, we examine the firm's equity multiplier and ROA results in more detail. The equity multiplier value of 2.02, versus the benchmark value of 1.40, suggests that Diaz Manufacturing is using more leverage than the average firm in the benchmark sample. Management is comfortable with the higher-than-average leverage. Conversations with the firm's investment banker, however, indicate that the company's debt could become a problem if the economy deteriorated and went into a recession.

Without the higher equity multiplier and management's willingness to bear additional risk, Diaz Manufacturing's ROE would be much lower. To illustrate this point, suppose management reduced the company's leverage to the peer group average equity multiplier of 1.40 (see Exhibit 4.7). With an equity multiplier of 1.40, the firm's ROE would be only 8.78 percent (0.0627 × 1.40 = 0.0878, or 8.78 percent); this is 3.86 percent below the firm's current ROE of 12.64 percent and 4.29 percent below the peer group benchmark. Thus, the use of higher leverage has, to some extent, masked the severity of the firm's problem with ROA.

EXHIBIT 4.7 **Peer Group Analysis for Diaz Manufacturing**

Examining the differences between the ratios of a firm and its peer group is a good way to spot areas that require further analysis.

	(1) Diaz Ratio	(2) Peer Group Ratio	(3) Difference (Column 1 – Column 2)
DuPont Ratios:			
Return on equity (%)	12.64	13.07	(0.43)
Return on assets (%)	6.27	9.34	(3.07)
Equity multiplier (%)	2.02	1.40	0.62
Net profit margin (%)	7.58	10.74	(3.16)
Total asset turnover	0.83	0.87	(0.04)
Profit Margins:			
Gross profit margin (%)	30.86	26.80	4.06
Operating margin (%)	10.77	12.00	(1.23)
Net profit margin (%)	7.58	10.74	(3.16)
Asset Ratios:			
Current ratio	2.75	2.10	0.65
Fixed asset turnover	3.92	3.50	0.42
Inventory turnover	2.55	5.40	(2.85)
Accounts receivable turnover	5.11	4.90	0.21

Recall that ROA equals the product of the net profit margin and total asset turnover. Diaz's net profit margin is 3.16 percent lower than the benchmark value (7.58 − 10.74 = −3.16), and its total asset turnover ratio is slightly below the benchmark value (0.83 versus 0.87). Thus, both ratios that comprise ROA are below the peer group benchmark standard, but the net profit margin appears to be the larger problem.

Turning to the asset turnover ratios shown in Exhibit 4.7, we find that the ratios for Diaz are generally similar to the corresponding peer group ratios. An exception is the inventory turnover ratio, which is substantially below the benchmark: 2.55 for Diaz versus 5.40 for the benchmark. Diaz's management needs to investigate why the inventory turnover ratio is off the mark.

Because Diaz Manufacturing's net profit margin is low, we next look at the various profit margins shown in Exhibit 4.7 to gain insight into this situation. Diaz Manufacturing's gross profit margin is 4.06 percentage points above the benchmark value (30.86 − 26.80 = 4.06), which is good news. Since gross profit margin is a factor of sales and the cost of goods sold, we can conclude that there is no problem with the price the firm is charging for its products or with its cost of goods sold.

Diaz's problems begin with its operating margin of 10.77 percent, which is 1.23 percentage points below the peer group benchmark of 12.00 percent (10.77 − 12.00 = −1.23). The major controllable expense here is selling and administrative costs, and management needs to investigate why these expenses appear to be out of line.

In sum, the DuPont analysis of Diaz Manufacturing has identified two areas that warrant detailed investigation by management: (1) the larger-than-average inventory (slow inventory turnover) and (2) the above-average selling and administrative expenses. Management must now investigate each of these areas and come up with a course of action. Management may also want to give careful consideration to the firm's high degree of financial leverage and whether it represents a prudent degree of risk.

Financial ratio analysis is an excellent diagnostic tool. It helps management identify the problem areas in the firm—the symptoms. However, it does not tell management what the causes of the problems are or what course of action should be taken. Management must drill down into the accounting data, talk with managers in the field, and if appropriate, talk with people outside the firm, such as suppliers, to understand what is causing the problems and how best to fix them.

Ron's Jewelry Store and the Missing Data

PROBLEM: Ron Roberts has owned and managed a profitable jewelry business in San Diego County for the past five years. He believes his jewelry store is one of the best managed in the county, and he is considering opening several new stores.

When Ron started the store, he supplied all the equity financing himself and financed the rest with personal loans from friends and family members. To open more stores, Ron needs a bank loan. The bank will want to examine his financial statements and know something about the competition he faces.

Ron has asked his brother-in-law, Dennis O'Neil, a CPA, to analyze the financials. Ron has also gathered some financial information about a company he considers the chief competition in the San Diego County market. The competitor has been in business for 25 years, has a number of stores, and is widely admired for its owners' management skills. Dennis organizes the available information in the following table:

Financial Ratio/Data	Ron's Store	Competitor
Net sales ($ thousands)	$240	$300
Net income ($ thousands)	$ 6	—
ROE	13.13%	—
Net profit margin	—	5.84%
Asset turnover	1.5	1.5
Equity multiplier	—	1.5
Debt-to-equity ratio	2.5	—

LEARNING BY DOING

APPLICATION 4.5

(continued)

Calculate the missing values for the financial data above.

APPROACH: Use the ratio equations discussed in the text to calculate the missing financial ratios for both Ron's store and the competitor.

SOLUTION:
Ron's jewelry store:

1. $\text{Net profit margin} = \dfrac{\text{Net income}}{\text{Net sales}} = \dfrac{\$6}{\$240} = 0.025, \text{ or } 2.5\%$

2. Equity multipier = 1 + Debt-to-equity ratio = 1 + 2.5 = 3.5

Competitor:
1. Net income = Net profit margin × Net sales = 0.0584 × $300 = $17.52

2. ROE = Net profit margin × Asset turnover × Equity multiplier
= 0.0584 × 1.5 × 1.5 = 0.1314, or 13.14%

3. $\text{Debt-to-equity ratio} = \dfrac{\text{Debt}}{\text{Equity}} = \dfrac{\$66.82}{\$133.1} = 0.50$

(a) $\text{Equity} = \dfrac{\text{NI}}{\text{ROE}} = \dfrac{\$17.5}{0.1314} = \$133.18$

(b) $\text{Assets} = \dfrac{\text{Net sales}}{\text{Asset turnover}} = \dfrac{\$300}{1.5} = \$200.00$

(c) Debt = Assets − Equity = $200.00 − $133.18 = $66.82

DECISION MAKING

EXAMPLE 4.3

Ron's Jewelry Store and the DuPont Analysis

SITUATION: Let's continue with our analysis of Ron's jewelry store, introduced in Learning by Doing Application 4.5. Brother-in-law Dennis has been asked to analyze the company's financials. He decides to use the DuPont system of analysis as a framework. He arranges the critical information as follows:

Financial Ratios	Ron's Store	Competitor
ROE	13.13%	13.14%
ROA	3.75%	8.76%
Net profit margin	2.50%	5.84%
Asset turnover	1.5	1.5
Equity multiplier	3.5	1.5
Debt-to-equity ratio	2.5	0.5
Net sales ($ thousands)	$240	$300
Net income ($ thousands)	$ 6.0	$ 17.5

Given the above financial ratios, what recommendations should Dennis make regarding Ron's jewelry store and its management?

DECISION: The good news is that Ron is able to earn about the same ROE as his major competitor. Unfortunately for Ron, it's pretty much downhill from there. Turning to the first two DuPont system ratios, we can see that Ron's ROA of 3.75 percent is much lower than his major competitor's ROA of 8.76 percent. Ron's business is also very highly leveraged, with an equity multiplier of 3.5 times, compared with 1.5 times for the competitor. In fact, the only reason Ron's ROE is comparable to the competitor's is the high leverage. Ron's debt-to-equity ratio is 2.5 whereas the competitor's is only 0.5.

Breaking the ROA into its components, we find that Ron's asset turnover ratio is the same as the competitor's, 1.5. However, the profitability of Ron's store is extremely poor as measured by the firm's net profit margin of 2.50 percent, compared with the competitor's margin of 5.84 percent. One possible explanation is that to stimulate sales and maintain asset turnover, Ron has been selling his merchandise at too low a price.

In summary, Ron's jewelry store is not well managed. Ron needs to either increase his net profit margin or increase his inventory turnover to bring his ROA into line with that of his major competitor. Ron may also need to reduce his dependence on financial leverage, but it makes sense to review interest coverage ratios before deciding whether he should do so.

Limitations of Financial Statement Analysis

Financial statement and ratio analysis as discussed in this chapter presents two major problems. First, it depends on accounting data based on historical costs. As we discussed in Chapter 3, knowledgeable financial managers would prefer to use financial statements in which all of the firm's assets and liabilities are valued at market. Financial statements based on current market values more closely reflect a firm's true economic condition than do statements based on historical cost.

Second, there is little theory to guide us in making judgments based on financial statement and ratio analysis. That is why it is difficult to say a current ratio of 2.0 is good or bad or to say whether ROE or ROA is a more important ratio. The lack of theory explains, in part, why rules of thumb are often used as decision rules in financial statement analysis. The problem with decision rules based on experience and "common sense" rather than theory is that they may work fine in a stable economic environment but may fail when a significant shift takes place. For example, if you were in an economic environment with low inflation, you could develop a set of decision rules to help manage your business. However, if the economy became inflationary, more than likely many of your decision rules would fail.

Despite the limitations, we know that financial managers and analysts routinely use financial statements and ratio analysis to evaluate a firm's performance and to make a variety of decisions about the firm. These financial statements and the resulting analysis are the primary means by which financial information is communicated both inside and outside of firms. The availability of market value data is limited for public corporations and not available for privately held firms and other entities such as government units.

Thus, practically speaking, historical accounting information often represents the best available information. However, times are changing. As the accounting profession becomes more comfortable with the use of market data and as technology increases its availability and reliability and lowers its cost, we expect to see an increase in the use of market-based financial statements.

> ## BEFORE YOU GO ON

1. Explain how the DuPont identity allows us to evaluate a firm's performance.

2. What are the limitations on traditional financial statement analysis?

3. List some of the problems that financial analysts confront when analyzing financial statements.

SUMMARY OF Learning Objectives

1 Explain the three perspectives from which financial statements can be viewed.

Financial statements can be viewed from the owners', managers', or creditors' perspective. All three groups are ultimately interested in a firm's profitability, but each group takes a different view. Stockholders want to know how much cash they can expect to receive for their stock, what their return on investment will be, and how much their stock is worth in the market. Managers are concerned with maximizing the firm's long-term value through a series of day-to-day management decisions; thus, they need to see the impact of their decisions on the financial statements to confirm that things are going as planned. Creditors monitor the firm's use of debt and

are concerned with how much debt the firm is using and whether the firm will have enough cash to meet its debt obligations.

2 Describe common-size financial statements, explain why they are used, and be able to prepare and use them to analyze the historical performance of a firm.

Common-size financial statements are financial statements in which each number has been scaled by a common measure of firm size: balance sheets are expressed as a percentage of total assets, and income statements are expressed as a percentage of net sales. Common-size financial statements make it easier to evaluate changes in a firm's performance and financial condition over time.

They are also useful when comparing firms that are significantly different in size. The preparation of common-size financial statements and their use are illustrated for Diaz Manufacturing in Section 4.2.

3 Discuss how financial ratios facilitate financial analysis and be able to compute and use them to analyze a firm's performance.

Financial ratios are used in financial analysis because they eliminate problems caused by comparing two or more companies of different size, or when looking at the same company over time as the size changes. Financial ratios can be divided into five categories: (1) Liquidity ratios measure the ability of a company to cover its current bills. (2) Efficiency ratios tell how efficiently the firm uses its assets. (3) Leverage ratios tell how much debt a firm has in its capital structure and whether the firm can meet its long-term financial obligations. (4) Profitability ratios focus on the firm's earnings. (5) Market value indicators look at a company based on market data as opposed to historical data used in financial statements. The computation and analysis of major financial ratios are presented in Section 4.3 (also see the Summary of Key Equations that follows).

4 Describe the DuPont system of analysis and be able to use it to evaluate a firm's performance and identify corrective actions that may be necessary.

The DuPont system of analysis is a diagnostic tool that uses financial ratios to assess a firm's financial strength. Once the financial ratios are calculated and the assessment is complete, management can focus on correcting the problems within the context of maximizing the firm's ROE. For analysis, the DuPont system breaks ROE into three components: net profit margin, which measures operating efficiency; total asset turnover, which measures how efficiently the firm's assets are being used; and the equity multiplier, which measures financial leverage. A diagnostic analysis of a firm's performance using the DuPont system is illustrated in Section 4.4.

5 Explain what benchmarks are, describe how they are prepared, and discuss why they are important in financial statement analysis.

Benchmarks are used to provide a standard for evaluating the financial performance of a firm. In financial statement analysis, a number of benchmarks are used. Most often, benchmark comparisons involve competitors that are roughly the same size and that offer a similar range of products. Another form of benchmarking is time-trend analysis, which compares a firm's current financial ratios against the same ratios from past years. Time-trend analysis tells us whether a ratio is increasing or decreasing over time. The preparation and use of peer group benchmark data are illustrated in Section 4.6.

6 Identify the major limitations in using financial statement analysis.

The major limitations to financial statement and ratio analysis are the use of historical accounting data and the lack of theory to guide the decision maker. The lack of theory explains, in part, why there are so many rules of thumb. Though rules of thumb are useful in that they may also work under certain conditions, they may also lead to poor decisions if circumstances or the economic environment have changed.

SUMMARY OF Key Equations

Equation	Description	Formula
4.1	Liquidity Ratio	$\text{Current ratio} = \dfrac{\text{Current assets}}{\text{Current liabilities}}$
4.2	Liquidity Ratio	$\text{Quick ratio} = \dfrac{\text{Current assets} - \text{Inventory}}{\text{Current liabilities}}$
4.3	Efficiency Ratio	$\text{Inventory turnover} = \dfrac{\text{Cost of goods sold}}{\text{Inventory}}$
4.4	Efficiency Ratio	$\text{Day's sales in inventory} = \dfrac{\text{365 Days}}{\text{Inventory turnover}}$
4.5	Efficiency Ratio	$\text{Accounts receivable turnover} = \dfrac{\text{Net sales}}{\text{Accounts receivable}}$
4.6	Efficiency Ratio	$\text{Day's sales outstanding} = \dfrac{\text{365 days}}{\text{Accounts receivable turnover}}$
4.7	Efficiency Ratio	$\text{Total asset turnover} = \dfrac{\text{Net sales}}{\text{Total assets}}$
4.8	Efficiency Ratio	$\text{Fixed asset turnover} = \dfrac{\text{Net sales}}{\text{Net fixed assets}}$
4.9	Leverage Ratio	$\text{Total debt ratio} = \dfrac{\text{Total debt}}{\text{Total assets}}$
4.10	Leverage Ratio	$\text{Debt-to-equity ratio} = \dfrac{\text{Total debt}}{\text{Total equity}}$
4.11	Leverage Ratio	$\text{Equity multiplier} = \dfrac{\text{Total assets}}{\text{Total equity}}$

Equation	Description	Formula
4.12	Leverage Ratio	Times interest earned $= \dfrac{\text{EBIT}}{\text{Interest expense}}$
4.13	Leverage Ratio	Cash coverage $= \dfrac{\text{EBITDA}}{\text{Interest expense}}$
4.14	Profitability Ratio	Gross profit margin $= \dfrac{\text{Net sales} - \text{Cost of goods sold}}{\text{Net sales}}$
4.15	Profitability Ratio	Operating profit margin $= \dfrac{\text{EBIT}}{\text{Net sales}}$
4.16	Profitability Ratio	Net profit margin $= \dfrac{\text{Net income}}{\text{Net sales}}$
4.17	Profitability Ratio	EBIT return on assets(EROA) $= \dfrac{\text{EBIT}}{\text{Total assets}}$
4.18	Profitability Ratio	Return on assets(ROA) $= \dfrac{\text{Net income}}{\text{Total assets}}$
4.19	Profitability Ratio	Return on equity(ROE) $= \dfrac{\text{Net income}}{\text{Total equity}}$
4.20	Market Value Indicator	Earning per share $= \dfrac{\text{Net income}}{\text{Shares outstanding}}$
4.21	Market Value Indicator	Price-earnings ratio $= \dfrac{\text{Price per share}}{\text{Earnings per share}}$
4.22	Market Value Indicator	Market-to-book ratio $= \dfrac{\text{Market value of equity per share}}{\text{Book value of equity per share}}$
4.23	ROA Breakdown	ROA $=$ Net profit margin $\times$ Total asset turnover
4.24	ROE Breakdown	ROE $=$ ROA $\times$ Equity multiplier
4.25	DuPont Equation	ROE $=$ Net profit margin $\times$ Total asset turnover $\times$ Equity multiplier
4.26	DuPont Equation	ROE $= \dfrac{\text{Net income}}{\text{Net sales}} \times \dfrac{\text{Net sales}}{\text{Total assets}} \times \dfrac{\text{Total assets}}{\text{Total equity}}$

Self-Study Problems

4.1 The Abercrombie Supply Company reported the following information for 2013. Prepare a common-size income statement for the year ended June 30, 2013.

Abercrombie Supply Company
Income Statement for the Fiscal Year Ended June 30, 2013 ($ thousands)

Net sales	$2,110,965
Cost of goods sold	1,459,455
Selling and administrative expenses	312,044
Nonrecurring expenses	27,215
Earnings before interest, taxes, depreciation, and amortization (EBITDA)	$ 312,251
Depreciation	112,178
Earnings before interest and taxes (EBIT)	$ 200,073
Interest expense	117,587
Earnings before taxes (EBT)	$ 82,486
Taxes (35%)	28,870
Net income	$ 53,616

4.2 Prepare a common-size balance sheet from the following information for Abercrombie Supply Company.

Abercrombie Supply Company
Balance Sheet as of June 30, 2013 ($ thousands)

Assets:		Liabilities and Equity:	
Cash and marketable securities	$ 396,494	Accounts payable	$ 817,845
Accounts receivable	708,275	Notes payable	101,229
Inventories	1,152,398	Accrued income taxes	41,322
Other current assets	42,115	Total current liabilities	$ 960,396
Total current assets	$2,299,282	Long-term debt	1,149,520
Net plant and equipment	1,978,455	Total liabilities	$2,109,916
		Common stock	1,312,137
		Retained earnings	855,684
		Total common equity	$2,167,821
Total assets	$4,277,737	Total liabilities and equity	$4,277,737

4.3 Using the 2013 data for the Abercrombie Supply Company, calculate the following liquidity ratios:
a. Current ratio.
b. Quick ratio.

4.4 Refer to the balance sheet and income statement for Abercrombie Supply Company for the year ended June 30, 2013. Calculate the following ratios:
a. Inventory turnover ratio.
b. Days' sales outstanding.
c. Total asset turnover.
d. Fixed asset turnover.
e. Total debt ratio.
f. Debt-to-equity ratio.
g. Times-interest-earned.
h. Cash coverage.

4.5 Refer to the balance sheet and income statement for Abercrombie Supply Company for the fiscal year ended June 30, 2013. Use the DuPont equation to calculate the return on equity (ROE). In the process, calculate the following ratios: profit margin, EBIT return on assets, return on assets, equity multiplier, and total asset turnover.

Solutions to Self-Study Problems

4.1 The common-size income statement for Abercrombie Supply Company should look like the following one:

Abercrombie Supply Company
Income Statement for the Fiscal Year Ended June 30, 2013 ($ thousands)

		% of Net Sales
Net sales	$2,110,965	100.0
Cost of goods sold	1,459,455	69.1
Selling and administrative expenses	312,044	14.8
Nonrecurring expenses	27,215	1.3
Earnings before interest, taxes, depreciation and amortization (EBITDA)	$ 312,251	14.8
Depreciation	112,178	5.3
Earnings before interest and taxes (EBIT)	$ 200,073	9.5
Interest expense	117,587	5.6
Earnings before taxes (EBT)	$ 82,486	3.9
Taxes (35%)	28,870	1.4
Net income	$ 53,616	2.5

4.2 Abercrombie Supply's common-size balance sheet is as follows:

Abercrombie Supply Company
Balance Sheet as of June 30, 2013 ($ thousands)

Assets		% of Assets	Liabilities and Equity:		% of Assets
Cash and marketable sec.	$ 396,494	9.3	Accounts payable and accruals	$ 817,845	19.1
Accounts receivable	708,275	16.5	Notes payable	101,229	2.4
Inventories	1,152,398	26.9	Accrued income taxes	41,322	1.0
Other current assets	42,115	1.0	Total current liabilities	$ 960,396	22.4
Total current assets	$2,299,282	53.7	Long-term debt	1,149,520	26.9
Net plant and equipment	1,978,455	46.2	Total liabilities	$2,109,916	49.3
			Common stock	1,312,137	30.7
			Retained earnings	855,684	20.0
			Total common equity	$2,167,821	50.7
Total asssets	$4,277,737	100.0	Total liabilities and equity	$4,277,737	100.0

4.3 Abercrombie Supply's current ratio and quick ratio are calculated as follows:

a. Current ratio $= \dfrac{\$2,299,282}{\$960,396} = 2.39$

b. Quick ratio $= \dfrac{\$2,299,282 - \$1,152,375}{\$960,396} = 1.19$

4.4 The ratios are calculated as shown in the following table:

Ratio	Calculation	Value
Inventory turnover ratio	$1,459,455 / 1,152,398	1.27
Days' sales outstanding	$708,275 / ($2,110,965/365)	122.5 days
Total asset turnover	$2,110,965 / $4,277,737	0.49
Fixed asset turnover	$2,110,965 / $1,978,455	1.07
Total debt ratio	$2,109,916 / $4,277,737	0.493
Debt-to-equity ratio	$2,109,916 / $2,167,821	0.974
Times-interest-earned	$200,073 / $117,587	1.7
Cash coverage	$312,251 / $117,587	2.66

4.5 Following are the calculations for the ROE and associated ratios:

$$\text{Net profit margin} = \frac{\text{Net income}}{\text{Net sales}} = \frac{\$53,616}{\$2,110,965} = 0.0254, \text{ or } 2.54\%$$

$$\text{EBIT ROA} = \frac{\text{EBIT}}{\text{Total assets}} = \frac{\$200,073}{\$4,277,737} = 0.0468, \text{ or } 4.68\%$$

$$\text{Return on assets} = \frac{\text{Net income}}{\text{Total assets}} = \frac{\$53,616}{\$4,277,737} = 0.0125, \text{ or } 1.25\%$$

$$\text{Equity multiplier} = \frac{\text{Total assets}}{\text{Total equity}} = \frac{\$4,277,737}{\$2,167,821} = 1.97$$

$$\text{Total asset turnover} = \frac{\text{Net sales}}{\text{Total assets}} = \frac{\$2,110,965}{\$4,277,737} = 0.49$$

DuPont identity:

$$\begin{aligned}
\text{ROE} &= \text{ROA} \times \text{Equity multiplier} \\
&= \text{Net profit margin} \times \text{Total asset turnover ratio} \times \text{Equity multiplier} \\
&= \frac{\text{Net income}}{\text{Net sales}} \times \frac{\text{Net sales}}{\text{Total assets}} \times \frac{\text{Total assets}}{\text{Total equity}} \\
&= 0.0254 \times 0.49 \times 1.97 \\
&= 0.0245, \text{ or } 2.45\%
\end{aligned}$$

Critical Thinking Questions

4.1 What does it mean when a company's return on assets (ROA) is equal to its return on equity (ROE)?

4.2 Why is too much liquidity not a good thing?

4.3 Inventory is excluded when the quick ratio or acid-test ratio is calculated because inventory is the most difficult current asset to convert to cash without loss of value. What types of inventory are likely to be most easily converted to cash without loss of value?

4.4 What does a very high inventory turnover ratio signify?

4.5 How would one explain a low receivables turnover ratio?

4.6 What additional information does the fixed asset turnover ratio provide over the total asset turn-over ratio? For which industries does it carry greater significance?

4.7 How does financial leverage help stockholders?

4.8 Why is ROE generally much higher than ROA for banks relative to other industries?

4.9 Why is the ROE a more appropriate proxy of wealth maximization for smaller firms rather than for larger ones?

4.10 Why is it not enough for an analyst to look at just the short-term and long-term debt on a firm's balance sheet?

Questions and Problems

BASIC ▷ **4.1 Liquidity ratios:** Explain why the quick ratio or acid-test ratio is a better measure of a firm's liquidity than the current ratio.

4.2 Liquidity ratios: Flying Penguins Corp. has total current assets of $11,845,175, current liabilities of $5,311,020, and a quick ratio of 0.89. How much inventory does it have?

4.3 Efficiency ratio: If Newton Manufacturers has an accounts receivable turnover of 4.8 times and net sales of $7,812,379, what would its receivables be?

4.4 Efficiency ratio: Bummel and Strand Corp. has a gross profit margin of 33.7 percent, sales of $47,112,365, and inventory of $14,595,435. What is its inventory turnover ratio?

4.5 Efficiency ratio: Sorenson Inc. has sales of $3,112,489, a gross profit margin of 23.1 percent, and inventory of $833,145. What are the company's inventory turnover ratio and days' sales in inventory?

4.6 Leverage ratios: Breckenridge Ski Company has total assets of $422,235,811 and a debt ratio of 29.5 percent. Calculate the company's debt-to-equity ratio and equity multiplier.

4.7 Leverage ratios: Norton Company has a debt-to-equity ratio of 1.65, ROA of 11.3 percent, and total equity of $1,322,796. What are the company's equity multiplier, debt ratio, and ROE?

4.8 DuPont equation: The Rangoon Timber Company has the following ratios:

Net sales/Total assets = 2.23   ROA = 9.69%   ROE = 16.4%

What are Rangoon's profit margin and debt ratios?

4.9 DuPont Equation: Lemmon Enterprises has a total asset turnover of 2.1 and a net profit margin of 7.5%. If its equity multiplier is 1.90, what is the ROE for Lemmon Enterprises?

4.10 Benchmark analysis: List the ways a company's financial manager can benchmark the company's own performance.

4.11 Benchmark analysis: Trademark Corp.'s financial manager collected the following information for its peer group to compare its performance against that of its peers.

Ratios	Trademark	Peer Group
DSO	33.5 days	27.9 days
Total asset turnover	2.3	3.7
Inventory turnover	1.8	2.8
Quick ratio	0.6	1.3

a. Explain how Trademark is doing relative to its peers.

b. How do the industry ratios help Trademark's management?

4.12 Market-value ratios: Rockwell Jewelers management has announced that the company had net earnings of $6,481,778 for this year. The company has 2,543,800 shares outstanding, and the year-end stock price is $54.21. What are Rockwell's earnings per share and P/E ratio?

4.13 Market-value ratios: Chisel Corporation has 3 million shares outstanding at a price per share of $3.25. If the debt-to-equity ratio is 1.7 and total book value of debt equals $12,400,000, what is the market-to-book ratio for Chisel Corporation?

4.14 Liquidity ratios: Laurel Electronics has a quick ratio of 1.15, current liabilities of $5,311,020, and inventories of $7,121,599. What is the firm's current ratio? ◁ INTERMEDIATE

4.15 Efficiency ratio: Lambda Corporation has current liabilities of $450,000, a quick ratio of 1.8, inventory turnover of 5.0, and a current ratio of 3.5. What is the cost of goods sold for Lambda Corporation?

4.16 Efficiency ratio: Norwood Corp. currently has accounts receivable of $1,223,675 on net sales of $6,216,900. What are its accounts receivable turnover ratio and days' sales outstanding (DSO)?

4.17 Efficiency ratio: If Norwood Corp.'s management wants to reduce the DSO from that calculated in Problem 4.16 to an industry average of 56.3 days and its net sales are expected to decline by about 12 percent, what would be the new level of receivables?

4.18 Coverage ratios: Nimitz Rental Company had depreciation expenses of $108,905, interest expenses of $78,112, and an EBIT of $1,254,338 for the year ended June 30, 2013. What are the times-interest-earned and cash coverage ratios for this company?

4.19 Leverage ratios: Conseco, Inc., has a debt ratio of 0.56. What are the company's debt-to-equity ratio and equity multiplier?

4.20 Profitability ratios: Cisco Systems has total assets of $35.594 billion, total debt of $9.678 billion, and net sales of $22.045 billion. Its net profit margin for the year is 20 percent, while the operating profit margin is 30 percent. What are Cisco's net income, EBIT ROA, ROA, and ROE?

4.21 Profitability ratios: Procter & Gamble reported the following information for its fiscal year end: On net sales of $51.407 billion, the company earned net income after taxes of $6.481 billion. It had a cost of goods sold of $25.076 billion and EBIT of $9.827 billion. What are the company's gross profit margin, operating profit margin, and net profit margin?

4.22 Profitability ratios: Wal-Mart, Inc., has net income of $9,054,000 on net sales of $256,329,812. The company has total assets of $104,912,112 and stockholders' equity of $43,623,445. Use the extended DuPont identity to find the return on assets and return on equity for the firm.

4.23 Profitability ratios: Xtreme Sports Innovations has disclosed the following information:

EBIT = $25,664,300   Net income = $13,054,000   Net sales = $83,125,336
Total debt = $20,885,753   Total assets = $71,244,863

Compute the following ratios for this firm using the DuPont identity: debt-to-equity ratio, EBIT ROA, ROA, and ROE.

4.24 Market-value ratios: Cisco Systems had net income of $4.401 billion and, at year end, 6.735 billion shares outstanding. Calculate the earnings per share for the company.

4.25 Market-value ratios: Use the information for Cisco Systems in Problem 4.24. In addition, the company's EBITDA was $6.834 billion and its share price was $22.36. Compute the firm's price-earnings ratio and the price-EBITDA ratio.

4.26 DuPont equation: Carter, Inc., a manufacturer of electrical supplies, has an ROE of 23.1 percent, a profit margin of 4.9 percent, and a total asset turnover ratio of 2.6 times. Its peer group also has an ROE of 23.1 percent but has outperformed Carter with a net profit margin of 5.3 percent and a total asset turnover ratio of 3.0 times. Explain how Carter managed to achieve the same level of profitability as reflected by the ROE.

4.27 DuPont equation: Grossman Enterprises has an equity multiplier of 2.6 times, total assets of $2,312,000, an ROE of 14.8 percent, and a total asset turnover ratio of 2.8 times. Calculate the firm's sales and ROA.

ADVANCED > **4.28** Complete the balance sheet of Flying Roos Corporation.

Flying Roos Corporation
Balance Sheet as of December 31, 2013

Assets:		Liabilities and Equity:	
Cash and marketable securities		Accounts payable and accruals	
Accounts receivable		Notes payable	$ 300,000
Inventories	_____	Total current liabilities	
Total current assets			
		Long-term debt	$2,000,000
Net plant and equipment		Common stock	
		Retained earnings	$1,250,000
Total assets	$8,000,000	Total liabilities and equity	

You have the following information:

Debt ratio = 40%   DSO = 39 days
Current ratio = 1.5   Inventory turnover ratio = 3.375
Net sales = $2.25 million   Cost of goods sold = $1.6875 million

4.29 For the year ended June 30, 2013, Northern Clothing Company has total assets of $87,631,181, ROA of 11.67 percent, ROE of 21.19 percent, and a net profit margin of 11.59 percent. What are the company's net income and net sales? Calculate the firm's debt-to-equity ratio.

4.30 Blackwell Automotive's balance sheet at the end of its most recent fiscal year shows the following information:

Blackwell Automotive
Balance Sheet as of March 31, 2013

Assets:		Liabilities and Equity:	
Cash and marketable sec.	$ 23,015	Accounts payable and accruals	$ 163,257
Accounts receivable	141,258	Notes payable	21,115
Inventories	212,444	Total current liabilities	$ 184,372
Total current assets	$ 376,717		
		Long-term debt	168,022
Net plant and equipment	711,256	Total liabilities	$ 352,394
Goodwill and other assets	89,899	Common stock	313,299
		Retained earnings	512,159
Total assets	$1,177,852	Total liabilities and equity	$1,177,852

In addition, it was reported that the firm had a net income of $156,042 on net sales of $4,063,589.
a. What are the firm's current ratio and quick ratio?
b. Calculate the firm's days' sales outstanding, total asset turnover ratio, and fixed asset turnover ratio.

4.31 The following are the financial statements for Nederland Consumer Products Company for the fiscal year ended September 30, 2013.

Nederland Consumer Products Company
Income Statement for the Fiscal Year
Ended September 30, 2013

Net sales	$51,407
Cost of products sold	25,076
Gross margin	$26,331
Marketing, research, administrative exp.	15,746
Depreciation	758
Operating income (loss)	$ 9,827
Interest expense	477
Earnings (loss) before income taxes	$ 9,350
Income taxes	2,869
Net earnings (loss)	$ 6,481

Nederland Consumer Products Company
Balance Sheet as of September 30, 2013

Assets:		Liabilities and Equity:	
Cash and marketable securities	$ 5,469	Accounts payable	$ 3,617
Investment securities	423	Accrued and other liabilities	7,689
Accounts receivable	4,062	Taxes payable	2,554
Total inventories	4,400	Debt due within one year	8,287
Deferred income taxes	958	Total current liabilities	$22,147
Prepaid expenses and other		Long-term debt	12,554
receivables	1,803	Deferred income taxes	2,261
Total current assets	$17,115	Other noncurrent liabilities	2,808
Property, plant, and equipment,	25,304	Total liabilities	$39,770
at cost		Convertible class A preferred	1,526
Less: Accumulated depreciation	11,196	stock	
Net property, plant, and equipment	$14,108	Common stock	2,141
Net goodwill and other intangible	23,900	Retained earnings	13,611
assets		Total stockholders' equity	$17,278
Other noncurrent assets	1,925	(deficit)	
Total assets	$57,048	Total liabilities and equity	$57,048

Calculate all the ratios, for which industry figures are available below, for Nederland and compare the firm's ratios with the industry ratios.

Ratio	Industry Average
Current ratio	2.05
Quick ratio	0.78
Gross margin	23.9%
Net profit margin	12.3%
Debt ratio	0.23
Long-term debt to equity	0.98
Interest coverage	5.62
ROA	5.3%
ROE	18.8%

4.32 Refer to the preceding information for Nederland Consumer Products Company. Compute the firm's ratios for the following categories and briefly evaluate the company's performance using these numbers.
  a. Efficiency ratios.
  b. Asset turnover ratios.
  c. Leverage ratios.
  d. Coverage ratios.

4.33 Refer to the earlier information for Nederland Consumer Products Company. Using the DuPont identity, calculate the return on equity for Nederland, after calculating the ratios that make up the DuPont identity.

4.34 Nugent, Inc., has a gross profit margin of 31.7 percent on net sales of $9,865,214 and total assets of $7,125,852. The company has a current ratio of 2.7 times, accounts receivable of $1,715,363, cash and marketable securities of $315,488, and current liabilities of $870,938.
  a. What is Nugent's total current assets?
  b. How much inventory does the firm have? What is the inventory turnover ratio?
  c. What is Nugent's days' sales outstanding?
  d. If management sets a target DSO of 30 days, what should Nugent's accounts receivable be?

4.35 Recreational Supplies Co. has net sales of $11,655,000, an ROE of 17.64 percent, and a total asset turnover of 2.89 times. If the firm has a debt-to-equity ratio of 1.43, what is the company's net income?

4.36 Nutmeg Houseware Inc. has an operating profit margin of 10.3 percent on revenues of $24,547,125 and total assets of $8,652,352.
  a. Calculate the company's total asset turnover ratio and its operating profit (EBIT).
  b. The company's management has set a target for the total asset turnover ratio of 3.25 for next year. If there is no change in the total assets of the company, what will the new net sales level

have to be next year? Calculate the dollar change in sales necessary and the percentage change in sales necessary.

c. If the operating profit margin declines to 10 percent, what will be the EBIT at the new level of net sales?

4.37 Modern Appliances Corporation has reported its financial results for the year ended December 31, 2013.

Modern Appliances Corporation
Income Statement for the Fiscal
Year Ended December 31, 2013

Net sales	$5,398,412,000
Cost of goods sold	3,432,925,255
Gross profit	$1,965,486,745
Selling, general, and administrative expenses	1,036,311,231
Depreciation	299,928,155
Operating income	$ 629,247,359
Interest expense	35,826,000
EBT	$ 593,421,359
Income taxes	163,104,554
Net earnings	$ 430,316,805

Modern Appliances Corporation
Balance Sheet as of December 31, 2013

Assets:		Liabilities and Equity:	
Cash and cash equivalents	$ 514,412,159	Short-term borrowings	$ 117,109,865
Accounts receivable	1,046,612,233	Trade accounts payable	466,937,985
Inventories	981,870,990	Other current liabilities	994,289,383
Other current assets	313,621,610	Total current liabilities	$1,578,337,233
Total current assets	$2,856,516,992	Long-term debt	1,200,691,565
Net fixed assets	754,660,275	Common stock	397,407,352
Goodwill	118,407,710	Retained earnings	1,218,207,588
Other assets	665,058,761		
Total assets	$4,394,643,738	Total liabilities and equity	$4,394,643,738

Using the information from the financial statements, complete a comprehensive ratio analysis for Modern Appliances Corporation.

a. Calculate these liquidity ratios: current and quick ratios.
b. Calculate these efficiency ratios: inventory turnover, accounts receivable turnover, DSO.
c. Calculate these asset turnover ratios: total asset turnover, fixed asset turnover.
d. Calculate these leverage ratios: total debt ratio, debt-to-equity ratio, equity multiplier.
e. Calculate these coverage ratios: times interest earned, cash coverage.
f. Calculate these profitability ratios: gross profit margin, net profit margin, ROA, ROE.
g. Use the DuPont identity, and after calculating the component ratios, compute the ROE.

CFA PROBLEMS **4.38** Common-size analysis is used in financial analysis to:
a. evaluate changes in a company's operating cycle over time.
b. predict changes in a company's capital structure using regression analysis.
c. compare companies of different sizes or compare a company with itself over time.
d. restate each element in a company's financial statement as a proportion of the similar account for another company in the same industry.

4.39 The TBI Company has a number of days of inventory of 50. Therefore, the TBI Company's inventory turnover is closest to:
a. 4.8 times.
b. 7.3 times.
c. 8.4 times.
d. 9.6 times.

4.40 DuPont analysis involves breaking return-on-assets ratios into their:
- **a.** profit components.
- **b.** marginal and average components.
- **c.** operating and financing components.
- **d.** profit margin and turnover components.

4.41 If a company's net profit margin is −5 percent, its total asset turnover is 1.5 times, and its financial leverage ratio is 1.2 times, its return on equity is closest to:
- **a.** −9.0 percent.
- **b.** −7.5 percent.
- **c.** −3.2 percent.
- **d.** 1.8 percent.

Sample Test Problems

4.1 Morgan Sports Equipment Company has accounts payable of $1,221,669, cash of $677,423, inventory of $2,312,478, accounts receivable of $845,113, and net working capital of $2,297,945. What are the company's current ratio and quick ratio?

4.2 Southwest Airlines, Inc., has total operating revenues of $6.53 million on total assets of $11.337 million. The company's property, plant, and equipment, including ground equipment and other assets, are listed at a historical cost of $11.921 million, while its accumulated depreciation and amortization amount to $3.198 million. What are Southwest's total asset turnover and fixed asset turnover ratios?

4.3 Haugen Enterprises has an equity multiplier of 2.5. What is its debt ratio?

4.4 Centennial Chemical Corp. has a gross profit margin of 31.4 percent on revenues of $13,144,680 and EBIT of $2,586,150. What are the company's cost of goods sold and operating profit margin?

4.5 National City Bank has 646,749,650 shares of common stock outstanding that are currently priced at $37.55 per share. If its net income is $2,780,955,000, what are National City's earnings per share and price-earnings ratio?

A SAD TALE: The Demise of Arthur Andersen

In January 2002, there were five major public accounting firms: Arthur Andersen, Deloitte Touche, KPMG, Pricewaterhouse-Coopers, and Ernst & Young. By late fall of that year, the number had been reduced to four. Arthur Andersen became the first major public accounting firm to be found guilty of a felony (a conviction later overturned), and as a result it virtually ceased to exist.

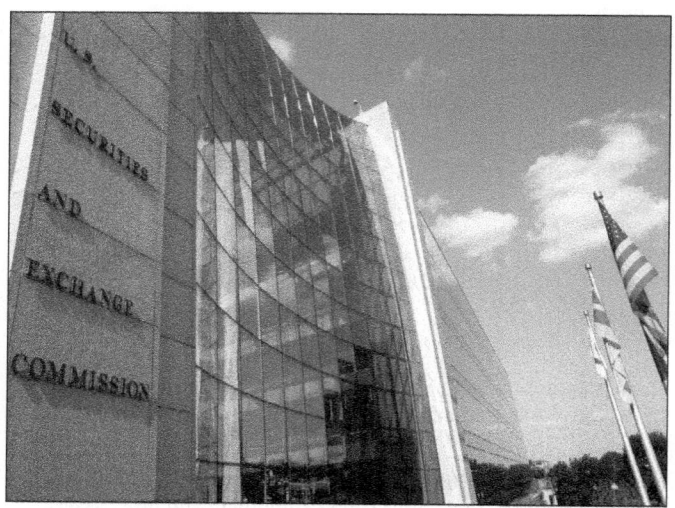

©Jim Bourg/Reuters/©Corbis

That such a fate could befall Andersen is especially sad given its early history. When Andersen and Company was established in 1918, it was led by Arthur Andersen, an acknowledged man of principle, and the company had a credo that became firmly embedded in the culture: "Think Straight and Talk Straight." Andersen became an industry leader partly on the basis of high ethical principles and integrity.

How did a one-time industry leader find itself in a position where it received a corporate death penalty over ethical issues? First, the market changed. During the 1980s, a boom in mergers and acquisitions and the emergence of information technology fueled the growth of an extremely profitable consulting practice at Andersen. The profits from consulting contracts soon exceeded the profits from auditing, Andersen's core business. Many of the consulting clients were also audit clients, and the firm found that the audit relationship was an ideal bridge for selling consulting services. Soon the audit fees became "loss leaders" to win audits, which allowed the consultants to sell more lucrative consulting contracts.

Tension between Audit and Consulting

At Andersen, tension between audit and consulting partners broke into open and sometimes public warfare. At the heart of the problem was how to divide the earnings from the consulting practice between the two groups. The resulting conflict ended in divorce, with the consultants leaving to form their own firm. The firm, Accenture, continues to thrive today.

Once the firm split in two, Andersen began to rebuild a consulting practice as part of the accounting practice. Consulting continued to be a highly profitable business, and audit partners were now asked to sell consulting services to other clients, a role that many auditors found uncomfortable.

Although the accountants were firmly in charge, the role of partners as salespersons compounded an already existing ethical issue—that of conflict of interest. It is legally well established that the fiduciary responsibility of a certified public accounting (CPA) firm is to the investors and creditors of the firm being audited. CPA firms are supposed to render an opinion as to whether a firm's financial statements are reasonably accurate and whether the firm has applied generally accepted accounting principles in a consistent manner over time so as not to distort the financial statements. To meet their fiduciary responsibilities, auditors must maintain independence from the firms they audit.

What might interfere with the objective judgment of the public accounting firms? One problem arises because it is the audited companies themselves that pay the auditors' fees. Auditors might not be completely objective when auditing a firm because they fear losing consulting business. This is an issue that regulators and auditors have not yet solved. But another problem arises in situations where accounting firms provide consulting services to the companies they audit. Although all of the major accounting firms were involved in this practice to some extent, Andersen had developed an aggressive culture for engaging partners to sell consulting services to audit clients.

Andersen's Problems Mount

The unraveling of Andersen began in the 1990s with a series of accounting scandals at Sunbeam, Waste Management, and Colonial Realty—all firms that Andersen had audited. But scandals involving the energy giant Enron proved to be the firm's undoing. The account was huge. In 2000 alone, Andersen received $52 million in fees from Enron, approximately 50 percent for auditing and 50 percent for other consulting services, especially tax services. The partner in charge of the account and his entire 100-person team worked out of Enron's Houston office. Approximately 300 of Enron's senior and middle managers had been Andersen employees.

Enron went bankrupt in December 2001 after large-scale accounting irregularities came to light, prompting an investigation by the Securities and Exchange Commission (SEC).

It soon became clear that Enron's financial statements for some time had been largely the products of accounting fraud, showing the company to be in far better financial condition than was actually the case. The inevitable question was asked: Why hadn't the auditors called attention to Enron's questionable accounting practices? The answer was a simple one. Andersen had major conflicts of interest. Indeed, when one member of Andersen's Professional Standards Group objected to some of Enron's accounting practices, Andersen removed him from auditing responsibilities at Enron—in response to a request from Enron management.

Playing Hardball and Losing

The SEC was determined to make an example of Andersen. The U.S. Justice Department began a criminal investigation, but investigators were willing to explore some "settlement options" in return for Andersen's cooperation. However, Andersen's senior management appeared arrogant and failed to grasp the political mood in Congress and in the country after a series of business scandals that had brought more than one large company to bankruptcy.

After several months of sparring with the Andersen senior management team, the Justice Department charged Andersen with a felony offense—obstruction of justice. Andersen was found guilty in 2002 of illegally instructing its employees to destroy documents relating to Enron, even as the government was conducting inquiries into Enron's finances. During the trial, government lawyers argued that by instructing its staff to "undertake an unprecedented campaign of document destruction," Andersen had obstructed the government's investigation.

Since a firm convicted of a felony cannot audit a publicly held company, the conviction spelled the end for Andersen. But even before the guilty verdict, there had been a massive defection of Andersen clients to other accounting firms. The evidence presented at trial showed a breakdown in Andersen's internal controls, a lack of leadership, and an environment in Andersen's Houston office that fostered recklessness and unethical behavior by some partners.

In 2005, the United States Supreme Court unanimously overturned the Andersen conviction on the grounds that the jury was given overly broad instructions by the federal judge who presided over the case. But by then it was too late. Most of the Andersen partners had either retired or gone to work for former competitors, and the company had all but ceased to exist.

DISCUSSION QUESTIONS

1. To what extent do market pressures encourage unethical behavior? Can the demise of Andersen be blamed on the fact that the market began rewarding consulting services of the kind Andersen could provide?
2. How serious are the kinds of conflicts of interest discussed in this case? Did Sarbanes-Oxley eliminate the most serious conflicts?
3. Was it fair for the government to destroy an entire company because of the misdeeds of some of its members, or had Andersen become such a serious offender that such an action on the part of the government was justified?

5

The Time Value of Money, Discounted Cash Flows, and Valuation

CHAPTER FIVE

Learning Objectives

1. Explain what the time value of money is and why it is so important in the field of finance.

2. Explain the concept of future value, including the meaning of the terms principal, simple interest, and compound interest, and use the future value formula to make business decisions.

3. Explain the concept of present value and how it relates to future value, and use the present value formula to make business decisions.

4. Explain why cash flows occurring at different times must be adjusted to reflect their value as of a common date before they can be compared, and compute the present value and future value for multiple cash flows.

5. Explain the difference between an ordinary annuity and an annuity due, and calculate the present value and the future value of an ordinary annuity and an annuity due.

6. Explain what a perpetuity is and where we see them in business, and calculate the value of a perpetuity.

7. Discuss growing annuities and perpetuities, as well as their application in business, and calculate their values.

8. Discuss why the effective annual interest rate (EAR) is the appropriate way to annualize interest rates, and calculate the EAR.

© AP/Wide World Photos

When you buy a piece of equipment for a business, the decision of whether to pay cash or to use debt financing can affect the price that you pay. For example, vehicle manufacturers often offer customers a choice between a cash rebate and low-cost financing. Both of these alternatives affect the cost, but one alternative can be worth more than the other to the buyer.

For example, consider the following. In September 2012, the automobile manufacturer Ford Motor Company wanted to sell its remaining inventory of 2012 Ford F-350 Super Duty pickup trucks. These trucks are commonly used in commercial businesses such as construction companies, landscape companies, and ranching operations, among others.

In an effort to increase sales of F-350 trucks, Ford offered buyers a choice between (1) receiving $3,000 off a base price of $38,090 if they paid cash and (2) receiving 0 percent financing on a five-year loan if they paid the base price. For a business that had enough cash to buy the truck outright and did not need the cash for other uses, the decision of whether to pay cash or finance the purchase of an F-350 depended on the rate of return that could be earned by investing the cash. On the one hand, if it was only possible to earn a 1 percent interest rate, the buyer was better off paying cash. On the other hand, if it was possible to earn a 5 percent interest rate, the buyer was better off taking the financing. With a 3.325 percent interest rate, the buyer would have been indifferent between the two alternatives.

As with most business transactions, a crucial element in the analysis of the alternatives offered by Ford is the value of the expected cash flows. Because the cash flows for the two alternatives take place in different time periods, they must be adjusted to account for the time value of money before they can be compared. The buyer of the truck in the preceding example wants to select the alternative with the cash flows that have the lowest value (price). This chapter provides the knowledge and tools you need to make the correct decision (as well as to calculate the rate of return at which the buyer would be indifferent). You will learn that at the bank, in the boardroom, or in the vehicle showroom, money has a time value—dollars today are worth more than dollars in the future—and you must account for this when making financial decisions.

CHAPTER PREVIEW

This chapter describes time value of money concepts and tools. As noted in the chapter opener, these concepts and tools are a central part of much of the analysis we do in finance. Businesses routinely use time value of money calculations to make decisions which require comparing cash flows that occur at different points in time. The chapter opener illustrates such a decision—whether to pay cash or use a loan to finance a truck. In that example, we assumed the decision had already been made to purchase a truck and side-stepped the investment decision. As you might suspect, the decision of whether to even purchase the truck also requires comparison of cash flows that occur at different points in time. Such a comparison is necessary to determine whether the benefits of the investment exceed the costs. To understand and correctly use the valuation models presented in this book, you must know how to adjust for the time value of money.

We begin this chapter with discussions of key time value of money concepts and time value of money calculations that involve a single cash flow. We describe future value calculations, which tell us how funds will grow if they are invested at a particular interest rate, and present value calculations,

through which we determine the value today of a cash payment that is to be received in the future. These discussions will help you understand why dollars today are more valuable than dollars to be received in the future, as well as the basics of simple interest, compound interest, future value, and present value calculations.

We then extend our discussion to include key time value of money concepts and future value and present value calculations that are crucial to making decisions that involve multiple cash flows. Understanding these concepts and calculations is important because business investment and financing decisions typically involve determining the value of a series of cash flows. This discussion first introduces the general concepts and calculations necessary for evaluating multiple cash flows. It then covers common situations in which future cash flows are level or grow at a constant rate over time.

Finally, we describe the effective annual interest rate and compare it with the annual percentage rate (APR), which is a rate that is used to describe the interest rate in consumer loans.

5.1 THE TIME VALUE OF MONEY

In financial decision making, one basic problem managers face is determining the value of (or price to pay for) cash flows expected in the future. Why is this a problem? Consider as an example the popular Mega Millions lottery game.[1] In Mega Millions, the jackpot continues to build up until some lucky person buys a winning ticket—the payouts for a number of jackpot winning tickets have exceeded $100 million.

If you won $100 million, headlines would read "Lucky Student Wins $100 Million Jackpot!" Does this mean that your ticket is worth $100 million on the day you win? The answer is no. A

LEARNING OBJECTIVE ❶

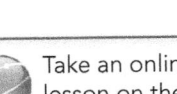

Take an online lesson on the time value of money from TeachMeFinance.com at http://teachmefinance .com/timevalueofmoney .html.

---

[1]Mega Millions is operated by a consortium of the state lottery commissions in 41 states plus the District of Columbia. To play the game, a player pays one dollar and picks five numbers from 1 to 56 and one additional number from 1 to 46 (the Mega Ball number). Twice a week a machine mixes numbered balls and randomly selects six balls (five white balls and one Mega Ball), which determines the winning combination for that drawing. There are various winning combinations, but a ticket that matches all six numbers, including the Mega Ball number, is the jackpot winner.

Mega Millions jackpot is paid either as a series of 26 payments over 25 years or as a cash lump sum. If you win "$100 million" and choose to receive the series of payments, the 26 payments will total $100 million. If you choose the lump sum option, Mega Millions will pay you less than the stated value of $100 million. This amount was about $58.7 million in October 2012. Thus, the value, or market price, of a "$100 million" winning Mega Millions ticket is really about $58.7 million because of the time value of money and the timing of the 26 cash payments. An appropriate question to ask now is "What is the time value of money?"

Consuming Today or Tomorrow

time value of money
the difference in value between a dollar in hand today and a dollar promised in the future; a dollar today is worth more than a dollar in the future

The **time value of money** is based on the idea that people prefer to consume goods today rather than wait to consume similar goods in the future. Most people would prefer to have a large-screen TV today than to have one a year from now, for example. Money has a time value because a dollar in hand today is worth more than a dollar to be received in the future. This makes sense because if you had the dollar today, you could buy something with it—or, instead, you could invest it and earn interest. For example, if you had $100,000, you could buy a one-year bank certificate of deposit paying 5 percent interest and earn $5,000 interest for the year. At the end of the year, you would have $105,000 ($100,000 + $5,000 = $105,000). The $100,000 today is worth $105,000 a year from today. If the interest rate was higher, you would have even more money at the end of the year.

> **BUILDING INTUITION**
>
> **THE VALUE OF MONEY CHANGES WITH TIME**
>
> The term *time value of money* reflects the notion that people prefer to consume things today rather than at some time in the future. For this reason, people require compensation for deferring consumption. The effect is to make a dollar in the future worth less than a dollar today.

Based on this example, we can make several generalizations. First, the value of a dollar invested at a positive interest rate grows over time. Thus, the further in the future you receive a dollar, the less it is worth today. Second, the trade-off between money today and money at some future date depends in part on the rate of interest you can earn by investing. The higher the rate of interest, the more likely you will elect to invest your funds and forgo current consumption. Why? At the higher interest rate, your investment will earn more money.

In the next two sections, we look at two views of time value—future value and present value. First, however, we describe time lines, which are pictorial aids that help us solve future and present value problems.

Time Lines as Aids to Problem Solving

time zero
the beginning of a transaction; often the current point in time

Time lines are an important tool for analyzing problems that involve cash flows over time. They provide an easy way to visualize the cash flows associated with investment decisions. A time line is a horizontal line that starts at time zero and shows cash flows as they occur over time. The term **time zero** is used to refer to the beginning of a transaction in time value of money problems. Time zero is often the current point in time (today).

Exhibit 5.1 shows the time line for a five-year investment opportunity and its cash flows. Here, as in most finance problems, cash flows are assumed to occur at the end of the period. The project involves a $10,000 initial investment (cash outflow), such as the purchase of a new machine, that is expected to generate cash inflows over a five-year period: $5,000 at the end of year 1, $4,000 at the end of year 2, $3,000 at the end of year 3, $2,000 at the end of year 4, and

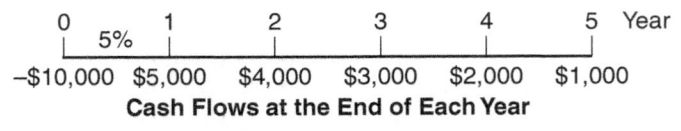

Cash Flows at the End of Each Year

EXHIBIT 5.1
Five-Year Time Line for a $10,000 Investment

Time lines help us to correctly identify the size and timing of cash flows—critical tasks in solving time value problems. This time line shows the cash flows generated over five years by a $10,000 investment where the relevant interest rate is 5 percent.

$1,000 at the end of year 5. Because of the time value of money, it is critical that you identify not only the size of the cash flows, but also the timing.

If it is appropriate, the time line will also show the relevant interest rate for the problem. In Exhibit 5.1 this is shown as 5 percent. Also, note in Exhibit 5.1 that the initial cash flow of $10,000 is represented by a negative number. It is conventional that cash outflows from the firm, such as for the purchase of a new machine, are treated as negative values on a time line and that cash inflows to the firm, such as revenues earned, are treated as positive values. The −$10,000 therefore means that there is a cash outflow of $10,000 at time zero. As you will see, it makes no difference how you label cash inflows and outflows as long as you are consistent. That is, if *all* cash outflows are given a negative value, then *all* cash inflows must have a positive value. If the signs get "mixed up"—if some cash inflows are negative and some positive—you will get the wrong answer to any problem you are trying to solve.

Financial Calculator

We recommend that students purchase a financial calculator for this course. A financial calculator will provide the computational tools to solve most problems in the book. A financial calculator is just an ordinary calculator that has preprogrammed future value and present value algorithms. Thus, all the variables you need to make financial calculations exist on the calculator keys. To solve problems, all you have to do is press the proper keys. The instructions in this book are generally meant for Texas Instruments calculators, such as the TI BAII Plus. If you are using an HP or Sharp calculator, consult the user's manual for instructions.

It may sound as if the financial calculator will solve problems for you. It won't. To get the correct answer, you must first analyze the problem correctly and then identify the cash flows (size and timing), placing them correctly on a time line. Only then will you enter the correct inputs into the financial calculator.

A calculator can help you eliminate computation errors and save you a great deal of time. However, it is important that you understand the calculations that the calculator is performing. For this reason we recommend when you first start using a financial calculator that you solve problems without using the calculator's financial functions and then use the financial functions to check your answers.

To help you master your financial calculator, throughout this chapter we provide helpful hints on how to best use the calculator. We also recognize that some professors or students may want to solve problems using one of the popular spreadsheet programs. In this chapter and a number of other chapters, we provide solutions to several problems that lend themselves to spreadsheet analysis. In solving these problems, we used Microsoft Excel. The analysis and basic commands are similar for other spreadsheet programs. We also provide spreadsheet solutions for additional problems on the book's Web site. Since spreadsheet programs are commonly used in industry, you should make sure to learn how to use one of these programs early in your studies and become proficient with it before you graduate.

> **BEFORE YOU GO ON**

   1. Why is a dollar today worth more than a dollar one year from now?

   2. What is a time line, and why is it important in financial analysis?

5.2 FUTURE VALUE AND COMPOUNDING

The **future value (FV)** of an investment is what the investment will be worth after earning interest for one or more time periods. The process of converting the initial amount into future value is called *compounding*. We will define this term more precisely later. First, though, we illustrate the concepts of future value and compounding with a simple example.

LEARNING OBJECTIVE

future value (FV)
the value of an investment after it earns interest for one or more periods

Single-Period Investment

Suppose you place $100 in a bank savings account that pays interest at 10 percent a year. How much money will you have in one year? Go ahead and make the calculation. Most people can intuitively arrive at the correct answer, $110, without the aid of a formula. Your calculation could have looked something like this:

$$
\begin{aligned}
\text{Future value at the end of year 1} &= \text{Principal} + \text{Interest earned} \\
&= \$100 + (\$100 \times 0.10) \\
&= \$100 \times (1 + 0.10) \\
&= \$100 \times (1.10) \\
&= \$110
\end{aligned}
$$

This approach computes the amount of interest earned ($100 × 0.10) and then adds it to the initial, or *principal*, amount ($100). Notice that when we solve the equation, we factor out the $100. Recall from algebra that if you have the equation $y = c + (c \times x)$, you can factor out the common term c and get $y = c \times (1 + x)$. By doing this in our future value calculation, we arrived at the term $(1 + 0.10)$. This term can be stated more generally as $(1 + i)$, where i is the interest rate. As you will see, this is a pivotal term in all time value of money calculations.

Let's use our intuitive calculation to generate a more general formula. First, we need to define the variables used to calculate the answer. In our example, $100 is the principal amount (P_0), which is the amount of money deposited (invested) at the beginning of the transaction (time zero); the 10 percent is the simple interest rate (i); and the $110 is the future value (FV_1) of the investment after one year. We can write the formula for a single-period investment as follows:

$$
\begin{aligned}
FV_1 &= P_0 + (P_0 \times i) \\
&= P_0 \times (1 + i)
\end{aligned}
$$

Looking at the formula, we more easily see mathematically what is happening in our intuitive calculation. P_0 is the principal amount invested at time zero. If you invest for one period at an interest rate of i, your investment, or principal, will grow by $(1 + i)$ per dollar invested. The term $(1 + i)$ is the *future value interest factor*—often called simply the *future value factor*—for a single period, such as one year. To test the equation, we plug in our values:

$$
\begin{aligned}
FV_1 &= \$100 \times (1 + 0.10) \\
&= \$100 \times 1.10 \\
&= \$110
\end{aligned}
$$

Good, it works!

Two-Period Investment

We have determined that at the end of one year (one period), your $100 investment has grown to $110. Now let's say you decide to leave this new principal amount (FV_1) of $110 in the bank for another year earning 10 percent interest. How much money would you have at the end of the second year (FV_2)? To arrive at the value for FV_2, we multiply the new principal amount by the future value factor $(1 + i)$. That is, $FV_2 = FV_1 \times (1 + i)$. Since $FV_1 = P_0 \times (1 + i)$ we can write this as:

$$
\begin{aligned}
FV_2 &= FV_1 \times (1 + i) \\
&= [P_0 \times (1 + i)] \times (1 + i) \\
&= P_0 \times (1 + i)^2
\end{aligned}
$$

The future value of your $110 at the end of the second year (FV_2) is as follows:

$$
\begin{aligned}
FV_2 &= P_0 \times (1 + i)^2 \\
&= \$100 \times (1 + 0.10)^2 \\
&= 100 \times (1.10)^2 \\
&= \$100 \times 1.21 \\
&= \$121
\end{aligned}
$$

Another way of thinking of a two-period investment is that it is two single-period investments back to back.

Turning to Exhibit 5.2, we can see what is happening to your $100 investment over the two years we have already discussed and beyond. The future value of $121 at year 2 consists of three parts. First is the initial *principal* of $100 (first row of column 2). Second is the $20 ($10 + $10 = $20) of *simple interest* earned at 10 percent for the first and second years (first and second rows of column 3). Third is the $1 interest earned during the second

EXHIBIT 5.2   **Future Value of $100 at 10 Percent**

With compounding, interest earned on an investment is reinvested so that, in future periods, interest is earned on interest as well as on the principal amount. Here, interest on interest begins accruing in year 2.

Year (1)	Value at Beginning of Year (2)	Simple Interest (3)		Interest on Interest (4)		Total (Compound) Interest (5)	Value at End of Year (6)
				Interest Earned			
1	$100.00	$10.00	+	$ 0.00	=	$10.00	$110.00
2	110.00	10.00	+	1.00	=	11.00	121.00
3	121.00	10.00	+	2.10	=	12.10	133.10
4	133.10	10.00	+	3.31	=	13.31	146.41
5	146.41	10.00	+	4.64	=	14.64	161.05
Five-year total	$100.00	$50.00	+	$11.05	=	$61.05	$161.05

year on the $10 of interest from the first year ($10 × 0.10 = $1.00) (second row of column 4). This is called *interest on interest*. The total amount of interest earned is $21 ($10 + $11 = $21), which is shown in column 5 and is called *compound interest*.

We are now in a position to formally define some important terms already mentioned in our discussion. The **principal** is the amount of money on which interest is paid. In our example, the principal amount is $100. **Simple interest** is the amount of interest paid on the original principal amount. With simple interest, the interest earned each period is paid only on the original principal. In our example, the simple interest is $10 per year or $20 for the two years. **Interest on interest** is the interest earned on the reinvestment of previous interest payments. In our example, the interest on interest is $1. **Compounding** is the process by which interest earned on an investment is reinvested so that in future periods, interest is earned on the interest previously earned as well as the principal. In other words, with compounding you are able to earn **compound interest**, which consists of both simple interest and interest on interest.

principal
the amount of money on which interest is paid

simple interest
interest earned on the original principal amount only

interest on interest
interest earned on interest that was earned in previous periods

compounding
the process by which interest earned on an investment is reinvested, so in future periods interest is earned on the interest as well as the principal

compound interest
interest earned both on the original principal amount and on interest previously earned

The Future Value Equation

Let's continue our bank example. Suppose you decide to leave your money in the bank for three years. Looking back at equations for a single-period and a two-period investment, you can probably guess that the equation for the future value of money invested for three years would be:

$$FV_3 = P_0 \times (1 + i)^3$$

With this pattern clearly established, we can see that the general equation to find the future value after any number of periods is as follows:

$$FV_n = P_0 \times (1 + i)^n$$

which is often written as:

$$FV_n = PV \times (1 + i)^n \qquad (5.1)$$

where:
FV_n = future value of investment at the end of period n
PV = original principal (P_0); this is often called the present value, or PV
i = the rate of interest per period
n = the number of periods; a period can be a year, a quarter, a month, a day, or some other unit of time
$(1 + i)^n$ = the future value factor

Let's test our general equation. Say you leave your $100 invested in the bank savings account at 10 percent interest for five years. How much would you have in the bank at the end of five years? Applying Equation 5.1 yields the following:

$$FV_5 = \$100 \times (1 + 0.10)^5$$
$$= \$100 \times (1.10)^5$$
$$= \$100 \times 1.6105$$
$$= \$161.05$$

Exhibit 5.2 shows how the interest is earned on a year-by-year basis. Notice that the total compound interest earned over the five-year period is $61.05 (column 5) and that it is made up of two parts: (1) $50.00 of simple interest (column 3) and (2) $11.05 of interest on interest (column 4). Thus, the total compound interest can be expressed as follows:

$$\text{Total compound interest} = \text{Total simple interest} + \text{Total interest on interest}$$
$$= \$50.00 + \$11.05$$
$$= \$61.05$$

The simple interest earned is $100 \times 0.10 = \$10.00$ per year, and thus the total simple interest for the five-year period is $50.00 (5 years $\times$ $10.00 = $50.00). The remaining balance of $11.05 ($61.05 $-$ $50.00 = $11.05) comes from earning interest on interest.

A helpful equation for calculating the simple interest can be derived by using the future value equation for a single-period investment and solving for the term $FV_1 - P_0$:

$$FV_1 = P_0 + (P_0 \times i)$$
$$FV_1 - P_0 = P_0 \times i$$
$$SI = P_0 \times i$$

where:

SI = the simple interest earned
i = the simple interest rate for the period, usually one year
P_0 = the initial or original principal amount

Thus, the calculation for simple interest is:[2]

$$SI = P_0 \times i = \$100 \times 0.10 = \$10.00$$

Notice in Exhibit 5.2 that the simple interest earned each year remains constant at $10 per year but that the amount of interest on interest increases every year. The reason, of course, is that interest on interest increases with the cumulative interest that has been earned. As more and more interest is earned, the compounding of interest accelerates the growth of the interest on interest and therefore the total interest earned.

An interesting observation about Equation 5.1 is that the higher the interest rate, the faster the investment will grow. This fact can be seen in Exhibit 5.3, which shows the growth in the future value of $1.00 at different interest rates and for different time periods into the future. First, notice that the growth in the future value over time is exponential, not linear. The dollar value of the invested funds does not increase by the same dollar amount from year to year. It increases by a greater amount each year. In other words, the growth of the invested funds is accelerated by the compounding of interest. Second, the higher the interest rate is, the more the

CNNMoney's Web site has a savings calculator at http://cgi.money.cnn.com/tools/savingscalc/savingscalc.html.

EXHIBIT 5.3
Future Value of $1 for Different Periods and Interest Rates

The higher the interest rate, the faster the value of an investment will grow, and the larger the amount of money that will accumulate over time. Because of compounding, the growth over time is not linear but exponential—the dollar increase in the future value is greater in each subsequent period.

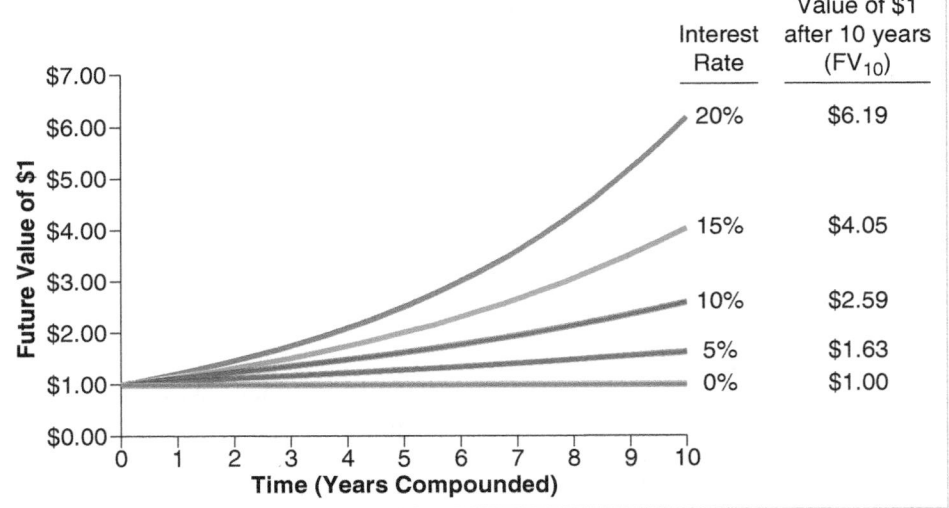

money accumulated for any time period. Looking at the right side of the exhibit, you can see the difference in total dollars accumulated if you invest a dollar for 10 years: At 5 percent, you will have $1.63; at 10 percent, you will have $2.59; at 15 percent, you will have $4.05; and at 20 percent, you will have $6.19. Finally, as you should expect, if you invest a dollar at 0 percent for 10 years, you will only have a dollar at the end of 10 years.

The Future Value Factor

To solve a future value problem, we need to know the future value factor, $(1 + i)^n$. Fortunately, almost any calculator suitable for college-level work has a power key (the y^x key) that we can use to make this computation. For example, to compute $(1.08)^{10}$, we enter 1.08, press the y^x key and enter 10, and press the = key. The number 2.159 should emerge. Give it a try with your calculator.

Future Value Factor Tables

Before calculators and computer spreadsheets became widely available, a financial analyst would typically use a future value factor table to obtain the factor for a future value calculation. Doing this reduced the necessary calculation to the simple multiplication of the present value by the future value factor—something that could easily be done by hand. A future value factor table, an example of which is provided in Table A-1 in Appendix A at the back of this book, provides future value factors for a range of interest rates and years. While such tables are no longer commonly used, you might find the one at the back of this book useful in checking some of the calculations that you do throughout this course.

Applying the Future Value Formula

Next, we will review a number of examples of future value problems to illustrate the typical types of problems you will encounter in business and in your personal life.

The Power of Compounding

Our first example illustrates the effects of compounding. Suppose you have an opportunity to make a $5,000 investment that pays 15 percent per year. How much money will you have at the end of 10 years? The time line for the investment opportunity is:

```
 0    15%   1      2      3      9      10   Year
 |    ___   |      |      |  /\   |
 -$5,000                         FV₁₀ = ?
```

where the $5,000 investment is a cash outflow and the future value you will receive in 10 years is a cash inflow.

We can apply Equation 5.1 to find the future value of $5,000 invested for 10 years at 15 percent interest. We want to multiply the original principal amount (PV) times the appropriate future value factor for 10 years at 15 percent, which is $(1 + 0.15)^{10}$; thus:

$$FV_n = PV \times (1 + i)^n$$
$$FV_{10} = \$5,000 \times (1 + 0.15)^{10}$$
$$= \$5,000 \times 4.045558$$
$$= \$20,227.79$$

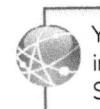 You can find a compound interest calculator at SmartMoney.com:
http://www.smartmoney.com/compoundcalc.

Now let's determine how much of the interest is from simple interest and how much is from interest on interest. The total compound interest earned is $15,227.79 ($20,227.79 − $5,000.00 = $15,227.79). The simple interest is the amount of interest paid on the original principal amount: $SI = P_0 \times i = \$5,000 \times 0.15 = \$750$ per year, which over 10 years is $750 × 10 = $7,500. The interest on interest must be the difference between the total compound interest earned and the simple interest: $15,227.79 − $7,500 = $7,727.79. Notice how quickly the value of an investment increases and how the reinvestment of interest earned impacts the total compound interest when the interest rate is high.

The relative importance of interest earned on
interest is especially great for long-term investments. For many people, retirement savings include the longest investments they will make. As
you might expect, interest earned on interest has
a great impact on how much money people ultimately have for their retirement. For example, consider someone who inherits and invests $10,000 on
her 25th birthday and earns 8 percent per year for
the next 40 years. This investment will grow to:

$$\$10,000 \times (1 + 0.80)^{40} = \$217,245.22$$

by the investor's 65th birthday. In contrast, if the same individual waited until her 35th birthday to invest the $10,000, she would have only:

$$\$10,000 \times (1 + 0.08)^{30} = \$100,626.57$$

when she turned 65.

Of the $116,618.65 difference in these amounts, the difference in simple interest accounts
for only $8,000 (10 years × $10,000 × 0.08 = $8,000). The remaining $108,618.65 is attributable to the difference in interest earned on interest. This example illustrates both the importance
of compounding for investment returns and the importance on getting started early when saving for retirement. The sooner you start saving, the better off you will be when you retire.

Compounding More Frequently Than Once a Year

Interest can, of course, be compounded more frequently than once a year. In Equation 5.1, the
term n represents the number of periods and can describe annual, semiannual, quarterly, monthly,
or daily payments. The more frequently interest payments are compounded, the larger the
future value of $1 for a given time period. Equation 5.1 can be rewritten to explicitly recognize
different compounding periods:

$$FV_n = PV \times (1 + i/m)^{m \times n} \tag{5.2}$$

where m is the number of times per year that interest is compounded and n is the number of
periods specified in years.

Let's say you invest $100 in a bank account that pays a 5 percent interest rate semiannually
(2.5 percent twice a year) for two years. In other words, the annual rate quoted by the bank
is 5 percent, but the bank calculates the interest it pays you based on a six-month rate of 2.5
percent. In this example there are four six-month periods, and the amount of principal and
interest you would have at the end of the four periods would be:

$$
\begin{aligned}
FV_2 &= \$100 \times (1 + 0.05/2)^{2 \times 2} \\
&= \$100 \times (1 + 0.025)^{4} \\
&= \$100 \times 1.1038 \\
&= \$110.38
\end{aligned}
$$

 Moneychimp
.com provides a
compound interest
calculator at http://
www.moneychimp
.com/calculator/
compound_interest_
calculator.htm.

It is not necessary to memorize Equation 5.2; using Equation 5.1 will do fine. All you have
to do is determine the interest paid per compounding period (i/m) and calculate the total
number of compounding periods ($m \times n$) as the exponent for the future value factor. For example, if the bank compounds interest quarterly, then both the interest rate and compounding
periods must be expressed in quarterly terms: ($i/4$) and ($4 \times n$).

If the bank in the preceding example paid interest annually instead of semiannually, you
would have:

$$FV_2 = \$100 \times (1 + 0.05)^2 = \$110.25$$

at the end of the two-year period. The difference between this amount and the $110.38 is due
to the additional interest earned on interest when the compounding period is shorter and the
interest payments are compounded more frequently.

During the late 1960s, the effects of compounding periods became an issue in banking. At that time, the interest rates that banks and thrift institutions could pay on consumer savings accounts were limited by regulation. However, financial institutions discovered they could keep their rates within the legal limit and pay their customers additional interest by increasing the compounding frequency. Prior to this, banks and thrifts had paid interest on savings accounts quarterly. You can see the difference between quarterly and daily compounding in Learning by Doing Application 5.1.

Changing the Compounding Period

LEARNING BY DOING

APPLICATION 5.1

NEED MORE HELP?

WileyPLUS

PROBLEM: Your grandmother has $10,000 she wants to put into a bank savings account for five years. The bank she is considering is within walking distance, pays 5 percent annual interest compounded quarterly (5 percent per year/4 quarters per year = 1.25 percent per quarter), and provides free coffee and doughnuts in the morning. Another bank in town pays 5 percent interest compounded daily. Getting to this bank requires a bus trip, but your grandmother can ride free as a senior citizen. More important, though, this bank does not serve coffee and doughnuts. Which bank should your grandmother select?

APPROACH: We need to calculate the difference between the two banks' interest payments. Bank A, which compounds quarterly, will pay one-fourth of the annual interest per quarter, 0.05/4 = 0.0125, and there will be 20 compounding periods over the five-year investment horizon (5 years × 4 quarters per year = 20 quarters). The time line for quarterly compounding is as follows:

Bank B, which compounds daily, has 365 compounding periods per year. Thus, the daily interest rate is 0.000137 (0.05/365 = 0.000137), and there are 1,825 (5 years × 365 days per year = 1,825 days) compounding periods. The time line for daily compounding is:

We use Equation 5.2 to solve for the future values the investment would generate at each bank. We then compare the two.

SOLUTION:

Bank A:
$$FV_n = PV \times (1 + i/m)^{m \times n}$$
$$FV_{qtrly} = \$10{,}000 \times (1 + 0.05/4)^{4 \times 5}$$
$$= \$10{,}000 \times (1 + 0.0125)^{20}$$
$$= \$12{,}820.37$$

Bank B:
$$FV_n = PV \times (1 + i/m)^{m \times n}$$
$$FV_{daily} = \$10{,}000 \times (1 + 0.05/365)^{365 \times 5}$$
$$= \$10{,}000 \times (1 + 0.000137)^{1{,}825}$$
$$= \$12{,}840.03$$

With daily compounding, the additional interest earned by your grandmother is $19.66:

$$\$12{,}840.03 - \$12{,}820.37 = \$19.66$$

Given that the interest gained by daily compounding is less than $20, your grandmother should probably select her local bank and enjoy the daily coffee and doughnuts. (If she is on a diet, of course, she should take the higher interest payment and walk to the other bank).

It is worth noting that the longer the investment period, the greater the additional interest earned from daily compounding vs. quarterly compounding. For example, if $10,000 was invested for 40 years instead of five years, the additional interest would increase to $900.23. (You should confirm this by doing the calculation.)

Continuous Compounding

We can continue to divide the compounding interval into smaller and smaller time periods, such as minutes and seconds, until, at the extreme, we would compound continuously. In this case, m in Equation 5.2 would approach infinity (∞). The formula to compute the future value for continuous compounding (FV_∞) is stated as follows:

$$FV_\infty = PV \times e^{i \times n} \qquad (5.3)$$

where e is the exponential function, which has a known mathematical value of about 2.71828, n is the number of periods specified in years, and i is the annual interest rate. Although the formula may look a little intimidating, it is really quite easy to apply. Look for a key on your calculator labeled e^x. If you don't have the key, you still can work the problem.

Let's go back to the example in Learning by Doing Application 5.1, in which your grandmother wants to put $10,000 in a savings account at a bank. How much money would she have at the end of five years if the bank paid 5 percent annual interest compounded continuously? To find out, we enter these values into Equation 5.3:

$$
\begin{aligned}
FV_\infty &= PV \times e^{i \times n} \\
&= \$10,000 \times e^{0.05 \times 5} \\
&= \$10,000 \times e^{0.25} \\
&= \$10,000 \times 2.71828^{0.25} \\
&= \$10,000 \times 1.284025 \\
&= \$12,840.25
\end{aligned}
$$

If your calculator has an exponent key, all you have to do to calculate $e^{0.25}$ is enter the number 0.25, then hit the e^x key, and the number 1.284025 should appear (depending on your calculator, you may have to press the equal [=] key for the answer to appear). Then multiply 1.284025 by $10,000, and you're done! If your calculator does not have an exponent key, then you can calculate $e^{0.25}$ by inputting the value of e (2.71828) and raising it to the 0.25 power using the y^x key, as described earlier in this chapter.

Let's look at your grandmother's $10,000 bank balance at the end of five years with several different compounding periods: yearly, quarterly, daily, and continuous:[3]

(1) Compounding Period	(2) Total Earnings	(3) Compound Interest	(4) Additional Interest
Yearly	$12,762.82	$2,762.82	—
Quarterly	$12,820.37	$2,820.37	$57.55 more than yearly compounding
Daily	$12,840.03	$2,840.03	$19.66 more than quarterly compounding
Continuous	$12,840.25	$2,840.25	$0.22 more than daily compounding

Notice that your grandmother's total earnings get larger as the frequency of compounding increases, as shown in column 2, but the earnings increase at a decreasing rate, as shown in column 4. The biggest gain comes when the compounding period goes from an annual interest payment to quarterly interest payments. The gain from daily compounding to continuous compounding is small on a modest savings balance such as your grandmother's. Twenty-two cents over five years will not buy grandmother a cup of coffee, let alone a doughnut. However, for businesses and governments with very large dollar balances at financial institutions, the difference in compounding periods can be substantial.

---

[3] The future value calculation for annual compounding is: $FV_{yearly} = \$10,000 \times (1.05)^5 = \$12,762.82$.

Which Bank Offers Depositors the Best Deal?

SITUATION: You have just received a bonus of $10,000 and are looking to deposit the money in a bank account for five years. You investigate the annual deposit rates of several banks and collect the following information:

Bank	Compounding Frequency	Annual Rate
A	Annually	5.00%
B	Quarterly	5.00%
C	Monthly	4.80%
D	Daily	4.85%

You understand that the more frequently interest is earned in each year, the more you will have at the end of your five-year investment horizon. To determine which bank you should deposit your money in, you calculate how much money you will have at the end of five years at each bank. You apply Equation 5.2 and come up with the following results. Which bank should you choose?

Bank	Investment Amount	Compounding Frequency	Rate	Value after 5 Years
A	$10,000	Annually	5.00%	$12,762.82
B	$10,000	Quarterly	5.00%	$12,820.37
C	$10,000	Monthly	4.80%	$12,706.41
D	$10,000	Daily	4.85%	$12,744.11

DECISION: Without making any calculations, we can exclude Bank A from consideration because we know that Bank B's CD will have a higher value at the end of 5 years. The reason is that the CDs from Banks A and B have the same investment amount ($10,000), maturity (5 years), and annual interest rate (5 percent); they differ only in their compounding frequency. Bank B's quarterly compounding will result in a higher value than Bank A's annual compounding. Since the CDs from Banks B, C, and D differ in both their annual rates and compounding frequencies, there is no way to determine the most attractive among them without doing future value calculations. These calculations reveal that the CD from Bank B will provide the highest value at the end of five years. You should choose Bank B.

Calculator Tips for Future Value Problems

As we have mentioned, all types of future value calculations can be done easily on a financial calculator. Here we discuss how to solve these problems, and we identify some potential problem areas to avoid.

A financial calculator includes the following five basic keys for solving future value and present value problems:

The keys represent the following inputs:

- **N** is the number of periods. The periods can be years, quarters, months, days, or some other unit of time.
- **i** is the interest rate per period, expressed as a percentage.
- **PV** is the present value or the original principal (P_0).
- **PMT** is the amount of any recurring payment.[4]
- **FV** is the future value.

Given any four of these inputs, the financial calculator will solve for the fifth. Note that the interest rate key i differs with different calculator brands: Texas Instruments uses the I/Y key; Hewlett-Packard an i, %i, or I/Y key; and Sharp the i key.

---

[4]The PMT key is used for annuity calculations, which we will discuss later in this chapter.

For future value problems, we need to use only four of the five keys: N for the number of periods, i for the interest rate (or growth rate), PV for the present value (at time zero), and FV for the future value in n periods. The PMT key is not used at this time, but, when doing a problem, always enter a zero for PMT to clear the register.

To solve a future value problem, enter the known data into your calculator. For example, if you know that the number of periods is five, key in 5 and press the N key. Repeat the process for the remaining known values. Once you have entered *all* of the values you know, then press the key for the unknown quantity, and you have your answer. Note that with some calculators, including the TI BAII Plus, you get the answer by first pressing the key labeled CPT (compute).

Let's try a problem to see how this works. Suppose we invest $5,000 at 15 percent for 10 years. How much money will we have in 10 years? To solve the problem, we enter data on the keys as displayed in the following calculation and solve for FV. Note that the initial investment of $5,000 is a negative number because it represents a cash outflow. Use the $+/-$ key to make a number negative.

Enter	10	15	−5,000	0	
	N	i	PV	PMT	FV
Answer					20,227.79

If you did not get the correct answer of $20,227.79, you may need to consult the instruction manual that came with your financial calculator. However, before you do that, you may want to look through Exhibit 5.4, which lists the most common problems with using financial calculators. Also, note again that PMT is entered as zero to clear the register.

EXHIBIT 5.4   Tips for Using Financial Calculators

Following these tips will help you avoid problems that sometimes arise in solving time value of money problems with a financial calculator.

Use the Correct Compounding Period. Make sure that your calculator is set to compound one payment per period or per year. Because financial calculators are often used to compute monthly payments, some will default to monthly payments unless you indicate otherwise. You will need to consult your calculator's instruction manual because procedures for changing settings vary by manufacturer. Most of the problems you will work in other chapters of this book will compound annually.

Clear the Calculator Before Starting. Be sure you clear the data from the financial register before starting to work a problem because most calculators retain information between calculations. Since the information may be retained even when the calculator is turned off, turning the calculator off and on will not solve this problem. Check your instruction manual for the correct procedure for clearing the financial register of your calculator.

Negative Signs on Cash Outflows. For certain types of calculations, it is critical that you input a negative sign for all cash outflows and a positive sign for all cash inflows. Otherwise, the calculator cannot make the computation, and the answer screen will display some type of error message.

Putting a Negative Sign on a Number. To create a number with a negative sign, enter the number first and then press the "change of sign key." These keys are typically labeled "CHS" or "$+/-$".

Interest Rate as a Percentage. Most financial calculators require that interest rate data be entered in percentage form, not in decimal form. For example, enter 7.125 percent as 7.125 and not 0.07125. Unlike nonfinancial calculators, financial calculators assume that rates are stated as percentages.

Rounding Off Numbers. Never round off any numbers until all your calculations are complete. If you round off numbers along the way, you can generate significant rounding errors.

Adjust Decimal Setting. Most calculators are set to display two decimal places. You will find it convenient at times to display four or more decimal places when making financial calculations, especially when working with interest rates or present value factors. Again, consult your instruction manual.

Have Correct BEG or END Mode. In finance, most problems that you solve will involve cash payments that occur at the end of each time period, such as with the ordinary annuities discussed in Chapter 6. Most calculators normally operate in this mode, which is usually designated as "END" mode. However, for annuities due, which are also discussed in Chapter 6, the cash payments occur at the beginning of each period. This setting is designated as the "BEG" mode. Most leases and rent payments fall into this category. When your financial calculator was purchased, it was set in the END mode. Financial calculators allow you to switch between the END and BEG modes.

TIME VALUE OF MONEY

Spreadsheet computer programs are popular tools for setting up and solving finance and accounting problems. Throughout this book, we will show you how to structure and calculate some problems using the Microsoft Excel spreadsheet program. Spreadsheet programs are like your financial calculator but are especially efficient at doing repetitive calculations. For example, once the spreadsheet program is set up, it will allow you to make computations using preprogrammed formulas. Thus, you can simply change any of the input cells, and the preset formula will automatically recalculate the answer based on the new input values. For this reason, we recommend that you use formulas whenever possible.

We begin our spreadsheet applications with time value of money calculations. As with the financial calculator approach, there are five variables used in these calculations,

and knowing any four of them will let you calculate the fifth one. Excel includes preset formulas for you to use. These are as follows:

Solving for	Formula
Present Value	= PV(RATE, NPER, PMT, FV)
Future Value	= FV(RATE, NPER, PMT, PV)
Discount Rate	= RATE(NPER, PMT, PV, FV)
Payment	= PMT(RATE, NPER, PV, FV)
Number of Periods	= NPER(RATE, PMT, PV, FV)

To enter a formula, all you have to do is type in the equal sign, the abbreviated name of the variable you want to compute, and an open parenthesis, and Excel will automatically prompt you to enter the rest of the variables. Here is an example of what you would type to compute the future value:

1. =
2. FV
3. (

Here are a few important things to note when entering the formulas: (1) be consistent with signs for cash inflows and outflows; (2) enter the rate of return as a decimal number, not a percentage; and (3) enter the amount of an unknown payment as zero.

To see how a problem is set up and how the calculations are made using a spreadsheet, let's return to Learning by Doing Application 5.1. The spreadsheet for that application is on the left.

	A	B	C	D	E	F
1						
2			**Time Value of Money Calculations**			
3						
4	Your grandmother wants to put $10,000 into a bank savings account for five years. Bank A pays 5 percent					
5	interest compounded quarterly, while Bank B offers 5 percent compounded daily. Which bank should your					
6	grandmother choose?					
7						
8	To answer the question, we need to solve for the future value.					
9						
10	**Problem setup and solution:**					
11						
12		**Bank A**	**Bank B**	Comment		
13	Present value	($10,000)	($10,000)	Value given		
14	Interest rate	0.01250	0.00014	Interest rate/# compounding periods per year		
15	Number of periods	20	1825	# years × # compounding periods per year		
16	**Future value**	**$12,820.37**	**$12,840.03**	See note below		
17						
18	The formula entered to calculate the future value for Bank A in cell B16 is =FV(B14, B15, 0, B13). Similarly, the					
19	formula to calculate the future value for Bank B in cell C16 is =FV(C14, C15, 0, C13). Since there are no					
20	payments, we enter PMT as zero. Also, notice that to be consistent with what we have said about cash inflows					
21	and outflows so far, the present value is entered as a negative number. Finally, the formulas in more recent					
22	versions of Excel contain additional variables like "type" or "guess". You can ignore these for now.					
23						

> **BEFORE YOU GO ON**

1. What is compounding, and how does it affect the future value of an investment?

2. What is the difference between simple interest and compound interest?

3. How does changing the compounding period affect the amount of interest earned on an investment?

5.3 PRESENT VALUE AND DISCOUNTING

LEARNING OBJECTIVE **3**

In our discussion of future value, we asked the question "If you put $100 in a bank savings account that pays 10 percent annual interest, how much money would accumulate in one year?" Another type of question that arises frequently in finance concerns present value. This question asks, "What is the value today of a cash flow promised in the future?" We'll illustrate the present value concept with a simple example.

Single-Period Investment

Suppose that a rich uncle gives you a bank certificate of deposit (CD) that matures in one year and pays $110. The CD pays 10 percent interest annually and cannot be redeemed until maturity. Being a student, you need the money and would like to sell the CD. What would be a fair price if you sold the CD today?

From our earlier discussion, we know that if we invest $100 in a bank at 10 percent for one year, it will grow to a future value of $110 = $100 × (1 + 0.10). It seems reasonable to conclude that if a CD has an interest rate of 10 percent and will have a value of $110 a year from now, it is worth $100 today.

More formally, to find the present value of a future cash flow, or its value today, we "reverse" the compounding process and divide the future value ($110) by the future value factor (1 + 0.10). The result is $100 = $110/(1 + 0.10), which is the same answer we derived from our intuitive calculation. If we write the calculations above as a formula, we have a one-period model for calculating the present value of a future cash flow:

$$PV = \frac{FV_1}{1 + i}$$

The numerical calculation for the present value (PV) from our one-period model follows:

$$
\begin{aligned}
PV &= \frac{FV_1}{1 + i} \\
&= \frac{\$110}{1 + 0.10} \\
&= \frac{\$110}{1.10} \\
&= \$100
\end{aligned}
$$

We have noted that while future value calculations involve *compounding* an amount forward into the future, *present value* calculations involve the reverse. That is, present value calculations involve determining the current value (or present value) of a future cash flow. The process of calculating the present value is called **discounting**, and the interest rate i is known as the **discount rate**. Accordingly, the **present value (PV)** can be thought of as the *discounted value of a future amount*. The present value is simply the current value of a future cash flow that has been discounted at the appropriate discount rate.

Just as we have a future value factor, (1 + i), we also have a *present value factor*, which is more commonly called the *discount factor*. The discount factor, which is 1/(1 + i), is the reciprocal of the future value factor. This expression may not be obvious in the equation above, but note that we can write that equation in two ways:

1. $PV = \dfrac{FV}{1 + i}$

2. $PV = FV_1 \times \dfrac{1}{1 + i}$

These equations amount to the same thing; the discount factor is explicit in the second one.

discounting
the process by which the present value of future cash flows is obtained

discount rate
the interest rate used in the discounting process to find the present value of future cash flows

present value (PV)
the current value of future cash flows discounted at the appropriate discount rate

Multiple-Period Investment

Now suppose your uncle gives you another 10 percent CD, but this CD matures in two years and pays $121 at maturity. Like the other CD, it cannot be redeemed until maturity. From the previous section, we know that if we invest $100 in a bank at 10 percent for two years, it will grow to a future value of $121 = $100 × (1 + 0.10)². To calculate the present value, or today's price, we divide the future value by the future value factor. If we write this as an equation, the result is a two-period model for computing the present value of a future cash flow:

$$PV = \frac{FV_2}{(1 + i)^2}$$

Plugging the data from our example into the equation yields:

$$PV = \frac{FV_2}{(1 + i)^2}$$
$$= \frac{\$121}{(1 + 0.10)^2}$$
$$= \frac{\$121}{1.21}$$
$$= \$100$$

By now, you know the drill. We can extend the equation to a third year as:

$$PV = \frac{FV_3}{(1 + i)^3}$$

and so on for the fourth year and beyond.

The Present Value Equation

Given the pattern shown above, we can see that the general formula for the present value is:[5]

$$PV = \frac{FV_n}{(1 + i)^n} \tag{5.4}$$

where:
    PV = the value today ($t = 0$) of a cash flow
    FV_n = the future value at the end of period n
      i = the discount rate, which is the interest rate per period
      n = the number of periods, which can be years, quarters, months, days, or some other
          unit of time

Note that Equation 5.4 can be written in slightly different ways, which we will sometimes do in this book. The first form, introduced earlier, separates out the discount factor, $1/(1 + i)$:

$$PV = FV_n \times \frac{1}{(1 + i)^n}$$

In the second form, DF_n is the discount factor for the nth period: $DF_n = 1/(1 + i)^n$:

$$PV = FV_n \times DF_n$$

Future and Present Value Equations Are the Same

Equation 5.4 is just a restatement of the future value equation, Equation 5.1. That is, to get the future value (FV_n) of funds invested for n years, we multiply the original investment by $(1 + i)^n$. To find the present value of a future payment (PV), we divide FV_n by $(1 + i)^n$. Stated another way, we can start with the future value equation (Equation 5.1), $FV_n = PV \times (1 + i)^n$, and then solve it for PV; the resulting equation is the present value equation (Equation 5.4), $PV = FV_n/(1 + i)^n$.

    Exhibit 5.5 illustrates the relation between the future value and present value calculations for $100 invested at 10 percent interest. You can see from the exhibit that present value and future value are just two sides of the same coin. The formula used to calculate the present value is really the same as the formula for future value, just rearranged.

Applying the Present Value Formula

Let's work through some examples to see how the present value equation is used. Suppose you are interested in buying a new BMW sports coupe a year from now. You estimate that the car

---

[5]Equation 5.4 can also be written as $PV = FV_n \times (1 + i)^{-n}$.

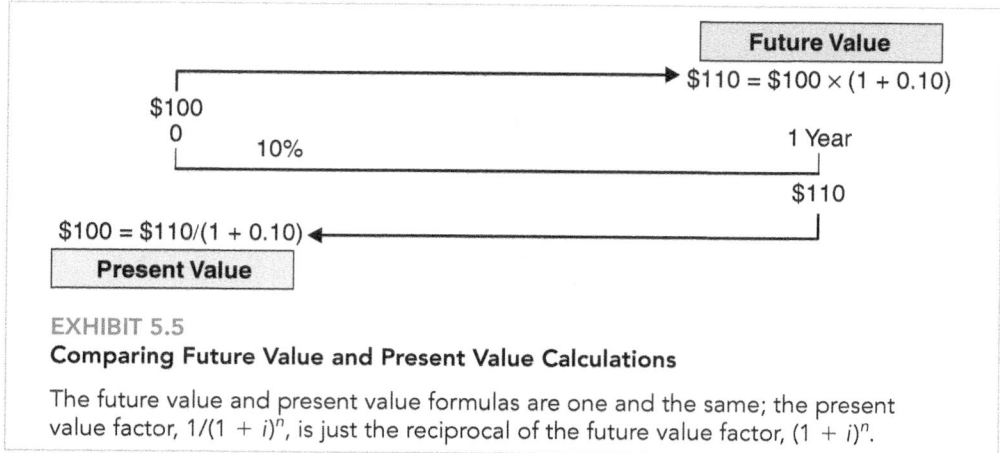

EXHIBIT 5.5

Comparing Future Value and Present Value Calculations

The future value and present value formulas are one and the same; the present value factor, $1/(1 + i)^n$, is just the reciprocal of the future value factor, $(1 + i)^n$.

will cost $40,000. If your local bank pays 5 percent interest on savings deposits, how much money will you need to save in order to buy the car as planned? The time line for the car purchase problem is as follows:

Solving this problem involves a direct application of Equation 5.4. What we want to know is how much money you have to put in the bank today to have $40,000 a year from now to buy your BMW. To find out, we compute the present value of $40,000 using a 5 percent discount rate:

$$PV = \frac{FV_1}{1 + i}$$
$$= \frac{\$40,000}{1 + 0.05}$$
$$= \frac{\$40,000}{1.05}$$
$$= \$38,095.24$$

SmartMoney's personal finance Web site provides a lot of useful information for day-to-day finance dealings at http://www.smartmoney.com/pf/?nav=dropTab.

If you put $38,095.24 in a bank savings account at 5 percent today, you will have the $40,000 to buy the car in one year.

Since that's a lot of money to come up with, your mother suggests that you leave the money in the bank for two years instead of one year. If you follow her advice, how much money do you need to invest? The time line is as follows:

For a two-year waiting period, assuming the car price will stay the same, the calculation is:

$$PV = \frac{FV_2}{(1 + i)^2}$$
$$= \frac{\$40,000}{(1 + 0.05)^2}$$
$$= \frac{\$40,000}{1.1025}$$
$$= \$36,281.18$$

Given the time value of money, the result is exactly what we would expect. The present value of $40,000 two years out is lower than the present value of $40,000 one year out—$36,281.18 compared with $38,095.24. Thus, if you are willing to leave your money in the bank for two years instead of one, you can make a smaller initial investment to reach your goal.

Now suppose your rich neighbor says that if you invest your money with him for one year, he will pay you 15 percent interest. The time line is:

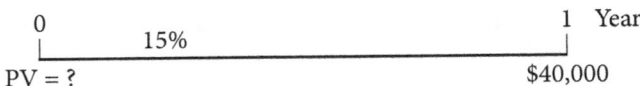

```
0                                          1   Year
|            15%                            |
PV = ?                                   $40,000
```

The calculation for the initial investment at this new rate is as follows:

$$PV = \frac{FV_1}{1 + i}$$
$$= \frac{\$40,000}{1 + 0.15}$$
$$= \frac{\$40,000}{1.15}$$
$$= \$34,782.61$$

Thus, when the interest rate, or discount rate, is 15 percent, the present value of $40,000 to be received in a year's time is $34,782.61, compared with $38,095.24 at a rate of 5 percent and a period of one year. Holding maturity constant, an increase in the discount rate decreases the present value of the future cash flow. This makes sense because when interest rates are higher, it is more valuable to have dollars in hand today to invest; thus, dollars in the future are worth less.

European Graduation Fling

PROBLEM: Suppose you plan to take a "graduation vacation" to Europe when you finish college in two years. If your savings account at the bank pays 6 percent, how much money do you need to set aside today to have $8,000 when you leave for Europe?

APPROACH: The money you need today is the present value of the amount you will need for your trip in two years. Thus, the value of FV_2 is $8,000. The interest rate is 6 percent. Using these values and the present value equation, we can calculate how much money you need to put in the bank at 6 percent to generate $8,000. The time line is:

```
0              1              2   Year
|      6%       |              |
PV = ?                      $8,000
```

SOLUTION:

$$PV = FV_n \times \frac{1}{(1 + i)^n}$$
$$= FV_2 \times \frac{1}{(1 + i)^2}$$
$$= \$8,000 \times \frac{1}{(1.06)^2}$$
$$= \$8,000 \times 0.889996$$
$$= \$7,119.97$$

Thus, if you invest $7,119.97 in your savings account today, at the end of two years you will have exactly $8,000.

The Relations Among Time, the Discount Rate, and Present Value

From our discussion so far, we can see that (1) the farther in the future a dollar will be received, the less it is worth today, and (2) the higher the discount rate, the lower the present value of a dollar to be received in the future. Let's look a bit more closely at these relations.

Recall from Exhibit 5.3 that the future value of a dollar increases with time because of compounding. In contrast, the present value of a dollar becomes smaller the farther into the future that dollar is to be received. The reason is that the present value factor $1/(1 + i)^n$ is the reciprocal of the future value factor $(1 + i)^n$. Thus, the present value of $1 must become smaller the farther into the future that dollar is to be received.

Exhibit 5.6 shows the present values of $1 for different time periods and discount rates. For example, the present value of $1 discounted at 5 percent for 10 years is 61 cents, at 10 percent it is 39 cents, and at 20 percent, 16 cents. Thus, the higher the discount rate, the lower the present value of $1 for a given time period. Exhibit 5.6 also shows that, just as with future value, the relation between the present value of $1 and time is not linear but exponential. Finally, it is interesting to note that if interest rates are zero, the present value of $1 is $1; that is, there is no time value of money. In this situation, $1,000 today has the same value as $1,000 a year from now or, for that matter, 10 years from now.

Calculator Tips for Present Value Problems

Calculating the discount factor (present value factor) on a calculator is similar to calculating the future value factor but requires an additional keystroke on most calculators. The discount factor, $1/(1 + i)^n$, is the reciprocal of the future value factor, $(1 + i)^n$. The additional keystroke involves the use of the reciprocal key $(1/x)$ to find the discount factor. For example, to compute $1/(1.08)^{10}$, first enter 1.08, press the y^x key and enter 10, then press the equal (=) key. The number on the screen should be 2.159. This is the future value factor. It is a calculation you have made before. Now press the $1/x$ key, then the equal key, and you have the present value factor, 0.463!

Calculating present value (PV) on a financial calculator is the same as calculating the future value (FV_n) except that you solve for PV rather than FV_n. For example, what is the present

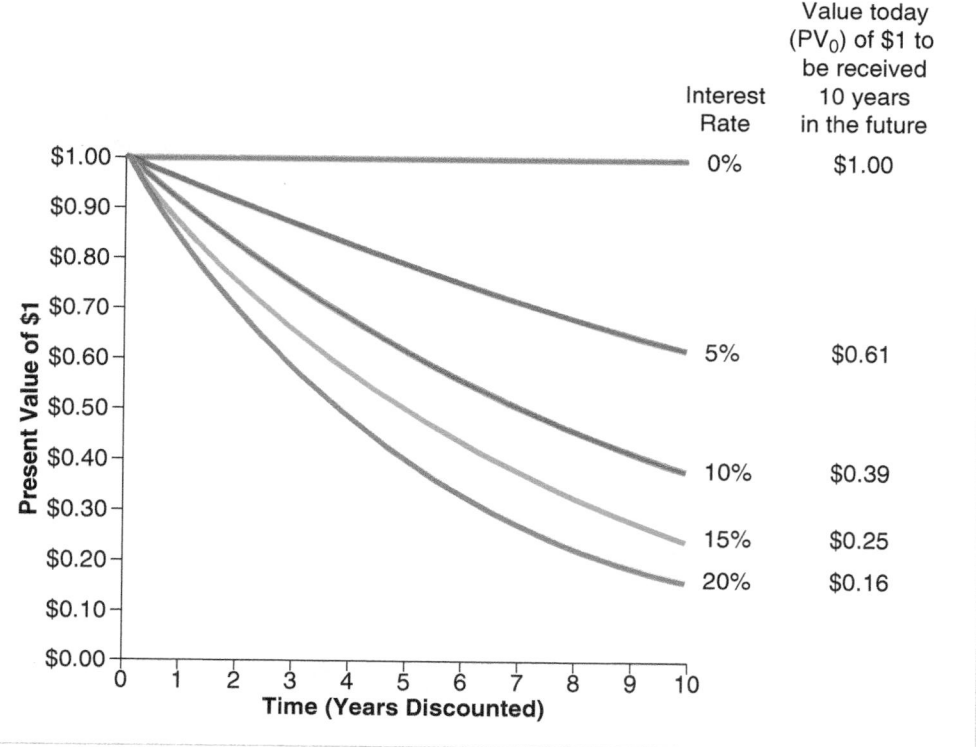

EXHIBIT 5.6
Present Value of $1 for Different Time Periods and Discount Rates

The higher the discount rate, the lower the present value of $1 for a given time period. Just as with future value, the relation between the present value and time is not linear but exponential.

Interest Rate	Value today (PV_0) of $1 to be received 10 years in the future
0%	$1.00
5%	$0.61
10%	$0.39
15%	$0.25
20%	$0.16

value of $1,000 received 10 years from now at a 9 percent discount rate? To find the answer on your financial calculator, enter the following keystrokes:

Enter	10	9		0	1,000
	N	i	PV	PMT	FV
Answer			−422.41		

then solve for the present value (PV), which is −$422.41. Notice that the answer has a negative sign. As we discussed previously, the $1,000 represents an inflow, and the $442.41 represents an outflow.

Note that, just as financial analysts used future value factor tables to help with calculations before calculators and computer spreadsheets became widely available, they also used present value factor tables. Table A-2 in Appendix A at the back of this book is an example of such a table.

Future Value Versus Present Value

We can analyze financial decisions using either future value or present value techniques. Although the two techniques approach the decision differently, both yield the same result. Both techniques focus on the valuation of cash flows received over time. In corporate finance, future value problems typically measure the value of cash flows at the end of a project, whereas present value problems measure the value of cash flows at the start of a project (time zero).

Picking the Best Lottery Payoff Option

DECISION MAKING

EXAMPLE 5.2

SITUATION: Congratulations! You have won the $1 million lottery grand prize. You have been presented with several payout alternatives, and you have to decide which one to accept. The alternatives are as follows:

- $1 million today
- $1.2 million lump sum in two years
- $1.5 million lump sum in five years
- $2 million lump sum in eight years

You are intrigued by the choice of collecting the prize money today or receiving double the amount of money in the future. Which payout option should you choose?

Your cousin, a stockbroker, advises you that over the long term you should be able to earn 10 percent on an investment portfolio. Based on that rate of return, you make the following calculations:

Alternative	Future Value	Present Value
Today	$1 million	$1 million
2 years	$1.2 million	$991,736
5 years	$1.5 million	$931,382
8 years	$2 million	$933,015

DECISION: As appealing as the higher amounts may sound, waiting for the big payout is not worthwhile in this case. Applying the present value formula has enabled you to convert future dollars into present, or current, dollars. Now the decision is simple—you can directly compare the present values. Given the choices here, you should take the $1 million today.

Finding the Interest Rate

In finance, some situations require you to determine the interest rate (or discount rate) for a given future cash flow. These situations typically arise when you want to determine the return on an investment. Consider a *zero coupon bond*, which is essentially a loan that pays no periodic interest. The issuer (the firm that borrows the money) makes a single payment when the bond matures (the loan is due) that includes repayment of the amount borrowed plus all of the interest. Needless to say, the issuer must prepare in advance to have the cash to pay off bondholders.

Suppose a firm is planning to issue $10 million worth of zero coupon bonds with 20 years to maturity. The bonds are issued in denominations of $1,000 and are sold for $90 each. In other words, you buy the bond today for $90, and 20 years from now the firm pays you $1,000. If you bought one of these bonds, what would be your return on investment?

To find the return, we need to solve Equation 5.1, the future value equation, for i, the interest, or discount, rate. The $90 you pay today is the PV (present value), the $1,000 you get in 20 years is the FV (future value), and 20 years is n (the compounding period). The resulting calculation is as follows:

$$FV_n = PV \times (1 + i)^n$$
$$\$1,000 = \$90 \times (1 + i)^{20}$$
$$(1 + i)^{20} = \frac{\$1,000}{\$90}$$
$$1 + i = \left(\frac{\$1,000}{\$90}\right)^{1/20}$$
$$i = (11.1111)^{1/20} - 1$$
$$= 1.1279 - 1$$
$$= 0.1279, \text{ or } 12.79\%$$

The rate of return on your investment, compounded annually, is 12.79 percent. Using a financial calculator, we arrive at the following solution:

Finding How Many Periods It Takes an Investment to Grow a Certain Amount

Up to this point we have used variations of Equation 5.1:

$$FV_n = PV \times (1 + i)^n$$

to calculate the future value of an investment (FV_n), the present value of an investment (PV), and the interest rate necessary for an initial investment (the present value) to grow to a specific value (the future value) over a certain number of periods (i). Note that Equation 5.1 has a total of four variables. You may have noticed that in all of the previous calculations, we took advantage of the mathematical principle that if we know the values of three of these variables we can calculate the value of the fourth.

The same principle allows us to calculate the number of periods (n) that it takes an investment to grow a certain amount. This is a more complicated calculation than the calculations of the values of the other three variables, but it is an important one for you to know and understand.

Suppose that you would like to purchase a new cross-country motorcycle to ride on dirt trails near campus. The motorcycle dealer will finance the bike that you are interested in if you make a down payment of $1,175. Right now you only have $1,000. If you can earn 5 percent by investing your money, how long will it take for your $1,000 to grow to $1,175?

To find this length of time, we must solve Equation 5.1, the future value equation, for n.

$$FV_n = PV \times (1 + i)^n$$

$$\$1,175 = \$1,000 \times (1 + 0.05)^n$$

$$\frac{\$1,175}{\$1,000} = (1 + 0.05)^n$$

$$\ln\left(\frac{\$1,175}{\$1,000}\right) = n \times \ln(1 + 0.05)$$

$$n = \frac{\ln\left(\dfrac{\$1,175}{\$1,000}\right)}{\ln(1 + 0.05)}$$

$$n = \frac{0.16127}{0.04879}$$

$$n = 3.31 \text{ years}$$

It will take 3.31 years for your investment to grow to $1,175. If you don't want to wait this long to get your motorcycle, you cannot rely on your investment earnings alone. You will have to put aside some additional money.

Note that because n is an exponent in the future value formula, we have to take the natural logarithm, $\ln(x)$, of both sides of the equation in the fourth line of the preceding calculations to compute the value of n directly. Your financial calculator should have a key that allows you to calculate natural logarithms. Just enter the value in the parentheses and then hit the LN key.

Using a financial calculator, we obtain the same solution.

Enter	5	−1,000	0	1,175
	N	i	PV	PMT	FV

Answer   **3.31**

> **BEFORE YOU GO ON**

1. What is the present value, and when is it used?

2. What is the discount rate? How does the discount rate differ from the interest rate in the future value equation?

3. What is the relation between the present value factor and the future value factor?

4. Explain why you would expect the discount factor to become smaller the longer the time to payment.

5.4 MULTIPLE CASH FLOWS

Future Value of Multiple Cash Flows

LEARNING OBJECTIVE ④

WileyPLUS

TIME VALUE OF MONEY:
AN ANIMATED TUTORIAL

Earlier in this chapter we worked through several examples that involved the future value of a lump sum of money invested in a savings account that paid 10 percent interest per year. But suppose you are investing more than one lump sum. Let's say you put $1,000 in your bank savings account today and another $1,000 a year from now. If the bank continues to pay 10 percent interest per year, how much money will you have at the end of two years?

To solve this future value problem, we can use Equation 5.1: $FV_n = PV \times (1 + i)^n$. First, however, we construct a time line so that we can see the magnitude and timing of the cash

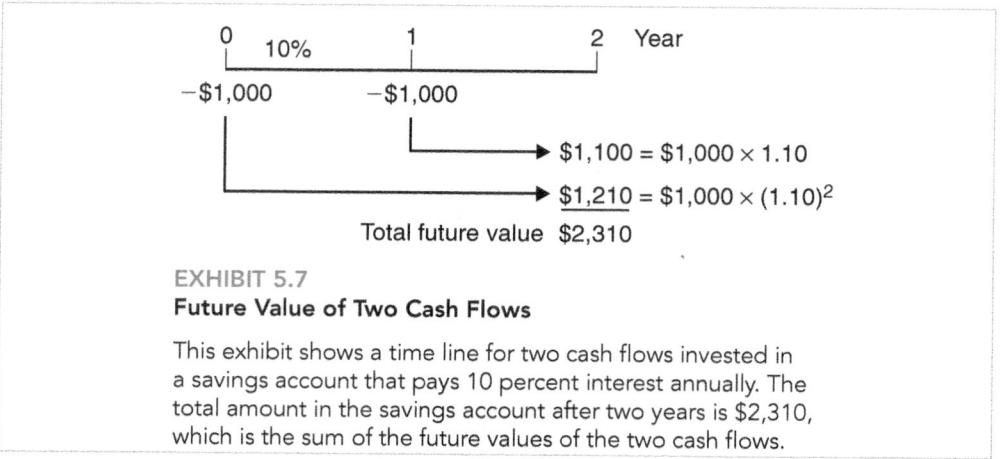

EXHIBIT 5.7

Future Value of Two Cash Flows

This exhibit shows a time line for two cash flows invested in a savings account that pays 10 percent interest annually. The total amount in the savings account after two years is $2,310, which is the sum of the future values of the two cash flows.

flows. As Exhibit 5.7 shows, there are two cash flows into the savings plan. The first cash flow is invested for two years and compounds to a future value as follows:

$$
\begin{aligned}
FV_2 &= PV \times (1 + i)^2 \\
&= \$1,000 \times (1 + 0.10)^2 \\
&= \$1,000 \times 1.21 \\
&= \$1,210
\end{aligned}
$$

The second cash flow earns simple interest for a single period only and grows to:

$$
\begin{aligned}
FV_1 &= PV \times (1 + i) \\
&= \$1,000 \times (1 + 0.10) \\
&= \$1,000 \times 1.10 \\
&= \$1,100
\end{aligned}
$$

The total amount of money in the savings account after two years is the sum of these two amounts, which is $2,310 ($1,100 + $1,210 = $2,310).

Now suppose that you expand your investment horizon to three years and invest $1,000 today, $1,000 a year from now, and $1,000 at the end of two years. How much money will you have at the end of three years? First, we draw a time line to be sure that we have correctly identified the time period for each cash flow. This is shown in Exhibit 5.8. Then we compute the future value of each of the individual cash flows using Equation 5.1. Finally, we add up the future values. The total future value is $3,641. The calculations are as follows:

$$
\begin{aligned}
FV_1 &= PV \times (1 + i) &&= \$1,000 \times (1 + 0.10) &&= \$1,000 \times 1.100 &&= \$1,100 \\
FV_2 &= PV \times (1 + i)^2 &&= \$1,000 \times (1 + 0.10)^2 &&= \$1,000 \times 1.210 &&= \$1,210 \\
FV_3 &= PV \times (1 + i)^3 &&= \$1,000 \times (1 + 0.10)^3 &&= \$1,000 \times 1.331 &&= \underline{\$1,331} \\
&&&&&\text{Total future value} &&\overline{\$3,641}
\end{aligned}
$$

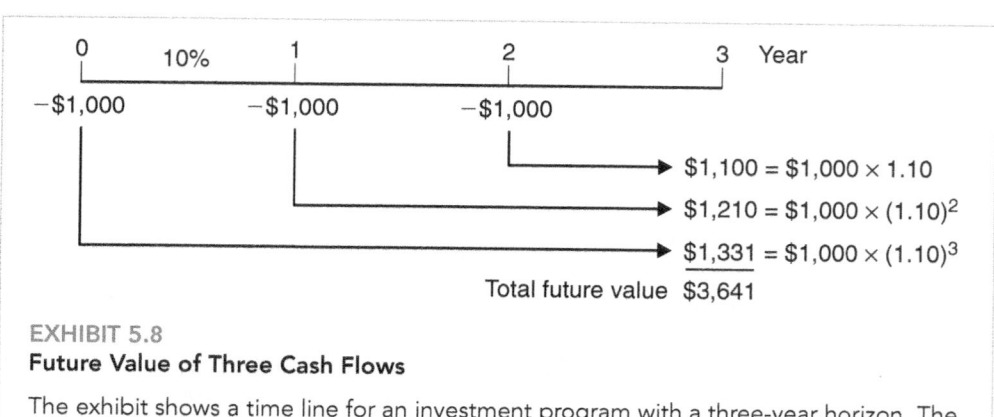

EXHIBIT 5.8

Future Value of Three Cash Flows

The exhibit shows a time line for an investment program with a three-year horizon. The value of the investment at the end of three years is $3,641, the sum of the future values of the three separate cash flows.

To summarize, solving future value problems with multiple cash flows involves a simple process. First, draw a time line to make sure that each cash flow is placed in the correct time period. Second, calculate the future value of each cash flow for its time period. Third, add up the future values.

Let's use this process to solve a practical problem. Suppose you want to buy a condominium in three years and estimate that you will need $20,000 for a down payment. If the interest rate you can earn at the bank is 8 percent and you can save $3,000 now, $4,000 at the end of the first year, and $5,000 at the end of the second year, how much money will you have to come up with at the end of the third year to have a $20,000 down payment?

The time line for the future value calculation in this problem looks like this:

To solve the problem, we need to calculate the future value for each of the cash flows, add up these values, and find the difference between this amount and the $20,000 needed for the down payment. Using Equation 5.1, we find that the future values of the cash flows at the end of the third year are:

$$FV_1 = PV \times (1 + i) = \$5,000 \times 1.08 = \$5,000 \times 1.0800 = \$\ 5,400.00$$
$$FV_2 = PV \times (1 + i)^2 = \$4,000 \times (1.08)^2 = \$4,000 \times 1.1664 = \$\ 4,665.60$$
$$FV_3 = PV \times (1 + i)^3 = \$3,000 \times (1.08)^3 = \$3,000 \times 1.2597 = \underline{\$\ 3,779.14}$$
$$\text{Total future value}\quad \$13,844.74$$

At the end of the third year, you will have $13,844.74, so you will need an additional $6,155.26 ($20,000 − $13,844.74 = $6,155.26) at that time to make the down payment.

Bidding on a Contract to Rebuild a Bridge

PROBLEM: The firm you work for is considering bidding on a government contract to rebuild an old bridge that has reached the end of its useful life. The two-year contract will pay the firm $11,000 at the end of the second year. The firm's estimator believes that the project will require an initial expenditure of $7,000 for equipment. The expenses for years 1 and 2 are estimated at $1,500 per year. Because the cash inflow of $11,000 at the end of the contract exceeds the total cash outflows of $10,000 ($7,000 + $1,500 + $1,500 = $10,000), the estimator believes that the firm should accept the job. Drawing on your knowledge of finance from college, you point out that the estimator's decision process ignores the time value of money. Not fully understanding what you mean, the estimator asks you how the time value of money should be incorporated into the decision process. Assume that the appropriate interest rate is 8 percent.

APPROACH: First, construct the time line for the costs in this problem, as shown here:

```
 0            8%          1                    2     Year
 ├───────────────────────┼────────────────────┤
-$7,000                -$1,500              -$1,500  FV = ?
```

Second, use Equation 5.1 to convert all of the cash outflows into year-two dollars. This will make all the cash flows comparable. Finally, compare the sum of the cash outflows, stated in year-two dollars, to the $11,000 that you would receive under the contract in year two.

SOLUTION:

$$FV_2 = PV \times (1 + i)^2 = -\$7,000 \times (1.08)^2 = -\$7,000 \times 1.1664 = -\$\ 8,165$$
$$FV_1 = PV \times (1 + i) = -\$1,500 \times 1.08 = -\$1,500 \times 1.0800 = -\$\ 1,620$$
$$FV_0 = PV \times (1 + i)^0 = -\$1,500 \times (1.08)^0 = -\$1,500 \times 1.0000 = \underline{-\$\ 1,500}$$
$$\text{Total net future value}\quad -\$11,285$$

Once the future value calculations have been made, the decision is self-evident. With all the dollars stated as year-two dollars, the cash inflow (benefits) is $11,000 and the cash outflow (costs) is $11,285. Thus, the costs exceed the benefits, and the firm's management should reject the contract. If management accepts the contract, the value of the firm will decline by $285 ($11,000 − $11,285 = −$285).

LEARNING BY DOING

APPLICATION 5.3

NEED MORE HELP?

WileyPLUS

Calculator Tip: Calculating the Future Value of Multiple Cash Flows

To calculate the future value of multiple cash flows with a financial calculator, we can use exactly the same process we used earlier in this chapter. We simply calculate the future value of each of the individual cash flows, write down each computed future value, and add them up.

Alternatively, we can generally use a shortcut. More than likely, your financial calculator has a memory where you can store numbers; refer to your calculator's instruction manual for the keys to use. For the preceding example, you would use your financial calculator's memory (M) as follows: Calculate the future value of the first number, then store the value in the memory (M1); compute the second value, and store it in the memory (M2); compute the third value, and store it in the memory (M3). Finally, retrieve the three numbers from the memory and add them up (M1 + M2 + M3).

Present Value of Multiple Cash Flows

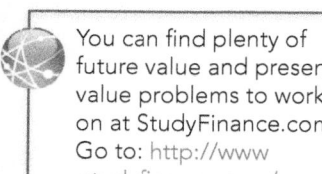
You can find plenty of future value and present value problems to work on at StudyFinance.com. Go to: http://www .studyfinance.com/ lectures/timevalue/ index.mv.

In business situations, we often need to compute the present value of a series of future cash flows. We do this, for example, to determine the market price of a bond, to decide whether to purchase a new machine, or to determine the value of a business. Solving present value problems involving multiple cash flows is similar to solving future value problems involving multiple cash flows. First, we prepare a time line so that we can see the magnitude and timing of the cash flows. Second, we calculate the present value of each individual cash flow using Equation 5.4: $PV = FV_n/(1 + i)^n$. Finally, we add up the present values. The sum of the present values of a stream of future cash flows is their current market price, or value. There is nothing new here!

Using the Present Value Equation

Let's work through some examples to see how we can use Equation 5.4 to find the present value of multiple cash flows. Suppose that your best friend needs cash and offers to pay you $1,000 at the end of each of the next three years if you will give him $3,000 cash today. You realize, of course, that because of the time value of money, the cash flows he has promised to pay are worth less than $3,000. If the interest rate on similar loans is 7 percent, how much should you pay for the cash flows your friend is offering?

To solve the problem, we first construct a time line, as shown in Exhibit 5.9.

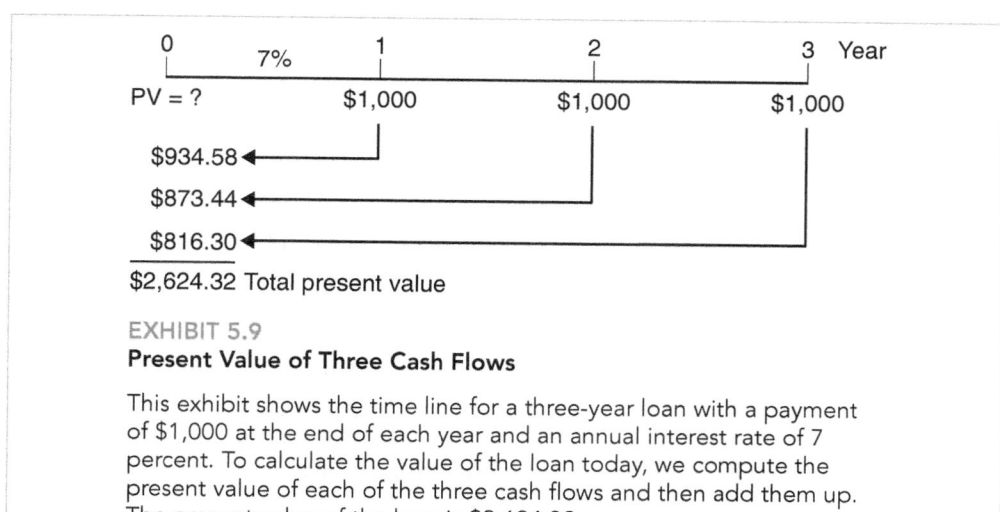

EXHIBIT 5.9
Present Value of Three Cash Flows

This exhibit shows the time line for a three-year loan with a payment of $1,000 at the end of each year and an annual interest rate of 7 percent. To calculate the value of the loan today, we compute the present value of each of the three cash flows and then add them up. The present value of the loan is $2,624.32.

Then, using Equation 5.4, we calculate the present value for each of the three cash flows, as follows:

$$PV = FV_1 \times 1/(1 + i) = FV_1 \times 1/1.07 = \$1,000 \times 0.9346 = \$\ 934.58$$
$$PV = FV_2 \times 1/(1 + i)^2 = FV_2 \times 1/(1.07)^2 = \$1,000 \times 0.8734 = \$\ 873.44$$
$$PV = FV_3 \times 1/(1 + i)^3 = FV_3 \times 1/(1.07)^3 = \$1,000 \times 0.8163 = \$\ 816.30$$
$$\text{Total present value} \quad \$2,624.32$$

If you view this transaction from a purely business perspective, you should not give your friend more than $2,624.32, which is the sum of the individual discounted cash flows.

Now let's consider another example. Suppose you have the opportunity to buy a small business while you are in school. The business involves selling sandwiches, soft drinks, and snack foods to students from a truck that you drive around campus. The annual cash flows from the business have been predictable. You believe you can expand the business, and you estimate that cash flows will be as follows: $2,000 in the first year, $3,000 in the second and third years, and $4,000 in the fourth year. At the end of the fourth year, the business will be closed down because the truck and other equipment will need to be replaced. The total of the estimated cash flows is $12,000. You did some research and found that a 10 percent discount rate would be appropriate. How much should you pay for the business?

To value the business, we compute the present value of the expected cash flows, discounted at 10 percent. The time line for the investment is:

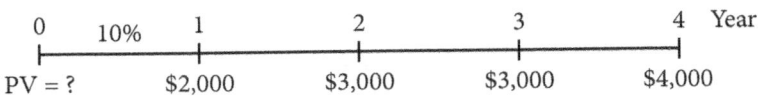

We compute the present value of each cash flow and then add them up:

$$PV = FV_1 \times 1/(1 + i) = \$2,000 \times 1/1.10 = \$2,000 \times 0.9091 = \$1,818.18$$
$$PV = FV_2 \times 1/(1 + i)^2 = \$3,000 \times 1/(1.10)^2 = \$3,000 \times 0.8264 = \$2,479.34$$
$$PV = FV_3 \times 1/(1 + i)^3 = \$3,000 \times 1/(1.10)^3 = \$3,000 \times 0.7513 = \$2,253.94$$
$$PV = FV_4 \times 1/(1 + i)^4 = \$4,000 \times 1/(1.10)^4 = \$4,000 \times 0.6830 = \$2,732.05$$
$$\text{Total present value} \quad \$9,283.51$$

This tells us that the present value of the expected cash flows is $9,283.51. If you pay $9,283.51 for the business, you will earn a return of exactly 10 percent. Of course, you should buy the business for the lowest price possible, but you should never pay more than the $9,283.51 value today of the expected cash flows. If you do, you will be paying more than the investment is worth.

You should note that from this point forward we will use a different notation. Up to this point, we have used the notation FV_n to represent a cash flow in period n. We have done this to stress that, for $n > 0$, we were referring to a future value. From this point on, we will use the notation CF_n instead of FV_n, because the CF_n notation is more commonly used by financial analysts. When you work through Learning by Doing Application 5.4, you will see the new notation.

Calculator Tip: Calculating the Present Value of Multiple Cash Flows

To calculate the present value of future cash flows with a financial calculator, we use exactly the same process we used in finding the future value, except that we solve for the present value instead of the future value. We can compute the present values of the individual cash flows, save them in the calculator's memory, and then add them up to obtain the total present value.

Buying a Used Car—Help!

PROBLEM: For a student—or anyone else—buying a used car can be a harrowing experience. Once you find the car you want, the next difficult decision is choosing how to pay for it—cash or a loan. Suppose the cash price you have negotiated for the car is $5,600, but that amount will stretch your budget for the year. The dealer says, "No problem. The car is yours for $4,000 down and payments of $1,000 per year for the next two years. Or you can put $2,000 down and pay $2,000 per year for two years. The choice is yours." Which offer is the best deal? The interest rate you can earn on your money is 8 percent.

APPROACH: In this problem, there are three alternative streams of cash flows. We need to convert all of the cash flows (CF_n) into today's dollars (present value) and select the alternative with the lowest present value (price). The time line for the three alternatives, along with the cash flows for each, is as follows:

```
   0            8%          1                    2  Year
   ├────────────────────────┼────────────────────┤
Cash price or down payment  CF₁                  CF₂
```

The cash flows at time zero represent the cash price of the car in the case of alternative A and the down payment in the cases of alternatives B and C.

	Cash Price or Down Payment	CF_1	CF_2	Total
Alternative A	−$5,600	—	—	−$5,600
Alternative B	−$4,000	−$1,000	−$1,000	−$6,000
Alternative C	−$2,000	−$2,000	−$2,000	−$6,000

Now we can use Equation 5.4 to find the present value of each alternative.

SOLUTION:

Alternative A:

$$-\$5,600 \times 1/(1.08)^0 = -\$5,600.00$$

Alternative B:

$$-\$4,000 \times 1/(1.08)^0 = -\$4,000.00$$
$$-\$1,000 \times 1/1.08 = -\$ \ 925.93$$
$$-\$1,000 \times 1/(1.08)^2 = -\$ \ 857.34$$
$$\text{Total} \quad -\$5,783.27$$

Alternative C:

$$-\$2,000 \times 1/(1.08)^0 = -\$2,000.00$$
$$-\$2,000 \times 1/1.08 = -\$1,851.85$$
$$-\$2,000 \times 1/(1.08)^2 = -\$1,714.68$$
$$\text{Total} \quad -\$5,566.53$$

Once we have converted the three cash flow streams to present values, the answer is clear. Alternative C has the lowest cost, in present value terms, and is the alternative you should choose.

> **BEFORE YOU GO ON**

1. Explain how to calculate the future value of a stream of cash flows.

2. Explain how to calculate the present value of a stream of cash flows.

3. Why is it important to adjust all cash flows to a common date?

5.5 LEVEL CASH FLOWS: ANNUITIES AND PERPETUITIES

LEARNING OBJECTIVE   5

In finance we commonly encounter contracts that call for the payment of equal amounts of cash over several time periods. For example, most business term loans and insurance policies require the holder to make a series of equal payments, usually monthly. Similarly, nearly all consumer loans, such as auto, personal, and home mortgage loans, call for equal monthly payments. Any financial contract that calls for equally spaced and level cash flows over a finite number of periods is called an **annuity**. If the cash flow payments continue forever, the contract is called a **perpetuity**. Most annuities are structured so that cash payments are received at the end of each period. Because this is the most common structure, these annuities are often called **ordinary annuities**.

annuity
a series of equally spaced and level cash flows extending over a finite number of periods

perpetuity
a series of level cash flows that continue forever

ordinary annuity
an annuity in which payments are made at the ends of the periods

Present Value of an Annuity

We frequently need to find the **present value of an annuity (PVA)**. Suppose, for example, that a financial contract pays $2,000 at the end of each year for three years and the appropriate discount rate is 8 percent. The time line for the contract is:

present value of an annuity (PVA)
the present value of the cash flows from an annuity, discounted at the appropriate discount rate

```
 0      8%      1            2            3   Year
 ├──────────────┼────────────┼────────────┤
PV = ?        $2,000       $2,000       $2,000
```

What is the most we should pay for this annuity? We have worked problems like this one before. All we need to do is calculate the present value of each individual cash flow (CF_n) and add them up. Using Equation 5.4, we find that the present value of the three-year annuity (PVA_3) at 8 percent interest is:

$$PVA_3 = \left[CF_1 \times \frac{1}{1+i} \right] + \left[CF_2 \times \frac{1}{(1+i)^2} \right] + \left[CF_3 \times \frac{1}{(1+i)^3} \right]$$

$$= \left[\$2{,}000 \times \frac{1}{1.08} \right] + \left[\$2{,}000 \times \frac{1}{(1.08)^2} \right] + \left[\$2{,}000 \times \frac{1}{(1.08)^3} \right]$$

$$= \$1{,}851.85 + \$1{,}714.68 + \$1{,}587.66$$

$$= \$5{,}154.19$$

This approach to computing the present value of an annuity works as long as the number of cash flows is relatively small. In many situations that involve annuities, however, the number of cash flows is large, and doing the calculations by hand would be tedious. For example, a typical 30-year home mortgage has 360 monthly payments (12 months per year $\times$ 30 years = 360 months).

Fortunately, our problem can be simplified because the cash flows (CF) for an annuity are all the same ($CF_1 = CF_2 = \cdots = CF_n = CF$). Thus, the present value of an annuity (PVA_n) with n equal cash flows (CF) at interest rate i is the sum of the individual present value calculations:

$$PVA_n = \left[CF \times \frac{1}{1+i} \right] + \left[CF \times \frac{1}{(1+i)^2} \right] + \cdots + \left[CF \times \frac{1}{(1+i)^n} \right]$$

With some mathematical manipulations that are beyond the scope of this discussion, we can simplify this equation to yield a useful formula for the present value of an annuity:

$$PVA_n = \frac{CF}{i} \times \left[1 - \frac{1}{(1+i)^n} \right] \tag{5.5}$$

$$= CF \times \left[\frac{1 - 1/(1+i)^n}{i} \right]$$

WileyPLUS

TIME VALUE OF MONEY:
AN ANIMATED TUTORIAL

where:

PVA_n = present value of an n period annuity
CF = level and equally spaced cash flow
i = discount rate, or interest rate
n = number of periods (often called the annuity's maturity)

Notice in Equation 5.5 that $1/(1 + i)^n$ is a term you have already encountered: It is the present value factor. Thus, we can also write Equation 5.5 as follows:

$$PVA_n = CF \times \frac{1 - \text{Present value factor}}{i}$$

where the term on the right is what we call the PV annuity factor:

$$PV\,\text{annuity factor} = \frac{1 - \text{Present value factor}}{i}$$

It follows that yet another way to state Equation 5.5 is:

$$PVA_n = CF \times PV\,\text{annuity factor}$$

Visit New York Life Insurance Company's Web site to learn more about investment products that pay out annuities: http://www .newyorklife.com.

Let's apply Equation 5.5 to the example involving a three-year annuity with a $2,000 annual cash flow. To solve for PVA_n, we first compute the PV annuity factor for three years at 8 percent. The calculation is made in two steps:

1. Calculate the present value factor for three years at 8 percent:

$$\begin{aligned}
\text{Present value factor} &= \frac{1}{(1 + i)^n} \\
&= \frac{1}{(1 + 0.08)^3} \\
&= \frac{1}{1.2597} \\
&= 0.7938
\end{aligned}$$

2. Use the present value factor to calculate the PV annuity factor:

$$\begin{aligned}
PV\,\text{annuity factor} &= \frac{1 - \text{Present value factor}}{i} \\
&= \frac{1 - 0.7938}{0.08} \\
&= 2.577
\end{aligned}$$

Investopedia is a great Web site for learning about a variety of finance topics. For example, you can find a discussion of annuities at
http://www.investopedia .com/articles/03/101503 .asp.

We now can calculate PVA_3 by plugging our values into the equation:

$$\begin{aligned}
PVA_3 &= CF \times PV\,\text{annuity factor} \\
&= \$2,000 \times 2.577 \\
&= \$5,154.00
\end{aligned}$$

This is almost the same as the $5,154.19 we calculated by hand earlier. The difference is due to rounding.

Calculator Tip: Finding the Present Value of an Annuity

There are four variables in a present value of an annuity equation (PVA_n, CF, n, and i), and if you know three of them, you can solve for the fourth in a few seconds with a financial calculator. The calculator key that you have not used so far is the PMT (payment) key, which is the key for level cash flows over the life of an annuity.

To illustrate problem solving with a financial calculator, we will revisit the financial contract that paid $2,000 per year for three years, discounted at 8 percent. To find the present value of the contract, we enter 8 percent for the interest rate (i), $2,000 for the payment (PMT), and 3 for the number of periods (N). The key for FV is not relevant for this calculation, so we enter zero into this register to clear it. The key entries and the answer are as follows:

Enter	3	8		2,000	0
	N	i	PV	PMT	FV
Answer			−5,154.19		

The price of the contract is $5,154.19, which agrees with our other calculations. As discussed earlier, the negative sign on the financial calculator box indicates that $5,154.19 is a cash outflow.

Computing a PV Annuity Factor

PROBLEM: Compute the PV annuity factor for 30 years at a 10 percent interest rate.

APPROACH: First, we calculate the present value factor at 10 percent for 30 years. Then, using this value, we calculate the PV annuity factor.

SOLUTION:

$$
\text{Present value factor} = \frac{1}{(1 + i)^n}
$$

$$
= \frac{1}{(1.10)^{30}}
$$

$$
= \frac{1}{17.4494}
$$

$$
= 0.0573
$$

Using this value, we calculate the PV annuity factor to be:

$$
\text{PV annuity factor} = \frac{1 - \text{Present value factor}}{i}
$$

$$
= \frac{1 - 0.0573}{0.10}
$$

$$
= 9.427
$$

We worked through the tedious calculations to show where the numbers come from and how the calculations are made. Financial analysts typically use financial calculators or spreadsheet programs for these calculations. You might check the answer to this problem using your calculator.

PV Annuity Factor Tables

Just as financial analysts used to use future value and present value factor tables to help with future value and present value calculations, they also used PV annuity factor tables, which contain PV annuity factors for a range of interest rates and annuity lengths. Table A-4 in Appendix A is an example of a PV annuity factor table.

Finding Monthly or Yearly Payments

A very common problem in finance is determining the payment schedule for a loan on a consumer asset, such as a car or a home that was purchased on credit. Nearly all consumer loans call for equal monthly payments. Suppose, for example, that you have just purchased a $450,000 condominium in Miami's South Beach district. You were able to put $50,000 down and obtain a 30-year fixed rate mortgage at 6.125 percent for the balance. What are your monthly payments?

In this problem we know the present value of the annuity. It is $400,000, the price of the condominium less the down payment ($450,000 − $50,000 = $400,000). We also know the number of payments; since the payments will be made monthly for 30 years, you will make 360 payments (12 months per year × 30 years = 360 months). Because the payments are monthly, both the interest rate and maturity must be expressed in monthly terms. For consumer loans, to get the monthly interest rate, we divide the annual interest rate by 12. Thus, the monthly interest rate equals 0.51042 percent (6.125 percent per year/12 months per year = 0.51042 percent per month). What we need to calculate is the monthly cash payment (CF) over the loan period. The time line looks like the following:

To find CF (remember that $CF_1 = CF_2 = \cdots = CF_{360} = CF$), we use Equation 5.5. We need to make two preliminary calculations:

1. First, we calculate the present value factor for 360 months at 0.51042 percent per month (or, in decimal form, 0.0051042):

$$
\begin{aligned}
\text{Present value factor} &= \frac{1}{(1 + i)^n} \\
&= \frac{1}{(1.0051042)^{360}} \\
&= \frac{1}{6.25160595} \\
&= 0.1599589
\end{aligned}
$$

2. Next, we solve for the PV annuity factor:

$$
\begin{aligned}
\text{PV annuity factor} &= \frac{1 - \text{Present value factor}}{i} \\
&= \frac{1 - 0.1599589}{0.0051042} \\
&= \frac{0.8400411}{0.0051042} \\
&= 164.578406
\end{aligned}
$$

We can now plug all the data into Equation 5.5 and solve it for CF:

$$
\begin{aligned}
\text{PVA}_n &= CF \times \text{PV annuity factor} \\
\$400,000 &= CF \times 164.578406 \\
CF &= \frac{\$400,000}{164.578406} \\
CF &= \$2,430.45
\end{aligned}
$$

Your mortgage payments will be about $2,430.45 per month.

Solving the problem on a financial calculator takes only a few seconds once the time line is prepared. The most common error students make when using financial calculators is failing to convert all contract variables to be consistent with the compounding period. If the contract calls for monthly payments, the interest rate and contract duration must be stated in monthly terms.

Having converted our data to monthly terms, we enter the following into the calculator: N = 360 months (30 years × 12 months per year = 360 months), i = 0.51042 (6.125 percent per year/12 months per year = 0.51042 percent per month), PV = $400,000, and FV = 0 (to clear the register). Then, pressing the payment button (PMT), we find the answer, which is −$2,430.44. The keystrokes are:

Enter	360	0.51042	400,000		0
	N	i	PV	PMT	FV
Answer				−2,430.44	

Notice that the hand and financial calculator answers differ by only 1 cent ($2,430.45 − $2,430.44 = $0.01). The answers are so close because when doing the hand calculation, we carried six to eight decimal places through the entire set of calculations. Had we rounded off each number as the calculations were made, the difference between the answers from the two calculation methods would have been about $2.00. The more numbers that are rounded during the calculations, the greater the possible rounding error.

Preparing a Loan Amortization Schedule

Once you understand how to calculate a monthly or yearly loan payment, you have all of the tools that you need to prepare a loan amortization schedule. The term *amortization* describes the way in which the principal (the amount borrowed) is repaid over the life of a loan. With an

What Are Your Monthly Car Payments?

PROBLEM: You have decided to buy a new car, and the dealer's best price is $16,000. The dealer agrees to provide financing with a five-year auto loan at 3 percent interest. Using a financial calculator, calculate your monthly payments.

APPROACH: All the problem data must be converted to monthly terms. The number of periods is 60 months (5 years × 12 months per year = 60 months), and the monthly interest charge is 0.25 percent (3 percent per year/12 months per year = 0.25 percent per month). The time line for the car purchase is as follows:

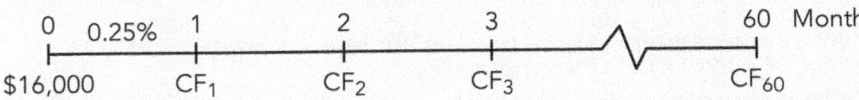

Having converted our data to monthly terms, we enter the following values into the calculator: N = 60 months, i = 0.25, PV = $16,000, and FV = 0 (to clear the register). Pressing the payment key (PMT) will give us the answer.

SOLUTION:

Note that since we entered $16,000 as a positive number (because it is a cash inflow to you), the monthly payment of $287.50 is a negative number.

---

amortizing loan, some portion of each month's loan payment goes to paying down the principal. When the final loan payment is made, the unpaid principal is reduced to zero and the loan is paid off. The other portion of each loan payment is interest, which is payment for the use of outstanding principal (the amount of money still owed). Thus, with an **amortizing loan**, each loan payment contains some repayment of principal and an interest payment. Nearly all loans to consumers are amortizing loans.

A loan **amortization schedule** is just a table that shows the loan balance at the beginning and end of each period, the payment made during that period, and how much of that payment represents interest and how much represents repayment of principal. To see how an amortization schedule is prepared, consider an example. Suppose that to purchase a car you have just borrowed $10,000 at a 5 percent interest rate from a bank. Typically, you would make monthly payments on such a loan. For simplicity, however, we will assume that the bank allows you to make annual payments and that the loan will be repaid over five years. Exhibit 5.10 shows the amortization schedule for this loan.

To prepare a loan amortization schedule, we must first compute the loan payment. Since, for consumer loans, the amount of the loan payment is fixed, all the payments are identical in amount. Applying Equation 5.5 we calculate the payment as follows:

$$PVA_n = CF \times \frac{1 - 1/(1 + i)^n}{i}$$

$$\$10,000 = CF \times \frac{1 - 1/(1 + 0.05)^5}{0.05}$$

$$\$10,000 = CF \times 4.329$$

$$CF = \frac{\$10,000}{4.329}$$

$$CF = \$2,310.00 \text{ per year}$$

Alternatively, we enter in a financial calculator the values N = 5 years, i = 5 percent, and PV = $10,000 and then press the PMT key to solve for the loan payment amount. The answer

amortizing loan
a loan for which each loan payment contains repayment of some principal and a payment of interest that is based on the remaining principal to be repaid

amortization schedule
a table that shows the loan balance at the beginning and end of each period, the payment made during that period, and how much of that payment represents interest and how much represents repayment of principal

Year	(1) Beginning Principal Balance	(2) Total Annual Payment[a]	(3) Interest Paid[b]	(4) Principal Paid (2)–(3)	(5) Ending Principal Balance (1)–(4)
1	$10,000.00	$2,309.75	$500.00	$1,809.75	$8,190.25
2	8,190.25	2,309.75	409.51	1,900.24	6,290.02
3	6,290.02	2,309.75	314.50	1,995.25	4,294.77
4	4,294.77	2,309.75	214.74	2,095.01	2,199.76
5	2,199.76	2,309.75	109.99	2,199.76	0.00

[a]The total annual payment is calculated using the formula for the present value of an annuity, Equation 5.5. The total annual payment is CF in $PVA_n = CF \times PV$ annuity factor.

[b]Interest paid equals the beginning balance times the interest rate.

EXHIBIT 5.10

Amortization Table for a Five-Year, $10,000 Loan at 5 Percent Interest

A loan amortization table shows how regular payments of principal and interest are applied to repay a loan. The exhibit is an amortization table for a five-year, $10,000 loan with an interest rate of 5 percent and annual payments of $2,309.75. Notice that the interest paid declines with each payment, while the principal paid increases.

is −$2,309.75 per year. The difference between the two answers results from rounding. For the amortization table calculation, we will use the more precise answer from the financial calculator.

Turning to Exhibit 5.10, we can work through the amortization schedule to see how the table is prepared. For the first year, the values are determined as follows:

1. The amount borrowed, or the beginning principal balance (P_0), is $10,000.

2. The annual loan payment, as calculated earlier, is $2,309.75.

3. The interest payment for the first year is $500 and is calculated as follows:

$$\text{Interest payment} = i \times P_0 = 0.05 \times \$10,000 = \$500$$

4. The principal paid for the year is $1,809.75, calculated as follows:

$$\text{Principal paid} = \text{Loan payment} - \text{Interest payment} = \$2,309.75 - \$500 = \$1,809.75$$

5. The ending principal balance is $8,190.25, computed as follows:

$$\text{Ending principal balance} = \text{Begining principal balance} - \text{Principal paid}$$
$$= \$10,000 - \$1,809.75$$
$$= 8,190.25$$

Note that the ending principal balance for the first year ($8,190.25) becomes the beginning principal balance for the second year ($8,190.25), which in turn is used in calculating the interest payment for the second year:

$$\text{Interest payment} = i \times P_1 = 0.05 \times \$8,190.25 = \$409.51$$

This calculation makes sense because each loan payment includes some principal repayment. This is why the interest in column 3 declines each year. We repeat the calculations until the loan is fully amortized, at which point the principal balance goes to zero and the loan is paid off.

Note, in Exhibit 5.10, the amounts of interest and principal that are paid each year change over time. Interest payments are greatest in the early years of an amortizing loan because much of the principal has not yet been repaid (see columns 1 and 3). However, as the principal balance is reduced over time, the interest payments decline and more of each payment goes toward paying down the principal (see columns 3 and 4).

LOAN AMORTIZATION TABLE

Loan amortization tables are most easily constructed using a spreadsheet program. Here, we have reconstructed the loan amortization table shown in Exhibit 5.10 using Excel.

Notice that all the values in the amortization table are obtained by using formulas. Once you have built an amortization table like this one, you can change any of the input variables, such as the loan amount or the interest rate, and all of the other numbers will automatically be updated.

	A	B	C	D	E	F	G	H	I	J	K	L	M
1													
2							Loan Amortization Table						
3													
4		Loan amount		$10,000									
5		Interest rate		0.05									
6		Loan period		5									
7		PMT		$2,309.75									
8						Total							
9		Year		Beginning Balance		Annual Payment		Simple Interest Paid		Principal Paid		Ending Balance	
10		1		$10,000.00		$2,309.75		$500.00		$1,809.75		$8,190.25	
11		2		8,190.25		2,309.75		409.51		1,900.24		6,290.02	
12		3		6,290.02		2,309.75		314.50		1,995.25		4,294.77	
13		4		4,294.77		2,309.75		214.74		2,095.01		2,199.76	
14		5		2,199.76		2,309.75		109.99		2,199.76		0.00	
15													
16	Corresponding formulas:												
17													
18		PMT		=PMT(D5, D6, -D4)									
19						Total							
20		Year		Beginning Balance		Annual Payment		Simple Interest Paid		Principal Paid		Ending Balance	
21		1		=D4		=$D$7		=D10*$D$5		=F10-H10		=D10-J10	
22		2		=L10		=$D$7		=D11*$D$5		=F11-H11		=D11-J11	
23		3		=L11		=$D$7		=D12*$D$5		=F12-H12		=D12-J12	
24		4		=L12		=$D$7		=D13*$D$5		=F13-H13		=D13-J13	
25		5		=L13		=$D$7		=D14*$D$5		=F14-H14		=D14-J14	
26													

If we were preparing an amortization table for monthly payments, all of the principal balances, loan payments, and interest rates would have to be adjusted to a monthly basis. For example, to calculate monthly payments for our auto loan, we would make the following adjustments: $n = 60$ payments (12 months per year $\times$ 5 years $=$ 60 months), $i = 0.4167$ percent (5 percent per year/12 months per year $=$ 0.4167 percent per month), and monthly payment $=$ \$188.71.

Finding the Interest Rate

Another important calculation in finance is determining the interest, or discount, rate for an annuity. The interest rate tells us the rate of return on an annuity contract. For example, suppose your parents are getting ready to retire and decide to convert some of their retirement portfolio, which is invested in the stock market, into an annuity that guarantees them a fixed annual income. Their insurance agent asks for $350,000 for an annuity that guarantees to pay them $50,000 a year for 10 years. What is the rate of return on the annuity?

As we did when we found the payment amount, we can insert these values into Equation 5.5:

$$PVA_n = CF \times \frac{1 - 1/(1 + i)^n}{i}$$

$$\$350,000 = \$50,000 \times \frac{1 - 1/(1 + i)^{10}}{i}$$

To determine the rate of return for the annuity, we need to solve the equation for the unknown value i. Unfortunately, it is not possible to solve the resulting equation for i algebraically. The only way to solve the problem is by trial and error. We normally solve this kind of problem using a financial calculator or computer spreadsheet program that finds the solution for us. However, it is important to understand how the solution is arrived at by trial and error, so let's work this problem without such aids.

To start the process, we must select an initial value for i, plug it into the right side of the equation, and solve the equation to see if the present value of the annuity stream equals $350,000, which is the left side of the equation. If the present value of the annuity is too large (PVA > $350,000), we need to select a higher value for i. If the present value of the annuity stream is too small (PVA < $350,000), we need to select a smaller value. We continue the trial-and-error process until we find the value of i for which PVA = $350,000.

The key to getting started is to make the best guess we can as to the possible value of the interest rate given the information and data available to us. We will assume that the current bank savings rate is 4 percent. Since the annuity rate of return should exceed the bank rate, we will start our calculations with a 5 percent discount rate. The present value of the annuity is:

$$PVA = \$50,000 \times \frac{1 - 1/(1 + 0.05)^{10}}{0.05} = \$50,000 \times 7.722 = \$386,100$$

That's a pretty good first guess, but our present value is greater than $350,000, so we need to try a higher discount rate.[6] Let's try 7 percent:

$$PVA = \$50,000 \times \frac{1 - 1/(1 + 0.07)^{10}}{0.07} = \$50,000 \times 7.024 = \$351,200$$

The present value of the annuity is still slightly higher than $350,000, so we still need a larger value of i. How about 7.10 percent:

$$PVA = \$50,000 \times \frac{1 - 1(1 + 0.071)^{10}}{0.071} = \$50,000 \times 6.991 = \$349,550$$

The value is too small, but we now know that i is between 7.00 and 7.10 percent. On the next try, we need to use a slightly smaller value of i—say, 7.07 percent:

$$PVA = \$50,000 \times \frac{1 - 1/(1 + 0.0707)^{10}}{0.0707} = \$50,000 \times 7.001 = \$350,050$$

Since this value is slightly too high, we should try a number for i that is only slightly greater than 7.07 percent. We'll try 7.073 percent:

$$PVA = \$50,000 \times \frac{1 - 1/(1 + 0.07073)^{10}}{0.07073} = \$50,000 \times 7.000 = \$350,000$$

The cost of the annuity, $350,000, is now exactly the same as the present value of the annuity stream ($350,000); thus, 7.073 percent is the rate of return earned by the annuity.

It often takes more guesses to solve for the interest rate than it did in this example. Our "guesses" were good because we knew the answer before we started guessing! Clearly, solving for i by trial and error can be a long and tedious process. Fortunately, as mentioned, these types of problems are easily solved with a financial calculator or computer spreadsheet program. Next, we describe how to compute the interest rate or rate of return on an annuity on a financial calculator.

Calculator Tip: Finding the Interest Rate

To illustrate how to find the interest rate for an annuity on a financial calculator, we will enter the information from the previous example. We know the number of periods (N = 10), the payment amount (PMT = $50,000), and the present value (PV = −$350,000), and we want to solve for the interest rate (i):

Enter	10		−350,000	50,000	0
	N	i	PV	PMT	FV
Answer		7.073			

As with our calculations above, the interest rate is 7.073 percent.

---

[6]Notice that we have rounded the PV annuity factor to three decimal places (7.722). If we use a financial calculator and do not round, we get a more precise answer of $386,086.75.

Return on Investments: Good Deal or Bad?

PROBLEM: With some business opportunities you know the price of a financial contract and the promised cash flows, and you want to calculate the interest rate or rate of return on the investment. For example, suppose you have a chance to invest in a small business. The owner wants to borrow $200,000 from you for five years and will make yearly payments of $60,000 at the end of each year. Similar types of investment opportunities will pay 5 percent. Is this a good investment opportunity?

APPROACH: First, we draw a time line for this loan:

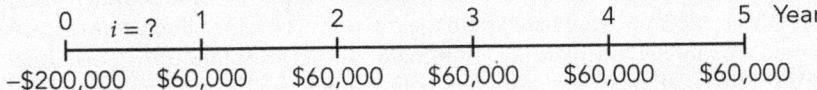

```
      0    i = ?   1        2        3        4        5  Year
      ├──────────┼────────┼────────┼────────┼────────┤
  -$200,000   $60,000  $60,000  $60,000  $60,000  $60,000
```

To compute the rate of return on the investment, we need to compute the interest rate that equates the initial investment of $200,000 to the present value of the promised cash flows of $60,000 per year. We can use the trial-and-error approach with Equation 5.5, a financial calculator, or a spreadsheet program (for example, using the RATE function in Excel) to solve this problem. Here we will use a financial calculator.

SOLUTION: The financial calculator steps are:

Enter   5   −200,000   60,000   0

Answer   15.24

The return on this investment is 15.24 percent, well above the market interest rate of 5 percent. It is a good investment opportunity.

The Pizza Dough Machine

SITUATION: As the owner of a pizza parlor, you are considering whether to buy a fully automated pizza dough preparation machine. Your staff is wildly supportive of the purchase because it would eliminate a tedious part of their work. Your accountant provides you with the following information:

- The cost, including shipping, for the pizza dough machine is $25,000.
- Cash savings, including labor, raw materials, and tax savings due to depreciation, are $3,500 per year for 10 years.
- The present value of the cash savings is $21,506 at a 10 percent discount rate.[7]

Given the above data, what should you do?

DECISION: As you arrive at the pizza parlor in the morning, the staff is in a festive mood because word has leaked out that the new machine will save the shop $35,000 and only cost $25,000.

With a heavy heart, you explain that the analysis done at the water cooler by some of the staff is incorrect. To make economic decisions involving cash flows, even for a small business such as your pizza parlor, you cannot compare cash values from different time periods unless they are adjusted for the time value of money. The present value formula takes into account the time value of money and converts the future cash flows into current dollars. The cost of the machine is already in current dollars.

The correct analysis is as follows: the machine costs $25,000, and the present value of the cost savings is $21,506. Thus, the cost of the machine exceeds the benefits; the correct decision is not to buy the new dough preparation machine.

---

[7]The annuity present value factor for 10 years at 10 percent is 6.1446. Thus, $PVA_{10} = CF \times$ Annuity factor $= \$3,500 \times 6.1446 = \$21,506.10$. Using a financial calculator, $PVA_{10} = \$21,505.98$. The difference is due to rounding errors.

Future Value of an Annuity

future value of an annuity (FVA)

the value of an annuity at some point in the future

Generally, when we are working with annuities, we are interested in computing their present value. On occasion, though, we need to compute the **future value of an annuity (FVA)**. Such computations typically involve some type of saving activity, such as a monthly savings plan. Another application is computing terminal values for retirement or pension plans with constant contributions.

We will start with a simple example. Suppose that you plan to save $1,000 at the end of every year for four years with the goal of buying a racing bicycle. The bike you want is a Colnago C50, a top-of-the-line Italian racing bike that costs around $4,500. If your bank pays 8 percent interest a year, will you have enough money to buy the bike at the end of four years?

To solve this problem, we can first lay out the cash flows on a time line, as we discussed earlier in this chapter. We can then calculate the future value for each cash flow using Equation 5.1, which is $FV_n = PV \times (1 + i)^n$. Finally, we can add up all the cash flows. The time line and calculations are shown in Exhibit 5.11. Given that the total future value of the four deposits is $4,506.11, as shown in the exhibit, you should have enough money to buy the bike.

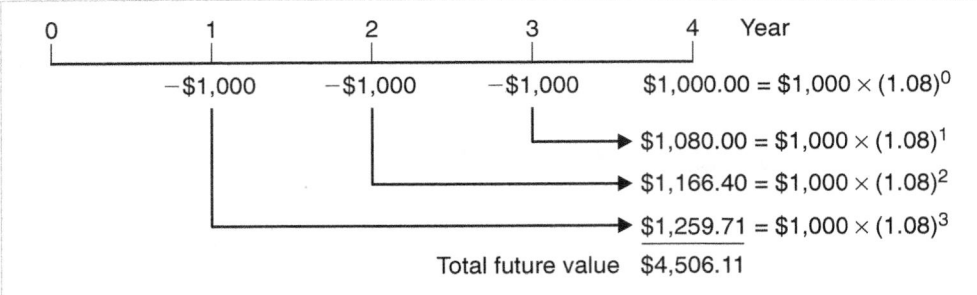

EXHIBIT 5.11
Future Value of a Four-Year Annuity: Colnago C50 Bicycle

The exhibit shows a time line for a savings plan to buy a Colnago C50 bicycle. Under this savings plan, $1,000 is invested at the end of each year for four years at an annual interest rate of 8 percent. We find the value at the end of the four-year period by adding the future values of the separate cash flows, just as in Exhibits 5.7 and 5.8.

Future Value of Annuity Equations

Of course, most business applications involve longer periods of time than the Colnago bike example. One way to solve more complex problems involving the future value of an annuity is first to calculate the present value of the annuity, PVA, using Equation 5.5, and then to use Equation 5.1 to calculate the future value of the PVA. In practice, many analyses condense this calculation into a single step by using the future value of annuity (FVA) formula, which we obtain by substituting PVA for PV in Equation 5.1.

$$FVA_n = PVA_n \times (1 + i)^n \tag{5.6}$$

$$= \frac{CF}{i} \times \left[1 - \frac{1}{(1 + i)^n} \right] \times (1 + i)^n$$

$$= \frac{CF}{i} \times \left[(1 + i)^n - 1 \right]$$

$$= CF \times \frac{(1 + i)^n - 1}{i}$$

where:

FVA_n = future value of an annuity at the end of n periods
PVA_n = present value of an n period annuity
CF = level and equally spaced cash flow
i = discount rate, or interest rate
n = number of periods

We can rearrange Equation 5.6 to write it in terms of the future value factor and the FV annuity factor:

$$FVA_n = CF \times \frac{(1 + i)^n - 1}{i}$$

$$= CF \times \frac{\text{Future value factor} - 1}{i}$$

$$= CF \times FV \text{ annuity factor}$$

As with PV annuity factors, there are tables listing FV annuity factors. Appendix A, at the back of this book, includes a table (Table A-3) that shows the future value annuity factor for various interest rates and annuity lengths (years).

Using Equation 5.6 to compute FVA for the Colnago bike problem is straightforward. The calculation and process are similar to those we developed for PVA problems. That is, we first calculate the FV annuity factor for four years at 8 percent:

$$\text{Future value factor} = (1 + i)^n = (1.08)^4 = 1.36049$$

$$FV \text{ annuity factor} = \frac{\text{Future value factor} - 1}{i} = \frac{1.36049 - 1}{0.08} = 4.5061$$

We then compute the future value of the annuity by multiplying the constant cash flow (CF) by the FV annuity factor. We plug our computed values into the equation:

$$FVA_n = CF \times FV \text{ annuity factor} = \$1,000 \times 4.5061 = \$4,506.10$$

This value differs slightly from the one we calculated in Exhibit 5.11 because of rounding.

Calculator Tip: Finding the Future Value of an Annuity

The procedure for calculating the future value of an annuity on a financial calculator is precisely the same as the procedure for calculating the present value of an annuity discussed earlier. The only difference is that we use the FV (future value) key instead of the PV (present value) key. The PV key is entered as a zero to clear the register.

Let's work the Colnago bicycle problem on a calculator. Recall that we decided to put $1,000 in the bank at the end of each year for four years. The bank pays 8 percent interest. Clear the financial register and make the following entries:

Enter	4	8	0	−1,000	
	N	i	PV	PMT	FV
Answer					4,506.11

The calculated value of $4,506.11 is the same as in Exhibit 5.11.

Perpetuities

LEARNING OBJECTIVE ⑥

A perpetuity is a constant stream of cash flows that goes on forever. Perpetuities in the form of bonds were used by the British Treasury Department to pay off the debt incurred by the government to finance the Napoleonic wars. These perpetual bonds, called *consols,* have no maturity date and are still traded in the international bond markets today. They will only be retired when the British Treasury repurchases them all in the open market.

The most important perpetuities in the securities markets today are preferred stock issues. The issuer of preferred stock promises to pay investors a fixed dividend forever unless a retirement date for the perferred stock has been set. Since, as we discussed in Chapter 1, a corporation can have an indefinite life, the expected cash flows from a corporation might also go on forever. When these expected cash flows are constant, they can be viewed as a perpetuity.

From Equation 5.5, we can calculate the present value of a perpetuity by setting n, which is the number of periods, equal to infinity (∞). When that is done, the value of the term $1/(1 + i)^\infty$ approaches 0, and thus the value of a perpetuity that begins next period (PVP) equals:

$$
\begin{aligned}
\text{PVP} &= \frac{\text{CF}}{i} \times \left[1 - \frac{1}{(1 + i)^\infty} \right] \qquad (5.7) \\
&= \frac{\text{CF}}{i} \times [1 - 0] \\
&= \frac{\text{CF}}{i}
\end{aligned}
$$

As you can see, the present value of a perpetuity is the promised constant cash payment (CF) divided by the interest rate (i). A nice feature of the final equation (PVP = CF/i) is that it is algebraically very simple to work with, since it allows us to solve for i directly rather than by trial and error, as is required with Equations 5.5 and 5.6.

To see how we use the perpetuity model, suppose you had a great experience during your studies at the school of business and decided to endow a scholarship fund for finance students. The goal of the fund is to provide the university with $100,000 of financial support each year forever. If the rate of interest is 8 percent, how much money will you have to give the university to provide the desired level of support? Using Equation 5.7, we find that the present value of the perpetuity is:

$$
\text{PVP} = \frac{\text{CF}}{i} = \frac{\$100,000}{0.08} = \$1,250,000
$$

Thus, a gift of $1.25 million will provide constant annual funding of $100,000 to the university forever.

Before we finish our discussion of perpetuities, we should point out that the present value of a perpetuity is typically not very different from the present value of a very long annuity. For example, suppose that instead of funding the scholarship forever, you only plan to fund it for 100 years.

LEARNING BY DOING

APPLICATION 5.8

Preferred Stock Dividends

PROBLEM: Suppose that you are the CEO of a public company and your investment banker recommends that you issue some preferred stock at $50 per share. Similar preferred stock issues are yielding 6 percent. What annual cash dividend does the firm need to offer to be competitive in the marketplace? In other words, what cash dividend paid annually forever would be worth $50 with a 6 percent discount rate?

APPROACH: As we have already mentioned, preferred stock is a type of perpetuity; thus, we can solve this problem by applying Equation 5.7. As usual, we begin by laying out the time line for the cash flows:

For preferred stock, PVP is the value of a share of stock, which is $50 per share. The discount rate is 6 percent. CF is the fixed-rate cash dividend, which is the unknown value. Knowing all this information, we can use Equation 5.7 and solve for CF.

SOLUTION:

$$
\text{PVP} = \frac{\text{CF}}{i}
$$

$$
\text{CF} = \text{PVP} \times i = \$50 \times 0.06 = \$3
$$

The annual dividend on the preferred stock would be $3 per share.

If you compute the present value of a 100-year annuity of $100,000 using an interest rate of 8 percent, you will find that it equals $1,249,431.76, which is only slightly less than the $1,250,000 value of the perpetuity. Making your gift a perpetuity would only cost you an additional $568.24. This is because the present value of the cash flows to be received after 100 years is extremely small. The key point here is that cash flows that are to be received far in the future can have very small present values.

Annuities Due

So far we have discussed annuities whose cash flow payments occur at the end of the period, so-called *ordinary annuities*. Another type of annuity that is fairly common in business is known as an **annuity due**. Here, cash payments start immediately, at the beginning of the first period. For example, when you rent an apartment, the first rent payment is typically due immediately. The second rent payment is due the first of the second month, and so on. In this kind of payment pattern, you are effectively prepaying for the service.

annuity due
an annuity in which payments are made at the beginning of each period

Exhibit 5.12 compares the cash flows for an ordinary annuity and an annuity due. Note that both annuities are made up of four $1,000 cash flows and carry an 8 percent interest rate.

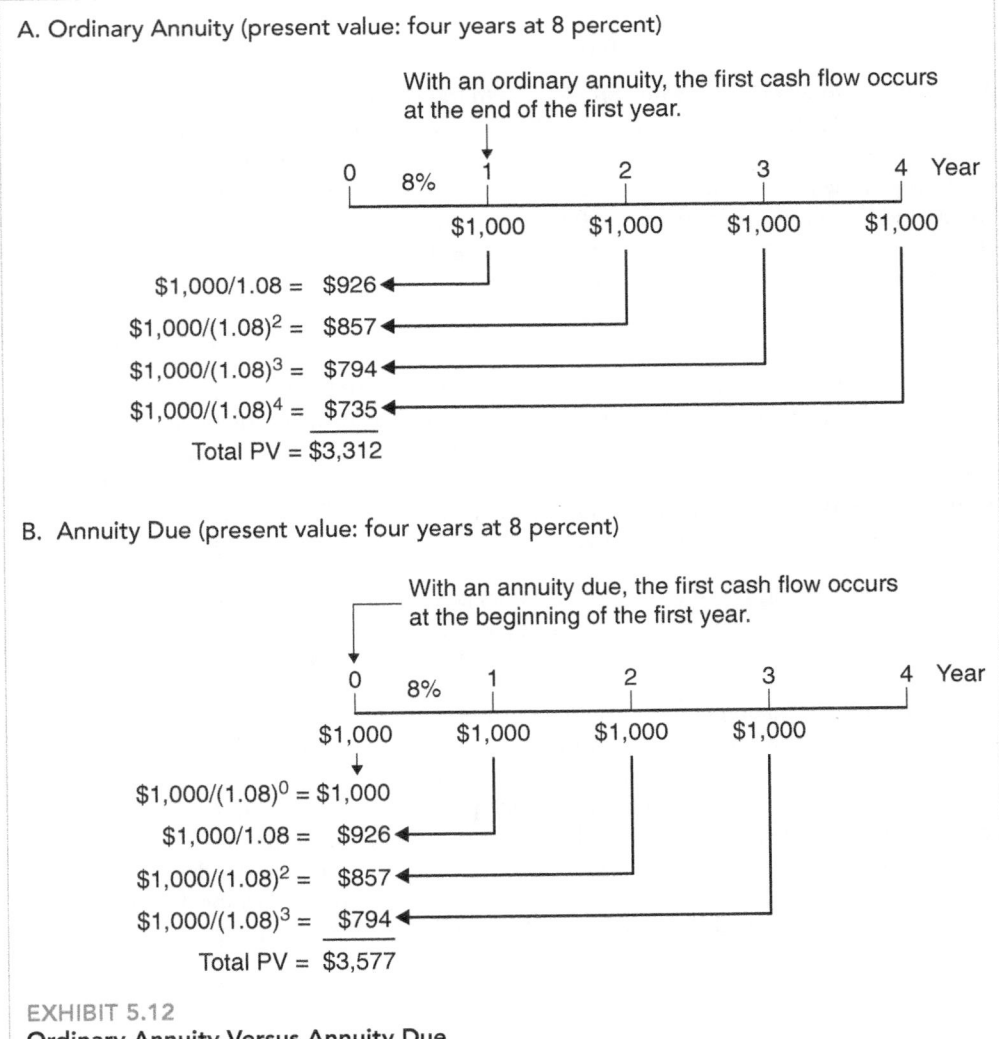

EXHIBIT 5.12
Ordinary Annuity Versus Annuity Due

The difference between an ordinary annuity (part A) and an annuity due (part B) is that with an ordinary annuity, the cash flows take place at the end of each period, while with an annuity due, the cash flows take place at the beginning of each period. As you can see in this example, the PV of the annuity due is larger than the PV of the ordinary annuity. The reason Is that the cash flows of the annuity due are shifted forward one year and thus are discounted less.

Part A shows an ordinary annuity, in which the cash flows take place at the end of the period, and part B shows an annuity due, in which the cash flows take place at the beginning of the period. There are several ways to calculate the present and future values of an annuity due, and we discuss them next.

Present Value Method

One way to compute the present value of an annuity due is to discount each individual cash flow to the present, as shown in Exhibit 5.12B. Note that since the first $1,000 cash flow takes place now, that cash flow is already in present value terms. The present value of the cash flows for the annuity due is $3,577.

Compare this present value with the present value of the cash flows for the ordinary annuity, $3,312, as calculated in Exhibit 5.12A. It should be no surprise that the present value of the annuity due is larger than the present value of the ordinary annuity ($3,577 > $3,312), even though both annuities have four $1,000 cash flows. The reason is that the cash flows of the annuity due are shifted forward one year and, thus, are discounted less.

Annuity Transformation Method

An easier way to work annuity due problems is to transform our formula for the present value of an annuity (Equation 5.5) so that it will work for annuity due problems. To do this, we pretend that each cash flow occurs at the end of the period (although it actually occurs at the beginning of the period) and use Equation 5.5. Since Equation 5.5 discounts each cash flow by one period too many, we then correct for the extra discounting by multiplying our answer by $(1 + i)$, where i is the discount rate or interest rate. The relation between an ordinary annuity and an annuity due can be formally expressed as:

$$\text{Annuity due value} = \text{Ordinary annuity value} \times (1 + i) \qquad (5.8)$$

Let's calculate the value of the annuity due shown in Exhibit 5.12B using Equation 5.8, the transformation technique. First, we restate the time line as if the problem were an ordinary annuity; the revised time line looks like the one in Exhibit 5.12A. Second, we calculate the present value of the annuity as if the problem involved an ordinary annuity. The value of the ordinary annuity is $3,312, as shown in part A of the exhibit. Finally, we use Equation 5.8 to make the adjustment to an annuity due:

$$
\begin{aligned}
\text{Annuity due value} &= \text{Ordinary annuity value} \times (1 + i) \\
&= \$3,312 \times 1.08 \\
&= \$3,577
\end{aligned}
$$

As they should, the answers for the two methods of calculation agree.

Another easy way to calculate the present value or future value of an annuity due is by using the BEG/END switch on your financial calculator. All financial calculators have a key that switches the cash flow from the end of each period to the beginning of each period. The keys are typically labeled "BEG" for cash flows at the beginning of the period and "END" for the cash flows at the end of the period. To calculate the PV of an annuity due: (1) switch the calculator to the BEG mode, (2) enter the data, and (3) press the PV key for the answer. As an example, work the problem from Exhibit 5.12B using your financial calculator.

> **BEFORE YOU GO ON**

1. How do an ordinary annuity, an annuity due, and a perpetuity differ?

2. Give two examples of perpetuities.

3. What is the annuity transformation method?

5.6 CASH FLOWS THAT GROW AT A CONSTANT RATE

So far, we have been examining level cash flow streams. Often, though, management needs to value a cash flow stream that increases at a constant rate over time. These cash flow streams are called growing annuities or growing perpetuities.

LEARNING OBJECTIVE ⑦

Growing Annuity

Financial managers often need to compute the value of multiyear product or service contracts with cash flows that increase each year at a constant rate. These are called **growing annuities**. For example, you may want to value the cost of a 25-year lease that adjusts annually for the expected rate of inflation over the life of the contract. Equation 5.9 can be used to compute the present value of an annuity growing at a constant rate for a finite time period:[8]

growing annuity
an annuity in which the cash flows increase at a constant rate

$$PVA_n = \frac{CF_1}{i - g} \times \left[1 - \left(\frac{1 + g}{1 + i} \right)^n \right]$$ (5.9)

where:

PVA_n = present value of a growing annuity with n periods
CF_1 = cash flow one period in the future ($t = 1$)
i = interest rate, or discount rate
g = constant growth rate per period

You should be aware of several important points when applying Equation 5.9. First, the cash flow (CF_1) used is not the cash flow for the current period (CF_0); rather, it is the cash flow to be received in the next period ($t = 1$). The relation between these two cash flows is $CF_1 = CF_0 \times (1 + g)$. Second, a necessary condition for using Equation 5.9 is that $i > g$. If this condition is not met ($i \leq g$) the calculations from the equation will be meaningless, as you will get a negative or infinite value for finite positive cash flows. A negative value essentially says that someone would have to pay you money to get you to accept a positive cash flow.

As an example of how Equation 5.9 is applied, suppose you work for a company that owns a number of coffee shops in the New York City area. One coffee shop is located in the Empire State Building, and your boss wants to know how much it is worth.[9] The coffee shop has a 50-year lease, so we will assume that it will be in business for 50 years. It produced cash flows of $300,000 after all expenses this year, and the discount rate used by similar businesses is 15 percent. You estimate that, over the long term, cash flows will grow at 2.5 percent per year because of inflation. Thus, you calculate that the coffee shop's cash flow next year (CF_1) will be $307,500, or $300,000 \times (1 + 0.025)$.

Plugging the values from the coffee shop example into Equation 5.9 yields the following result:

$$PVA_n = \frac{\$307,500}{0.15 - 0.025} \times \left[1 - \left(\frac{1.025}{1.15} \right)^{50} \right]$$

$$= \$2,460,000 \times 0.9968$$

$$= \$2,452,128$$

The estimated value of the coffee shop is $2,452,128.

Growing Perpetuity

Sometimes cash flows are expected to grow at a constant rate indefinitely. In this case the cash flow stream is called a **growing perpetuity**. The formula to compute the present value for a growing perpetuity that begins next period (PVP) is as follows:

growing perpetuity
a cash flow stream that grows at a constant rate forever

$$PVP = \frac{CF_1}{i - g}$$ (5.10)

---

[8]In Equation 5.9 we represent the present value of a growing annuity of n periods using the same notation (PVA_n) that we use for a regular annuity in Equation 5.5. We do this because the regular annuity is just a special case of the growing annuity, where $g = 0$. Equation 5.9 is the more general form of the annuity formula.
[9]For those interested, the Empire State Building has three coffee shops.

As before, CF_1 is the cash flow occurring at the end of the first period, i is the discount or interest rate, and g is the constant rate of growth of the cash flow (CF). Equation 5.10 is an easy equation to work with, and it is used widely in the valuation of common stock for firms that have a policy and history of paying dividends that grow at a constant rate. It is also widely used in the valuation of entire companies.

Notice that we can derive Equation 5.10 from Equation 5.9 by setting n equal to ∞. If i is greater than g, as we said it must be, the term $[(1 + g)/(1 + i)]^\infty$ is equal to 0, leading to the following result:

$$\begin{aligned} PVP &= \frac{CF_1}{i - g} \times \left[1 - \left(\frac{1 + g}{1 + i} \right)^\infty \right] \\ &= \frac{CF_1}{i - g} \times [1 - 0] \\ &= \frac{CF_1}{i - g} \end{aligned}$$

This makes sense, of course, since Equation 5.9 describes a growing annuity and Equation 5.10 describes a growing cash flow stream that goes on forever. Notice that both Equations 5.9 and 5.10 are exactly the same as Equations 5.5 and 5.7 when g equals zero.

To illustrate a growing perpetuity, we will consider an example. Suppose that, after graduating from college, you started a health and athletic club. Your concept included not only providing workout facilities, such as weights, treadmills, and elliptical trainers, but also promoting a healthy lifestyle through a focus on cooking and nutrition. The concept has proved popular, and after only five years, you have seven clubs in operation. Your accountant reports that the firm's cash flow last year was $450,000, and the appropriate discount rate for the club is 18 percent. You expect the firm's cash flows to increase by 5 percent per year, which includes 2 percent for expected inflation. Since the business is a corporation, you can assume it will continue operating indefinitely into the future. What is the value of the firm?

We can use Equation 5.10 to solve this problem. Although the equation is very easy to use, a common mistake is using the current period's cash flow (CF_0) and not the *next* period's cash flow (CF_1). Since the cash flow is growing at a constant growth rate, g, we simply multiply CF_0 by $(1 + g)$ to get the value of CF_1. Thus,

$$CF_1 = CF_0 \times (1 + g)$$

We can then substitute the result into Equation 5.10, which yields a helpful variant of this equation:

$$PVP = \frac{CF_1}{i - g} = \frac{CF_0 \times (1 + g)}{i - g}$$

Now we can insert the values for the health club into the equation and solve for PVP:

$$\begin{aligned} PVP &= \frac{CF_0 \times (1 + g)}{i - g} \\ &= \frac{\$450,000 \times (1 + 0.05)}{0.18 - 0.05} \\ &= \$3,634,615 \end{aligned}$$

The business is worth $3,634,615.

The growing annuity and perpetuity formulas are useful, and we will be applying them later on in this book. Unfortunately, even though advanced financial calculators have special programs for annuities and perpetuities with constant cash flows, typical financial calculators do not include programs for growing annuities and perpetuities.

> **BEFORE YOU GO ON**

　1. What is the difference between a growing annuity and a growing perpetuity?

5.7 THE EFFECTIVE ANNUAL INTEREST RATE

LEARNING OBJECTIVE 8

So far in this chapter, there has been little question about which interest rate to use in a particular computation. In most cases, a single interest rate has been supplied. When working with real market data, however, the situation is not so clear-cut. We often encounter interest rates that can be computed in different ways. In this final section, we try to untangle some of the issues that can cause problems.

Why the Confusion?

To better understand why interest rates can be so confusing, consider the following situation. Suppose you borrow $100 on your bank credit card and plan to keep the balance outstanding for one year. The credit card's stated interest rate is 1 percent per month. The federal Truth-in-Lending Act requires the bank and other financial institutions to disclose to consumers the **annual percentage rate (APR)** charged on a loan. The APR is the annualized interest rate using *simple interest*. It ignores the interest earned on interest associated with compounding periods of less than one year. Thus, the APR is defined as the simple interest charged per period multiplied by the number of periods per year. For the bank credit card loan, the APR is 12 percent (1 percent per month × 12 months = 12 percent).

> **annual percentage rate (APR)**
> the simple interest rate charged per period multiplied by the number of periods per year

At the end of the year, you go to pay off the credit card balance as planned. It seems reasonable to assume that with an APR of 12 percent your credit card balance at the end of one year would be $112 (1.12 × $100 = $112). Wrong! The bank's *actual* interest rate is 1 percent per month, meaning that the bank will compound your credit card balance monthly, 12 times over the year. The bank's calculation for the balance due is $112.68 [$100 × $(1.01)^{12}$ = $112.68].[10] The bank is actually charging you 12.68 percent per year, and the total interest paid for the one-year loan is $12.68 rather than $12.00. This example raises a question: What is the correct way to annualize an interest rate?

> Many useful financial calculators, including an APR calculator, can be found at eFunda .com. Go to http://www .efunda.com/formulae/ finance/apr_calculator .cfm.

Calculating the Effective Annual Interest Rate

In making financial decisions, the correct way to annualize an interest rate is to compute the effective annual interest rate. The **effective annual interest rate (EAR)** is defined as the annual interest rate that takes compounding into account. Mathematically, the EAR can be stated as follows:

$$\text{EAR} = \left[1 + \frac{\text{Quoted interest rate}}{m} \right]^m - 1 \qquad (5.11)$$

> **effective annual interest rate (EAR)**
> the annual interest rate that reflects compounding within a year

where m is the number of compounding periods during a year. The **quoted interest rate** is by definition a *simple* annual interest rate, like the APR. That means that the quoted interest rate has been annualized by multiplying the rate per period by the number of periods per year. The EAR conversion formula accounts for the number of compounding periods and, thus, effectively adjusts the annualized quoted interest rate for the time value of money. Because the EAR is the true cost of borrowing and lending, it is the rate that should be used for making all finance decisions.

> **quoted interest rate**
> a simple annual interest rate, such as the APR

We will use our bank credit card example to illustrate the use of Equation 5.11. Recall that the credit card has an APR of 12 percent (1 percent per month). The APR is the quoted interest rate, and the number of compounding periods (m) is 12. Applying Equation 5.11, we find that the effective annual interest rate is:

$$
\begin{aligned}
\text{EAR} &= \left(1 + \frac{\text{Quoted interest rate}}{m} \right)^m - 1 \\
&= \left(1 + \frac{0.12}{12} \right)^{12} - 1 \\
&= (1.01)^{12} - 1 \\
&= 1.1268 - 1 \\
&= 0.1268, \text{ or } 12.68\%
\end{aligned}
$$

---

[10]If you have any doubt about the total credit card debt at the end of one year, make the calculation 12 times on your calculator: the first month is $100 × 1.01 = 101.00; the second month is $101.00 × 1.01 = $102.01; the third month is $102.01 × 1.01 = $103.03; and so on for 12 months.

The EAR value of 12.68 percent is the true cost of borrowing the $100 on the bank credit card for one year. The EAR calculation adjusts for the effects of compounding and, hence, the time value of money.

Finally, notice that interest rates are quoted in the marketplace in three ways:

1. *The quoted interest rate.* This is an interest rate that has been annualized by multiplying the rate per period by the number of compounding periods. The APR is an example. All consumer borrowing and lending rates in the U.S. are annualized in this manner.

2. *The interest rate per period.* The bank credit card rate of 1 percent per month is an example of this kind of rate. You can find the interest rate per period by dividing the quoted interest rate by the number of compounding periods.

3. *The effective annual interest rate (EAR).* This is the interest rate actually paid (or earned) after accounting for compounding. Sometimes it is difficult to distinguish a quoted rate from an EAR. Generally, however, an annualized consumer rate is an APR rather than an EAR.

Comparing Interest Rates

When borrowing or lending money, it is sometimes necessary to compare and select among interest rate alternatives. Quoted interest rates are comparable when they cover the same overall time period, such as one year, and have the same number of compounding periods. If quoted interest rates are *not* comparable, we must adjust them to a common time period. The easiest way to make interest rates comparable for making finance decisions is to convert them to effective annual interest rates. Consider an example.

Suppose you are the chief financial officer of a manufacturing company. The company is planning a $1 billion plant expansion and will finance it by borrowing money for five years. Three financial institutions have submitted interest rate quotes; all are APRs:

Lender A: 10.40 percent compound monthly
Lender B: 10.90 percent compounded annually
Lender C: 10.50 percent compounded quarterly

Although all the loans have the same maturity, the loans are not comparable because the APRs have different compounding periods. To make the adjustments for the different time periods, we apply Equation 5.11 to convert each of the APR quotes into an EAR:

$$\text{Lender A: EAR} = \left(1 + \frac{0.1040}{12}\right)^{12} - 1$$
$$= (1.0087)^{12} - 1 = 1.1091 - 1 = 0.1091, \text{ or } 10.91\%$$

$$\text{Lender B: EAR} = \left(1 + \frac{0.1090}{1}\right)^{1} - 1$$
$$= 1.1090 - 1 = 0.1090, \text{ or } 10.90\%$$

$$\text{Lender C: EAR} = \left(1 + \frac{0.1050}{4}\right)^{4} - 1$$
$$= (1.0263)^{4} - 1 = 1.1092 - 1 = 0.1092, \text{ or } 10.92\%$$

As shown, Lender B offers the lowest interest cost at 10.90 percent.

Notice the shift in rankings that takes place as a result of the EAR calculations. When we initially looked at the APR quotes, it appeared that Lender A offered the lowest rate and Lender B had the highest. After computing the EAR, we find that when we account for the effect of compounding, Lender B actually offers the lowest interest rate.

Another important point is that if all the interest rates are quoted as APRs with the same annualizing period, such as monthly, the interest rates are comparable and you can select the correct rate by simply comparing the quotes. That is, the lowest APR corresponds with the lowest cost of funds. Thus, it is correct for borrowers or lenders to make economic decisions with APR data as long as interest rates have the same maturity and the same compounding period. To find the true cost of the loan, however, it is still necessary to compute the EAR.

Consumer Protection Acts and Interest Rate Disclosure

In 1968 Congress passed the **Truth-in-Lending Act** to ensure that all borrowers receive meaningful information about the cost of credit so that they can make intelligent economic decisions.[11] The act applies to all lenders that extend credit to consumers, and it covers credit card loans, auto loans, home mortgage loans, home equity loans, home improvement loans, and some small-business loans. Similar legislation, the so-called **Truth-in-Savings Act,** applies to consumer savings vehicles such as certificates of deposit (CDs). These two pieces of legislation require by law that the APR be disclosed on all consumer loans and savings plans and that it be prominently displayed on advertising and contractual documents.

We know that the EAR, not the APR, represents the true economic interest rate. So why did the Truth-in-Lending and Truth-in-Savings Acts specify that the APR must be the disclosed rate? The APR was selected because it's easy to calculate and easy to understand. When the legislation was passed in 1969, PCs and handheld calculators did not exist. Down at the auto showroom, salespeople needed an easy way to explain and annualize the monthly interest charge, and the APR provided just such a method. And most important, if all the auto lenders quoted monthly APR, consumers could use this rate to select the loan with the lowest economic interest cost.

Today, although lenders and borrowers are legally required to quote the APR, they run their businesses using interest rate calculations based on the present value and future value formulas. Consumers are bombarded with both APR and EAR rates, and confusion reigns. At the car dealership, for example, you may find that your auto loan's APR is 5 percent but the actual borrowing rate is 5.12 percent. And at the bank where your grandmother gets free coffee and doughnuts, she may be told that the bank's one-year CD has an APR of 3 percent, but it really pays 3.04 percent. Because of confusion arising from conflicting interest rates in the marketplace, some observers believe that the APR calculation has outlived its usefulness and should be replaced by the EAR.

The Appropriate Interest Rate Factor

Here is a final question to consider: What is the appropriate interest rate to use when making future or present value calculations? The answer is simple: use the EAR. Under no circumstance should the APR or any other quoted rate be used as the interest rate in present or future value calculations. Consider an example of using the EAR in such a calculation.

Petra, an MBA student at Georgetown University, has purchased from a small consumer finance company a $100 savings note with a two-year maturity. The contract states that the note has a 20 percent APR and pays interest quarterly. The quarterly interest rate is thus 5 percent (20 percent APR/4 quarters per year = 5 percent per quarter). Petra has several questions about the note: (1) What is the note's effective annual interest rate (EAR)? (2) How much money will she have at the end of two years? (3) When making the future value calculation, should she use the quarterly interest rate or the EAR?

To answer Petra's questions, we first compute the EAR, which is the actual interest earned on the note:

$$\text{EAR} = \left(1 + \frac{\text{APR}}{m}\right)^m - 1$$
$$= \left(1 + \frac{0.20}{4}\right)^4 - 1$$
$$= (1 + 0.05)^4 - 1$$
$$= 1.21551 - 1$$
$$= 0.21551, \text{ or } 21.551\%$$

Next, we calculate the future value of the note using the EAR. Because the EAR is an annual rate, for this problem we use a total of two compounding periods. The calculation is as follows:

$$FV_2 = PV \times (1 + i)^n$$
$$= \$100 \times (1 + 0.21551)^2$$
$$= \$100 \times 1.4775$$
$$= \$147.75$$

Truth-in-Lending Act
a federal law requiring lenders to fully inform borrowers of important information related to loans, including the annual percentage rate charged

Truth-in-Savings Act
a federal law requiring institutions offering consumer savings vehicles, such as certificates of deposit (CDs), to fully inform consumers of important information about the savings vehicles, including the annual percentage rate paid

 You can read more about credit protection laws, including those passed after the 2007 financial crisis at the Federal Reserve web site http://federalreserve .gov/creditcard/regs .html.

---

[11]The Truth-in-Lending Act is Title I of the Consumer Credit Protection Act.

We can also calculate the future value using the quarterly rate of interest of 5 percent with a total of eight compounding periods. In this case, the calculation is as follows:

$$FV_2 = \$100 \times (1 + 0.050)^8$$
$$= \$100 \times 1.4775$$
$$= \$147.75$$

The two calculation methods yield the same answer: $147.75.

In summary, any time you do a future value or present value calculation, you must use either the interest rate per period (quoted rate/m) or the EAR as the interest rate factor. It does not matter which of these you use. Both will properly account for the impact of compounding on the value of cash flows. Interest rate proxies such as the APR should never be used as interest rate factors for calculating future or present values, because they do not properly account for the number of compounding periods.

> **BEFORE YOU GO ON**

1. What is the APR, and why are lending institutions required to disclose this rate?

2. What is the correct way to annualize an interest rate in financial decision making?

3. Distinguish between quoted interest rate, interest rate per period, and effective annual interest rate.

SUMMARY OF Learning Objectives

1 **Explain what the time value of money is and why it is so important in the field of finance.**

The idea that money has a time value is one of the most fundamental concepts in the field of finance. The concept is based on the idea that most people prefer to consume goods today rather than wait to have similar goods in the future. Since money buys goods, they would rather have money today than in the future. Thus, a dollar today is worth more than a dollar received in the future. Another way of viewing the time value of money is that your money is worth more today than at some point in the future because, if you had the money now, you could invest it and earn interest. Thus, the time value of money is the opportunity cost of forgoing consumption today.

Applications of the time value of money focus on the trade-off between current dollars and dollars received at some future date. This is an important element in financial decisions because most investment decisions require the comparison of cash invested today with the value of expected future cash inflows. Time value of money calculations facilitate such comparisons by accounting for both the magnitude and timing of cash flows. Investment opportunities are undertaken only when the value of future cash inflows exceeds the cost of the investment (the initial cash outflow).

2 **Explain the concept of *future value*, including the meaning of the terms *principal*, *simple interest*, and *compound interest*, and use the future value formula to make business decisions.**

The future value is the sum to which an investment will grow after earning interest. The principal is the amount of the

investment. Simple interest is the interest paid on the original investment; the amount of simple interest remains constant from period to period. Compound interest includes not only simple interest, but also interest earned on the reinvestment of previously earned interest, the so-called interest earned on interest. For future value calculations, the higher the interest rate, the faster the investment will grow. The application of the future value formula in business decisions is presented in Section 5.2.

3 **Explain the concept of present value and how it relates to future value, and use the present value formula to make business decisions.**

The present value is the value today of a future cash flow. Computing the present value involves discounting future cash flows back to the present at an appropriate discount rate. The process of discounting cash flows adjusts the cash flows for the time value of money. Computationally, the present value factor is the reciprocal of the future value factor, or $1/(1 + i)$. The calculation and application of the present value formula in business decisions is presented in Section 5.3.

4 **Explain why cash flows occurring at different times must be adjusted to reflect their value as of a common date before they can be compared, and compute the present value and future value for multiple cash flows.**

When making decisions involving cash flows over time, we should first identify the magnitude and timing of the cash flows and then adjust each individual cash flow to reflect its value as of a common date. For example, the process of discounting (compounding) cash flows adjusts them for the time value of money because today's dollars are not equal in value to dollars in the future. Once all of the cash flows are in present (future) value terms, they can be compared to make decisions. Section 5.4 discusses the computation of present values and future values of multiple cash flows.

5 **Explain the difference between an ordinary annuity and an annuity due, and calculate the present value and the future value of an ordinary annuity and an annuity due.**

An ordinary annuity is a series of equally spaced, level cash flows over time. The cash flows for an ordinary annuity are assumed to take place at the end of each period. To find the present value of an ordinary annuity, we multiply the present value of an annuity factor, which is equal to (1 − present value factor)/*i*, by the amount of the constant cash flow. We multiply the present value of an ordinary annuity by (1 + *i*)^n to calculate its future value in *n* periods.

An annuity due is an annuity in which the cash flows occur at the beginning of each period. A lease is an example of an annuity due. In this case, we are effectively prepaying for the service. To calculate the value of an annuity due, we calculate the present value (or future value) as though the cash flows are from an ordinary annuity. We then multiply the ordinary annuity value times (1 + *i*). Section 5.5 discusses the calculation of the present value and future value of an ordinary annuity and annuity due.

6 **Explain what a perpetuity is and where we see them in business, and calculate the value of a perpetuity.**

A perpetuity is like an annuity except that the cash flows are perpetual—they never end. British Treasury Department bonds, called consols, were the first widely used securities of this kind. The most common example of a perpetuity today is preferred stock. The issuer of preferred stock promises to pay fixed-rate dividends forever. The cash flows from corporations can also look like perpetuities. To calculate the present value of a perpetuity, we simply divide the constant cash flow (CF) by the interest rate (*i*).

7 **Discuss growing annuities and perpetuities, as well as their application in business, and calculate their values.**

Financial managers often need to value cash flow streams that increase at a constant rate over time. These cash flow streams are called growing annuities or growing perpetuities. An example of a growing annuity is a 10-year lease with an annual adjustment for the expected rate of inflation over the life of the contract. If the cash flows continue to grow at a constant rate indefinitely, this cash flow stream is called a growing perpetuity. Application and calculation of cash flows that grow at a constant rate are discussed in Section 5.6.

8 **Discuss why the effective annual interest rate (EAR) is the appropriate way to annualize interest rates, and calculate the EAR.**

The EAR is the annual growth rate that takes compounding into account. Thus, the EAR is the true cost of borrowing or lending money. When we need to compare interest rates, we must make sure that the rates to be compared have the same time and compounding periods. If interest rates are not comparable, they must be converted into common terms. The easiest way to convert rates to common terms is to calculate the EAR for each interest rate. The use and calculation of EAR are discussed in Section 5.7.

SUMMARY OF **Key Equations**

Equation	Description	Formula
5.1	Future value of an *n*-period investment	$FV_n = PV \times (1 + i)^n$
5.2	Future value with compounding more than annually	$FV_n = PV \times (1 + i/m)^{m \times n}$
5.3	Future value with continuous compounding	$FV_\infty = PV \times e^{i \times n}$
5.4	Present value of an *n*-period investment	$PV = \dfrac{FV_n}{(1 + i)^n}$
5.5	Present value of an ordinary annuity	$PVA_n = \dfrac{CF}{i} \times \left[1 - \dfrac{1}{(1 + i)^n} \right]$ $= CF \times \dfrac{1 - 1/(1 + i)^n}{i}$ $= CF \times \dfrac{1 - \text{Present value factor}}{i}$ $= CF \times PV \text{ annuity factor}$

Equation	Description	Formula
5.6	Future value of an ordinary annuity	$FVA_n = \dfrac{CF}{i} \times [(1 + i)^n - 1]$
		$= CF \times \dfrac{(1 + i)^n - 1}{i}$
		$= CF \times \dfrac{\text{Future value factor} - 1}{i}$
		$= CF \times \text{FV annuity factor}$
5.7	Present value of a perpetuity	$PVP = \dfrac{CF}{i}$
5.8	Value of an annuity due	$\text{Annuity due value} = \text{Ordinary annuity value} \times (1 + i)$
5.9	Present value of a growing annuity	$PVA_n = \dfrac{CF_1}{i - g} \times \left[1 - \left(\dfrac{1 + g}{1 + i} \right)^n \right]$
5.10	Present value of a growing perpetuity	$PVP = \dfrac{CF_1}{i - g}$
5.11	Effective annual interest rate	$EAR = \left(1 + \dfrac{\text{Quoted interest rate}}{m} \right)^m - 1$

Self-Study Problems

5.1 Amit Patel is planning to invest $10,000 in a bank certificate of deposit (CD) for five years. The CD will pay interest of 9 percent. What is the future value of Amit's investment?

5.2 Megan Gaumer expects to need $50,000 as a down payment on a house in six years. How much does she need to invest today in an account paying 7.25 percent?

5.3 Kelly Martin has $10,000 that she can deposit into a savings account for five years. Bank A compounds interest annually, Bank B twice a year, and Bank C quarterly. Each bank has a stated interest rate of 4 percent. What amount would Kelly have at the end of the fifth year if she left all the interest paid on the deposit in each bank?

5.4 Kronka, Inc., is expecting cash inflows of $13,000, $11,500, $12,750, and $9,635 over the next four years. What is the present value of these cash flows if the appropriate discount rate is 8 percent?

5.5 Mike White is planning to save up for a trip to Europe in three years. He will need $7,500 when he is ready to make the trip. He plans to invest the same amount at the end of each of the next three years in an account paying 6 percent. What is the amount that he will have to save every year to reach his goal of $7,500 in three years?

5.6 Becky Scholes has $150,000 to invest. She wants to be able to withdraw $12,500 every year forever without using up any of her principal. What interest rate would her investment have to earn in order for her to be able to do so?

Solutions to Self-Study Problems

5.1 Present value of Amit's investment = PV = $10,000
Interest rate = i = 9%
Number of years = n = 5

$FV_n = PV \times (1 + i)^n$
$FV_5 = \$10,000 \times (1 + 0.09)^5$
$\quad\ = \$15,386.24$

5.2 Amount Megan will need in six years = FV_6 = $50,000
Number of years = $n = 6$
Interest rate = $i = 7.25\%$
Amount needed to be invested now = PV = ?

$$PV = \frac{FV_n}{(1 + i)^n}$$
$$= \frac{\$50,000}{(1 + 0.0725)^6}$$
$$= \$32,853.84$$

5.3 Present value of Kelly's deposit = PV = $10,000
Number of years = $n = 5$
Interest rate = $i = 4\%$
Compound period (m):

$A = 1$
$B = 2$
$C = 4$

Amount at the end of five years = FV_5 = ?

Bank A: $FV_n = PV \times (1 + i/m)^{m \times n}$
$FV_5 = \$10,000 \times (1 + 0.04/1)^{1 \times 5}$
$= \$12,166.53$

Bank B: $FV_5 = \$10,000 \times (1 + 0.04/2)^{2 \times 5}$
$= \$12,189.94$

Bank C: $FV_5 = \$10,000 \times (1 + 0.04/4)^{4 \times 5}$
$= \$12,201.90$

5.4 The time line for Kronka's cash flows and their present value is as follows:

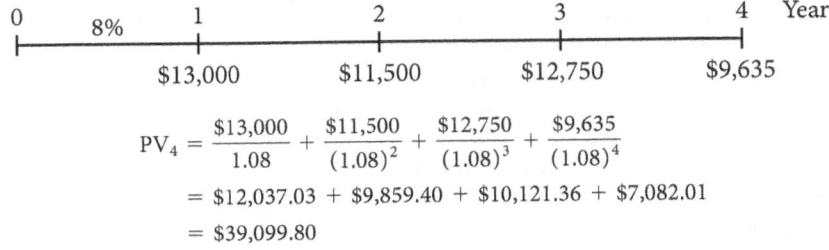

$$PV_4 = \frac{\$13,000}{1.08} + \frac{\$11,500}{(1.08)^2} + \frac{\$12,750}{(1.08)^3} + \frac{\$9,635}{(1.08)^4}$$
$$= \$12,037.03 + \$9,859.40 + \$10,121.36 + \$7,082.01$$
$$= \$39,099.80$$

5.5 Amount Mike White will need in three years = FVA_3 = $7,500
Number of years = $n = 3$
Interest rate on investment = $i = 6.0\%$
Amount that Mike needs to invest every year = PMT = ?

$$FVA_n = CF \times \frac{(1 + i)^n - 1}{i}$$
$$\$7,500 = CF \times \frac{(1 + 0.06)^3 - 1}{0.06}$$
$$= CF \times 3.1836$$
$$CF = \frac{\$7,500}{3.1836}$$
$$= \$2,355.82$$

Mike will have to invest $2,355.82 every year for the next three years.

5.6 Present value of Becky Scholes's investment = $150,000
Amount needed annually = $12,500
This is a perpetuity!

$$PVP = \frac{CF}{i}$$

$$i = \frac{CF}{PVP} = \frac{\$12,500}{\$150,000}$$

$$i = 8.33\%$$

Critical Thinking Questions

5.1 Explain the phrase "A dollar today is worth more than a dollar tomorrow."

5.2 Explain the difference between future value and present value.

5.3 Explain the difference between compounding and discounting.

5.4 Explain how compound interest differs from simple interest.

5.5 What is the key economic principle involved in calculating the present value and future value of multiple cash flows?

5.6 Raymond Bartz is trying to choose between two equally risky annuities, each paying $5,000 per year for five years. One is an ordinary annuity, the other is an annuity due. Which of the following statements is most correct?

   a. The present value of the ordinary annuity must exceed the present value of the annuity due, but the future value of an ordinary annuity may be less than the future value of the annuity due.

   b. The present value of the annuity due exceeds the present value of the ordinary annuity, while the future value of the annuity due is less than the future value of the ordinary annuity.

   c. The present value of the annuity due exceeds the present value of the ordinary annuity, and the future value of the annuity due also exceeds the future value of the ordinary annuity.

   d. If interest rates increase, the difference between the present value of the ordinary annuity and the present value of the annuity due remains the same.

5.7 Which of the following investments will have the highest future value at the end of three years? Assume that the effective annual rate for all investments is the same.

   a. You earn $3,000 at the end of three years (a total of one payment).

   b. You earn $1,000 at the end of every year for the next three years (a total of three payments).

   c. You earn $1,000 at the beginning of every year for the next three years (a total of three payments).

5.8 Explain whether or not each of the following statements is correct.

   a. A 15-year mortgage will have larger monthly payments than a 30-year mortgage of the same amount and same interest rate.

   b. If an investment pays 10 percent interest compounded annually, its effective rate will also be 10 percent.

5.9 Why is the effective annual rate (EAR) superior to the annual percentage rate (APR) in measuring the true economic cost or return? When will the EAR and the APR be the same?

5.10 Suppose three investments have equal lives and multiple cash flows. A high discount rate tends to favor:

   a. The investment with large cash flows early.

   b. The investment with large cash flows late.

   c. The investment with even cash flows.

   d. None of the investments since they have equal lives.

Questions and Problems

BASIC ▶ **5.1** **Future value:** Ted Rogers is investing $7,500 in a bank CD that pays a 6 percent annual interest. How much will the CD be worth at the end of five years?

EXCEL®
More interactive Excel®
exercises available in
WileyPLUS

5.2 **Future value:** Your aunt is planning to invest in a bank CD that will pay 7.5 percent interest semiannually. If she has $5,000 to invest, how much will she have at the end of four years?

5.3 **Future value:** Your birthday is coming up, and, instead of other presents, your parents promised to give you $1,000 in cash. Since you have a part-time job and, thus, don't need the cash immediately, you decide to invest the money in a bank CD that pays an annual rate of 5.2 percent, compounded quarterly, for the next two years. How much money can you expect to earn in this period of time?

5.4 Present value: Roy Gross is considering an investment that pays 7.6 percent. How much will he have to invest today so that the investment will be worth $25,000 in six years?

5.5 Present value: Maria Addai has been offered a future payment of $750 two years from now. If she can earn 6.5 percent compounded annually on her investment, what should she pay for this investment today?

5.6 Present value: Tracy Chapman is saving to buy a house in five years. She plans to put 20 percent down at that time, and she believes that she will need $35,000 for the down payment. If Tracy can invest in a fund that pays 9.25 percent annually, how much will she need to invest today?

5.7 Interest rate: You are in desperate need of cash and turn to your uncle, who has offered to lend you some money. You decide to borrow $1,300 and agree to pay back $1,500 in two years. Alternatively, you could borrow from your bank that is charging 6.5 percent interest annually. Should you borrow from your uncle or the bank?

5.8 Number of periods: You invest $150 in a mutual fund today that pays 9 percent interest annually. How long will it take to double your money?

5.9 Future value with multiple cash flows: Ben Woolmer has an investment that will pay him the following cash flows over the next five years: $2,350, $2,725, $3,128, $3,366, and $3,695. If his investments typically earn 7.65 percent, what is the future value of the investment's cash flows at the end of five years?

5.10 Future value with multiple cash flows: You are a freshman in college and are planning a trip to Europe when you graduate from college at the end of four years. You plan to save the following amounts annually, starting today: $625, $700, $700, and $750. If the account pays 5.75 percent annually, how much will you have at the end of four years?

5.11 Present value with multiple cash flows: Saul Cervantes has just purchased some equipment for his landscaping business. For this equipment he must pay the following amounts at the end of each of the next five years: $10,450, $8,500, $9,675, $12,500, and $11,635. If the appropriate discount rate is 10.875 percent, what is the cost in today's dollars of the equipment Saul purchased today?

5.12 Present value with multiple cash flows: Jeremy Fenloch borrowed some money from his friend and promised to repay him the amounts of $1,225, $1,350, $1,500, $1,600, and $1,600 over the next five years. If the friend normally discounts investment cash flows at 8 percent annually, how much did Jeremy borrow?

5.13 Present value of an ordinary annuity: Dynamics Telecommunications Corp. has made an investment in another company that will guarantee it a cash flow of $22,500 each year for the next five years. If the company uses a discount rate of 15 percent on its investments, what is the present value of this investment?

5.14 Future value of an ordinary annuity: Cecelia Thomas is a sales executive at a Baltimore firm. She is 25 years old and plans to invest $3,000 every year in an IRA account, beginning at the end of this year until she turns 65 years old. If the IRA investment will earn 9.75 percent annually, how much will she have in 40 years, when she turns 65?

5.15 Future value of an annuity due: Refer to Problem 5.14. If Cecelia invests at the beginning of each year, how much will she have at age 65?

5.16 Computing annuity payment: The Elkridge Bar & Grill has a seven-year loan of $23,500 with Bank of America. It plans to repay the loan in seven equal installments starting today. If the rate of interest is 8.4 percent, how much will each payment be?

5.17 Perpetuity: Calculate the annual cash flows for each of the following investments:
   a. $250,000 invested at 6 percent.
   b. $50,000 invested at 12 percent.
   c. $100,000 invested at 10 percent.

5.18 Growing perpetuity: You are evaluating a growing perpetuity investment from a large financial services firm. The investment promises an initial payment of $20,000 at the end of this year and subsequent payments that will grow at a rate of 3.4 percent annually. If you use a 9 percent discount rate for investments like this, what is the present value of this growing perpetuity?

5.19 Effective annual interest rate: Raj Krishnan bought a Honda Civic for $17,345. He put down $6,000 and financed the rest through the dealer at an APR of 4.9 percent for four years. What is the effective annual interest rate (EAR) if the loan payments are made monthly?

5.20 Effective annual interest rate: Cyclone Rentals borrowed $15,550 from a bank for three years. If the quoted rate (APR) is 6.75 percent, and the compounding is daily, what is the effective annual interest rate (EAR)?

INTERMEDIATE > **5.21 Future Value:** CelebNav, Inc., had sales last year of $700,000, and the analysts are predicting a good year for the start-up, with sales growing 20 percent a year for the next three years. After that, the sales should grow 11 percent per year for two years, at which time the owners are planning to sell the company. What are the projected sales for the last year before the sale?

5.22 Present value: Congress and the president have decided to increase the federal tax rate in an effort to reduce the budget deficit. Suppose that Caroline Weslin will pay 35 percent of her bonus to the federal government for taxes if she accepts the bonus today and 40 percent if she receives her bonus in two years. Will the increase in tax rates affect her decision?

5.23 Multiple compounding periods: Find the future value of an investment of $2,500 made today for the following rates and periods:

a. 6.25 percent compounded semiannually for 12 years.
b. 7.63 percent compounded quarterly for six years.
c. 8.9 percent compounded monthly for 10 years.
d. 10 percent compounded daily for three years.
e. 8 percent compounded continuously for two years.

5.24 Multiple compounding periods: Find the present value of $3,500 under each of the following rates and periods:

a. 8.9 percent compounded monthly for five years.
b. 6.6 percent compounded quarterly for eight years.
c. 4.3 percent compounded daily for four years.
d. 5.7 percent compounded continuously for three years.

5.25 Multiple compounding periods: Samantha plans to invest some money so that she has $5,500 at the end of three years. How much should she invest today given the following choices?

a. 4.2 percent compounded daily.
b. 4.9 percent compounded monthly.
c. 5.2 percent compounded quarterly.
d. 5.4 percent compounded annually.

5.26 Time to grow: You have just inherited $550,000. You plan to save this money and continue to live off the money that you are earning in your current job. If you can invest the money in a bond that pays 4.6 percent interest annually, how long will it be before your inheritance is worth $1 million?

5.27 Future value with multiple cash flows: Stephanie Watson plans to make the following investments beginning next year. She will invest $3,125 in each of the next three years and will then make investments of $3,650, $3,725, $3,875, and $4,000 over the following four years. If the investments are expected to earn 11.5 percent annually, how much will Stephanie have at the end of the seven years?

5.28 Present value with multiple cash flows: Carol Jenkins, a lottery winner, will receive the following payments over the next seven years. If she can invest her cash flows in a fund that will earn 10.5 percent annually, what is the present value of her winnings?

1	2	3	4	5	6	7	Year
$200,000	$250,000	$275,000	$300,000	$350,000	$400,000	$550,000	

5.29 Computing annuity payment: Gary Whitmore is a high school sophomore. He currently has $7,500 in a savings account that pays 5.65 percent annually. Gary plans to use his current savings plus what he can save over the next four years to buy a car. He estimates that the car will cost $12,000 in four years. How much money should Gary save each year if he wants to buy the car?

5.30 Growing annuity: Modern Energy Company owns several gas stations. Management is looking to open a new station in the western suburbs of Baltimore. One possibility management is evaluating is to take over a station located at a site that has been leased from the county. The lease, originally for 99 years, currently has 73 years before expiration. The gas station generated a net cash flow of $92,500 last year, and the current owners expect an annual growth rate of 6.3 percent. If Modern Energy uses a discount rate of 14.5 percent to evaluate such businesses, what is the present value of this growing annuity?

5.31 Future value of annuity due: Jeremy Denham plans to save $5,000 every year for the next eight years, starting today. At the end of eight years, Jeremy will turn 30 years old and plans to use his savings toward the down payment on a house. If his investment in a mutual fund will earn him 10.3 percent annually, how much will he have saved in eight years when he buys his house?

5.32 Present value of an annuity due: You wrote a piece of software that does a better job of allowing computers to network than any other program designed for this purpose. A large networking company wants to incorporate your software into its systems and is offering to pay you $500,000 today, plus $500,000 at the end of each of the following six years, for permission to do this. If the appropriate interest rate is 6 percent, what is the present value of the cash flow stream that the company is offering you?

5.33 Present value of an annuity: Suppose that the networking company in Problem 5.32 will not start paying you until the first of the new systems that uses your software is sold in two years. What is the present value of that annuity? Assume that the appropriate interest rate is still 6 percent.

5.34 Effective annual interest rate: You are considering three alternative investments: (1) a three-year bank CD paying 7.5 percent compounded quarterly; (2) a three-year bank CD paying 7.3 percent compounded monthly; and (3) a three-year bank CD paying 7.75 percent compounded annually. Which investment has the highest effective annual interest rate (EAR)?

< **ADVANCED**

5.35 You have $2,500 you want to invest in your classmate's start-up business. You believe the business idea to be great and hope to get $3,700 back at the end of three years. If all goes according to plan, what will be the return on your investment?

5.36 You have $12,000 in cash. You can deposit it today in a mutual fund earning 8.2 percent semiannually, or you can wait, enjoy some of it, and invest $11,000 in your brother's business in two years. Your brother is promising you a return of at least 10 percent on your investment. Whichever alternative you choose, you will need to cash in at the end of 10 years. Assume your brother is trustworthy and both investments carry the same risk. Which one will you choose?

5.37 Surmec, Inc., reported sales of $2.1 million last year. The company's primary business is the manufacture of nuts and bolts. Since this is a mature industry, analysts are confident that sales will grow at a steady rate of 7 percent per year. The company's net income equals 23 percent of sales. Management would like to buy a new fleet of trucks but can only do so once the net income reaches $620,000 a year. At the end of what year will Surmec be able to buy the trucks? What will sales be in that year?

5.38 You have been offered the opportunity to invest in a project expected to provide you with the following cash flows: $4,000 in one year, $12,000 in two years, and $8,000 in three years. If the appropriate interest rates are 6 percent for the first year, 8 percent for the second year, and 12 percent for the third year, what is the present value of these cash flows?

5.39 Tirade Owens, a professional athlete, currently has a contract that will pay him a large amount in the first year of his contract and smaller amounts thereafter. He and his agent have asked the team to restructure the contract. The team, though reluctant, obliged. Tirade and his agent came up with a counteroffer. What are the present values of each of the contracts using a 14 percent discount rate? Which of the three contacts has the highest present value?

Year	Current Contract	Team's Offer	Counteroffer
1	$8,125,000	$4,000,000	$5,250,000
2	$3,650,000	$3,825,000	$7,550,000
3	$2,715,000	$3,850,000	$3,625,000
4	$1,822,250	$3,925,000	$2,800,000

5.40 Gary Kornig will be 30 years old next year and wants to retire when he is 65. So far he has saved (1) $6,950 in an IRA account in which his money is earning 8.3 percent annually and (2) $5,000 in a money market account in which he is earning 5.25 percent annually. Gary wants to have $1 million when he retires. Starting next year, he plans to invest the same amount of money every year until he retires in a mutual fund in which he expects to earn 9 percent annually. How much will Gary have to invest every year to achieve his savings goal?

5.41 The top prize for the state lottery is $100,000,000. You have decided it is time for you to take a chance and purchase a ticket. Before you purchase the ticket, you must decide whether to choose the cash option or the annual payment option. If you choose the annual payment option and win, you will receive $100,000,000 in 25 equal payments of $4,000,000—one payment today and one payment at the end of each of the next 24 years. If you choose the cash payment, you will receive a one-time lump sum payment of $59,194,567.18. If you can invest the proceeds and earn 6 percent, which option should you choose?

5.42 At what interest rate would you be indifferent between the cash and annual payment options in Problem 5.41?

5.43 Babu Baradwaj is saving for his son's college tuition. His son is currently 11 years old and will begin college in seven years. Babu has an index fund investment worth $7,500 that is earning 9.5 percent annually. Total expenses at the University of Maryland, where his son says he plans to go, currently total $15,000 per year, but are expected to grow at roughly 6 percent each year. Babu plans to invest in a mutual fund that will earn 11 percent annually to make up the difference between the college expenses and his current savings. In total, Babu will make seven equal investments with the first starting today and with the last being made a year before his son begins college.

a. What will be the present value of the four years of college expenses at the time that Babu's son starts college? Assume a discount rate of 5.5 percent.

b. What will be the value of the index mutual fund when his son just starts college?

c. What is the amount that Babu will have to have saved when his son turns 18 if Babu plans to cover all of his son's college expenses?

d. How much will Babu have to invest every year in order to have enough funds to cover all his son's expenses?

5.44 You are now 50 years old and plan to retire at age 65. You currently have a stock portfolio worth $150,000, a 401(k) retirement plan worth $250,000, and a money market account worth $50,000. Your stock portfolio is expected to provide annual returns of 12 percent, your 401(k) investment will earn 9.5 percent annually, and the money market account earns 5.25 percent, compounded monthly.

a. If you do not save another penny, what will be the total value of your investments when you retire at age 65?

b. Assume you plan to invest $12,000 every year in your 401(k) plan for the next 15 years (starting one year from now). How much will your investments be worth when you retire at age 65?

c. Assume that you expect to live 25 years after you retire (until age 90). Today, at age 50, you take all of your investments and place them in an account that pays 8 percent (use the scenario from part b in which you continue saving). If you start withdrawing funds starting at age 66, how much can you withdraw every year (e.g., an ordinary annuity) and leave nothing in your account after a 25th and final withdrawal at age 90?

d. You want your current investments, which are described in the problem statement, to support a perpetuity that starts a year from now. How much can you withdraw each year without touching your principal?

5.45 Trevor Díaz is looking to purchase a Mercedes Benz SL600 Roadster, which has an invoice price of $121,737 and a total cost of $129,482. Trevor plans to put down $20,000 and will pay the rest by taking on a 5.75 percent five-year bank loan. What is the monthly payment on this auto loan? Prepare an amortization table using Excel.

Sample Test Problems

5.1 Michael Carter is expecting an inheritance of $1.25 million in four years. If he had the money today, he could earn interest at an annual rate of 7.35 percent. What is the present value of this inheritance?

5.2 What is the future value of an investment of $3,000 after three years with compounding at the following rates and frequencies? What is the effective annual interest rate in each case?

a. 8.75 percent compounded monthly.

b. 8.625 percent compounded daily.

c. 8.5 percent compounded continuously.

5.3 Twenty-five years ago, Amanda Cortéz invested $10,000 in an account paying an annual interest rate of 5.75 percent. What is the value of the investment today? How much interest on interest did she earn on this investment?

5.4 Freisinger, Inc., is expecting a new project to start paying off, beginning at the end of next year. It expects cash flows to be as follows:

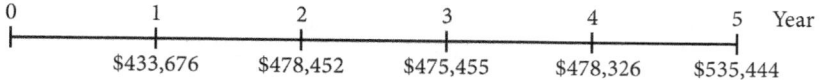

0	1	2	3	4	5 Year
	$433,676	$478,452	$475,455	$478,326	$535,444

If Freisinger can reinvest these cash flows to earn a return of 7.8 percent, what is the future value of this cash flow stream at the end of five years? What is its present value?

5.5 Sochi, Russia, is the site of the next Winter Olympics in 2014. City officials plan to build a new multi-purpose stadium. The projected cost of the stadium in 2014 dollars is $7.5 million. Assume that it is the end of 2011 and city officials intend to invest an equal amount of money at the end of each of the next three years in an account that will pay 8.75 percent. What is the annual investment necessary to meet the projected cost of the stadium?

Buy It on Credit and Be True to Your School

At the start of every school year, major banks offer students "free" credit cards. There are good reasons for banks to solicit students' business even though most students have neither steady jobs nor credit histories. First, students have a better record of paying their bills than the general public, because if they can't pay, usually their parents will. Second, students turn into loyal customers. Studies have shown that

© AP/Wide World Photos

students keep their first credit card for an average of 15 years. That enables banks to sell them services over time, such as car loans, first mortgages, and (somewhat ironically) debt consolidation loans. Third and perhaps most important, students are ideal customers because they do not tend to pay off their credit balances each month. A 2009 study by Sallie Mae, the largest student loan provider, found that among undergraduates who have credit cards, the credit card balances of only 18 percent are paid off each month. The other 82 percent carry a balance and pay interest charges. Sallie Mae also found that the percentage of undergraduates with at least one credit card increased from 76 percent in 2004 to 84 percent in 2009. Furthermore, students with credit cards had an average of 4.6 cards and owed an average of $3,173 in 2009. Seniors owed the most, with average debt of $4,100. Nineteen percent of students with credit cards owed over $7,000 on those cards!

Concern over Growing Student Debt

Concern has been growing that students cannot handle the debt they are taking on. In addition to credit card debt, the average graduating senior in the class of 2009 had $24,000 in student educational loan debt and 10 percent had more than $40,000 of such debt. The average student loan debt among graduating seniors in 2009 was almost twice as large as the average in 1996. Many students fail to realize that when they apply for a car loan or a mortgage, the total ratio of debt to income is usually the most important factor determining whether they get the loan. Student educational loans are added to credit card debt, and that, in turn, is added to the requested loan amount to determine eligibility. When all the debt is summed up, many do not qualify for the loan they want. In many cases, people are forced to postpone marriage or the purchase of a house because of their outstanding student loans and credit card debt.

To understand how students get into this kind of situation, consider the following hypothetical case. Suppose a student has a balance of $2,000 on a credit card. She makes the minimum payment every month but does not make any other purchases. Assuming a typical rate of interest, it would take 6.5 years to pay off the credit card debt, and the student would have incurred interest charges of $2,500. As one observer noted, students like this one "will still be paying for all that pizza they bought in college when they are 30 years old." A book published in 2000, *Credit Card Nation: The Consequences of America's Addiction to Credit*, was particularly critical of marketing credit cards to college students. The author, Robert Manning, identified a wide range of concerns, such as lowering of the age at which students can obtain credit cards, increasing credit limits on credit cards, students financing their education with credit card debt, and students using credit cards to conceal activities their parents might not approve of. Critics also point out that some of the advertising and marketing practices of the credit card companies are deceptive. In one case, for example, a credit card was touted as having no interest. That was true for the first month, but the annual percentage rate (APR) soared to 21 percent in the second month. Finally, many—including the students themselves—say that students do not receive sufficient education about how to manage credit card debt.

Supporters of credit card programs counter that most students do not "max out" their credit limits and that the three most common reasons for taking out a credit card are the establishment of a credit history, convenience, and emergency protection—all laudable goals.

The Credit Card Act of 2009, passed by Congress and signed by President Obama in 2009, includes a provision that is aimed at limiting the ability of credit card companies to market cards to students and other young adults. This provision, effective February 22, 2010, prohibits credit card companies from issuing credit cards to anyone under 21 unless that person can produce either (1) proof of a sufficiently high independent income to pay the credit card loans or (2) a willing co-signer who is over the age of 21. It remains to be seen whether this provision helps reverse the trend toward greater student credit card debt.

Affinity Credit Cards

The marketing of credit cards to students took a new twist in the 1990s. Banks began to compete fiercely to sign up students for their credit cards, and some banks entered into exclusive arrangements with universities for the right to issue an affinity card—a credit card that features the university's name and logo. The card issuer may be willing to support the university to the tune of several million dollars to gain the exclusive right to issue the affinity card and to keep other banks off campus.

The "Report to the Congress on College Credit Card Agreements," which was required by the Credit Card Act of 2009, revealed for the first time in October 2010 exactly how pervasive this practice had become. In 2009 alone, banks paid $83 million to U.S. colleges, universities, and affiliated organizations for the right to market their credit cards to students and alumni. Universities usually receive 0.5 percent of the purchase value when the card is used. Often, they receive a fee for each new account, and sometimes they receive a small percentage of the loans outstanding. Every time a student uses the credit card, the university benefits. The total benefits to individual universities can be substantial. For example, in 2009 alone, the University of Notre Dame du Lac received $1,860,000, the University of Southern California received $1,502,850, and the University of Tennessee received $1,428,571 from credit card agreements. In previous years, some universities received even larger direct payments from credit card issuers seeking to do business with students and alumni. Georgetown University, for example, received $2 million from MBNA for a career counseling center; Michigan State received $5.5 million from MBNA for athletic and academic scholarship programs; and the University of Tennessee received $16 million from First USA primarily for athletics and scholarships.

Universities have been facing difficult financial times, and it is easy to understand why they enter into these arrangements. However, the price the university pays is that it becomes ensnared in the ethical issue of contributing to the rising level of student credit card debt. Moreover, universities with affinity credit cards cannot escape a conflict of interest: the higher student credit card debt climbs, the greater the revenues the university earns from the bank. As a result of these issues, some universities have increased the amount of information they provide to students about handling credit card debt, both through counseling and formal courses.

Certainly, learning to responsibly manage credit card purchases and any resulting debt is a necessary part of the passage to adulthood. We can applaud the fact that universities educate students about the dangers of excessive credit card debt. However, if universities make money on that debt, we must question whether they have less incentive to educate students about the associated problems.

DISCUSSION QUESTIONS

1. Should universities enter into agreements to offer affinity credit cards to students?
2. Whether or not a university has an affinity credit card, does it have an obligation to educate students about credit card misuse and debt management?
3. Does the existence of an affinity credit card create a conflict of interest for a university if and when it adopts an education program on credit card misuse and debt management?
4. To what extent are students themselves responsible for their predicament?

Sources: "Big Cards on Campus," *Business Week*, September 20, 1999, pp. 136–137; Marilyn Gardner, "A Generation Weighed Down by Debt," *Christian Science Monitor*, November 24, 2004; "Survey Reveals Aggressive Marketing of Credit Cards Continues on Many Maryland College Campuses," U.S. PIRG press release, February 19, 2004; "Golden Eggs," *Boston Globe*, June 25, 2006; "How Undergraduate Students Use Credit Cards: Sallie Mae's National Study of Usage Rates and Trends, 2009," Sallie Mae, 2009; "Student Debt and the Class of 2009," Project on Student Debt, 2009; "Federal Reserve Board of Governors Report to the Congress on College Credit Card Agreements," Board of Governors of the Federal Reserve System, October 2010.

David Paul Morris/Bloomberg via Getty Images

Risk and Return 6

When Blockbuster Inc. filed for bankruptcy protection in September 2010, it looked like Netflix was unstoppable. With the demise of its major competitor in the video rental market, Netflix had become the most successful company in that market through its strategy of renting videos exclusively online and avoiding the high costs associated with operating video rental stores. On the day of the Blockbuster filing, Netflix's stock price closed at $160.47 per share, up from $46.85 just a year earlier. By early July of the following year, its shares were trading for as much as $304.79.

Then Netflix managers made a decision that did not turn out as expected. On July 12, 2011, they announced a new pricing strategy that would raise prices by as much as 60 percent for millions of Netflix subscribers who wanted to both rent DVDs by mail and watch video on the internet. Those two services would be un-bundled and, instead of paying $10 per month for both, customers would have to buy them separately at a cost of at least $16 per month. Customers and investors reacted swiftly and negatively to this announcement. During the fiscal quarter from July to September 2011, Netflix lost 800,000 U.S. subscribers and its stock price dropped to $113.27.

While Netflix managers did announce on October 10, 2011, that they were reversing their decision to unbundle the DVD rentals and video streaming, the damage had been done. The company's stock price continued to drift down, finishing the year at $70 per share. Perhaps sensing that Netflix was especially vulnerable after the events of 2011, Verizon Communications and Coinstar Inc. announced plans to work together to bundle streaming video and DVD rentals in direct competition with Netflix. By September 2012, Netflix shares were trading for less than $60.

This chapter discusses risk and return and the relation between them. The large increase in Netflix's share price prior to the July 2011 announcement and the subsequent decline illustrate a challenge faced by all investors—determining how volatile the value of their investments will be. Netflix shares were considered a risky investment, yet few investors would have thought that the price of those shares could go up or decline as quickly as they did. How should investors have viewed the risks of investing in Netflix? How are these risks related to the returns that investors might expect to earn? How does diversification reduce the overall risk of an investor's portfolio? These are among the topics that we discuss in this chapter.

CHAPTER PREVIEW

Up to this point, we have often mentioned the rate of return that we use to discount cash flows, but we have not explained how that rate is determined. We have now reached the point where it is time to examine key concepts underlying the discount rate. This chapter introduces a quantitative framework for measuring risk and return. This framework will help you develop an intuitive understanding of how risk and return are related and what risks matter to investors. The relation between risk and return has implications for the rate we use to discount cash flows because the time value of money concepts that we discussed in Chapter 5 are directly related to the returns that investors require. We must understand these concepts in order to determine the correct present value for a series of cash flows and to be able to make investment decisions that create value for stockholders.

We begin this chapter with a discussion of the general relation between risk and return to introduce the idea that investors require a higher rate of return from riskier assets. This is one of the most fundamental relations in finance. We next develop the statistical concepts required to quantify holding period returns, expected returns, and risk. We then apply these concepts to portfolios with a single asset and with more than one asset to illustrate the benefit of diversification. From this discussion, you will see how investing in more than one asset enables an investor to reduce the total risk associated with his or her investment portfolio, and you will learn how to quantify this benefit.

Once we have discussed the concept of diversification, we examine what it means for the relation between risk and return. We find that the total risk associated with an investment consists of two components: (1) unsystematic risk and (2) systematic risk. Diversification enables investors to eliminate the unsystematic risk associated with an individual asset. Investors do not require higher returns for the unsystematic risk that they can eliminate through diversification. Only systematic risk—risk that cannot be diversified away—affects expected returns on an investment. The distinction between unsystematic and systematic risk and the recognition that unsystematic risk can be diversified away are extremely important in finance. After reading this chapter, you will understand precisely what the term *risk* means in finance and how it is related to the rates of return that investors require.

6.1 RISK AND RETURN

LEARNING OBJECTIVE

The rate of return that investors require for an investment depends on the risk associated with that investment. The greater the risk, the larger the return investors require as compensation for bearing that risk. This is one of the most fundamental relations in finance. The *rate of return* is what you earn on an investment, stated in percentage terms. We will be more specific later, but for now you might think of *risk* as a measure of how certain you are that you will receive a particular return. Higher risk means you are less certain.

To get a better understanding of how risk and return are related, consider an example. You are trying to select the best investment from among the following three stocks:

Stock	Expected Return (%)	Risk Level (%)
A	12	12
B	12	16
C	16	16

Which would you choose? If you were comparing only Stocks A and B, you should choose Stock A. Both stocks have the same expected return, but Stock A has less risk. It does not make sense to invest in the riskier stock if the expected return is the same. Similarly, you can see that Stock C is clearly superior to Stock B. Stocks B and C have the same level of risk, but Stock C has a higher expected return. It would not make sense to accept a lower return for taking on the same level of risk.

But what about the choice between Stocks A and C? This choice is less obvious. Making it requires understanding the concepts that we discuss in the rest of this chapter.

> **MORE RISK MEANS A HIGHER EXPECTED RETURN**
>
> The greater the risk associated with an investment, the greater the return investors expect from it. A corollary to this idea is that investors want the highest return for a given level of risk or the lowest risk for a given level of return. When choosing between two investments that have the same level of risk, investors prefer the investment with the higher return. Alternatively, if two investments have the same expected return, investors prefer the less risky alternative.
>
> **BUILDING INTUITION**

6.2 QUANTITATIVE MEASURES OF RETURN

Before we begin a detailed discussion of the relation between risk and return, we should define more precisely what these terms mean. We begin with measures of return.

LEARNING OBJECTIVE 2

Holding Period Returns

When people refer to the return from an investment, they are generally referring to the total return over some *investment period,* or *holding period.* The **total holding period return** consists of two components: (1) capital appreciation and (2) income. The capital appreciation component of a return, R_{CA}, arises from a change in the price of the asset over the investment or holding period and is calculated as follows:

total holding period return the total return on an asset over a specific period of time or holding period

$$R_{CA} = \frac{\text{Capital appreciation}}{\text{Initial price}} = \frac{P_1 - P_0}{P_0} = \frac{\Delta P}{P_0}$$

where P_0 is the price paid for the asset at time zero and P_1 is the price at a later point in time.

The income component of a return arises from income that an investor receives from the asset while he or she owns it. For example, when a firm pays a cash dividend on its stock, the income component of the return on that stock, R_I, is calculated as follows:

$$R_I = \frac{\text{Cash flow}}{\text{Initial price}} = \frac{CF_1}{P_0}$$

where CF_1 is the cash flow from the dividend.

The total holding period return, R_T, is simply the sum of the capital appreciation and income components of return:

$$R_T = R_{CA} + R_I = \frac{\Delta P}{P_0} + \frac{CF_1}{P_0} = \frac{\Delta P + CF_1}{P_0} \tag{6.1}$$

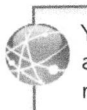

You can download actual realized investment returns for a large number of stock market indexes at the Callan Associates Web site, http://www.callan.com/research/periodic/.

Let's consider an example of calculating the total holding period return on an investment. One year ago today, you purchased a share of Dell Inc. stock for $12.50. Today it is worth $13.90. What total return did you earn on this stock over the past year if Dell paid no dividend?

Since Dell paid no dividend, and assuming you received no other income from holding the stock, the total return for the year equals the return from the capital appreciation. The total return is calculated as follows:

$$R_T = R_{CA} + R_I = \frac{P_1 - P_0 + CF_1}{P_0}$$
$$= \frac{\$13.90 - \$12.50 + \$0.00}{\$12.50}$$
$$= 0.112, \text{ or } 11.2\%$$

What return would you have earned if Dell had paid a $1 dividend and today's price was $12.90? With the $1 dividend and a correspondingly lower price, the total return is the same:

$$R_T = R_{CA} + R_I = \frac{P_1 - P_0 + CF_1}{P_0} = \frac{\$12.90 - \$12.50 + \$1.00}{\$12.50} = 0.112, \text{ or } 11.2\%$$

You can see from this example that a dollar of capital appreciation is worth the same as a dollar of income.

LEARNING BY DOING

APPLICATION 6.1

NEED MORE HELP?

WileyPLUS

Calculating the Return on an Investment

PROBLEM: You purchased a beat-up 1974 Datsun 240Z sports car a year ago for $1,500. Datsun is what Nissan, the Japanese car company, was called in the 1970s. The 240Z was the first in a series of cars that led to the Nissan 370Z that is being sold today. Recognizing that a mint-condition 240Z is a much sought-after car, you invested $7,000 and a lot of your time fixing up the car. Last week, you sold it to a collector for $18,000. Not counting the value of the time you spent restoring the car, what is the total return you earned on this investment over the one-year holding period?

APPROACH: Use Equation 6.1 to calculate the total holding period return. To calculate R_T using Equation 6.1, you must know P_0, P_1, and CF_1. In this problem, you can assume that the $7,000 was spent at the time you bought the car to purchase parts and materials. Therefore, your initial investment, P_0, was $1,500 + $7,000 = $8,500. Since there were no other cash inflows or outflows between the time that you bought the car and the time that you sold it, CF_1 equals $0.

SOLUTION: The total holding period return is:

$$R_T = R_{CA} + R_I = \frac{P_1 - P_0 + CF_1}{P_0} = \frac{\$18,000 - \$8,500 + \$0}{\$8,500} = 1.118, \text{ or } 111.8\%$$

Expected Returns

3 LEARNING OBJECTIVE

Suppose that you are a senior who plays college baseball and that your team is in the College World Series. Furthermore, suppose that you have been drafted by the Washington Nationals and are coming up for what you expect to be your last at-bat as a college player. The fact that you expect this to be your last at-bat is important because you just signed a very unusual contract with the Nationals. Your signing bonus will be determined solely by whether you get a hit in your final collegiate at-bat. If you get a hit, then your signing bonus will be $800,000. Otherwise, it will be $400,000. This past season, you got a hit 32.5 percent of the times you were at bat (you did not get a hit 67.5 percent of the time), and you believe this percentage reflects the likelihood that you will get a hit in your last collegiate at-bat.[1]

What is the expected value of your bonus? If you have taken a statistics course, you might recall that an expected value represents the sum of the products of the possible outcomes and

[1]For simplicity, let's ignore the possibility of your hitting a sacrifice fly and other such outcomes.

the probabilities that those outcomes will be realized. In our example the expected value of the bonus can be calculated using the following formula:

$$E(Bonus) = (p_H \times B_H) + (p_{NH} \times B_{NH})$$

where $E(Bonus)$ is your expected bonus, p_H is the probability of a hit, p_{NH} is the probability of no hit, B_H is the bonus you receive if you get a hit, and B_{NH} is the bonus you receive if you get no hit. Since p_H equals 0.325, p_{NH} equals 0.675, B_H equals \$800,000, and B_{NH} equals \$400,000, the expected value of your bonus is:

$$\begin{aligned} E(Bonus) &= (p_H \times B_H) + (p_{NH} \times B_{NH}) \\ &= (0.325 \times \$800{,}000) + (0.675 \times \$400{,}000) = \$530{,}000 \end{aligned}$$

Notice that the expected bonus of \$530,000 is not equal to either of the two possible payoffs. Neither is it equal to the simple average of the two possible payoffs. This is because the expected bonus takes into account the probability of each event occurring. If the probability of each event had been 50 percent, then the expected bonus would have equaled the simple average of the two payoffs:

$$E(Bonus) = (0.5 \times \$800{,}000) + (0.5 \times \$400{,}000) = \$600{,}000$$

However, since it is more likely that you will not get a hit (a 67.5 percent chance) than that you will get a hit (a 32.5 percent chance), and the payoff is lower if you do not get a hit, the expected bonus is less than the simple average.

What would your expected payoff be if you got a hit 99 percent of the time? We intuitively know that the expected bonus should be much closer to \$800,000 in this case. In fact, it is:

$$E(Bonus) = (0.99 \times \$800{,}000) + (0.01 \times \$400{,}000) = \$796{,}000$$

The key point here is that the expected value reflects the relative likelihoods of the possible outcomes.

We calculate an **expected return** in finance in the same way that we calculate any expected value. The expected return is a weighted average of the possible returns from an investment, where each of these returns is weighted by the probability that it will occur. In general terms, the expected return on an asset, $E(R_{Asset})$, is calculated as follows:

expected return
an average of the possible returns from an investment, where each return is weighted by the probability that it will occur

$$E(R_{Asset}) = \sum_{i=1}^{n} (p_i \times R_i) = (p_1 \times R_1) + (p_2 \times R_2) + \cdots + (p_n \times R_n) \qquad (6.2)$$

where R_i is possible return i and p_i is the probability that you will actually earn R_i. The summation symbol in this equation

$$\sum_{i=1}^{n}$$

is mathematical shorthand indicating that n values are added together. In Equation 6.2, each of the n possible returns is multiplied by the probability that it will be realized, and these products are then added together to calculate the expected return.

It is important to make sure that the sum of the n individual probabilities, the p_i's, always equals 1, or 100 percent, when you calculate an expected value. The sum of the probabilities cannot be less than 100 percent because you must account for all possible outcomes in the calculation. On the other hand, as you may recall from statistics, the sum of the probabilities of all possible outcomes cannot exceed 100 percent. For example, notice that the sum of the p_i's equals 1 in each of the expected bonus calculations that we discussed earlier ($0.325 + 0.625 = 1$ in the first calculation, $0.5 + 0.5 = 1$ in the second, and $0.99 + 0.01 = 1$ in the third).

The expected return on an asset reflects the return that you can expect to receive from investing in that asset over the period that you plan to own it. It is your best estimate of this return, given the possible outcomes and their associated probabilities.

Note that if each of the possible outcomes is equally likely (that is, $p_1 = p_2 = p_3 = \cdots = p_n = p = 1/n$), this formula reduces to the formula for a simple (equally weighted) average of the possible returns:

$$E(R_{Asset}) = \frac{\sum_{i=1}^{n} (R_i)}{n} = \frac{R_1 + R_2 + \cdots + R_n}{n}$$

To see how we calculate the expected return on an asset, suppose you are considering purchasing Dell, Inc. stock for $13.90 per share. You plan to sell the stock in one year. You estimate that there is a 30 percent chance that Dell stock will sell for $13.40 at the end of one year, a 30 percent chance that it will sell for $14.90, a 30 percent chance that it will sell for $15.40, and a 10 percent chance that it will sell for $16.00. If Dell pays no dividends on its shares, what is the return that you expect from this stock in the next year?

With no dividends, the total return on Dell's stock equals the return from capital appreciation:

$$R_T = R_{CA} = \frac{P_1 - P_0}{P_0}$$

Therefore, we can calculate the return from owning Dell stock under each of the four possible outcomes using the approach we used for the similar Dell problem we solved earlier in the chapter. These returns are calculated as follows:

Dell Stock Price in One Year	Total Return
(1) $13.40	$\frac{\$13.40 - \$13.90}{\$13.90} = -0.0360$, or -3.60%
(2) $14.90	$\frac{\$14.90 - \$13.90}{\$13.90} = 0.0719$, or 7.19%
(3) $15.40	$\frac{\$15.40 - \$13.90}{\$13.90} = 0.1079$, or 10.79%
(4) $16.00	$\frac{\$16.00 - \$13.90}{\$13.90} = 0.1511$, or 15.11%

Applying Equation 6.2, the expected return on Dell stock over the next year is therefore 5.83 percent, calculated as follows:

$$E(R_{Dell}) = \sum_{i=1}^{4} (p_i \times R_i) = (p_1 \times R_1) + (p_2 \times R_2) + (p_3 \times R_3) + (p_4 \times R_4)$$
$$= (0.3 \times -0.0360) + (0.3 \times 0.0719) + (0.3 \times 0.1079) + (0.1 \times 0.1511)$$
$$= -0.01080 + 0.02157 + 0.03237 + 0.01511 = 0.0583, \text{ or } 5.83\%$$

Notice that the negative return is entered into the formula just like any other. Also notice that the sum of the p_i's equals 1.

LEARNING
BY
DOING

NEED MORE HELP?

WileyPLUS

APPLICATION 6.2

Calculating Expected Returns

PROBLEM: You have just purchased 100 railroad cars that you plan to lease to a large railroad company. Demand for shipping goods by rail has recently increased dramatically due to the rising price of oil. You expect oil prices, which are currently at $98.81 per barrel, to reach $115.00 per barrel in the next year. If this happens, railroad shipping prices will increase, thereby driving up the value of your railroad cars as increases in demand outpace the rate at which new cars are being produced.

Given your oil price prediction, you estimate that there is a 30 percent chance that the value of your railroad cars will increase by 15 percent, a 40 percent chance that their value will increase by 25 percent, and a 30 percent chance that their value will increase by 30 percent in the next year. In addition to appreciation in the value of your cars, you expect to earn 10 percent on your investment over the next year (after expenses) from leasing the railroad cars. What total return do you expect to earn on your railroad car investment over the next year?

APPROACH: Use Equation 6.1 first to calculate the total return that you would earn under each of the three possible outcomes. Next use these total return values, along with the associated probabilities, in Equation 6.2 to calculate the expected total return.

SOLUTION: To calculate the total returns using Equation 6.1,

$$R_T = R_{CA} + R_I = \frac{\Delta P}{P_0} + \frac{CF_1}{P_0}$$

you must recognize that $\Delta P/P_0$ is the capital appreciation under each outcome and that CF_1/P_0 equals the 10 percent that you expect to receive from leasing the rail cars. The expected returns for the three outcomes are:

Increase in Value of Rail Cars in One Year	Return from Leases	Total Return
15%	10%	$R_T = \frac{\Delta P}{P_0} + \frac{CF_1}{P_0} = 0.15 + 0.10 = 0.25$, or 25%
25%	10%	$R_T = \frac{\Delta P}{P_0} + \frac{CF_1}{P_0} = 0.25 + 0.10 = 0.35$, or 35%
30%	10%	$R_T = \frac{\Delta P}{P_0} + \frac{CF_1}{P_0} = 0.30 + 0.10 = 0.40$, or 40%

You can then use Equation 6.2 to calculate the expected return for your rail car investment:

$$E(R_{Rail\ cars}) = \sum_{i=1}^{3} (\rho_i \times R_i) = (\rho_1 \times R_1) + (\rho_2 \times R_2) + (\rho_3 \times R_3)$$
$$= (0.3 \times 0.25) + (0.4 \times 0.35) + (0.3 \times 0.40)$$
$$= 0.335, \text{ or } 33.5\%$$

Alternatively, since there is a 100 percent probability that the return from leasing the railroad cars is 10 percent, you could have simply calculated the expected increase in value of the railroad cars:

$$E\left(\frac{\Delta P}{P_0}\right) = (0.3 \times 0.15) + (0.4 \times 0.25) + (0.3 \times 0.30)$$
$$= 0.235, \text{ or } 23.5\%$$

and added the 10 percent to arrive at the answer of 33.5 percent. Of course, this simpler approach only works if the return from leasing is known with certainty.

Using Expected Values in Decision Making

SITUATION: You are deciding whether you should advertise your pizza business on the radio or on billboards placed on local taxicabs. For $1,000 per month, you can either buy 20 one-minute ads on the radio or place your ad on 40 taxicabs.

There is some uncertainty regarding how many new customers will visit your restaurant after hearing one of your radio ads. You estimate that there is a 30 percent chance that 35 people will visit, a 45 percent chance that 50 people will visit, and a 25 percent chance that 60 people will visit. Therefore, you expect the following number of new customers to visit your restaurant in response to each radio ad:

$$E(\text{New customers per ad}_{Radio}) = (0.30 \times 35) + (0.45 \times 50) + (0.25 \times 60) = 48$$

This means that you expect 20 one-minute ads to bring in $20 \times 48 = 960$ new customers.

(continued)

Similarly, you estimate that there is a 20 percent chance you will get 20 new customers in response to an ad placed on a taxi, a 30 percent chance you will get 30 new customers, a 30 percent chance that you will get 40 new customers, and a 20 percent chance that you will get 50 new customers. Therefore, you expect the following number of new customers in response to each ad that you place on a taxi:

$$E(\text{New customers per ad}_{Taxi}) = (0.2 \times 20) + (0.3 \times 30) + (0.3 \times 40) + (0.2 \times 50)$$
$$= 35$$

Placing ads on 40 taxicabs is therefore expected to bring in $40 \times 35 = 1,400$ new customers.

Which of these two advertising options is more attractive? Is it cost effective?

DECISION: You should advertise on taxicabs. For a monthly cost of $1,000, you expect to attract 1,400 new customers with taxicab advertisements but only 960 new customers if you advertise on the radio.

The answer to the question of whether advertising on taxicabs is cost effective depends on how much the gross profits (profits after variable costs) of your business are increased by those 1,400 customers. Monthly gross profits will have to increase by $1,000, or average 72 cents per new customer ($1,000/1,400 = $0.72) to cover the cost of the advertising campaign.

> **BEFORE YOU GO ON**

1. What are the two components of a total holding period return?

2. How is the expected return on an investment calculated?

6.3 VARIANCE AND STANDARD DEVIATION AS MEASURES OF RISK

4 LEARNING OBJECTIVE

We turn next to a discussion of the two most basic measures of risk used in finance—variance and standard deviation. These are the same variance and standard deviation measures that you studied if you took a course in statistics.

Calculating Variance and Standard Deviation

Let's begin by returning to our College World Series example. Recall that you will receive a bonus of $800,000 if you get a hit in your final collegiate at-bat and a bonus of $400,000 if you do not. The expected value of your bonus is $530,000. Suppose you want to measure the risk, or uncertainty, associated with the bonus. How can you do this? One approach would be to compute a measure of how much, on average, the bonus payoffs deviate from the expected value. The underlying intuition here is that the greater the difference between the actual bonus and the expected value, the greater the risk. For example, you might calculate the difference between each possible bonus payment and the expected value, and sum these differences. If you do this, you will get the following result:

$$\text{Risk} = (\$800,000 - \$530,000) + (\$400,000 - \$530,000)$$
$$= \$270,000 + (-130,000)$$
$$= \$140,000$$

Unfortunately, using this calculation to obtain a measure of risk presents two problems. First, since one difference is positive and the other difference is negative, one difference partially cancels the other. As a result, you are not getting an accurate measure of total risk. Second, this calculation does not take into account the number of potential outcomes or the probability of each outcome.

A better approach would be to square the differences (squaring the differences makes all the numbers positive) and multiply each squared difference by its associated probability before summing them up. This calculation yields the **variance (σ^2)** of the possible outcomes. The variance does not suffer from the two problems associated with the above calculation and provides a measure of risk that has a consistent interpretation across different situations or assets. For the original bonus arrangement, the variance is:

variance (σ^2)
a measure of the uncertainty associated with an outcome

$$\begin{aligned} \text{Var}(\text{Bonus}) = \sigma^2_{(\text{Bonus})} &= \{p_\text{H} \times [\text{B}_\text{H} - \text{E}(\text{Bonus})]^2\} \\ &\quad + \{p_\text{NH} \times [\text{B}_\text{NH} - \text{E}(\text{Bonus})]^2\} \\[6pt] &= [0.325 \times (\$800,\!000 - \$530,\!000)^2] \\ &\quad + [0.675 \times (\$400,\!000 - \$530,\!000)^2] \\[6pt] &= 35,\!100,\!000,\!000 \text{ dollars}^2 \end{aligned}$$

Note that the square of the Greek symbol sigma, σ^2, is generally used to represent the variance.

Because it is somewhat awkward to work with units of squared dollars, in a calculation such as this we would typically take the square root of the variance. The square root gives us the **standard deviation (σ)** of the possible outcomes. For our example, the standard deviation is:

standard deviation (σ)
the square root of the variance

$$\sigma_{(\text{Bonus})} = (\sigma^2_{(\text{Bonus})})^{1/2} = (35,\!100,\!000,\!000 \text{ dollars}^2)^{1/2} = \$187,\!349.94$$

As you will see when we discuss the normal distribution, the standard deviation has a natural interpretation that is very useful for assessing investment risks.

The general formula for calculating the variance of returns can be written as follows:

$$\text{Var}(\text{R}) = \sigma^2_\text{R} = \sum_{i=1}^{n} \{p_i \times [\text{R}_i - \text{E}(\text{R})]^2\} \tag{6.3}$$

Equation 6.3 simply extends the calculation illustrated above to the situation where there are n possible outcomes. Like the expected return calculation (Equation 6.2), Equation 6.3 can be simplified if all of the possible outcomes are equally likely. In this case it becomes:

$$\sigma^2_\text{R} = \frac{\sum_{i=1}^{n} [\text{R}_i - \text{E}(\text{R})]^2}{n}$$

In both the general case and the case where all possible outcomes are equally likely, the standard deviation is simply the square root of the variance $\sigma_\text{R} = (\sigma^2_\text{R})^{1/2}$.

Interpreting Variance and Standard Deviation

The variance and standard deviation are especially useful measures of risk for variables that are normally distributed—those that can be represented by a normal distribution. The **normal distribution** is a symmetric frequency distribution that is completely described by its mean (average) and standard deviation. Exhibit 6.1 illustrates what this distribution looks like. Even if you have never taken a statistics course, you have already encountered the normal distribution. It is the "bell curve" on which instructors often base their grade distributions. SAT scores and IQ scores are also based on normal distributions.

normal distribution
a symmetric frequency distribution that is completely described by its mean and standard deviation; also known as a bell curve due to its shape

This distribution is very useful in finance because the returns for many assets are approximately normally distributed. This makes the variance and standard deviation practical measures of the uncertainty associated with investment returns. Since the standard deviation is more easily interpreted than the variance, we will focus on the standard deviation as we discuss the normal distribution and its application in finance.

In Exhibit 6.1, you can see that the normal distribution is symmetric: the left and right sides are mirror images of each other. The mean falls directly in the center of the distribution, and the probability that an outcome is less than or greater than a particular distance from the mean is the same whether the outcome is on the left or the right side of the distribution. For example, if the mean is 0, the probability that a particular outcome is −3 or less is the same as the probability that it is +3 or more (both are 3 or more units from the mean).

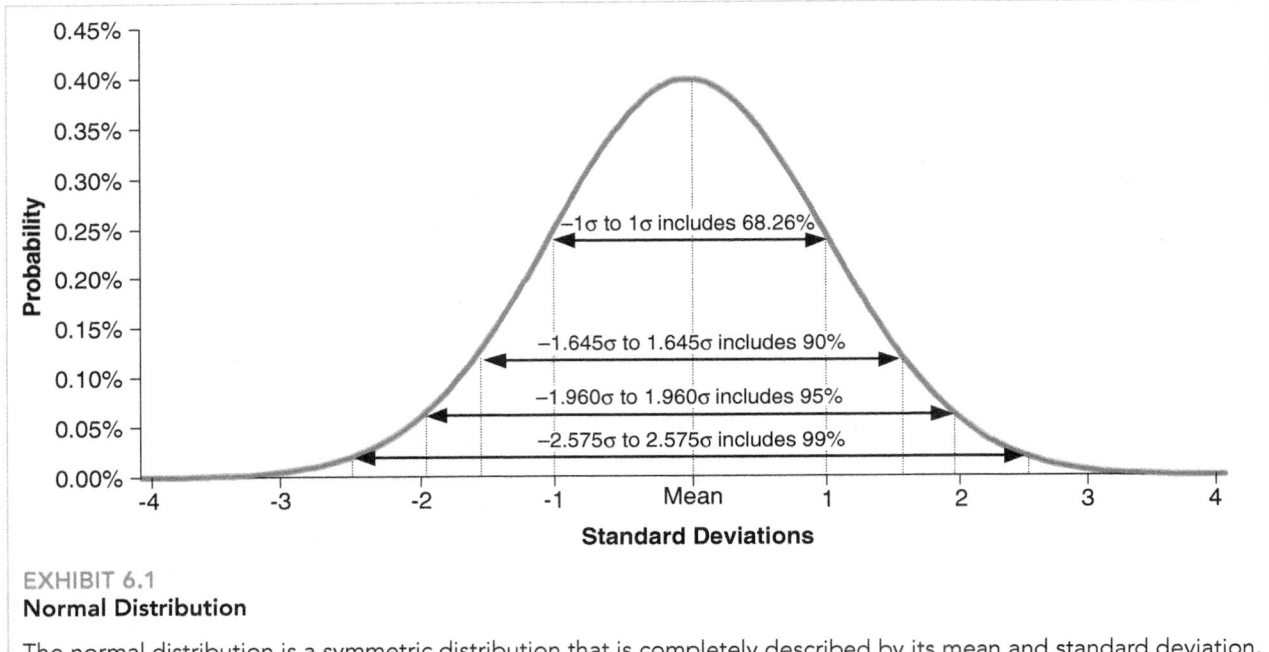

EXHIBIT 6.1
Normal Distribution

The normal distribution is a symmetric distribution that is completely described by its mean and standard deviation. The mean is the value that defines the center of the distribution, and the standard deviation, σ, describes the dispersion of the values centered around the mean.

This enables us to use a single measure of risk for the normal distribution. That measure is the standard deviation.

The standard deviation tells us everything we need to know about the width of the normal distribution or, in other words, the variation in the individual values. This variation is what we mean when we talk about risk in finance. In general terms, risk is a measure of the range of potential outcomes. The standard deviation is an especially useful measure of risk because it tells us the probability that an outcome will fall a particular distance from the mean, or within a particular range. You can see this in the following table, which shows the fraction of all observations in a normal distribution that are within the indicated number of standard deviations from the mean.

Number of Standard Deviations from the Mean	Fraction of Total Observations
1.000	68.26%
1.645	90%
1.960	95%
2.575	99%

Since the returns on many assets are approximately normally distributed, the standard deviation provides a convenient way of computing the probability that the return on an asset will fall within a particular range. In these applications, the expected return on an asset equals the mean of the distribution, and the standard deviation is a measure of the uncertainty associated with the return.

For example, if the expected return for a real estate investment in Miami, Florida, is 10 percent with a standard deviation of 2 percent, there is a 90 percent chance that the actual return will be within 3.29 percent of 10 percent. How do we know this? As shown in the table above, 90 percent of all outcomes in a normal distribution have a value that is within 1.645 standard deviations of the mean value, and 1.645 × 2 percent = 3.29 percent. This tells us that there is a 90 percent chance that the realized return on the investment in Miami will be between 6.71 percent (10 percent − 3.29 percent = 6.71 percent) and 13.29 percent (10 percent + 3.29 percent = 13.29 percent), a range of 6.58 percent (13.29 percent − 6.71 percent = 6.58 percent).

You may be wondering what is *standard* about the standard deviation. The answer is that this statistic is standard in the sense that it can be used to directly compare the uncertainties (risks) associated with the returns on different investments. For instance, suppose you are comparing the real estate investment in Miami with a real estate investment in Fresno, California. Assume that the expected return on the Fresno investment is also 10 percent. If the standard deviation for the returns on the Fresno investment is 3 percent, there is a 90 percent chance that the actual return is within 4.935 percent (1.645 × 3 percent = 4.935 percent) of 10 percent. In other words, 90 percent of the time, the return will be between 5.065 percent (10 percent − 4.935 percent = 5.065 percent) and 14.935 percent (10 percent + 4.935 percent = 14.935 percent), a range of 9.87 percent (14.935 percent − 5.065 percent = 9.87 percent).

This range is exactly 9.87 percent/6.58 percent = 1.5 times as large as the range for the Miami investment opportunity. Notice that the ratio of the two standard deviations also equals 1.5 (3 percent/2 percent = 1.5). This is not a coincidence. We could have used the standard deviations to directly compute the relative uncertainty associated with the Fresno and Miami investment returns. The relation between the standard deviation of returns and the width of a normal distribution (the uncertainty) is illustrated in Exhibit 6.2.

Let's consider another example of how the standard deviation is interpreted. Suppose customers at your pizza restaurant have complained that there is no consistency in the number of slices of pepperoni that your cooks are putting on large pepperoni pizzas. One night you decide to work in the area where the pizzas are made so that you can count the number of pepperoni slices on the large pizzas to get a better idea of just how much variation there is. After counting the slices of pepperoni on 50 pizzas, you estimate that, on average, your pies have 18 slices of pepperoni and that the standard deviation is 3 slices.

With this information, you estimate that 95 percent of the large pepperoni pizzas sold in your restaurant have between 12.12 and 23.88 pepperoni slices. You are able to estimate this range because you know that 95 percent of the observations in a normal distribution fall within 1.96 standard deviations of the mean. With a standard deviation of three slices, this implies that the number of pepperoni slices on 95 percent of your pizzas is within 5.88 slices of the mean (3 slices × 1.96 = 5.88 slices). This, in turn, indicates a range of 12.12 (18 − 5.88 = 12.12) to 23.88 (18 + 5.88 = 23.88) slices.

Since you put only whole slices of pepperoni on your pizzas, 95 percent of the time the number of slices is somewhere between 12 and 24. No wonder your customers are up in arms! In response to this information, you decide to implement a standard policy regarding the number of pepperoni slices that go on each type of pizza.

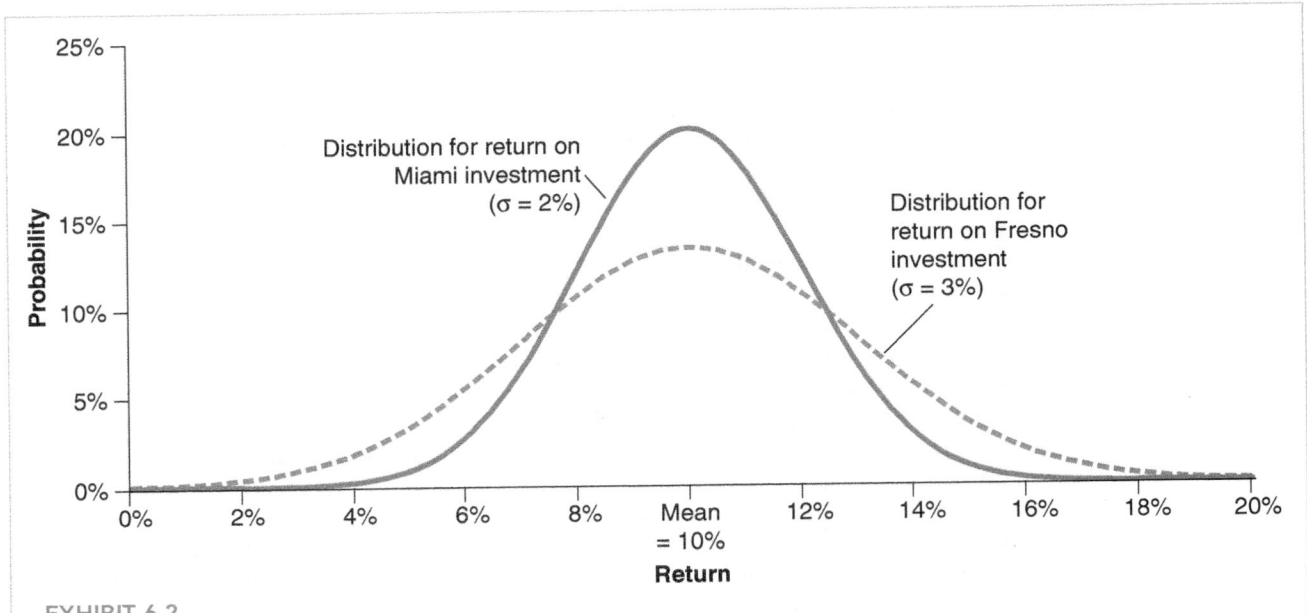

EXHIBIT 6.2
Standard Deviation and Width of the Normal Distribution

The larger standard deviation for the return on the Fresno investment means that the Fresno investment is riskier than the Miami investment. The actual return for the Fresno investment is more likely to be further from its expected return.

Understanding the Standard Deviation

PROBLEM:　You are considering investing in a share of Google Inc. stock and want to evaluate how risky this potential investment is. You know that stock returns tend to be normally distributed, and you have calculated the expected return on Google stock to be 4.67 percent and the standard deviation of the annual return to be 23 percent. Based on these statistics, within what range would you expect the return on this stock to fall during the next year? Calculate this range for a 90 percent level of confidence (that is, 90 percent of the time, the returns will fall within the specified range).

APPROACH:　Use the values in the previous table or Exhibit 6.1 to compute the range within which Google's stock return will fall 90 percent of the time. First, find the number of standard deviations associated with a 90 percent level of confidence in the table or Exhibit 6.1 and then multiply this number by the standard deviation of the annual return for Google's stock. Then subtract the resulting value from the expected return (mean) to obtain the lower end of the range and add it to the expected return to obtain the upper end.

SOLUTION:　From the table, you can see that we would expect the return over the next year to be within 1.645 standard deviations of the mean 90 percent of the time. Multiplying this value by the standard deviation of Google's stock (23 percent) yields 23 percent × 1.645 = 37.835 percent. This means that there is a 90 percent chance that the return will be between −33.165 percent (4.67 percent − 37.835 percent = −33.165 percent) and 42.505 percent (4.67 percent + 37.835 percent = 42.505 percent).

　　While the expected return of 4.67 percent is relatively low, the returns on Google stock vary considerably, and there is a reasonable chance that the stock return in the next year could be quite high or quite low (even negative). As you will see shortly, this wide range of possible returns is similar to the range we observe for typical shares in the U.S. stock market.

Historical Market Performance

Now that we have discussed how returns and risks can be measured, we are ready to examine the characteristics of the historical returns earned by securities such as stocks and bonds. Exhibit 6.3 illustrates the distributions of historical returns for some securities in the United States and shows the average and standard deviations of these annual returns for the period from 1926 to 2011.

　　Note that the statistics reported in Exhibit 6.3 are for indexes that represent total *average* returns for the indicated types of securities, not total returns on individual securities. We generally use indexes to represent the performance of the stock or bond markets. For instance, when news services report on the performance of the stock market, they often report that the Dow Jones Industrial Average (an index based on 30 large stocks), the S&P 500 Index (an index based on 500 large stocks), or the NASDAQ Composite Index (an index based on all stocks that are traded on NASDAQ) went up or down on a particular day. These and other indexes are discussed in Chapter 8.

　　The plots in Exhibit 6.3 are arranged in order of decreasing risk, which is indicated by the decreasing standard deviation of the annual returns. The top plot shows returns for a small-stock index that represents the 10 percent of U.S. firms that have the lowest total equity value (number of shares multiplied by price per share). The second plot shows returns for the S&P 500 Index, representing large U.S. stocks. The remaining plots show three different types of government debt: long-term government bonds that mature in 20 years, intermediate-term government bonds that mature in five years, and U.S. Treasury bills, which are short-term debts of the U.S. government, that mature in 30 days.

EXHIBIT 6.3

Distributions of Annual Total Returns for U.S. Stocks and Bonds from 1926 to 2011

Higher standard deviations of returns have historically been associated with higher returns. For example, between 1926 and 2011, the standard deviation of the annual returns for small stocks was higher than the standard deviations of the returns earned by other types of securities, and the average return that investors earned from small stocks was also higher. At the other end of the spectrum, the returns on Treasury bills had the smallest standard deviation, and Treasury bills earned the smallest average return.

Source: Data from Morningstar, 2012 SBBI Yearbook

    The key point to note in Exhibit 6.3 is that, on average, annual returns have been higher for riskier securities. Small stocks, which have the largest standard deviation of total returns, at 32.51 percent, also have the largest average annual return, 16.51 percent. On the other end of the spectrum, Treasury bills have the smallest standard deviation, 3.10 percent, and the smallest average annual return, 3.62 percent. Returns for small stocks in any particular year may have been higher or lower than returns for the other types of securities, but on average, they were higher. This is evidence that investors require higher returns for investments with greater risks.

The statistics in Exhibit 6.3 describe actual investment returns, as opposed to expected returns. In other words, they represent what has happened in the past. Financial analysts often use historical numbers such as these to estimate the returns that might be expected in the future. That is exactly what we did in the baseball example earlier in this chapter. We used the percentage of at-bats in which you got a hit this past season to estimate the likelihood that you would get a hit in your last collegiate at-bat. We assumed that your past performance was a reasonable indicator of your future performance.

To see how historical numbers are used in finance, let's suppose that you are considering investing in a fund that mimics the S&P 500 Index (this is what we call an *index fund*) and that you want to estimate what the returns on the S&P 500 Index are likely to be in the future. If you believe that the 1926 to 2011 period provides a reasonable indication of what we can expect in the future, then the average historical return on the S&P 500 Index of 11.77 percent provides a perfectly reasonable estimate of the return you can expect from your investment in the S&P 500 Index fund. In Chapter 11 we will explore in detail how historical data can be used in this way to estimate the discount rate for evaluating projects in the capital budgeting process.

Comparing the historical returns for an individual stock with the historical returns for an index can also be instructive. Exhibit 6.4 shows such a comparison for Apple Inc. and the S&P 500 Index using monthly returns for the period from August 2007 to August 2012. Notice in the exhibit that the returns on Apple stock are much more volatile than the average returns on the firms represented in the S&P 500 Index. In other words, the standard deviation of returns for Apple stock is higher than that for the S&P 500 Index. This is not a coincidence; we will discuss shortly why returns on individual stocks tend to be riskier than returns on indexes.

One last point is worth noting while we are examining historical returns: the value of a $1.00 investment in 1926 would have varied greatly by 2011, depending on where that dollar was invested. Exhibit 6.5 shows that $1.00 invested in U.S. Treasury bills in 1926 would have been worth $20.56 by 2011. In contrast, that same $1.00 invested in small stocks would have

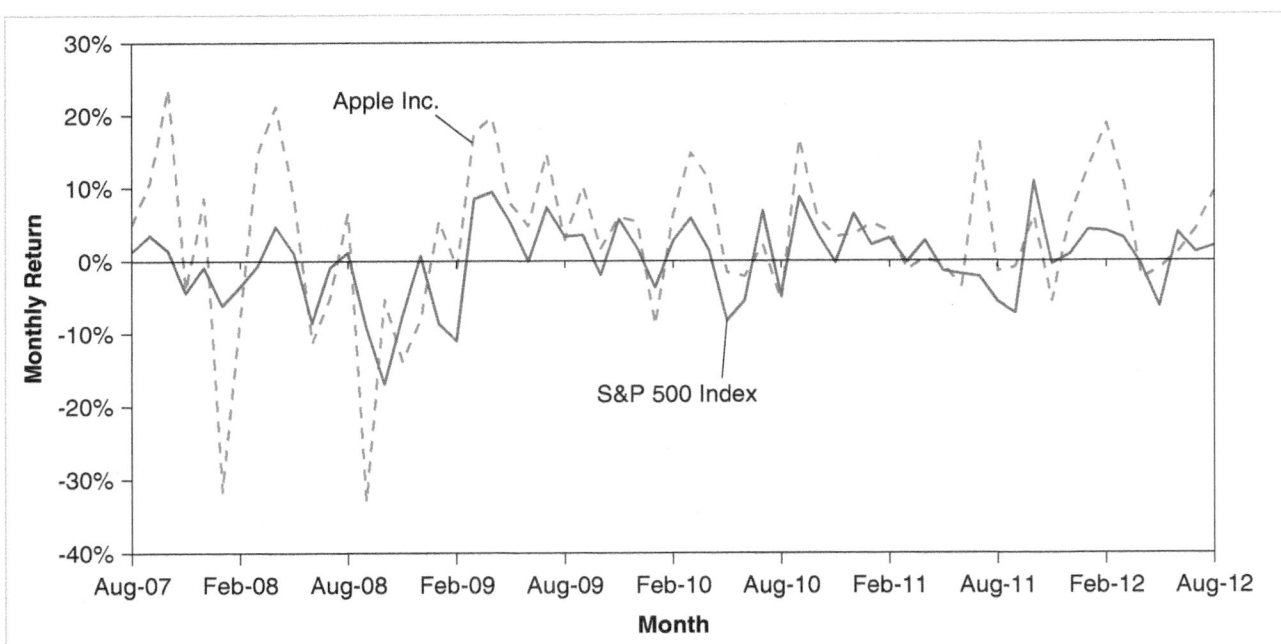

EXHIBIT 6.4

Monthly Returns for Apple Inc. stock and the S&P 500 Index from August 2007 through August 2012

The returns on shares of individual stocks tend to be much more volatile than the returns on portfolios of stocks, such as the S&P 500.

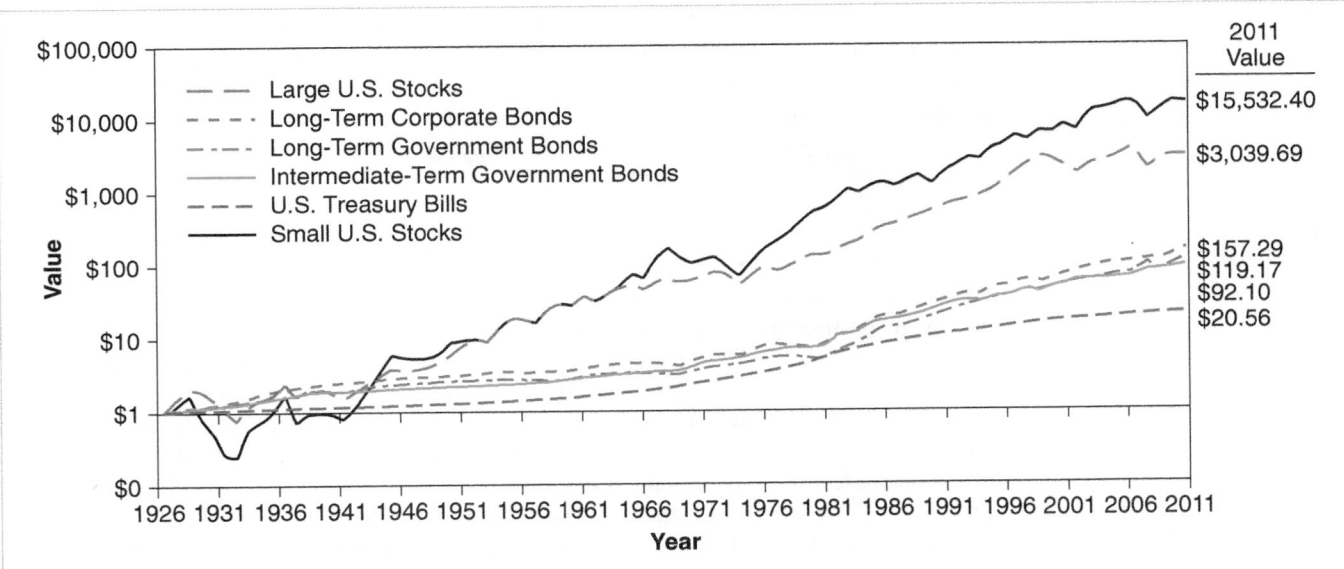

EXHIBIT 6.5
Cumulative Value of $1 Invested in 1926

The value of a $1 investment in stocks, small or large, grew much more rapidly than the value of a $1 investment in bonds or Treasury bills over the 1926 to 2011 period. This graph illustrates how earning a higher rate of return over a long period of time can affect the value of an investment portfolio. Although annual stock returns were less certain between 1926 and 2011, the returns on stock investments were much greater.

Source: Data from Morningstar, 2012 SBBI Yearbook

been worth $15,532.40 by 2011.[2] Over a long period of time, earning higher rates of return can have a dramatic impact on the value of an investment. This huge difference reflects the impact of compounding of returns (returns earned on returns), much like the compounding of interest we discussed in Chapter 5.

> **BEFORE YOU GO ON**

1. What is the relation between the variance and the standard deviation?

2. What relation do we generally observe between risk and return when we examine historical returns?

3. How would we expect the standard deviation of the return on an individual stock to compare with the standard deviation of the return on a stock index?

6.4 RISK AND DIVERSIFICATION

It does not generally make sense to invest all of your money in a single asset. The reason is directly related to the fact that returns on individual stocks tend to be riskier than returns on indexes. By investing in two or more assets whose values do not always move in the same direction at the same time, an investor can reduce the risk of his or her collection of investments, or **portfolio**. This is the idea behind the concept of **diversification**.

LEARNING OBJECTIVE 5

portfolio
the collection of assets an investor owns

diversification
reducing risk by investing in two or more assets whose values do not always move in the same direction at the same time

---

[2]From a practical standpoint, it would not really have been possible to grow $1.00 to $15,532.40 by investing in small U.S. stocks because this increase assumes that an investor is able to rebalance the stock portfolio by buying and selling shares as necessary at no cost. Since buying and selling shares are costly endeavors, the final wealth would have been lower. Nevertheless, even after transaction costs, it would have been much more profitable to invest in small stocks than in U.S. Treasury bills.

This section develops the tools necessary to evaluate the benefits of diversification. We begin with a discussion of how to quantify risk and return for a single-asset portfolio, and then we discuss more realistic and complicated portfolios that have two or more assets. Although our discussion focuses on stock portfolios, it is important to recognize that the concepts discussed apply equally well to portfolios that include a range of assets, such as stocks, bonds, gold, art, and real estate, among others.

Single-Asset Portfolios

Returns for individual stocks from one day to the next have been found to be largely independent of each other and approximately normally distributed. In other words, the return for a stock on one day is largely independent of the return on that same stock the next day, two days later, three days later, and so on. Each daily return can be viewed as having been randomly drawn from a normal distribution where the probability associated with the return depends on how far it is from the expected value. If we know what the expected value and standard deviation are for the distribution of returns for a stock, it is possible to quantify the risks and expected returns that an investment in the stock might yield in the future.

To see how we might do this, assume that you are considering investing in one of two stocks for the next year: Advanced Micro Devices (AMD) or Intel. Also, to keep things simple, assume that there are only three possible economic conditions (outcomes) a year from now and that the returns on AMD and Intel under each of these outcomes are as follows:

Economic Outcome	Probability	AMD Return	Intel Return
Poor	0.2	−0.13	−0.10
Neutral	0.5	0.10	0.07
Good	0.3	0.25	0.22

With this information, we can calculate the expected returns for AMD and Intel by using Equation 6.2:

$$E(R_{AMD}) = (p_{Poor} \times R_{Poor}) + (p_{Neutral} \times R_{Neutral}) + (p_{Good} \times R_{Good})$$
$$= (0.2 \times -0.13) + (0.5 \times 0.10) + (0.3 \times 0.25)$$
$$= 0.099, \text{ or } 9.9\%$$

and

$$E(R_{Intel}) = (p_{Poor} \times R_{Poor}) + (p_{Neutral} \times R_{Neutral}) + (p_{Good} \times R_{Good})$$
$$= (0.2 \times -0.10) + (0.5 \times 0.07) + (0.3 \times 0.22)$$
$$= 0.081, \text{ or } 8.1\%$$

Similarly, we can calculate the standard deviations of the returns for AMD and Intel in the same way that we calculated the standard deviation for our baseball bonus example in Section 6.2:

$$\sigma^2_{R_{AMD}} = \{p_{Poor} \times [R_{Poor} - E(R_{AMD})]^2\} + \{p_{Neutral} \times [R_{Neutral} - E(R_{AMD})]^2\}$$
$$+ \{p_{Good} \times [R_{Good} - E(R_{AMD})]^2\}$$
$$= [0.2 \times (-0.13 - 0.099)^2] + [0.5 \times (0.10 - 0.099)^2] + [0.3 \times (0.25 - 0.099)^2]$$
$$= 0.01733$$
$$\sigma_{R_{AMD}} = (\sigma^2_{R_{AMD}})^{1/2} = (0.01733)^{1/2} = 0.13164, \text{ or } 13.164\%$$

and

$$\sigma^2_{R_{Intel}} = \{p_{Poor} \times [R_{Poor} - E(R_{Intel})]^2\} + \{p_{Neutral} \times [R_{Neutral} - E(R_{Intel})]^2\}$$
$$+ \{p_{Good} \times [R_{Good} - E(R_{Intel})]^2\}$$
$$= [0.2 \times (-0.10 - 0.081)^2] + [0.5 \times (0.07 - 0.081)^2] + [0.3 \times (0.22 - 0.081)^2]$$
$$= 0.01241$$
$$\sigma_{R_{Intel}} = (\sigma^2_{R_{Intel}})^{1/2} = (0.01241)^{1/2} = 0.11140, \text{ or } 11.140\%$$

Having calculated the expected returns and standard deviations for the expected returns on AMD and Intel stock, the natural question to ask is which provides the highest risk-adjusted return. Before we answer this question, let's return to the example at the beginning of Section 6.1. Recall that, in this example, we proposed choosing among three stocks: A, B, and C. We stated that investors would prefer the investment that provides the highest expected return for a given level of risk or the lowest risk for a given expected return. This made it fairly easy to choose between Stocks A and B, which had the same return but different risk levels, and between Stocks B and C, which had the same risk but different returns. We were stuck when trying to choose between Stocks A and C, however, because they differed in both risk and return. Now, armed with tools for quantifying expected returns and risk, we can at least take a first pass at comparing stocks such as these.

The **coefficient of variation (CV)** is a measure that can help us in making comparisons such as that between Stocks A and C. The coefficient of variation for stock i is calculated as:

$$CV_i = \frac{\sigma_{R_i}}{E(R_i)} \tag{6.4}$$

> **coefficient of variation (CV)** a measure of the risk associated with an investment for each 1 percent of expected return

In this equation, CV is a measure of the risk associated with an investment for each 1 percent of expected return.

Recall that Stock A has an expected return of 12 percent and a risk level of 12 percent, while Stock C has an expected return of 16 percent and a risk level of 16 percent. If we assume that the risk level given for each stock is equal to the standard deviation of its return, we can find the coefficients of variation for the stocks as follows:

$$CV_A = \frac{0.12}{0.12} = 1.00 \quad \text{and} \quad CV_C = \frac{0.16}{0.16} = 1.00$$

Since these values are equal, the coefficient of variation measure suggests that these two investments are equally attractive on a risk-adjusted basis.

While this analysis appears to make sense, there is a conceptual problem with using the coefficient of variation to compute the amount of risk an investor can expect to realize for each 1 percent of expected return. This problem arises because investors expect to earn a positive return even when assets are completely risk free. For example, as shown in Exhibit 6.3, from 1926 to 2011 investors earned an average return of 3.62 percent each year on 30-day Treasury bills, which are considered to be risk free.[3] If investors can earn a positive risk-free rate without bearing any risk, then it really only makes sense to compare the risk of the investment, σ_{R_i}, with the return that investors expect to earn over and above the risk-free rate. As we will discuss in detail in Section 6.6, the expected return over and above the risk-free rate is a measure of the return that investors expect to earn for bearing risk.

This suggests that we should use the difference between the expected return, $E(R_i)$, and the risk-free rate, R_{rf}, instead of $E(R_i)$ alone in the coefficient of variation calculation. With this change, Equation 6.4 would be written as:

$$CV_i^* = \frac{\sigma_{R_i}}{E(R_i) - R_{rf}}$$

where CV_i^* is a modified coefficient of variation that is computed by subtracting the risk-free rate from the expected return.

Let's compute this modified coefficient of variation for the AMD and Intel example. If the risk-free rate equals 0.03, or 3 percent, the modified coefficients of variation for the two stocks are:

$$CV_{AMD}^* = \frac{\sigma_{R_{AMD}}}{E(R_{AMD}) - R_{rf}} = \frac{0.13164}{0.099 - 0.03} = 1.908$$

$$CV_{Intel}^* = \frac{\sigma_{R_{Intel}}}{E(R_{Intel}) - R_{rf}} = \frac{0.11140}{0.081 - 0.03} = 2.184$$

We can see that the modified coefficient of variation for AMD is smaller than the modified coefficient of variation for Intel. This tells us that an investment in AMD stock is expected to

---

[3]On August 5, 2011, Standard and Poor's, the credit rating agency, lowered its rating on U.S. Treasury securities from AAA to AA+, indicating that it considered these securities to have a very small amount of default risk. The other two large credit rating agencies, Moody's and Fitch, decided not to lower their ratings of U.S. Treasury securities at that time, suggesting that if there was any default risk, it remained extremely small.

have less risk for each 1 percent of return. Since investors prefer less risk for a given level of return, the AMD stock is a more attractive investment.

A popular version of this modified coefficient of variation calculation is known as the Sharpe Ratio. This ratio is named after 1990 Nobel Prize Laureate William Sharpe who developed the concept and was one of the originators of the capital asset pricing model that is discussed in Section 6.7. The **Sharpe Ratio** is simply the inverse of the modified coefficient of variation:

Sharpe Ratio
A measure of the return per unit of risk for an investment

$$\text{Sharpe Ratio} = S = \frac{E(R_i) - R_{rf}}{\sigma_{R_i}} \tag{6.5}$$

For the stocks of AMD and Intel, the Sharpe Ratios are:

$$S_{AMD} = \frac{1}{CV^*_{AMD}} = \frac{E(R_{AMD}) - R_{rf}}{\sigma_{R_{AMD}}} = \frac{0.099 - 0.03}{0.13164} = 0.524$$

$$S_{Intel} = \frac{1}{CV^*_{Intel}} = \frac{E(R_{Intel}) - R_{rf}}{\sigma_{R_{Intel}}} = \frac{0.081 - 0.03}{0.11140} = 0.458$$

You can read more about the Sharpe Ratio and other ratios that are used to measure risk-adjusted returns for investments at the following Web site: http://en.wikipedia.org/wiki/sharpe-ratio.

This tells us that investors in AMD stock can expect to earn 0.524 percent for each one standard deviation of return while investors in Intel stock can expect to earn 0.458 percent for each one standard deviation of return. Many people find the Sharpe Ratio to be a more intuitive measure than the coefficient of variation because they find it easier to think about the return per unit of risk than risk per unit of return.

LEARNING BY DOING

APPLICATION 6.4

Calculating and Interpreting the Sharpe Ratio

PROBLEM: You are trying to choose between two investments. The first investment, a painting by Picasso, has an expected return of 14 percent with a standard deviation of 30 percent over the next year. The second investment, a pair of blue suede shoes once worn by Elvis, has an expected return of 20 percent with a standard deviation of return of 40 percent. The risk-free rate of interest is 3 percent. What is the Sharpe Ratio for each of these investments, and what do these ratios tell us?

APPROACH: Use Equation 6.5 to compute the Sharpe Ratios for the two investments.

SOLUTION: The Sharpe Ratios are:

$$S_{painting} = \frac{0.14 - 0.03}{0.3} = 0.367 \quad \text{and} \quad S_{shoes} = \frac{0.2 - 0.03}{0.4} = 0.425$$

The Sharpe Ratio for Elvis's blue suede shoes is larger than the Sharpe Ratio for the painting. This indicates that the return for each one standard deviation of risk is greater for Elvis's shoes than for the painting. The blue suede shoes are a better investment.

Portfolios with More Than One Asset

It may seem like a good idea to evaluate investments by calculating a measure of risk for each 1 percent of expected return or the expected return per unit of risk. However, the coefficient of variation and the Sharpe Ratio have a critical shortcoming that is not quite evident when we are considering only a single asset. In order to explain this shortcoming, we must discuss the more realistic setting in which an investor has constructed a portfolio with more than one asset.

Expected Return on a Portfolio with More than One Asset

Suppose you own a portfolio that consists of $500 of AMD stock and $500 of Intel stock and that over the next year you expect to earn returns on the AMD and Intel shares of 9.9 percent and 8.1 percent, respectively. How would you calculate the expected return for the overall portfolio?

Let's try to answer this question using our intuition. If half of your funds are invested in each stock, it would seem reasonable that the expected return for this portfolio should be a 50–50 mixture of the expected returns from the two stocks, or:

$$E(R_{Portfolio}) = (0.5 \times 0.099) + (0.5 \times 0.081) = 0.09, \text{ or } 9.0\%$$

Notice that this formula is just like the expected return formula for an individual stock. However, in this case, instead of multiplying outcomes by their associated probabilities, we are multiplying expected returns for individual stocks by the fraction of the total portfolio value that each of these stocks represents. In other words, the formula for the expected return for a two-stock portfolio is:

$$E(R_{Portfolio}) = x_1 E(R_1) + x_2 E(R_2)$$

where x_i represents the fraction of the portfolio invested in asset i. The corresponding equation for a portfolio with n assets is:

$$E(R_{Portfolio}) = \sum_{i=1}^{n} [x_i \times E(R_i)] \tag{6.6}$$
$$= [x_1 \times E(R_1)] + [x_2 \times E(R_2)] + \cdots + [x_n \times E(R_n)]$$

This equation is just like Equation 6.2, except that (1) the returns are expected returns for individual assets and (2) instead of multiplying by the probability of an outcome, we are multiplying by the fraction of the portfolio invested in each asset. Note that this equation can be used only if you have already calculated the expected return for each stock.

To see how Equation 6.6 is used to calculate the expected return on a portfolio with more than two assets, consider an example. Suppose that you were recently awarded a $500,000 grant from a national foundation to pursue your interest in advancing the art of noodling—a popular pastime in some parts of the country in which people catch 40- to 50-pound catfish by putting their hands into catfish holes and wiggling their fingers like noodles to attract the fish.[4] Since your grant is intended to support your activities for five years, you kept $100,000 to cover your expenses for the next year and invested the remaining $400,000 in U.S. Treasury bonds and stocks. Specifically, you invested $100,000 in Treasury bonds (TB) that yield 4.5 percent; $150,000 in Procter & Gamble stock (P&G), which has an expected return of 7.5 percent; and $150,000 in Exxon Mobil Corporation stock (EMC), which has an expected return of 9.0 percent. What is the expected return on this $400,000 portfolio?

In order to use Equation 6.6, we must first calculate x_i, the fraction of the portfolio invested in asset i, for each investment. These fractions are as follows:

$$x_{TB} = \frac{\$100,000}{\$400,000} = 0.25$$

$$x_{P\&G} = x_{EMC} = \frac{\$150,000}{\$400,000} = 0.375$$

Therefore, the expected return on the portfolio is:

$$E(R_{Portfolio}) = [x_{TB} \times E(R_{TB})] + [x_{P\&G} \times E(R_{P\&G})] + [x_{EMC} \times E(R_{EMC})]$$
$$= (0.25 \times 0.045) + (0.375 \times 0.075) + (0.375 \times 0.090)$$
$$= 0.0731, \text{ or } 7.31\%$$

Risk of a Portfolio with More than One Asset

Now that we have calculated the expected return on a portfolio with more than one asset, the next question is how to quantify the risk of such a portfolio. Before we discuss the mechanics of how to do this, it is important to have some intuitive understanding of how volatility in the returns for different assets interact to determine the volatility of the overall portfolio.

---

[4]For more information on noodling, see the April 21, 2006, *New York Times* article titled "In the Jaws of a Catfish," by Ethan Todras-Whitehill and the May 16, 2011, *Wall Street Journal* article titled "Long Arm of the Law Penalizes Texans Who Nab Catfish by Hand," by Ana Campoy.

LEARNING
BY
DOING

APPLICATION 6.5

Calculating the Expected Return on a Portfolio

PROBLEM: You have become concerned that you have too much of your money invested in your pizza restaurant and have decided to diversify your personal portfolio. Right now the pizza restaurant is your only investment. To diversify, you plan to sell 45 percent of your restaurant and invest the proceeds from the sale, in equal proportions, into a stock market index fund and a bond market index fund. Over the next year, you expect to earn a return of 15 percent on your remaining investment in the pizza restaurant, 12 percent on your investment in the stock market index fund, and 8 percent on your investment in the bond market index fund. What return will you expect from your diversified portfolio over the next year?

APPROACH: First, calculate the fraction of your portfolio that will be invested in each type of asset after you have diversified. Then use Equation 6.6 to calculate the expected return on the portfolio.

SOLUTION: After you have diversified, 55 percent (100 percent − 45 percent = 55 percent) of your portfolio will be invested in your restaurant, 22.5 percent (45 percent × 0.50 = 22.5 percent) will be invested in the stock market index fund, and 22.5 percent (45 percent × 0.50 = 22.5 percent) will be invested in the bond market index fund. Therefore, from Equation 6.6, we know that the expected return for your portfolio is:

$$E(R_{Portfolio}) = [x_{Rest} \times E(R_{Rest})] + [x_{Stock} \times E(R_{Stock})] + [x_{Bond} \times E(R_{Bond})]$$
$$= (0.550 \times 0.15) + (0.225 \times 0.12) + (0.225 \times 0.08)$$
$$= 0.1275, \text{ or } 12.75\%$$

At 12.75 percent, the expected return is an average of the returns on the individual assets in your portfolio, weighted by the fraction of your portfolio that is invested in each.

The prices of two stocks in a portfolio will rarely, if ever, change by the same amount and in the same direction at the same time. Normally, the price of one stock will change by more than the price of the other. In fact, the prices of two stocks will frequently move in different directions. These differences in price movements affect the total volatility of the returns for a portfolio.

Exhibit 6.6 shows monthly returns for the stock of Southwest Airlines and Netflix over the period from August 2007 through August 2012. Notice that the returns on these shares are generally different and that the prices of the shares can move in different directions in a given month (one stock has a positive return when the other has a negative return). When the stock prices move in opposite directions, the change in the price of one stock offsets at least some of the change in the price of the other stock. As a result, the level of risk for a portfolio of the two stocks is less than the average of the risks associated with the individual shares.

This means that we *cannot* calculate the variance of a portfolio containing two assets simply by calculating the weighted average of the variances of the individual stocks. We have to account for the fact that the returns on different shares in a portfolio tend to partially offset each other. For a two-asset portfolio, we calculate the variance of the returns using the following formula:

$$\sigma^2_{R_{2\,Asset\ portfolio}} = x_1^2 \sigma^2_{R_1} + x_2^2 \sigma^2_{R_2} + 2x_1 x_2 \sigma_{R_{1,2}} \qquad (6.7)$$

covariance of returns
a measure of how the returns on two assets covary, or move together

where x_i represents the fraction of the portfolio invested in stock i, $\sigma^2_{R_i}$ is the variance of the return of stock i, and $\sigma_{R_{1,2}}$ is the covariance of the returns between stocks 1 and 2. The **covariance of returns** is a measure of how the returns on two assets covary, or move together. The third term in Equation 6.7 accounts for the fact that returns from the two assets will offset each other to some extent. The covariance of returns is calculated using the following formula:

$$Cov(R_1, R_2) = \sigma_{R_{1,2}} = \sum_{i=1}^{n} \{p_i \times [R_{1,i} - E(R_1)] \times [R_{2,i} - E(R_2)]\} \qquad (6.8)$$

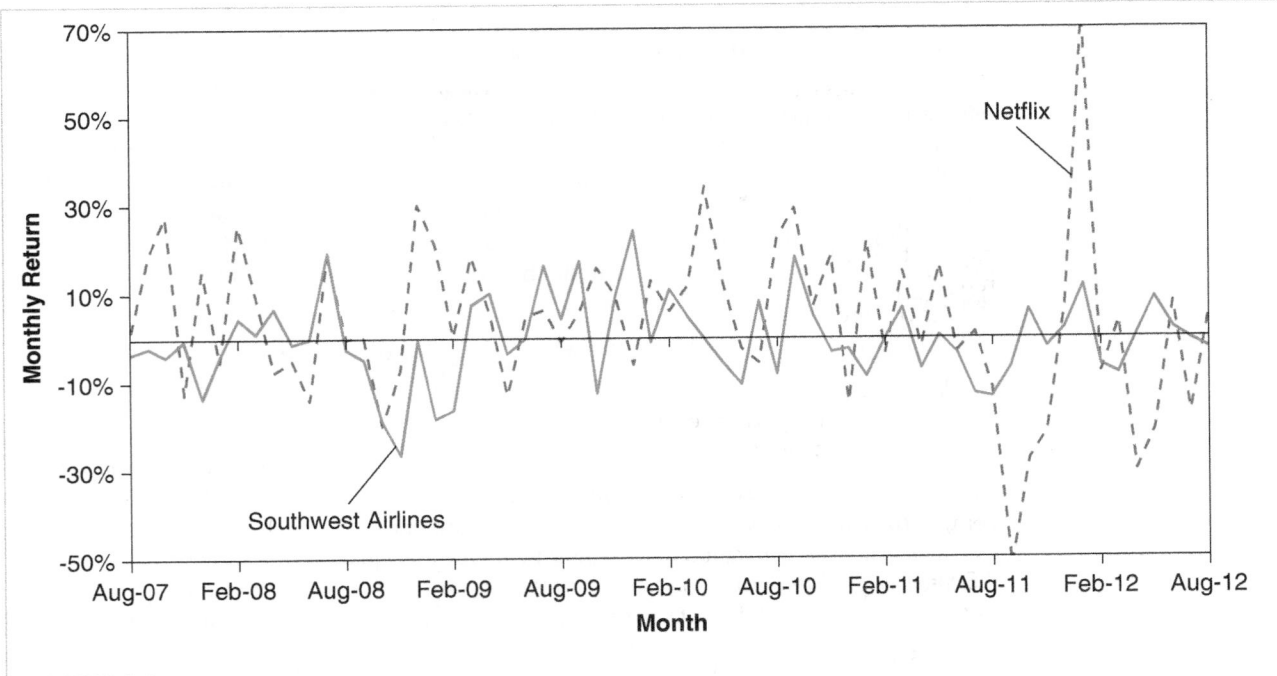

EXHIBIT 6.6

Monthly Returns for Southwest Airlines and Netflix Stock from August 2007 through August 2012

The returns on two stocks are generally different. In some periods, the return on one stock is positive, while the return on the other is negative. Even when the returns on both are positive or negative, they are rarely exactly the same.

where i represents outcomes rather than assets. Compare this equation with Equation 6.3, reproduced here:

$$\text{Var}(R) = \sigma_R^2 = \sum_{i=1}^{n} \{p_i \times [R_i - E(R)]^2\}$$

You can see that the covariance calculation is very similar to the variance calculation. The difference is that, instead of squaring the difference between the return from each outcome and the expected return for an individual asset, we calculate the product of this difference for two different assets.

Just as it is difficult to directly interpret the variance of the returns for an asset—recall that the variance is in units of squared dollars—it is difficult to directly interpret the covariance of returns between two assets. We get around this problem by dividing the covariance of returns by the product of the standard deviations of the returns for the two assets. This gives us the correlation, ρ, between the returns on those assets:

$$\rho_{R_{1,2}} = \frac{\sigma_{R_{1,2}}}{\sigma_{R_1}\sigma_{R_2}} \tag{6.9}$$

The correlation between the returns on two assets will always have a value between -1 and $+1$. This makes the interpretation of this variable straightforward. A *negative correlation* means that the returns tend to have opposite signs. For example, when the return on one asset is positive, the return on the other asset tends to be negative. If the correlation is exactly -1, the returns on the two assets are perfectly negatively correlated. In other words, when the return on one asset is positive, the return on the other asset will always be negative. A *positive correlation* means that when the return on one asset is positive, the return on the other asset also tends to be positive. If the correlation is exactly equal to $+1$, then the returns of the two assets are said to be perfectly positively correlated. The return on one asset will always be positive when the return on the other asset is positive. Finally, a *correlation of 0* means that the returns on the assets are not correlated. In this case, the fact that the return on one asset is positive or negative tells you nothing about how likely it is that the return on the other asset will be positive or negative.

Let's work an example to see how Equation 6.7 is used to calculate the variance of the returns on a portfolio that consists of 50 percent Southwest Airlines stock and 50 percent Netflix stock. Using the data plotted in Exhibit 6.6, we can calculate the variance of the annual returns for the Southwest Airlines and Netflix stocks, σ_R^2, to be 0.1166 and 0.4229, respectively. The covariance between the annual returns on these two stocks is 0.0389. We do not show the calculations for the variances and the covariance because each of these numbers was calculated using 60 different monthly returns. These calculations are too cumbersome to illustrate. Rest assured, however, that they were calculated using Equations 6.3 and 6.8.[5] With these values, we can calculate the variance of a portfolio that consists of 50 percent Southwest Airlines (SW) stock and 50 percent Netflix stock as:

$$
\begin{aligned}
\sigma_{R_{\text{Portfolio of SW and Netflix}}}^2 &= x_{\text{SW}}^2 \sigma_{R_{\text{SW}}}^2 + x_{\text{Netflix}}^2 \sigma_{R_{\text{Netflix}}}^2 + 2x_{\text{SW}}x_{\text{Netflix}}\sigma_{R_{\text{SW, Netflix}}} \\
&= (0.5)^2(0.1166) + (0.5)^2(0.4229) + 2(0.5)(0.5)(0.0389) \\
&= 0.1543
\end{aligned}
$$

You can see that this portfolio variance is smaller than the average of the variances of the returns on the Southwest Airlines and Netflix stocks [(0.1166 + 0.4229)/2 = 0.2698]. This is because their returns are not perfectly positively correlated.

If we calculate the standard deviations by taking the square roots of the variances, we find that the standard deviations for Southwest Airlines stock, Netflix stock, and the portfolio consisting of those two stocks are 0.341 (34.1 percent), 0.650 (65.0 percent), and 0.393 (39.3 percent), respectively.

Exhibit 6.7 illustrates the monthly returns for the portfolio of Southwest Airlines and Netflix stock, along with the monthly returns for the individual stocks. You can see in this exhibit that the returns on the portfolio vary quite a bit. However, as noted above, this variation is less than the average variation in the returns for the individual company shares.

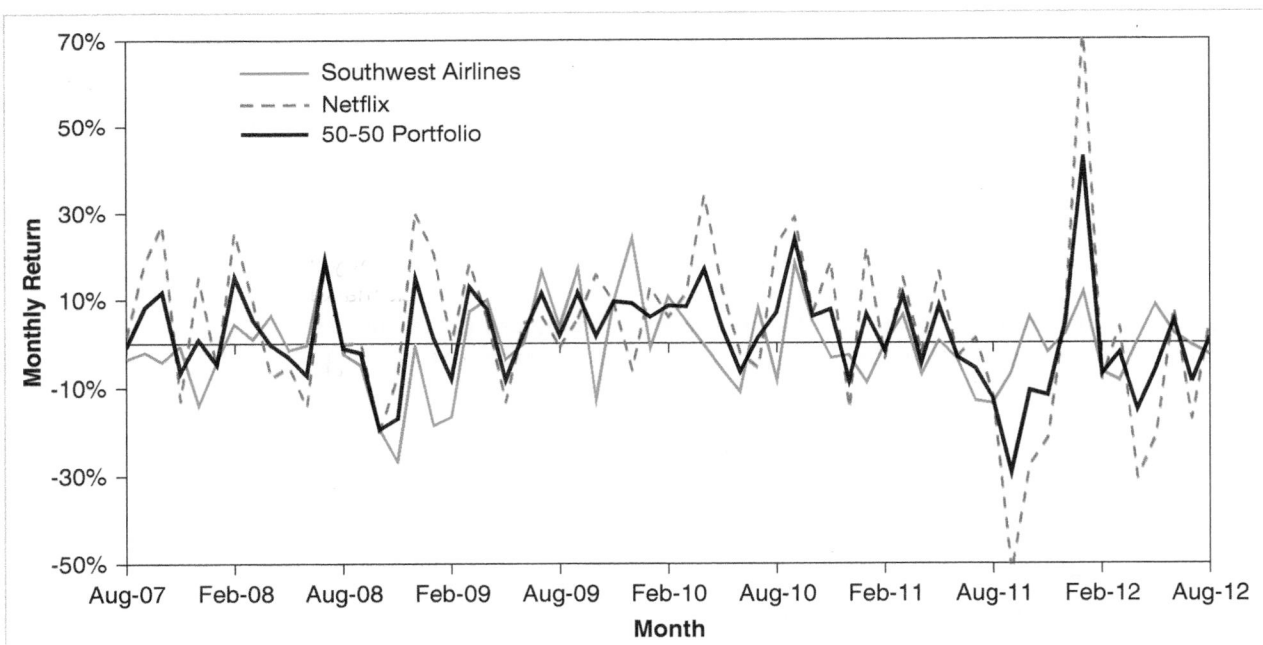

EXHIBIT 6.7

Monthly Returns for Southwest Airlines and Netflix Stock and for a Portfolio with 50 Percent of the Value in Each of These Two Stocks from August 2007 through August 2012

The variation in the returns from a portfolio that consists of Southwest Airlines and Netflix stock in equal proportions is less than the variation in the returns from either of those stocks alone.

---

[5]The only adjustment that we had to make was to account for the fact that our calculations used monthly returns rather than annual returns. This adjustment simply required us to multiply each number we calculated by 12 because there are 12 months in a year.

Using Equation 6.9, we can calculate the correlation of the returns between Southwest Airlines and Netflix stock as:

$$\rho_{R_{SW, Netflix}} = \frac{\sigma_{R_{SW, Netflix}}}{\sigma_{R_{SW}}\sigma_{R_{Netflix}}} = \frac{0.0389}{0.341 \times 0.650} = 0.176$$

The positive correlation tells us that the prices of Southwest Airlines and Netflix stock tend to move in the same direction. However, the correlation of less than one tells us that they do not always do so. The fact that the prices of these two shares do not always move together is the reason that the returns on a portfolio of the two stocks have less variation than the average of the returns on the individual company shares. This example illustrates the benefit of *diversification*—how holding more than one asset with different risk characteristics can reduce the risk of a portfolio. Note that if the correlation of the returns between Southwest Airlines and Netflix stock equaled one, holding these two stocks would not reduce risk because their prices would always move up or down together. Also, the standard deviation of the returns on the portfolio would equal the average of the standard deviations of the returns on the individual stocks.[6]

As we add more and more assets to a portfolio, calculating the variance using the approach illustrated in Equation 6.7 becomes increasingly complex. The reason for this is that we have to account for the covariance between each pair of assets. These more extensive calculations are beyond the scope of this book, but they are conceptually the same as those for a portfolio with two assets.

Calculating the Variance of a Two-Asset Portfolio

LEARNING BY DOING

APPLICATION 6.6

NEED MORE HELP?
WileyPLUS

PROBLEM: You are still planning to sell 45 percent of your pizza restaurant in order to diversify your personal portfolio. However, you have now decided to invest all of the proceeds in the stock market index fund. After you diversify, you will have 55 percent of your wealth invested in the restaurant and 45 percent invested in the stock market index fund. You have estimated the variances of the returns for these two investments and the covariance between their returns to be as follows:

$\sigma^2_{R_{Restaurant}}$	0.0625
$\sigma^2_{R_{Stock\,market\,index}}$	0.0400
$\sigma_{R_{Restaurant,\,Stock\,market\,index}}$	0.0250

What will be the variance and standard deviation of returns in your portfolio after you have sold the ownership interest in your restaurant and invested in the stock market index fund?

APPROACH: Use Equation 6.7 to calculate the variance of the portfolio returns and then take the square root of this value to obtain the standard deviation.

SOLUTION: The variance of the portfolio returns is:

$$\sigma^2_{R_{Portfolio}} = x^2_{R_{Restaurant}}\sigma^2_{R_{Restaurant}} + x^2_{R_{Stock\,market\,index}}\sigma^2_{R_{Stock\,market\,index}}$$
$$+ 2x_{Restaurant}x_{Stock\,market\,index}\sigma_{R_{Restaurant,\,Stock\,market\,index}}$$
$$= [(0.55)^2 \times 0.0625] + [(0.45)^2 \times 0.0400] + (2 \times 0.55 \times 0.45 \times 0.0250)$$
$$= 0.0394$$

and the standard deviation is $(0.0394)^{1/2} = 0.1985$, or 19.85 percent.

Comparing the variance of the portfolio returns of 0.0394 with the variances of the restaurant returns, 0.0625, and the stock market index fund returns, 0.0400, shows that a portfolio with two or more assets can actually have a smaller variance of returns (and thus a smaller standard deviation of returns) than any of the individual assets in the portfolio.

---

[6]You can see this by using Equation 6.9 to solve for $\sigma_{R_{1,2}} = \rho_{R_{1,2}}\sigma_{R_1}\sigma_{R_2}$, substituting for $\sigma_{R_{1,2}}$ in Equation 6.7, and then solving for $\sigma_{R_{2Asset\,portfolio}}$ by using algebra to solve for the square root of $\sigma^2_{R_{2Asset\,portfolio}}$.

<table>
<tr><td>

BUILDING
INTUITION
</td><td>

DIVERSIFIED PORTFOLIOS ARE LESS RISKY

Diversified portfolios generally have less risk for a given level of return than the individual risky assets in the portfolio. This is because the values of individual assets rarely change by the same amount and in the same direction at the same time. As a result, some of the variation in an asset's value can be diversified away by owning another asset at the same time. This is important because it tells us that investors can eliminate some of the risk associated with individual investments by holding them in a diversified portfolio.
</td></tr>
</table>

The Limits of Diversification

In the sample calculations for the portfolio containing Southwest Airlines and Netflix stock, we saw that the standard deviation of the returns for a portfolio consisting of equal investments in those two stocks was 39.3 percent from August 2007 through August 2012 and that this figure was lower than the average of the standard deviation of returns for the individual stocks. You might wonder how the standard deviation for the portfolio is likely to change if we increase the number of assets in the portfolio. The answer is simple. If the returns on the individual stocks added to our portfolio do not all change in the same way, then increasing the number of stocks in the portfolio will reduce the standard deviation of the portfolio returns even further.

Let's consider a simple example to illustrate this point. Suppose that all assets have a standard deviation of returns that is equal to 40 percent and that the covariance between the returns for each pair of assets is 0.048. If we form a portfolio in which we have an equal investment in two assets, the standard deviation of returns for the portfolio will be 32.25 percent. If we add a third asset, the portfolio standard deviation of returns will decrease to 29.21 percent. It will be even lower, at 27.57 percent, for a four-asset portfolio. Exhibit 6.8 illustrates how the standard deviation for the portfolio declines as more stocks are added.

In addition to showing how increasing the number of assets decreases the overall risk of a portfolio, Exhibit 6.8 illustrates three other very important points. First, the decrease in the standard deviation for the portfolio gets smaller and smaller as more assets are added. You can see this effect by looking at the distance between the straight horizontal line and the plot of the standard deviation of the portfolio returns.

The second important point is this: as the number of assets becomes very large, the portfolio standard deviation does not approach zero; it decreases only so far. In the example in Exhibit 6.8, it approaches 21.9 percent. The standard deviation does not approach zero because we are assuming that the variations in the asset returns do not completely cancel each other out. This is a realistic assumption because in practice investors can rarely diversify away all risk. They can diversify away risk that is unique to the individual assets, but they cannot diversify away risk that is common to all assets. The risk investors can diversify away is called **unsystematic or diversifiable risk**, and the risk they cannot diversify away is called **systematic or nondiversifiable risk**. In the next section, we will discuss systematic risk in detail.

unsystematic or diversifiable risk
risk that can be eliminated through diversification

systematic or nondiversifiable risk
risk that cannot be eliminated through diversification

EXHIBIT 6.8
Total Risk in a Portfolio as the Number of Assets Increases

The total risk of a portfolio decreases as the number of assets increases. This is because the amount of unsystematic risk in the portfolio decreases. The diversification benefit from adding another asset declines as the total number of assets in the portfolio increases and the unsystematic risk approaches zero. Most of the diversification benefit can often be achieved with as few as 15 or 20 assets.

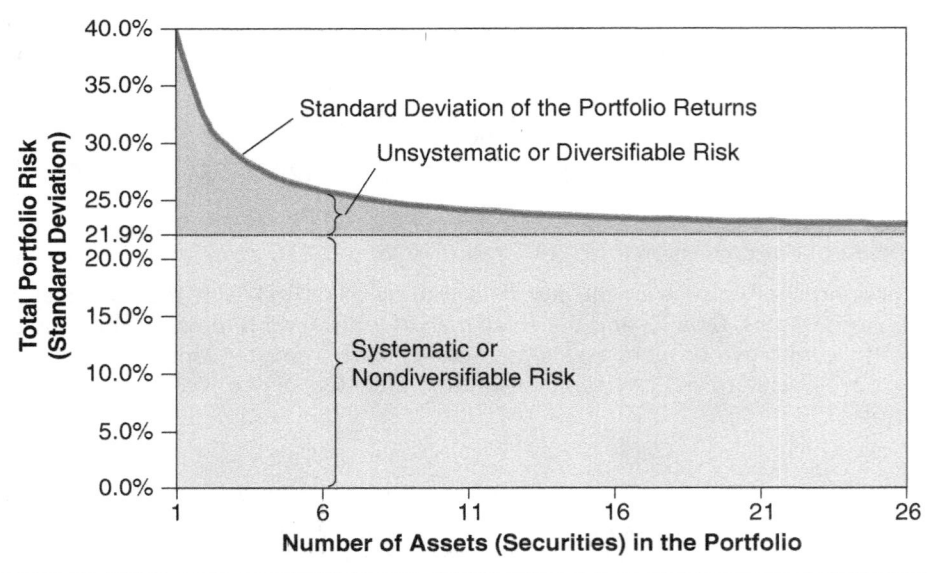

The third key point illustrated in Exhibit 6.8 is that most of the risk-reduction benefits from diversification can be achieved in a portfolio with 15 to 20 assets. Of course, the number of assets required to achieve a high level of diversification depends on the covariances between the assets in the portfolio. However, in general, it is not necessary to invest in a very large number of different assets.

> **BEFORE YOU GO ON**

1. What does the coefficient of variation tell us, and how is it related to the Sharpe Ratio?

2. What are the two components of total risk?

3. Why does the total risk of a portfolio not approach zero as the number of assets in a portfolio becomes very large?

6.5 SYSTEMATIC RISK

The objective of diversification is to eliminate variation in returns that is unique to individual assets. We diversify our investments across a number of different assets in the hope that these unique variations will cancel each other out. With complete diversification, all of the unsystematic risk is eliminated from the portfolio. An investor with a diversified portfolio still faces systematic risk, however, and we now turn our attention to that form of risk.

LEARNING OBJECTIVE 6

Why Systematic Risk Is All That Matters

The idea that unsystematic risk can be diversified away has direct implications for the relation between risk and return. If the transaction costs associated with constructing a diversified portfolio are relatively low, then rational, informed investors, such as the students who are taking this class, will prefer to hold diversified portfolios.

Diversified investors face only systematic risk, whereas investors whose portfolios are not well diversified face systematic risk plus unsystematic risk. Because they face less risk, the diversified investors will be willing to pay higher prices for individual assets than the other investors. Therefore, expected returns on individual assets will be lower than the total risk (systematic plus unsystematic risk) of those assets suggests they should be.

To illustrate, consider two individual investors, Emily and Jane. Each of them is trying to decide if she should purchase stock in your pizza restaurant. Emily holds a diversified portfolio and Jane does not. Assume your restaurant's stock has five units of systematic risk and nine units of total risk. You can see that Emily faces less risk than Jane and will require a lower expected rate of return. Consequently, Emily will be willing to pay a higher price than Jane.

If the market includes a large number of diversified investors such as Emily, competition among these investors will drive the price of your restaurant's shares up further. This competition will ultimately push the price up to the point where the expected return just compensates all investors for the systematic risk associated with your stock. The bottom line is this: because of competition among diversified investors, all investors are only rewarded for bearing systematic risk in asset markets. For this reason, we are concerned only about systematic risk when we think about the relation between risk and return in finance.

SYSTEMATIC RISK IS THE RISK THAT MATTERS

The required rate of return on an asset depends only on the systematic risk associated with that asset. Because unsystematic risk can be diversified away, investors can and will eliminate their exposure to this risk. Competition among diversified investors will drive the prices of assets to the point where the expected returns will compensate investors for only the systematic risk that they bear.

BUILDING INTUITION

Measuring Systematic Risk

If systematic risk is all that matters when we think about expected returns, then we cannot use the standard deviation as a measure of risk.[7] The standard deviation is a measure of total risk. We need a way of quantifying the systematic risk of individual assets.

A natural starting point for doing this is to recognize that the most diversified portfolio possible will come closest to eliminating all unsystematic risk. Such a portfolio provides a natural benchmark against which we can measure the systematic risk of an individual asset. What is the most diversified portfolio possible? The answer is simple. It is the portfolio that consists of all assets, including stocks, bonds, real estate, precious metals, commodities, art, baseball cards, and so forth from all over the world. In finance, we call this the **market portfolio**.

Unfortunately, we do not have very good data for most of these assets for most of the world, so we use the next best thing: the U.S. public stock market. A large number of stocks from a broad range of industries trade in this market. The companies that issue these stocks own a wide range of assets all over the world. These characteristics, combined with the facts that the U.S. market has been operating for a very long time and that we have very reliable and detailed information on prices for U.S. stocks, make the U.S. stock market a natural benchmark for estimating systematic risk.

Since systematic risk is, by definition, risk that cannot be diversified away, the systematic risk of an individual asset is really just a measure of the relation between the returns on the individual asset and the returns on the market. In fact, systematic risk is often referred to as **market risk**. To see how we might use data from the U.S. public stock market to estimate the systematic risk of an individual asset, look at Exhibit 6.9, which plots 60 historical monthly returns for General Electric Company (GE) against the corresponding monthly returns for the S&P 500 index (a proxy for the U.S. stock market). In this plot, you can see that returns on GE stock tend to be higher when returns on the S&P 500 tend to be higher. The measure of systematic risk that we use in finance is a statistical measure of this relation.

We quantify the relation between the returns on GE stock and the market by finding the slope of the line that best represents the relation illustrated in Exhibit 6.9. Specifically, we estimate the slope of the *line of best fit*. We do this using the statistical technique called regression analysis. If you are not familiar with regression analysis, don't worry; the details are beyond the scope of this course. All you have to know is that this technique gives us the line that fits the data best.

market portfolio
the portfolio of all assets

market risk
a term commonly used to refer to nondiversifiable, or systematic, risk

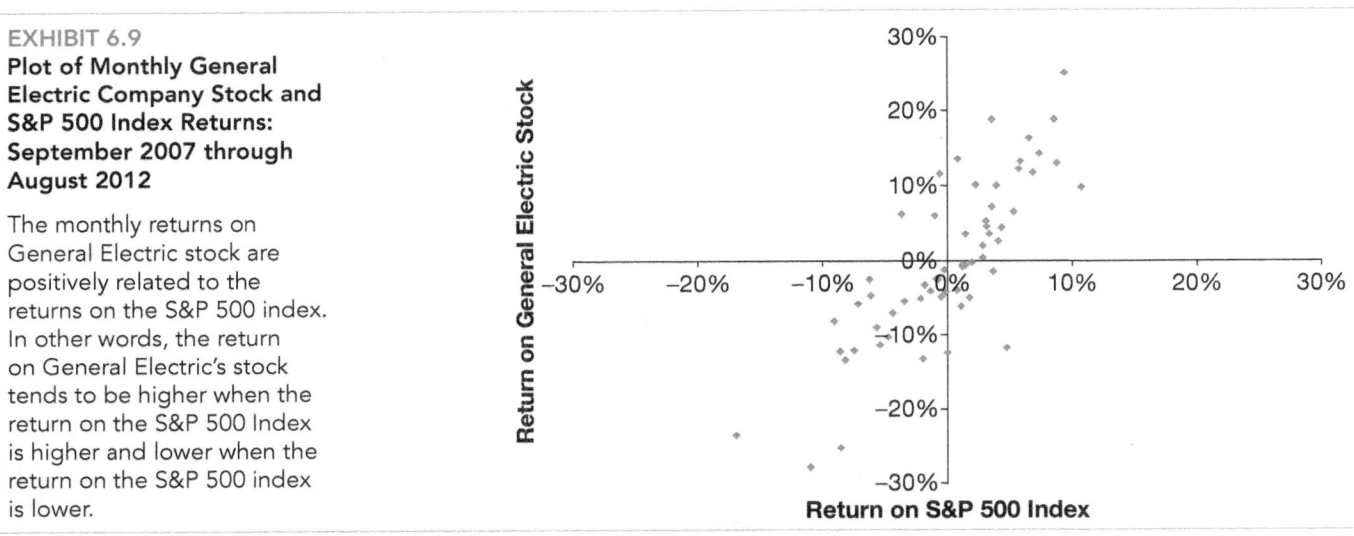

EXHIBIT 6.9

Plot of Monthly General Electric Company Stock and S&P 500 Index Returns: September 2007 through August 2012

The monthly returns on General Electric stock are positively related to the returns on the S&P 500 index. In other words, the return on General Electric's stock tends to be higher when the return on the S&P 500 Index is higher and lower when the return on the S&P 500 index is lower.

---

[7]This statement is true in the context of how expected returns are determined. However, the standard deviation is still a very useful measure of the risk faced by an individual investor who does not hold a diversified portfolio. For example, the owners of most small businesses have much of their personal wealth tied up in their businesses. They are certainly concerned about the total risk because it is directly related to the probability that they will go out of business and lose much of their wealth.

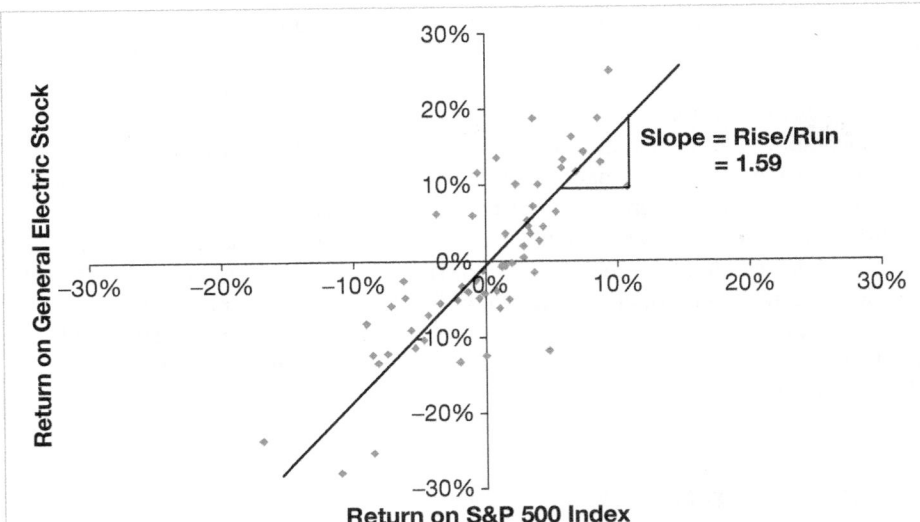

EXHIBIT 6.10
Slope of Relation between General Electric Company Monthly Stock Returns and S&P 500 Index Returns: September 2007 through August 2012

The line shown In the exhibit best represents the relation between the monthly returns on General Electric stock and the returns on the S&P 500 index. The slope of this line, which equals 1.59, indicates that the return on General Electric stock tends to equal about 1.59 times the return on the S&P 500 index.

Exhibit 6.10 illustrates the line that was estimated for the data in Exhibit 6.9 using regression analysis. Note that the slope of this line is 1.59. Recall from your math classes that the slope of a line equals the ratio of the rise (vertical distance) divided by the corresponding run (horizontal distance). In this case, the slope is the change in the return on GE stock divided by the change in the return on the U.S. stock market. A slope of 1.59 therefore means that, on average, the change in the return on GE stock was 1.59 times as large as the change in the return on the S&P 500 index. Thus, if the S&P 500 index goes up 1 percent, the average increase in GE's stock is 1.59 percent. This is a measure of systematic risk because it tells us that the volatility of the returns on GE stock is 1.59 times as large as that for the S&P 500 as a whole.

To explore this idea more completely, let's consider another, simpler example. Suppose that you have data for Nike stock and for the U.S. stock market (S&P 500 index) for each of the past two years. In the first year, the return on the market was 10 percent, and the return on Nike stock was 15 percent. In the second year, the return on the market was 12 percent, and the return on Nike stock was 19 percent. From this information, we know that the return on Nike stock increased by 4 percent while the return on the market increased 2 percent. If we plotted the returns for Nike stock and for the market for each of the last two periods, as we did for GE stock and the market in Exhibits 6.9 and 6.10, and estimated the line that best fit the data, it would be a line that connected the dots for the two periods. The slope of this line would equal 2, calculated as follows:

$$\text{Slope} = \frac{\text{Rise}}{\text{Run}} = \frac{\text{Change in Nike return}}{\text{Change in market return}} = \frac{19\% - 15\%}{12\% - 10\%} = \frac{4\%}{2\%} = 2$$

Although we have to be careful about drawing conclusions when we have only two data points, we might interpret the slope of 2 to indicate that new information that causes the market return to increase by 1 percent will tend to cause the return on Nike stock to increase by 2 percent. Of course, the reverse might also be true. That is, new information that causes the market return to decrease by 1 percent may also cause the return on Nike stock to go down by 2 percent. To the extent that the same information is driving the changes in returns on Nike stock and on the market, it would not be possible for an investor in Nike stock to diversify this risk away. It is nondiversifiable, or systematic, risk.

In finance, we call the slope of the line of best fit **beta**. Often we simply use the corresponding Greek letter, β, to refer to this measure of systematic risk. As shown below, a beta of 1 tells us that an asset has just as much systematic risk as the market. A beta higher than or lower than 1 tells us that the asset has more or less systematic risk than the market, respectively. A beta of 0 indicates a risk-free security, such as a U.S. Treasury bill.

beta (β)
a measure of nondiversifiable, systematic, or market, risk

$\beta = 1$ Same systematic risk as market
$\beta > 1$ More systematic risk than market
$\beta < 1$ Less systematic risk than market
$\beta = 0$ No systematic risk

A convenient place to find betas for individual companies is MSN Money Central at http://moneycentral.msn.com. Just enter the stock symbol in the "Get Quote" box near the top of the page and hit "Enter" on your computer (try the railroad company CSX, for example). You will get prices, an estimate of the beta, and other financial information.

Now you might ask yourself what happened to the unsystematic risk of GE or Nike stock. This is best illustrated by the GE example, where we have more than two observations. As you can see in Exhibit 6.10, the line of best fit does not go through each data point. That is because some of the change in GE's stock price each month reflected information that did not affect the S&P 500 as a whole. That information is the unsystematic component of the risk of GE's stock. The vertical distance between each data point and the line of best fit represents variation in GE's stock return that can be attributed to this unsystematic risk.

The positive slope (β) of the regression line in Exhibit 6.10 tells us that returns for the S&P 500 and for GE stock will tend to move in the same direction. The return on the S&P 500 and the return on GE's stock will not always change in the same direction, however, because the unsystematic risk associated with GE stock can more than offset the effect of the market in any particular period. In the next section, we will discuss the implications of beta for the level (as opposed to the change) in the expected return for a stock such as GE.

> **BEFORE YOU GO ON**

1. Why are returns on the stock market used as a benchmark in measuring systematic risk?

2. How is beta estimated?

3. How would you interpret a beta of 1.5 for an asset? A beta of 0.75?

6.6 COMPENSATION FOR BEARING SYSTEMATIC RISK

Now that we have identified the measure of the risk that diversified investors care about—systematic risk—we are in a position to examine how this measure relates to expected returns. Earlier, in our discussion of the coefficient of variation and the Sharpe Ratio, we asserted that the expected return over and above the risk-free rate is the return that investors expect to earn for bearing risk. To see why this must be true, think about the rate of return that you would require for an investment. First, you would want to make sure that you were compensated for inflation. It would not make sense to invest if you expected the investment to return an amount that did not at least allow you to have the same purchasing power that the money you invested had when you made the investment. Second, you would want some compensation for the fact that you are giving up the use of your money for a period of time. This compensation may be very small if you are forgoing the use of your money for only a short time, such as when you invest in a 30-day Treasury bill, but it might be relatively large if you are investing for several years. Finally, you would also require compensation for the systematic risk associated with the investment.

When you invest in a U.S. government security such as a Treasury bill, note, or bond, you are investing in a security that has no risk of default. After all, the U.S. government can always increase taxes or print more money to pay you back. Changes in economic conditions and other factors that affect the returns on other assets do not affect the default risk of U.S. government securities. As a result, these securities do not have systematic risk, and their returns can be viewed as risk free. In other words, returns on government bonds reflect the compensation required by investors to account for the impact of inflation on purchasing power and for their inability to use the money during the life of the investment.

It follows that the difference between required returns on government securities and required returns for risky investments represents the compensation investors require for taking risk. Recognizing this allows us to write the expected return for an asset i as:

$$E(R_i) = R_{rf} + \text{Compensation for taking risk}_i$$

where R_{rf} is the return on a security with a risk-free rate of return, which analysts typically estimate by looking at returns on government securities. The compensation for taking risk, which varies with the risk of the asset, is added to the risk-free rate of return to get an estimate of the expected rate of return for an asset. If we recognize that the compensation for taking risk varies with asset risk and that systematic risk is what matters, we can write the preceding equation as follows:

$$E(R_i) = R_{rf} + (\text{Units of systematic risk}_i \times \text{Compensation per unit of systematic risk})$$

where units of systematic risk$_i$ is the number of units of systematic risk associated with asset i. Finally, if beta, β, is the appropriate measure for the number of units of systematic risk, we can also define compensation for taking risk as follows:

$$\text{Compensation for taking risk}_i = \beta_i \times \text{Compensation per unit of systematic risk}$$

where β_i is the beta for asset i.

Remember that beta is a measure of systematic risk that is directly related to the risk of the market as a whole. If the beta for an asset is 2, that asset has twice as much systematic risk as the market. If the beta for an asset is 0.5, then the asset has half as much systematic risk as the market. Recognizing this natural interpretation of beta suggests that the appropriate "unit of systematic risk" is the level of risk in the market as a whole and that the appropriate "compensation per unit of systematic risk" is the expected return required for the level of systematic risk in the market as a whole. The required rate of return on the market, over and above that of the risk-free return, represents compensation required by investors for bearing a market (systematic) risk. This suggests that:

$$\text{Compensation per unit of systematic risk} = E(R_m) - R_{rf}$$

where $E(R_m)$ is the expected return on the market. The term $E(R_m) - R_{rf}$ is called the *market risk premium*. Consequently, we can now write the equation for expected return as:

$$E(R_i) = R_{rf} + \beta_i[E(R_m) - R_{rf}] \tag{6.10}$$

6.7 THE CAPITAL ASSET PRICING MODEL

In deriving Equation 6.10, we intuitively arrived at the **Capital Asset Pricing Model (CAPM)**. Equation 6.10 is the CAPM, a model that describes the relation between risk and expected return. We will discuss the predictions of the CAPM in more detail shortly, but first let's look more closely at how it works.

Suppose that you want to estimate the expected return for a stock that has a beta of 1.5 and that the expected return on the market and risk-free rate are 10 percent and 4 percent, respectively. We can use Equation 6.10 (the CAPM) to find the expected return for this stock:

$$E(R_i) = R_{rf} + \beta_i[E(R_m) - R_{rf}]$$
$$= 0.04 + [1.5 \times (0.10 - 0.04)] = 0.13, \text{ or } 13\%$$

Note that we must have three pieces of information in order to use Equation 6.10: (1) the risk-free rate, (2) beta, and (3) either the market risk premium or the expected return on the market. Recall that the market risk premium is the difference between the expected return on the market and the risk-free rate $[E(R_m) - R_{rf}]$, which is 6 percent in the above example.

While the expected return on the market is known in the above example, we actually cannot observe it in practice. For this reason, financial analysts estimate the market risk premium using historical data. We discuss how they do this in Chapter 11.

The Security Market Line

Exhibit 6.11 displays a plot of Equation 6.10 to illustrate how the expected return on an asset varies with systematic risk. This plot shows that the relation between the expected return on an asset and beta is positive and linear. In other words, it is a straight line with a positive slope. The line in Exhibit 6.11 is known as the **Security Market Line (SML)**.

LEARNING OBJECTIVE ⑦

Capital Asset Pricing Model (CAPM)
a model that describes the relation between risk and expected return

Security Market Line (SML)
a plot of the relation between expected return and systematic risk

EXHIBIT 6.11
The Security Market Line

The Security Market Line (SML) is the line that shows the relation between expected return and systematic risk, as measured by beta. When beta equals zero and there is no systematic risk, the expected return equals the risk-free rate. As systematic risk (beta) increases, the expected return increases. This is an illustration of the positive relation between risk and return. The SML shows that it is systematic risk that matters to investors.

$$E(R_i) = R_{rf} + \beta[E[R_m] - R_{rf}]$$

E(R_m)

Security Market Line

Market Portfolio

R_{rf}

E(R_i)

Beta: 0.0   0.5   1.0   1.5   2.0

In Exhibit 6.11 you can see that the expected rate of return equals the risk-free rate when beta equals 0. This makes sense because when investors do not face systematic risk, they will only require a return that reflects the expected rate of inflation and the fact that they are giving up the use of their money for a period of time. Exhibit 6.11 also shows that the expected return on an asset equals the expected return on the market when beta equals 1. This is not surprising given that both the asset and the market would have the same level of systematic risk if this were the case.

It is important to recognize that the SML illustrates what the CAPM predicts the expected total return should be for various values of beta. The actual expected total return depends on the price of the asset. You can see this from Equation 6.1:

$$R_T = \frac{\Delta P + CF_1}{P_0}$$

where P_0 is the price that the asset is currently selling for. If an asset's price implies that the expected return is greater than that predicted by the CAPM, that asset will plot above the SML in Exhibit 6.11. This means that the asset's price is lower than the CAPM suggests it should be. Conversely, if the expected return on an asset plots below the SML, this implies that the asset's price is higher than the CAPM suggests it should be. The point at which a particular asset plots relative to the SML, then, tells us something about whether the price of that asset might be low or high. Recognizing this fact can be helpful in evaluating the attractiveness of an investment such as the General Electric stock in Learning by Doing Application 6.7.

LEARNING BY DOING

APPLICATION 6.7

Expected Returns and Systematic Risk

PROBLEM: You are considering buying 100 shares of General Electric stock. The Yahoo Finance Web site reports that the beta for General Electric is 1.59. The risk-free rate is 4 percent, and the market risk premium is 6 percent. What is the expected rate of return on General Electric stock according to the CAPM?

APPROACH: Use Equation 6.10 to calculate the expected return on General Electric stock.

SOLUTION: The expected return is:

$$E(R_{GE}) = R_{rf} + \beta_{GE}[E(R_m) - R_{rf}]$$
$$= 0.04 + (1.59 \times 0.06) = 0.1354, \text{ or } 13.54\%$$

The Capital Asset Pricing Model and Portfolio Returns

The expected return for a portfolio can also be estimated using the CAPM. The expected return on a portfolio with n assets is calculated using the relation:

$$E(R_{n \text{ Asset portfolio}}) = R_{rf} + \beta_{n \text{ Asset portfolio}}[E(R_m) - R_{rf}]$$

Of course, this should not be surprising since investing in a portfolio is simply an alternative to investing in a single asset.

The fact that the SML is a straight line turns out to be rather convenient if we want to estimate the beta for a portfolio. Recall that the equation for the expected return for a portfolio with n assets was given by Equation 6.6:

$$E(R_{\text{Portfolio}}) = \sum_{i=1}^{n} [x_i \times E(R_i)]$$
$$= [x_1 \times E(R_1)] + [x_2 \times E(R_2)] + \cdots + [x_n \times E(R_n)]$$

If we substitute Equation 6.10 into Equation 6.6 for each of the n assets and rearrange the equation, we find that the beta for a portfolio is simply a weighted average of the betas for the individual assets in the portfolio. In other words:

$$\beta_{n \text{ Asset portfolio}} = \sum_{i=1}^{n} x_i\beta_i = x_1\beta_1 + x_2\beta_2 + x_3\beta_3 + \cdots + x_n\beta_n \qquad (6.11)$$

where x_i is the proportion of the portfolio value that is invested in asset i, β_i is the beta of asset i, and n is the number of assets in the portfolio. This formula makes it simple to calculate the beta of any portfolio of assets once you know the betas of the individual assets. As an exercise, you might prove this to yourself by using Equations 6.6 and 6.10 to derive Equation 6.11.

Let's consider an example to see how Equation 6.11 is used. Suppose that you invested 25 percent of your wealth in a fully diversified market fund, 25 percent in risk-free Treasury bills, and 50 percent in a house with twice as much systematic risk as the market. What is the beta of your overall portfolio? What rate of return would you expect to earn from this portfolio if the risk-free rate is 4 percent and the market risk premium is 6 percent?

We know that the beta for the market must equal 1 by definition and that the beta for a risk-free asset equals 0. The beta for your home must be 2 since it has twice the systematic risk of the market. Therefore, the beta of your portfolio is:

$$\beta_{\text{Portfolio}} = x_{\text{Fund}}\beta_{\text{Fund}} + x_{\text{TB}}\beta_{\text{TB}} + x_{\text{House}}\beta_{\text{House}}$$
$$= (0.25 \times 1.0) + (0.25 \times 0.0) + (0.50 \times 2.0)$$
$$= 1.25$$

Your portfolio has 1.25 times as much systematic risk as the market. Based on Equation 6.10, you would, therefore, expect to earn a return of 11.5 percent, calculated as follows:

$$E(R_{\text{Portfolio}}) = R_{rf} + \beta_{\text{Portfolio}}[E(R_m) - R_{rf}]$$
$$= 0.04 + (1.25 \times 0.06) = 0.115, \text{ or } 11.5\%$$

Up to this point, we have focused on calculating the expected rate of return for an investment in any asset from the perspective of an investor, such as a stockholder. A natural question that might arise is how these concepts relate to the rate of return that should be used within a firm to evaluate a project. The short answer is that they are the same. The rate of return used to discount the cash flows for a project with a particular level of systematic risk is exactly the same as the rate of return that an investor would expect to receive from an investment in any asset having the same level of systematic risk. In Chapter 11 we will explore the relation between the expected return and the rate used to discount project cash flows in much more detail. By the time we finish that discussion, you will understand thoroughly how businesses determine the rate that they use to discount the cash flows from their investments.

APPLICATION 6.8

Portfolio Risk and Expected Return

PROBLEM: You have recently become very interested in real estate. To gain some experience as a real estate investor, you have decided to get together with nine of your friends to buy three small cottages near campus. If you and your friends pool your money, you will have just enough to buy the three properties. Since each investment requires the same amount of money and you will have a 10 percent interest in each, you will effectively have one-third of your portfolio invested in each cottage.

While the cottages cost the same, they are different distances from campus and in different neighborhoods. You believe that this causes them to have different levels of systematic risk, and you estimate that the betas for the individual cottages are 1.2, 1.3, and 1.5. If the risk-free rate is 4 percent and the market risk premium is 6 percent, what will be the expected return on your real estate portfolio after you make all three investments?

APPROACH: There are two approaches that you can use to solve this problem. First, you can estimate the expected return for each cottage using Equation 6.10 and then calculate the expected return on the portfolio using Equation 6.6. Alternatively, you can calculate the beta for the portfolio using Equation 6.11 and then use Equation 6.10 to calculate the expected return.

SOLUTION: Using the first approach, we find that Equation 6.10 gives us the following expected returns:

$$E(R_i) = R_{rf} + \beta_i[E(R_m) - R_{rf}]$$
$$= 0.04 + (1.2 \times 0.06) = 0.112, \text{ or } 11.2\%, \text{ for cottage 1}$$
$$= 0.04 + (1.3 \times 0.06) = 0.118, \text{ or } 11.8\%, \text{ for cottage 2}$$
$$= 0.04 + (1.5 \times 0.06) = 0.130, \text{ or } 13.0\%, \text{ for cottage 3}$$

Therefore, from Equation 6.6, the expected return on the portfolio is:

$$E(R_{Portfolio}) = [x_1 \times E(R_1)] + [x_2 \times E(R_2)] + [x_3 \times E(R_3)]$$
$$= (1/3 \times 0.112) + (1/3 \times 0.118) + (1/3 \times 0.13) = 0.12, \text{ or } 12.0\%$$

Using the second approach, from Equation 6.11, the beta of the portfolio is:

$$\beta_{Portfolio} = x_1\beta_1 + x_2\beta_2 + x_3\beta_3 = (1/3)(1.2) + (1/3)(1.3) + (1/3)(1.5) = 1.33333$$

and from Equation 6.10, the expected return is:

$$E(R_{Portfolio}) = R_{rf} + \beta_{Portfolio}[E(R_m) - R_{rf}]$$
$$= 0.04 + (1.33333 \times 0.06) = 0.120, \text{ or } 12.0\%$$

DECISION
MAKING

EXAMPLE 6.2

Choosing between Two Investments

SITUATION: You are trying to decide whether to invest in one or both of two different stocks. Stock 1 has a beta of 0.8 and an expected return of 7.0 percent. Stock 2 has a beta of 1.2 and an expected return of 9.5 percent. You remember learning about the CAPM in school and believe that it does a good job of telling you what the appropriate expected return should be for a given level of risk. Since the risk-free rate is 4 percent and the market risk premium is 6 percent, the CAPM tells you that the appropriate expected rate of return for an asset with a beta of 0.8 is 8.8 percent. The corresponding return for an asset with a beta of 1.2 is 11.2 percent. Should you invest in either or both of these stocks?

DECISION: You should not invest in either stock. The expected returns for both of them are below the values predicted by the CAPM for investments with the same level of risk. In other words, both would plot below the line in Exhibit 6.11. This implies that they are both overpriced.

> **BEFORE YOU GO ON**

1. How is the expected return on an asset related to its systematic risk?

2. What name is given to the relation between risk and expected return implied by the CAPM?

3. If an asset's expected return does not plot on the line in question 2 above, what does that imply about its price?

SUMMARY OF Learning Objectives

1 Explain the relation between risk and return.

Investors require greater returns for taking greater risk. They prefer the investment with the highest possible return for a given level of risk or the investment with the lowest risk for a given level of return.

2 Describe the two components of a total holding period return, and calculate this return for an asset.

The total holding period return on an investment consists of a capital appreciation component and an income component. This return is calculated using Equation 6.1. It is important to recognize that investors do not care whether they receive a dollar of return through capital appreciation or as a cash dividend. Investors value both sources of return equally.

3 Explain what an expected return is and calculate the expected return for an asset.

The expected return is a weighted average of the possible returns from an investment, where each of these returns is weighted by the probability that it will occur. It is calculated using Equation 6.2.

4 Explain what the standard deviation of returns is and why it is very useful in finance, and calculate it for an asset.

The standard deviation of returns is a measure of the total risk associated with the returns from an asset. It is useful in evaluating returns in finance because the returns on many assets tend to be normally distributed. The standard deviation of returns provides a convenient measure of the dispersion of returns. In other words, it tells us about the probability that a return will fall within a particular distance from the expected value or within a particular range. To calculate the standard deviation, the variance is first calculated using Equation 6.3. The standard deviation of returns is then calculated by taking the square root of the variance.

5 Explain the concept of diversification.

Diversification is reducing risk by investing in two or more assets whose values do not always move in the same direction at the same time. Investing in a portfolio containing assets whose prices do not always move together reduces risk because some of the changes in the prices of individual assets offset each other. This can cause the overall volatility in the value of an investor's portfolio to be lower than if it consisted of only a single asset.

6 Discuss which type of risk matters to investors and why.

Investors care about only systematic risk. This is because they can eliminate unsystematic risk by holding a diversified portfolio. Diversified investors will bid up prices for assets to the point at which they are just being compensated for the systematic risks they must bear.

7 Describe what the Capital Asset Pricing Model (CAPM) tells us and how to use it to evaluate whether the expected return of an asset is sufficient to compensate an investor for the risks associated with that asset.

The CAPM tells us that the relation between systematic risk and return is linear and that the risk-free rate of return is the appropriate return for an asset with no systematic risk. From the CAPM we know what rate of return investors will require for an investment with a particular amount of systematic risk (beta). This means that we can use the expected return predicted by the CAPM as a benchmark for evaluating whether expected returns for individual assets are sufficient. If the expected return for an asset is less than that predicted by the CAPM, then the asset is an unattractive investment because its return is lower than the CAPM indicates it should be. By the same token, if the expected return for an asset is greater than that predicted by the CAPM, then the asset is an attractive investment because its return is higher than it should be.

SUMMARY OF Key Equations

Equation	Description	Formula
6.1	Total holding period return	$R_T = R_{CA} + R_I = \dfrac{P_1 - P_0}{P_0} + \dfrac{CF_1}{P_0} = \dfrac{\Delta P + CF_1}{P_0}$
6.2	Expected return on an asset	$E(R_{Asset}) = \displaystyle\sum_{i=1}^{n} (P_i \times R_i)$

Equation	Description	Formula
6.3	Variance of return on an asset	$\text{Var}(R) = \sigma_R^2 = \sum_{i=1}^{n} \{p_i \times [R_i - E(R)]^2\}$
6.4	Coefficient of variation	$CV_i = \dfrac{\sigma_{R_i}}{E(R_i)}$
6.5	Sharpe Ratio	$S = \dfrac{E(R_i) - R_{rf}}{\sigma_{R_i}}$
6.6	Expected return for a portfolio	$E(R_{Portfolio}) = \sum_{i=1}^{n} [x_i \times E(R_i)]$
6.7	Variance for a two-asset portfolio	$\sigma_{R_{2Asset\,portfolio}}^2 = x_1^2 \sigma_{R_1}^2 + x_2^2 \sigma_{R_2}^2 + 2x_1 x_2 \sigma_{R_{1,2}}$
6.8	Covariance of returns between two assets	$\sigma_{R_{1,2}} = \sum_{i=1}^{n} \{p_i \times [R_{1,i} - E(R_1)] \times [R_{2,i} - E(R_2)]\}$
6.9	Correlation between the returns on two assets	$\rho_{R_{1,2}} = \dfrac{\sigma_{R_{1,2}}}{\sigma_{R_1} \sigma_{R_2}}$
6.10	Expected return and systematic risk	$E(R_i) = R_{rf} + \beta_i [E(R_m) - R_{rf}]$
6.11	Portfolio beta	$\beta_{n\,Asset\,portfolio} = \sum_{i=1}^{n} x_i \beta_i$

Self-Study Problems

6.1 Kaaran made a friendly wager with a colleague that involves the result from flipping a coin. If heads comes up, Kaaran must pay her colleague $15; otherwise, her colleague will pay Kaaran $15. What is Kaaran's expected cash flow, and what is the variance of that cash flow if the coin has an equal probability of coming up heads or tails? Suppose Kaaran's colleague is willing to handicap the bet by paying her $20 if the coin toss results in tails. If everything else remains the same, what are Kaaran's expected cash flow and the variance of that cash flow?

6.2 You know that the price of CFI, Inc., stock will be $12 exactly one year from today. Today the price of the stock is $11. Describe what must happen to the price of CFI, Inc., today in order for an investor to generate a 20 percent return over the next year. Assume that CFI does not pay dividends.

6.3 The expected value of a normal distribution of prices for a stock is $50. If you are 90 percent sure that the price of the stock will be between $40 and $60, then what is the variance of the stock price?

6.4 You must choose between investing in stock A or stock B. You have already used CAPM to calculate the rate of return you should expect to receive for each stock given each one's systematic risk and decided that the expected return for both exceeds that predicted by CAPM by the same amount. In other words, both are equally attractive investments for a diversified investor. However, since you are still in school and do not have a lot of money, your investment portfolio is not diversified. You have decided to invest in the stock that has the highest expected return per unit of total risk. If the expected return and standard deviation of returns for stock A are 10 percent and 25 percent, respectively, and the expected return and standard deviation of returns for stock B are 15 percent and 40 percent, respectively, which should you choose? Assume that the risk-free rate is 5 percent.

6.5 CSB, Inc., stock has a beta of 1.35. If the expected market return is 14.5 percent and the risk-free rate is 5.5 percent, what is the appropriate expected return for CSB stock (using the CAPM)?

Solutions to Self-Study Problems

6.1 Part 1: $E(\text{cash flow}) = (0.5 \times -\$15) + (0.5 \times \$15) = 0$

$\sigma_{Cash\,flow}^2 = [0.5 \times (-\$15 - \$0)^2] + [0.5 \times (\$15 - \$0)^2] = 225$

Part 2: $E(\text{cash flow}) = (0.5 \times -\$15) + (0.5 \times \$20) = \$2.50$

$\sigma_{Cash\,flow}^2 = [0.5 \times (-\$15 - \$2.50)^2] + [0.5 \times (\$20 - \$2.50)^2] = 306.25$

6.2 The expected return for CFI based on today's stock price is ($12 − $11)/$11 = 9.09 percent, which is lower than 20 percent. Since the stock price one year from today is fixed, the only way that you will generate a 20 percent return is if the price of the stock drops today. Consequently, the price of the stock today must drop to $10. It is found by solving the following: 0.2 = ($12 − x)/x, or x = $10.

6.3 Since you know that 1.645 standard deviations around the expected return captures 90 percent of the distribution, you can set up either of the following equations:

$$\$40 = \$50 - 1.645\sigma \quad \text{or} \quad \$60 = \$50 + 1.645\sigma$$

and solve for σ Doing this with either equation yields:

$$\sigma = \$6.079 \text{ and } \sigma^2 = 36.954$$

6.4 A comparison of the Sharpe Ratios for the two stocks will tell you which has the highest expected return per unit of total risk.

$$S_A = \frac{E(R_A) - R_{rf}}{\sigma_{R_A}} = \frac{0.10 - 0.05}{0.25} = 0.20$$

$$S_B = \frac{E(R_B) - R_{rf}}{\sigma_{R_B}} = \frac{0.15 - 0.05}{0.40} = 0.25$$

Stock B has the highest expected return per unit of risk.

6.5 $E(R_{CSB}) = R_{rf} + \beta_{CSB}[E(R_M) - R_{rf}] = 0.055 + [1.35 \times (0.145 - 0.055)] = 0.1765$ or, 17.65%

Critical Thinking Questions

6.1 Given that you know the risk as well as the expected return for two stocks, discuss what process you might utilize to determine which of the two stocks is a better buy. You may assume that the two stocks will be the only assets held in your portfolio.

6.2 What is the difference between the expected rate of return and the required rate of return? What does it mean if they are different for a particular asset at a particular point in time?

6.3 Suppose that the standard deviation of the returns on the shares of stock at two different companies is exactly the same. Does this mean that the required rate of return will be the same for these two stocks? How might the required rate of return on the stock of a third company be greater than the required rates of return on the stocks of the first two companies even if the standard deviation of the returns of the third company's stock is lower?

6.4 The correlation between stocks A and B is 0.50, while the correlation between stocks A and C is −0.5. You already own stock A and are thinking of buying either stock B or stock C. If you want your portfolio to have the lowest possible risk, would you buy stock B or C? Would you expect the stock you choose to affect the return that you earn on your portfolio?

6.5 The idea that we can know the return on a security for each possible outcome is overly simplistic. However, even though we cannot possibly predict all possible outcomes, this fact has little bearing on the risk-free return. Explain why.

6.6 Which investment category has shown the greatest degree of risk in the United States since 1926? Explain why that makes sense in a world where the value of an asset in this investment category is likely to be more sensitive to changes in market conditions than is the price of a corporate bond.

6.7 You are concerned about one of the investments in your fully diversified portfolio. You just have an uneasy feeling about the CFO, Iam Shifty, of that particular firm. You do believe, however, that the firm makes a good product and that it is appropriately priced by the market. Should you be concerned about the effect on your portfolio if Shifty embezzles a portion of the firm's cash?

6.8 The CAPM is used to price the risk (estimate the expected return) for any asset. Our examples have focused on stocks, but we could also use CAPM to estimate the expected rate of return for bonds. Explain why.

6.9 In recent years, investors have agreed that the market portfolio consists of more than just a group of U.S. stocks and bonds. If you are an investor who invests in only U.S. stocks, describe the effects on the risk in your portfolio.

6.10 You may have heard the statement that you should not include your home as an asset in your investment portfolio. Assume that your house will comprise up to 75 percent of your assets in the early part of your investment life. Evaluate the implications of omitting it when calculating the risk of your overall investment portfolio.

Questions and Problems

BASIC > **6.1** **Returns:** Describe the difference between a total holding period return and an expected return.

6.2 **Expected returns:** John is watching an old game show rerun on television called *Let's Make a Deal* in which the contestant chooses a prize behind one of two curtains. Behind one of the curtains is a gag prize worth $150, and behind the other is a round-the-world trip worth $7,200. The game show has placed a subliminal message on the curtain containing the gag prize, which makes the probability of choosing the gag prize equal to 75 percent. What is the expected value of the selection, and what is the standard deviation of that selection?

6.3 **Expected returns:** You have chosen biology as your college major because you would like to be a medical doctor. However, you find that the probability of being accepted to medical school is about 10 percent. If you are accepted to medical school, then your starting salary when you graduate will be $300,000 per year. However, if you are not accepted, then you would choose to work in a zoo, where you will earn $40,000 per year. Without considering the additional years you would spend in school if you study medicine or the time value of money, what is your expected starting salary as well as the standard deviation of that starting salary?

6.4 **Historical market:** Describe the general relation between risk and return that we observe in the historical bond and stock market data.

6.5 **Single-asset portfolios:** Stocks A, B, and C have expected returns of 15 percent, 15 percent, and 12 percent, respectively, while their standard deviations are 45 percent, 30 percent, and 30 percent, respectively. If you were considering the purchase of each of these stocks as the only holding in your portfolio and the risk-free rate is 0 percent, which stock should you choose?

6.6 **Diversification:** Describe how investing in more than one asset can reduce risk through diversification.

6.7 **Systematic risk:** Define systematic risk.

6.8 **Measuring systematic risk:** Susan is expecting the returns on the market portfolio to be negative in the near term. Since she is managing a stock mutual fund, she must remain invested in a portfolio of stocks. However, she is allowed to adjust the beta of her portfolio. What kind of beta would you recommend for Susan's portfolio?

6.9 **Measuring systematic risk:** Describe and justify what the value of the beta of a U.S. Treasury bill should be.

6.10 **Measuring systematic risk:** If the expected rate of return for the market is not much greater than the risk-free rate of return, what does this suggest about the general level of compensation for bearing systematic risk?

6.11 **CAPM:** Describe the Capital Asset Pricing Model (CAPM) and what it tells us.

6.12 **The Security Market Line:** If the expected return on the market is 10 percent and the risk-free rate is 4 percent, what is the expected return for a stock with a beta equal to 1.5? What is the market risk premium?

INTERMEDIATE > **6.13** **Expected returns:** José is thinking about purchasing a soft drink machine and placing it in a business office. He knows that there is a 5 percent probability that someone who walks by the machine will make a purchase from the machine, and he knows that the profit on each soft drink sold is $0.10. If José expects a thousand people per day to pass by the machine and requires a complete return of his investment in one year, then what is the maximum price that he should be willing to pay for the soft drink machine? Assume 250 working days in a year, and ignore taxes and the time value of money.

6.14 **Interpreting the variance and standard deviation:** The distribution of grades in an introductory finance class is normally distributed, with an expected grade of 75. If the standard deviation of grades is 7, in what range would you expect 95 percent of the grades to fall?

6.15 **Calculating the variance and standard deviation:** Kate recently invested in real estate with the intention of selling the property one year from today. She has modeled the returns on that investment based on three economic scenarios. She believes that if the economy stays healthy, then her investment will generate a 30 percent return. However, if the economy softens, as predicted, the return will be 10 percent, while the return will be −25 percent if the economy slips into a recession. If the probabilities of the healthy, soft, and recessionary states are 0.4, 0.5, and 0.1, respectively, then what are the expected return and the standard deviation of the return on Kate's investment?

6.16 **Calculating the variance and standard deviation:** Barbara is considering investing in a stock and is aware that the return on that investment is particularly sensitive to how the economy is performing. Her analysis suggests that four states of the economy can affect the return on the investment. Using the table of returns and probabilities below, find the expected return and the standard deviation of the return on Barbara's investment.

	Probability	Return
Boom	0.1	25.00%
Good	0.4	15.00%
Level	0.3	10.00%
Slump	0.2	−5.00%

6.17 Calculating the variance and standard deviation: Ben would like to invest in gold and is aware that the returns on such an investment can be quite volatile. Use the following table of states, probabilities, and returns to determine the expected return and the standard deviation of the return on Ben's gold investment.

	Probability	Return
Boom	0.1	40.00%
Good	0.2	30.00%
OK	0.3	15.00%
Level	0.2	2.00%
Slump	0.2	−12.00%

6.18 Single-asset portfolios: Using the information from Problems 6.15, 6.16, and 6.17, calculate the coefficient of variation for each of the investments in those problems.

6.19 Portfolios with more than one asset: Emmy is analyzing a two-stock portfolio that consists of a utility stock and a commodity stock. She knows that the return on the utility stock has a standard deviation of 40 percent and the return on the commodity stock has a standard deviation of 30 percent. However, she does not know the exact covariance in the returns of the two stocks. Emmy would like to plot the variance of the portfolio for each of three cases—covariance of 0.12, 0, and −0.12—in order to understand what the variance of the portfolio would be for a range of covariances. Do the calculation for all three cases (0.12, 0, and −0.12), assuming an equal proportion of each stock in the portfolio.

6.20 Portfolios with more than one asset: Given the returns and probabilities for the three possible states listed below, calculate the covariance between the returns of Stock A and Stock B. For convenience, assume that the expected returns of Stock A and Stock B are 11.75 percent and 18 percent, respectively.

	Probability	Return on A	Return on B
Good	0.35	0.30	0.50
OK	0.50	0.10	0.10
Poor	0.15	−0.25	−0.30

6.21 Compensation for bearing systematic risk: You have constructed a diversified portfolio of stocks such that there is no unsystematic risk. Explain why the expected return of that portfolio should be greater than the expected return of a risk-free security.

6.22 Compensation for bearing systematic risk: Write out the equation for the covariance in the returns of two assets, Asset 1 and Asset 2. Using that equation, explain the easiest way for the two asset returns to have a covariance of zero.

6.23 Compensation for bearing systematic risk: Evaluate the following statement: "By fully diversifying a portfolio, such as by buying every asset in the market, we can completely eliminate all types of risk, thereby creating a synthetic Treasury bill."

6.24 CAPM: Damien knows that the beta of his portfolio is equal to 1, but he does not know the risk-free rate of return or the market risk premium. He also knows that the expected return on the market is 8 percent. What is the expected return on Damien's portfolio?

6.25 CAPM: In February 2013 the risk-free rate was 4.75 percent, the market risk premium was 6 percent, and the beta for Dell stock was 1.31. What is the expected return that was consistent with the systematic risk associated with the returns on Dell stock?

6.26 CAPM: The market risk premium is 6 percent, and the risk-free rate is 5 percent. If the expected return on a bond is 6.5 percent, what is its beta?

6.27 David is going to purchase two stocks to form the initial holdings in his portfolio. Iron stock has an expected return of 15 percent, while Copper stock has an expected return of 20 percent. If David plans to invest 30 percent of his funds in Iron and the remainder in Copper, what will be the expected return from his portfolio? What if David invests 70 percent of his funds in Iron stock?

◄ ADVANCED

6.28 Sumeet knows that the covariance in the return on two assets is -0.0025. Without knowing the expected return of the two assets, explain what that covariance means.

6.29 In order to fund her retirement, Glenda requires a portfolio with an expected return of 12 percent per year over the next 30 years. She has decided to invest in Stocks 1, 2, and 3, with 25 percent in Stock 1, 50 percent in Stock 2, and 25 percent in Stock 3. If Stocks 1 and 2 have expected returns of 9 percent and 10 percent per year, respectively, then what is the minimum expected annual return for Stock 3 that will enable Glenda to achieve her investment requirement?

6.30 Tonalli is putting together a portfolio of 10 stocks in equal proportions. What is the relative importance of the variance for each stock versus the covariance for the pairs of stocks in her portfolio? For this exercise, ignore the actual values of the variance and covariance terms and explain their importance conceptually.

6.31 Explain why investors who have diversified their portfolios will determine the price and, consequently, the expected return on an asset.

6.32 Brad is about to purchase an additional asset for his well-diversified portfolio. He notices that when he plots the historical returns of the asset against those of the market portfolio, the line of best fit tends to have a large amount of prediction error for each data point (the scatter plot is not very tight around the line of best fit). Do you think that this will have a large or a small impact on the beta of the asset? Explain your opinion.

6.33 Draw the Security Market Line (SML) for the case where the market risk premium is 5 percent and the risk-free rate is 7 percent. Now suppose an asset has a beta of -1.0 and an expected return of 4 percent. Plot it on your graph. Is the security properly priced? If not, explain what we might expect to happen to the price of this security in the market. Next, suppose another asset has a beta of 3.0 and an expected return of 20 percent. Plot it on the graph. Is this security properly priced? If not, explain what we might expect to happen to the price of this security in the market.

6.34 If the CAPM describes the relation between systematic risk and expected returns, can both an individual asset and the market portfolio of all risky assets have negative expected real rates of return? Why or why not?

6.35 You have been provided the following data on the securities of three firms and the market:

Security	E[R$_i$]	σ_{R_i}	ρ	β_i
Stock A	0.15		1.0	1.5
Stock B	0.15	0.18	0.5	
Stock C	0.10	0.02		0.5
Market portfolio	0.10	0.04		
Treasury bills	0.05	0		

Assume the CAPM and SML are true and fill in the missing values in the table. Would you invest in the stock of any of the three firms? If so, which one(s) and why?

Sample Test Problems

6.1 Friendly Airlines stock is selling at a current price of $37.50 per share. If the stock does not pay a dividend and has a 12 percent expected return, what is the expected price of the stock one year from today?

6.2 Stefan's parents are about to invest their nest egg in a stock that he has estimated to have an expected return of 9 percent over the next year. If the return on the stock is normally distributed with a 3 percent standard deviation, in what range will the stock return fall 95 percent of the time?

6.3 Elaine has narrowed her investment alternatives to two stocks (at this time she is not worried about diversifying): Stock M, which has a 23 percent expected return, and Stock Y, which has an 8 percent expected return. If Elaine requires a 16 percent return on her total investment, then what proportion of her portfolio will she invest in each stock?

6.4 You have just prepared a graph similar to Exhibit 6.9, comparing historical data for Pear Computer Corp. and the general market. When you plot the line of best fit for these data, you find that the slope of that line is 2.5. If you know that the market generated a return of 12 percent and that the risk-free rate is 5 percent, then what would your best estimate be for the return of Pear Computer during that same time period?

6.5 The CAPM predicts that the return of MoonBucks Tea Corp. is 23.6 percent. If the risk-free rate of return is 8 percent and the expected return on the market is 20 percent, then what is MoonBucks's beta?

Bond Valuation and the Structure of Interest Rates

7

© George Atsametakis/Age Fotostock America, Inc.

Learning Objectives

1 Describe the market for corporate bonds and three types of corporate bonds.

2 Explain how to calculate the value of a bond and why bond prices vary negatively with interest rate movements.

3 Distinguish between a bond's coupon rate, yield to maturity, and effective annual yield.

4 Explain why investors in bonds are subject to interest rate risk and why it is important to understand the bond theorems.

5 Discuss the concept of default risk and know how to compute a default risk premium.

6 Describe the factors that determine the level and shape of the yield curve.

On April 23, 2010, the Greek government officially asked the European Union and International Monetary Fund for a bailout package that would consist of loans totaling €45 billion ($61 billion U.S.). This bailout, which would amount to more than $5,500 for every one of Greece's 11 million people, reflected the dire financial situation that the Greek people had gotten themselves into. A few days later Standard & Poors, the bond rating firm, lowered Greece's debt rating to BB+, officially placing the country's debt into the "junk debt" category.

The financial conditions that led to the request for the bailout package had developed over a long period. Greece's financial situation had already been deteriorating, and the recession that began in December 2007 pushed the country over the edge. The challenge facing the Greek people and their government was enormous. The government had spent money freely and done a poor job of collecting taxes for many years. Government efforts to lower spending by reducing wages and cutting retirement benefits were met with riots and protests in the streets of Athens. Efforts to improve tax collections were equally challenging. The Greek shadow economy, the economy on which taxes are illegally avoided, was estimated to be over 25 percent of Greece's GDP (vs. 7.2 percent in U.S.), and uncollected taxes were estimated to total €15 billion ($20.5 billion U.S.) annually.

The yield on long-term Greek government bonds was already increasing steadily in early 2010 as the extent of the country's financial difficulties was becoming known. On the day after Standard & Poors downgraded Greece's debt, the yield jumped an additional 1.56 percent to 11.24 percent. This yield was 8.22 percent higher than the 3.02 percent yield on German government bonds. A year earlier, Greek bond yields had exceeded German bond yields by only 1 percent.

The yields on Greek bonds were increasing because the prices that investors were willing to pay for the country's bonds were going down. The prices that investors pay for bonds reflect the value of the interest and principal payments that ownership of the bonds entitles them to receive. When a bond issuer gets into financial difficulty, investors are less likely to receive the interest and principal payments that they have been promised, and so they place less value on them. This chapter discusses the characteristics of bonds, how bonds are valued, and the factors that determine bond prices and yields.

CHAPTER PREVIEW

This chapter is all about bonds and how they are valued, or priced, in the marketplace. As you might suspect, the bond valuation models presented in this chapter are derived from the present value concepts discussed in Chapter 5. The market price of a bond is simply the present value of the promised cash flows (interest and principal payments), discounted at the current market rate of interest for bonds of similar risk.

In this chapter we first discuss the corporate bond market, bond price information that is available, and the types of bonds found in the market. Then we develop the basic equation used to calculate bond prices and show how to compute the following characteristics of a bond: (1) yield to maturity and (2) effective annual yield. We next discuss interest rate risk and identify three bond theorems that describe how bond prices respond to changes in interest rates. Finally, we explain why firms have different borrowing costs. We find that four factors affect a firm's cost of borrowing: (1) the debt's marketability, (2) default risk, (3) call risk, and (4) term to maturity.

7.1 CORPORATE BONDS

In this section we discuss the market for corporate bonds and some of the types of bonds that firms issue.

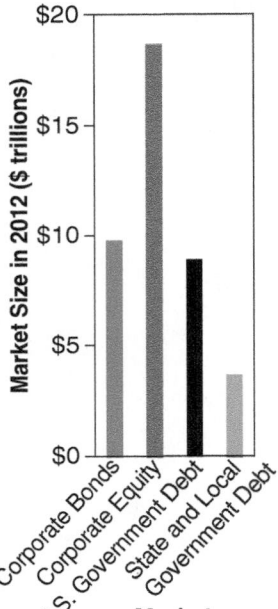

Market for Corporate Bonds

The market for corporate bonds is enormous. At the beginning of June 2012, for example, the value of corporate bonds outstanding in the United States was $9.8 trillion, almost 65 percent as large as the total U.S. gross domestic product of $15.1 trillion. By comparison, the market for corporate equity was the largest part of the U.S. capital market with a value of $18.7 trillion and U.S. government long-term Treasury securities totaled $8.9 trillion. State and local government debt markets were much smaller at $3.7 trillion. The most important investors in corporate bonds are big institutional investors such as life insurance companies, pension funds, and mutual funds. Because the primary investors are so big, trades in this market tend to involve very large blocks of securities.

Most secondary market transactions for corporate bonds take place through dealers in the over-the-counter (OTC) market. An interesting characteristic of the corporate bond market is that there are a large number of different bond issues that trade in the market. The reason is that while a corporation typically has a single issue of common stock outstanding, it may have a dozen or more different notes and bonds outstanding. Therefore, despite the large overall trading volume of corporate bonds, the bonds from any particular issue will not necessarily trade on a given day. As a result, the market for corporate bonds is thin compared to the market for corporate stocks or money market securities. On Wall Street, the term *thin* means that secondary market trades of individual securities are relatively infrequent. Thus, corporate bonds are less marketable than the securities that have higher daily trading volumes.

Prices in the corporate bond market also tend to be more volatile than prices of securities sold in markets with greater trading volumes. This is because a few large trades can have a larger impact on a security's price than numerous trades of various sizes. The result of this is that the market for corporate bonds is not as efficient (new information does not get incorporated into corporate bond prices as efficiently) as those for highly marketable stocks or money market instruments, such as U.S. Treasury securities.

Bond Price Information

The corporate bond market also has little *transparency* because it is almost entirely an OTC market. A financial market is transparent if it is easy to view prices and trading volume. An example of a transparent market is the New York Stock Exchange (NYSE), where price information on every trade and trade size are available for every transaction during the day. In contrast, corporate bond market transactions are widely dispersed, with dealers located all over the country, and there are an enormous number of different securities. Furthermore, many corporate bond transactions are negotiated directly between the buyer and the seller and there is little centralized reporting of these sales. As a result, information on individual corporate bond transactions is not widely published as the transactions occur. This is another reason that the corporate bond market is not as efficient as the stock or money markets.

 A primer on bonds can be found at the Yahoo! Finance Web site at http://finance.yahoo.com/bonds/bonds_101. Investinginbonds.com is another Web site providing educational information about bonds and their markets. Go to http://www.investinginbonds.com.

Types of Corporate Bonds

Corporate bonds are long-term IOUs that represent claims against a firm's assets. Unlike stockholders' returns, most bondholders' returns are *fixed*; they receive only the interest payments that are promised plus the repayment of the loan amount when the bond matures. Debt instruments where the interest paid to investors is fixed for the life of the contract are called **fixed-income securities**. We examine three types of fixed-income securities in this section.

fixed-income securities
debt instruments that pay interest in amounts that are fixed for the life of the contract

Vanilla Bonds

The most common bonds issued by corporations have coupon payments that are fixed for the life of the bond, and at maturity the entire original principal is paid and the bonds are retired. These bonds, which are known as vanilla bonds, have no unusual features.

The time line above shows the cash payments for a three-year vanilla bond with a $1,000 face value and an 8 percent coupon (interest) rate. P_B is the price (value) of the bond, which will be discussed in the next section. The $80 cash payments ($1,000 × 8 percent = $80) made each year are called the coupon payments. **Coupon payments** are the interest payments made to bondholders. These payments are usually made annually or semiannually, and the payment amount (or rate) remains fixed for the life of the bond contract, which for our example is three years. The **face value**, or **par value**, for most corporate bonds is $1,000, and it is the principal amount owed to the bondholder at maturity. Finally, the bond's **coupon rate** is the annual coupon payment (C) divided by the bond's face value (F). Our vanilla bond pays $80 of coupon interest annually and has a face value of $1,000. The coupon rate is thus:

coupon payments
the interest payments made to bondholders

face value, or **par value**
the amount on which interest is calculated and that is owed to the bondholder when a bond reaches maturity

coupon rate
the annual coupon payment of a bond divided by the bond's face value

$$
\begin{aligned}
\text{Coupon rate} &= \frac{C}{F} \\
&= \frac{\$80}{\$1,000} \\
&= 0.08, \text{ or } 8\%
\end{aligned}
$$

Zero Coupon Bonds

At times, corporations issue bonds that have no coupon payments but promise a single payment at maturity. The interest paid to a bondholder is the difference between the price paid for the bond and the face value received at maturity. These bonds are sold at a price below the amount that the investor receives at maturity because all of the interest is paid when the bonds are retired at maturity rather than in semiannual or yearly coupon payments. The face value of a zero coupon bond is different from that of a vanilla bond in that it includes both the interest and principal.

The most frequent and regular issuer of zero coupon securities is the U.S. Department of Treasury, and perhaps the best-known zero coupon bond is a United States Saving Bond. Corporations also issue zero coupon bonds from time to time. Firms that are expanding operations but have little cash available to make interest payments are especially likely to use zero coupon bonds for funding. In the 1990s, the bond market was flooded with zero coupon bonds issued by telecommunications firms. These firms were spending huge amounts to build fiber-optic networks, which generated few cash inflows until they were completed.

You can find information about zero coupon bonds at http:// beginnersinvest .about.com/od/ zerocouponbonds.

Convertible Bonds

Corporate convertible bonds can be converted into shares of common stock at some predetermined ratio at the discretion of the bondholder. For example, a $1,000 face-value bond may be convertible into 100 shares of common stock. A conversion feature is valuable to bondholders because it allows them to share in the good fortunes of the firm if the firm's stock price rises above a certain level. Specifically, the bondholders profit if they exchange their bonds for the company's stock when the market value of the stock they receive exceeds the market value of the bonds.

Typically, the conversion ratio is set so that the firm's stock price must appreciate at least 15 to 20 percent before it is profitable to convert the bonds into stock. As you would expect from our discussion, since a conversion feature is valuable to bondholders, firms that issue convertible bonds can do so at a lower interest rate. This reduces the amount of cash that the firms must use to make interest payments.

> **BEFORE YOU GO ON**

1. What are the main differences between the bond markets and stock markets?

2. A bond has a 7 percent coupon rate, a face value of $1,000, and a maturity of four years. On a time line, lay out the cash flows for the bond.

3. Explain what a convertible bond is.

7.2 BOND VALUATION

LEARNING OBJECTIVE

We turn now to the topic of bond valuation—how bonds are priced. Throughout this book, we have stressed that the value, or price, of any asset is the present value of its future cash flows. The steps necessary to value an asset are as follows:

1. Estimate the expected future cash flows.
2. Determine the required rate of return, or discount rate. This rate depends on the riskiness of the future cash flows.
3. Compute the present value of the future cash flows. This present value is what the asset is worth at a particular point in time.

For bonds, the valuation procedure is relatively easy. The cash flows (coupon and principal payments) are contractual obligations of the firm and are known by market participants, since they are stated in the bond contract. Thus, market participants know the magnitude and timing of the expected cash flows as promised by the borrower (the bond issuer). The required rate of return, or discount rate, for a bond is the market interest rate, called the bond's *yield to maturity* (or more commonly, simply its *yield*). This rate is determined from the market prices of bonds that have features similar to those of the bond being valued; by *similar*, we mean bonds that have the same term to maturity, have the same bond rating (default risk class), and are similar in other ways.

Notice that the required rate of return is the **opportunity cost** for the investors who purchase the bond. An opportunity cost is the highest alternative return that is given up when an investment is made. For example, if bonds identical to the bond being valued—having the same risk—yield 9 percent annually, the threshold yield or required return on the bond being valued is 9 percent. Why? An investor would not buy a bond with an 8 percent yield when an identical bond yielding 9 percent is available.

opportunity cost
the return from the best alternative investment with similar risk that an investor gives up when he or she makes a certain investment

Given the above information, we can compute the current value, or price, of a bond (P_B) by calculating the present value of the bond's expected cash flows:

$$P_B = PV(\text{Coupon payments}) + PV(\text{Principal payment})$$

Next, we examine this calculation in detail.

The Bond Valuation Formula

To begin, refer to Exhibit 7.1, which shows the cash flows for a three-year corporate bond (a bond with three years to maturity) with an 8 percent coupon rate and a $1,000 face value. If the market rate of interest on similar bonds is 10 percent and interest payments are made annually, what is the market price of the bond? In other words, how much should you be willing to pay for the promised cash flow stream?

There are a number of ways to solve this problem. Probably the simplest is to write the bond valuation formula in terms of the individual cash flows. Thus, the price of the bond (P_B) is the sum of the present value calculations for the coupon payments (C) and the principal amount (F), discounted at the required rate (i). That calculation is:

$$
\begin{aligned}
P_B &= PV\ (\text{Each coupon payment}) + PV\ (\text{Principle payment}) \\
&= \left[C_1 \times \frac{1}{1+i} \right] + \left[C_2 \times \frac{1}{(1+i)^2} \right] + \left[C_3 \times \frac{1}{(1+i)^3} \right] + \left[F_3 \times \frac{1}{(1+i)^3} \right] \\
&= \left[\$80 \times \frac{1}{1.10} \right] + \left[\$80 \times \frac{1}{(1.10)^2} \right] + \left[\$80 \times \frac{1}{(1.10)^3} \right] + \left[\$1{,}000 \times \frac{1}{(1.10)^3} \right] \\
&= [\$80 \times 0.9091] + [\$80 \times 0.8264] + [\$80 \times 0.7513] + [\$1{,}000 \times 0.7513] \\
&= \$72.73 + \$66.11 + \$60.10 + \$751.30 \\
&= \$950.24
\end{aligned}
$$

Notice that you could have simplified the calculation by combining the final coupon payment and the principal payment ($C_3 + F_3$), since both cash flows occur at time $t = 3$.

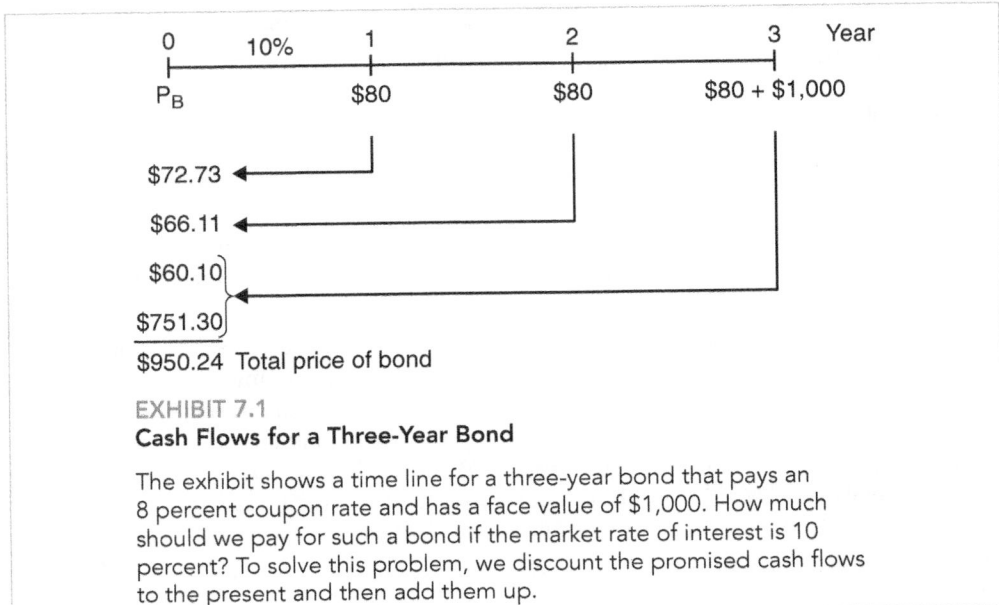

EXHIBIT 7.1

Cash Flows for a Three-Year Bond

The exhibit shows a time line for a three-year bond that pays an 8 percent coupon rate and has a face value of $1,000. How much should we pay for such a bond if the market rate of interest is 10 percent? To solve this problem, we discount the promised cash flows to the present and then add them up.

To develop the general bond pricing formula, we can write the equations for the price of a four-year, five-year, and six-year maturity bond, as follows:

$$P_B = \left[C_1 \times \frac{1}{1+i} \right] + \left[C_2 \times \frac{1}{(1+i)^2} \right] + \cdots + \left[(C_4 + F_4) + \frac{1}{(1+i)^4} \right]$$

$$= \left[C_1 \times \frac{1}{1+i} \right] + \left[C_2 \times \frac{1}{(1+i)^2} \right] + \cdots + \left[(C_5 + F_5) + \frac{1}{(1+i)^5} \right]$$

$$= \left[C_1 \times \frac{1}{1+i} \right] + \left[C_2 \times \frac{1}{(1+i)^2} \right] + \cdots + \left[(C_6 + F_6) + \frac{1}{(1+i)^6} \right]$$

If we continue the process for n periods to maturity, we arrive at the general equation for the price of the bond:

$$P_B = \left[C_1 \times \frac{1}{1+i} \right] + \left[C_2 \times \frac{1}{(1+i)^2} \right] + \cdots + \left[(C_n + F_n) \times \frac{1}{(1+i)^n} \right]$$

In practice, the bond pricing equation is usually written with C_n divided by $(1+i)^n$ rather than with C_n multiplied by $1/(1+i)^n$. Thus, the general equation for the price of a bond can be written as follows:

$$P_B = \frac{C_1}{1+i} + \frac{C_2}{(1+i)^2} + \cdots + \frac{C_n + F_n}{(1+i)^n} \qquad (7.1)$$

where:

P_B = the price of the bond, or present value of the stream of cash payments
C_t = the coupon payment in period t, where $t = 1, 2, 3, \ldots, n$
F_n = par value or face value (principal amount) to be paid at maturity
i = market interest rate (discount rate or yield)
n = number of periods to maturity

Note that there are five variables in the bond pricing equation. If we know any four of them, we can solve for the fifth.

Calculator Tip: Bond Valuation Problems

We can easily calculate bond prices using a financial calculator or a spreadsheet program. We solve for bond prices and bond yields in exactly the same way we solved for the present value (bond price) and discount rate (bond yield) in Chapter 5. We solve our example problem on a financial calculator as follows:

Enter	3	10		80	1,000
	N	i	PV	PMT	FV
Answer			−950.26		

Several points are worth noting:

1. Always draw a time line for the cash flows. This simple step will significantly reduce mistakes.

2. The PMT key enters the dollar amount of an ordinary annuity for n periods. In our example, keying in 3 with the N key and $80 with the PMT key enters an $80 annuity with the final payment made at the end of year 3.

3. Be sure that you enter the coupon and the principal payments separately. Do not enter the final coupon payment ($80) and principal amount ($1,000) as a single entry of $1,080 on the FV key. The reason is that the PMT key is the annuity key, and when you enter N = 3, the $80 is entered in the calculator as a three-year ordinary annuity with a final payment of $80 in period $t = 3$. If you then enter $1,080 on the FV key, you will have an extra $80 in the final period ($t = 3$). For the example problem, we correctly entered the $80 coupon payments with the PMT key and the $1,000 principal payment with the FV key.

4. Finally, as we have mentioned in earlier chapters, you must be consistent throughout a problem in how you enter the signs (positive or negative) for cash inflows and cash

outflows. For example, if you are a bond investor and decide to enter all cash inflows with a positive sign, then you must enter all coupon and principal payments with a positive sign. The price you paid for the bond, which is a cash outflow, must be entered as a negative number. This is the convention we will follow.

Par, Premium, and Discount Bonds

One of the mathematical properties of the bond pricing equation is that whenever a bond's coupon rate is equal to the market rate of interest on similar bonds (the bond's yield), the bond will sell at par value. We call such bonds **par-value bonds**. For example, suppose that you own a three-year bond with a face value of $1,000 and an annual coupon rate of 5 percent, when the yield or market rate of interest on similar bonds is 5 percent. The price of your bond, based on Equation 7.1, is:

$$P_B = \frac{\$50}{1.05} + \frac{\$50}{(1.05)^2} + \frac{\$1,050}{(1.05)^3}$$
$$= \$47.62 + \$45.35 + \$907.03$$
$$= \$1,000$$

par-value bonds
bonds that sell at par value, or face value; whenever a bond's coupon rate is equal to the market rate of interest on similar bonds, the bond will sell at par (face) value

As predicted, the bond's price equals its par value.

Now assume that the market rate of interest rises overnight to 8 percent. What happens to the price of the bond? Will the bond's price be below, above, or at par value?

$$P_B = \frac{\$50}{1.08} + \frac{\$50}{(1.08)^2} + \frac{\$1,050}{(1.08)^3}$$
$$= \$46.30 + \$42.87 + \$833.52$$
$$= \$922.69$$

When i is equal to 8 percent, the price of the bond declines to $922.69. The bond sells at a price below par value; such bonds are called **discount bonds**.

Whenever a bond's coupon rate is lower than the market rate of interest on similar bonds, the bond will sell at a discount. This is true because of the fixed nature of a bond's coupon payments. Let's return to our 5 percent coupon bond. If the market rate of interest is 8 percent and our bond pays only 5 percent, no economically rational person would buy the bond at its par value. This would be like choosing a bond with a 5 percent yield over one with an 8 percent yield. We cannot change the coupon rate to 8 percent because it is fixed for the life of the bond. That is why bonds are referred to as fixed-income securities. The only way to increase our bond's yield to 8 percent is to reduce the price of the bond to $922.69. At this price, the bond's yield will be precisely 8 percent, which is the current market rate for similar bonds. Through the price reduction of $77.31 ($1,000 − $922.69 = $77.31), the seller provides the new owner with additional "interest" in the form of a capital gain.

discount bonds
bonds that sell at prices below par (face) value

What would happen to the price of the bond if interest rates on similar bonds declined to 2 percent and the coupon rate remained at 5 percent? The price would rise to $1,086.52. At this price, the bond's yield would be precisely 2 percent, which is the current market yield. The $86.52 ($1,086.52 − $1,000 = $86.52) premium adjusts the bond's yield to 2 percent, which is the current market yield for similar bonds. Bonds that sell at prices above par are called **premium bonds**. Whenever a bond's coupon rate is higher than the market rate of interest, the bond will sell at a premium.

premium bonds
bonds that sell at prices above par (face) value

Our discussion of bond pricing can be summarized as follows, where i is the market rate of interest:

1. $i >$ coupon rate—the bond sells for a discount
2. $i <$ coupon rate—the bond sells for a premium
3. $i =$ coupon rate—the bond sells at par value

This negative relation between changes in the level of interest rates and changes in the price of a bond (or any fixed-income security) is one of the most fundamental relations in corporate finance. The relation exists because the coupon payments on most bonds are fixed and the only way bonds can pay the current market rate of interest to investors is through an adjustment in the price of the bond. This is exactly what happened to the Greek government bonds discussed at the beginning of this chapter. As the risk of those bonds increased, their prices declined so that investors received a market rate of interest that reflected the bond's higher risk.

LEARNING BY DOING

APPLICATION 7.1

Pricing a Bond

PROBLEM: Your stockbroker is trying to sell you a 15-year bond with a 7 percent coupon, and the interest, or yield, on similar bonds is 10 percent. Is the bond selling for a premium, at par, or at a discount? Answer the question without making any calculations, and then prove that your answer is correct. The time line is as follows:

APPROACH: Since the market rate of interest is greater than the coupon rate ($i >$ coupon rate), the bond must sell at a discount.

SOLUTION: To prove the answer is correct (or wrong), we can compute the bond's price with a financial calculator.

The bond is selling at a discount, and it should. Why? The market rate of interest is 10 percent, and the bond is paying only 7 percent. Since the bond's coupon rate is fixed, the only way we can bring the bond's yield up to the current market rate of 10 percent is to reduce the price of the bond to $771.82.

USING EXCEL

BOND PRICES AND YIELDS

Calculating bond prices and yields using a spreadsheet may seem daunting at first. However, understanding the terminology used in the formulas will make the calculations a matter of common sense:

   Settlement date—the date a buyer purchases the bond.

   Maturity date—the date the bond expires. If you know only the "*n*" (number of years remaining) of the bond, use a date that is *n* years in the future in this field.

Redemption—the security's redemption value per $10 face value. In other words, if the bond has a par value of $1,000, you enter 100 in this field.

Frequency—the number of coupon payments per year.

   Here is a spreadsheet showing the setup for calculating the price of the discount bond described in Learning by Doing Application 7.1.

   We first use the =PRICE(settlement, maturity, rate, yield, redemption, frequency) formula in Excel to calculate the bond price as a percentage of par. We then multiply this percentage (77.18 percent in the above example) by $1,000 to obtain the bond price in dollars. A bond yield, which is discussed in the next section, is calculated in a similar manner, using the "=YIELD (settlement, maturity, rate, price, redemption, frequency)" formula.

	A	B	C	D
1				
2		**Bond Price Calculations**		
3	**Inputs**			
4	Settlement date	1/1/00		
5	Maturity date	1/1/15		
6	Rate	0.07		
7	Yield	0.10		
8	Redemption (% of par)	100		
9	Frequency	1		
10				
11	**Bond Price**		**Formulas Used**	
12	Bond price as % of par	77.18	=PRICE(B4,B5,B6,B7,B8,B9)	
13	Par value	$1,000.00		
14	Bond price	$771.82	=B12%*B13	
15				

Semiannual Compounding

In Europe, bonds generally pay coupon interest on an annual basis. In contrast, in the United States, most bonds pay coupon interest semiannually—that is, twice a year. Thus, if a bond has an 8 percent coupon rate (paid semiannually), the bondholder will in one year receive two coupon payments of $40 each, totaling $80 ($40 × 2 = $80). We can modify Equation 7.1 as follows to adjust for coupon payments made more than once a year:

$$P_B = \frac{C/m}{1 + i/m} + \frac{C/m}{(1 + i/m)^2} + \frac{C/m}{(1 + i/m)^3} + \cdots + \frac{C/m + F_{mn}}{(1 + i/m)^{mn}} \tag{7.2}$$

where C is the annual coupon payment, m is the number of times coupon payments are made each year, n is the number of years to maturity, and i is the annual market interest rate. In the case of a bond with semiannual coupon payments, m equals 2.

Whether we are computing bond prices annually, semiannually, quarterly, or for some other period, the computation is the same. We need only be sure that the bond's yield, coupon payment, and maturity are adjusted to be consistent with the bond's stated compounding period. Once that information is converted to the correct compounding period, it can simply be entered into Equation 7.1. Thus, there is really no need to memorize or use Equation 7.2 unless you find it helpful. Let's work an example to demonstrate.

Earlier we determined that a three-year, 5 percent coupon bond will sell for $922.69 when the market rate of interest is 8 percent. Our computation assumed that coupon payments were made annually. What is the price of the bond if the coupon payments are made semiannually? The time line for the semiannual bond situation follows:

0	8%/2	1		2		3		4		5		6	Semiannual period
P_B		$50/2		$50/2		$50/2		$50/2		$50/2		$50/2 + $1,000	

We convert the bond data to semiannual compounding as follows: (1) the market yield is 4 percent semiannually (8 percent per year/2 = 4 percent), (2) the coupon payment is $25 semiannually ($50 per year/2 = $25), and (3) the total number of coupon payments is 6 (2 payments per year × 3 years = 6 payments). Plugging the data into Equation 7.1, we find that the bond price is:

$$P_B = \frac{\$25}{1.04} + \frac{\$25}{(1.04)^2} + \frac{\$25}{(1.04)^3} + \frac{\$25}{(1.04)^4} + \frac{\$25}{(1.04)^5} + \frac{\$1,025}{(1.04)^6}$$

$$= \$921.37$$

Notice that the price of the bond is slightly less with semiannual compounding than with annual compounding ($921.37 < $922.69). The slight difference in price reflects the change in the timing of the cash flows and the interest rate adjustment.[1]

Zero Coupon Bonds

As previously mentioned, zero coupon bonds have no coupon payments but promise a single payment at maturity. The price (or yield) of a zero coupon bond is simply a special case of Equation 7.2 in which all the coupon payments are equal to zero.

Hence, the pricing equation for a zero coupon bond is:

$$P_B = \frac{F_{mn}}{(1 + i/m)^{mn}} \tag{7.3}$$

where:

P_B = the price of the bond
F_{mn} = the amount of the cash payment at maturity (face value)
i = annual market interest rate (discount rate or yield)
n = number of years until the payment is due
m = number of times interest is compounded each year

---

[1]If the bond sold at a premium, the reverse would be true; that is, the price with semiannual compounding would be slightly more than the price with annual compounding.

Bond Pricing with Semiannual Coupon Payments

PROBLEM: A corporate treasurer decides to purchase a 20-year Treasury bond with a 4 percent coupon rate. If the current market rate of interest for similar Treasury securities is 4.5 percent, what is the price of the bond?

APPROACH: Treasury securities pay interest semiannually, so this problem is best worked on a financial calculator because of the large number of compounding periods. We can convert the bond data to semiannual compounding as follows: (1) the bond's semiannual yield is 2.25 percent (4.5 percent per year/2 = 2.25 percent), (2) the semiannual coupon payment is $20 [($1,000 × 4 percent)/2 = $40/2 = $20], and (3) the total number of compounding periods is 40 (2 periods per year × 20 years = 40 periods). Note that at maturity, the bond principal, or face value, of $1,000 is paid to the investor. Thus, the bond's time line for the cash payments is as follows:

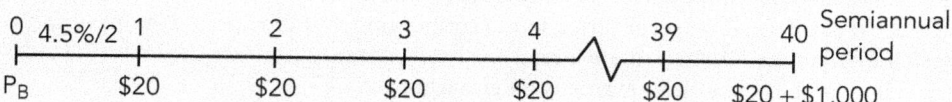

SOLUTION: We can enter the appropriate values on the financial calculator and solve for the present value:

The bond sells for a discount, and its price is $934.52.

Notice that if a zero coupon bond compounds annually, $m = 1$ and Equation 7.3 becomes:

$$P_B = \frac{F_n}{(1 + i)^n}$$

Now let's work an example. What is the price of a zero coupon bond with a $1,000 face value, 10-year maturity, and semiannual compounding when the market interest rate is 12 percent? Since the bond compounds interest semiannually, the number of compounding periods is 20 ($m \times n = 2 \times 10 = 20$). The semiannual interest is 6 percent (12 percent/2 = 6 percent). The time line for the cash flows is as follows:

Plugging the data into Equation 7.3, we find that the price of the bond is:

$$P_B = \frac{\$1,000}{(1.06)^{20}}$$
$$= \$1,000 \times 0.3118 = \$311.80$$

Notice that the zero coupon bond is selling at a very large (deep) discount. This should come as no surprise, since the bond has no coupon payment and all the dollars paid to investors are paid at maturity. Why are zero coupon bonds so heavily discounted compared with similar bonds that do have coupon payments? From Chapter 5, we know that because of the time value of money, dollars to be received in the future have less value than current dollars. Thus, zero coupon bonds, for which all the cash payments are made at maturity, must sell for less than similar bonds that make coupon payments before maturity.

The Price of a Bond

PROBLEM: An investor is considering buying a U.S. corporate bond with an eight-year maturity and a coupon rate of 6 percent. Similar bonds in the marketplace yield 14 percent. How much should the investor be willing to pay for the bond? Using Equation 7.1 (or 7.2), set up the equation to be solved, and then solve the problem using your financial calculator. Note that the discount rate used in the problem is the 14 percent market yield on similar bonds (bonds of similar risk), which is the investor's opportunity cost.

APPROACH: Since U.S. corporate bonds pay coupon interest semiannually, we first need to convert all of the bond data to reflect semiannual compounding: (1) the annual coupon payment is $60 per year (6 percent × $1,000 = $60) and the semiannual payment is $30 per period ($60/2 = $30); (2) the appropriate semiannual yield is 7 percent (14 percent/2 = 7 percent); and (3) the total number of compounding periods is 16 (2 periods per year × 8 years = 16 periods). The time line for the semiannual cash flows is as follows:

SOLUTION: Using Equation 7.1 (or 7.2), the setup is as follows:

$$P_B = \frac{\$30}{1.07} + \frac{\$30}{(1.07)^2} + \cdots + \frac{\$1,030}{(1.07)^{16}}$$

To solve the problem using a financial calculator, we enter the appropriate values and solve for PV:

Enter	16	7		30	1,000
	N	i	PV	PMT	FV
Answer			−622.13		

The investor should be willing to pay $622.13 because the bond's yield at this price would be exactly 14 percent, which is the current market yield on similar bonds. If the bond price was more than $622.13, the investment would yield a return of less than 14 percent. In this situation an investor would be better off buying the similar bonds in the market that yield 14 percent. Of course, if the investor can buy the bond for less than $622.13, the price is a bargain, and the return on investment will be greater than the market yield.

> **BEFORE YOU GO ON**

1. Explain conceptually how bonds are priced.

2. What is the compounding period for most bonds sold in the United States?

3. What are zero coupon bonds, and how are they priced?

7.3 BOND YIELDS

We frequently know a bond's price from an offer to sell it, but not its yield to maturity. In this section, we discuss how to compute the yield to maturity and some other important bond yields.

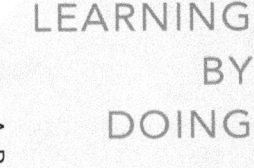

LEARNING OBJECTIVE ③

Yield to Maturity

The **yield to maturity** of a bond is the discount rate that makes the present value of the coupon and principal payments equal to the price of the bond. The yield to maturity can be viewed as a *promised yield* because it is the annual yield that the investor earns if the bond is held to maturity and all the coupon and principal payments are made as promised. A bond's yield to maturity changes daily as interest rates increase or decrease, but its calculation is always based on the issuer's promise to make interest and principal payments as stipulated in the bond contract.

Let's work through an example to see how a bond's yield to maturity is calculated. Suppose you decide to buy a three-year bond with a 6 percent coupon rate for $960.99. For simplicity, we will assume that the coupon payments are made annually. The time line for the cash flows is as follows:

```
0          i = ?        1              2              3    Year
├───────────────────────┼──────────────┼──────────────┤
-$960.99                $60            $60        $60 + $1,000
```

To compute the yield to maturity, we apply Equation 7.1 and solve for i. We can set up the problem using Equation 7.1 as follows:

$$\$960.99 = \frac{\$60}{1 + i} + \frac{\$60}{(1 + i)^2} + \frac{\$1,060}{(1 + i)^3}$$

As we discussed in Chapter 5, we cannot solve for i mathematically; we must find it by trial and error. We know that the bond is selling for a discount because its price is below par, so the yield must be higher than the 6 percent coupon rate. Let's try 7 percent.

$$\$973.76 = \frac{\$60}{1.07} + \frac{\$60}{(1.07)^2} + \frac{\$1,060}{(1.07)^3}$$

The computed price of $973.76 is still greater than our market price of $960.99; thus, we need to use a slightly larger discount rate. Let's try 7.7 percent

$$\$955.95 = \frac{\$60}{1.077} + \frac{\$60}{(1.077)^2} + \frac{\$1,060}{(1.077)^3}$$

Our computed value of $955.95 is now less than the market price of $960.99, so we need a lower discount rate. We'll try 7.5 percent.

$$\$960.99 = \frac{\$60}{1.075} + \frac{\$60}{(1.075)^2} + \frac{\$1,060}{(1.075)^3}$$

At a discount rate of 7.5 percent, the price of the bond is exactly equal to the market price, and thus, the bond's yield to maturity is 7.5 percent.

We can, of course, also compute the bond's yield to maturity using a financial calculator. Computing the yield in this way is no different from computing the price, except that the unknown is the bond's yield. As with calculating the price of a bond, the major source of computational errors is failing to make sure that all the bond data are consistent with the bond's compounding period. The three variables that may require adjustment are (1) the coupon payment, (2) the yield, and (3) the bond maturity.

For the three-year corporate bond discussed earlier, the bond data are already in a form that is consistent with the annual compounding period, so we enter it into the calculator and solve for i, which is the yield to maturity:

The bond's yield to maturity is 7.5 percent, which is identical to the answer from our hand calculation.

Effective Annual Yield

Up to now, when pricing a bond with a semiannual compounding period, we assumed the bond's annual yield to be twice the semiannual yield. This is the convention used on Wall Street and by other practitioners who deal in bonds. However, notice that bond yields quoted in this manner are just like the APRs discussed in Chapter 5. For example, in Section 5.7 we showed that the APR for a bank credit card with a 1 percent monthly interest rate is simply the monthly interest rate multiplied by the number of months in a year, or 12 percent. As you recall, interest rates (or yields) annualized in this manner do not take compounding into account. Hence, the values calculated are not the true cost of funds, and their use can lead to decisions that are economically incorrect.

As a result, annualized yields calculated by multiplying a yield per period by the number of compounding periods is only acceptable for decision-making purposes when comparing bonds that have the same compounding frequencies. For example, an investor must be careful when comparing yields of European and U.S. bonds, since interest on a European bond is compounded annually while interest on a U.S. bond compounds twice a year.

The correct way to annualize an interest rate to make an economic decision is to compute the effective annual interest rate (EAR). On Wall Street, the EAR is called the **effective annual yield (EAY)**; thus, EAR = EAY. Drawing on Equation 5.11 (see Chapter 5), we find that the correct way to annualize the yield on a bond is as follows:

effective annual yield (EAY)
the annual yield that takes compounding into account; another name for the *effective annual interest rate (EAR)*

$$EAY = \left(1 + \frac{\text{Quoted interest rate}}{m}\right)^m - 1$$

where: Quoted interest rate = simple annual yield (semiannual yield × 2)
m = the number of compounding periods per year

Let's work through an example to see how the EAY differs from the yield to maturity. Suppose an investor buys a 30-year bond with a $1,000 face value for $800. The bond's coupon rate is 8 percent, and interest payments are made semiannually. What is the bond's yield to maturity, and what is its EAY? To find out, we first need to convert the bond's annual data into semiannual data: (1) the 30-year bond has 60 compounding periods (30 years × 2 periods per year = 60 periods) and (2) the bond's semiannual coupon payment is $40 [($1,000 × 0.08)/2 = $80/2 = $40]. The time line for this bond is:

We can set up the problem using Equation 7.1 (or 7.2) as:

$$\$800 = \frac{\$40}{1 + i/2} + \frac{\$40}{(1 + i/2)^2} + \frac{\$40}{(1 + i/2)^3} + \cdots + \frac{\$40}{(1 + i/2)^{59}} + \frac{\$1,040}{(1 + i/2)^{60}}$$

However, solving an equation with so many terms can be time consuming. Therefore, we will solve for the yield to maturity using the yield function in a financial calculator as follows:

The answer is 5.07 percent. We then multiply the semiannual yield by 2 to convert it to an annual yield: 2 × 5.07 percent = 10.14 percent. This is the bond's yield to maturity.

If, instead of multiplying 5.07 percent by 2 we calculate the EAY for the semiannual yield of 5.07 percent, we will get:

$$\begin{aligned} \text{EAY} &= \left(1 + \frac{\text{Quoted interest rate}}{m}\right)^{m} - 1 \\ &= \left(1 + \frac{0.1014}{2}\right)^{2} - 1 \\ &= (1.0507)^{2} - 1 = 0.1040, \text{ or } 10.40\% \end{aligned}$$

The EAY of 10.40 percent is greater than the annual yield to maturity of 10.14 percent because the EAY takes into account the effects of compounding—earning interest on interest. As mentioned earlier, calculating the EAY is the economically correct way to annualize a bond's yield because it takes compounding into account.

Choosing Between Bonds with Different Coupon Payment Frequencies

PROBLEM: You can purchase a U.S. corporate bond from your broker for $1,099.50. The bond has six years to maturity, and an annual coupon rate of 5 percent. Another broker offers you a dollar Eurobond (a dollar-denominated bond sold overseas) with a yield of 3.17 percent, which is denominated in U.S. dollars and has the same maturity and credit rating as the U.S. corporate bond. Which bond should you buy?

APPROACH: Solving this problem involves two steps. First, we must compute the U.S. bond's yield to maturity. The bond pays coupon interest semiannually, so we have to convert the bond data to semiannual periods: (1) the number of compounding periods is 12 (6 years × 2 periods per year = 12 periods) and (2) the semiannual coupon payment is $25 [($1,000 × 0.05)/2 = $50/2 = $25]. Second, we must annualize the yield for the U.S. bond so that we can compare its yield with that of the Eurobond.

SOLUTION: We can solve for the yield to maturity using a financial calculator:

Enter	12		−1,099.50	25	1,000
	N	i	PV	PMT	FV
Answer		1.5831			

The answer, 1.5831 percent, is the semiannual yield. Since the Eurobond's yield, 3.17 percent, is an annualized yield because of that bond's yearly compounding, we must annualize the yield on the U.S. bond in order to compare the two.[2] We annualize the yield on the U.S. bond by computing its effective annual yield:

$$\begin{aligned} \text{EAY} &= \left(1 + \frac{\text{Quoted interest rate}}{m}\right)^{m} - 1 \\ &= \left(1 + \frac{0.031662}{2}\right)^{2} - 1 \\ &= (1.015831)^{2} - 1 = 0.03191, \text{ or } 3.191\% \end{aligned}$$

The U.S. corporate bond is a better deal because of its higher EAY (3.191 percent > 3.170 percent). Notice that if we had just annualized the yield on the U.S. bond by multiplying the semiannual yield by 2 (1.5831 percent × 2 = 3.1661 percent) and compared the simple yields for the Eurobond and the U.S. bond (3.170 percent > 3.1661 percent), we would have selected the Eurobond. This would have been the wrong economic decision.

---

[2]Notice that, for annual compounding, the yield to maturity equals the EAY; for the Eurobond, the yield to maturity = 3.17 percent and EAY = $(1 + \text{Quoted interest rate}/m)^{m} - 1 = (1 + 0.0317/1)^{1} - 1 = (1 + 0.0317) - 1 = 0.0317$, or 3.17 percent.

Realized Yield

The yield to maturity (or promised yield) tells the investor the return on a bond if the bond is held to maturity and all the coupon and principal payments are made as promised. Quite often, however, the investor will sell the bond before maturity. The **realized yield** is the return earned on a bond given the cash flows *actually received* by the investor. More formally, it is the interest rate at which the present value of the actual cash flows from the investment equal the bond's price. The realized yield allows investors to see the return they actually earned on their investment. It is the same as the holding period return discussed in Chapter 6.

realized yield
for a bond, the interest rate at which the present value of the actual cash flows from a bond equals the bond's price

Let's return to the situation involving a three-year bond with a 6 percent coupon that was purchased for $960.99 and had a promised yield of 7.5 percent. Suppose that interest rates increased sharply and the price of the bond plummeted. Disgruntled, you sold the bond for $750.79 after having owned it for two years. The time line for the realized cash flows looks like this:

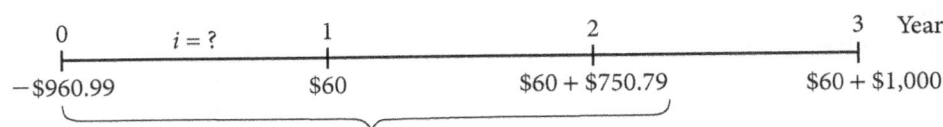

Substituting the cash flows into Equation 7.1 yields the following:

$$P_B = \$960.99 = \frac{\$60}{1 + i} + \frac{\$60}{(1 + i)^2} + \frac{\$750.79}{(1 + i)^2}$$

We can solve this equation for i either by trial and error or with a financial calculator, as described earlier. Using a financial calculator, the solution is as follows:

The result is a realized yield of negative 4.97 percent. The difference between the promised yield of 7.50 percent and the realized yield of negative 4.97 percent is 12.47 percent [7.50 percent − (−4.97 percent) = 12.47 percent], which can be accounted for by the capital loss of $210.20 ($960.99 − $750.79 = $210.20) from the decline in the bond price.

> **BEFORE YOU GO ON**
>
> 1. Explain how bond yields are calculated.

7.4 INTEREST RATE RISK

As discussed previously, the prices of bonds fluctuate with changes in interest rates, giving rise to **interest rate risk**. Anyone who owns bonds is subject to interest rate risk because interest rates are always changing in financial markets. A number of relations exist between bond prices and changes in interest rates. These are often called the bond theorems, but they apply to all fixed-income securities. It is important that investors and financial managers understand these theorems.

LEARNING OBJECTIVE **4**

interest rate risk
uncertainty about future bond values that is caused by the unpredictability of interest rates

Bond Theorems

1. **Bond prices are negatively related to interest rate movements.** As interest rates decline, the prices of bonds rise; and as interest rates rise, the prices of bonds decline. As mentioned

earlier, this negative relation exists because the coupon rate on most bonds is fixed at the time the bonds are issued. Note that this negative relation is observed not only for bonds but also for all other financial claims that pay a fixed rate of interest to investors, such as bank loans and home mortgages.

2. **For a given change in interest rates, the prices of long-term bonds will change more than the prices of short-term bonds.** In other words, long-term bonds have greater price volatility (risk) than short-term bonds because, all other things being equal, long-term bonds have greater interest rate risk than short-term bonds. Exhibit 7.2 illustrates the fact that bond values are not equally affected by changes in market interest rates. The exhibit shows how the prices of a 1-year bond and a 30-year bond change with changing interest rates. As you can see, the long-term bond has much wider price swings than the short-term bond. Why? The answer is that long-term bonds receive most of their cash flows farther into the future, and because of the time value of money, these cash flows are heavily discounted. This makes the 30-year bond riskier than the 1-year bond.

3. **For a given change in interest rates, the prices of lower-coupon bonds change more than the prices of higher-coupon bonds.** Exhibit 7.3 illustrates the relation between bond price volatility and coupon rates. The exhibit shows the prices of three 10-year bonds: a zero coupon bond, a 5 percent coupon bond, and a 10 percent coupon bond. Initially, the bonds are priced to yield 5 percent (see column 2). The bonds are then priced at yields of 6 and 4 percent (see columns 3 and 6). The dollar price changes for each bond given the appropriate interest rate change are recorded in columns 4 and 7, and percentage price changes (price volatilities) are shown in columns 5 and 8.

As shown in column 5, when interest rates increase from 5 to 6 percent, the zero coupon bond experiences the greatest percentage price decline, and the 10 percent bond

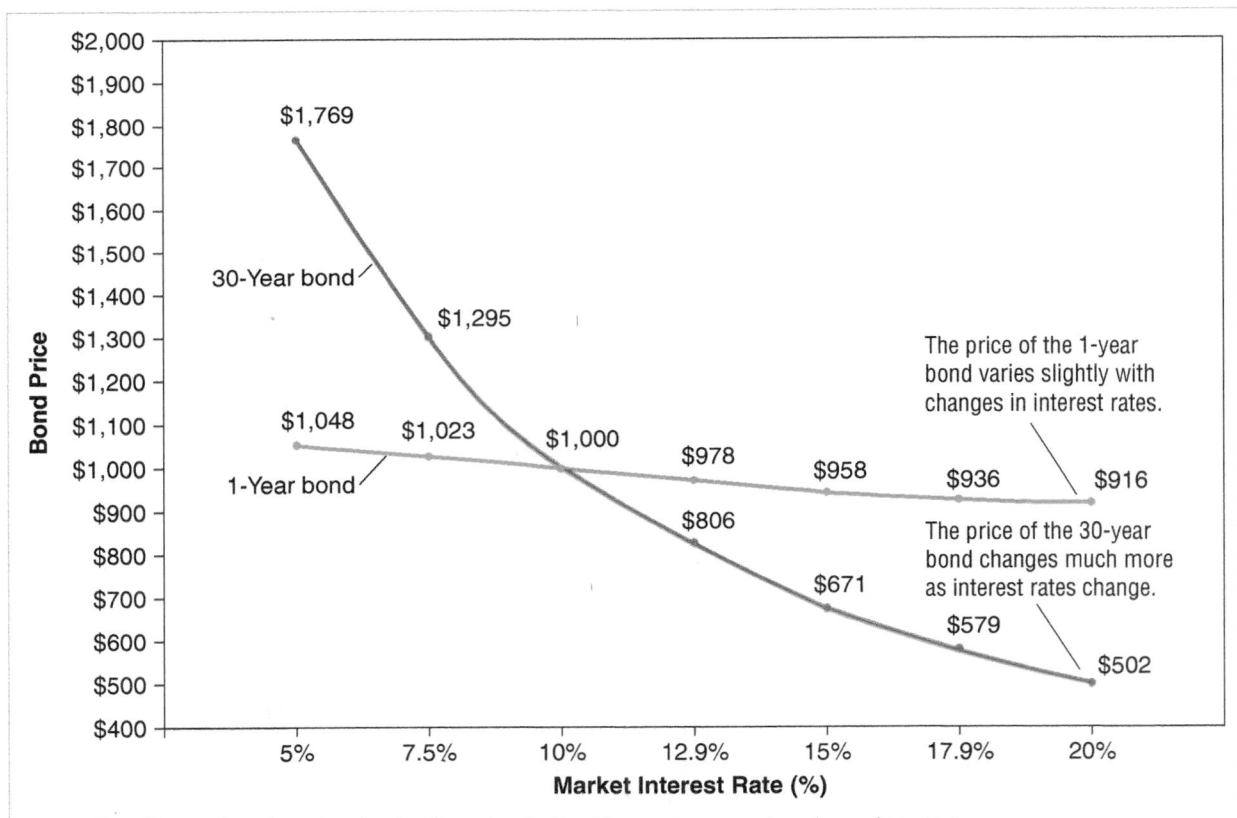

Note: Plots are for a 1-year bond and a 30-year bond with a 10 percent coupon rate and annual payment

EXHIBIT 7.2
Relation between Bond Price Volatility and Maturity

The prices of a 1-year and a 30-year bond respond differently to changes in market interest rates. The long-term bond has much wider price swings than the short-term bond, as predicted by the second bond theorem.

EXHIBIT 7.3 **Relation between Bond Price Volatility and the Coupon Rate**

The exhibit shows the prices of three 10-year bonds: a zero coupon bond, a 5 percent coupon bond, and a 10 percent coupon bond. Initially, the bonds are priced at a 5 percent yield (column 2). The bonds are then priced at yields of 6 and 4 percent (columns 3 and 6). The price changes shown are consistent with the third bond theorem: the smaller the coupon rate, the greater the percentage price change for a given change in interest rates.

		Price Change if Yield Increases from 5% to 6%			Price Change if Yield Decreases from 5% to 4%		
(1)	(2)	(3)	(4)	(5)	(6)	(7)	(8)
Coupon Rate	Bond Price at 5% Yield	Bond Price at 6%	Loss from Increase in Yield	% Price Change	Bond Price at 4%	Gain from Decrease in Yield	% Price Change
0%	$613.91	$588.39	$25.52	−9.04%	$675.56	$61.65	10.04%
5%	$1,000.00	$926.40	$73.60	−7.36%	$1,081.11	$81.11	8.11%
10%	$1,386.09	$1,294.40	$91.69	−6.62%	$1,486.65	$100.56	7.25%

Note: Calculations are based on a bond with a $1,000 face value and a 10-year maturity and assume annual compounding.

experiences the smallest percentage price decline. Similar results are shown in column 8 for interest rate decreases. In sum, the lower a bond's coupon rate, the greater its price volatility, and hence, lower-coupon bonds have greater interest rate risk.

The reason for the higher interest rate risk for low-coupon bonds is essentially the same as the reason for the higher interest rate risk for long-term bonds. The lower the bond's coupon rate, the greater the proportion of the bond's total cash flows investors will receive at maturity. This is clearly seen with a zero coupon bond, where all of the bond's cash flows are received at maturity. The farther into the future the cash flows are to be received, the greater the impact of a change in the discount rate on their present value. Thus, all other things being equal, a given change in interest rates will have a greater impact on the price of a low-coupon bond than a higher-coupon bond with the same maturity.

Bond Theorem Applications

The bond theorems provide important information about bond price behavior for financial managers. For example, if you are the treasurer of a firm and are investing cash temporarily—say, for a few days—the last security you want to purchase is a long-term zero coupon bond. In contrast, if you are an investor and you expect interest rates to decline, you may well want to invest in a long-term zero coupon bond. This is because as interest rates decline, the prices of long-term zero coupon bonds will increase more than those of any other type of bond.

Make no mistake, forecasting interest rate movements and investing in long-term bonds is a very high-risk strategy. In 1990, for example, executives at Shearson Lehman Hutton made a huge bet on interest rate movements and lost. Specifically, over a number of months, the firm made investments in long-term bonds that totaled $480 million. The bet was that interest rates would decline. When interest rates failed to decline and losses mounted, the Shearson team sold the bonds at a loss totaling $115 million. The executives responsible were fired for "lack of judgment."

The moral of the story is simple. Long-term bonds carry substantially more interest rate risk than short-term bonds, and investors in long-term bonds need to fully understand the magnitude of the risk involved. Furthermore, no one can predict interest rate movements consistently, including the Federal Reserve Bank (Fed)—and it controls the money supply.

> **BEFORE YOU GO ON**

1. What is interest rate risk?

2. Explain why long-term bonds with zero coupons are riskier than short-term bonds that pay coupon interest.

DECISION MAKING

EXAMPLE 7.1

Risk Taking

SITUATION: You work for the treasurer of a large manufacturing corporation where earnings are down substantially for the year. The treasurer's staff is convinced that interest rates are going to decline over the next three months, and they want to invest in fixed-income securities to make as much money as possible for the firm. The staff recommends investing in one of the following securities:

- Three-month T-bill
- 20-year corporate bond
- 20-year zero coupon Treasury bond

The treasurer asks you to answer the following questions about the staff's plan: (1) What is the underlying strategy of the proposed plan? (2) Which investment should be selected if the plan were to be executed? (3) What should the treasurer do?

DECISION: First, the staff's strategy is based on the negative relation between interest rates and bond prices. Thus, if interest rates decline, bond prices will rise, and the firm will earn a capital gain. Second, to maximize earnings, the treasurer should select bonds that will have the largest price swing for a given change in interest rates. Bond theorems 2 and 3 suggest that for a given change in interest rates, low-coupon, long-term bonds will have the largest price swing. Thus, the treasurer should invest in the 20-year zero coupon Treasury bond. With respect to the plan's merits, the intentions are good, but the investment plan is pure folly. Generating "earnings" from risky financial investments is not the firm's line of business or one of its core competencies. As was discussed in Chapter 1, the treasurer's primary investment function is to invest idle cash in safe investments such as money market instruments that have very low default and interest rate risk.

7.5 THE STRUCTURE OF INTEREST RATES

LEARNING OBJECTIVE

In Chapter 2 we discussed the economic forces that determine the level of interest rates, and so far in this chapter, we have discussed how to price various types of debt securities. Armed with this knowledge, we now explore why, on the same day, different business firms have different borrowing costs. As you will see, market analysts have identified four risk characteristics of debt instruments that are responsible for most of the differences in corporate borrowing costs: the security's marketability, call provision, default risk, and term to maturity.

Marketability

The interest rate, or yield, on a security varies with its degree of marketability. Recall from Chapter 2 that marketability refers to the ease with which an investor can sell a security quickly at a low transaction cost. The transaction costs include all fees and the cost of searching for information. The lower the costs, the greater a security's marketability. Because investors prefer marketable securities, they must be paid a premium to purchase otherwise similar securities that are less marketable. The difference in interest rates or yields between a highly marketable security ($i_{\text{high mkt}}$) and a less marketable security ($i_{\text{low mkt}}$) is known as the *marketability risk premium* (MRP).

$$\text{MRP} = i_{\text{low mkt}} - i_{\text{high mkt}} > 0$$

U.S. Treasury bills have the largest and most active secondary market and are considered to be the most marketable of all securities. Investors can sell virtually any dollar amount of Treasury securities quickly without disrupting the market. Similarly, the securities of many well-known businesses enjoy a high degree of marketability, especially firms whose securities are traded on the major exchanges. For thousands of other firms whose securities are not traded actively, marketability can pose a problem and can raise borrowing costs substantially.

Call Provision

Most corporate bonds contain a call provision in their contract. A call provision gives the firm issuing the bonds the option to purchase the bond from an investor at a predetermined price (the call price). The investor must sell the bond at that price to the firm when the firm exercises this option. Bonds with a call provision pay higher yields than comparable noncallable bonds. Investors require the higher yields because call provisions work to the benefit of the borrower and the detriment of the investor. For example, if interest rates decline after the bond is issued, the issuer can call (retire) the bonds at the call price and refinance with a new bond issued at the lower prevailing market rate of interest. The issuing firm is delighted because the refinancing has lowered its interest expense. However, investors are less gleeful. When bonds are called, investors suffer a financial loss because they are forced to surrender their high-yielding bonds and reinvest their funds at the lower prevailing market rate of interest.

The difference in interest rates between a callable bond and a comparable noncallable bond is called the *call interest premium* (CIP) and can be defined as follows:

$$CIP = i_{call} - i_{ncall} > 0$$

where CIP is the call interest premium, i_{call} is the yield on a callable bond, and i_{ncall} is the yield on a noncallable bond of the same marketability, default risk, and term to maturity. Thus, the more likely a bond is to be called, the higher the CIP and the higher the bond's market yield. Bonds issued during periods when interest rates are high are likely to be called when interest rates decline, and as a result, these bonds have a large CIP. Conversely, bonds sold when interest rates are relatively low are less likely to be called and have a smaller CIP.

Default Risk

Recall that any debt, such as a bond or a bank loan, is a formal promise by the borrower to make periodic interest payments and pay the principal as specified in the debt contract. Failure on the borrower's part to meet any condition of the debt or loan contract constitutes default. As discussed in Chapter 4, default risk refers to the risk that the borrower will not be able to pay its debt obligations as they come due.

The Default Risk Premium

Because investors are risk averse, they must be paid a premium to purchase a security that exposes them to default risk. The size of the premium has two components: (1) compensation for the expected loss if a default occurs and (2) compensation for bearing the risk that a default could occur. The degree of default risk for a security can be measured as the difference between the interest rate on the risky security and the interest rate on a default-free security—all other factors, such as marketability, the existence of a call provision, or term to maturity are held constant. The *default risk premium* (DRP) is defined as follows:

$$DRP = i_{dr} - i_{rf} > 0$$

where i_{dr} is the interest rate (yield) on the security that has default risk and i_{rf} is the interest rate (yield) on a risk-free security. U.S. Treasury securities are the best proxy measure for the risk-free rate. The larger the default risk premium, the higher the probability of default, and the higher the security's market yield.

Bond Ratings

Many investors, especially individuals and smaller businesses, do not have the expertise to formulate the probabilities of default themselves, so they must rely on credit rating agencies to provide this information. The three most prominent credit rating agencies are Moody's Investors Service (Moody's), Standard & Poor's (S&P), and Fitch. All three credit rating services rank bonds in order of their expected probability of default and publish the ratings as letter grades. The rating schemes used are shown in Exhibit 7.4. The highest-grade bonds, those with the lowest default risk, are rated Aaa (or AAA). The default risk premium on corporate bonds increases as the bond rating becomes lower.

 Fidelity Investment Company's Web site provides information on bond ratings at http:// personal.fidelity.com/ products/fixedincome/ bondratings.shtml.

EXHIBIT 7.4 **Corporate Bond Rating Systems**

Moody's has a slightly different notation in their ratings of corporate bonds than do Standard & Poor's and Fitch, but the interpretation is the same. Bonds with the highest credit standing are rated Aaa (or AAA) and have the lowest default risk. The credit rating declines as the default risk of the bonds increases.

Explanation	Moody's	Standard & Poor's/Fitch	Default Risk Premium	Regulatory Designation
Best quality, smallest degree of risk	Aaa	AAA	Lowest	Investment Grade
High quality, slightly more long-term risk than top rating	Aa	AA		
Upper-medium grade, possible impairment in the future	A	A		
Medium grade, lacks outstanding investment characteristics	Baa	BBB		
Speculative, protection may be very moderate	Ba	BB		Noninvestment Grade
Very speculative, may have small assurance of interest and principal payments	B	B		
Issues in poor standing, may be in default	Caa	CCC		
Speculative to a high degree, with marked shortcomings	Ca	CC		
Lowest quality, poor prospects of attaining real investment standing	C	C	Highest	

investment-grade bonds
bonds with low risk of default that are rated Baa (BBB) or above

noninvestment-grade bonds
bonds rated below Baa (or BBB) by rating agencies; often called *speculative-grade bonds, high-yield bonds, or junk bonds*

Exhibit 7.4 also shows that bonds in the top four rating categories are called **investment-grade bonds**. Moody's calls bonds rated below Baa (or BBB) **noninvestment-grade bonds**, but most Wall Street practitioners refer to them as *speculative-grade bonds, high-yield bonds,* or *junk bonds.* The distinction between investment-grade and noninvestment-grade bonds is important because state and federal laws typically require commercial banks, insurance companies, pension funds, other financial institutions, and government agencies to purchase securities rated only as investment grade.

Exhibit 7.5 shows default risk premiums associated with selected bonds with investment-grade bond ratings in September 2012. The premiums are the differences between yields on Treasury securities—which, as mentioned, are the proxy for the risk-free rate—and yields on riskier securities of similar maturity. The 0.43 percent default risk premium on Aaa-rated corporate bonds represents the market consensus of the amount investors must be compensated to induce them to purchase typical Aaa-rated bonds instead of a risk-free security. As credit quality declines from Aaa to Baa, the default risk premiums increase from 0.43 percent to 1.86 percent.

EXHIBIT 7.5 **Default Risk Premiums for Selected Bond Ratings**

The default risk premium (DRP) measures the yield difference between the yield on Treasury securities (the risk-free rate) and the yields on riskier securities of the same maturity.

Security: Moody's Credit Rating	Security Yield (%) (1)	Risk-Free Rate[a] (%) (2)	Default Risk: Premium (%) (1) − (2)
Aaa	3.48	3.05	0.43
Aa	3.86	3.05	0.81
A	4.09	3.05	1.04
Baa	4.91	3.05	1.86

[a]30-year Treasury bond yield as of September 17, 2012.
Sources: Federal Reserve Statistical Release H.15 (http://www.federalreserve.gov) and Yahoo Finance (http://finance .yahoo.com).

The Term Structure of Interest Rates

The term to maturity of a loan is the length of time until the principal amount is payable. The relation between yield to maturity and term to maturity is known as the **term structure of interest rates**. We can view the term structure visually by plotting the **yield curve**, a graph with term to maturity on the horizontal axis and yield to maturity on the vertical axis. Yield curves show graphically how market yields vary as term to maturity changes.

For yield curves to be meaningful, the securities used to plot the curves should be similar in all features (for example, marketability, call provisions, and default risk) except for maturity. We do not want to confound the relation of yield and term to maturity with other factors that also affect interest rates. We can see the term structure relation by examining yields on U.S. Treasury securities with different maturities because their other features are similar.

Exhibit 7.6 shows data and yield curve plots for Treasury securities at various points in time in the 2000s. As you can see, the shape of the yield curve is not constant over time. As the general level of interest rises and falls, the yield curve shifts up and down and has different slopes. We can observe three basic shapes (slopes) of yield curves in the marketplace. First is the ascending, or upward-sloping, yield curve (May 2003 and February 2005), which is the yield curve most commonly observed. Second, descending, or downward-sloping, yield curves (September 2006) appear periodically and are characterized by short-term yields (for example, the six-month yield) exceeding long-term yields (for example, the 20-year yield).

term structure of interest rates
the relation between yield to maturity and term to maturity

yield curve
a graph representing the term structure of interest rates, with the term to maturity on the horizontal axis and the yield on the vertical axis

Smart Money's Web site gives a good overview of yield curves. Go to http://www.smartmoney.com/Investing/Bonds/The-Living-Yield-Curve-7923.

The September 2006 yield curve is downward sloping, which means that yields are higher for shorter-term (6 month and 1 year) securities than for longer-term securities.

September 2006

February 2005

The other two yield curves are upward sloping, which means that yields are higher for longer-term securities than for shorter-term securities. This is the more common situation.

May 2003

Years to Maturity

Terms to Maturity	Interest Rate (%)		
	September 2006	February 2005	May 2003
6 months	5.10	2.86	1.08
1 year	4.99	3.05	1.14
5 year	4.68	3.78	2.33
10 years	4.73	4.16	3.34
20 years	4.95	4.60	4.28

EXHIBIT 7.6

Yield Curves for Treasury Securities at Three Different Points in Time

The shape, or slope, of the yield curve is not constant over time. The exhibit shows two shapes: (1) the curves for May 2003 and February 2005 are upward sloping, which is the shape most commonly observed, and (2) the curve for September 2006 is downward sloping for maturities out to 5 years.

Downward-sloping yield curves often appear before the beginning of a recession. Finally, relatively flat yield curves are not common but do occur from time to time. Three factors affect the level and the shape (the slope) of the yield curve over time: the real rate of interest, the expected rate of inflation, and interest rate risk.

The real rate of interest is the base interest rate in the economy and is determined by individuals' time preference for consumption; that is, it tells us how much individuals must be paid to forgo spending their money today. The real rate of interest varies with the business cycle, with the highest rates seen at the end of a period of business expansion and the lowest at the bottom of a recession. The real rate is not affected by the term to maturity. Thus, the real rate of interest affects the level of interest rates but not the shape of the yield curve.

The expected rate of inflation can influence the shape of the yield curve. If investors believe that inflation will be increasing in the future, the yield curve will be upward sloping because long-term interest rates will contain a larger inflation premium than short-term interest rates. The inflation premium is the market's best estimate of future inflation. Conversely, if investors believe inflation will be subsiding in the future, the prevailing yield will be downward sloping.

Finally, the presence of interest rate risk affects the shape of the yield curve. As discussed earlier, long-term bonds have greater price volatility than short-term bonds. Because investors are aware of this risk, they demand compensation in the form of an interest rate premium. It follows that the longer the maturity of a security, the greater its interest rate risk, and the higher the interest rate. It is important to note that the interest rate risk premium always adds an upward bias to the slope of the yield curve.

In sum, the cumulative effect of three economic factors determines the level and shape of the yield curve: (1) the cyclical movements of the real rate of interest affect the level of the yield curve, (2) the expected rate of inflation can bias the slope of the yield curve either positively or negatively, depending on market expectations of inflation, and (3) interest rate risk always provides an upward bias to the slope of the yield curve.

> **BEFORE YOU GO ON**

1. What are default risk premiums, and what do they measure?

2. Describe the three most prominent bond rating systems.

3. What are the key factors that most affect the level and shape of the yield curve?

SUMMARY OF Learning Objectives

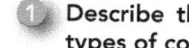 **Describe the market for corporate bonds and three types of corporate bonds.**

The market for corporate bonds is a very large market in which the most important investors are large institutions. Most trades take place through dealers in the OTC market, making the corporate bond market relatively thin. Prices of corporate bonds tend to be more volatile than prices of securities that trade more frequently, such as stock and money market instruments, and the corporate bond market tends to be less efficient than markets for these other securities.

A vanilla bond pays fixed regular coupon payments over the life of the bond, and the entire principal is repaid at maturity. A zero coupon bond pays all interest and all principal at maturity. Since there are no payments before maturity, zero coupon bonds are issued at prices below their face value. Convertible bonds can be exchanged for common stock at a predetermined ratio.

 Explain how to calculate the value of a bond and why bond prices vary negatively with interest rate movements.

The value of a bond is equal to the present value of the future cash flows (coupon payments and principal repayment) discounted at the market rate of interest for bonds with similar risk. Bond prices vary negatively with interest rates because the coupon rate on most bonds is fixed at the time the bond is issued. As market interest rates go up, the prices of bonds with fixed coupon payments will be bid down by investors, driving up the yields of those bonds to market levels. When interest rates decline, the yield on fixed-income securities will be higher relative to yield on similar securities price to market; the favorable yield will increase investor demand for these securities, increasing their price and lowering their yield to the market yield.

3 **Distinguish between a bond's coupon rate, yield to maturity, and effective annual yield.**

A bond's coupon rate is the interest rate on the bond, relative to its face value, when it is issued. U.S. bonds typically pay interest semiannually, whereas European bonds pay once a year. The yield to maturity is the expected return on a bond if it is held to its maturity date. The effective annual yield is the yield an investor actually earns in one year, adjusting for the effects of compounding. If the bond pays coupon payments more often than annually, the effective annual yield will be higher than the simple annual yield because of compounding. Work through Learning by Doing Applications 7.2, 7.3, and 7.4 to master these calculations.

4 **Explain why investors in bonds are subject to interest rate risk and why it is important to understand the bond theorems.**

Because interest rates are always changing in the market, all investors who hold bonds are subject to interest rate risk. Interest rate risk is uncertainty about future bond values caused by fluctuations in interest rates. Three of the most important bond theorems can be summarized as follows:

1. Bond prices are negatively related to interest rate movements.
2. For a given change in interest rates, the prices of long-term bonds will change more than the prices of short-term bonds.
3. For a given change in interest rates, the prices of lower-coupon bonds will change more than the prices of higher-coupon bonds.

Understanding these theorems is important because it helps investors better understand why bond prices change and, thus, make better decisions regarding the purchase or sale of bonds and other fixed-income securities.

5 **Discuss the concept of default risk and know how to compute a default risk premium.**

Default risk is the risk that the issuer will be unable to pay its debt obligation. Since investors are risk averse, they must be paid a premium to purchase a security that exposes them to default risk. The default risk premium has two components: (1) compensation for the expected loss if a default occurs and (2) compensation for bearing the risk that a default could occur. All factors held constant, the degree of default risk a security possesses can be measured as the difference between the interest rate on a risky security and the interest rate on a default-free security. The default risk is also reflected in the company's bond rating. The highest-grade bonds, those with the lowest default risk, are rated Aaa (or AAA). The default risk premium on corporate bonds increases as the bond rating becomes lower.

6 **Describe the factors that determine the level and shape of the yield curve.**

The level and shape of the yield curve are determined by three factors: (1) the real rate of interest, (2) the expected rate of inflation, and (3) interest rate risk. The real rate of interest is the base interest rate in the economy and varies with the business cycle. The real rate of interest affects only the level of the yield curve and not its shape. The expected rate of inflation does affect the shape of the yield curve. If investors believe inflation will be increasing in the future, for example, the curve will be upward sloping, as long-term rates will contain a larger inflation premium than short-term rates. Finally, interest rate risk, which increases with a security's maturity, adds an upward bias to the slope of the yield curve.

SUMMARY OF Key Equations

Equation	Description	Formula
7.1	Price of a bond	$P_B = \dfrac{C_1}{1+i} + \dfrac{C_2}{(1+i)^2} + \cdots + \dfrac{C_n + F_n}{(1+i)^n}$
7.2	Price of a bond making multiple payments each year	$P_B = \dfrac{C/m}{1+i/m} + \dfrac{C/m}{(1+i/m)^2} + \dfrac{C/m}{(1+i/m)^3} + \cdots + \dfrac{C/m + F_{mn}}{(1+i/m)^{mn}}$
7.3	Price of zero coupon bond	$P_B = \dfrac{F_{mn}}{(1+i/m)^{mn}}$

Self-Study Problems

7.1 Calculate the price of a five-year bond that has a coupon of 6.5 percent paid annually. The current market rate is 5.75 percent.

7.2 Bigbie Corp. issued a five-year bond one year ago with a coupon of 8 percent. The bond pays interest semiannually. If the yield to maturity on this bond is 9 percent, what is the price of the bond?

7.3 Rockwell Industries has a three-year bond outstanding that pays a 7.25 percent coupon and is currently priced at $913.88. What is the yield to maturity of this bond? Assume annual coupon payments.

7.4 Hindenberg, Inc., has a 10-year bond that is priced at $1,100.00. It has a coupon of 8 percent paid semiannually. What is the yield to maturity on this bond?

7.5 Highland Corp., a U.S. company, has a five-year bond whose yield to maturity is 6.5 percent. The bond has no coupon payments. What is the price of this zero coupon bond?

Solutions to Self-Study Problems

7.1 The time line and calculations for the five-year bond are as follows:

$$P_B = \frac{C_1}{1+i} + \frac{C_2}{(1+i)^2} + \frac{C_3}{(1+i)^3} + \frac{C_4}{(1+i)^4} + \frac{C_5+F_5}{(1+i)^5}$$

$$= \frac{\$65}{1.0575} + \frac{\$65}{(1.0575)^2} + \frac{\$65}{(1.0575)^3} + \frac{\$65}{(1.0575)^4} + \frac{\$65+\$1,000}{(1.0575)^5}$$

$$= \$61.47 + \$58.12 + \$54.96 + \$51.95 + \$805.28$$

$$= \$1,031.81$$

7.2 We can find the price of Bigbie Corp.'s bond as follows:

$$P_B = \frac{C/m}{1+i/m} + \frac{C/m}{(1+i/m)^2} + \frac{C/m}{(1+i/m)^3} + \cdots + \frac{C/m+F_8}{(1+i/m)^8}$$

$$= \frac{\$40}{1.045} + \frac{\$40}{(1.045)^2} + \frac{\$40}{(1.045)^3} + \cdots + \frac{(\$40+\$1,000)}{(1.045)^8}$$

$$= \$38.28 + \$36.63 + \$35.05 + \$33.54 + \$32.10 + \$30.72 + \$29.39 + \$731.31$$

$$= \$967.02$$

Alternatively, we can use the present value of an ordinary annuity equation (Equation 5.5) and the present value equation (Equation 5.4) from Chapter 5 to solve for the price of the bond.

$$P_B = C \times \left[\frac{1 - \frac{1}{(1+i/m)^{mn}}}{i/m}\right] + \frac{F_n}{(1+i/m)^{mn}} = \$40 \times \left[\frac{1 - \frac{1}{(1+0.045)^8}}{0.045}\right] + \frac{\$1,000}{(1.045)^8}$$

$$= \$263.84 + \$703.19 = \$967.03$$

7.3 We start with a time line for Rockwell's bond:

$$\begin{array}{c}
0 \qquad\quad i = ? \qquad\quad 1 \qquad\qquad\qquad 2 \qquad\qquad\qquad 3 \quad \text{Year} \\
\vdash\!\!\!\!-\!\!\!\!-\!\!\!\!-\!\!\!\!-\!\!\!\!-\!\!\!\!-\!\!\!\!-\!\!\!\!-\!\!\!\!-\!\!\!\!-\!\!\!\!-\!\!\!\!-\!\!\!\!-\!\!\!\!-\dashv \\
P_B = -\$913.88 \qquad\quad \$72.50 \qquad\qquad \$72.50 \qquad\qquad \$1,072.50
\end{array}$$

Use trial and error to solve for the yield to maturity (YTM). Since the bond is selling at a discount, we know that the yield to maturity is higher than the coupon rate.

Try YTM = 10%.

$$P_B = \frac{C_1}{1+i} + \frac{C_2}{(1+i)^2} + \frac{C_3+F_3}{(1+i)^3}$$

$$\$913.88 = \frac{\$72.50}{1.10} + \frac{\$72.50}{(1.10)^2} + \frac{\$72.50+\$1,000}{(1.10)^3}$$

$$= \$65.91 + \$59.92 + \$805.79$$

$$\neq \$931.61$$

Try a higher rate, say YTM = 11%.

$$P_B = \frac{C_1}{1+i} + \frac{C_2}{(1+i)^2} + \frac{C_3+F_3}{(1+i)^3}$$

$$\$913.88 = \frac{\$72.50}{1.11} + \frac{\$72.50}{(1.11)^2} + \frac{\$72.50+\$1,000}{(1.11)^3}$$

$$= \$65.32 + \$58.84 + \$784.20$$

$$\neq \$908.36$$

Since this is less than the price of the bond, we know that the YTM is between 10 and 11 percent and closer to 11 percent.

Try YTM = 10.75%.

$$P_B = \frac{C_1}{1 + i} + \frac{C_2}{(1 + i)^2} + \frac{C_3 + F_3}{(1 + i)^3}$$

$$\$913.88 = \frac{\$72.50}{1.1075} + \frac{\$72.50}{(1.1075)^2} + \frac{\$72.50 + \$1,000}{(1.1075)^3}$$

$$= \$65.46 + \$59.11 + \$789.53$$

$$\cong \$914.09$$

Alternatively, we can use Equation 5.5 and Equation 5.4 to solve for the price of the bond.

$$P_B = C \times \left[\frac{1 - \frac{1}{(1 + i)^n}}{i} \right] + \frac{F_n}{(1 + i)^n}$$

$$\$913.88 = \$72.50 \times \left[\frac{1 - \frac{1}{(1 + 0.1075)^3}}{0.1075} \right] + \frac{\$1,000}{(1.1075)^3}$$

$$= \$177.94 + \$736.15$$

$$\cong \$914.09$$

Thus, the YTM is approximately 10.75 percent. Using a financial calculator provides an exact YTM of 10.7594%.

7.4 The time line for Hindenberg's 10-year bond looks like this:

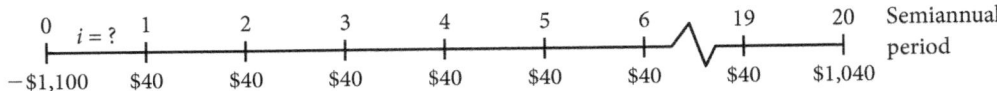

The easiest way to calculate the yield to maturity is with a financial calculator. The inputs are as follows:

The answer we get is 3.31 percent, which is the semiannual interest rate. To obtain an annualized yield to maturity, we multiply this by two:

$$\text{YTM} = 3.31\% \times 2$$

$$\text{YTM} = 6.62\%$$

7.5 You have the following information about Highland's bonds:

$$\text{YTM} = 6.5\%$$

No coupon payments

Most U.S. bonds pay interest semiannually. Thus $m \times n = 2 \times 5 = 10$ and $i/2 = 0.065/2 = 0.0325$. Using Equation 7.3, we obtain the following:

$$P_B = \frac{F_{mn}}{(1 + i/m)^{mn}}$$

$$= \frac{\$1,000}{(1 + 0.0325)^{10}}$$

$$= \$726.27$$

Critical Thinking Questions

7.1 Because the conversion feature in a convertible bond is valuable to bondholders, convertible bond issues have lower coupon payments than otherwise similar bonds that are not convertible. Does this mean that a company can lower its cost of borrowing by selling convertible debt? Explain.

7.2 What economic conditions would prompt investors to take advantage of a bond's convertibility feature?

7.3 We know that a vanilla bond with a coupon rate below the market rate of interest will sell for a discount and that a vanilla bond with a coupon rate above the market rate of interest will sell for a premium. What kind of bond or loan will sell at its par value regardless of what happens to the market rate of interest?

7.4 Define *yield to maturity*. Why is it important?

7.5 Define *interest rate risk*. How can CFOs manage this risk?

7.6 Explain why bond prices and interest rates are negatively related. What are the roles of the coupon rate and the term to maturity in this relation?

7.7 If interest rates are expected to increase, should investors look to long-term bonds or short-term securities? Explain.

7.8 Explain what you would assume the yield curve would look like during economic expansion and why.

7.9 An investor holds a 10-year bond paying a coupon of 9 percent. The yield to maturity of the bond is 7.8 percent. Would you expect the investor to be holding a par-value, premium, or discount bond? What if the yield to maturity were 10.2 percent? Explain.

7.10 a. Investor A holds a 10-year bond, while investor B holds an 8-year bond. If the interest rate increases by 1 percent, which investor has the higher interest rate risk? Explain.

b. Investor A holds a 10-year bond paying 8 percent a year, while investor B also has a 10-year bond that pays a 6 percent coupon. Which investor has the higher interest rate risk? Explain.

Questions and Problems

BASIC > **7.1** **Bond price:** BA Corp is issuing a 10-year bond with a coupon rate of 8 percent. The interest rate for similar bonds is currently 6 percent. Assuming annual payments, what is the value of the bond?

EXCEL®
More interactive Excel® exercises available in
WileyPLUS

7.2 **Bond price:** Pierre Dupont just received a cash gift from his grandfather. He plans to invest in a five-year bond issued by Venice Corp. that pays an annual coupon of 5.5 percent. If the current market rate is 7.25 percent, what is the maximum amount Pierre should be willing to pay for this bond?

7.3 **Bond price:** Knight, Inc., has issued a three-year bond that pays a coupon of 6.10 percent. Coupon payments are made semiannually. Given the market rate of interest of 5.80 percent, what is the market value of the bond?

7.4 **Bond price:** Regatta Inc. has seven-year bonds outstanding that pay a 12 percent coupon rate. Investors buying these bonds today can expect to earn a yield to maturity of 8.875 percent. What is the current value of these bonds? Assume annual coupon payments.

7.5 **Bond price:** You are interested in investing in a five-year bond that pays a 7.8 percent coupon with interest to be received semiannually. Your required rate of return is 8.4 percent. What is the most you would be willing to pay for this bond?

7.6 **Zero coupon bonds:** Diane Carter is interested in buying a five-year zero coupon bond with a face value of $1,000. She understands that the market interest rate for similar investments is 9 percent. Assume annual coupon payments. What is the current value of this bond?

7.7 **Zero coupon bonds:** Ten-year zero coupon bonds issued by the U.S. Treasury have a face value of $1,000 and interest is compounded semiannually. If similar bonds in the market yield 10.5 percent, what is the value of these bonds?

7.8 Zero coupon bonds: Northrop Real Estate Company management is planning to fund a development project by issuing 10-year zero coupon bonds with a face value of $1,000. Assuming semiannual compounding, what will be the price of these bonds if the appropriate discount rate is 14 percent?

7.9 Yield to maturity: Ruth Hornsby is looking to invest in a three-year bond that makes semi-annual coupon payments at a rate of 5.875 percent. If these bonds have a market price of $981.13, what yield to maturity and effective annual yield can she expect to earn?

7.10 Yield to maturity: Rudy Sandberg wants to invest in four-year bonds that are currently priced at $868.43. These bonds have a coupon rate of 6 percent and make semiannual coupon payments. What is the current market yield on this bond?

7.11 Realized yield: Josh Kavern bought 10-year, 12 percent coupon bonds issued by the U.S. Treasury three years ago at $913.44. If he sells these bonds, for which he paid the face value of $1,000, at the current price of $804.59, what is his realized yield on the bonds? Assume similar coupon-paying bonds make annual coupon payments.

7.12 Realized yield: Four years ago, Lisa Stills bought six-year, 5.5 percent coupon bonds issued by the Fairways Corp. for $947.68. If she sells these bonds at the current price of $894.52, what will be her realized yield on the bonds? Assume similar coupon-paying bonds make annual coupon payments.

7.13 Bond price: The International Publishing Group is raising $10 million by issuing 15-year bonds **< INTERMEDIATE** with a coupon rate of 8.5 percent. Coupon payments will be made annually. Investors buying the bonds today will earn a yield to maturity of 8.5 percent. At what price will the bonds sell in the marketplace? Explain.

7.14 Bond price: Pullman Corp issued 10-year bonds four years ago with a coupon rate of 9.375 percent. At the time of issue, the bonds sold at par. Today bonds of similar risk and maturity must pay an annual coupon of 6.25 percent to sell at par value. Assuming semiannual coupon payments, what will be the current market price of the firm's bonds?

7.15 Bond price: Marshall Company is issuing eight-year bonds with a coupon rate of 6.5 percent and semiannual coupon payments. If the current market rate for similar bonds is 8 percent, what will be the bond price? If company management wants to raise $1.25 million, how many bonds does the firm have to sell?

7.16 Bond price: Rockne, Inc., has outstanding bonds that will mature in six years and pay an 8 percent coupon semiannually. If you paid $1,036.65 today and your required rate of return was 6.6 percent, did you pay the right price for the bond?

7.17 Bond price: Nanotech, Inc., has a bond issue maturing in seven years that is paying a coupon rate of 9.5 percent (semiannual payments). Management wants to retire a portion of the issue by buying the securities in the open market. If it can refinance at 8 percent, how much will Nanotech pay to buy back its current outstanding bonds?

7.18 Zero coupon bonds: Kintel, Inc., management wants to raise $1 million by issuing six-year zero coupon bonds with a face value of $1,000. The company's investment banker states that investors would use an 11.4 percent discount rate to value such bonds. At what price would these bonds sell in the marketplace? How many bonds would the firm have to issue to raise $1 million? Assume semiannual coupon payments.

7.19 Zero coupon bonds: Rockinghouse Corp. management plans to issue seven-year zero coupon bonds. It has learned that these bonds will sell today at a price of $439.76. Assuming annual coupon payments, what is the yield to maturity on these bonds?

7.20 Yield to maturity: Electrolex, Inc., has four-year bonds outstanding that pay a coupon rate of 6.6 percent and make coupon payments semiannually. If these bonds are currently selling at $914.89, what is the yield to maturity that an investor can expect to earn on these bonds? What is the effective annual yield?

7.21 Yield to maturity: Serengeti Corp. has five-year bonds outstanding that pay a coupon of 8.8 percent. If these bonds are priced at $1,064.86, what is the yield to maturity on these bonds? Assume semiannual coupon payments. What is the effective annual yield?

7.22 Yield to maturity: Adrienne Dawson is planning to buy 10-year zero coupon bonds issued by the U.S. Treasury. If these bonds have a face value of $1,000 and are currently selling at $404.59, what is the expected return on them? Assume that interest compounds semiannually on similar coupon paying bonds.

7.23 **Realized yield:** Brown & Co. issued seven-year bonds two years ago that can be called after two years. The bonds make semiannual coupon payments at a coupon rate of 7.875 percent. Each bond has a market value of $1,053.40, and the call price is $1,078.75. If an investor purchased the bonds at par value when they were originally issued and the bonds are called by the firm today, what is the investor's realized yield?

7.24 **Realized yield:** Trevor Price bought 10-year bonds issued by Harvest Foods five years ago for $936.05. The bonds make semiannual coupon payments at a rate of 8.4 percent. If the current price of the bonds is $1,048.77, what is the yield that Trevor would earn by selling the bonds today?

7.25 **Realized yield:** You bought a six-year bond issued by Runaway Corp. four years ago. At that time, you paid $974.33 for the bond. The bond pays a coupon rate of 7.375 percent, and coupon payments are made semiannually. Currently, the bond is priced at $1,023.56. What yield can you expect to earn on this bond if you sell it today?

ADVANCED ▷ **7.26** Lopez Information Systems management is planning to issue 10-year bonds. The going market yield for such bonds is 8.125 percent. Assume that coupon payments will be made semiannually. Management is trying to decide between issuing an 8 percent coupon bond or a zero coupon bond. Lopez needs to raise $1 million.
   a. What will be the price of an 8 percent coupon bond?
   b. How many 8 percent coupon bonds would have to be issued?
   c. What will be the price of a zero coupon bond?
   d. How many zero coupon bonds will have to be issued?

7.27 Showbiz, Inc., has issued eight-year bonds with a coupon of 6.375 percent and semiannual coupon payments. The market's required rate of return on such bonds is 7.65 percent.
   a. What is the market price of these bonds?
   b. If the above bond is callable after five years at an 8.5 percent premium on the face value, what is the expected return on this bond?

7.28 Peabody Corp. has seven-year bonds outstanding. The bonds pay a coupon of 8.375 percent semi-annually and are currently worth $1,063.49. The bonds can be called in three years at a price of $1,075.
   a. What is the yield to maturity of these bonds?
   b. What is the effective annual yield?
   c. What is the realized yield on the bonds if they are called?
   d. If you plan to invest in one of these bonds today, what is the expected yield on the investment? Explain.

7.29 The Maryland Department of Transportation has issued 25-year bonds that make semiannual coupon payments at a rate of 9.875 percent. The current market rate for similar securities is 11 percent.
   a. What is the current market value of one of these bonds?
   b. What will be the bond's price if rates in the market (i) decrease to 9 percent or (ii) increase to 12 percent?
   c. Refer to your answers in part b. How do the interest rate changes affect premium bonds and discount bonds?
   d. Suppose the bond were to mature in 12 years. How do the interest rate changes in part b affect the bond prices?

7.30 Rachette Corp. has 18-year bonds outstanding. These bonds, which pay interest semiannually, have a coupon rate of 9.735 percent and a yield to maturity of 7.95 percent.
   a. Compute the current price of these bonds.
   b. If the bonds can be called in five years at a premium of 13.5 percent over par value, what is the investor's realized yield?
   c. If you bought one of these bonds today, what is your expected rate of return? Explain.

7.31 Zippy Corporation just sold $30 million of convertible bonds with a conversion ratio of 40. Each $1,000 bond is convertible into 25 shares of Zippy's stock.
   a. What is the conversion price of Zippy's stock?
   b. If the current price of Zippy's stock is $15 and the company's annual stock return is normally distributed with a standard deviation of $5, what is the probability that investors will find it attractive to convert the bond into Zippy stock in the next year?

Sample Test Problems

7.1 Torino Foods issued 10-year bonds three years ago with a coupon of 6 percent. If the current market rate is 8.5 percent and the bonds make annual coupon payments, what is the current market value of one of these bonds?

7.2 Kim Sundaram recently bought a 20-year zero coupon bond that compounds interest semiannually. If the current market rate is 7.75 percent, what is the maximum price he should have paid for this bond?

7.3 Five-year bonds issued by Infotech Corporation are currently priced at $1,065.23. They make semi-annual coupon payments of 8.5 percent. If you bought these bonds today, what would be the yield to maturity and effective annual yield that you would earn?

7.4 The Gold Company is applying for a five-year term loan from its bank. The lender determines that the firm should pay a default risk premium of 1.75 percent over the Treasury rate. The five-year Treasury rate is currently 5.65 percent. The firm must also pay a marketability risk premium of 0.80 percent. What is the total borrowing cost to the firm?

7.5 Trojan Corp. has issued seven-year bonds with a 7 percent semiannual coupon payment. If the opportunity cost for an investor is 8.25 percent, what is the maximum price that the investor should be willing to pay for this bond?

THE SUBPRIME MORTGAGE MARKET MELTDOWN:
How Did It Happen?

The U.S. economy appeared strong throughout the first half of 2007, but many observers saw clouds on the horizon in the form of trouble brewing in the subprime home mortgage market. Fear of the coming storm had been intensifying as housing prices dropped, home foreclosures increased, major subprime mortgage lenders filed for bankruptcy, and investors took losses on

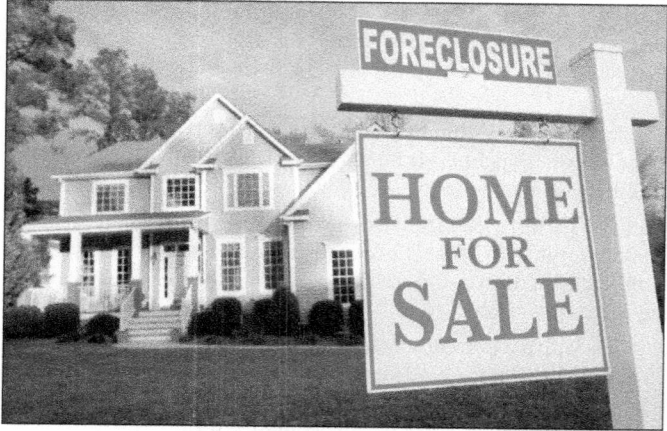

Ariel Skelley Agency/Corbis Premium RF/Alamy Limited

mortgage-backed securities. By the end of the year, many were predicting a serious economic downturn.

"It's not like a bottle of water," said Senator Charles E. Schumer, chairman of the Joint Economic Committee of the U.S. Congress. "It's much more like a pond where ripples start and can spread quickly. . . . The subprime ripple leads to another ripple of lower housing prices and a credit crunch for banks and financial markets. Another ripple driven by consumer anxiety causes lower consumer spending, which makes up nearly two-thirds of our economic growth, and leads to an even larger ripple that may end up causing a recession."[1]

What Are Subprime Mortgages?

The subprime mortgages at the center of all this turmoil were made to borrowers who had poor credit histories or who were considered high credit risks for other reasons. Subprime mortgages are a relatively recent phenomenon because, prior to the 1980s, usury laws limited the ability of lenders to charge interest rates that adequately compensated them for the risks associated with these loans. As a result, subprime mortgage loans were simply not made before the usury laws were relaxed.

Several new federal laws were passed in the 1980s that, among other things, eliminated interest rate caps and made it possible for high-risk borrowers to obtain home mortgages. The subprime market experienced ups and downs in the 1990s, but by the early 2000s it had become an important part of the broader mortgage market. Loans originated in the subprime market made up less than

5 percent of mortgage loans in 1994 but increased to 13 percent in 2000 and to more than 20 percent in 2005 and 2006.[2] The increase after 2000 accompanied a rapid rise in home prices in many real estate markets throughout the United States. Higher prices resulted in larger mortgage loans, which in turn increased the average risk of new loans, because incomes were not rising as quickly as home prices.

The emergence of the subprime market was accompanied by a number of changes in the structure of mortgage lending. Traditionally, a person who wanted a mortgage loan dealt with a bank or a savings and loan institution, which granted the loan (or refused to grant it), financed the loan with deposits, collected the payments, and foreclosed on the property if the payments weren't made. Today, these activities are much more likely to be carried out by separate institutions. For example, a majority of subprime mortgages are originated by mortgage brokers—intermediaries that earn a fee by bringing borrowers and lenders together. Once the loans are made, the lenders often resell the resulting mortgages.

Beginning in the 1990s, the *securitization* of mortgage loans became quite popular. This practice involves bundling groups of loans with similar characteristics and selling claims on the cash flows from these bundles, called mortgage-backed securities (MBSs). Most commonly, MBSs are sold to institutional investors by investment banks. Investors in mortgage-backed securities include insurance companies, mutual funds, pension funds, and hedge funds, among others. The securitization of subprime loans increased from about 32 percent of all such loans in 1994 to about 78 percent in 2006.[3] This development meant that much of the relatively high risk associated with subprime loans was spread among a large number of investors, rather than a relatively small number of lending institutions.

Over the same period a number of new kinds of mortgages were developed to supplement the traditional fixed-rate mortgage. Especially important in the subprime

[1]Senator Charles E. Schumer, "A Call to Action on the Subprime Mortgage Crisis," remarks on the state of the economy, as prepared for delivery to the Brookings Institution, December 19, 2007.

[2]James R. Barth et al., "A Short History of the Subprime Mortgage Market Meltdown" (Milken Institute, January 2008), p. 3.

[3]Brenda B. White, "A Short History of Subprime (Mortgage Industry)," *Mortgage Banking*, March 1, 2006.

market are various kinds of adjustable-rate mortgages (ARMs). The interest rate in an ARM changes (resets) at regular intervals—once a year, for example—in response to changes in some index, such as the prime rate. Many subprime ARMs are hybrids that start with low "teaser" rates that remain constant for a certain period, typically two or three years. After that period is over, the mortgage "resets." Thereafter, it is adjusted periodically.

In addition, no-documentation loans appeared in the early 2000s as housing prices began their rapid rise. With these loans, lenders do not even ask for verification of the borrower's income.

What Went Wrong?

Many observers touted the benefits of subprime loans in enabling previously disadvantaged groups, such as those living in poor or minority neighborhoods, to become homeowners. In addition, lenders initially earned large profits by charging these borrowers high interest rates and, because so many of the mortgages were securitized, a relatively large number of investors earned high returns.

So how did this evidently great idea turn into an economic disaster? Remember that subprime borrowers are risky borrowers—they're considered more likely to default on their loans. And that's just what happened. Beginning in 2006, more and more subprime borrowers fell behind on their loan payments, and many of them ended up defaulting. This began a long upward trend in foreclosures that showed little sign of slowing even by the end of 2010. Several economic conditions contributed to the high rate of defaults. For one thing, the prime rate of interest, which had been declining or holding steady since 2001, began to rise in 2004, affecting the rate to which interest on ARMs was reset. To further complicate the situation, housing prices, which had been increasing steadily, began to drop in 2006, leaving some buyers owing more than the current value of their homes.

As a result of the large number of defaults, subprime lenders found themselves in deep financial trouble, and some top lenders filed for bankruptcy. Lenders were originating fewer loans and were finding it difficult to sell those that they had originated. Investment bankers who had purchased loans and securitized them, also suffered. In order to get the highest possible prices, they had retained some exposure to the riskiest parts of the loan bundles that they sold. As the default rates on loans underlying MBSs increased, the investment bankers suffered losses, as did the investors who bought the securities.

As investors in other types of fixed-income securities saw what was happening to the values of securitized subprime mortgages, they became concerned about the values of similar securitized debt instruments, such as collateralized loan obligations (CLOs). CLOs are securitized business loans, which included business loans that had been used to fund leveraged buyouts and were therefore also quite risky. Investors' concerns caused prices for CLOs to decline rapidly. In addition, banks and other lenders began to tighten their credit standards, which made it more difficult for businesses and individuals to get loans, further contributing to a general weakening of the economy.

Who's to Blame?

Inevitably, observers looked around for someone to blame for the subprime crisis. And they came up with a long list of candidates, from the homebuyers themselves (who should have been more prudent) to the SEC and the Federal Reserve (who should have been paying closer attention). Few disagree, though, that those promoting subprime mortgages—such as mortgage brokers and lenders—must bear at least a part of the blame.

Motivated by the potential to earn a lot of money in a rapidly expanding market, many of these players turned their backs on ethical standards. "In the feeding frenzy for housing loans," according to one writer, "basic quality controls were ignored in the mortgage business, while the big Wall Street investment banks that backed these firms looked the other way."[4] Problems existed at many levels, as a few examples show:

- Mortgage lenders did not adequately monitor what the mortgage brokers were doing. In fact, some allege that they were willing to make virtually any loan that brokers sent their way. With little oversight, the brokers did not have a strong incentive to carefully evaluate the ability of borrowers to repay the mortgages. They filled out the loan paperwork that they submitted to the lenders without verifying all of the information and, it has been alleged, in some cases actually misrepresented the facts.
- Appraisers inflated the market value of houses, causing consumers to take out mortgages that did not reflect their houses' true value. According to several national studies, lenders commonly pressured appraisers to value a property at whatever amount was needed to allow a high-priced sale to close.[5] Willingness to inflate appraisals also made some appraisers attractive to unscrupulous mortgage brokers, who

---

[4]David Cho, "Pressure at Mortgage Firm Led to Mass Approval of Bad Loans," *Washington Post*, May 7, 2007.
[5]Kenneth R. Harney, "Appraisal Inflation," *Washington Post*, April 21, 2007.

were an important source of their business. The attorneys general of several states filed suit against mortgage and appraisal firms, claiming that they engaged in this practice.

- Mortgage companies lured buyers with teaser rates and other loan terms that appeared favorable but, in the longer run, were not. (Some have called these terms "toxic.") Mortgage agreements often included prepayment penalties that would make it very expensive for buyers to refinance later. Many subprime buyers weren't experienced or sophisticated enough to fully understand the terms, but lenders and brokers were interested in pushing through the loans—not in explaining the loan terms.

- Many subprime mortgages were "no-doc" loans, which required little or no documentation of income. These loans, claimed one observer, "were available to anyone with a pulse." Opportunities for abuse are obvious—and not restricted to borrowers. A former employee of Ameriquest Mortgage Corp. stated that it was "a common and open practice at Ameriquest for account executives to forge or alter borrower information or loan documents. . . . I saw account executives openly engage in conduct such as altering borrowers' W-2 forms or pay stubs, photocopying borrower signatures and copying them onto other, unsigned documents, and similar conduct."[6]

- As bonds backed by subprime mortgages became more popular and profitable, investment banks—eager to bundle more mortgages—loosened their standards. The quality of the loans being bundled began to slide as the popularity of subprime mortgages grew, according to the consultants (called due-diligence firms) hired by the bankers to evaluate loan quality. However, many investment banking firms overlooked the problem—and, as a result, passed ever-higher risk along to the investors who bought their mortgage-backed securities.

- Investors in the MBSs did not fully understand the risks associated with them. The way in which the mortgages were bundled made it difficult for investors to value the MBSs. They were so complex that many investors apparently relied on investment bankers to tell them what they were worth. The investment bankers apparently did not understand or simply failed to inform investors of all the risks. Some investors probably also got a bit greedy.

DISCUSSION QUESTIONS

1. What were the responsibilities of the mortgage brokers to borrowers? To lenders? To investors? How well did they fulfill their responsibilities? Why?
2. Did some subprime lenders behave unethically? If so, how? Whose interests did the subprime lenders have a responsibility to represent? Did they adequately represent those interests?
3. What motivated the investment bankers to get involved in the subprime market? Did they behave appropriately? Why or why not?
4. Should the borrowers (homeowners) share in the blame? If so, how?
5. What about the investors in MBSs? What could they have done differently?
6. What can be done to prevent future blowups like the one that occurred in the subprime market?

[6]Bob Irvy, "Subprime 'Liar Loans' Fuel Bust with $1 Billion Fraud (Update 1)," Bloomberg.com, updated April 25, 2007.

Sources: Associated Press, "Regulators' Cases Targeting Wall Street's Role in Subprime Market," Boston.com, February 18, 2008; James R. Barth, Tong Li, Triphon Phumiwasana, and Glenn Yago, "A Short History of the Subprime Mortgage Market Meltdown" (Milken Institute, January 2008), p. 3; Souphala Chomsisengphet and Anthony Pennington-Cross, "The Evolution of the Subprime Mortgage Market," Federal Reserve Bank of St. Louis Review, January/February 2006; Patrick Rucker, "Wall Street Often Shelved Damaging Subprime Reports," *International Herald Tribune*, August 1, 2007; Robert J. Samuelson, "The Catch-22 of Economics," *Newsweek*, updated September 15, 2007; Time/CNN, "A Sub-Prime Primer," March 15, 2007; Faten Sabry and Thomas Schopflocher, "The Subprime Meltdown: A Primer," Part I of NERA Insights Series, June 21, 2007; Brenda B. White, "A Short History of Subprime (Mortgage Industry)," *Mortgage Banking*, March 1, 2006.

Stock Valuation

Lucas Jackson/Reuters/Landov LLC

F inding the actual market price of a share of publicly traded stock is easy. You can just look it up online at Yahoo! Finance or MSN Money Central. But don't expect the market price to stay the same; stock prices change all the time—sometimes dramatically.

Consider what happened in the U.S. stock markets on Thursday, May 6, 2010. The U.S. stock market indices were down sharply by early afternoon on May 6 as investors drove prices down over concerns that the Greek debt crisis would spill over into other countries, such as Spain, Portugal, and Ireland, and send the world back into a severe recession. The Dow Jones Industrial average (the Dow) was down over 300 points (3 percent) at 2:42 P.M. when the markets went into a free-fall that lasted about five minutes. By 2:47 P.M. the Dow was 998.5 points (9.2 percent) lower for the day. Fortunately for investors who owned stocks at 2:42 P.M., the market promptly reversed direction, and by 3:07 P.M. the Dow was almost back to the same level that it was at when the free-fall began. At the end of the day, the Dow was down 348 points, or 3.2 percent.

While the stock market decline during the "flash crash," the name by which the sudden drop on May 6 has come to be known,

Learning Objectives

1. List and describe the four types of secondary markets.

2. Explain why many financial analysts treat preferred stock as a special type of bond rather than as an equity security.

3. Describe how the general dividend-valuation model values a share of stock.

4. Discuss the assumptions that are necessary to make the general dividend-valuation model easier to use, and use the model to compute the value of a firm's stock.

5. Explain why g must be less than R in the constant-growth dividend model.

6. Explain how valuing preferred stock with a stated maturity differs from valuing preferred stock with no maturity, and calculate the price of a share of preferred stock under both conditions.

appears to have been caused by unusual trading activity rather than a sudden change in investor estimates of what stocks were worth, people who traded during the crash made or lost real money because of it. In contrast, the 348-point decline in the Dow over the entire day reflected changes in investor expectations regarding the value of the cash flows that ownership of stocks would entitle them to receive. On that one day, investors decided that the stocks in the Dow index were worth 3.2 percent less than they had thought just the day before.

When stock prices rise or fall, how do investors or financial managers know when it is time to sell or buy? In other words, how can they tell if the market price of a stock reflects its value? One approach is to develop a stock-valuation model and compare the value estimate from the model with the market price. If the market price is below the estimate, the stock may be undervalued, in which case an investor might buy the stock. (Of course, other factors may also weigh into the final decision to buy.) In this chapter, we develop and apply stock-valuation models that enable us to estimate a stock's value. The models are very similar to those used by Wall Street firms.

CHAPTER PREVIEW

This chapter focuses on equity securities (stocks) and how they are valued. We describe the market in which stocks trade and discuss several valuation models. These models tell us what a stock's price *should* be. We can compare our estimates from such models with the *actual* market price to better understand how the market is valuing an individual stock.

Why are stock-valuation formulas important for you to study in a corporate finance course? First, management may want to know if the firm's stock is undervalued or overvalued. This knowledge can affect the decisions that managers make. For example, if the stock is undervalued, management may want to repurchase shares of stock to reissue in the future or postpone an equity offering until the stock price increases. Second, as we mentioned in Chapter 1, the overarching goal of financial managers is to maximize the current value of the

firm's stock. To make investment or financing decisions that increase stockholder wealth, you must understand the fundamental factors that determine the market value of the firm's stock.

We begin this chapter with a discussion of the secondary markets for stocks and their efficiency, describe the major U.S. stock market indexes, explain how to read stock market price listings in the newspaper, and introduce the types of equity securities that firms typically issue. We then develop a general valuation model and demonstrate that the value of a share of stock is the present value of *all* expected future cash dividends. We use some simplifying assumptions about dividend payments to implement this valuation model. These assumptions correspond to actual practice and allow us to develop several specific valuation models.

8.1 THE MARKET FOR STOCKS

Equity securities, which are certificates of ownership of a corporation, are the most visible securities on the financial landscape. In June 2012, $18.7 trillion worth of public equity securities were outstanding in the United States alone. Every day Americans eagerly track the ups and downs of the stock market. Most people instinctively believe that the performance of the stock market is an important barometer of the country's economic health. Also fueling interest is the large number of people who actually own equity securities through their pension or retirement plans. The stocks owned by households represent about 35 percent of the total value of all corporate equity.

Secondary Markets

1 LEARNING OBJECTIVE

Recall from Chapter 2 that the stock market consists of primary and secondary markets. In the primary market, firms sell new shares of stock to investors to raise money. In secondary markets, outstanding shares of stock are bought and sold among investors. We will discuss the primary markets for bonds and stocks further in Chapter 13. Our focus here is on secondary markets.

Any trade of a security after its primary offering is said to be a secondary market transaction. Most secondary market transactions do not directly affect the firm that issues the securities.

For example, when an investor buys 100 shares of AT&T stock on the New York Stock Exchange (NYSE), the exchange of money is only between the investors buying and selling the securities; no money flows into or out of AT&T.

The presence of a secondary market does, however, affect the issuer indirectly. As discussed in Chapter 2, investors will pay a higher price for primary securities that have an active secondary market. The reason is that, with an active secondary market, investors face lower transaction costs and are more likely to receive a price that reflects the true value of their securities when they sell them. As a result, firms whose securities trade on a secondary market can sell their new debt or equity issues at a lower cost than can firms selling similar securities that have no secondary market.

Secondary Markets and Their Efficiency

In the United States, most secondary market transactions take place on one of the many stock exchanges, the two most important being the NYSE and NASDAQ.

New York Stock Exchange. Chapter 2 described a traditional securities exchange as an organized market that provides a physical meeting place and communication facilities for members to buy and sell securities under a specific set of rules and regulations. The oldest, largest, and best-known exchange of this kind in the United States is the NYSE, which was founded in 1792. The exchange lists the common and preferred stocks of more than three thousand companies, as well as eight hundred bonds. Collectively, the companies whose securities are traded on the NYSE had a market capitalization (total stock value) of about $14.0 trillion in January 2012.

 Learn more about the NYSE by visiting its Web site at http://www. nyse.com.

Stocks that are traded on an exchange are said to be *listed* on that exchange. For a firm's stocks to be listed on an exchange, the firm must pay a fee and meet the exchange's requirements for membership. Requirements include a minimum asset size, total stock value, a minimum number of shares of stock outstanding, and a minimum number of stockholders. Because of the prestige associated with being listed on the "big board," as the NYSE is known, it has the most stringent listing requirements. As a result, companies listed on the NYSE tend to be large, well-known firms.

NASDAQ. The NASDAQ (pronounced "Naz-dak") is one of the world's largest electronic stock markets, listing over three thousand companies. NASDAQ was created in 1971 by the National Association of Securities Dealers (NASD), and its odd name is an acronym for National Association of Securities Dealers Automated Quotation (NASDAQ) system.

 Find out about over-the-counter markets and NASDAQ at http://www. nasdaq.com.

NASDAQ is an OTC market because it does not have a physical location where trading takes place. Nevertheless, NASDAQ has achieved the stature of a major exchange. In fact, thanks to its sophisticated electronic trading system, NASDAQ is the second-largest stock market in the United States. The companies whose shares trade on NASDAQ had an aggregate market capitalization of $4.0 trillion in January 2012. Only the NYSE is larger. Although the OTC market has generally traded in the stocks of small firms that would not qualify to be listed on a major exchange, only 20 percent of the firms traded on NASDAQ are considered small.

The World's Stock Exchanges/Markets. Although we have focused on the NYSE and NASDAQ, it is important to recognize that there are approximately 100 equity stock exchanges/markets located throughout the world. The NYSE and NASDAQ are two of the top three based on the market value of the shares that trade in them. The largest exchanges/markets outside the United States in 2012 were the Tokyo Stock Exchange, NYSE Euronext, the London Stock Exchange, the Shanghai Stock Exchange, the Hong Kong Stock Exchange, and the Toronto Stock Exchange.

Furthermore, over the last decade there has been significant restructuring and consolidation of the exchanges and markets through mergers and acquisitions. Some examples in the last five years are the purchase of Euronext by the NYSE, the merger of NASDAQ with the OMX Group, and the merger of the Chicago Mercantile Exchange with the Chicago Board of Trade. The consolidation among the world's major exchanges/markets is driven by (1) new technologies that provide faster executions of trades and access to more markets and more products, (2) increased competition, which has reduced profit margins, and (3) the need to increase size in order to achieve greater economies of scale and operational efficiencies.

The role of the NYSE, NASDAQ, and other secondary markets is to bring together buyers and sellers. Ideally, we would like them to do this as efficiently as possible. As discussed in Chapter 2, markets are efficient when the current market prices of securities that are trading reflect all available information relevant to the valuation of those securities. When this happens, security prices will be near or at their true (intrinsic) value. The more efficient the market, the more likely this is to happen.

There are four types of secondary markets, and each type differs according to the amount of price information available to investors, which in turn affects the efficiency of the market. We discuss the four types of secondary markets—direct search, broker, dealer, and auction—in the order from least to most efficient.

Direct Search. The secondary markets furthest from the ideal of complete availability of price information are those in which buyers and sellers must seek each other out directly. In these markets, individuals bear the full cost of locating and negotiating with a buyer or seller, and it is typically too costly for them to conduct a thorough search to locate the best price. Securities that sell in direct search markets are usually bought and sold so infrequently that few third parties, such as a brokers or dealers, find it profitable enough to serve the market. In these markets, sellers often rely on word-of-mouth communication to find interested buyers. The common stock of small private companies is a good example of a security that trades in this manner.

Broker. When trading in a security issue becomes sufficiently heavy, brokers find it profitable to offer specialized search services to market participants. Brokers bring together buyers and sellers to earn a fee, called a commission. To provide investors with an incentive to hire them, brokers may charge a commission that is less than the cost of a direct search. Brokers are not passive agents but aggressively seek out buyers or sellers and try to negotiate an acceptable transaction price for their clients. The presence of active brokers increases market efficiency because brokers are in frequent contact with market participants and are likely to know what constitutes a "fair" price for a security.

Dealer. If the trading in a given security has sufficient volume, market efficiency is improved when there is someone in the marketplace who provides continuous bidding (selling or buying) for the security. Dealers do this by holding inventories of securities, which they own, and then buying and selling from the inventory to earn a profit. Unlike brokers, dealers have capital at risk. Dealers earn their profits from the *spread* on the securities they trade—the difference between their **bid price** (the price at which they buy) and their **offer (ask) price** (the price at which they sell). NASDAQ is the best-known example of a dealer market in the United States.

The advantage of a dealer over a broker market is that brokers cannot guarantee that an order to buy or sell will be executed promptly. This uncertainty about the speed of execution creates price risk. During the time a broker is trying to sell a security, its price may change and the person trying to sell the security could suffer a loss. A dealer market eliminates the need for time-consuming searches for a fair deal because buying and selling take place immediately from the dealer's inventory of securities.

Dealers make markets in securities using electronic computer networks to quote prices at which they are willing to buy or sell a particular security. These networks enable dealers to electronically survey the prices quoted by different dealers to help establish their sense of a fair price and to trade. A major development in the 1990s was the opening of the so-called electronic communications network (ECN). An ECN is an electronic network that allows individual investors to trade securities directly with one another, much like dealers.

Auction. In an auction market, buyers and sellers confront each other directly and bargain over price. The participants can communicate orally if they are located in the same place, or the information can be transmitted electronically. The NYSE is the best-known example of an auction market in the United States. In the NYSE, the auction for a security takes place at a specific location on the floor of the exchange, called a **post**. The auctioneer in this case is the **specialist**, who is designated by the exchange to represent orders placed by public customers. Specialists, as the name implies, specialize in orders for a small set of securities and are also allowed to act as dealers. Thus, in reality, the NYSE is an auction market that also has some features of a

bid price
the price a securities dealer will pay for a given stock

offer (ask) price
the price at which a securities dealer seeks to sell a given stock

post
a specific location on the floor of a stock exchange at which auctions for a particular security take place

specialist
the trader designated by an exchange to represent orders placed by public customers at auctions of securities; specialists handle a small set of securities and are also allowed to act as dealers

dealer market. In recent years, the NYSE has been moving toward electronic trading with the SuperDOT system (DOT stands for "designated order turnaround"), which allows orders to be transmitted electronically to specialists.

Stock Market Indexes

Stock market indexes are used to measure the performance of the stock market—whether stock prices on average are moving up or down. The indexes are watched closely not only to track economic activity but also to measure the performance of specific firms. A wide variety of general and specialized indexes is available. Here, we discuss some of the better-known indexes.

- *Dow Jones Industrial Average.* The most widely quoted stock market index is the Dow Jones Industrial Average (DJIA), which was first published in 1896. The index consists of 30 companies that represent about 20 percent of the market value of all U.S. stocks. Dow Jones also publishes specialized indexes for industrial, transportation, and utility companies. These specialized indexes tell us how stocks in a particular segment of the economy are performing.
- *New York Stock Exchange Index.* The NYSE composite index, published since 1966, includes all of the common and preferred stocks listed on the NYSE. This index provides information on the performance of many of the largest and most well-known firms in the U.S. economy.
- *Standard and Poor's 500 Index.* The Standard and Poor's 500 Index, which consists of 500 stocks, was created in 1926 and is regarded as the best index for measuring the performance of the largest companies in the U.S. economy. The stocks in the S&P 500 are selected by the Standard and Poor's Index Committee and represent more than 70 percent of the total market capitalization (market value) of all stocks traded in the United States.
- *NASDAQ Composite Index.* The NASDAQ Composite Index consists of all of the common stocks listed on the NASDAQ stock exchange. Currently, the index includes more than three thousand firms, many of which are in the technology sector of the economy. Thus, the NASDAQ Composite Index is considered a barometer of performance in the high-tech sector.

The Web site http://www.bigcharts.com offers a real-time summary of all the major market indexes.

Reading the Stock Market Listings

The *Wall Street Journal,* the *Financial Times,* and other newspapers provide stock listings for the major stock exchanges, such as the NYSE, NASDAQ, and the relevant regional exchanges. Exhibit 8.1 shows a small section of a listing from the *Wall Street Journal* online (WSJ.com) for the NYSE.

In the exhibit, go to the entry for Adams Resources & Energy, which is highlighted. Adams is a Houston-based company that markets crude oil, natural gas, and petroleum products. Look at column 2, which provides the trading (ticker) symbol of the company—AE. The trading symbol is used in requesting price quotes or company information and in placing a trade. Columns 4 and 5 show the high price ($37.05 per share) and low price ($36.44 per share) for the day, and column 6 shows that AE's closing price at the end of the day was $36.44 per share. The closing price, which is the price at which the last trade took place, was a $0.03 increase from the close on the previous day (column 7). The trading volume of shares for the day, which for AE is 7,539 shares of stock, is listed in column 9. Column 10 shows the firm's highest price ($75.13 per share) and Column 11 its lowest price ($18.73 per share) over the past 52 weeks.

Column 12 shows AE's annual cash dividend per share, which is $0.57. Although the annual dividend is shown here, most firms, including AE, pay dividends quarterly, or four times a year. Column 13 shows AE's **dividend yield**, which is 1.56 percent. The dividend yield is calculated by dividing the annual dividend payout by the current market price. For AE, that calculation is $0.57/$36.44 = 0.0156, or 1.56 percent. If you scan the dividend yields, you will see that most of the firms pay no dividend at all; for those that pay dividends, the dividend yields range from 1.56 percent to 2.52 percent. Investors are willing to accept low dividend

To monitor stocks trading on the New York Stock Exchange, visit the NYSE EURONEXT Web site at http://usequities.nyse.com/.

dividend yield
a stock's annual dividend divided by its current price

EXHIBIT 8.1　NYSE Stock Listings from the Wall Street Journal

(1) Company Name	(2) Symbol	(3) Open	(4) High	(5) Low	(6) Close	(7) Net Chg
Accelr8 Technology	AXK	3.08	3.10	3.05	3.09	0.09
Acme United	ACU	11.00	11.10	11.00	11.10	0.10
Acquity Group ADS	AQ	10.02	10.35	9.59	10.35	0.33
Adams Resources & Energy	AE	36.72	37.05	36.44	36.44	0.03
AdCare Health Systems	ADK	4.95	4.99	4.87	4.95	0.01
Advanced Photonix	API	0.75	0.76	0.74	0.75	0.01
ADVENTRX Pharmaceuticals	ANX	0.68	0.69	0.67	0.68	−0.01
Aerocentury	ACY	12.85	12.85	12.85	12.85	0.35
Aerosonic	AIM	3.17	3.32	3.17	3.32	0.12
Alderon Iron Ore	AXX	2.11	2.24	2.11	2.17	0.08
Alexco Resource	AXU	4.40	4.64	4.40	4.56	0.24
Allied Nevada Gold	ANV	38.03	39.40	38.03	39.11	1.08
Almaden Minerals	AAU	2.96	3.05	2.86	2.89	−0.01

Source: Wall Street Journal Online, Friday, September 14, 2012.

payouts, or none at all, as long as they expect higher cash dividends and/or a higher stock price in the future.

Column 14 shows AE's price-earnings (P/E) ratio, which—as you may recall from Chapter 4—is the stock's current price per share divided by its earnings per share. For AE, the P/E ratio is 6.07. This tells us that investors are currently willing to pay a price per share 6.07 times the earnings per share for AE stock. A P/E ratio of 6.07 is fairly low. A low P/E ratio suggests that investors believe that the firm is unlikely to have rapid earnings growth in the future. We will have more to say about the P/E ratio in later chapters. Finally, Column 15 shows the percentage change in price for the stock for the calendar year. In AE's case the price has gone up by 25.18 percent.

Common and Preferred Stock

common stock

an equity share that represents the basic ownership claim in a corporation; the most common type of equity security

Equity securities take several forms. The most prevalent type of equity security, as its name implies, is **common stock**. Common stock represents the basic ownership claim in a corporation. One of the basic rights of the owners is to vote on all important matters that affect the company, such as the election of the board of directors or a proposed merger or acquisition. Owners of common stock are not guaranteed any dividend payments and have the lowest-priority claim on the firm's assets in the event of bankruptcy. Legally, common stockholders enjoy limited liability; that is, their losses are limited to the original amount of their investment in the firm, and their personal assets cannot be taken to satisfy the obligations of the corporation. Finally, common stocks are perpetuities in the sense that they have no maturity. Common stock can be retired only if management buys it in the open market from investors or if the firm is liquidated, in which case its assets are sold, as described in the next section.

preferred stock

an equity share in a corporation that entitles the owner to preferred treatment over owners of common stock with respect to dividend payments and claims against the firm's assets in the event of bankruptcy or liquidation, but that typically has no voting rights

Like common stock, **preferred stock** represents an ownership interest in the corporation, but as the name implies, preferred stock receives preferential treatment over common stock. Specifically, preferred stockholders take precedence over common stockholders in the payment of dividends and in the distribution of corporate assets in the event of liquidation. Unlike the interest payments on bonds, which are contractual obligations, preferred stock dividends are declared by the board of directors, and if a dividend is not paid, the lack of payment is not legally viewed as a default.

Preferred stock is legally a form of equity. Thus, preferred stock dividends are paid by the issuer with after-tax dollars. Even though preferred stock is an equity security, the owners have no voting privileges unless the preferred stock is convertible into common stock. Preferred stocks are generally viewed as perpetuities because they have no maturity. However, most preferred stocks are not true perpetuities because their share contracts often contain call provisions and can even include *sinking fund* provisions, which require management to retire (purchase) a certain percentage of the stock issue annually until the entire issue is retired.

(8)	(9)	(10)	(11)	(12)	(13)	(14)	(15)
% Chg	Volume	52 Wk High	52 Wk Low	Div	Yield	P/E	YTD % Chg
3.00	11,500	3.90	0.76	...	...	...	155.37
0.91	6,239	11.54	8.52	0.28	2.52	10.68	16.84
3.29	227,161	10.75	5.54	...	...	...	80
0.08	7,539	75.13	18.73	0.57	1.56	6.07	25.18
0.20	39,011	5.00	3.15	...	...	...	24.37
1.30	41,232	1.15	0.48	...	...	...	33.14
−1.45	203,406	1.21	0.45	...	...	...	15.25
2.80	100	15.60	5.30	...	...	6.16	108.94
3.72	600	4.44	2.07	...	...	11.02	3.72
3.76	14,590	3.83	1.69	...	...	...	−17.78
5.56	588,569	9.13	3.21	...	...	54.29	−33.04
2.84	876,707	45.90	23.69	...	...	69.71	29.16
−0.34	503,021	3.67	1.55	...	...	16.72	14.68

Preferred Stock: Debt or Equity?

An ongoing debate in finance is whether preferred stock is debt or equity. A strong case can be made that preferred stock is a special type of bond rather than equity. The argument behind this view is as follows. First, regular (nonconvertible) preferred stock confers no voting rights. Second, preferred stockholders receive a fixed dividend, regardless of the firm's earnings, and if the firm is liquidated, they receive a stated value (usually par) and not a residual value. Third, preferred stocks often have credit ratings that are similar in nature to those issued to bonds. Fourth, preferred stock is sometimes convertible into common stock. Finally, most preferred stock issues have a retirement date and, thus, are not true perpetuities.

LEARNING OBJECTIVE

> **BEFORE YOU GO ON**

1. What is NASDAQ?

2. How do dealers differ from brokers?

3. List the major stock market indexes and explain what they tell us.

4. What does the price-earnings ratio tell us?

5. Why do some people view preferred stock as a special type of a bond rather than a stock?

8.2 COMMON STOCK VALUATION

In earlier chapters we emphasized that the value of any asset is the present value of its future cash flows. The steps in valuing an asset are as follows:

1. Estimate the expected future cash flows.

2. Determine the required rate of return, or discount rate, which reflects the riskiness of the future cash flows.

3. Compute the present value of the future cash flows to determine what the asset is worth.

It is relatively straightforward to apply these steps in valuing a bond because the cash flows are stated as part of the bond contract and the required rate of return or discount rate is just the yield to maturity on bonds with comparable risk. However, common stock valuation is more difficult for several reasons. First, while the expected cash flows for bonds are well documented and easy to determine, common stock dividends are much less certain. Dividends are

You can read about
stock-valuation models
at the Motley Fool:
http://www.fool.com/
research/2000/
features000406.htm.

declared by the board of directors, and a board may or may not decide to pay a cash dividend at a particular time. Thus, the size and the timing of dividend cash flows are less certain. Second, common stocks are true perpetuities in that they have no final maturity date. Thus, firms never have to redeem them. In contrast, with the exception of the consol bonds mentioned in Chapter 5, bonds have a finite maturity. Finally, unlike the rate of return, or yield, on bonds, the rate of return on common stock is not directly observable. Thus, grouping common stocks into risk classes is more difficult than grouping bonds. Keeping these complexities in mind, we now turn to a discussion of common stock valuation.

A One-Period Model

Let's assume that you have a genie that can tell the future with perfect certainty. Also, suppose that you are thinking about buying a share of stock and selling it after a year. The genie volunteers that in one year the price (P_1) you can sell the stock for will be $100 and it will pay an $8 dividend ($D_1$) at the end of the year. The time line for the transaction is:

0	1 Year
Buy stock	$8 + $100

If you and the other investors require a 20 percent return on investments in securities in this risk class, what price would you be willing to pay for the stock today?

The value of the stock is the present value of the future cash flows you can expect to receive from it. The cash flows you will receive are as follows: (1) the $8 dividend and (2) the $100 sale price. Using a 20 percent rate of return, we see that the value of the stock equals the present value (PV) of the dividend plus the present value of the cash received from the sale of the stock:

$$PV(\text{stock}) = PV(\text{dividend}) + PV(\text{sale price})$$
$$= \frac{\$8}{1 + 0.2} + \frac{\$100}{1 + 0.2}$$
$$= \frac{\$8 + \$100}{1.2} = \frac{\$108}{1.2}$$
$$= \$90$$

Thus, the value of the stock today is $90. If you pay $90 for the stock, you will have a one-year holding period return of exactly 20 percent. More formally, the time line and the current value of the stock for our one-period model can be as shown:

0	1 Year
P_0	$D_1 + P_1$

$$P_0 = \frac{D_1 + P_1}{1 + R}$$

where:
P_0 = the current value, or price, of the stock
D_1 = dividend paid at the end of the period
P_1 = price of the stock at the end of the period
R = required return on common stock, or discount rate, in a particular risk class

Note that P_0 denotes time zero, which is today; P_1 is the price one period later; P_2 is the price two periods in the future; and so on. Note also that when we speak of the price (P_t) in this context, we mean the value—what we have determined is what the price *should* be, given our model—not the actual market price. Our one-period model provides an estimate of what the market price should be.

Now what if at the beginning of year 2, we are again asked to determine the price of a share of common stock with the same dividend pattern and a one-year holding period. As in our first calculation, the current price (P_1) of the stock is the present value of the dividend and the stock's sale price, both received at the end of the year (P_2). Specifically, our time line and the stock pricing formula are as follows:

```
1                                    2    Year
├────────────────────────────────────┤
P₁                                   D₂ + P₂
```

$$P_1 = \frac{D_2 + P_2}{1 + R}$$

If we repeat the process again at the beginning of year 3, the result is similar:

$$P_2 = \frac{D_3 + P_3}{1 + R}$$

and at the beginning of year 4:

$$P_3 = \frac{D_4 + P_4}{1 + R}$$

Each single-period model discounts the dividend and sale price at the end of the period by the required return.

A Perpetuity Model

Unfortunately, although our one-period model is correct, it is not very realistic. We need a stock-valuation formula for a perpetuity, not for one or two periods. However, we can string together a series of one-period stock pricing models to arrive at a stock perpetuity model. Here is how we do it.

First, we construct a two-period stock-valuation model. The time line for the two-period model follows:

```
0                    1                    2    Period
├──────────────────────┼────────────────────┤
P₀ ←──────────────── (D₁ + P₁)
                     P₁ ←──────────────── (D₂ + P₂)
```

To construct our two-period model, we start with our initial single-period valuation model:

$$P_0 = \frac{D_1 + P_1}{1 + R}$$

Now we substitute into this equation the expression derived earlier for P_1 [$P_1 = (D_2 + P_2)/(1 + R)$] and obtain the following:

$$P_0 = \frac{D_1 + [(D_2 + P_2)/(1 + R)]}{1 + R}$$

Rearranging this equation results in a stock-valuation model for two periods:

$$P_0 = \frac{D_1}{1 + R} + \frac{D_2}{(1 + R)^2} + \frac{P_2}{(1 + R)^2}$$

Finally, we combine the second-period terms to obtain:

$$P_0 = \frac{D_1}{1 + R} + \frac{D_2 + P_2}{(1 + R)^2}$$

This equation shows that the price of a share of stock that is held for two periods is the present value of the dividend in period 1 (D_1) plus the present value of the dividend and sale price in period 2 (D_2 and P_2).

Now let's construct a three-period model. The time line for the three-period model is:

```
0                1                2                3    Period
├─────────────────┼────────────────┼────────────────┤
P₀ ←─────── (D₁ + P₁)
            P₁ ←─────── (D₂ + P₂)
                        P₂ ←─────── (D₃ + P₃)
```

If we substitute the equation for P_2 into the two-period valuation model shown above, we have a three-period model, which is as follows. Recall that $P_2 = (D_3 + P_3)/(1 + R)$.

$$
\begin{aligned}
P_0 &= \frac{D_1}{1 + R} + \frac{D_2}{(1 + R)^2} + \frac{P_2}{(1 + R)^2} \\
&= \frac{D_1}{1 + R} + \frac{D_2}{(1 + R)^2} + \frac{(D_3 + P_3)/(1 + R)}{(1 + R)^2} \\
&= \frac{D_1}{1 + R} + \frac{D_2}{(1 + R)^2} + \frac{D_3}{(1 + R)^3} + \frac{P_3}{(1 + R)^3} \\
&= \frac{D_1}{1 + R} + \frac{D_2}{(1 + R)^2} + \frac{D_3 + P_3}{(1 + R)^3}
\end{aligned}
$$

By now, it should be clear that we could go on to develop a four-period model, a five-period model, a six-period model, and so on, ad infinitum. The ultimate result is the following equation:

$$
P_0 = \frac{D_1}{1 + R} + \frac{D_2}{(1 + R)^2} + \frac{D_3}{(1 + R)^3} + \cdots + \frac{D_t}{(1 + R)^t} + \frac{P_t}{(1 + R)^t}
$$

Here, t is the time period, which can be any number from one to infinity (∞). We will use t, instead of n, to denote the time period from this point forward because it is more commonly used in pricing equations. n will still be used to denote the number of periods.

In summary, we have developed a model showing that the value, or price, of a share of stock today (P_0) is the present value of all future dividends and the stock's sale price in the future. Although theoretically sound, this model is not practical to apply because the number of dividends could be infinite. It is unlikely that we can successfully forecast an infinite number of dividend payments or a stock's sale price far into the future. What we need are some realistic simplifing assumptions.

The General Dividend Valuation Model

 LEARNING OBJECTIVE

In the preceding equation, notice that the final term, as in the earlier stock valuation models, is always the sale price of the stock in period t (P_t) and that t can be any number, including infinity. The model assumes that we can forecast the sale price of the stock far into the future, which does not seem very likely in real life. However, as a practical matter, as P_t moves further out in time toward infinity, the value of the P_t approaches zero. Why? No matter how large the sale price of the stock, the present value of P_t will approach zero because the discount factor approaches zero. Therefore, if we go out to infinity, we can ignore the $P_t/(1 + R)^t$ term and write our final equation as:

$$
\begin{aligned}
P_0 &= \frac{D_1}{1 + R} + \frac{D_2}{(1 + R)^2} + \frac{D_3}{(1 + R)^3} + \frac{D_4}{(1 + R)^4} + \frac{D_5}{(1 + R)^5} + \cdots + \frac{D_\infty}{(1 + R)^\infty} \\
&= \sum_{t=1}^{\infty} \frac{D_t}{(1 + R)^t}
\end{aligned}
\qquad (8.1)
$$

where:

P_0 = the current value, or price, of the stock
D_t = the dividend received in period t, where $t = 1, 2, 3, \ldots, \infty$
R = the required return on the common stock or discount rate

Equation 8.1 is a general expression for the value of a share of stock. It says that the price of a share of stock is the present value of *all* expected future dividends:

$$\text{Stock price} = \text{PV(All expected dividends)}$$

The formula does not assume any specific pattern for future dividends, such as a constant growth rate. Nor does it make any assumption about when the share of stock is going to be sold in the future. Furthermore, the model says that to compute a stock's current value, we need to forecast an infinite number of dividends, which is a daunting task.

Equation 8.1 provides some insights into why stock prices are changing all the time and why, at certain times, price changes can be dramatic. Equation 8.1 implies that the underlying value of a share of stock is determined by the market's expectations of the future cash flows (from dividends) that the firm can generate. In efficient markets, stock prices change constantly as new information becomes available and is incorporated into the firm's market price. For publicly traded companies, the market is inundated with facts and rumors, such as when a firm fails to meet sales projections, the CEO resigns or is fired, or a class-action suit is filed against the firm because of a defect in one of its products. Some events may have little or no impact on the firm's expected cash flows and, hence, its stock price. Others can have very large effects on expected cash flows. Examples include the effects of the subprime mortgage market collapse in 2007, which led to a sharp slowdown in the economy in 2008, or the effect of the 2010 Gulf oil spill on the cash flows of BP p.l.c., the large oil company.

The Growth Stock Pricing Paradox

An interesting issue concerning growth stocks arises out of the fact that the stock-valuation equation is based on dividend payments. *Growth stocks* are typically defined as the stocks of companies whose earnings are growing at above-average rates and are expected to continue to do so for some time. A company of this type typically pays little or no dividends on its stock because management believes that the company has a number of high-return investment opportunities and that both the company and its investors will be better off if earnings are reinvested rather than paid out as dividends.

To illustrate the problem with valuing growth stocks, let's suppose that the earnings of Acme Corporation are growing at an exceptionally high rate. The company's stock pays no dividends, and management states that there are no plans to pay any dividends. Based on our stock-valuation equation, what is the value of Acme's stock?

Obviously, since all the dividend values are zero, the value of our growth stock is zero!

$$P_0 = \frac{0}{1 + R} + \frac{0}{(1 + R)^2} + \frac{0}{(1 + R)^3} + \cdots = 0$$

How can the value of a growth stock be zero? What is going on here?

The problem is that our definition of growth stocks was less than precise. Our application of Equation 8.1 assumes that Acme will never pay a dividend. If Acme had a charter that stated it would *never* pay dividends and would *never* liquidate itself (unless it went bankrupt), the value of its stock would indeed be zero. Equation 8.1 predicts and common sense says that if you own stock in a company that will *never* pay you any cash, the market value of those shares of stock are worth absolutely nothing. As you may recall, this is a point we emphasized in Chapter 1.

What we should have said is that a growth stock is stock in a company that *currently* has exceptional investment opportunities and thus is not *currently* paying dividends because it is reinvesting earnings. At some time in the future, growth stock companies will pay dividends or will liquidate themselves (for example, by selling out to other companies) and pay a single large cash dividend. People who buy growth stocks expect rapid price appreciation because management reinvests the cash flows from earnings internally in investment projects believed to have high rates of return. If the internal investments succeed, the stock's price should go up significantly, and investors can sell their stock at a price that is higher than the price they paid.

> **BEFORE YOU GO ON**

1. What is the general formula used to calculate the price of a share of a stock? What does it mean?

2. What are growth stocks, and why do they typically pay little or no dividends?

8.3 STOCK VALUATION: SOME SIMPLIFYING ASSUMPTIONS

Conceptually, the general dividend valuation model (Equation 8.1) is consistent with the notion that the value of an asset is the discounted value of future cash flows. Unfortunately, at a practical level, the model is not easy to use because of the difficulty of estimating future dividends over a long period of time. We can, however, make some simplifying assumptions about the pattern of dividends that make the model more manageable. Fortunately, these assumptions closely resemble the way many firms manage their dividend payments. We have a choice among three different assumptions: (1) Dividends remain constant over time; that is, they have a growth rate of zero. (2) Dividends grow at a constant rate; for example, they grow at 3 percent per year. (3) Dividends exhibit a mixed growth rate pattern; that is, dividends have one growth pattern and then switch to another. We discuss each of these assumptions in turn.

Zero-Growth Dividend Model

The simplest assumption is that dividends will have a growth rate of zero. Thus, the dividend payment pattern remains constant over time:

$$D_1 = D_2 = D_3 = \cdots = D_\infty$$

In this case the dividend-discount model (Equation 8.1) becomes:

$$P_0 = \frac{D}{1+R} + \frac{D}{(1+R)^2} + \frac{D}{(1+R)^3} + \frac{D}{(1+R)^4} + \frac{D}{(1+R)^5} + \cdots + \frac{D}{(1+R)^\infty}$$

This cash flow pattern is a perpetuity with a constant cash flow. You may recall that we developed an equation for such a perpetuity in Chapter 5. Equation 5.7 said that the present value of a perpetuity with a constant cash flow is CF/i, where CF is the constant cash flow and i is the interest rate. In terms of our stock-valuation model, we can present the same relation as follows:

$$P_0 = \frac{D}{R} \tag{8.2}$$

where:

　　P_0 = the current value, or price, of the stock
　　D = the constant cash dividend received in each time period
　　R = the required return on the common stock or discount rate

This model fits the dividend pattern for common stock of a company that is not growing and has little growth potential or for preferred stock, which we discuss in the next section.

For example, the Del Mar Corporation is a small printing company that serves a rural three-county area near San Diego, California. The county's economic base has remained constant over the years, and Del Mar's sales and earnings reflect this trend. The firm pays a $5 dividend per year, and the board of directors has no plans to change the dividend. If the firm's investors are mostly local businesspeople who expect a 20 percent return on their investment, what should be the price of the firm's stock?

Since the cash dividend payments are constant, we can use Equation 8.2 to find the price of the stock:

$$P_0 = \frac{D}{R} = \frac{\$5}{0.20} = \$25 \text{ per share}$$

Constant-Growth Dividend Model

Under the next dividend growth assumption, cash dividends do not remain constant but instead grow at some average rate g from one period to the next forever. The rate of growth can be positive or negative. And, as it turns out, a constant-growth rate is not a bad approximation of the actual dividend pattern for some firms. Constant dividend growth is often an appropriate assumption for mature companies with a history of stable growth.

The Value of a Small Business

PROBLEM: For the past 15 years, a family has operated the gift shop in a luxury hotel near Rodeo Drive in Los Angeles. The hotel management wants to sell the gift shop to the family members rather than paying them to operate it. The family's accountant will incorporate the new business and estimates that it will generate an annual cash dividend of $150,000 for the stockholders. The hotel will provide the family with an infinite guarantee for use of the space and a generous buyout plan in the unlikely event that the hotel closes its doors. The accountant estimates that a 20 percent discount rate is appropriate. What is the value of the stock?

APPROACH: Assuming that the business will operate indefinitely, that its growth is constrained by its circumstances, and that inflation will be negligible, the zero-growth discount model can be used to value the stock. Thus, we can use Equation 8.2. Since the number of shares outstanding is not known, we can simply interpret P_0 as being the total value of the outstanding stock.

SOLUTION: Applying Equation 8.2:

$$P_0 = \frac{D}{R} = \frac{\$150,000}{0.20} = \$750,000$$

You may have concerns about the assumption of an infinite time horizon. In practice, though, it does not present a problem. It is true that most companies do not live on forever. We know, however, that the further in the future a cash flow will occur, the smaller its present value. Thus, far-distant dividends have a small present value and contribute very little to the price of the stock. For example, as shown in Exhibit 8.2, with constant dividends and a 15 percent

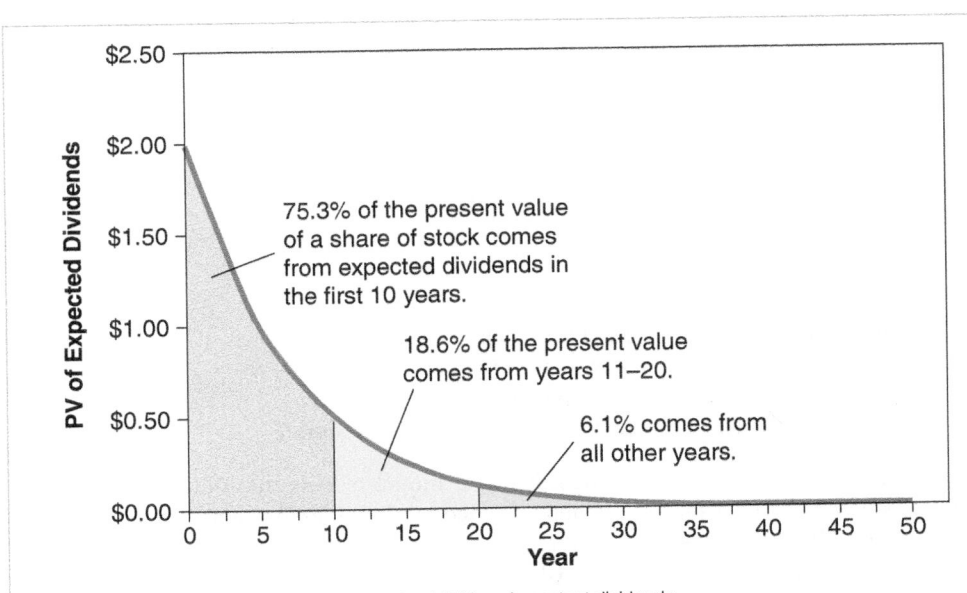

75.3% of the present value of a share of stock comes from expected dividends in the first 10 years.

18.6% of the present value comes from years 11–20.

6.1% comes from all other years.

Note: Calculations based on discount rate of 15% and constant dividends.

EXHIBIT 8.2

Impact on Stock Prices of Near and Distant Future Dividends

Dividends expected far in the future have a smaller present value than dividends expected in the next few years, and so they have less effect on the price of the stock. As you can see in the exhibit, with constant dividends more than 75 percent of the current price of a share of stock comes from expected dividends in the first 10 years.

discount rate, dividends paid during the first 10 years account for more than 75 percent of the value of a share of stock, while dividends paid after the twentieth year contribute only about 6 percent of the value.

Identifying and applying the constant-growth dividend model is fairly straightforward. First, we need a model that can be used to compute the value of a dividend payment for any future period. If we assume that cash dividends grow at a constant rate g from one period to the next, we can use the future value formula, Equation 5.1, to obtain such a model:

$$FV_n = PV \times (1 + i)^n$$

To apply this formula to dividend payments, we replace FV_n with D_t, PV with D_0, i with g, and n with t:

$$D_t = D_0 \times (1 \times g)^t \tag{8.3}$$

where:

D_t = dividend payment in period t, where $t = 1, 2, 3, \ldots, \infty$
D_0 = dividend paid in the current period, $t = 0$
g = the constant-growth rate for dividends

Equation 8.3 allows us to compute the dividend payment for any time period. For example, the next dividend, paid at time $t = 1$, is D_1, which is just the current dividend (D_0) multiplied by the growth factor, $(1 + g)$. Thus, $D_1 = D_0 \times (1 + g)$.

Notice that to compute the dividend payment for any future period, we multiply D_0 by the growth rate factor to some power, but we *always* start with D_0.

We can now develop the constant-growth dividend model, which is easy to do because it is just an application of Equation 5.10 from Chapter 5. Equation 5.10 says that the present value of a growing perpetuity (PVP) equals the cash flow value from period 1 (CF_1), divided by the difference between the discount rate (i) and the rate of growth (g) of the cash flow (CF_1):

$$PVP = \frac{CF_1}{i - g}$$

We can represent this same relation for stock valuation as follows:

$$P_0 = \frac{D_1}{R - g} \tag{8.4}$$

where:

P_0 = the current value, or price, of the stock
D_1 = the dividend paid in the next period ($t = 1$)
g = the constant-growth rate for dividends
R = the required return on the common stock or discount rate

In other words, the constant-growth dividend model tells us that the current price of a share of stock is the next period dividend divided by the difference between the discount rate and the dividend growth rate. Note that PVP is the current value of the stock (P_0), which equals the present value of the dividend cash flows.

As discussed in Chapter 5, the growing-perpetuity model is valid only if the growth rate is less than the discount rate, or required rate of return. In terms of Equation 8.4, then, the value of g must be less than the value of R ($g < R$). If the equation is used in situations where R is equal to or less than g ($R \leq g$), the computed results will be meaningless.

Finally, notice that if $g = 0$, there is no dividend growth and the dividend payment pattern is simply a constant no-growth dividend stream. In this case, Equation 8.4 becomes $P_0 = D/R$, which is precisely the same as Equation 8.2, the zero-growth dividend model. Thus, Equation 8.2 is just a special case of Equation 8.4 where $g = 0$.

Let's work through an example using the constant-growth dividend model. Big Red Automotive is a regional auto parts supplier based in Oklahoma City. At the firm's year-end stockholders' meeting, the CFO announces that this year's dividend will be $4.81. The announcement conforms to Big Red's dividend policy, which sets dividend growth at a 4 percent annual rate. Investors who own stock in similar types of firms expect to earn a return of 18 percent. What is the value of the firm's stock?

First, we need to compute the cash dividend payment for next year (D_1). Applying Equation 8.3 for $t = 1$ yields the following:

$$D_1 = D_0 \times (1 + g) = \$4.81 \times (1 + 0.04) = \$4.81 \times 1.04 = \$5.00$$

Next, we apply Equation 8.4 to compute the value of the firm's stock, which is $35.71 per share:

$$
\begin{aligned}
P_0 &= \frac{D_1}{R - g} \\
&= \frac{\$5.00}{0.18 - 0.04} \\
&= \frac{\$5.00}{0.14} \\
&= \$35.71
\end{aligned}
$$

Big Red Grows Faster

LEARNING BY DOING

APPLICATION 8.2

PROBLEM: Using the information given in the text, compute the value of Big Red's stock if dividends grow at 6 percent rather than 4 percent. Explain why the answer makes sense.

APPROACH: First compute the cash dividend payment for next year (D_1) using the 6 percent growth rate (g) in Equation 8.3. Then apply Equation 8.4 to solve for the firm's stock price.

SOLUTION:

$$
\begin{aligned}
D_1 &= D_0 \times (1 + g) \\
D_1 &= \$4.81 \times 1.06 = \$5.10 \\
P_0 &= \frac{D_1}{R - g} \\
P_0 &= \frac{\$5.10}{0.18 - 0.06} = \frac{\$5.10}{0.12} = \$42.50
\end{aligned}
$$

The higher stock value of $42.50 is no surprise because dividends are now growing at a rate of 6 percent rather than 4 percent. Hence, the value of the cash payments to investors (dividends) is expected to be larger.

Computing Future Stock Prices

The constant-growth dividend model (Equation 8.4) can be modified to determine the value, or price, of a share of stock at any point in time. In general, the price of a share of stock, P_t, can be expressed in terms of the dividend in the next period (D_{t+1}), g, and R, when the dividends from D_{t+1} forward are expected to grow at a constant rate. Thus, the price of a share of stock at time t is as follows:

$$P_t = \frac{D_{t+1}}{R - g} \tag{8.5}$$

Notice that Equation 8.4 is just a special case of Equation 8.5 in which $t = 0$. To be sure that you understand this, set up Equation 8.5 to compute a stock's current price at $t = 0$. When you are done, the resulting equation should look exactly like Equation 8.4.

An example will illustrate how Equation 8.5 is used. Suppose that a firm has a current dividend (D_0) of $2.50, R is 15 percent, and g is 5 percent. What is the price of the stock today (P_0), and what will it be in five years (P_5)? To help visualize the problem, we will lay out a time line and identify some of the important variables necessary to solve the problem:

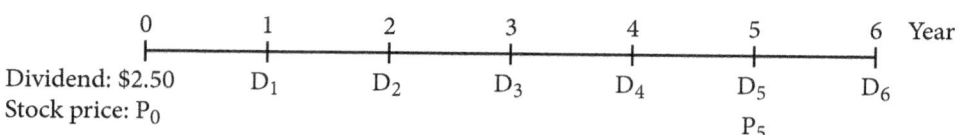

To find the current stock price, we can apply Equation 8.4, but we must first compute the dividend for the next period (D_1), which is at $t = 1$. Using Equation 8.3, we compute the firm's dividend for next year:

$$D_1 = D_0 \times (1 + g) = \$2.50 \times 1.05 = \$2.625$$

Now we can use Equation 8.4 to find the price of the stock today:

$$P_0 = \frac{D_1}{R - g} = \frac{\$2.625}{0.15 - 0.05} = \frac{\$2.625}{0.10} = \$26.25$$

We next find the value of the stock in five years. In this situation Equation 8.5 is expressed as:

$$P_5 = \frac{D_6}{R - g}$$

We need to compute D_6, and we do so by using Equation 8.3:

$$D_6 = D_0 \times (1 + g)^6 = 2.50 \times (1.05)^6 = 2.50 \times 1.34 = \$3.35$$

The price of the stock in five years is therefore:

$$P_5 = \frac{\$3.35}{0.15 - 0.05} = \frac{\$3.35}{0.10} = \$33.50$$

Finally, note that $\$33.50/(1.05)^5 = \$26.25$, which is the value today.

A P P L I C A T I O N   8 . 3

Procter & Gamble's Current Stock Price

PROBLEM: Suppose that the current cash dividend on Procter & Gamble's common stock is $1.84. Financial analysts expect the dividends to grow at a constant rate of 5 percent per year, and investors require an 8 percent return on stocks with the same level of risk. What should be the current price of a share of Procter & Gamble stock?

APPROACH: In this scenario, $D_0 = \$1.84$, R = 0.08, and $g = 0.05$. We first compute D_1 using Equation 8.3. We then calculate the value of a share using Equation 8.4.

SOLUTION:

$$\text{Dividend: } D_1 = D_0 \times (1 + g) = \$1.84 \times 1.05 = \$1.93$$

$$\text{Value of a share: } P_0 = \frac{D_1}{R - g} = \frac{\$1.93}{0.08 - 0.05} = \frac{\$1.93}{0.03} = \$64.33$$

Procter & Gamble's Future Stock Price

PROBLEM: Continuing the example in Learning by Doing Application 8.3, what should Procter & Gamble's stock price be seven years from now (P_7)?

APPROACH: This is an application of Equation 8.5. We first must calculate Procter & Gamble's dividend in period 8, using Equation 8.3. Then we can apply Equation 8.5 to compute the estimated price of the stock seven years in the future.

SOLUTION:

Dividend in period 8: $D_8 = D_0 \times (1 + g)^8 = \$1.93 \times (1.05)^8 = \$1.93 \times 1.477 = \$2.85$

Price of a share in 7 years: $P_7 = \dfrac{D_8}{R - g} = \dfrac{\$2.85}{0.08 - 0.05} = \dfrac{\$2.85}{0.03} = \$95.00$

The Relation between R and g

We previously mentioned that the divided growth model provides valid solutions only when $g < R$. Students frequently ask what happens to Equation 8.4 or 8.5 if this condition does not hold (if $g \geq R$). Mathematically, as g approaches R, the stock price becomes larger and larger, and when $g = R$, the value of the stock is infinite, which is, of course, nonsense. When the growth rate (g) is larger than the discount rate (R), the constant-growth dividend model tells us that the value of the stock is negative. However, this is not possible. The value of a share of stock can never be negative because, as we discussed in Section 1.2, stockholders have limited liability.

From a practical perspective, the growth rate in the constant-growth dividend model cannot be greater than the sum of the long-term rate of inflation and the long-term real growth rate of the economy. Since this model assumes that the firm will grow at a constant rate forever, any growth rate that is greater than this sum would imply that the firm will eventually take over the entire economy. Of course, we know this is not possible. Since the sum of the long-term rate of inflation and the long-term real growth rate has historically been less than 6 to 7 percent, the growth rate (g) is virtually always less than the discount rate (R) for the stocks that we would want to use the constant-growth dividend model to value.

It is possible for firms to grow faster than the long-term rate of inflation plus the real growth rate of the economy—just not forever. A firm that is growing at such a high rate is said to be growing at a supernormal growth rate. We must use a different model to value the stock of a firm like this. We discuss one such model next.

Mixed (Supernormal) Growth Dividend Model

For many firms, it is not appropriate to assume that dividends will grow at a constant rate. Firms typically go through life cycles and, as a result, exhibit different dividend patterns over time.

During the early part of their lives, successful firms experience a supernormal rate of growth in earnings. These firms tend to pay lower dividends or no dividends at all because many good investment projects are available to them and management wants to reinvest earnings in the firm to take advantage of these opportunities. If a growth firm does not pay regular dividends, investors receive their returns from capital appreciation of the firm's stock (which reflects increases in expected future dividends), from a cash or stock payout if the firm is acquired, or possibly from a large special cash dividend. As a firm matures, it will settle into a growth rate at or below the long-term rate of inflation plus the long-term real growth rate of the economy. When a firm reaches this stage, it will often be paying a fairly predictable regular dividend.

Exhibit 8.3 shows several dividend growth patterns. In the top curve, dividends exhibit a supernormal growth rate of 25 percent for four years, then a more sustainable nominal growth rate of 5 percent (this might, for example, be made up of 2.5 percent growth from inflation plus a 2.5 percent real growth rate). By comparison, the remaining curves show dividends with a constant nominal growth rate of 5 percent, a zero-growth rate, and a negative 10 percent growth rate. In

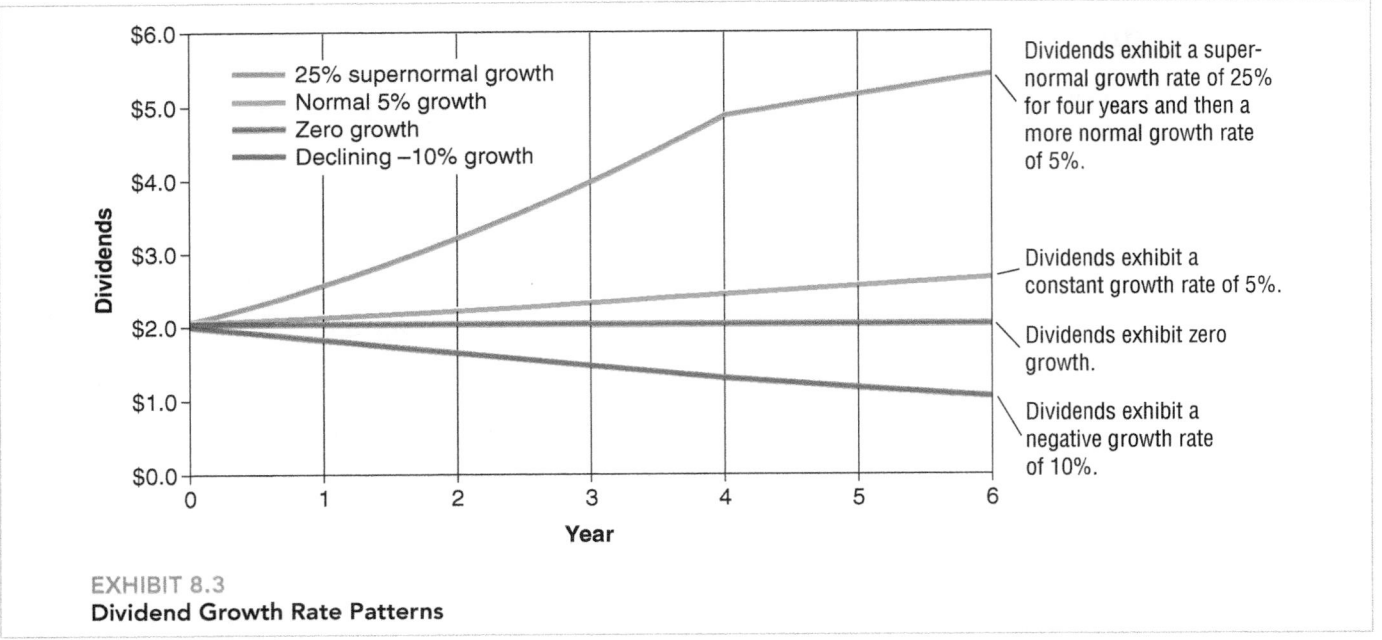

EXHIBIT 8.3
Dividend Growth Rate Patterns

addition to the constant growth rates illustrated in Exhibit 8.3, it is also possible for the dividend growth rate to vary during the early years. We refer to this as a mixed dividend growth pattern.

As mentioned earlier, successful companies often experience supernormal growth early in their life cycles. During the last decade, for example, firms such as Google, Facebook, and Netflix have experienced supernormal growth. Older companies that reinvent themselves with new products or strategies may also experience periods of supernormal growth. In the early 2000s, Steve Jobs repositioned Apple from primarily a manufacturer of computers into a firm that is now also a market leader in the manufacture of telecommunications devices and music players, and in the sale of digital music. Under Job's leadership, Apple's stock generated huge returns for investors, rising from less than $10 per share in 2003 to $666.80 per share on October 4, 2012.[1]

To value a share of stock for a firm with a mixed (supernormal) dividend growth pattern, we do not have to develop any new equations. Instead, we can apply Equation 8.1, our general dividend model, and Equation 8.5, which gives us the price of a share of stock with constant dividend growth at any point in time.

We will illustrate with an example. Suppose a company's expected dividend pattern for three years is as follows: $D_1 = \$1$, $D_2 = \$2$, $D_3 = \$3$. After three years, the dividends are expected to grow at a constant rate of 6 percent a year. What should the current price (P_0) of the firm's stock be if the required rate of return demanded by investors is 15 percent?

We begin by drawing a time line, as shown in Exhibit 8.4. We recommend that you prepare a time line whenever you solve a problem with a complex dividend pattern so that you can

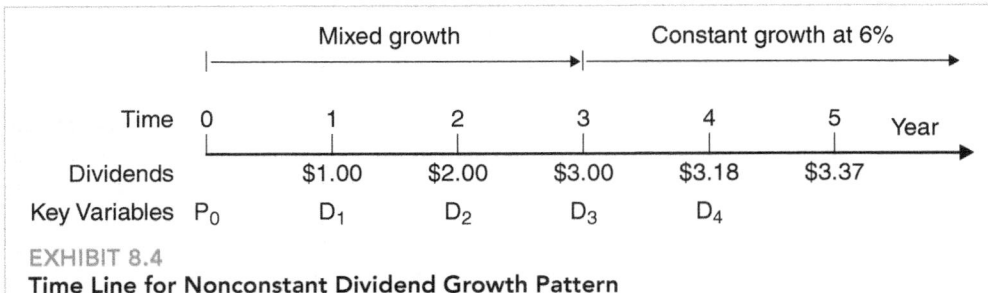

EXHIBIT 8.4
Time Line for Nonconstant Dividend Growth Pattern

The exhibit shows a time line for a nonconstant dividend growth pattern. The time line makes it easy to see that we have two different dividend growth patterns. For three years, the dividends are expected to grow at a mixed rate; after that, they are expected to grow at a constant rate of 6 percent.

---

[1] Steve Job's unfortunate death on October 5, 2012 raised the question of whether Steve's successor, Tim Cook, would be able to maintain the company's leadership position in its industry.

be sure the cash flows are placed in the proper time periods. The critical element in working these problems is to correctly identify when the constant growth starts and to value it properly.

Looking at Exhibit 8.4, it is easy to see that we have two different dividend patterns: (1) D_1 through D_3 represent a mixed dividend growth pattern, which can be valued using Equation 8.1, the general dividend-valuation model. (2) After the third year, dividends grow at a constant rate of 6 percent and can be valued using Equation 8.5, the constant-growth dividend-valuation model. Thus, our valuation model is:

$$P_0 = PV(\text{Mixed dividend growth}) + PV(\text{Constant dividend growth})$$

Combining these present values yields the following formula:

$$P_0 = \underbrace{\frac{D_1}{(1 + R)} + \frac{D_2}{(1 + R)^2} + \frac{D_3}{(1 + R)^3}}_{\substack{\text{PV of mixed-growth} \\ \text{dividend payments}}} + \underbrace{\frac{P_3}{(1 + R)^3}}_{\substack{\text{Value of constant-growth} \\ \text{dividend payments}}}$$

The value of the constant-growth dividend stream is P_3, which is the value, or price, at time $t = 3$. More specifically, P_3 is the value of the future cash dividends discounted to time period $t = 3$. With a required rate of return of 15%, the value of these dividends is calculated as follows:

$$D_4 = D_3 \times (1 + g) = \$3.00 \times 1.06 = \$3.18$$

$$P_3 = \frac{D_4}{R - g} = \frac{\$3.18}{0.15 - 0.06}$$

$$= \frac{\$3.18}{0.09}$$

$$= \$35.33$$

We find the value of P_3 using Equation 8.5, which allows us to compute stock prices in the future for stocks with constant dividend growth. Note that the equation gives us the value, as of year 3, of a constant-growth perpetuity that begins in year 4. This formula always gives us the value as of one period before the first cash flow.

Now, since P_3 is at time period $t = 3$, we must discount it back to the present ($t = 0$). This is accomplished by dividing P_3 by $(1 + R)^3$.

Plugging the values for the dividends, P_3, and R into the above mixed-growth equation results in the following:

$$P_0 = \frac{\$1.00}{1.15} + \frac{\$2.00}{(1.15)^2} + \frac{\$3.00}{(1.15)^3} + \frac{\$35.33}{(1.15)^3}$$

$$= \$0.87 + \$1.51 + \$1.97 + \$23.23$$

$$= \$27.58$$

Thus, the value of the stock is $27.58.

We can write a general equation for the mixed (supernormal) growth situation, where dividends grow first at a mixed or high constant rate until period t, and then at a constant rate thereafter, as follows:

$$P_0 = \frac{D_1}{1 + R} + \frac{D_2}{(1 + R)^2} + \cdots + \frac{D_t}{(1 + R)^t} + \frac{P_t}{(1 + R)^t} \tag{8.6}$$

If the mixed or high growth period ends and dividends grow at a constant rate, g, then P_t can be calculated using Equation 8.5:

$$P_t = \frac{D_{t+1}}{R - g}$$

The two preceding equations can also be applied when dividends are constant over time, since we know that $g = 0$ is just a special case of the constant-growth dividend model ($g > 0$).

Let's look at another example, this time using Equation 8.6. Suppose that Redteck is a high-tech medical device firm located in Lincoln, Nebraska. The company is three years old and has experienced spectacular growth since its inception. You are a financial analyst for a stock brokerage firm and have just returned from a two-day visit to the company. You learned that Redteck plans to pay no dividends for the next five years. In year 6, management plans to pay a large, special cash dividend, which you estimate to be $25 per share. Then, beginning in year 7, management plans to pay a constant annual dividend of $6 per share for the foreseeable future. The appropriate discount rate for the stock is 12 percent, and the current market price is $25 per share. Your boss doesn't think the stock is worth the price. You think that it's a bargain and that you should recommend it to the firm's clients. Who is right?

Our first step in answering this question is to lay out the expected dividend payments on a time line:

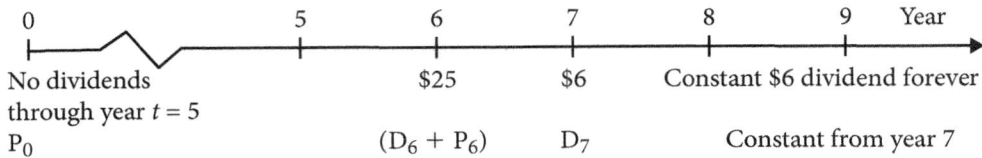

Equation 8.6, the mixed (supernormal) dividend model, can be used to determine the value of the stock. There are two different dividend cash streams: (1) the mixed dividends, which in this case comprise a single dividend paid in year 6 (Equation 8.1), and (2) the constant dividend stream ($g = 0$) of $6 per year forever (Equation 8.5). The value of the common stock can be computed as follows:

$$P_0 = PV(\text{Mixed dividend growth}) + PV(\text{Constant dividends with no growth})$$

Applying Equation 8.6 to the cash flows presented in the problem yields:

$$P_0 = \frac{D_1}{1 + R} + \frac{D_2}{(1 + R)^2} + \cdots + \frac{D_t}{(1 + R)^t} + \frac{P_t}{(1 + R)^t}$$

$$= \frac{D_6}{(1 + R)^6} + \frac{P_6}{(1 + R)^6}$$

$$= \frac{D_6 + P_6}{(1 + R)^6}$$

Note that the first term in the second line computes the present value of the large $25 dividend paid in year 6. In the second term, P_6 is the discounted value of the constant $6 dividend payments made in perpetuity, as of period $t = 6$. To compute the present value of P_6, we divide it by the appropriate discount factor, which is $(1 + R)^6$.

Plugging the data given earlier into the above equation yields:

$$P_0 = \frac{\$25 + P_6}{(1.12)^6}$$

We can see from this relation that we still need to compute the value of P_6 using Equation 8.5:

$$P_t = \frac{D_{t+1}}{R - g}$$

Equation 8.5 is easy to apply since the dividend payments remain constant over time. Since $D_{t+1} = \$6$ and $g = 0$, P_6 is calculated as follows:

$$P_6 = \frac{D_7}{R - g} = \frac{\$6}{0.12 - 0} = \frac{\$6}{0.12}$$

$$= \$50$$

and the calculation for P_0 is, therefore:

$$P_0 = \frac{\$25 + \$50}{(1.12)^6}$$

$$= \frac{\$75}{1.9738}$$

$$= \$38.00$$

The stock's current market price is $25, and if your estimates of dividend payments are correct, the stock's value is $38 per share. This suggests that the stock is a bargain and that your boss is incorrect.

> **BEFORE YOU GO ON**

1. What three different models are used to value stocks based on different dividend patterns?

2. Explain why the growth rate g must always be less than the rate of return R.

8.4 VALUING PREFERRED STOCK

LEARNING OBJECTIVE 6

As mentioned earlier in this chapter, preferred stocks are hybrid securities, falling someplace between bonds and common stock. For example, preferred stock has a higher-priority claim on the firm's assets than common stock but a lower-priority claim than the firm's creditors in the event of default. In computing the value of preferred stock, however, the critical issue is whether the preferred stock has a fixed maturity. If the preferred stock contract has a sinking fund that calls for the mandatory retirement of the stock over a scheduled period of time, financial analysts will tend to treat the stock as if it were a bond with a fixed maturity.

The most significant difference between preferred stock with a fixed maturity and a bond is the risk of default. Bond coupon payments are a legal obligation of the firm, and failure to pay them results in default, whereas preferred stock dividends are declared by the board of directors, and failure to pay dividends does not result in default. Even though it is not a legal default, the failure to pay a preferred stock dividend as promised is not a trivial event. It is a noteworthy financial breach which can signal to the market that the firm is in serious financial difficulty. As a result, managers make every effort to pay preferred stock dividends as promised.

 Riskglossary.com offers a good discussion of preferred stock, including its valuation. Go to http://www.riskglossary.com/link/preferred_stock.htm.

Preferred Stock with a Fixed Maturity

Because preferred stock with a fixed maturity is considered similar to a bond, we can use the bond valuation model developed in Chapter 7 to determine its price, or value. Applying Equation 7.2 requires only that we recognize that the coupon payments (C) are equivalent to dividend payments (D) and the preferred stock dividends are paid quarterly. Thus, Equation 7.2 can be restated as the price of a share of preferred stock (PS_0):

$$\text{Preferred stock price} = \text{PV(Dividend payments)} + \text{PV(Par value)}$$

$$PS_0 = \frac{D/m}{1 + i/m} + \frac{D/m}{(1 + i/m)^2} + \frac{D/m}{(1 + i/m)^3} + \cdots + \frac{D/m + P_{mn}}{(1 + i/m)^{mn}} \qquad (8.7)$$

where:

D = the annual preferred stock dividend payment
P = the stated (par) value of the preferred stock
i = the yield to maturity of the preferred stock
m = the number of times dividend payments are made each year
n = the number of years to maturity

For preferred stock with quarterly dividend payments, m equals 4.

Consider an example of how this equation is used. Suppose that a utility company's preferred stock has an annual dividend payment of $10 (paid quarterly), a stated (par) value of $100, and a maturity of 20 years owing to a sinking fund requirement. If similar preferred stock issues have market yields of 8 percent, what is the value of the preferred stock?

First, we convert the data to quarterly compounding as follows: (1) the market yield is 2 percent quarterly (8 percent per year/4 quarters per year = 2 percent per quarter), (2) the dividend payment is $2.50 quarterly ($10 per year/4 quarters per year = $2.50 per quarter), and (3) the total number of dividend payments is 80 (4 payments per year × 20 years = 80 payments). Plugging the data into Equation 8.7, we find that the value of the preferred stock is:

$$PS_0 = \frac{\$2.50}{1.02} + \frac{\$2.50}{(1.02)^2} + \cdots + \frac{\$102.50}{(1.02)^{80}}$$

$$= \$119.87$$

We can, of course, also solve this problem on a financial calculator. The keystrokes are as follows:

Enter   80   2   2.50   100

N   i   PV   PMT   FV

Answer   −119.87

Computing the Yield on Preferred Stock

PROBLEM: San Diego Gas and Electric (SDG&E) has a preferred stock issue outstanding that has a stated value of $100, will be retired by the company in 15 years, and pays a $2 dividend each quarter. If the preferred stock is currently selling for $95, what is the stock's yield to maturity?

APPROACH: We compute the yield to maturity on this preferred stock in exactly the same way we compute the yield to maturity on a bond. We already know that the quarterly dividend rate is $2, but we must convert the number of periods to allow for quarterly compounding. The total number of compounding periods is 60 (4 periods per year × 15 years = 60 periods). Using Equation 8.7, we can enter the data and find i, the stock's yield to maturity through trial and error. Alternatively, we can solve the problem easily on a financial calculator.

SOLUTION: Applying Equation 8.7:

$$\$95 = \frac{\$2}{1+i} + \frac{\$2}{(1+i)^2} + \frac{\$2}{(1+i)^3} + \cdots + \frac{\$102}{(1+i)^{60}}$$

Financial calculator steps:

Enter   60   −95   2   100

N   i   PV   PMT   FV

Answer   2.15

The preferred stock's yield is 2.15 percent per quarter, and the annual yield is 8.60 percent (2.15 percent per quarter × 4 quarters per year = 8.60 percent per year).

LEARNING BY DOING

APPLICATION 8.5

NEED MORE HELP?

WileyPLUS

Preferred Stock with No Maturity

Some preferred stock issues have no maturity. These securities have dividends that are constant over time ($g = 0$) and that go on forever. Thus, these preferred stocks can be valued as perpetuities, using Equation 8.2:

$$P_0 = \frac{D}{R}$$

where D is a constant cash dividend and R is the interest rate, or required rate of return.

Let's work an example. Suppose that Delta Airlines has a perpetual preferred stock issue that pays a dividend of $5 per year and that investors require an 8 percent return on such an investment. What is the value of the preferred stock? Applying Equation 8.2, we find that the value is:

$$P_0 = \frac{D}{R} = \frac{\$5.00}{0.08} = \$62.50$$

> **BEFORE YOU GO ON**

1. Why can skipping payment of a preferred dividend be a bad signal?

2. How is a preferred stock with a fixed maturity valued?

SUMMARY OF **Learning Objectives**

1 List and describe the four types of secondary markets.

The four types of secondary markets are (1) direct search, (2) broker, (3) dealer, and (4) auction. In direct search markets, buyers and sellers seek out each other directly. In broker markets, brokers bring together buyers and sellers for a fee. Trades in dealer markets go through dealers who buy securities at one price and sell at a higher price. The dealers face the risk that prices could decline while they own the securities. Auction markets have a fixed location where buyers and sellers confront each other directly and bargain over the transaction price.

2 Explain why many financial analysts treat preferred stock as a special type of bond rather than as an equity security.

Preferred stock represents ownership in a corporation and entitles the owner to a dividend, which must be paid before dividends are paid to common stockholders. Similar to bonds, preferred stock issues have credit ratings, are sometimes convertible to common stock, and are often callable. Unlike owners of common stock, owners of nonconvertible preferred stock do not have voting rights and do not participate in the firm's profits beyond the fixed dividends they receive. It is because of their strong similarity to bonds that many financial analysts treat preferred stock which are not true perpetuities as a form of debt rather than equity.

3 Describe how the general dividend-valuation model values a share of stock.

The general dividend-valuation model values a share of stock as the present value of all future cash dividend payments, where the dividend payments are discounted using the rate of return required by investors for investments with a similar level of risk.

4 Discuss the assumptions that are necessary to make the general dividend-valuation model easier to use, and use the model to compute the value of a firm's stock.

The problems with the general dividend-valuation model are that future dividends are uncertain and some companies do not pay dividends at all. To make the model easier to apply, we make

assumptions about the dividend payment patterns of firms. These simplifying assumptions allow the development of more manageable models, and they also conform with the actual dividend policies of many firms. Dividend patterns include the following: (1) Dividends are constant (zero growth), as computed in Learning by Doing Application 8.1. (2) Dividends have a constant-growth pattern (they grow forever at a constant rate g), as computed in Learning by Doing Application 8.2. (3) Dividends grow first at a nonconstant rate rather than at a constant rate, as computed in the Redteck example at the end of Section 8.3.

5 Explain why g must be less than R in the constant-growth dividend model.

The constant-growth dividend model assumes that dividends will grow at a constant rate forever. With the constant-growth model, if $g = R$, the value of the denominator is zero and the value of the stock is infinite, which of course is nonsense. If $g > R$, the value of the denominator is negative, as is the value of the stock, which also does not make economic sense. Thus, g must always be less than R ($g < R$).

6 Explain how valuing preferred stock with a stated maturity differs from valuing preferred stock with no maturity, and calculate the price of a share of preferred stock under both conditions.

When preferred stock has a stated maturity, financial analysts value it as they value any other fixed obligation—that is, like a bond. To value such preferred stock, we can use the bond valuation model from Chapter 7. Before using the model, we need to recognize that we will be using dividends in the place of coupon payments and that the stated (par) value of the preferred stock will replace the par value of the bond. In addition, while bond coupons are paid semiannually in the United States, preferred dividends are paid quarterly. When a preferred stock has no stated maturity, it becomes a perpetuity, with the dividend becoming a constant payment that goes on forever. We use the perpetuity valuation model represented by Equation 8.2 to price such stocks. The calculations appear in Learning by Doing Application 8.5 and the Delta Airlines example at the end of Section 8.4.

SUMMARY OF **Key Equations**

Equation	Description	Formula
8.1	General dividend valuation model	$P_0 = \dfrac{D_1}{1+R} + \dfrac{D_2}{(1+R)^2} + \dfrac{D_3}{(1+R)^3} + \dfrac{D_4}{(1+R)^4} + \dfrac{D_5}{(1+R)^5} + \cdots + \dfrac{D_\infty}{(1+R)^\infty}$ $= \displaystyle\sum_{t=1}^{\infty} \dfrac{D_t}{(1+R)^t}$
8.2	Zero-growth dividend model	$P_0 = \dfrac{D}{R}$
8.3	Value of a dividend at time t with constant-growth	$D_t = D_0 \times (1+g)^t$

8.4	Constant-growth dividend model	$P_0 = \dfrac{D_1}{R - g}$
8.5	Value of a stock at time t when dividends grow at a constant rate	$P_t = \dfrac{D_{t+1}}{R - g}$
8.6	Mixed (supernormal) growth dividend model	$P_0 = \dfrac{D_1}{1 + R} + \dfrac{D_2}{(1 + R)^2} + \cdots + \dfrac{D_t}{(1 + R)^t} + \dfrac{P_t}{(1 + R)^t}$
8.7	Value of preferred stock with a fixed maturity	$PS_0 = \dfrac{D/m}{1 + i/m} + \dfrac{D/m}{(1 + i/m)^2} + \dfrac{D/m}{(1 + i/m)^3} + \cdots + \dfrac{D/m + P_{mn}}{(1 + i/m)^{mn}}$

Self-Study Problems

8.1 Ted McKay has just bought the common stock of Ryland Corp. The company expects to grow at the following rates for the next three years: 30 percent, 25 percent, and 15 percent. Last year the company paid a dividend of $2.50. Assume a required rate of return of 10 percent. Compute the expected dividends for the next three years and also the present value of these dividends.

8.2 Merriweather Manufacturing Company has been growing at a rate of 6 percent for the past two years, and the company's CEO expects it to continue to grow at this rate for the next several years. The company paid a dividend of $1.20 last year. If your required rate of return is 14 percent, what is the maximum price that you would be willing to pay for this company's stock?

8.3 Clarion Corp. has been selling electrical supplies for the past 20 years. The company's product line has changed very little in the past five years, and the company's management does not expect to add any new items for the foreseeable future. Last year, the company paid a dividend of $4.45 to its common stockholders. The company is not expected to increase its dividends for the next several years. If your required rate of return for such firms is 13 percent, what is the current value of this company's stock?

8.4 Barrymore Infotech is a fast-growing communications company. The company did not pay a dividend last year and is not expected to do so for the next two years. Last year the company's growth accelerated, and management expects to grow the business at a rate of 35 percent for the next five years before growth slows to a more stable rate of 7 percent. In the third year, management has forecasted a dividend payment of $1.10. Dividends will grow with the company thereafter. Calculate the value of the company's stock at the end of its rapid growth period (i.e., at the end of five years). The required rate of return for such stocks is 17 percent. What is the current value of this stock?

8.5 You are interested in buying the preferred stock of a bank that pays a dividend of $1.80 every quarter. If you discount such cash flows at 8 percent, what is the value of this stock?

Solutions to Self-Study Problems

8.1 Expected dividends for Ryland Corp and their present value:

$g_1 = 30\%$ $\qquad g_2 = 25\%$ $\qquad g_3 = 15\%$

$D_1 = D_0 \times (1 + g_1) = \$2.50 \times (1 + 0.30) = \$3.25$
$D_2 = D_1 \times (1 + g_2) = \$3.25 \times (1 + 0.25) = \$4.06$
$D_3 = D_2 \times (1 + g_3) = \$4.06 \times (1 + 0.15) = \$4.67$

Present value of the dividends $= PV(D_1) + PV(D_2) + PV(D_3)$

$\qquad\qquad = \$2.96 + \$3.36 + \$3.51$

$\qquad\qquad = \$9.83$

8.2 Present value of Merriweather stock:

$g = 6\%$

$D_1 = D_0 \times (1 + g)$
$\quad = \$1.20 \times (1 + 0.06)$
$\quad = \$1.27$

$P_0 = \dfrac{D_1}{R - g}$

$\quad = \dfrac{\$1.27}{0.14 - 0.06}$

$\quad = \$15.88$

The maximum price you should be willing to pay for this stock is \$15.88.

8.3 Present value of Clarion Corp. stock:

$g = 0\%$

Since the company's dividends are not expected to grow,

$D_0 = D_1 = D_2 = \ldots = D_\infty = \$4.45 = D$

Current value of the stock $= \dfrac{D}{R}$

$\qquad\qquad\qquad\qquad = \$4.45/0.13$

$\qquad\qquad\qquad\qquad = \$34.23$

8.4 Present value of Barrymore Infotech stock:

g_1 to $g_5 = 35\%$ $\qquad\qquad g_6$ and beyond $= 7\%$

$D_0 = D_1 = D_2 = 0$
$D_3 = \$1.100$
$D_4 = D_3 \times (1 + g_4) = \$1.10 \ \times (1 + 0.35) = \$1.485$
$D_5 = D_4 \times (1 + g_5) = \$1.485 \times (1 + 0.35) = \$2.005$
$D_6 = D_5 \times (1 + g_6) = \$2.005 \times (1 + 0.07) = \$2.145$

Value of stock at $t = 5$:

$$P_5 = \dfrac{D_6}{R - g}$$

$$\quad = \dfrac{\$2.145}{0.17 - 0.07}$$

$$\quad = \$21.45$$

Present value of the dividends in years 1 to 5 $= PV(D_1) + PV(D_2) + PV(D_3) + PV(D_4) + PV(D_5)$
$\qquad\qquad\qquad\qquad\qquad\qquad\qquad\quad = \$0 + \$0 + \$0.69 + \$0.79 + \ \$0.91$
$\qquad\qquad\qquad\qquad\qquad\qquad\qquad\quad = \$2.39$

Current value of stock:

$$P_0 = PV(\text{Dividends}) + PV(P_5)$$

$$\quad = \$2.39 + \dfrac{\$21.45}{(1.17)^5}$$

$$\quad = \$2.39 + \$9.78$$

$$\quad = \$12.17$$

8.5 Present value of bank preferred stock:

Quarterly dividend on preferred stock = D = $1.80
Required rate of return = 8%
Current value of stock:

$$P_0 = \frac{D}{R}$$
$$= \frac{\$1.80 \times 4}{0.08}$$
$$= \$90.00$$

Critical Thinking Questions

8.1 Why can the market price of a stock differ from its true (intrinsic) value?

8.2 Why are investors and managers concerned about stock market efficiency?

8.3 Why are common stockholders considered to be more at risk than the holders of other types of securities?

8.4 Under what conditions does it make sense to use the constant-growth dividend model to value a stock?

8.5 What does it mean when a company has a very high P/E ratio? Give examples of industries in which you believe high P/E ratios are justified.

8.6 Explain why preferred stock is considered to be a hybrid of equity and debt securities.

8.7 Why is stock valuation more difficult than bond valuation?

8.8 You are currently thinking about investing in a stock valued at $25.00 per share. The stock recently paid a dividend of $2.25 and its dividend is expected to grow at a rate of 5 percent for the foreseeable future. You normally require a return of 14 percent on stocks of similar risk. Is the stock overpriced, underpriced, or correctly priced?

8.9 Stock A and Stock B are both priced at $50 per share. Stock A has a P/E ratio of 17, while Stock B has a P/E ratio of 24. Which is the more attractive investment, considering everything else to be the same, and why?

8.10 Facebook does not pay dividends. How can it have a positive stock price?

Questions and Problems

BASIC ▶ **8.1** **Stock market index:** What is a stock market index?

8.2 **Stock market index:** What is the Dow Jones Industrial Average?

8.3 **Stock market index:** What does NASDAQ stand for? What is NASDAQ?

8.4 **Dividend yield:** What is a dividend yield? What does it tell us?

8.5 **Present value of dividends:** Fresno Corp. is a fast-growing company whose management expects it to grow at a rate of 30 percent over the next two years and then to slow to a growth rate of 18 percent for the following three years. If the last dividend paid by the company was $2.15, estimate the dividends for the next five years. Compute the present value of these dividends if the required rate of return is 14 percent.

8.6 **Zero growth:** Nynet, Inc., paid a dividend of $4.18 last year. The company's management does not expect to increase its dividend in the foreseeable future. If the required rate of return is 18.5 percent, what is the current value of the stock?

8.7 **Zero growth:** Knight Supply Corp. has not grown for the past several years, and management expects this lack of growth to continue. The firm last paid a dividend of $3.56. If you require a rate of return of 13 percent, what is the current value of this stock to you?

8.8 **Zero growth:** Ron Santana is interested in buying the stock of First National Bank. While the bank's management expects no growth in the near future, Ron is attracted by the dividend income. Last year the bank paid a dividend of $5.65. If Ron requires a return of 14 percent on such stocks, what is the maximum price he should be willing to pay for a share of the bank's stock?

8.9 **Zero growth:** The current stock price of Largent, Inc., is $44.72. If the required rate of return is 19 percent, what is the dividend paid by this firm if the dividend is not expected to grow in the future?

8.10 Constant growth: Moriband Corp. paid a dividend of $2.15 yesterday. The company's dividend is expected to grow at a steady rate of 5 percent for the foreseeable future. If investors in stocks of companies like Moriband require a rate of return of 15 percent, what should be the market price of Moriband stock?

8.11 Constant growth: Nyeil, Inc., is a consumer products firm that is growing at a constant rate of 6.5 percent. The firm's last dividend was $3.36. If the required rate of return is 18 percent, what is the market value of this stock if dividends grow at the same rate as the firm?

8.12 Constant growth: Reco Corp. is expected to pay a dividend of $2.25 next year. The forecast for the stock price a year from now is $37.50. If the required rate of return is 14 percent, what is the current stock price? Assume constant growth.

8.13 Constant growth: Proxicam, Inc., is expected to grow at a constant rate of 7 percent. If the company's next dividend, which will be paid in a year, is $1.15 and its current stock price is $22.35, what is the required rate of return on this stock?

8.14 Preferred stock valuation: X-Centric Energy Company has issued perpetual preferred stock with a stated (par) value of $100 and a dividend of 4.5 percent. If the required rate of return is 8.25 percent, what is the stock's current market price?

8.15 Preferred stock valuation: The First Bank of Ellicott City has issued perpetual preferred stock with a $100 par value. The bank pays a quarterly dividend of $1.65 on this stock. What is the current price of this preferred stock given a required rate of return of 11.6 percent?

8.16 Preferred stock valuation: The preferred stock of Axim Corp. is currently selling at $47.13. If the required rate of return is 12.2 percent, what is the dividend paid by this stock?

8.17 Preferred stock valuation: Each quarter, Sirkota, Inc., pays a dividend on its perpetual preferred stock. Today the stock is selling at $63.37. If the required rate of return for such stocks is 15.5 percent, what is the quarterly dividend paid by this firm?

8.18 Constant growth: Kay Williams is interested in purchasing the common stock of Reckers, Inc., < INTERMEDIATE which is currently priced at $37.45. The company is expected to pay a dividend of $2.58 next year and to increase its dividend at a constant rate of 7 percent.
  a. What should the market value of the stock be if the required rate of return is 14 percent?
  b. Is this a good buy? Why or why not?

8.19 Constant growth: The required rate of return is 23 percent. Ninex Corp. has just paid a dividend of $3.12 and is expected to increase its dividend at a constant rate of 5 percent. What is the expected price of the stock three years from now?

8.20 Constant growth: Jenny Banks is interested in buying the stock of Fervan, Inc., which is increasing its dividends at a constant rate of 6 percent. Last year the firm paid a dividend of $2.65. The required rate of return is 16 percent. What is the current value of this stock? What should be the price of the stock in year 5?

8.21 Constant growth: You own shares of Old World DVD Company and are interested in selling them. With so many people downloading music these days, sales, profits, and dividends at Old World have been declining 6 percent per year. The firm just paid a dividend of $1.15 per share. The required rate of return for a stock this risky is 15 percent. If dividends are expected to decline at 6 percent per year, what is a share of the stock worth today?

8.22 Nonconstant growth: You own a company that competes with Old World DVD Company (in the previous problem). Instead of selling DVDs, however, your company sells music downloads from a Web site. Things are going well now, but you know that it is only a matter of time before someone comes up with a better way to distribute music. Your company just paid a $1.50 per share dividend, and you expect to increase the dividend 10 percent next year. However, you then expect your dividend growth rate to begin going down—to 5 percent the following year, 2 percent the next year, and to -3 percent per year thereafter. Based upon these estimates, what is the value of a share of your company's stock? Assume that the required rate of return is 12 percent.

8.23 Nonconstant growth: Tre-Bien, Inc., is a fast-growing technology company. Management projects rapid growth of 30 percent for the next two years, then a growth rate of 17 percent for the following two years. After that, a constant-growth rate of 8 percent is expected. The firm expects to pay its first dividend of $2.45 a year from now. If dividends will grow at the same rate as the firm and the required rate of return on stocks with similar risk is 22 percent, what is the current value of the stock?

8.24 Nonconstant growth: Management of ProCor, a biotech firm, forecasted the following growth rates for the next three years: 35 percent, 28 percent, and 22 percent. Management then expects the company to grow at a constant rate of 9 percent forever. The company paid a dividend of $1.75 last week. If the required rate of return is 20 percent, what is the value of this stock?

8.25 Nonconstant growth: Revarop, Inc., is a fast-growth company that is expected to grow at a rate of 23 percent for the next four years. It is then expected to grow at a constant rate of 6 percent. Revarop's first dividend, of $4.25, will be paid in year 3. If the required rate of return is 17 percent, what is the current value of the stock if dividends are expected to grow at the same rate as the company?

8.26 Nonconstant growth: Quansi, Inc., management expects to pay no dividends for the next six years. It has projected a growth rate of 25 percent for the next seven years. After seven years, the firm will grow at a constant rate of 5 percent. Its first dividend, to be paid in year 7, will be $3.25. If the required rate of return is 24 percent, what is the stock worth today?

8.27 Nonconstant growth: Staggert Corp. will pay dividends of $5.00, $6.25, $4.75, and $3.00 in the next four years. Thereafter, management expects the dividend growth rate to be constant at 6 percent. If the required rate of return is 18.5 percent, what is the current value of the stock?

8.28 Nonconstant growth: Diaz Corp. is expected to grow rapidly at a rate of 35 percent for the next seven years. The company's first dividend, to be paid three years from now, will be $5. After seven years, the company (and the dividends it pays) will grow at a rate of 8.5 percent. What is the value of Diaz stock with a required rate of return of 14 percent?

8.29 Nonconstant growth: Tin-Tin Waste Management, Inc., is growing rapidly. Dividends are expected to grow at rates of 30 percent, 35 percent, 25 percent, and 18 percent over the next four years. Thereafter, management expects dividends to grow at a constant rate of 7 percent. The stock is currently selling at $47.85, and the required rate of return is 16 percent. Compute the dividend for the current year (D_0).

ADVANCED > **8.30** Equation 8.4 shows the relation between a stock's value and the dividend that is expected next year if dividends grow at a constant rate forever. If a firm pays all of its earnings as dividends, show how Equation 8.4 can be rearranged to calculate that firm's P/E ratio. What does this tell us about the factors that determine a firm's P/E ratio?

8.31 Riker Departmental Stores management has forecasted a growth rate of 40 percent for the next two years, followed by growth rates of 25 percent and 20 percent for the following two years. It then expects growth to stabilize at a constant rate of 7.5 percent forever. The firm paid a dividend of $3.50 recently. If the required rate of return is 18 percent, what is the current value of Riker's stock?

8.32 Courtesy Bancorp issued perpetual preferred stock a few years ago. The bank pays an annual dividend of $4.27 and your required rate of return is 12.2 percent.
a. What is the value of the stock given your required rate of return?
b. Should you buy this stock if its current market price is $34.41? Explain.

8.33 Rhea Kirby owns shares in Ryoko Corp. Currently, the market price of the stock is $36.34. Management expects dividends to grow at a constant rate of 6 percent for the foreseeable future. Its last dividend was $3.25. Rhea's required rate of return for such stocks is 16 percent. She wants to find out whether she should sell her shares or add to her holdings.
a. What is the value of this stock?
b. Based on your answer to part a, should Rhea buy additional shares in Ryoko Corp? Why or why not?

8.34 Perry, Inc., paid a dividend of $2.50 yesterday. You are interested in investing in this company, which has forecasted a constant-growth rate of 7 percent for its dividends, forever. The required rate of return is 18 percent.
a. Compute the expected dividends D_1, D_2, D_3, and D_4.
b. Compute the present value of these four dividends.
c. What is the expected value of the stock four years from now (P_4)?
d. What is the value of the stock today based on the answers to parts b and c?
e. Use the equation for constant growth (Equation 8.4) to compute the value of the stock today.

8.35 Zweite Pharma is a fast-growing drug company. Management forecasts that in the next three years, the company's dividend growth rates will be 30 percent, 28 percent, and 24 percent, respectively. Last week it paid a dividend of $1.67. After three years, management expects dividend growth to stabilize at a rate of 8 percent. The required rate of return is 14 percent.
a. Compute the dividends for each of the next three years, and calculate their present value.
b. Calculate the price of the stock at the end of year 3, when the firm settles to a constant-growth rate.
c. What is the current price of the stock?

8.36 Triton Inc., is expected to grow at a rate of 22 percent for the next five years and then settle to a constant growth rate of 6 percent. The company recently paid a dividend of $2.35. The required rate of return is 15 percent.
  a. Find the present value of the dividends during the rapid-growth period if dividends grow at the same rate as the company.
  b. What is the value of the stock at the end of year 5?
  c. What is the value of the stock today?

8.37 Ceebros Builders is expanding very fast and is expected to grow at a rate of 25 percent for the next four years. The company recently paid a dividend of $3.60 but is not expected to pay any dividends for the next three years. In year 4, management expects to pay a $5 dividend and thereafter to increase the dividend at a constant rate of 6 percent. The required rate of return on such stocks is 20 percent.
  a. Calculate the present value of the dividends during the fast-growth period.
  b. What is the value of the stock at the end of the fast-growth period (P_4)?
  c. What is the value of the stock today?
  d. Would today's stock value be affected by the length of time you intend to hold the stock?

Sample Test Problems

8.1 Mason Corp. is a manufacturer of consumer staples and has experienced no growth for the past five years while paying a dividend of $3.50 every year. The CFO expects the firm to have no growth and for dividends to remain constant for the foreseeable future. If the required rate of return is 10 percent, what should be the price of this stock today?

8.2 Bucknell, Inc., recently paid a dividend of $2.10. Management forecasts dividend growth of 6 percent per year for the foreseeable future. What is the value of the stock today with a discount rate of 13 percent?

8.3 Bradley Corp. is growing at a constant rate of 7.2 percent every year. Last week the company paid a dividend of $1.85. If dividends are expected to grow at the same rate as the firm and the required rate of return is 15 percent, what should be the stock's price four years from now?

8.4 Wichita Technologies is expected to grow at a rate of 35 percent for the next three years and then stabilize with annual growth of 7 percent. The company will pay no dividend for the first two years and will pay a dividend of $1.25 in year 3. What will be the value of the company's stock when the company's supernormal growth ends? What is the value of the stock today? Assume that dividends will grow at the same rate as the firm once Wichita starts paying them. The required rate of return is 12 percent.

8.5 UNC Bancorp has issued preferred stock with no maturity date. It has a par value of $100 and pays a quarterly dividend of $2.25. If the required rate of return is 8 percent, what is the value of the stock today?

INSIDER TRADING: Have I Got a Stock Tip for You!

Everyone would like to get a stock tip that will yield a huge return on a small investment. That's human nature. But stock tips can be mixed blessings. Consider the following example: Dr. Sam Waksal developed a promising cancer drug called Erbitux. As the CEO of ImClone, Waksal was an entrepreneur as well as an immunologist. Waksal sold an interest in Erbitux to the pharmaceutical company Bristol Myers for $42 million.

Ramin Talaie/Corbis Images

It was a Bristol Myers executive who informed Waksal that the Federal Drug Administration (FDA) was not going to approve the drug because there were insufficient data to determine its effectiveness; thus, new clinical trials were needed. Investors had expected approval, and once the FDA decision was made public, ImClone stock was certain to face a sharp decline in price. At least in the short term, some people were going to lose a lot of money.

One of those people was, of course, Waksal himself. He had millions of shares of ImClone. So did his family. Waksal told his daughter and father to sell their shares. In addition, Waksal transferred 79,000 of his own shares to his daughter to sell. Waksal knew that it was illegal under federal law for him or his family members to trade on inside information. And in the end, all three were indicted and later convicted of violating federal security laws.

Waksal was guilty of insider trading. As we pointed out in Chapter 1, insider trading results from information asymmetry, which arises when one party in a business transaction has information that is unavailable to the other parties in the transaction. To be legally actionable, insider trading must involve information that has not been publicly announced, as you might expect. In addition, the information must be material. *Material* means that the information will cause a significant change in the stock price—the price will go either up or down as a result of the event the information concerns. Examples of material corporate events include the introduction of a new product line, an acquisition, a divestiture, a key executive appointment, and the failure or success of a product under development.

Martha Stewart Enters the Picture

Waksal's conviction is not the only part of this story. Waksal was friends with the celebrity Martha Stewart, who also owned ImClone stock. On the day before the negative FDA announcement, Stewart sold 4,000 shares of ImClone worth $230,000. Did Stewart sell her shares on the basis of inside information regarding the FDA decision? Stewart's sale certainly looked suspicious, and the Securities and Exchange Commission (SEC) started an investigation and asked her to explain her sale. In her discussions with the SEC, Stewart did not admit to insider trading.

Stewart claimed that she had a prearranged order in place to sell her ImClone stock when it dipped below $60 per share. The stock did dip below $60 the day before the FDA announcement. Federal prosecutors, however, alleged that she and her broker, Peter Bacanovic, had doctored stock transaction records to support her story. In the SEC indictment, it was clear that they did not believe her explanation.

It is also interesting to note that Stewart is not alleged to have received a tip from Waksal himself. Indeed, she contacted Waksal only after the sale, when she called him to ask what was happening to the company. However, it is alleged that her broker, Bacanovic, received a tip that Waksal and his daughter had placed orders to sell shares of ImClone.

Martha Stewart was eventually convicted in a criminal trial, but convicted of what? The most serious charges, which involved securities fraud and insider trading, were thrown out of court. She was convicted only of lying to investigators. However, Stewart was also charged in a civil suit, and in that suit the insider trading charge would have been allowed in court. After serving a jail term, Stewart eventually reached an agreement with the SEC to settle the insider trading accusations. Under the agreement, she had to pay $195,000, covering her gains from the trading and penalties, although she did not admit to any wrongdoing.

Conclusions

What can we conclude about insider trading? The ethical issues can be analyzed at two levels: At the institutional level, we can ask whether the insider trading laws are ethical. At the individual level, we can ask why a person would engage in this illegal behavior.

Institutional Level. Fairness is the ethical basis of the insider trading laws. If the competitive system is to work, it must operate on an even playing field. If insiders have material financial information not available to the public, then the playing field is not level. Note what the SEC said in its press release: "It is fundamentally unfair for someone to have an edge on the market just because she has a stock-broker who is willing to break the rules and give her an illegal tip. It's worse still when the individual engaging in the insider trading is the Chairman and CEO of a public company." However, not everyone is convinced by this argument. Using a utilitarian framework, others argue that persons acting on insider information bring information to the market more quickly and thus make the market more efficient for the benefit of all.

Both sides have a point. One of the keystone propositions of efficient financial markets is that no participant should possess a significant *unfair* advantage over others. If you believe that the deck of cards is stacked against you and that some people who trade have access to inside information, you will collect your money and invest it elsewhere. Conversely, without inside information, there would be little reason for trading securities. Unless you know some information that affects securities' prices that others do not know, why trade? Furthermore, how would information relevant to security prices be released to the market unless some traded on that information?

The bottom line is that too much or too little inside information trading seems to be detrimental to financial markets. The critical question is how much inside information is optimal. There is no consensus among economists on an answer.

Individual Level. At the individual level, we must evaluate the motivation of the inside traders. Waksal, for example, knew that insider trading was illegal. Why did he do it? In an interview on CBS's *60 Minutes*, Waksal admitted that he did not think that he would get caught. Investigation showed that Waksal had been guilty of a number of ethical lapses in his life. He had been dismissed from a number of academic and research positions for questionable conduct. Aristotle would say he had a weak character. If Stewart had not tried to obscure what she did and simply told the truth to investigators, most legal experts are convinced she would not have been convicted of anything.

DISCUSSION QUESTIONS

1. Discuss whether it would be unethical to buy a stock based on some information you found in the trash that had been thrown away by mistake.
2. Suppose you are the printer who has been given the job of preparing the official announcement of the FDA report. Can you use that information for personal gain? Why or why not?
3. Some argue that insider trading brings information to the market more quickly and thus is morally acceptable on the grounds of efficiency. Do you agree with that argument? Why or why not?

Sources: Press release from Securities and Exchange Commission, June 4, 2003; *CBS News*, www.cbsnews.com/2005/19/02/60minutes/main576328.shtml; CNNMoney.com, money.cnn.com/2004/03/05/news/companies/martha_verdict; Landon Thomas, Jr., "The Return of Martha Stewart, the Civil Case." *New York Times*, May 25, 2006, Section C, p. 1; and Landon Thomas, Jr., "Stewart Deal Resolves Stock Case," *New York Times*, August 8, 2006, www.nytimes.com/2006/08/08/business.

9 The Fundamentals of Capital Budgeting

AFP/Getty Images, Inc.

CHAPTER NINE

..... Learning Objectives

1. Discuss why capital budgeting decisions are the most important investment decisions made by a firm's management.

2. Explain the benefits of using the net present value (NPV) method to analyze capital expenditure decisions and calculate the NPV for a capital project.

3. Describe the strengths and weaknesses of the payback period as a capital expenditure decision-making tool and compute the payback period for a capital project.

4. Explain why the accounting rate of return (ARR) is not recommended for use as a capital expenditure decision-making tool.

5. Compute the internal rate of return (IRR) for a capital project and discuss the conditions under which the IRR technique and the NPV technique produce different results.

6. Explain how the profitability index can be used to rank projects when a firm faces capital rationing and describe the limitations that apply to the profitability index.

7. Explain the benefits of postaudit and ongoing reviews of capital projects.

In October 2010, Intel Corporation's newly built 300-mm wafer fabrication plant in Dalian, China, began regular production. The Dalian plant is Intel's first chipset factory in Asia and is part of a network of eight such facilities worldwide. A $2.5 billion project that was expected to eventually employ 4,000 people, the Dalian plant is Intel's single largest investment in China.

Even before construction of the fabrication plant was completed, Intel was developing plans for a $3.5 billion addition to the project. This second phase would consist of investments in supporting facilities, including four assembly and testing plants, an R&D center, and a sales division. To place the anticipated $6.0 billion cost of the two Dalian project phases in perspective, Intel's total worldwide capital expenditures during fiscal year 2008 were $5.2 billion.

Intel's investment in the Dalian fabrication plant illustrates not only the large amount of corporate resources that can be committed to a major capital project, but also the strategic importance such an investment can have. When the project was originally announced in March 2007, Intel's president and CEO, Paul Otellini, pointed out that China was Intel's fastest-growing major market. It was imperative, said Otellini, that Intel make investments in markets that provide for future growth.

The Dalian project involves significant risks for Intel. Construction of the fabrication plant was a three-year endeavor that unexpectedly coincided with a worldwide financial and economic crisis. A project of Dalian's scale represented a potential source of excess capacity for Intel as the growth in demand for chipsets declined worldwide during 2008 and 2009. In addition, political or economic instability in China could have severe financial consequences for Intel.

While few companies make capital investments as large as Intel's investment in Dalian, China, all companies must routinely invest capital in projects that are critical to their success. These investment opportunities must be carefully scrutinized, and their costs and benefits carefully weighed. How do firms make these important capital budgeting decisions? In this chapter we examine this decision-making process and introduce some financial models used to make investment decisions.

CHAPTER PREVIEW

This chapter is about capital budgeting, a topic we first visited in Chapter 1. Capital budgeting is the process of deciding which capital investments the firm should make.

We begin the chapter with a discussion of the types of capital projects that firms undertake and how the capital budgeting process is managed within the firm. When making capital investment decisions, management's goal is to select projects that will increase the value of the firm.

Next we examine some of the techniques used to evaluate capital budgeting decisions. We first discuss the net present value (NPV) method, which is the capital budgeting approach recommended in this book. The NPV method takes into account the time value of money and provides a direct measure of how much a capital project will increase the value of the firm.

We then examine the payback method and the accounting rate of return. As methods of selecting capital projects, both of these have some serious deficiencies. We also discuss the internal rate of return (IRR), which is the expected rate of return for a capital project when the project's NPV is equal to zero. The IRR is a very popular and important alternative to the NPV technique. However, in certain circumstances, the IRR can lead to incorrect decisions. We next discuss how to select projects when there is not enough money to invest in all attractive projects. Finally, we present evidence on which techniques financial managers actually use when making capital budgeting decisions.

9.1 AN INTRODUCTION TO CAPITAL BUDGETING

We begin with an overview of capital budgeting, followed by a discussion of some important concepts you will need to understand in this and later chapters.

LEARNING OBJECTIVE 1

The Importance of Capital Budgeting

Capital budgeting decisions are the most important investment decisions made by management. The objective of these decisions is to select investments in productive assets that will increase the value of the firm. These investments *create value* when they are worth more than they cost. Capital investments are important because they can involve substantial cash outlays and, once made, are not easily reversed. They also define what the company is all about—the firm's lines of business and its inherent business risk. For better or worse, capital investments produce most of a typical firm's revenues for years to come.

Capital budgeting *techniques* help management systematically analyze potential business opportunities in order to decide which are worth undertaking. As you will see, not all capital budgeting techniques are equal. The best techniques are those that determine the value of a capital project by discounting all of the cash flows generated by the project and thus account for the time value of money.

In the final analysis, capital budgeting is really about management's search for the best capital projects—those that add the greatest value to the firm. Over the long term, the most

capital budgeting
the process of choosing the productive assets in which the firm will invest

successful firms are those whose managements consistently search for and find capital investment opportunities that increase firm value.

The Capital Budgeting Process

The capital budgeting process starts with a firm's strategic plan, which spells out its strategy for the next three to five years. Division managers then convert the firm's strategic objectives into business plans. These plans have a one- to two-year time horizon, provide a detailed description of what each division should accomplish during the period covered by the plan, and have quantifiable targets that each division is expected to achieve. Behind each division's business plan is a capital budget that details the resources management believes it needs to get the job done.

The capital budget is generally prepared jointly by the CFO's staff and financial staffs at the divisional and lower levels and reflects, in large part, the activities outlined in the divisional business plans. Many of these proposed expenditures are routine in nature, such as the repair or purchase of new equipment at existing facilities. Less frequently, firms face broader strategic decisions, such as whether to launch a new product, build a new plant, enter a new market, or buy a business. Exhibit 9.1 identifies some reasons that firms initiate capital projects.

EXHIBIT 9.1 Key Reasons for Making Capital Expenditures

Capital budgeting decisions are the most important investment decisions made by management. Many of these decisions are routine in nature, but from time to time, managers face broader strategic decisions that call for significant capital investments.

Reason	Description
Renewal:	Over time, equipment must be repaired, overhauled, rebuilt, or retrofitted with new technology to keep the firm's manufacturing or service operations going. For example, a company that has a fleet of delivery trucks may decide to overhaul the trucks and their engines rather than purchase new trucks. Renewal decisions typically do not require an elaborate analysis and are made on a routine basis.
Replacement:	At some point, an asset will have to be replaced rather than repaired or overhauled. The major decision is whether to replace the asset with a similar piece of equipment or purchase equipment that would require a change in the production process. Sometimes, replacement decisions involve equipment that is operating satisfactorily but has become obsolete. The new or retrofitted equipment may provide cost savings with respect to labor or material usage and/or may improve product quality. These decisions typically originate at the plant level.
Expansion:	Strategically, the most important motive for capital expenditures is to expand the level of operating output. One type of expansion decision involves increasing the output of existing products. This may mean new equipment to produce more products or expansion of the firm's distribution system. These types of decisions typically require a more complex analysis than a renewal or replacement decision. Another type of expansion decision involves producing a new product or entering a new market. This type of expansion often involves large dollar amounts and significant business risk and requires the approval of the firm's board of directors.
Regulatory:	Some capital expenditures are required by federal and state regulations. These mandatory expenditures usually involve meeting workplace safety standards and environmental standards.
Other:	This category includes items such as parking facilities, office buildings, and executive aircraft. Many of these capital expenditures are hard to analyze because it is difficult to estimate their cash inflows. Ultimately, the decisions can be more subjective than analytical.

Sources of Information

Where does management get all of the information it needs to make capital budgeting decisions? Most of the information is generated within the firm, and, for expansion decisions, it often starts with sales representatives and marketing managers who are in the marketplace talking to potential and current customers on a day-to-day basis. For example, a sales manager with a new product idea might present the idea to management. If the product looks promising, the firm's marketing research group will estimate the size of the market and a market price. If the product requires new technology, the firm's research and development group must decide whether to develop the technology or to buy it. Next, cost accountants and production engineers will determine the cost of producing the product and any capital expenditures necessary to manufacture it. Finally, the CFO's staff will take the data and estimate the total cost of the project and the cash flows it will generate over time. The project is a viable candidate for the capital budget if the present value of the expected cash benefits exceeds the present value of the project's cost.

Classification of Investment Projects

Potential capital budgeting projects can be classified into three types: (1) independent projects, (2) mutually exclusive projects, and (3) contingent projects.

Independent Projects

Projects are independent when their cash flows are unrelated. With **independent projects**, accepting or rejecting one project does not eliminate other projects from consideration (assuming the firm has unlimited funds to invest). For example, suppose a firm has unlimited funding and management wants to (1) build a new parking ramp at its headquarters; (2) acquire a small competitor; and (3) add manufacturing capacity to one of its plants. Since the cash flows for each project are unrelated, accepting or rejecting one of the projects will have no effect on the others.

independent projects
projects whose cash flows are unrelated

Mutually Exclusive Projects

When projects are mutually exclusive, acceptance of one project precludes acceptance of others. Typically, **mutually exclusive projects** perform the same function, and thus only one project needs to be accepted. For example, when BMW decided to manufacture automobiles in the United States, it considered three possible manufacturing sites (or capital projects). Once BMW management selected the Spartanburg, South Carolina, site, the other two possible locations were out of the running. Since some projects are mutually exclusive, it is very important that a capital budgeting method allow us to choose the best project when we are faced with two or more alternatives.

mutually exclusive projects
projects for which acceptance of one precludes acceptance of the other

Contingent Projects

With **contingent projects**, the acceptance of one project is contingent on the acceptance of another. There are two types of contingency situations. In the first type of situation, the contingent product is *mandatory*. For example, when a public utility company (such as your local electric company) builds a power plant, it must also invest in suitable pollution control equipment to meet federal environmental standards. The pollution control investment is a mandatory contingent project. When faced with mandatory contingent projects, it is best to treat all of the projects as a single investment for the purpose of evaluation. This provides management with the best measure of the value created by these projects.

contingent projects
projects whose acceptance depends on the acceptance of other projects

In the second type of situation, the contingent project is *optional*. For example, suppose Dell invests in a new computer for the home market. This computer has a feature that allows Dell to bundle a proprietary gaming system. The gaming system is a contingent project but is an optional add-on to the new computer. In these situations, the optional contingent project should be evaluated *independently* and should be accepted or rejected on its own merits.

Basic Capital Budgeting Terms

In this section we briefly introduce two terms that you will need to be familiar with—*cost of capital* and *capital rationing*.

Cost of Capital

cost of capital
the required rate of return for a capital investment

The **cost of capital** is the rate of return that a capital project must earn to be accepted by management. The cost of capital can be thought of as an opportunity cost. Recall from Chapter 7 that an *opportunity cost* is the value of the most valuable alternative given up if a particular investment is made.

> **BUILDING INTUITION**
>
> **INVESTMENT DECISIONS HAVE OPPORTUNITY COSTS**
>
> When any investment is made, the opportunity to earn a return from an alternative investment is lost. The lost return can be viewed as a cost that arises from a lost opportunity. For this reason, it is called an *opportunity cost*. The opportunity cost of capital is the return an investor gives up when his or her money is invested in one asset rather than the best alternative asset. For example, suppose that a firm invests in a piece of equipment rather than returning money to stockholders. If stockholders could have earned an annual return of 12 percent on a stock with cash flows that are as risky as the cash flows the equipment will produce, this is the opportunity cost of capital associated with the investment in the piece of equipment.

Let's consider the opportunity cost concept in the context of capital budgeting decisions. When investors buy shares of stock in a company or loan money to a company, they are giving management money to invest on their behalf. Thus, when a firm's management makes capital investments in productive assets such as plant and equipment they are investing *stockholders' and creditors' money* in *real assets*. Since stockholders and creditors could have invested their money in *financial assets*, the minimum rate of return they are willing to accept on an investment in a real asset is the rate they could have earned investing in financial assets that have similar risk. The rate of return that investors can earn on financial assets with similar risk is an *opportunity cost* because investors lose the opportunity to earn that rate if the money is invested in a real asset instead. It is therefore the rate of return that investors will require for an investment in a capital project. In other words, this rate is the cost of capital. It is also known as the **opportunity cost of capital**. Chapter 11 discusses how we estimate the opportunity cost of capital in practice.

opportunity cost of capital
the return an investor gives up when his or her money is invested in one asset rather than the best alternative asset

Capital Rationing

When a firm has all the money it needs to invest in all the capital projects that meet its capital selection criteria, the firm is said to be operating without a *funding constraint,* or *resource constraint.* Firms are rarely in this position, especially growth firms. Typically, a firm has a fixed number of dollars available for capital expenditures, and the number of qualified projects that need funding exceeds the funds that are available. This funding constraint on investments means that some projects will be mutually exclusive, since investing in one project exhausts resources that might otherwise be invested in another. When faced with a resource constraint, the firm must allocate its funds to the subset of projects that provides the largest increase in stockholder value. The process of limiting, or rationing, capital expenditures in this way is called **capital rationing**. Capital rationing and its implications for capital budgeting are discussed in Section 9.6.

capital rationing
a situation where a firm does not have enough capital to invest in all attractive projects and must therefore ration capital

> **▷ BEFORE YOU GO ON**
>
> 1. Why are capital investments the most important decisions made by a firm's management?
>
> 2. What are the differences between capital projects that are independent, mutually exclusive, and contingent?

9.2 NET PRESENT VALUE

In this section we discuss a capital budgeting method that is consistent with this goal of financial management—to maximize the wealth of the firm's owners. It is called the **net present value (NPV) method**, and it is one of the most basic analytical methods underlying corporate finance. The NPV method tells us the amount by which the benefits from a capital expenditure exceed its costs. It is the capital budgeting technique recommended in this book.

LEARNING OBJECTIVE 2

net present value (NPV) method
a method of evaluating a capital investment project that measures the difference between its cost and the present value of its expected cash flows

Valuation of Real Assets

Throughout this book, we have emphasized that the value of any asset is the present value of its future cash flows. In Chapters 7 and 8, we developed valuation models for financial assets, such as bonds, preferred stock, and common stock. We now extend our discussion of valuation models from financial to real assets. The steps used in valuing an asset are the same whether the asset is real or financial:

1. Estimate the expected future cash flows.
2. Determine the required rate of return, or discount rate, which depends on the riskiness of the future cash flows.
3. Compute the present value of the future cash flows to determine what the asset is worth.

The valuation of real assets, however, is less straightforward than the valuation of financial assets, for several reasons.

First, in many cases, cash flows for financial assets are well documented in a legal contract. If they are not, we are at least able to make some reasonable assumptions about what they are. For real assets, much less information exists. Specialists within the firm, usually from the finance, marketing, and production groups, often prepare estimates of expected future cash flows for capital projects with only limited information.

Second, many financial securities are traded in public markets, and these markets are reasonably efficient. Thus, market data on rates of return are accessible. For real assets, no such markets exist. As a result, we must estimate required rates of return on real assets (opportunity costs) from market data on financial assets; this can be difficult to do.

NPV—The Basic Concept

The NPV of a project is the difference between the present value of the project's expected future cash flows and the present value of its cost. The NPV can be expressed as follows:

$$\text{NPV} = \text{PV (Project's expected future cash flows)} - \text{PV (Cost of the project)}$$

WileyPLUS

CAPITAL BUDGETING: AN ANIMATED TUTORIAL

If a capital project has a positive NPV, the value of the cash flows the project is expected to generate exceeds the project's cost. Thus, a positive NPV project increases the value of the firm and, hence, stockholders' wealth. If a capital project has a negative NPV, the value of the expected cash flows from the project is less than its cost. If accepted, a negative NPV project will decrease the value of the firm and stockholders' wealth.

To illustrate these important points, consider an example. Suppose a firm is considering building a new marina for pleasure boats. The firm has a genie who can tell the future with perfect certainty. The finance staff estimates that the marina will cost $3.50 million. The genie volunteers that the present value of the future cash flows from the marina is $4.25 million.

Assuming this information is correct, the NPV for the marina project is a positive $750,000 ($4.25 million − $3.50 million = $0.75 million). Management should accept the project because the excess of the value of the cash flows over cost increases the value of the firm by $750,000. Why is a positive NPV a *direct* measure of how much a capital project will increase the value of the firm? If management wanted to, the firm could sell the marina for $4.25 million, pay the $3.50 million in expenses, and deposit $750,000 in the bank. The value of the firm would increase by the $750,000 deposited in the bank. In sum, the NPV method tells us which capital projects to select and how much value they add to the firm.

NPV and Value Creation

We have just stated that any project with a positive NPV should be accepted because it will increase the value of the firm. Let's take a moment to think about this proposition. What makes a capital asset worth more than it costs? In other words, how does management create value with capital investments?

How Value Is Created

Suppose that when you were in college, you worked part time at a successful pizza parlor near campus. During this time, you learned a lot about the pizza business. After graduation, for $100,000 you purchased a pizza parlor that was in a good location but had been forced to close because of a lack of business. The owners had let the restaurant and the quality of the pizzas deteriorate, and the wait staff had been rude to customers. Once you purchased the restaurant, you immediately invested $40,000 to fix it up: you painted the building, spruced up the interior, replaced some of the dining room furniture, and added an eye-catching, 1950s-style neon sign to attract attention. You also spent $15,000 for a one-time advertising blitz to quickly build a customer base. More important, you improved the quality of the pizzas you sold, and you built a profitable takeout business. Finally, you hired your wait staff carefully and trained them to be customer friendly.

Almost immediately the restaurant was earning a substantial profit and generating substantial cash flows. The really good news was that several owners of local pizzerias wanted to buy your restaurant. After intense negotiations with several of the potential buyers, you accepted a cash offer of $475,000 for the business shortly after you purchased it.

What is the NPV for the pizza parlor? For this investment, the NPV is easy to calculate. We do not need to estimate future cash flows and discount them because we already have an estimate of the present value of the cash flows the pizza parlor is expected to produce—$475,000. Someone is willing to pay you $475,000 because he or she believes the future cash flows are worth that amount. The cost of your investment includes the purchase price of the restaurant, the cost to fix it up, and the cost of the initial advertising campaign, which totals $155,000 ($100,000 + $40,000 + $15,000 = $155,000). Thus, the NPV for the pizza parlor is:

$$
\begin{aligned}
\text{NPV} &= \text{PV (Project's future cash flows)} - \text{PV (Cost of the project)} \\
&= \$475{,}000 - \$155{,}000 \\
&= \$320{,}000
\end{aligned}
$$

The $475,000 price paid for the pizza parlor exceeds the cost ($155,000) by $320,000. You have created $320,000 in value. How did you do this? You did it by improving the food, customer service, and dining ambiance while keeping prices competitive. Your management skills and knowledge of the pizza business resulted in significant growth in the current year's cash flows and the prospect of even larger cash flows in the future.

Where did the $320,000 in value you created go? The NPV of your investment is the amount that your personal net worth increased because of the investment. For an ongoing business, the result would have been a $320,000 increase in the value of the firm.

How about the original owners? Why would they sell a business worth $475,000 to you for $100,000? The answer is simple; if they could have transformed the business as you did, they would have done so. Instead, when they ran the business, it lost money! They sold it to you because you offered them a price reflecting its value to them.

Market Data versus Discounted Cash Flows

Our pizza parlor example is greatly simplified by the fact that we can observe the price that someone is willing to pay for the asset. In most capital project analyses, we have to estimate the market value of the asset by forecasting its future cash flows and discounting them by the cost of capital. The discounted value of a project's future cash flows is an estimate of its value, or the market price for which it can be sold.

Framework for Calculating NPV

We now describe a framework for analyzing capital budgeting decisions using the NPV method. As you will see, the NPV technique uses the discounted cash flow technique developed in

Time line	0	1	2	3	4	5 Year

Cash Flows:

Initial cost	$-CF_0$					
Cash inflows (CIF)		CIF_1	CIF_2	CIF_3	CIF_4	CIF_5
Cash outflows (COF)		$-COF_1$	$-COF_2$	$-COF_3$	$-COF_4$	$-COF_5$
Salvage value (SV)						SV
Net cash flow	$-NCF_0$	NCF_1	NCF_2	NCF_3	NCF_4	NCF_5

$$NPV = -NCF_0 + \sum_{t=1}^{5} \frac{NCF_t}{(1 + k)^t}$$

EXHIBIT 9.2

Sample Worksheet for Net Present Value Analysis

In addition to following the five-step framework for solving NPV analysis problems, we recommend that you use a worksheet with a time line like the one shown here to help you determine the proper cash flows for each period.

Chapter 5 and applied in Chapters 7 and 8. The good news, then, is that the NPV method requires only the application of what you already know.

The five-step framework discussed in this section and the accompanying cash flow worksheet (Exhibit 9.2) can help you systematically organize a project's cash flow data and compute its NPV. Most mistakes people make when working capital budgeting problems result from problems with cash flows: not identifying a cash flow, getting a cash flow in the wrong time period, or assigning the wrong sign to a cash flow. What can make cash flow analysis difficult in capital budgeting is this: there are often multiple cash flows in a single time period, and some are cash inflows and others are cash outflows.

As always, we recommend that you prepare a time line when doing capital budgeting problems. A sample time line is shown in Exhibit 9.2, along with an identification of the cash flows for each period. Our goal is to compute the net cash flow (NCF) for each time period t, where NCF_t = Total cash inflows − Total cash outflows for the period t. For a capital project, the time periods (t) are usually in years, and t varies from the current period ($t = 0$) to some finite time period that is the estimated life of the project ($t = n$). Recall that getting the correct sign on each cash flow is critical to getting the correct answer to a problem. As you have seen in earlier chapters, the convention in finance problem solving is that cash inflows carry a positive sign and cash outflows carry a negative sign. Finally, note that all cash flows in this chapter are on an after-tax basis. We will make adjustments for tax consequences on specific transactions such as the calculation of a project's salvage value.

Our five-step framework for analysis is as follows:

 CCH Business Owner's Toolkit is a valuable Web source for information about running a business, including capital budget analysis. Go to http://www.toolkit.cch .com/text/p06_6500.asp.

1. **Determine the initial cost of starting the project.** We first need to identify and add up all the cash flows related to the initial cost of starting the project. In most cases, the initial cost of a project is incurred at the start; hence the cash flows are already in current dollars. These cash flows typically include any property, plant, and equipment outlays for production as well as employee hiring and training costs. In some cases, like Intel's investment in the Dalian fabrication plant, these initial outlays can be made over several years before the project is up and running. Of course, any future cash flows must be discounted to obtain their present value. Turning to Exhibit 9.2, we have incurred a single negative cash flow ($-CF_0$) as our initial cost of starting the project; thus NCF_0 has a negative value.

2. **Estimate the project's future cash flows over its expected life.** Once they are up and running, capital projects typically generate some cash inflows from revenues (CIF_t) for each period, along with some cash outflows (COF_t) associated with costs incurred to generate the revenues. In most cases revenues exceed costs, and thus, NCF_t is positive. However, this may not always be the case. For example, if the project is the purchase of a piece of equipment, it is possible for NCF_3 to have a negative value ($CIF_3 < COF_3$) if the equipment is projected to need a major overhaul or must be replaced during the third year. Finally, you also need to pay attention to a project's final cash flow, which is $t = 5$ in Exhibit 9.2. There may be a salvage value (SV) at the end of the project, which is a cash inflow. In that case $NCF_5 = CIF_5 - COF_5 + SV$. The important point is that for each time period, we must identify all the cash flows that take place, assign each cash flow its proper sign, and add up all the cash flows.

3. **Determine the riskiness of the project and the appropriate cost of capital.** The third step is to identify for each project its risk-adjusted cost of capital, which takes into account the riskiness of the project's cash flows. The riskier the project, the higher its cost of capital. The cost of capital is the discount rate used in determining the present value of the future expected cash flows. In this chapter, the cost of capital and any risk adjustments will be supplied, and no calculations will be required for this step.

4. **Compute the project's NPV.** The NPV, as you know, is the present value of the net cash flows the project is expected to generate minus the cost of the project.

5. **Make a decision.** If the NPV is positive, the project should be accepted because all projects with a positive NPV will increase the value of the firm. If the NPV is negative, the project should be rejected; projects with negative NPVs will decrease the value of the firm.

You might be wondering about how to handle a capital project with an NPV of 0. Technically, management should be indifferent to accepting or rejecting projects such as this because they neither increase nor decrease the value of the firm. When the NPV = 0, the project is generating returns that are just equal to the opportunity cost of capital. At a practical level, projects rarely have an NPV equal to 0, and most firms have more good capital projects (with NPV > 0) than they can fund. Thus, this is not an issue that generates much interest among practitioners.

Net Present Value Techniques

The NPV of a capital project can be stated in equation form as the present value of all net cash flows (total cash inflows − total cash outflows) connected with the project, whether in the current period or in the future. The NPV equation can be written as follows:

$$\text{NPV} = \text{NCF}_0 + \frac{\text{NCF}_1}{1 + k} + \frac{\text{NCF}_2}{(1 + k)^2} + \cdots + \frac{\text{NCF}_n}{(1 + k)^n} \qquad (9.1)$$

$$= \sum_{t=0}^{n} \frac{\text{NCF}_t}{(1 + k)^t}$$

where:

NCF_t = net cash flow (total cash inflows − total cash outflows) in period t, where $t = 0, 1, 2, 3, \ldots, n$

k = the cost of capital

n = the project's estimated life

Next, we will work an example to see how the NPV is calculated for a capital project. Suppose you are the president of a small regional firm located in Chicago that manufactures frozen pizzas, which are sold to grocery stores and to firms in the hospitality and food service industry. Your market research group has developed an idea for a "pocket" pizza that can be used as an entrée with a meal or as an "on the go" snack. The sales manager believes that, with an aggressive advertising campaign, sales of the product will be about $300,000 per year. The cost to modify the existing production line will also be $300,000, according to the plant manager. The marketing and plant managers estimate that the cost to produce the pocket pizzas, to market and advertise them, and to deliver them to customers will be about $220,000 per year. The product's life is estimated to be five years, and the specialized equipment necessary for the project has an estimated salvage value of $30,000. The appropriate cost of capital is 15 percent.

When analyzing capital budgeting problems, we typically have a lot of data to sort through. The worksheet approach introduced in Exhibit 9.2 is helpful in keeping track of the data in an organized format. Exhibit 9.3 shows the time line and relevant cash flows for the pocket pizza project. The steps in analyzing the project's cash flows and determining its NPV are as follows:

1. *Determine the initial cost of starting the project.* The cost of the project is the cost to modify the existing production line, which is $300,000. This is a cash outflow (negative sign).

2. *Estimate the project's future cash flows over its expected life.* The project's future cash inflows come from sales of the new product. Sales are estimated at $300,000 per year (positive sign). The cash outflows are the costs to manufacture and distribute the new product, which are $220,000 per year (negative sign). The life of the project is five years. The project

Time line	0	1	2	3	4	5 Year

EXHIBIT 9.3
Pocket Pizza Project Time Line and Cash Flows ($ thousands)

Cash Flows:						
Initial cost	−$300					
Cash inflows		$300	$300	$300	$300	$300
Cash outflows		−$220	−$220	−$220	−$220	−$220
Salvage						$ 30
Net cash flow	−$300	$80	$80	$80	$80	$110

The worksheet approach introduced in Exhibit 9.2 is helpful in organizing the data given for the pocket pizza project.

has a salvage value of $30,000, which is a cash inflow (positive sign). The net cash flow (NCF) in a particular time period is just the sum of the cash inflows and cash outflows for that period. For example, the NCF for period $t = 0$ is −$300,000, the NCF for period $t = 1$ is $80,000, and so on, as you can see in Exhibit 9.3.

3. *Determine the riskiness of the project and the appropriate cost of capital.* The discount rate is the cost of capital, which is 15 percent.

4. *Compute the project's NPV.* To compute the project's NPV, we apply Equation 9.1 by plugging in the NCF values for each time period and using the cost of capital, 15 percent, as the discount rate. The equation looks like this (the figures are in thousands of dollars):

$$NPV = \sum_{t=0}^{n} \frac{NCF_t}{(1+k)^t}$$
$$= -\$300 + \frac{\$80}{1.15} + \frac{\$80}{(1.15)^2} + \frac{\$80}{(1.15)^3} + \frac{\$80}{(1.15)^4} + \frac{(\$80 + \$30)}{(1.15)^5}$$
$$= -\$300 + \$69.57 + \$60.49 + \$52.60 + \$45.74 + \$54.69$$
$$= -\$300 + \$283.09$$
$$= -\$16.91$$

The NPV for the pocket pizza project is therefore −$16,910.

5. *Make a decision.* The pocket pizza project has a negative NPV, which indicates that the project is not a good investment and should be rejected. If management undertook this project, the value of the firm would decrease by $16,910; and, if the firm had one hundred thousand shares of stock outstanding, we can estimate that the project would decrease the value of each share by about 17 cents ($16,910/100,000 shares = $0.1691 per share).

Calculating NPV with a Financial Calculator

Using a financial calculator is an easier way to calculate the present value of the future cash flows. In this example you should recognize that the cash flow pattern is a five-year ordinary annuity with an additional cash inflow in the fifth year. This is exactly the cash pattern for a bond with annual coupon payments and payment of principal at maturity we saw in Chapter 7. We can find the present value using a financial calculator, with $80 being the annuity stream for five years and $30 the salvage value at year 5:

Enter	5	15		80	30
	N	i	PV	PMT	FV
Answer			−283.09		

The PV of the future cash flows is −$283.09. With that information, we can compute the NPV using Equation 9.1 as follows:

$$NPV = \sum_{t=1}^{n} \frac{NCF_t}{(1+k)^t} - NCF_0$$
$$= \$283.09 - \$300.00$$
$$= -\$16.91$$

A P P L I C A T I O N   9 . 1

The Dough's Up: The Self-Rising Pizza Project

PROBLEM: Let's continue our frozen pizza example. Suppose the head of the research and development (R&D) group announces that R&D engineers have developed a breakthrough technology—self-rising frozen pizza dough that, when baked, rises and tastes exactly like fresh-baked dough.

The cost is $300,000 to modify the production line and the modifications will have a five year life. Sales of the new product are estimated at $200,000 for the first year, $300,000 for the next two years, and $500,000 for the final two years. It is estimated that production, sales, and advertising costs will be $250,000 for the first year and will then decline to a constant $200,000 per year. There is no salvage value at the end of the product's life, and the appropriate cost of capital is 15 percent. Is the project, as proposed, economically viable?

APPROACH: To solve the problem, work through the steps for NPV analysis given in the text.

SOLUTION: Exhibit 9.4 shows the project's cash flows.

1. The cost to modify the production line is $300,000, which is a cash outflow in Year 0 and the cost of the project.
2. The future cash flows over the expected life of the project are laid out on the time line in Exhibit 9.4. The project's life is five years. The NCFs for the capital project are negative at the beginning of the project and in the first year (−$300,000 and −$50,000) and thereafter are positive.
3. The appropriate cost of capital is 15 percent.
4. The values are substituted into Equation 9.1 to calculate the NPV:

$$NPV = NCF_0 + \frac{NCF_1}{1 + k} + \frac{NCF_2}{(1 + k)^2} + \cdots + \frac{NCF_n}{(1 + k)^n}$$

$$= -\$300,000 + \frac{-\$50,000}{1.15} + \frac{\$100,000}{(1.15)^2} + \frac{\$100,000}{(1.15)^3} + \frac{\$300,000}{(1.15)^4} + \frac{\$300,000}{(1.15)^5}$$

$$= -\$300,000 - \$43,478 + \$75,614 + \$65,752 + \$171,526 + \$149,153$$

$$= 118,567$$

5. The NPV for the self-rising pizza dough project is $118,567. Because the NPV is positive, management should accept the project. The project is estimated to increase the value of the firm by $118,567.

Time line	0	1	2	3	4	5 Year

Cash Flows:

	0	1	2	3	4	5
Initial cost	−$300					
Cash inflows		$200	$300	$300	$500	$500
Cash outflows		−$250	−$200	−$200	−$200	−$200
Salvage						
Net cash flow	−$300	−$50	$100	$100	$300	$300

EXHIBIT 9.4
Self-Rising Pizza Dough Project Time Line and Cash Flows ($ thousands)

The worksheet shows the time line and cash flows for the self-rising pizza dough project in Learning by Doing Application 9.1. As always, it is important to assign each cash flow to the appropriate year and to give it the proper sign. Once you have computed the net cash flow for each time period, solving for NPV is just a matter of plugging the data into the NPV formula.

NET PRESENT VALUE

Net present value problems are most commonly solved using a spreadsheet program. The program's design is good for keeping track of all the cash flows and the periods in which they occur. The spreadsheet setup for Learning by Doing Application 9.1, presented on the right, shows how to calculate the NPV for the self-rising pizza dough machine:

Notice that the NPV formula does not take into account the cash flow in year zero. Therefore, you only enter into the NPV formula the cash flows in years 1 through 5, along with the discount rate. You then add the cash flow in year zero to the total from the NPV formula calculation to get the NPV for the investment.

◇	A	B	C	D	E
1					
2		Net Present Value Calculations			
3					
4		Year		Cash Flow	
5		0		−$300,000	
6		1		−50,000	
7		2		100,000	
8		3		100,000	
9		4		300,000	
10		5		300,000	
11					
12		Cost of capital		0.15	
13					
14		NPV		$118,567	
15		Formula used		=NPV(D12, D6:D10)+D5	
16					

Mutually Exclusive Projects and NPV

Recall that investments are mutually exclusive if, by making one, another will not be undertaken. Projects may be mutually exclusive because they are substitutes for one another or because the firm has a funding constraint. A project's NPV provides an objective measure of its incremental value to the firm's investors, and thus makes it simple to choose between two or more mutually exclusive projects. When faced with such a choice, managers should allocate capital to the project that has the most positive dollar impact on the value of the firm—in other words, the project with the highest NPV.

The IS Department's Capital Projects

SITUATION: Suppose you are the manager of the information systems (IS) department of the frozen pizza manufacturer we have been discussing. Your department has identified four possible capital projects with the following NPVs: (1) $4,500, (2) $3,000, (3) $0.0, and (4) −$1,000. What should you decide about each project if the projects are independent? What should you decide if the projects are mutually exclusive?

DECISION: If the projects are independent, you should accept Projects 1 and 2, both of which have a positive NPV, and reject Project 4. Project 3, with an NPV of zero, could be either accepted or rejected without affecting the value of the firm. If the projects are mutually exclusive and you can accept only one of them, it should be Project 1, which has the largest NPV.

DECISION
MAKING

EXAMPLE 9.1

Concluding Comments on NPV

Some concluding comments about the NPV method are in order. First, as you may have noticed, the NPV computations are rather mechanical once we have estimated the cash flows and the cost of capital. The real difficulty is estimating or forecasting the future cash flows. Although this may seem to be a daunting task, managers with experience in producing and selling a particular type of product can usually generate fairly accurate estimates of sales volumes, prices, and production costs. Most business managers are routinely required to make decisions that involve expectations about future events. In fact, that is what business is really all about—dealing with uncertainty and making decisions that involve risk.

Second, estimating project cash flows over a long forecast period requires skill and judgment. There is nothing wrong with using estimates to make business decisions as long as they are based on informed judgments and not guesses. Problems can arise with the cash flow estimates when a project team becomes overly enamored with a project. In wanting a particular project to succeed, a project team can be too optimistic about the cash flow projections. It is therefore very important that capital budgeting decisions be subject to ongoing and post-audit review.

In conclusion, the NPV approach is the method we recommend for making capital investment decisions. It provides a direct (dollar) measure of how much a project will increase the value of the firm. NPV also makes it possible to correctly choose between mutually exclusive projects. The accompanying table summarizes NPV decision rules and the method's key advantages and disadvantages.

Summary of Net Present Value (NPV) Method

Decision Rule: NPV > 0 ⊳ Accept the project.
NPV < 0 ⊳ Reject the project.

Key Advantages	Key Disadvantage
1. Uses the discounted cash flow valuation technique to adjust for the time value of money.	1. Can be difficult to understand without an accounting and finance background.
2. Provides a direct (dollar) measure of how much a capital project will increase the value of the firm.	
3. Consistent with the goal of maximizing stockholder value.	

> **BEFORE YOU GO ON**

1. What is the NPV of a project?

2. If a firm accepts a project with a $10,000 NPV, what is the effect on the value of the firm?

3. What are the five steps used in NPV analysis?

9.3 THE PAYBACK PERIOD

 LEARNING OBJECTIVE

payback period
the length of time required to recover a project's initial cost

The payback period is one of the most widely used tools for evaluating capital projects. The **payback period** is defined as the number of years it takes for the cash flows from a project to recover the project's initial investment. With the payback method for evaluating projects, a project is accepted if its payback period is below some specified threshold. Although it has serious weaknesses, this method does provide some insight into a project's risk; the more quickly you recover the cash, the less risky is the project.

Computing the Payback Period

To compute the payback period, we need to know the project's cost and estimate its future net cash flows. The net cash flows and the project cost are the same values that we use to compute the NPV. The payback (PB) equation can be expressed as follows:

$$PB = \text{Years before cost recovery} + \frac{\text{Remaining cost to recover}}{\text{Cash flow during the year}} \qquad (9.2)$$

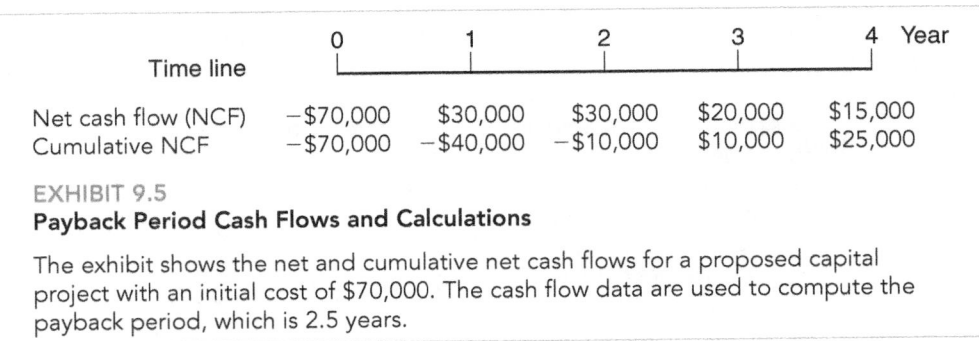

EXHIBIT 9.5
Payback Period Cash Flows and Calculations

The exhibit shows the net and cumulative net cash flows for a proposed capital project with an initial cost of $70,000. The cash flow data are used to compute the payback period, which is 2.5 years.

Exhibit 9.5 shows the net cash flows (row 1) and cumulative net cash flows (row 2) for a proposed capital project with an initial cost of $70,000. The payback period calculation for our example is:

$$PB = \text{Years before cost recovery} + \frac{\text{Remaining cost to recover}}{\text{Cash flow during the year}}$$

$$= 2 \text{ years} + \frac{\$70,000 - \$60,000}{\$20,000 \text{ per year}}$$

$$= 2 \text{ years} + \frac{\$10,000}{\$20,000 \text{ per year}}$$

$$= 2 \text{ years} + 0.5 \text{ years}$$

$$= 2.5 \text{ years}$$

Let's look at this calculation in more detail. Note in Exhibit 9.5 that the firm recovers cash flows of $30,000 in the first year and $30,000 in the second year, for a total of $60,000 over the two years. During the third year, the firm needs to recover only $10,000 ($70,000 − $60,000 = $10,000) to pay back the full cost of the project. The third-year cash flow is $20,000, so we will have to wait 0.5 year ($10,000/$20,000 = 0.5) to recover the final amount. Thus, the payback period for this project is 2.5 years (2 years + 0.5 year = 2.5 years).

The idea behind the payback period method is simple: the shorter the payback period, the faster the firm gets its money back and the more desirable the project. However, there is no economic rationale that links the payback method to stockholder value maximization. Firms that use the payback method accept all projects having a payback period under some threshold and reject those with a payback period over this threshold. If a firm has a number of projects that are mutually exclusive, the projects are selected in order of their payback rank: projects with the shortest payback period are selected first.

A Payback Calculation

PROBLEM: A firm has two capital projects, A and B, which are under review for funding. Both projects cost $500, and the projects have the following cash flows:

Year	Project A	Project B
0	−$500	−$500
1	100	400
2	200	300
3	200	200
4	400	100

What is the payback period for each project? If the projects are independent, which project should management select? If the projects are mutually exclusive, which project should management accept? The firm's payback cutoff point is two years.

APPROACH: Use Equation 9.2 to calculate the number of years it takes for the cash flows from each project to recover the project's initial investment. If the two projects are independent, you should accept the projects that have a payback period that is less than or equal to two years. If the projects are mutually exclusive, you should accept the project with the shortest payback period if that payback period is less than or equal to two years.

(continued)

LEARNING BY DOING

APPLICATION 9.2

NEED MORE HELP?
WileyPLUS

SOLUTION: Computing the payback for Project A requires only that we calculate the first term in Equation 9.2—Years before recovery: the first year recovers $100, the second year $200, and the third year $200, for a total of $500 ($100 + $200 + $200 = $500). Thus, in three years, the $500 investment is fully recovered, so PB_A = 3.00 years.

For Project B, the first year recovers $400 and the second year $300. Since we need only part of the second-year cash flow to recover the initial cost, we calculate both terms in Equation 9.2 to obtain the payback period.

$$PB = \text{Years before cost recovery} + \frac{\text{Remaining cost to recover}}{\text{Cash flow during the year}}$$

$$PB_A = 3 \text{ years}$$

$$PB_B = 1 \text{ year} + \frac{\$500 - \$400}{\$300 \text{ per year}}$$

$$= 1 \text{ year} + \frac{\$100}{\$300 \text{ per year}}$$

$$= 1.33 \text{ years}$$

Whether the projects are independent or mutually exclusive, management should accept only Project B since Project A's payback period exceeds the two-year cutoff point.

How the Payback Period Performs

We have worked through some simple examples of how the payback period is computed. Now we will consider several more complex situations to see how well the payback period performs as a capital budgeting rule. Exhibit 9.6 illustrates five different capital budgeting projects. The projects all have an initial investment of $500, but each one has a different cash flow pattern. The bottom part of the exhibit shows each project's payback period, along with its net present value for comparison. We will assume that management has set a payback period of two years as the cutoff point for an acceptable project.

Project A: The cash flows for Project A are $200 in the first year and $300 in the second, for a total of $500; thus, the project's payback period is two years. Under our acceptance criterion, management should accept this project. Project A also has a positive NPV of $450, so the two capital budgeting decision rules agree.

Project B: Project B never generates enough cash flows to pay off the original investment of $500: $300 + $100 + $50 = $450. Thus, the project payback period is infinite. With an infinite payback period, the project should be rejected. Also, as you would expect, project B's NPV is negative. So far, the payback period and NPV methods have agreed on which projects to accept.

Project C: Project C has a payback period of two years: $250 + $250 = $500. Thus, according to the payback criteria, it should be accepted. However, the project's NPV is a negative $115, which indicates that the project should be rejected. Why the conflict? Look

EXHIBIT 9.6   **Payback Period with Various Cash Flow Patterns**

Each of the five capital budgeting projects shown in the exhibit calls for an initial investment of $500, but all have different cash flow patterns. The bottom part of the exhibit shows each project's payback period, along with its net present value for comparison.

Year	A	B	C	D	E
0	−$500	−$500	−$500	−$500	−$500
1	200	300	250	500	200
2	300	100	250	0	200
3	400	50	−250	0	200
4	500	0	250	−5,000	5,000
Payback (years)	2.0	∞	2.0/4.0	1.0/∞	2.5
NPV	$450	−$131	−$115	−$2,924	$2,815

Cost of capital = 15%

at the cash flows after the payback period of two years. In year 3 the project requires an additional investment of $250 (a cash outflow) and now is in a deficit position; that is, the cumulative net cash balance is now only $250 ($250 + $250 − $250 = $250). Then, in the final year, the project earns an additional $250, recovering the cost of the total investment. The payback period analysis can lead to erroneous decisions because the rule does not consider cash flows after the payback period.

Projects D and E: Projects D and E dramatically illustrate the problem when a capital budgeting evaluation tool fails to consider cash flows after the payback period. Project D has a payback period of one year, suggesting that it should be accepted, and Project E has a payback period of 2.5 years, suggesting that it should be rejected. However, a simple look at the future cash flows suggests otherwise. It is clear that Project D, with a negative $5,000 cash flow in year 4, is a disaster and should be rejected, while Project E, with a positive $5,000 cash flow in year 4, should be accepted. Indeed, the NPV analysis confirms these conclusions: Project D has a negative NPV of $2,924, and Project E has a positive NPV of $2,815. In both instances, the payback rule led to the wrong economic decision. These examples illustrate that a rapid payback does not necessarily mean a good investment.

Discounted Payback Period

Another weakness of the ordinary payback period criteria is that it does not take into account the time value of money. All dollars received before the cutoff period are given equal weight. To address this problem, some financial managers use a variant of the payback period called the **discounted payback period**. This payback calculation is similar to the ordinary payback calculation except that the future cash flows are discounted by the cost of capital.

discounted payback period
the length of time required to recover a project's initial cost, accounting for the time value of money

The major advantage of the discounted payback approach is that it tells management how long it takes a project to reach an NPV of zero. Thus, any capital project that meets a firm's decision rule must also have a positive NPV. This is an improvement over the standard payback calculation, which can lead to accepting projects with negative NPVs. Regardless of the improvement, the discounted payback method is not widely used by businesses, and it also ignores all cash flows after the arbitrary cutoff period, which is a major flaw.

To see how the discounted payback period is calculated, turn to Exhibit 9.7. The exhibit shows the net cash flows for a proposed capital project along with both the cumulative and discounted cumulative cash flows; thus, we can compute both the ordinary and the discounted payback periods for the project and then compare them. The cost of capital is 10 percent.

The first two rows show the nondiscounted cash flows, and we can see by inspection that the ordinary payback period is two years. We do not need to make any additional calculations because the cumulative cash flows equal zero at precisely two years. Now let's turn our attention to the lower two rows, which show the project's discounted and cumulative discounted cash flows. Note that the first year's cash flow is $20,000 and its discounted value is $18,182 ($20,000 × 0.9091 = $18,182), and the second year's cash flow is also $20,000 and its discounted value is $16,529 ($20,000 × 0.8264 = $16,529). Now, looking at the cumulative discounted cash flows row, notice that it turns positive between two and three years. This means that the discounted payback period is two years plus some fraction of the third year's discounted cash flow. The exact discounted payback period computed value is 2 years + $5,289/$15,026 per year = 2 years + 0.35 years = 2.35 years.

	0	1	2	3 Year
Time line				
Net cash flow (NCF)	−$40,000	$20,000	$20,000	$20,000
Cumulative NCF	−$40,000	−$20,000	$0	$20,000
Discounted NCF (at 10%)	−$40,000	$18,182	$16,529	$15,026
Cumulative discounted NCF	−$40,000	−$21,818	−$5,289	$9,737

Payback period = 2 years + $0/$20,000 per year = 2 years
Discounted payback period = 2 years + $5,289/$15,026 per year = 2.35 years
Cost of capital = 10%
NPV = $49,737 − $40,000 = $9,737

EXHIBIT 9.7
Discounted Payback Period Cash Flows and Calculations

The exhibit shows the net and cumulative net cash flows for a proposed capital project with an initial cost of $40,000. The cash flow data are used to compute the discounted payback period for a 10 percent cost of capital, which is 2.35 years.

As expected, the discounted payback period is longer than the ordinary payback period (2 years < 2.35 years), and in 2.35 years the project will reach a NPV of $0. The project NPV is positive (NPV = $9,737); therefore, we should accept the project. But notice that the payback decision criteria are ambiguous. If we use 2.0 years as the payback criterion, we reject the project, and if we use 2.5 or 3.0 years as criterion, the project is accepted. The lack of a definitive decision rule remains a major problem with the payback period as a capital budgeting tool.

Evaluating the Payback Rule

The standard payback period is often calculated for projects because it provides an intuitive and simple measure of a project's liquidity risk. This makes sense because projects that pay for themselves quickly are less risky than projects whose paybacks occur farther in the future. There is a strong feeling in business that "getting your money back quickly" is an important standard when making capital investments. This intuition can be economically justified if the firm faces payments to creditors before the payback date, or if estimates of project cash flows beyond the payback date are very uncertain. Probably the greatest advantage of the payback period is its simplicity; it is easy to calculate and easy to understand.

When compared with the NPV method, however, the payback methods have some serious shortcomings. First, the standard payback calculation does not adjust or account for the timing or risk associated with future cash flows. Second, there is little economic justification for the choice of the payback cutoff criteria other than a liquidity motive. Who is to say that a particular cutoff, such as two years, is optimal with regard to maximizing stockholder value? Finally, perhaps the greatest shortcoming of the payback method is its failure to consider cash flows after the payback period. As a result, the payback method is biased toward shorter-term projects and may cause managers to reject important positive NPV projects where cash inflows tend to occur farther in the future, such as research and development investments, new product launches, and entry into new lines of business.

While the payback period is relatively simple to calculate, it is important to note that payback requires forecasts of future project cash flows up to the established cutoff period. Furthermore, discounted payback requires that managers identify a project's discount rate. Thus the inputs into the payback and NPV methods are virtually identical. Consequently, using a payback method may not even save much time and effort in evaluating a project. The table below summarizes key advantages and disadvantages of the payback method.

Summary of Payback Method

Decision Rule:
Payback period ≤ Payback cutoff point ⇨ Accept the project.
Payback period > Payback cutoff point ⇨ Reject the project.

Key Advantages	Key Disadvantages
1. Easy to calculate and understand for people without a strong accounting and finance background. 2. A simple measure of a project's liquidity risk.	1. Most common version does not account for time value of money. 2. Does not consider cash flows past the payback period. 3. Bias against long-term projects such as research and development and new product launches. 4. Arbitrary cutoff point.

> **BEFORE YOU GO ON**

1. What is the payback period?

2. Why does the payback period provide a measure of a project's liquidity risk?

3. What are the main shortcomings of the payback method?

9.4 THE ACCOUNTING RATE OF RETURN

LEARNING OBJECTIVE **4**

We turn next to a capital budgeting technique based on the **accounting rate of return (ARR)**, sometimes called the *book value rate of return*. This method computes the return on a capital project using accounting numbers—the project's net income (NI) and book value (BV)—rather than cash flow data. The ARR can be calculated in a number of ways, but the most common definition is:

$$ARR = \frac{\text{Average net income}}{\text{Average book value}} \tag{9.3}$$

where:

Average net income $= (NI_1 + NI_2 + \cdots + NI_n)/n$

Average book value $= (BV_0 + BV_1 + BV_2 + \cdots + BV_n)/(n + 1)$

n = the project's estimated life

BV_0 = the original cost of the asset

accounting rate of return (ARR)
a rate of return on a capital project based on average net income divided by average book value over the project's life; also called the *book value rate of return*

Although ARR is fairly easy to understand and calculate, as you probably guessed, it has major flaws as a tool for evaluating capital expenditure decisions. Instead of discounting a project's cash flows over time, it simply gives us a number based on average figures from the income statement and balance sheet. Thus, the ARR is based on accounting numbers and ignores the time value of money. Also, as with the payback method, there is no economic rationale that links a particular acceptance criterion to the goal of maximizing stockholder value.

Because of these major shortcomings, the ARR technique should not be used to evaluate the viability of capital projects under any circumstances. You may wonder why we even included the ARR technique in this book if it is a poor criterion for evaluating projects. The reason is simply that we want to be sure that if you run across the ARR method at work, you will recognize it and be aware of its shortcomings.

> **BEFORE YOU GO ON**
>
> 1. What are the major shortcomings of using the ARR method as a capital budgeting method?

9.5 INTERNAL RATE OF RETURN

LEARNING OBJECTIVE **5**

The **internal rate of return**, known in practice as the **IRR**, is an important alternative to the NPV method. The NPV and IRR techniques are closely related in that both involve discounting the cash flows from a project; thus, both account for the time value of money. When we use the NPV method to evaluate a capital project, the discount rate is the rate of return required by investors for investments with similar risk, which is the project's opportunity cost of capital. When we use the IRR, we are looking for the rate of return associated with a project so that we can determine whether this rate is higher or lower than the project's discount rate.

We can define the IRR as the discount rate that equates the present value of a project's cost to the present value of its expected cash inflows:

$$PV(\text{Cost of the project}) = PV(\text{Expected cash inflows})$$

This means that we can also describe the IRR as the discount rate that causes the NPV to equal zero. This relation can be written in a general form as follows:

internal rate of return (IRR)
the discount rate at which the present value of a project's expected cash inflows equals the present value of the project's outflows; it is the discount rate at which the project's NPV equals zero

$$NPV = NCF_0 + \frac{NCF_1}{1 + IRR} + \frac{NCF_2}{(1 + IRR)^2} + \cdots + \frac{NCF_n}{(1 + IRR)^n} \tag{9.4}$$

$$= \sum_{t=0}^{n} \frac{NCF_t}{(1 + IRR)^t} = 0$$

Because of their close relation, it may seem that the IRR and the NPV are interchangeable—that is, either should tell you to accept or reject the same capital projects. After all, both methods are based on whether the project's return exceeds the cost of capital and, hence, whether the project will add value to the firm. In many circumstances, the IRR and NPV methods do give us the same answer. As you will see later, however, some of the properties of the IRR equation can lead to incorrect decisions concerning whether to accept or reject a particular capital project.

Calculating the IRR

The IRR is an expected rate of return much like the yield to maturity we calculated for bonds in Chapter 7. Thus, in calculating the IRR, we need to apply the same trial-and-error method we used in Chapter 7. We will begin by doing some IRR calculations by trial and error so that you understand the process, and then we will switch to the financial calculator and computer spreadsheets, which provide an answer more quickly.

Trial-and-Error Method

Suppose that Ford Motor Company has an investment opportunity with cash flows as shown in Exhibit 9.8 and that the cost of capital is 12 percent. We want to find the IRR for this project. Using Equation 9.4, we will substitute various values for IRR into the equation to compute the project's IRR by trial and error. We continue this process until we find the IRR value that makes Equation 9.4 equal zero.

A good starting point is to use the cost of capital as the discount rate. Note that when we discount the NCFs by the cost of capital, we are calculating the project's NPV:

$$NPV = NCF_0 + \frac{NCF_1}{1 + IRR} + \frac{NCF_2}{(1 + IRR)^2} + \cdots + \frac{NCF_n}{(1 + IRR)^n}$$

$$NPV_{12\%} = -\$560 + \frac{\$240}{1.12} + \frac{\$240}{(1.12)^2} + \frac{\$240}{(1.12)^3} = \$16.44$$

Recall that the result we are looking for is zero. Because our result is $16.44, the discount rate of 12 percent is too low, and we must try a higher rate. Let's try 13 percent:

$$NPV_{13\%} = -\$560 + \frac{\$240}{1.13} + \frac{\$240}{(1.13)^2} + \frac{\$240}{(1.13)^3} = \$6.68$$

We are very close; let's try 14 percent:

$$NPV_{14\%} = -\$560 + \frac{\$240}{1.14} + \frac{\$240}{(1.14)^2} + \frac{\$240}{(1.14)^3} = -\$2.81$$

Because our result is now a negative number, we know the correct rate is between 13 and 14 percent, and looking at the magnitude of the numbers, we know that the answer is closer to 14 percent. Let's try 13.7 percent.

$$NPV_{13.7\%} = -\$560 + \frac{\$240}{1.137} + \frac{\$240}{(1.137)^2} + \frac{\$240}{(1.137)^3} = 0$$

	0	1	2	3 Year
Time line	L			J
Net cash flow	−$560	$240	$240	$240

Cost of capital = 12%
NPV = $576.44 − $560.00 = $16.44

EXHIBIT 9.8

Time Line and Expected Net Cash Flows for the Ford Project ($ thousands)

The cash flow data in the exhibit are used to compute the project's IRR. The project's NPV is a positive $16,440, which indicates that the IRR is greater than the cost of capital of 12 percent.

Good guess! This means that the NPV of Ford's capital project is zero at a discount rate of 13.7 percent. The required rate of return is the cost of capital, which is 12.0 percent. Since the project's IRR of 13.7 percent exceeds the cost of capital, the IRR criterion indicates that the project should be accepted.

The project's NPV is a positive $16,440, which also indicates that Ford should go ahead with the project. Thus, both the IRR and NPV suggest the same conclusion.

Calculating the IRR at Larry's Ice Cream Parlor

PROBLEM: Larry's Ice Cream Parlor in the DuPont Circle area of Washington, D.C., is famous for its gourmet ice cream. However, some customers have asked for a healthy, low-cal, soft yogurt. The machine that makes this confection is manufactured in Italy and costs $5,000 plus $1,750 for installation. Larry estimates that the machine will generate a net cash flow of $2,000 a year (the shop closes November through March of each year). Larry also estimates the machine's life to be 10 years and that it will have a $400 salvage value. His cost of capital is 15 percent. Larry thinks the machine is overpriced. Is he right?

APPROACH: The IRR for an investment is the discount rate at which the NPV is zero. Thus, we can use Equation 9.4 to solve for the IRR and then compare this value with Larry's cost of capital. If the IRR is greater than the cost of capital, the project has a positive NPV and should be accepted.

SOLUTION: The total cost of the machine is $6,750 ($5,000 + $1,750 = $6,750), and the final cash flow in year 10 is $2,400 ($2,000 + $400 = $2,400).

```
 0            1        2        3        9       10  Year
    15%
 |---------|--------|--------|------\/--|--------|
-$6,750   $2,000   $2,000   $2,000   $2,000   $2,400
```

The hand trial-and-error calculations are shown below. The first calculation uses 15 percent, the cost of capital, our recommended starting point, and the answer is $3,386.41 (which is also the project's NPV). Because the value is a positive number, we need to use a discount rate larger than 15 percent. Our guess is 27.08 percent. At that value the NPV equals zero; thus, the IRR for the yogurt machine is 27.08 percent.

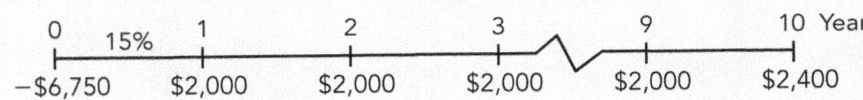

$$NPV = NCF_0 + \frac{NCF_1}{1 + IRR} + \frac{NCF_2}{(1 + IRR)^2} + \cdots + \frac{NCF_n}{(1 + IRR)^n} = 0$$

$$NPV_{15.00\%} = -\$6,750 + \frac{\$2,000}{1.15} + \frac{\$2,000}{(1.15)^2} + \cdots + \frac{\$2,400}{(1.15)^{10}} = \$3,386.41$$

$$NPV_{27.08\%} = -\$6,750 + \frac{\$2,000}{1.2708} + \frac{\$2,000}{(1.2708)^2} + \cdots + \frac{\$2,400}{(1.2708)^{10}} = \$0.00$$

Because the project's future cash flow pattern resembles that for a coupon bond, we can also solve for the IRR using a financial calculator, just as we would solve for the yield to maturity of a bond. Just enter the data directly into the corresponding keys on the calculator, press the interest key, and we have our answer: 27.08 percent.

Enter	10		−6,750	2,000	400
	N	i	PV	PMT	FV
Answer		27.08			

As with present value calculations, for projects with unequal cash flows, you should consult your financial calculator's manual.

Because the project's IRR exceeds Larry's cost of capital of 15 percent, the project should be accepted. Larry is wrong.

LEARNING
BY
DOING

APPLICATION 9.3

NEED MORE HELP?

WileyPLUS

INTERNAL RATE OF RETURN

You know that calculating IRR by hand can be tedious. The trial-and-error method can take a long time and can be quite frustrating. Knowing all the cash flows and an approximate rate will allow you to use a spreadsheet formula to get an answer instantly.

The accompanying spreadsheet shows the setup for calculating the IRR for the low-cal yogurt machine at Larry's Ice Cream Parlor that is described in Learning by Doing Application 9.3.

Here are a couple of important points to note about IRR calculations using spreadsheet programs:

1. Unlike the NPV formula, the IRR formula accounts for all cash flows, including the initial investment in year 0, so there is no need to add this cash flow later.
2. The syntax of the IRR function requires that you first provide the project's cash flows in order beginning at time zero. To calculate the IRR, you will also need to provide a "guess" value, or a number you estimate is close to the IRR. A good value to start with is the cost of capital. To learn more about why this value is needed, you should go to your spreadsheet's help manual and search for "IRR."

◇	A	B	C	D	E
1					
2		**IRR Calculations**			
3					
4		Year		Cash Flow	
5		0		−$6,750	
6		1		2,000	
7		2		2,000	
8		3		2,000	
9		4		2,000	
10		5		2,000	
11		6		2,000	
12		7		2,000	
13		8		2,000	
14		9		2,000	
15		10		2,400	
16					
17		Cost of capital		0.15	
18					
19		**IRR**		**27.08%**	
20		Formula used		=IRR(E5:E15, E17)	
21					
22	Remember to keep track of signs—cash outflows are negative, and cash inflows are positive.				
23					
24					

When the IRR and NPV Methods Agree

In the Ford example, the IRR and NPV methods agree. The two methods will *always* agree when you are evaluating *independent* projects and the projects' cash flows are *conventional*. As discussed earlier, an independent project is one that can be selected with no effect on the viability of any other project. A project with **conventional cash flows** is one with an initial cash outflow followed by one or more cash inflows. Put another way, after the initial investment is made (cash outflow), the net cash flow in each future year is positive (inflows). For example, the purchase of a bond involves conventional cash flows. You purchase the bond for a price (cash outflow), and in the future you receive coupon payments and a principal payment at maturity (cash inflows).

conventional cash flow
a cash flow pattern consisting of an initial cash outflow that is followed by one or more cash inflows

Let's look more closely at the kinds of situations in which the NPV and the IRR methods agree. A good way to visualize the relation between the IRR and NPV methods is to graph NPV as a function of the discount rate. The graph, called an **NPV profile**, shows the NPV of the project at various costs of capital.

NPV profile
a graph showing NPV as a function of the discount rate

Exhibit 9.9 shows the NPV profile for the Ford project. We have placed the NPVs on the vertical axis, or y-axis, and the discount rates on the horizontal axis, or x-axis. We used the calculations from our earlier example and made some additional NPV calculations at various discount rates as follows:

Discount Rate	NPV ($ thousands)
0%	$160
5	94
10	37
15	−12
20	−54
25	−92
30	−124

EXHIBIT 9.9
NPV Profile for the Ford Project

In the NPV profile for the Ford project, the NPV value is on the vertical (y) axis and the discount rate is on the horizontal (x) axis. You can see that as the discount rate increases, the NPV profile curve declines smoothly and intersects the x-axis at the point where the NPV is 0. The IRR of 13.7 percent is the point at which the NPV changes from a positive to a negative value. The NPV and IRR methods lead to identical accept-or-reject decisions for the Ford project.

As you can see, a discount rate of 0 percent corresponds with an NPV of $160,000, a discount rate of 5 percent with an NPV of $94,000, and so forth. As the discount rate increases, the NPV curve declines smoothly. Not surprisingly, the curve intersects the x-axis at precisely the point where the NPV is 0 and the IRR is 13.7 percent.

The NPV profile in Exhibit 9.9 illustrates why the NPV and IRR methods lead to identical accept-reject decisions for the Ford project. The IRR of 13.7 percent precisely marks the point at which the NPV changes from a positive to a negative value. Whenever a project is independent and has conventional cash flows, the result will be as shown in the exhibit. The NPV will decline as the discount rate increases, and the IRR and the NPV methods will result in the same capital expenditure decision.

When the NPV and IRR Methods Disagree

We have seen that the IRR and NPV methods lead to identical investment decisions for capital projects that are independent and that have conventional cash flows. However, if either of these conditions is not met, the IRR and NPV methods can produce different accept-reject decisions.

Unconventional Cash Flows

Unconventional cash flows can cause a conflict between the NPV and IRR decision rules. In some instances the cash flows for an unconventional project are just the reverse of those of a conventional project: the initial cash flow is positive, and all subsequent cash flows are negative. In this case, we need only reverse the IRR decision rule and accept the project if the IRR is *less* than the cost of capital to make the IRR and NPV methods agree.

When a project's future cash flows include both positive and negative cash flows, the situation is more complicated. An example of such a project is an assembly line that will require one or more major renovations over its lifetime. Another common business situation is a project that has conventional cash flows except for the final cash flow, which is negative. The final cash flow might be negative because extensive environmental cleanup is required at the end of the project, such as the cost for decommissioning a nuclear power plant, or because the equipment originally purchased has little or no salvage value and is expensive to remove.

Consider an example. Suppose a firm invests in a gold-mining operation that costs $55 million and has an expected life of two years. In the first year, the project generates a cash inflow of $150 million. In the second year, extensive environmental and site restoration is required, so the expected cash flow is a negative $100 million. The time line for these cash flows follows.

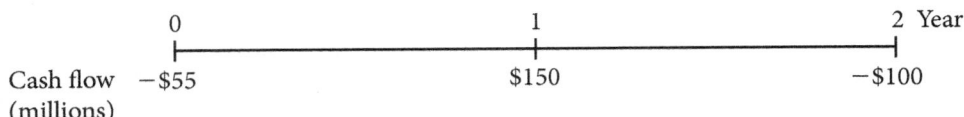

	0	1	2 Year
Cash flow (millions)	−$55	$150	−$100

Once again, the best way to understand the effect of these cash flows is to look at an NPV profile. Shown here are NPV calculations we made at various discount rates to generate the data necessary to plot the NPV profile shown in Exhibit 9.10:

Discount Rate	NPV ($ millions)
0%	−$5.00
10	−1.28
20	0.56
30	1.21
40	1.12
50	0.56
60	−0.31
70	−1.37

Looking at the data in the table, you can probably spot a problem. The NPV is initially negative (−$5.00); then, at a discount rate of 20 percent, switches to positive ($0.56); and then, at a discount rate of 60 percent, switches back to negative (−$0.31).

The NPV profile in Exhibit 9.10 shows the results of this pattern: we have two IRRs, one at 16.05 percent and the other at 55.65 percent. Which is the correct IRR, or are both correct? Actually, there is no correct answer; the results are meaningless, and you should not try to interpret them. Thus, in this situation, the IRR technique provides information that should not be used for decision making.

How many IRR solutions can there be for a given cash flow? The maximum number of IRR solutions is equal to the number of sign reversals in the cash flow stream. For a project with a conventional cash flow, there is only one cash flow sign reversal; thus, there is only one IRR solution. In our mining example, there are two cash flow sign reversals; thus, there are two IRR solutions.

Finally, for some cash flow patterns, it is impossible to compute an IRR. These situations can occur when the initial cash flow ($t = 0$) is either a cash inflow or outflow and is followed by cash flows with two or more sign reversals. An example of such a cash flow pattern is $NCF_0 = \$15$, $NCF_1 = -\$25$, and $NCF_2 = \$20$. This type of cash flow pattern might occur on

---

EXHIBIT 9.10

NPV Profile for Gold-Mining Operation with Multiple IRR Solutions

The gold-mining operation has unconventional cash flows. Because there are two cash flow sign reversals, we end up with two IRRs—16.05 percent and 55.65 percent—neither of them useful. In situations like this, the IRR provides a solution that is meaningless, and therefore, the results should not be used for capital budgeting decisions.

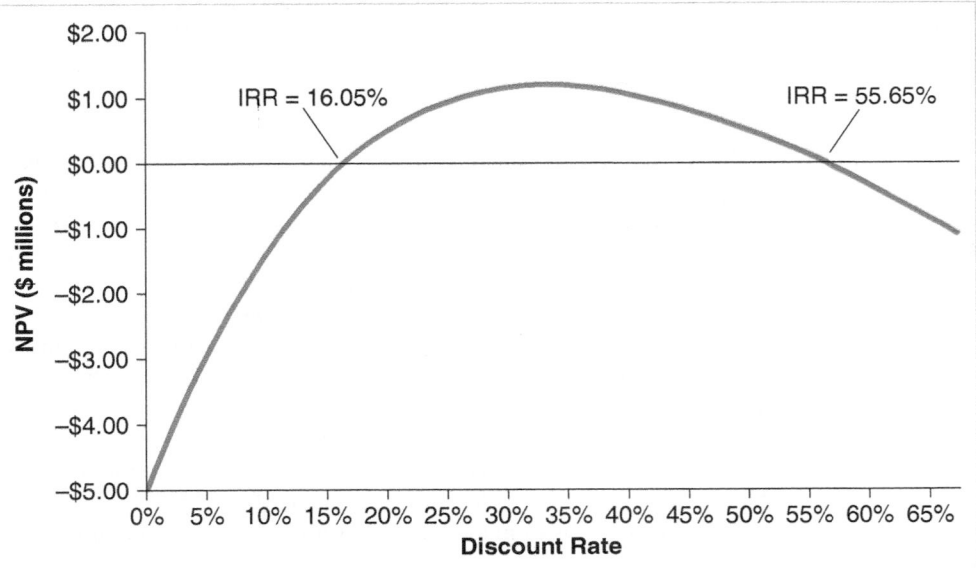

a building project where the contractor is given a prepayment, usually the cost of materials and supplies ($15); then does the construction and pays the labor cost ($25); and finally, upon completion of the work, receives the final payment ($20). Note that when it is not possible to compute an IRR, the project either has a positive NPV or a negative NPV for all possible discount rates. In this example, the NPV is always positive.

Mutually Exclusive Projects

The other situation in which the IRR can lead to incorrect capital budgeting decisions is when projects are mutually exclusive—that is, when accepting one project means rejecting the other. For example, suppose you own a small store in the business district of Seattle that is currently vacant. You are looking at two business opportunities: opening an upscale coffee house or opening a copy center. Since you cannot pursue both projects at the same location, they are mutually exclusive.

When you have mutually exclusive projects, how do you select the best alternative? If you are using the NPV method, the answer is easy. You select the project that has the highest NPV because it will increase the value of the firm by the largest amount. If you are using the IRR method, it would seem logical to select the project with the highest IRR. In this case, though, the logic is wrong! You cannot tell which mutually exclusive project to select just by looking at the projects' IRRs.

Let's consider another example to illustrate the problem. The cash flows for two projects, A and B, are as follows:

Year	Project A	Project B
0	−$100	−$100
1	50	20
2	40	30
3	30	50
4	30	65

The IRR is 20.7 percent for Project A and 19.0 percent for Project B. Because the two projects are mutually exclusive, only one project can be accepted. If you were following the IRR decision rule, you would accept Project A. However, as you will see, it turns out that Project B might be the better choice.

The following table shows the NPVs for the two projects at several discount rates:

Discount Rate	NPV of Project A	NPV of Project B
0%	$50.0	$65.0
5	34.5	42.9
10	21.5	24.9
13	14.8	15.7
15	10.6	10.1
20	1.3	−2.2
25	−6.8	−12.6
30	−13.7	−21.3
IRR	20.7%	19.0%

Notice that the NPV of each project depends on the rate of return used to discount the cash flows. Our example shows a conflict in the ranking order between the IRR and NPV methods at discount rates between 0 and 13 percent. In this range, Project B has the lower IRR, but it has the higher NPV and should be the project selected. If the discount rate is above 15 percent, however, Project A has the higher NPV as well as the higher IRR. In this range, there is no conflict between the two evaluation methods.

The relative IRR and NPV rankings change in this way because the cash inflows of Project B arrive later than those of Project A. Thus, higher discount rates have more of an impact on the value of Project B. In other words, changes in relative IRR and NPV rankings result from differences in the timing of project cash flows.

 To read an article that warns finance managers using the IRR about the method's pitfalls, visit www.cfo.com/printable/article.cfm/3304945?f=options.

EXHIBIT 9.11

NPV Profiles for Two Mutually Exclusive Projects

The NPV profiles for two projects often cross over each other. When evaluating mutually exclusive projects, it is helpful to know where this crossover point is. For Projects A and B in the exhibit, the crossover point is at 14.3 percent. For any cost of capital above 14.3 percent but below 20.7 percent, the NPV for Project A is higher than that for Project B and is positive; thus, Project A should be selected. For any cost of capital below the crossover point, the NPV of Project B is higher, and Project B should be selected.

crossover point
the discount rate at which the NPV profiles of two projects cross and, thus, at which the NPVs of the projects are equal

Now take a look at Exhibit 9.11, which shows the NPV profiles for Projects A and B. As you can see, there is a point, called the **crossover point**, at which the NPV profiles for Projects A and B intersect. The crossover point here is at a discount rate of 14.3 percent. For any cost of capital above 14.3 percent, the NPV for Project A is higher than that for Project B; thus, Project A should be selected if its NPV is positive. For any cost of capital below the crossover point, Project B should be selected.

Another conflict involving mutually exclusive projects concerns comparisons of projects that have significantly different costs. The IRR does not adjust for these differences in the scale of projects. What the IRR gives us is a rate of return on each dollar invested. In contrast, the NPV method computes the total dollar value created by the project. The difference in results can be significant, as can be seen in Decision-Making Example 9.2 on the next page.

Modified Internal Rate of Return (MIRR)

A major weakness of the IRR method compared with the NPV method concerns the rate at which the cash flows generated by a capital project are reinvested. The NPV method assumes that cash flows from a project are reinvested at the cost of capital, whereas the IRR technique assumes they are reinvested at the IRR. Determining which is the better assumption depends on which rate better represents the rate that firms can actually earn when they reinvest a project's cash flows over time. It is generally believed that the cost of capital, which is often lower than the IRR, better reflects the rate that firms are likely to earn. Using the IRR may thus involve overly optimistic assumptions regarding reinvestment rates.

modified internal rate of return (MIRR)
an internal rate of return (IRR) measure which assumes that cash inflows are reinvested at the opportunity cost of capital until the end of the project

To eliminate the reinvestment rate assumption of the IRR, some practitioners prefer to calculate the **modified internal rate of return (MIRR)**. In this approach, each operating cash flow is converted to a future value at the end of the project's life, compounded at the cost of capital. These values are then summed up to get the project's *terminal value (TV)*. The MIRR is the interest rate that equates the project's cost (PV_{Cost}), or cash outflows, with the future

The Lemonade Stand versus the Convenience Store

SITUATION: Suppose you work for an entrepreneur who owns a number of small businesses in Fresno, California, as well as a small piece of property near California State University at Fresno, which he believes would be an ideal site for a student-oriented convenience store. His 7-year-old son, who happens to be in the office after school, says he has a better idea: his father should open a lemonade stand. Your boss tells you to find the NPV and IRR for both projects, assuming a 10 percent discount rate. After collecting data, you present the following analysis:

Year	Lemonade Stand	Convenience Store
0	−$1,000	−$1,000,000
1	850	372,000
2	850	372,000
3	850	372,000
4	850	372,000
IRR	76.2%	18.0%
NPV	$1,694	$179,190

Assuming the projects are mutually exclusive, which should be selected?

DECISION: Your boss, who favors the IRR method, looks at the analysis and declares his son a genius. The IRR decision rule suggests that the lemonade stand, with its 76.2 percent rate of return, is the project to choose! You point out that the goal of capital budgeting is to select projects, or combinations of projects, that maximize the value of the firm, his business. The convenience store adds by far the greater value: $179,190 compared with only $1,694 for the lemonade stand. Although the lemonade stand has a high rate of return, its small size precludes it from being competitive against the larger project.

value of the projec's cash inflows at the end of the project (PV_{TV}).[1] Because each future value is computed using the cost of capital as the interest rate, the reinvestment rate problem is eliminated.

We can set up the equation for the MIRR in the same way we set up Equation 9.4 for the IRR:

$$PV(\text{Cost of the project}) = PV(\text{Expected cash inflows})$$
$$PV_{\text{Cost}} = PV_{TV}$$
$$PV_{\text{Cost}} = \frac{TV}{(1 + MIRR)^n} \tag{9.5}$$

To compute the MIRR, we have to make two preliminary calculations. First, we calculate the value of PV_{Cost}, which is the present value of the cash outflows that make up the investment cost of the project. Since for most capital projects, the investment cost cash flows are incurred at the beginning of the project, $t = 0$, there is often no need to calculate a present value. If investment costs are incurred over time $(t > 0)$, then the cash flows must be discounted at the cost of capital.

Second, we need to compute the terminal value (TV). To do this, we find the future value of each operating cash flow at the end of the project's life, compounded at the cost of capital.

---

[1]As we pointed out in Chapter 5, financial decision-making problems can be solved either by discounting cash flows to the beginning of the project or by using compounding to find the future value of cash flows at the end of a project's life.

We then sum up these future values to get the project's TV. Mathematically, the TV can be expressed as:

$$TV = [CF_1 \times (1 + k)^{n-1}] + [CF_2 \times (1 + k)^{n-2}] + \cdots + [CF_n \times (1 + k)^{n-n}]$$
$$= \sum_{t=1}^{n} CF_t \times (1 + k)^{n-t}$$

where:

TV = the project's terminal value
CF_t = cash flow from operations in period t
k = the cost of capital
n = the project life

Once we have computed the values of PV_{Cost} and TV, we use Equation 9.5 to compute the MIRR. Note that by combining intermediate cash flows into a single terminal value, MIRR has the added advantage of always yielding a conventional cash flow.

To illustrate, let's return to the Ford Motor Company example shown in Exhibit 9.8. Recall that the cost of the project is $560, incurred at $t = 0$, and that the discount rate is 12 percent. To determine the MIRR for the project, we start by calculating the terminal value of the cash flows, as shown on the following time line:

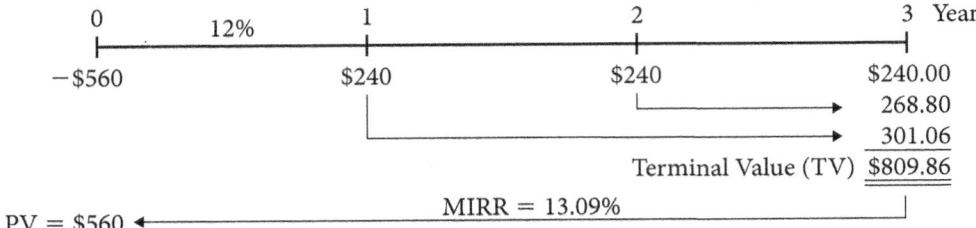

The terminal value of $809.86 equals the sum of the $240 in year 1 compounded at 12 percent for two years plus the $240 in year 2 compounded at 12 percent for 1 year plus the $240 in year 3. Mathematically, this calculation is:

$$TV = [CF_1 \times (1 + k)^{n-1}] + [CF_2 \times (1 + k)^{n-2}] + \cdots + [CF_n \times (1 + k)^{n-n}]$$
$$= [\$240 \times (1.12)^2] + [\$240 \times 1.12] + \$240 = \$809.86$$

With the information that the cost of the project is $560 and the TV is $809.86, we can calculate the MIRR using Equation 9.5:

$$PV_{Cost} = \frac{TV}{(1 + MIRR)^n}$$
$$\$560 = \frac{\$809.86}{(1 + MIRR)^3}$$
$$(1 + MIRR)^3 = \frac{\$809.86}{\$560} = 1.4462$$
$$(1 + MIRR) = (1.4462)^{1/3} = 1.1309$$
$$MIRR = 1.1309 - 1 = 0.1309$$
$$= 13.09\%$$

At 13.09 percent, the MIRR is higher than Ford's cost of capital of 12 percent, so the project should be accepted.

IRR versus NPV: A Final Comment

The IRR method, as noted, is an important alternative to the NPV method. As we have seen, it accounts for the time value of money, which is not true of methods such as the payback period and accounting rate of return. Furthermore, the IRR technique has great intuitive appeal. Many business practitioners are in the habit of thinking in terms of rates of return, whether the rates relate to their common-stock portfolios or their firms' capital expenditures. To these practitioners, the IRR method just seems to make sense. Indeed, we suspect that the IRR's popularity with business managers results more from its simple intuitive appeal than from its merit.

On the downside, we have seen that the IRR method has several flaws. For example, IRR can't be used effectively for projects with unconventional cash flows, and IRR can lead to incorrect investment decisions when it is used to choose between mutually exclusive projects. MIRR addresses some of the shortcomings of IRR; namely, it does not assume that project proceeds are reinvested at the IRR, and it eliminates issues associated with unconventional project cash flows. Nonetheless, we believe that NPV should be the primary method used to make capital budgeting decisions. Investment decisions made using NPV are always consistent with the goal of maximizing the value of the firm, even when discriminating between mutually exclusive projects. Finally, it is important to note that the IRR, MIRR, and NPV methods all require a set of projected cash flows over the life of the project and a discount rate. Thus, using IRR or MIRR, rather than NPV, does not require less effort from financial managers.

Summary of Internal Rate of Return (IRR) Method

Decision Rule: IRR > Cost of capital ⇨ Accept the project.
IRR < Cost of capital ⇨ Reject the project.

Key Advantages	Key Disadvantages
1. Intuitive and easy to understand.	1. With nonconventional cash flows, IRR approach can yield no usable answer or multiple answers.
2. Based on discounted cash flow technique.	2. A lower IRR can be better if a cash inflow is followed by cash outflows.
	3. With mutually exclusive projects, IRR can lead to incorrect investment decisions.
	4. IRR calculation assumes cash flows are reinvested at the IRR.

> **BEFORE YOU GO ON**

1. What is the IRR method?

2. In capital budgeting, what is a conventional cash flow pattern?

3. Why should the NPV method be the primary decision tool used in making capital investment decisions?

9.6 INVESTMENT DECISIONS WITH CAPITAL RATIONING

LEARNING OBJECTIVE 6

Our discussion of capital budgeting so far has focused on determining whether an individual project creates value for stockholders. Although the analytical methods we have discussed are critical components of the capital budgeting process, they do not tell us what to do when, as is often the case, a firm does not have enough money to invest in all available positive NPV projects. In other words, they do not tell us how to identify the *bundle* or combination of positive NPV projects that creates the greatest total value for stockholders when there are capital constraints or, as we called it earlier in this chapter, *capital rationing.*

In an ideal world, of course, we could accept all positive NPV projects because we would be able to finance them. If managers and investors agreed on which projects had positive NPVs, investors would provide capital to those projects because returns from them would be greater than the returns the investors could earn elsewhere in the capital markets. However, the world is not ideal, and firms often cannot invest in all of the available projects with positive NPVs. It can be difficult for outside investors to accurately assess the risks and returns associated with the firm's projects. Consequently, investors may require returns for their capital that are too high, and the firm may face capital constraints. Managers might be forced to reject positive NPV projects because investors are not providing enough capital to fund those projects at reasonable rates.

Capital Rationing in a Single Period

profitability index (PI)
a measure of the value a project generates for each dollar invested in that project

The basic principle that we follow in choosing the set of projects that creates the greatest value in a given period is to select the projects that yield the largest value *per dollar invested*. We can do this by computing the **profitability index (PI)** for each project and choosing the projects with the largest profitability indexes until we run out of money. The profitability index is computed as follows:

$$PI = \frac{Benefits}{Costs} = \frac{Present\ value\ of\ future\ free\ cash\ flows}{Initial\ investment} = \frac{NPV + Initial\ investment}{Initial\ investment} \quad (9.6)$$

where Initial investment is the up-front investment required to fund the project.

To illustrate, let's suppose you run a lawn mowing business and are trying to decide when to replace one of your lawn mowers. Assume that the new mower would cost $2,000 and would bring in net cash flows of $7,000 for four years. With a discount rate of 10 percent, the NPV of this mower is $20,189 and its PI is calculated as follows:

$$PI = (\$20,189 + \$2,000)/\$2,000 = 11.09$$

This means that an investment in the new mower is expected to generate $11.09 of value for every dollar invested.

Now consider the case in which we have several projects to choose from in a given year but do not have enough money to invest in all of them. For example, suppose that we have identified the four positive NPV projects listed in Exhibit 9.12 and have only $10,000 to invest. How do we choose from among the four projects when we cannot afford to invest in all of them?

Our objective in a case such as this is to identify the bundle or combination of positive NPV projects that creates the greatest total value for stockholders. The PI is helpful in such a situation because it helps us choose the projects that create the most value per dollar invested. We use the PI to do this by following a four-step procedure:

1. Calculate the PI for each project.
2. Rank the projects from highest PI to lowest PI.
3. Starting at the top of the list (the project with the highest PI) and working your way down (to the project with the lowest PI), select the projects that the firm can afford.
4. Repeat the third step by starting with the second project on the list, the third project on the list, and so on to make sure that a more valuable bundle cannot be identified.

Applying this process to the projects in Exhibit 9.12, we would choose to accept Projects A, B, and D. We would begin by choosing Projects A and B because they have the largest PIs and we have enough money to invest in both. Since choosing Projects A and B means we would no longer have enough money to invest in Project C, we would skip C and choose D, for which we do have enough money. Projects A, B, and D would generate a total of $7,500 in total value for stockholders. Following the fourth step reveals that no other combination of projects has a larger total NPV than Projects A, B, and D, so we would select these projects.

EXHIBIT 9.12   **Positive NPV Investments This Year**

With only $10,000 to invest, how do we choose among these four positive-NPV projects? The exhibit shows the yearly free cash flows, NPV, and profitability index (PI) for the projects. The PI values indicate the value of the expected future free cash flows per dollar invested in each project.

Project	Year 0	Year 1	Year 2	NPV @ 10%	PI
A	−$5,000	$5,500	$6,050	$5,000	2.000
B	−$3,000	$2,000	$3,850	$2,000	1.667
C	−$3,000	$4,400	$0	$1,000	1.333
D	−$2,000	$1,500	$1,375	$500	1.250

Ranking Projects Using the Profitability Index

PROBLEM: You have identified the following seven positive NPV investments for your in-home computer-support business. If you have $50,000 to invest this year, which projects should you accept?

Project	Investment	NPV @ 10%
Buy new notebook computer	$ 3,000	$ 500
Buy employee training program	8,000	4,000
Buy new tool set	500	1,000
Buy office condo	40,000	5,000
Buy used car	12,000	4,000
Paint existing cars	4,000	2,000
Buy new test equipment	10,000	2,000

APPROACH: Use the four-step procedure presented in the text to determine which projects you should accept.

SOLUTION: Calculating the PI and ranking the projects from highest to lowest PI yields the following:

Project	Investment	NPV @ 10%	PI
Buy new tool set	$ 500	$1,000	$1,500/$500 = 3.000
Buy employee training program	8,000	4,000	$12,000/$8,000 = 1.500
Paint existing cars	4,000	2,000	$6,000/$4,000 = 1.500
Buy used car	12,000	4,000	$16,000/$12,000 = 1.333
Buy new test equipment	10,000	2,000	$12,000/$10,000 = 1.200
Buy new notebook computer	3,000	500	$3,500/$3,000 = 1.167
Buy office condo	40,000	5,000	$45,000/$40,000 = 1.125

With $50,000 to invest, you should invest in all projects except the office condo. This strategy will require $37,500 and is expected to result in a total NPV of $13,500. The $12,500 that you have left over, which is not enough to buy the office condo, can be held in the business until an appropriate use for the money is identified, or it can be distributed to the stockholder (you).

LEARNING
BY
DOING

APPLICATION 9.4

NEED MORE HELP?

WileyPLUS

Capital Rationing across Multiple Periods

The PI concept is relatively straightforward and easy to apply if you are choosing among projects in a single period. However, if you are faced with capital rationing over several years, the investments you choose this year can affect your ability to make investments in future years. This can happen if you plan on reinvesting some or all of the cash flows generated by the projects you invest in this year. In such a situation, you cannot rely solely on the PI to identify the projects you should invest in this year. You must maximize the total NPV across all of the years in which you will be investing.

Let's look more closely at how multiperiod concerns can cause you to deviate from PI-based investment choices in a given year. Suppose you operate a business that will generate $10,000 per year for new investments. Furthermore, suppose that today (Year 0) you are choosing among Projects A, B, C, and D in Exhibit 9.13 and that, based on the PIs of the individual projects, you choose to invest in Projects A, B, and D. The total NPV from these projects will be $7,500, and the total Year 1 cash flow from them will be $9,000 ($5,500 + $2,000 + $1,500 = $9,000).

Now suppose that you expect Projects F, G, and H to be available next year (Year 1). If other operations yield $10,000 for investments next year, you will have a total of $19,000 to invest in Year 1. With this amount of money, you can invest in Projects F and H, which require

EXHIBIT 9.13   **Positive NPV Investments for Two Years**

Investment decision-making with capital rationing becomes more complex when multiple periods are involved. This exhibit shows the yearly free cash flows, NPV, and profitability index (PI) for the four positive NPV projects in Exhibit 9.12 and for three other positive-NPV projects that are expected to become available in Year 1.

Project	Year 0	Year 1	Year 2	Year 3	Year 0 NPV @ 10%	PI
A	−$5,000	$5,500	$6,050	$0	$5,000	2.000
B	−$3,000	$2,000	$3,850	$0	$2,000	1.667
C	−$3,000	$4,400	$0	$0	$1,000	1.333
D	−$2,000	$1,500	$1,375	$0	$500	1.250
F		−$10,000	$12,000	$11,000	$9,091	1.909
G		−$10,000	$8,000	$11,770	$6,364	1.636
H		−$5,000	$4,000	$2,255	$455	1.091

a total investment of $15,000 and have a combined NPV of $9,546 ($9,091 + $455 = $9,546). Therefore, in year 0 dollars, the total value created from investing activities over the two years will be $17,046 ($7,500 + $9,546 = $17,046).

While $17,046 is a lot of value for a total investment of $25,000 ($10,000 today and $15,000 in year 1), you could do better. Notice that if, instead of Projects A, B, and D, you invest in Projects A, C, and D today, you will have enough cash in Year 1 to invest in Projects F and G. This strategy would yield a total NPV of $21,955 ($5,000 + $1,000 + $500 + $9,091 + $6,364 = $21,955)! Ranking and selecting the projects today based on the PI would have yielded a bundle of projects over two years with a lower NPV. This illustrates an important limitation of the profitability index. It does not tell us enough to make informed decisions over multiple periods. Solving a multiple-period problem requires the application of more advanced analytical techniques, such as linear programming, that are beyond the scope of this book.

> If you have a strong math background and are interested, you can learn more about linear programming from http://www.purplemath.com/modules/linprog.htm.

> **BEFORE YOU GO ON**

1. What decision criteria should managers use in selecting projects when there is not enough money to invest in all available positive NPV projects?

2. What might cause a firm to face capital constraints?

3. How can the PI help in choosing projects when a firm faces capital constraints? What are its limitations?

9.7 CAPITAL BUDGETING IN PRACTICE

LEARNING OBJECTIVE

Capital expenditures are big-ticket items in the U.S. economy. According to the Department of Commerce, U.S. businesses invested $1.226 trillion in capital goods in 2011. Capital investments also represent large expenditures for individual firms, though the amount spent can vary widely from year to year. For example, AT&T invested heavily its wireless network capabilities in 2012, and its $19.7 billion in capital expenditures that year exceeded those of all but a very small number of firms in the world. More typical are the capital expenditure totals for Caterpillar, Microsoft, and Kellogg Company, which are shown in the following table. Given the large dollar amounts and the strategic importance of capital expenditures, it is no surprise that corporate managers spend considerable time and energy analyzing capital projects.

Company	2012 Capital Expenditures ($ billions)	2012 Sales ($ billions)	Capital Expenditures as a Percentage of Sales
AT&T, Inc.	$19.7	$127.4	15.5%
Caterpillar, Inc.	5.1	65.9	7.7
Microsoft Corp.	2.3	73.7	3.1
Kellogg Company	0.5	14.2	3.5

Practitioners' Methods of Choice

Because of the importance of capital budgeting, over the years a number of surveys have asked financial managers what techniques they actually use in making capital investment decisions. Exhibit 9.14, which summarizes the results from two such studies, reveals significant changes over time. As shown, in 1981 only 16.5 percent of the financial managers surveyed frequently used the NPV approach, and the payback period and accounting rate of return approaches were used even less frequently. Most firms, 65.3 percent, used the IRR method. However, practices changed in the 1980s and 1990s. By 1999, 74.9 percent of the firms surveyed were frequently using the NPV technique, 75.7 percent were using the IRR, and 56.7 percent were using the payback period method. As you can see, the most recent findings reflect a much better alignment between what practitioners do and the theory discussed in this chapter. As you can also see, many financial managers use multiple capital budgeting tools.

 An article that surveys the use of capital budgeting techniques by the CFOs of Fortune 500 companies can be found at http://faculty.fuqua.duke.edu/~jgraham/website/SurveyJACF.pdf.

EXHIBIT 9.14 **Capital Budgeting Techniques Used by Business Firms**

The exhibit summarizes evidence from two studies that examined the use of capital budgeting techniques by businesses. As you can see, over time more firms have come to use the NPV and IRR techniques. Surprisingly, though, even in 1999, 20.3 percent still computed the accounting rate of return.

Capital Budgeting Tool	Percent of Surveyed Firms That Use the Technique Frequently	
	1981	1999
Payback period	5.0%	56.7%
Accounting rate of return (ARR)	10.7	20.3
Internal rate of return (IRR)	65.3	75.7
Net persent value (NPV)	16.5	74.9

Sources: Stanley, Marjorie T., and Stanley B. Block, "A Survey of Multinational Capital Budgeting," *The Financial Review,* March 1984. Graham, John R., and Campbell R. Harvey, "The Theory and Practice of Corporate Finance," *Journal of Financial Economics,* May/June 2001.

Postaudit and Ongoing Reviews

Management should systematically review the status of all ongoing capital projects and perform postaudit reviews on all completed capital projects. In a **postaudit review**, management compares the actual performance of a project with what was projected in the capital budgeting proposal. For example, suppose a new microchip was expected to earn a 20 percent IRR, but the product's actual IRR turned out to be 9 percent. A postaudit examination would determine why the project failed to achieve its expected financial goals. Project reviews keep all people involved in the capital budgeting process honest because they know that the project and their performance will be reviewed and that they will be held accountable for the results.

Managers should also conduct *ongoing reviews* of capital projects in progress. Such a review should challenge the business plan, including the cash flow projections and the operating cost assumptions. For example, Intel has periodically reviewed the viability of its wafer fabrication plant in China and has made adjustments to reflect changing business conditions. Business plans are management's best estimates of future events at the time they are prepared, but as new information becomes available, the decision to undertake a capital project and the nature of that project must be reassessed.

Management must also evaluate the people responsible for implementing a capital project. They should monitor whether the project's revenues and expenses are meeting

postaudit review
an audit to compare actual project results with the results projected in the capital budgeting proposal

projections. If the project is not proceeding according to plan, the difficult task for management is to determine whether the problem is a flawed plan or poor execution by the implementation team.

> **BEFORE YOU GO ON**

1. What changes have taken place in the capital budgeting techniques used by U.S. companies?

SUMMARY OF Learning Objectives

1 Discuss why capital budgeting decisions are the most important investment decisions made by a firm's management.

Capital budgeting is the process by which management decides which productive assets the firm should invest in. Because capital expenditures involve large amounts of money, are critical to achieving the firm's strategic plan, define the firm's line of business over the long term, and determine the firm's profitability for years to come, they are considered the most important investment decisions made by management.

2 Explain the benefits of using the net present value (NPV) method to analyze capital expenditure decisions and calculate the NPV for a capital project.

The net present value (NPV) method leads to better investment decisions than other techniques because it (1) uses the discounted cash flow valuation approach, which accounts for the time value of money and (2) provides a direct measure of how much a capital project is expected to increase the dollar value of the firm. Thus, NPV is consistent with the top management goal of maximizing stockholder value. NPV calculations are described in Section 9.2 and Learning by Doing Application 9.1.

3 Describe the strengths and weaknesses of the payback period as a capital expenditure decision-making tool and compute the payback period for a capital project.

The payback period is the length of time it will take for the cash flows from a project to recover the cost of the project. The payback period is widely used, mainly because it is simple to apply and easy to understand. It also provides a simple measure of liquidity risk because it tells management how quickly the firm will get its money back. The payback period has a number of shortcomings, however. For one thing, the payback period, as most commonly computed, ignores the time value of money. We can overcome this objection by using discounted cash flows to calculate the payback period. Regardless of how the payback period is calculated, however, it fails to take account of cash flows recovered after the payback period. Thus, the payback period is biased in favor of short-lived projects. Also, the hurdle rate used to identify what payback period is acceptable is arbitrarily determined. Payback period calculations are described in Section 9.3 and Learning by Doing Application 9.2.

4 Explain why the accounting rate of return (ARR) is not recommended for use as a capital expenditure decision-making tool.

The ARR is based on accounting numbers, such as book value and net income, rather than cash flow data. As such, it is not a true rate of return. Instead of discounting a project's cash flows over time, it simply gives us a number based on average figures from the income statement and balance sheet. Furthermore, as with the payback method, there is no economic rationale for establishing the hurdle rate. Finally, the ARR does not account for the size of the projects when a choice between two projects of different sizes must be made.

5 Compute the internal rate of return (IRR) for a capital project and discuss the conditions under which the IRR technique and the NPV technique produce different results.

The IRR is the expected rate of return for an investment project; it is the discount rate that equates the present value of a project's expected cash inflows to the present value of the project's outflows—in other words, as the discount rate at which the NPV is equal to zero. Calculations are shown in Section 9.5 and Learning by Doing Application 9.3. If a project's IRR is greater than the required rate of return, the cost of capital, the project is accepted. The IRR rule often gives the same investment decision for a project as the NPV rule. However, the IRR method does have operational pitfalls that can lead to incorrect decisions. Specifically, when a project's cash flows are unconventional, the IRR calculation may yield no solution or more than one IRR. In addition, the IRR technique cannot be used to rank projects that are mutually exclusive because the project with the highest IRR may not be the project that would add the greatest value to the firm if accepted—that is, the project with the highest NPV.

6 Explain how the profitability index can be used to rank projects when a firm faces capital rationing and describe the limitations that apply to the profitability index.

The profitability index (PI) aids in the process of choosing the most valuable bundle of projects that the firm can afford. It is a measure of value received per dollar invested, which can be used to rank projects in a given period. The major limitation of the PI is that, although it can be used to rank projects in a given period, it can lead to misleading project choices in a multiperiod context.

7 Explain the benefits of postaudit and ongoing reviews of capital projects.

A postaudit review enables managers to determine whether a project's goals were met and to quantify the actual benefits or costs of the project. By conducting these reviews, managers can avoid making similar mistakes in future projects, learn to better recognize opportunities, and keep people involved in the budgeting process honest. An ongoing review enables managers to assess the impact of changing information and market conditions on the value of a project that is already underway. Unexpected changes in conditions can affect the viability of continuing such a project as originally conceived.

SUMMARY OF Key Equations

Equation	Description	Formula
9.1	Net present value	$$NPV = NCF_0 + \frac{NCF_1}{1+k} + \frac{NCF_2}{(1+k)^2} + \cdots + \frac{NCF_n}{(1+k)^n}$$ $$= \sum_{t=0}^{n} \frac{NCF_t}{(1+k)^t}$$
9.2	Payback period	$$PB = \text{Years before cost recovery} + \frac{\text{Remaining cost to recover}}{\text{Cash flow during the year}}$$
9.3	Accounting rate of return	$$ARR = \frac{\text{Average net income}}{\text{Average book value}}$$
9.4	Internal rate of return	$$NPV = \sum_{t=0}^{n} \frac{NCF_t}{(1+IRR)^t} = 0$$
9.5	Modified internal rate of return	$$PV_{Cost} = \frac{TV}{(1+MIRR)^n}$$
9.6	Profitability index	$$PI = \frac{NPV + \text{Initial investment}}{\text{Initial investment}}$$

Self-Study Problems

9.1 The management of Premium Manufacturing Company is evaluating two forklift systems to use in its plant that produces the towers for a windmill power farm. The costs and the cash flows from these systems are shown below. If the company uses a 12 percent discount rate for all projects, determine which forklift system should be purchased using the net present value (NPV) approach.

	Year 0	Year 1	Year 2	Year 3
Otis Forklifts	−$3,123,450	$979,225	$1,358,886	$2,111,497
Craigmore Forklifts	−$4,137,410	$875,236	$1,765,225	$2,865,110

9.2 Perryman Crafts Corp. management is evaluating two independent capital projects that will each cost the company $250,000. The two projects will provide the following cash flows:

Year	Project A	Project B
1	$ 80,750	$ 32,450
2	93,450	76,125
3	40,235	153,250
4	145,655	96,110

Which project will be chosen if the company's payback criterion is three years? What if the company accepts all projects as long as the payback period is less than five years?

9.3 Terrell Corp. management is considering purchasing a machine that will cost $117,250 and will be depreciated on a straight-line basis over a five-year period. The sales and expenses (excluding depreciation) for the next five years are shown in the following table. The company's tax rate is 34 percent.

	Year 1	Year 2	Year 3	Year 4	Year 5
Sales	$123,450	$176,875	$242,455	$255,440	$267,125
Expenses	$137,410	$126,488	$141,289	$143,112	$133,556

Terrell will accept all projects that provide an accounting rate of return (ARR) of at least 45 percent. Should the company accept this project?

9.4 Refer to Problem 9.1. Compute the IRR for each of the two systems. Is the investment decision different from the one indicated by NPV?

9.5 You are considering a project that has an initial outlay of $1 million. The profitability index of the project is 2.24. What is the NPV of the project?

Solutions to Self-Study Problems

9.1 NPVs for two forklift systems:

NPV for Otis Forklifts:

$$NPV_{Otis} = \sum_{t=0}^{n} \frac{NCF_t}{(1 + k)^t}$$

$$= -\$3,123,450 + \frac{\$979,225}{1.12} + \frac{\$1,358,886}{(1.12)^2} + \frac{\$2,111,497}{(1.12)^3}$$

$$= -\$3,123,450 + \$874,308 + \$1,083,296 + \$1,502,922$$

$$= \$337,076$$

NPV for Craigmore Forklifts:

$$NPV_{Craigmore} = \sum_{t=0}^{n} \frac{NCF_t}{(1 + k)^t}$$

$$= -\$4,137,410 + \frac{\$875,236}{1.12} + \frac{\$1,765,225}{(1.12)^2} + \frac{\$2,865,110}{(1.12)^3}.$$

$$= -\$4,137,410 + \$781,461 + \$1,407,227 + \$2,039,329$$

$$= \$90,607$$

Premium should purchase the Otis forklift since it has a larger NPV.

9.2 Payback periods for Perryman projects A and B:

	Project A	
Year	Cash Flow	Cumulative Cash Flows
0	($250,000)	($250,000)
1	80,750	(169,250)
2	93,450	(75,800)
3	40,235	(35,565)
4	145,655	110,090

	Project B	
Year	Cash Flow	Cumulative Cash Flows
0	($250,000)	($250,000)
1	32,450	(217,550)
2	76,125	(141,425)
3	153,250	11,825
4	96,110	107,935

Payback Period for Project A:

$$Payback\ period_A = Years\ before\ cost\ recovery + \frac{Remaining\ cost\ to\ recover}{Cash\ flow\ during\ the\ year}$$

$$= 3\ years + \frac{\$35,565}{\$145,655\ per\ year}$$

$$= 3.24\ years$$

Payback Period for Project B:

$$Payback\ period_B = Years\ before\ cost\ recovery + \frac{Remaining\ cost\ to\ recover}{Cash\ flow\ during\ the\ year}$$

$$= 2\ years + \frac{\$141,425}{\$153,250\ per\ year}$$

$$= 2.92\ years$$

If the payback period is three years, project B will be chosen. If the payback criterion is five years, both A and B will be chosen.

9.3 Evaluation of Terrell Corp. project:

	Year 1	Year 2	Year 3	Year 4	Year 5
Sales	$123,450	$176,875	$242,455	$255,440	$267,125
Expenses	137,410	126,488	141,289	143,112	133,556
Depreciation	23,450	23,450	23,450	23,450	23,450
EBIT	($ 37,410)	$ 26,937	$ 77,716	$ 88,878	$110,119
Taxes (34%)	12,719	9,159	26,423	30,219	37,440
Net Income	($ 24,691)	$ 17,778	$ 51,293	$ 58,659	$ 72,679
Beginning Book Value	117,250	93,800	70,350	46,900	23,450
Less: Depreciation	(23,450)	(23,450)	(23,450)	(23,450)	(23,450)
Ending Book Value	$ 93,800	$ 70,350	$ 46,900	$ 23,450	$ 0

$$\text{Average net income} = (-\$24,691 + \$17,778 + \$51,293 + \$58,659 + \$72,679)/5$$
$$= \$35,143.60$$
$$\text{Average book value} = (\$117,250 + \$93,800 + \$70,350 + \$46,900 + \$23,450 + \$0)/6$$
$$= \$58,625.00$$
$$\text{Accounting rate of return} = \$35,143.60/\$58,625.00$$
$$= 0.599, \text{ or } 59.9\%$$

The company should accept the project.

9.4 IRRs for two forklift systems:

Otis Forklifts:

First compute the IRR by the trial-and-error approach.

NPV (Otis) = $337,075 > 0

We should use a higher discount rate to get NPV = 0.

At $k = 15$ percent:

$$\text{NPV}_{\text{Otis}} = -\$3,123,450 + \frac{\$979,225}{1.15} + \frac{\$1,358,886}{(1.15)^2} + \frac{\$2,111,497}{(1.15)^3}$$
$$= -\$3,123,450 + \$851,500 + \$1,027,513 + \$1,388,344$$
$$= \$143,907$$

Try a higher rate. At $k = 17$ percent:

$$\text{NPV}_{\text{Otis}} = -\$3,123,450 + \$836,944 + \$992,685 + \$1,318,357$$
$$= \$24,536$$

Try a higher rate. At $k = 17.5$ percent:

$$\text{NPV}_{\text{Otis}} = -\$3,123,450 + \$833,383 + \$984,254 + \$1,301,598$$
$$= -\$4,215$$

Thus, the IRR for Otis is less than 17.5 percent. Using a financial calculator, you can find the exact rate to be 17.43 percent.

Craigmore Forklifts:

First compute the IRR using the trial-and-error approach.

NPV (Craigmore) = $90,606 > 0

We should use a higher discount rate to get NPV = 0.

At $k = 15$ percent:

$$\text{NPV}_{\text{Craigmore}} = -\$4,137,410 + \frac{\$875,236}{1.15} + \frac{\$1,765,225}{(1.12)^2} + \frac{\$2,865,110}{(1.12)^3}$$
$$= -\$4,137,410 + \$761,075 + \$1,334,764 + \$1,883,856$$
$$= -\$157,715$$

Try a lower rate. At $k = 13$ percent:

$$\text{NPV}_{\text{Craigmore}} = -\$4,137,410 + \$774,545 + \$1,382,430 + \$1,985,665$$
$$= \$5,230$$

Try a higher rate. At $k = 13.1$ percent:

$$\text{NPV}_{\text{Craigmore}} = -\$4,137,410 + \$773,860 + \$1,379,987 + \$1,980,403$$
$$= -\$3,161$$

Thus, the IRR for Craigmore is less than 13.1 percent. The exact rate is 13.06 percent. Based on the IRR, we would still choose the Otis system over the Craigmore system. The decision is the same as that indicated by NPV.

9.5 You can use Equation 9.6 to solve for the NPV:

$$PI = \frac{NPV + \text{Initial investment}}{\text{Initial investment}}$$

$$2.24 = \frac{NPV + \$1,000,000}{\$1,000,000}$$

Therefore:

$$NPV = \$1,240,000$$

Critical Thinking Questions

9.1 Explain why the cost of capital is referred to as the "hurdle" rate in capital budgeting.

9.2 a. Sykes, Inc. management is considering two projects: a plant expansion and a new computer system for the firm's production department. Classify these projects as independent, mutually exclusive, or contingent projects and explain your reasoning.

b. A company is building a new plant on the outskirts of Smallesville. The town has offered to donate the land, and as part of the agreement, the company will have to build an access road from the main highway to the plant. How will the project of building the road be classified in the capital budgeting analysis?

c. Your firm is currently considering the upgrading of the operating systems of all the firm's computers. One alternative is to choose the Linux operating system that a local computer services firm has offered to install and maintain. Microsoft has also put in a bid to install the new Windows operating system for businesses. What type of project is this?

9.3 In the context of capital budgeting, what is "capital rationing"?

9.4 Provide two conditions under which a set of projects might be characterized as mutually exclusive.

9.5 a. A firm invests in a project that is expected to earn a return of 12 percent. If the appropriate cost of capital is also 12 percent, did the firm make the right decision? Explain.

b. What is the impact on the firm if it accepts a project with a negative NPV?

9.6 Identify the weaknesses of the payback period method.

9.7 What are the strengths and weaknesses of the accounting rate of return approach?

9.8 Under what circumstances might the IRR and NPV approaches produce conflicting results?

9.9 The modified IRR (MIRR) alleviates two concerns with using the IRR method for evaluating capital investments. What are they?

9.10 Elkridge Construction Company has an overall (composite) cost of capital of 12 percent. This cost of capital reflects the cost of capital for an Elkridge Construction project with average risk. However, the firm takes on projects of various risk levels. The company's experience suggests that low-risk projects have a cost of capital of 10 percent and high-risk projects have a cost of capital of 15 percent. Which of the following projects should the company not select to maximize shareholder wealth?

Project	Expected Return	Risk
1. Single-family homes	13%	Low
2. Multifamily residential	12	Average
3. Commercial	18	High
4. Single-family homes	9	Low
5. Commercial	13	High

9.11 High Tech Monopoly Co. has plenty of cash to fund any conceivable positive NPV project. Can you describe a situation in which capital rationing could still occur?

9.12 The profitability index is a tool for measuring a project's benefits relative to its costs. How might this help to eliminate bias in project selection?

Questions and Problems

9.1 Net present value: Riggs Corp. management is planning to spend $650,000 on a new marketing campaign. They believe that this action will result in additional cash flows of $325,000 over the next three years. If the discount rate is 17.5 percent, what is the NPV on this project?

◁ BASIC

9.2 Net present value: Kingston, Inc. management is considering purchasing a new machine at a cost of $4,133,250. They expect this equipment to produce cash flows of $814,322, $863,275, $937,250, $1,017,112, $1,212,960, and $1,225,000 over the next six years. If the appropriate discount rate is 15 percent, what is the NPV of this investment?

9.3 Net present value: Crescent Industries management is planning to replace some existing machinery in its plant. The cost of the new equipment and the resulting cash flows are shown in the accompanying table. If the firm uses an 18 percent discount rate for projects like this, should management go ahead with the project?

Year	Cash Flow
0	−$3,300,000
1	875,123
2	966,222
3	1,145,000
4	1,250,399
5	1,504,445

9.4 Net present value: Management of Franklin Mints, a confectioner, is considering purchasing a new jelly bean-making machine at a cost of $312,500. They project that the cash flows from this investment will be $121,450 for the next seven years. If the appropriate discount rate is 14 percent, what is the NPV for the project?

9.5 Net present value: Blanda Incorporated management is considering investing in two alternative production systems. The systems are mutually exclusive, and the cost of the new equipment and the resulting cash flows are shown in the accompanying table. If the firm uses a 9 percent discount rate for production system projects, in which system should the firm invest?

Year	System 1	System 2
0	−$15,000	−$45,000
1	15,000	32,000
2	15,000	32,000
3	15,000	32,000

9.6 Payback: Refer to Problem 9.5. What are the payback periods for Production Systems 1 and 2? If the systems are mutually exclusive and the firm always chooses projects with the lowest payback period, in which system should the firm invest?

9.7 Payback: Quebec, Inc., is purchasing machinery at a cost of $3,768,966. The company's management expects the machinery to produce cash flows of $979,225, $1,158,886, and $1,881,497 over the next three years, respectively. What is the payback period?

9.8 Payback: Northern Specialties just purchased inventory-management computer software at a cost of $1,645,276. Cost savings from the investment over the next six years will produce the following cash flow stream: $212,455, $292,333, $387,479, $516,345, $645,766, and $618,325. What is the payback period on this investment?

9.9 Payback: Nakamichi Bancorp has made an investment in banking software at a cost of $1,875,000. Management expects productivity gains and cost savings over the next several years. If, as a result of this investment, the firm is expected to generate additional cash flows of $586,212, $713,277, $431,199, and $318,697 over the next four years, what is the investment's payback period?

9.10 Average accounting rate of return (ARR): Capitol Corp. management is expecting a project to generate after-tax income of $63,435 in each of the next three years. The average book value of the project's equipment over that period will be $212,500. If the firm's investment decision on any project is based on an ARR of 37.5 percent, should this project be accepted?

9.11 Internal rate of return: Refer to Problem 9.4. What is the IRR that Franklin Mints management can expect on this project?

9.12 Internal rate of return: Hathaway, Inc., a resort company, is refurbishing one of its hotels at a cost of $7.8 million. Management expects that this will lead to additional cash flows of $1.8 million for the next six years. What is the IRR of this project? If the appropriate cost of capital is 12 percent, should Hathaway go ahead with this project?

9.13 Profitability index: What is the profitability index, and why is it helpful in the capital rationing process?

INTERMEDIATE > **9.14 Net present value:** Champlain Corp. management is investigating two computer systems. The Alpha 8300 costs $3,122,300 and will generate cost savings of $1,345,500 in each of the next five years. The Beta 2100 system costs $3,750,000 and will produce cost savings of $1,125,000 in the first three years and then $2 million for the next two years. If the company's discount rate for similar projects is 14 percent, what is the NPV for the two systems? Which one should be chosen based on the NPV?

9.15 Net present value: Briarcrest Condiments is a spice-making firm. Recently, it developed a new process for producing spices. The process requires new machinery that would cost $1,968,450, have a life of five years, and would produce the cash flows shown in the following table. What is the NPV if the discount rate is 15.9 percent?

Year	Cash Flow
1	$512,496
2	−242,637
3	814,558
4	887,225
5	712,642

9.16 Net present value: Cranjet Industries is expanding its product line and its production capacity. The costs and expected cash flows of the two independent projects are given in the following table. The firm uses a discount rate of 16.4 percent for such projects.
a. What are the NPVs of the two projects?
b. Should both projects be accepted? or either? or neither? Explain your reasoning.

Year	Product Line Expansion	Production Capacity Expansion
0	−$2,575,000	−$8,137,250
1	600,000	2,500,000
2	875,000	2,500,000
3	875,000	2,500,000
4	875,000	3,250,000
5	875,000	3,250,000

9.17 Net present value: Emporia Mills management is evaluating two alternative heating systems. Costs and projected energy savings are given in the following table. The firm uses 11.5 percent to discount such project cash flows. Which system should be chosen?

Year	System 100	System 200
0	−$1,750,000	−$1,735,000
1	275,223	750,000
2	512,445	612,500
3	648,997	550,112
4	875,000	384,226

9.18 Payback: Creative Solutions, Inc., has just invested $4,615,300 in new equipment. The firm uses a payback period criteria of not accepting any project that takes more than four years to recover its costs. The company anticipates cash flows of $644,386, $812,178, $943,279, $1,364,997, $2,616,300, and $2,225,375 over the next six years. Does this investment meet the firm's payback criteria?

9.19 Discounted payback: Timeline Manufacturing Co. management is evaluating two projects. The company uses payback criteria of three years or less. Project A has a cost of $912,855, and Project

B's cost is $1,175,000. Cash flows from both projects are given in the following table. What are their discounted payback periods, and which will be accepted with a discount rate of 8 percent?

Year	Project A	Project B
1	$86,212	$586,212
2	313,562	413,277
3	427,594	231,199
4	285,552	

9.20 Payback: Regent Corp. management is evaluating three competing types of equipment. Costs and cash flow projections for all three are given in the following table. Which would be the best choice based on payback period?

Year	Type 1	Type 2	Type 3
0	−$1,311,450	−$1,415,888	−$1,612,856
1	212,566	586,212	786,212
2	269,825	413,277	175,000
3	455,112	331,199	175,000
4	285,552	141,442	175,000
5	121,396		175,000
6			175,000

9.21 Discounted payback: Nugent Communication Corp. is investing $9,365,000 in new technologies. The company's management expects significant benefits in the first three years after installation (as can be seen by the following cash flows), and smaller constant benefits in each of the next four years. What is the discounted payback period for the project assuming a discount rate of 10 percent?

	Year			
	1	2	3	4–7
Cash Flows	$2,265,433	$4,558,721	$3,378,911	$1,250,000

9.22 Modified internal rate of return (MIRR): Morningside Bakeries recently purchased equipment at a cost of $650,000. Management expects the equipment to generate cash flows of $275,000 in each of the next four years. The cost of capital is 14 percent. What is the MIRR for this project?

9.23 Modified internal rate of return (MIRR): Management of Sycamore Home Furnishings is considering acquiring a new machine that can create customized window treatments. The equipment will cost $263,400 and will generate cash flows of $85,000 over each of the next six years. If the cost of capital is 12 percent, what is the MIRR on this project?

9.24 Internal rate of return: Management of Great Flights, Inc., an aviation firm, is considering purchasing three aircraft for a total cost of $161 million. The company would lease the aircraft to an airline. Cash flows from the proposed leases are shown in the following table. What is the IRR of this project?

Years	Cash Flow
1–4	$23,500,000
5–7	72,000,000
8–10	80,000,000

9.25 Internal rate of return: Refer to Problem 9.5. Compute the IRR for both production System 1 and production System 2. Which has the higher IRR? Which production system has the higher NPV? Explain why the IRR and NPV rankings of Systems 1 and 2 are different.

9.26 Internal rate of return: Ancala Corporation management is considering investments in two new golf apparel lines for next season: golf hats and belts. Due to a funding constraint, these lines are mutually exclusive. A summary of each project's estimated cash flows over its three-year life, as well as the IRR and NPV of each, are outlined below. The CFO of the firm has decided to manufacture the belts; however, the CEO is questioning this decision given that the IRR is higher for manufacturing hats. Explain to the CEO why the IRRs and NPVs of the belt and hat projects disagree? Is the CFO's decision correct?

Year	Golf Belts	Golf Hats
0	−$1,000	−$500
1	1000	500
2	500	300
3	500	300
NPV	$697.97	$427.87
IRR	54%	61%

9.27 Internal rate of return: Compute the IRR on the following cash flow streams:
   a. An initial investment of $25,000 followed by a single cash flow of $37,450 in year 6.
   b. An initial investment of $1 million followed by a single cash flow of $1,650,000 in year 4.
   c. An initial investment of $2 million followed by cash flows of $1,650,000 and $1,250,000 in years 2 and 4, respectively.

9.28 Internal rate of return: Compute the IRR for the following project cash flows:
   a. An initial outlay of $3,125,000 followed by annual cash flows of $565,325 for the next eight years.
   b. An initial investment of $33,750 followed by annual cash flows of $9,430 for the next five years.
   c. An initial outlay of $10,000 followed by annual cash flows of $2,500 for the next seven years.

9.29 Profitability index: Suppose that you could invest in the following projects but have only $30,000 to invest. How would you make your decision and in which projects would you invest?

Project	Cost	NPV
A	$ 8,000	$4,000
B	11,000	7,000
C	9,000	5,000
D	7,000	4,000

9.30 Profitability index: Suppose that you could invest in the same projects as in the previous problem but have only $25,000 to invest. Which projects would you choose?

ADVANCED > **9.31** Management of Draconian Measures, Inc., is evaluating two independent projects. The company uses a 13.8 percent discount rate for such projects. The costs and cash flows for the projects are shown in the following table. What are their NPVs?

Year	Project 1	Project 2
0	−$8,425,375	−$11,368,000
1	3,225,997	2,112,589
2	1,775,882	3,787,552
3	1,375,112	3,125,650
4	1,176,558	4,115,899
5	1,212,645	4,556,424
6	1,582,156	
7	1,365,882	

9.32 Refer to Problem 9.31.
   a. What are the IRRs for the projects?
   b. Does the IRR criterion suggest a different decision than the NPV criterion?
   c. Explain how you would expect the management of Draconian Measures to decide.

9.33 Management of Dravid, Inc., is currently evaluating three projects that are independent. The cost of funds can be either 13.6 percent or 14.8 percent depending on their financing plan. All three projects cost the same at $500,000. Expected cash flow streams are shown in the following table. Which projects would be accepted at a discount rate of 14.8 percent? What if the discount rate was 13.6 percent?

Year	Project 1	Project 2	Project 3
1	$ 0	$ 0	$245,125
2	125,000	0	212,336
3	150,000	500,000	112,500
4	375,000	500,000	74,000

9.34 Management of Intrepid, Inc., is considering investing in three independent projects. The costs and the cash flows are given in the following table. The appropriate cost of capital is 14.5 percent. Compute the project IRRs and identify the projects that should be accepted.

Year	Project 1	Project 2	Project 3
0	−$275,000	−$312,500	−$500,000
1	63,000	153,250	212,000
2	85,000	167,500	212,000
3	85,000	112,000	212,000
4	100,000		212,000

9.35 Jekyll & Hyde Corp. management is evaluating two mutually exclusive projects. The cost of capital is 15 percent. Costs and cash flows for each project are given in the following table. Which project should be accepted?

Year	Project 1	Project 2
0	−$1,250,000	−$1,250,000
1	250,000	350,000
2	350,000	350,000
3	450,000	350,000
4	500,000	350,000
5	750,000	350,000

9.36 Management of Larsen Automotive, a manufacturer of auto parts, is considering investing in two projects. The company typically compares project returns to a cost of funds of 17 percent. Compute the IRRs based on the cash flows in the following table. Which project(s) will be accepted?

Year	Project 1	Project 2
0	−$475,000	−$500,000
1	300,000	117,500
2	110,000	181,300
3	125,000	244,112
4	140,000	278,955

9.37 Compute the IRR for each of the following projects:

Year	Project 1	Project 2	Project 3
0	−$10,000	−$10,000	−$10,000
1	4,750	1,650	800
2	3,300	3,890	1,200
3	3,600	5,100	2,875
4	2,100	2,750	3,400
5		800	6,600

9.38 Primus Corp. management is planning to convert an existing warehouse into a new plant that will increase its production capacity by 45 percent. The cost of this project will be $7,125,000. It will result in additional cash flows of $1,875,000 for the next eight years. The discount rate is 12 percent.
 a. What is the payback period?
 b. What is the NPV for this project?
 c. What is the IRR?

9.39 Quasar Tech Co. management is investing $6 million in new machinery that will produce the next-generation routers. Sales to its customers will amount to $1,750,000 for the next three years and then increase to $2.4 million for three more years. The project is expected to last six years and operating costs, excluding depreciation, will be $898,620 annually. The machinery will be depreciated to a salvage value of $0 over 6 years using the straight-line method. The company's tax rate is 30 percent, and the cost of capital is 16 percent.
 a. What is the payback period?
 b. What is the average accounting return (ARR)?
 c. Calculate the project NPV.
 d. What is the IRR for the project?

9.40 Management of Skywards, Inc., an airline caterer, is purchasing refrigerated trucks at a total cost of $3.25 million. After-tax net income from this investment is expected to be $750,000 for the next five years. Annual depreciation expense will be $650,000. The cost of capital is 17 percent.
  a. What is the discounted payback period?
  b. Compute the ARR.
  c. What is the NPV on this investment?
  d. Calculate the IRR.

9.41 Trident Corp. management is evaluating two independent projects. The costs and expected cash flows are given in the following table. The cost of capital is 10 percent.

Year	A	B
0	−$312,500	−$395,000
1	121,450	153,552
2	121,450	158,711
3	121,450	166,220
4	121,450	132,000
5	121,450	122,000

  a. Calculate the projects' NPV.
  b. Calculate the projects' IRR.
  c. Which project should be chosen based on NPV? Based on IRR? Is there a conflict?
  d. If you are the decision maker for the firm, which project or projects will be accepted? Explain your reasoning.

9.42 Management of Tyler, Inc., is considering switching to a new production technology. The cost of the required equipment will be $4 million. The discount rate is 12 percent. The cash flows that the firm expects the new technology to generate are as follows.

Years	CF
1–2	0
3–5	$ 845,000
6–9	$1,450,000

  a. Compute the payback and discounted payback periods for the project.
  b. What is the NPV for the project? Should the firm go ahead with the project?
  c. What is the IRR, and what would be the decision based on the IRR?

9.43 You are analyzing two proposed capital investments with the following cash flows:

Year	Project X	Project Y
0	−$20,000	−$20,000
1	13,000	7,000
2	6,000	7,000
3	6,000	7,000
4	2,000	7,000

The cost of capital for both projects is 10 percent. Calculate the profitability index (PI) for each project. Which project, or projects, should be accepted if you have unlimited funds to invest? Which project should be accepted if they are mutually exclusive?

CFA PROBLEMS ▷ **9.44** Given the following cash flows for a capital project, calculate the NPV and IRR. The required rate of return is 8 percent.

	Year					
	0	1	2	3	4	5
Cash Flow	−$50,000	$15,000	$15,000	$20,000	$10,000	$5,000

	NPV	IRR
a.	$1,905	10.9%
b.	$1,905	26.0%
c.	$3,379	10.9%
d.	$3,379	26.0%

9.45 Given the following cash flows for a capital project, calculate its payback period and discounted payback period. The required rate of return is 8 percent.

	Year					
	0	**1**	**2**	**3**	**4**	**5**
Cash Flow	−$50,000	$15,000	$15,000	$20,000	$10,000	$5,000

The discounted payback period is
a. 0.16 year longer than the payback period.
b. 0.80 year longer than the payback period.
c. 1.01 years longer than the payback period.
d. 1.85 years longer than the payback period.

9.46 An investment of $100 generates after-tax cash flows of $40 in Year 1, $80 in Year 2, and $120 in Year 3. The required rate of return is 20 percent. The net present value is closest to
a. $42.22
b. $58.33
c. $68.52
d. $98.95

9.47 An investment of $150,000 is expected to generate an after-tax cash flow of $100,000 in one year and another $120,000 in two years. The cost of capital is 10 percent. What is the internal rate of return?
a. 28.19 percent
b. 28.39 percent
c. 28.59 percent
d. 28.79 percent

9.48 An investment requires an outlay of $100 and produces after-tax cash flows of $40 annually for four years. A project enhancement increases the required outlay by $15 and the annual after-tax cash flows by $5. How will the enhancement affect the project's NPV profile? The vertical intercept of the NPV profile of the project shifts:
a. Up and the horizontal intercept shifts left.
b. Up and the horizontal intercept shifts right.
c. Down and the horizontal intercept shifts left.
d. Down and the horizontal intercept shifts right.

Sample Test Problems

9.1 Net present value: Techno Corp. management is considering developing new computer software. The cost of development will be $675,000, and management expects the net cash flow from sale of the software to be $195,000 for each of the next six years. If the discount rate is 14 percent, what is the net present value of this project?

9.2 Net present value: Raycom, Inc. needs a new overhead crane and two alternatives are available. Crane T costs $1.35 million and will produce cost savings of $765,000 in each of the next three years. Crane R will cost $1.675 million and will yield annual cost savings of $815,000 for the next three years. The required rate of return is 15 percent. Which of the two options should Raycom choose based on NPV criteria, and why?

9.3 Payback method: Parker Office Supplies management is considering replacing the company's outdated inventory-management software. The cost of the new software will be $168,000. Cost savings are expected to be $43,500 for each of the first three years and then drop to $36,875 for the following two years. What is the payback period for this project?

9.4 Internal rate of return: Refer to Sample Test Problem 9.1. What is the IRR on this project?

9.5 You are chairperson of the investment committee at your firm. Five projects have been submitted to your committee for approval this month. The investment required and the project profitability index for each of these projects are presented in the following table:

Project	Investment	PI
A	$20,000	2.500
B	50,000	2.000
C	70,000	1.750
D	10,000	1.000
E	80,000	0.800

If you have $500,000 available for investments, which of these projects would you approve? Assume that you do not have to worry about having enough resources for future investments when making this decision.

10 Cash Flows and Capital Budgeting

David Woo/© Corbis

Learning Objectives

1. Explain why incremental after-tax free cash flows are relevant in evaluating a project and calculate them for a project.

2. Discuss the five general rules for incremental after-tax free cash flow calculations and explain why cash flows stated in nominal (real) dollars should be discounted using a nominal (real) discount rate.

3. Describe how distinguishing between variable and fixed costs can be useful in forecasting operating expenses.

4. Explain the concept of equivalent annual cost and use it to compare projects with unequal lives.

CHAPTER TEN

On September 27, 2010, Southwest Airlines announced that it had agreed to purchase its smaller rival AirTran Airways for $1.4 billion in cash and stock. This would be the third large U.S. airline merger in two years. By the end of the day, Southwest's stock price was up 8.7 percent while the S&P 500 stock market index was down 0.5 percent. The 8.7 percent change in Southwest's stock price represented a nearly $800 million increase in the total value of its common stock. This increase, combined with the decrease in the value of the S&P 500 index, suggests that investors thought the acquisition of AirTran would have a very large positive impact on the wealth of Southwest stockholders.

When the managers of Southwest announced their plans to acquire AirTran, they were announcing a $1.4 billion investment. This investment was viewed by stock market investors from the same perspective as any capital project that a firm might pursue. Investors evaluated whether the Net Present Value (NPV) of the expected cash flows from the acquisition of AirTran would be positive or negative. The financial model used to estimate this NPV is the same one you saw in Chapter 9. The increase in the value of Southwest stock on the day of the announcement reflected investors' estimates of the NPV of the decision to purchase Airtran.

In Chapter 9 we stressed understanding the NPV concept and other project valuation models as well as the mechanics of discounting project cash flows. This chapter focuses on *what* project cash flows are discounted and *how* they are calculated and used in practice. The topics covered in this chapter are central to the goal of value creation. It is necessary to understand them in order to determine which capital projects have positive NPVs and which projects have negative NPVs. Only if you can do this will you be able to choose projects that create value.

CHAPTER PREVIEW

In Chapter 9 we saw that capital budgeting involves comparing the benefits and costs associated with a project to determine whether the project creates value for stockholders. These benefits and costs are reflected in the cash flows that the project is expected to produce. The NPV is a dollar measure of the amount by which the present value of the benefits exceeds the present value of the costs. Chapters 10 and 11 discuss how analysts actually apply the capital budgeting concepts introduced in Chapter 9. This chapter focuses on cash flows, while Chapter 11 covers concepts related to the discount rate.

We begin this chapter with a discussion of how to calculate the cash flows used to compute the NPV of a project. We then present five rules to follow when you calculate cash flows. We also address some concepts that will help you better understand cash flow calculations.

Next, we discuss how analysts actually forecast a project's cash flows. Since the cash flows generated by a project will almost certainly differ from the forecasts, it is important to have a framework that helps minimize errors and ensures that forecasts are internally consistent. We discuss such a framework in this part of the chapter.

Finally, in the last section we describe how analysts adjust cash flows to choose between projects that have different lives.

10.1 CALCULATING PROJECT CASH FLOWS

We begin our discussion of cash flows in capital budgeting by describing the mechanics of cash flow calculations and the rules for estimating the cash flows for individual projects. You will see that the approach we use to calculate project cash flows is similar to that used to calculate the cash flow to investors discussed in Chapter 3. However, there are two very important differences:

LEARNING OBJECTIVE **1**

1. Most important, the cash flows used in capital budgeting calculations are based on forecasts of *future* cash revenues, expenses, taxes, and investment outlays. In contrast, in Chapter 3 we focused on calculating historical cash flows to investors using accounting statements, rather than the future cash flows that might be generated by the firm.

2. In capital budgeting we focus on estimating the cash flows we expect an individual project to produce in the future, which we refer to as incremental after-tax free cash flows. In contrast, the cash flow to investors in Chapter 3 is a measure of the cash flows generated by the entire firm.

> **CAPITAL BUDGETING IS FORWARD LOOKING**
>
> **BUILDING INTUITION**
>
> In capital budgeting, we estimate the NPV of the cash flows that a project is *expected to produce in the future*. In other words, all of the cash flow estimates are forward looking. This is very different from using historical accounting statements to estimate cash flows.

Incremental After-Tax Free Cash Flows

incremental after-tax free cash flows
the difference between the total after-tax free cash flows at a firm with a project and the total after-tax free cash flows at the same firm without that project; a measure of a project's total impact on the free cash flows at a firm

The cash flows we discount in an NPV analysis are the **incremental after-tax free cash flows** that are expected from the project. The term *incremental* refers to the fact that these cash flows reflect how much the firm's total after-tax free cash flows will change if the project is adopted. Thus, we define the incremental after-tax free cash flows (FCF) for a project as the total after-tax free cash flows the firm would produce with the project, less the total after-tax free cash flows the firm would produce without the project.

$$\text{FCF}_{\text{Project}} = \text{FCF}_{\text{Firm with project}} - \text{FCF}_{\text{Firm without project}} \qquad (10.1)$$

In other words, $\text{FCF}_{\text{Project}}$ equals the net effect the project will have on the firm's cash revenues, costs, taxes, and investment outlays. These are the cash flows investors care about.

Throughout the rest of this chapter, we will refer to the total incremental after-tax free cash flows associated with a project simply as the FCF for the project. For convenience, we will drop the "Project" subscript from the FCF in Equation 10.1.

The FCF for a project is what we generically referred to as NCF in Chapter 9. The term *free cash flows*, which is commonly used in practice, refers to the fact that the firm is free to distribute these cash flows to creditors and stockholders because these are the cash flows that are left over after a firm has made necessary investments in working capital and long-term assets. The cash flows associated with financing a project (cash outflows or inflows to or from creditors or stockholders) are not included in the FCF calculation because, as we will discuss in Chapter 11, these are accounted for in the discount rate that is used in an NPV analysis. All of these points will become clearer as we discuss the FCF calculation next.

The FCF Calculation

The FCF calculation is illustrated in Exhibit 10.1. Let's begin with an overall review of how the calculation is done. After that, we will look more closely at details of the calculation.

incremental cash flow from operations (CF Opns)
the cash flow that a project generates after all operating expenses and taxes have been paid but before any cash outflows for investments

When we calculate the FCFs for a project, we first compute the **incremental cash flow from operations (CF Opns)** for each year during the project's life. This is the cash flow that the project is expected to generate after all operating expenses and taxes have been paid. To obtain the FCF, we then subtract the **incremental capital expenditures (Cap Exp)** and the **incremental additions to working capital (Add WC)** required for the project. Cap Exp and

incremental capital expenditures (Cap Exp)
the investments in property, plant, and equipment and other long-term assets that must be made if a project is pursued

incremental additions to working capital (Add WC)
the investments in working capital items, such as accounts receivable, inventory, and accounts payable, that must be made if the project is pursued

EXHIBIT 10.1 **The Free Cash Flow Calculation**

This exhibit shows how the incremental after-tax free cash flow (FCF) for a project is calculated. The FCF equals the change in the firm's cash income, excluding interest expense, that the project is responsible for, plus depreciation and amortization for the project, minus all required capital expenditures and investments in working capital. FCF also equals the incremental after-tax cash flow from operations minus the capital expenditures and investments in working capital required for the project.

Explanation	Calculation	Formula
The change in the firm's cash income, excluding interest expense, resulting from the project	Revenue	Revenue
	− Cash operating expenses	− Op Ex
	Earnings before interest, taxes, depreciation, and amortization	EBITDA
	− Depreciation and amortization	− D&A
	Operating profit	EBIT
	× (1 − Firm's marginal tax rate)	× (1 − *t*)
	Net operating profit after tax	NOPAT
Adjustments for the impact of depreciation and amortization and investments on FCF	+ Depreciation and amortization	+ D&A
	Cash flow from operations	CF Opns
	− Capital expenditures	− Cap Exp
	− Additions to working capital	− Add WC
	= Free cash flow	= FCF

Add WC represent the investments in long-term assets, such as property, plant, and equipment, and in working capital items, such as accounts receivable, inventory, and accounts payable, which must be made if the project is pursued.

As we noted earlier, the calculation of free cash flows for capital budgeting, which is summarized in Exhibit 10.1, is very similar to the calculation of the cash flows to investors that we discussed in Chapter 3. This should not be surprising since managers evaluate projects based on the present value of the cash flows they produce for their firms' investors. Nevertheless, there is an important computational difference between the cash flow calculations in Chapters 3 and 10. In Exhibit 10.1 the taxes for a project analysis are computed by multiplying the project's operating profit (EBIT) by the firm's marginal tax rate. This calculation gives us the taxes that the firm would owe on a project if no debt is used to finance that project. In contrast, the calculation in Chapter 3 uses the actual taxes paid by the firm, which includes the effect that interest deductions have on the taxes owed. It is true that interest payments will reduce the taxable income from a project if any debt financing is used. However, we ignore this reduction when evaluating a project for two reasons. First, we want to exclude the effects associated with how the project is financed in order to isolate the cash flows from the project itself. Second, as we discuss in Chapter 11, the cost of both debt and equity financing for a project, including the impact of using debt financing on the firm's tax obligations, are reflected in the discount rate. Doing the calculation this way makes it easier to estimate the NPV of a project under alternative financial structures.

Since the FCF calculation gives us the after-tax cash flows from operations over and above what is necessary to make any required investments, the FCFs for a project are the cash flows that the firm's investors can expect to receive from the project. This is why we discount the FCFs when we compute the NPV.

> ## BUILDING INTUITION
>
> ### INCREMENTAL AFTER-TAX FREE CASH FLOWS ARE WHAT STOCKHOLDERS CARE ABOUT IN CAPITAL BUDGETING
>
> When evaluating a project, managers focus on the FCF that the project is expected to produce because that is what stockholders care about. The FCFs reflect the impact of the project on the firm's overall cash flows. They also represent the additional cash flows that can be distributed to security holders if the project is accepted. Only after-tax cash flows matter because these are the cash flows that are actually available for distribution after taxes are paid to the government.

The formula for the FCF calculation can also be written as:

$$FCF = [(\text{Revenue} - \text{Op Ex} - \text{D\&A}) \times (1 - t)] + \text{D\&A} - \text{Cap Exp} - \text{Add WC} \quad (10.2)$$

where Revenue is the incremental revenue (net sales) associated with the project, D&A is the **incremental depreciation and amortization** associated with the project, and t is the **firm's marginal tax rate**.

Let's use Equation 10.2 to work through an example. Suppose you are considering purchasing a new truck for your plumbing business. This truck will increase revenues $50,000 and operating expenses $30,000 in the next year. Depreciation and amortization charges for the truck will equal $10,000 next year, and your firm's marginal tax rate will be 35 percent. Capital expenditures of $3,000 will be required to offset wear and tear on the truck, but no additions to working capital will be required. To calculate the FCF for the project in the next year, you can simply substitute the appropriate values into Equation 10.2:

$$
\begin{aligned}
FCF &= [(\text{Revenue} - \text{Op Ex} - \text{D\&A}) \times (1 - t)] + \text{D\&A} - \text{Cap Exp} - \text{Add WC} \\
&= [(\$50,000 - \$30,000 - \$10,000) \times (1 - 0.35)] + \$10,000 - \$3,000 - \$0 \\
&= \$13,500
\end{aligned}
$$

The FCF calculated with Equation 10.2 equals the total annual cash flow the firm will produce with the project less the total cash flow the firm will produce without the project. Even so, it is important to note that it is not necessary to actually estimate the firm's total cash flows in an NPV analysis. We need only estimate the cash outflows and inflows that arise as a direct result of the project in order to value it. The idea that we can evaluate the cash flows from a project independently of the cash flows for the firm is known as the **stand-alone principle**. The stand-alone principle says that we can treat the project as if it were a stand-alone firm that has its own revenue, expenses, and investment requirements. NPV analysis compares the present value of the FCF from this stand-alone firm with the cost of the project.

To fully understand the stand-alone principle, it is helpful to consider an example. Suppose that you own shares of stock in Dell, Inc., and that Dell's stock is currently selling for $13.90 per share. Now suppose that Dell's management announces it will immediately invest

incremental depreciation and amortization (D&A)
the depreciation and amortization charges that are associated with a project

firm's marginal tax rate (t)
the tax rate that is applied to each additional dollar of earnings at a firm

stand-alone principle
the principle that allows us to treat each project as a stand-alone firm when we perform an NPV analysis

$1.9 billion in a new production and distribution center that is expected to produce after-tax cash flows of $0.6 billion per year forever. Since Dell has 1.9 billion shares outstanding and uses no debt, this means that the investment will equal $1.00 per share ($1.9 billion/1.9 billion shares = $1.00 per share). The annual increase in the cash flows for Dell is expected to be $0.32 per share per year ($0.6 billion/1.9 billion shares = $0.32 per share). How should this announcement affect the value of a share of Dell stock?

If the appropriate cost of capital for the project is 10 percent, then from Equation 8.2 and the discussion in Chapter 9, we know that the value of a share of Dell's stocks should increase by D/R = $0.32/0.10 = $3.20 less the $1.00 invested, or $2.20, making each share of Dell stock worth $13.90 + $2.20 = $16.10 after the announcement. This example illustrates how the stand-alone principle allows us to simply add the value of a project's cash flows to the value of the firm's other cash flows to obtain the total value of the firm with the project.

Cash Flows from Operations

incremental net operating profits after tax (NOPAT)
a measure of the impact of a project on the firm's cash net income, excluding the effects of any interest expenses associated with financing the project

Let's examine Exhibit 10.1 in more detail to better understand why FCF is calculated as it is. First, note that the incremental cash flow from operations, CF Opns, equals the **incremental net operating profits after tax (NOPAT)** plus D&A.

If you refer back to the discussion of the income statement in Chapter 3, you will notice that NOPAT is essentially a cash flow measure of the incremental net income from the project without interest expenses. In other words, it is the impact of the project on the firm's cash flow, excluding the effects of any interest expenses associated with financing the project. We exclude interest expenses when calculating NOPAT because, as we mentioned earlier, the cost of financing a project is reflected in the discount rate.

We use the firm's marginal tax rate, t, to calculate NOPAT because the profits from a project are assumed to be incremental to the firm. Since the firm already pays taxes, the appropriate tax rate for FCF calculations is the tax rate that the firm will pay on any *additional* profits that are earned because the project is adopted. You may recall from Chapter 3 that this rate is the marginal tax rate. We will discuss taxes in more detail later in this chapter.

We add incremental depreciation and amortization, D&A, to NOPAT when calculating CF Opns because, as in the accounting statement of cash flows, D&A represents a noncash charge that reduces the firm's tax obligation. Note that we subtract D&A before computing the taxes that the firm would pay on the incremental earnings for the project. This accounts for the ability of the firm to deduct D&A when computing taxes. However, since D&A is a noncash charge, we have to add it back to NOPAT in order to get the cash flow from operations right.

The net effect of subtracting D&A, computing the taxes, and then adding back D&A is to reduce the taxes attributable to earnings from the project. For example, suppose that EBITDA for a project is $100.00, D&A is $50.00, and t is 35 percent. If we did not subtract D&A before computing taxes and add it back to compute CF Opns, the taxes owed for the project would be $100.00 \times 0.35 = $35.00 and CF Opns would be $100.00 − $35.00 = $65.00. This would understate CF Opns from this project by $17.50 since deducting D&A reduces the firm's tax obligation by this amount. With this deduction, the correct tax obligation is ($100.00 − $50.00) \times 0.35 = $17.50 and the correct CF Opns is $100.00 − $17.50 = $82.50. We get exactly this value when we compute CF Opns as shown in Exhibit 10.1 and Equation 10.2:

$$\text{CF Opns} = [(\text{Revenue} - \text{Op Ex} - \text{D\&A}) \times (1 - t)] + \text{D\&A}$$

since Revenue − Op Ex = EBITDA, as shown in Exhibit 10.1, we can write:

$$\begin{aligned}
\text{CF Opns} &= [(\text{EBITDA} - \text{D\&A}) \times (1 - t)] + \text{D\&A} \\
&= [(\$100.00 - \$50.00) \times (1 - 0.35)] + \$50.00 \\
&= 82.50
\end{aligned}$$

Cash Flows Associated with Capital Expenditures and Net Working Capital

tangible assets
physical assets such as property, plant, and equipment

Once we have estimated CF Opns, we simply subtract cash flows associated with the required investments to obtain the FCF for a project in a particular period. Investments can be required to purchase long-term **tangible assets**, such as property, plant, and equipment, to purchase

intangible assets, such as patents, mailing lists, or brand names, or to fund **current assets**, such as accounts receivables and inventories.

It is important to recognize that all investments that are incremental to a project must be accounted for. The most obvious investments are those in the land, buildings, and machinery and equipment that are acquired for the project. However, investments in intangible assets can also be required. For example, a manufacturing firm may purchase the right to use a particular production technology. Incremental investments in long-term tangible assets and intangible assets are collectively referred to as incremental capital expenditures (Cap Exp).

In addition to tangible and intangible assets, such as those described earlier, it is also necessary to account for incremental additions to working capital (Add WC). For example, if the product being produced is going to be sold on credit, thereby generating additional accounts receivable, the cost of providing that credit must be accounted for. Similarly, if it will be necessary to hold product in inventory, the cost of financing that inventory must be considered. Finally, it is important to consider any incremental changes in current liabilities associated with the project.

intangible assets
nonphysical assets such as patents, mailing lists, or brand names

current assets
assets, such as accounts receivable and inventories, that are expected to be liquidated (collected or sold) within one year

The FCF Calculation: An Example

Let's work a more comprehensive example to see how FCF is calculated in practice. Suppose that you work at an outdoor performing arts center and are evaluating a project to increase the number of seats by building four new box seating areas and adding 5,000 seats for the general public. Each box seating area is expected to generate $400,000 in incremental annual revenue, while each of the new seats for the general public will generate $2,500 in incremental annual revenue. The incremental expenses associated with the new boxes and seating will amount to 60 percent of the revenues. These expenses include hiring additional personnel to handle concessions, ushering, and security. The new construction will cost $10 million and will be fully depreciated (to a value of zero dollars) on a straight-line basis over the 10-year life of the project. The center will have to invest $1 million in additional working capital immediately, but the project will not require any other working capital investments during its life. This working capital will be recovered in the last year of the project. The center's marginal tax rate is 30 percent. What are the incremental cash flows from this project?

When evaluating a project, it is generally helpful to first organize your calculations by setting up a worksheet such as the one illustrated in Exhibit 10.2. A worksheet like this helps ensure that the calculations are completed correctly. The left-hand column in Exhibit 10.2 shows the actual calculations that will be performed. Other columns are included for each of the years during the life of the project, from Year 0 (today) through the last year in the life of the project (Year 10). In this example the cash flows will be exactly the same for Years 1 through 9; therefore, for illustration purposes, we will only include a single column to represent these years. If you were using a spreadsheet program, you would normally include one column for each year.

EXHIBIT 10.2 FCF Calculation Worksheet for the Performing Arts Center Project

A free cash flow (FCF) calculation table is useful in evaluating a project. It helps organize the calculations and ensure that they are completed correctly.

	Year 0	Years 1 to 9	Year 10
Revenue			
− Op Ex			
EBITDA			
− D&A			
EBIT			
× (1 − t)			
NOPAT			
+ D&A			
CF Opns			
− Cap Exp			
− Add WC			
= FCF			

Unless there is information to the contrary, we can assume that the investment outlay for this project will be made today (Year 0). We do this because in a typical project, no revenue will be generated and no expenses will be incurred until after the investment has been made. Consequently, the only cash flows in Year 0 are those for new construction (Cap Exp = $10,000,000) and additional working capital (Add WC = $1,000,000). The FCF in Year 0 will therefore equal −$11,000,000.

In Years 1 through 9, incremental revenue (Revenue) will equal:

Box seating ($400,000 × 4)	$ 1,600,000
Public seating ($2,500 × 5,000)	$12,500,000
Total incremental net revenue	$14,100,000

Incremental Op Ex will equal 0.60 × $14,100,000 = $8,460,000. Finally, depreciation (there is no amortization in this example) is computed as:

$$D\&A = (\text{Cap Exp} - \text{Salvage value of Cap Exp})/\text{Depreciable life of the investment}$$
$$= (\$10,000,000 - \$0)/10 \text{ years}$$
$$= \$1,000,000$$

Note that only the Cap Exp are depreciated and that these capital expenditures will be completely depreciated or written off over the 10-year life of the project because no salvage value is anticipated. Working capital is not depreciated because it will be recovered at the end of the project as the project's inventory is sold off, receivables are collected, and short-term liabilities are repaid.

The cash flows in Year 10 will be the same as those in Years 1 through 9 except that the $1 million invested in additional working capital will be recovered in the last year. The $1 million is added back to (or a negative number is subtracted from) the incremental cash flows from operations in the calculation of the Year 10 cash flows.

The completed cash flow calculation worksheet for this example is presented in Exhibit 10.3. We could have completed the calculations without the worksheet. However, as mentioned, a cash flow calculation worksheet is a useful tool because it helps us make sure we don't forget anything. Once we have set up the worksheet, calculating the incremental cash flows is simply a matter of filling in the blanks. As you will see in the following discussion, correctly filling in some blanks can be difficult at times, but the worksheet keeps us organized by reminding us which blanks have yet to be filled in.

Notice that with a discount rate of 10 percent, the NPV of the cash flows in Exhibit 10.3 is $15,487,664. As in Chapter 9, the NPV is obtained by calculating the present values of all of the cash flows and adding them up. You might confirm this by doing this calculation yourself.

EXHIBIT 10.3   **Completed FCF Calculation Worksheet for the Performing Arts Center Project**

The completed calculation table shows how the incremental after-tax free cash flows (FCF) for the performing arts center project are computed, along with the NPV for that project when the cost of capital is 10 percent.

	Year 0	Years 1 to 9	Year 10
Revenue		$14,100,000	$14,100,000
− Op Ex		8,460,000	8,460,000
EBITDA		$ 5,640,000	$ 5,640,000
− D&A		1,000,000	1,000,000
EBIT		$ 4,640,000	$ 4,640,000
× (1 − t)		0.70	0.70
NOPAT		$ 3,248,000	$ 3,248,000
+ D&A		1,000,000	1,000,000
CF Opns		$ 4,248,000	$ 4,248,000
− Cap Exp	$10,000,000	0	0
− Add WC	1,000,000	0	−1,000,000
= FCF	−$11,000,000	$ 4,248,000	$ 5,248,000
NPV @ 10%	$15,487,664		

USING EXCEL

PERFORMING ARTS CENTER PROJECT

Cash flow calculations for capital budgeting problems are best set up and solved using a spreadsheet application. Here is the setup for the performing arts center project:

	A	B	0	1	2	3	4	5	6	7	8	9	10
1	**Key Assumptions:**												
2	Life of the project (Years)	10											
3	Number of new boxes	4											
4	Annual incremental revenue per box	$400,000											
5	Number of new seats	5,000											
6	Annual incremental revenue per seat	$2,500											
7	Incremental expense (% of revenue)	60%											
8	Construction cost (Cap Exp)*	$10,000											
9	Depreciation (per year)*	$1,000											
10	Additional investment in Year 0 (Add WC)*	$1,000											
11	WC to be recovered in Year 10*	($1,000)											
12	Tax rate	30%											
13	Cost of capital	10%											
14	Note: * denotes figures in thousands of dollars												
15													
16	**Cash Flow Calculations for Performing Arts Center Project ($ thousands)**												
17								Year					
18			0	1	2	3	4	5	6	7	8	9	10
19	Revenue			$14,100	$14,100	$14,100	$14,100	$14,100	$14,100	$14,100	$14,100	$14,100	$14,100
20	Operating Expenses			8,460	8,460	8,460	8,460	8,460	8,460	8,460	8,460	8,460	8,460
21	EBITDA			$5,640	$5,640	$5,640	$5,640	$5,640	$5,640	$5,640	$5,640	$5,640	$5,640
22	Less: Depreciation & Amortization			1,000	1,000	1,000	1,000	1,000	1,000	1,000	1,000	1,000	1,000
23	EBIT			$4,640	$4,640	$4,640	$4,640	$4,640	$4,640	$4,640	$4,640	$4,640	$4,640
24	Less Taxes			1,392	1,392	1,392	1,392	1,392	1,392	1,392	1,392	1,392	1,392
25	NOPAT			$3,248	$3,248	$3,248	$3,248	$3,248	$3,248	$3,248	$3,248	$3,248	$3,248
26													
27	Plus: Depreciation & Amortization			1,000	1,000	1,000	1,000	1,000	1,000	1,000	1,000	1,000	1,000
28	Cash Flows from Operations			$4,248	$4,248	$4,248	$4,248	$4,248	$4,248	$4,248	$4,248	$4,248	$4,248
29	Less: Capital Expenditures		$10,000	0	0	0	0	0	0	0	0	0	0
30	Less: Changes in Working Capital		$1,000	0	0	0	0	0	0	0	0	0	($1,000)
31													
32	**Free Cash Flow**		($11,000)	$4,248	$4,248	$4,248	$4,248	$4,248	$4,248	$4,248	$4,248	$4,248	$5,248
33													
34	NPV	$15,488											
35													

The following is the formula setup for the performing arts center project. As we did in Exhibit 10.3, we have combined Years 1 through 9 in a single column to save space. As mentioned in previous chapters, notice that none of the values in the actual worksheet are hard coded but instead use references from the key assumptions list, or specific formulas. This allows for an easy analysis of the impact of changes in the assumptions.

	A	B	C	D	E	V
1	**Key Assumptions:**					
2	Life of the project (Years)	10				
3	Number of new boxes	4				
4	Annual incremental revenue per box	400000				
5	Number of new seats	5000				
6	Annual incremental revenue per seat	2500				
7	Incremental expense (% of revenue)	0.6				
8	Construction cost (Cap Exp)*	10000				
9	Depreciation (per year)*	=B8/B2				
10	Additional investment in Year 0 (Add WC)*	1000				
11	WC to be recovered in Year 10*	(1000)				
12	Tax rate	0.3				
13	Cost of capital	0.1				
14	Note: * denotes figures in millions of dollars					
15						
16	**Cash Flow Calculations for Performing Arts Center Project ($ thousands)**					
17				Year		
18		0		1-9		10
19	Revenue			=($B$3*$B$4+$B$5*$B$6)/1000		=($B$3*$B$4+$B$5*$B$6)/1000
20	Operating Expenses			=$B$7*D19		=$B$7*V19
21	EBITDA			=D19-D20		=V19-V20
22	Less: Depreciation & Amortization			=$B$9		=$B$9
23	EBIT			=D21-D22		=V21-V22
24	Less Taxes			=D23*$B$12		=V23*$B$12
25	NOPAT			=D23-D24		=V23-V24
26						
27	Plus: Depreciation & Amortization			=$B$9		=$B$9
28	Cash Flows from Operations			=D25+D27		=V25+V27
29	Less: Capital Expenditures	=B8		0		0
30	Less: Changes in Working Capital	=B10		0		=B11
31						
32	**Free Cash Flow**	=B28-B29-B30		=D28-D29-D30		=V28-V29-V30
33						
34	NPV	=NPV(B13, D32:V32)+B32				
35						

FCF versus Accounting Earnings

It is worth stressing again that the FCF we have been discussing in this section is what matters to investors. The impact of a project on a firm's overall value or on its stock price does not depend on how the project affects the company's accounting earnings. It depends only on how the project affects the company's FCF.

Recall that accounting earnings can differ from cash flows for a number of reasons, making accounting earnings an unreliable measure of the costs and benefits of a project. For example, as soon as a firm sells a good or provides a service, its income statement will reflect the associated revenue and expenses, regardless of whether the customer has paid cash.

Accounting earnings also reflect noncash charges, such as depreciation and amortization, which are intended to account for the costs associated with deterioration of the assets in a business as those assets are used. Depreciation and amortization rules can cause substantial differences between cash flows and reported income because the assets acquired for a project are generally depreciated over several years, even though the actual cash outflow for their acquisition typically takes place at the beginning of the project.

DECISION MAKING

EXAMPLE 10.1

Free Cash Flows

SITUATION: You have saved $6,000 and plan to use $5,500 to buy a motorcycle. However, just before you go visit the motorcycle dealer, a friend of yours asks you to invest your $6,000 in a local pizza delivery business he is starting. Assuming he can raise the money, your friend has two alternatives regarding how to market the business. As illustrated below, both of these alternatives have an NPV of $2,614 with an opportunity cost of capital of 12 percent. You will receive all free cash flows from the business until you have recovered your $6,000 plus 12 percent interest. After that, you and your friend will split any additional cash proceeds. If you decide to invest, which alternative would you prefer that your friend choose?

	Alternative 1			Alternative 2		
	Year 0	Year 1	Year 2	Year 0	Year 1	Year 2
Revenue		$12,000	$12,000		$16,000	$8,000
− Op Ex		4,000	6,000		8,000	4,240
EBITDA		$ 8,000	$ 6,000		$ 8,000	$3,760
− D&A		2,500	2,500		2,500	2,500
EBIT		$ 5,500	$ 3,500		$ 5,500	$1,260
× (1 − t)		0.75	0.75		0.75	0.75
NOPAT		$ 4,125	$ 2,625		$ 4,125	$ 945
+ D&A		2,500	2,500		2,500	2,500
CF Opns		$ 6,625	$ 5,125		$ 6,625	$3,445
− Cap Exp	$5,000	2,000	500	$5,000	500	500
− Add WC	1,000		(1,000)	1,000		(1,000)
= FCF	−$6,000	$ 4,625	$ 5,625	−$6,000	$ 6,125	$3,945
NPV at 12%	$2,614			$2,614		

DECISION: If you expect no cash from other sources during the next year, you should insist that your friend choose Alternative 2. This is the only alternative that will produce enough FCF next year to purchase the motorcycle. Alternative 1 will produce $6,625 in CF Opns but will require $2,000 in capital expenditures. You will not be able to take more than $4,625 from the business in Year 1 under Alternative 1 without leaving the business short of cash.

1. Why do we care about incremental cash flows at the firm level when we evaluate a project?

2. Why is D&A first subtracted and then added back in FCF calculations?

3. What types of investments should be included in FCF calculations?

10.2 ESTIMATING CASH FLOWS IN PRACTICE

Now that we have discussed what FCFs are and how they are calculated, we are ready to focus on some important issues that arise when we estimate FCFs in practice. The first of these issues is determining which cash flows are incremental to the project and which are not. In this section we begin with a discussion of five general rules that help us do this. We then discuss why it is important to distinguish between nominal and real cash flows. Next, we discuss some concepts regarding tax rates and depreciation that are crucial to the calculation of FCF in practice. Finally, we describe and illustrate special factors that must be considered when calculating FCF for the final year of a project.

LEARNING OBJECTIVE 2

Five General Rules for Incremental After-Tax Free Cash Flow Calculations

As discussed earlier, we must determine how a project would change the after-tax free cash flows of the firm in order to calculate its NPV. This is not always simple to do, especially in a large firm that has a complex accounting system and many other projects that are not independent of the project being considered. Fortunately, there are five rules that can help us isolate the FCFs specific to an individual project even under the most complicated circumstances.

Rule 1: Include cash flows and only cash flows in your calculations. Do not include allocated costs unless they reflect cash flows. Examples of allocated costs are charges that accountants allocate to individual businesses to reflect their share of the corporate overhead (the costs associated with the senior managers of the firm, centralized accounting and finance functions, and so forth).

To see how allocated costs can differ from actual costs (and cash flows), consider a firm with $3 million of annual corporate overhead expenses and two identical manufacturing plants. Each of these plants would typically be allocated one-half, or $1.5 million, of the corporate overhead when their accounting profitability is estimated.

Suppose now that the firm is considering building a third plant that would be identical to the other two. If this plant is built, it will have no impact on the annual corporate overhead cash expense. Someone in accounting might argue that the new plant should be able to support its "fair share" of the $3 million overhead, or $1 million, and that this overhead should be included in the cash flow calculation. Of course, this person would be wrong. Since total corporate overhead costs will not change if the third plant is built, no overhead should be included when calculating the incremental FCFs for this plant.

Rule 2: Include the impact of the project on cash flows from other product lines. If the product associated with a project is expected to affect sales of one or more other products at the firm, you must include the expected impact of the new project on the cash flows from the other products when computing the FCFs. For example, consider the analysis that analysts at Apple Inc. would have done before giving the go-ahead for the development of the iPhone. Since, like the iPod, the iPhone can store music, these analysts might have expected that the introduction of the iPhone would reduce annual iPod sales. If so, they would have had to account for the reduction in cash flows from lost iPod sales when they forecast the FCFs for the iPhone.

You can learn more about incremental free cash flows at Investopedia.com, http://www .investopedia.com.

Similarly, if a new product is expected to boost sales of another, complementary, product, then the increase in cash flows associated with the new sales from that complementary product line should also be reflected in the FCFs. For example, consider how the introduction of the Apple iPad might affect music and video downloads from Apple iTunes. Many of the people who purchase an iPad and who have not previously downloaded songs and other content from iTunes will begin to do so. The cash flows from downloads by these new users are not directly tied to iPad sales, but they are incremental to those sales. If Apple had not introduced the iPad device, it would not have these iTunes sales. The analysis of the iPad project should have included the estimated impact of that project on cash flows from iTunes.

Rule 3: Include all opportunity costs. By opportunity costs, we mean the cost of giving up the next best opportunity.[1] Opportunity costs can arise in many different ways. For example, a project may require the use of a building or a piece of equipment that could otherwise be sold or leased to someone else. To the extent that selling or leasing the building or piece of equipment would generate additional cash flow for the firm and the opportunity to realize that cash flow must be forgone if the project is adopted, it represents an opportunity cost.

To see why this is so, suppose that a project will require the use of a piece of equipment that the firm already has and that can be sold for $50,000 on the used-equipment market. If the project is accepted, the firm will lose the opportunity to sell the piece of equipment for $50,000. This is a $50,000 cost that must be included in the project analysis. Accepting the project reduces the amount of money that the firm can realize from selling excess equipment by this amount.

Rule 4: Forget sunk costs. Sunk costs are costs that have already been incurred. All that matters when you evaluate a project at a particular point in time is how much you have to invest in the future and what you can expect to receive in return for that investment. Past investments are irrelevant.

To see this, consider the situation in which your company has invested $10 million in a project that has not yet generated any cash inflows. Also assume that circumstances have changed so the project, which was originally expected to generate cash inflows with a present value of $20 million, is now expected to generate cash inflows with a value of only $2 million. To receive this $2 million, however, your company will have to invest another $1 million. Should your firm do it? Of course it should!

The sunk cost for this investment is $10 million. That money has been spent and is therefore not relevant for the decision of whether to invest $1 million now. Since the $1 million of new spending generates new cash flows worth $2 million, this is a project with a positive NPV of $1 million and it should be accepted. Another way to think about it is that if your company stops investing now, it will have lost $10 million. If it makes the investment, its total loss will be $9 million. Although neither is an attractive alternative, it should be clear that it is better to lose $9 million than it is to lose $10 million. The point here is that, while it is often painful to do, you should ignore sunk costs when computing project FCFs.

Rule 5: Include only after-tax cash flows in the cash flow calculations. The incremental pretax earnings of a project matter only to the extent that they affect the after-tax cash flows that the firm's investors receive. For an individual project, as mentioned earlier, we compute the after-tax cash flows using the firm's marginal tax rate because this is the rate that will be applied against the incremental cash flows generated by the project.

Let's use the performing arts center project to illustrate how these rules are applied in practice. Suppose the following requirements and costs are associated with this project:

1. The chief financial officer requires that each project be assessed 5 percent of the initial investment to account for costs associated with the accounting, marketing, and information technology departments.

---

[1]The concept of opportunity cost here is similar to that discussed in Chapter 9, in the context of the opportunity cost of capital.

2. It is very likely that increasing the number of seats will reduce revenues next door at the cinema that your employer also owns. Attendance at the cinema is expected to be lower only when the performing arts center is staging a big event. The total impact is expected to be a reduction of $500,000 each year, before taxes, in the operating profits (EBIT) of the cinema. The depreciation of the cinema's assets will not be affected.

3. If the project is adopted, the new seating will be built in an area where exhibits have been placed in the past when the center has hosted guest lectures by well-known painters or sculptors. The performing arts center will no longer be able to host such events, and revenue will be reduced by $600,000 each year as a result.

4. The center has already spent $400,000 researching demand for new seating.

5. You have just discovered that a new salesperson will be hired if the center goes ahead with the expansion. This person will be responsible for sales and service of the four new luxury boxes and will be paid $75,000 per year, including salary and benefits. The $75,000 is not included in the 60 percent figure for operating expenses that was previously mentioned.

What impact will these requirements and costs have on the FCFs for the project? Exhibit 10.4 shows their impact on the FCFs and NPV presented in Exhibit 10.3.

1. The 5 percent assessment sounds like an allocated overhead cost. To the extent that this assessment does not reflect an actual increase in cash costs, it should not be included. It is not relevant to the project. The analysis should include only incremental cash flows.

2. The impact of the expansion on the operating profits of the cinema is an example of how a project can erode or cannibalize business in another part of a firm. The $500,000 reduction in EBIT is relevant and should be included in the analysis.

3. The loss of the ability to use the exhibits area, the next best alternative to the new seating plan, represents a $600,000 opportunity cost. The center is giving up revenue from guest lecturers that require exhibit space in order to build the additional seating. This opportunity cost will be partially offset by elimination of the operating expenses associated with the guest lectures.

4. The $400,000 for research has already been spent. The decision of whether to accept or reject the project will not alter the amount spent for this research. This is a sunk cost that should not be included in the analysis.

EXHIBIT 10.4	Adjusted FCF Calculations and NPV for the Performing Arts Center Project

The adjustments described in the text result in changes in the FCF calculations and a different NPV for the performing arts center project.

	Year 0	Years 1 to 9	Year 10
Revenue		$13,500,000	$13,500,000
− Op Ex		8,100,000	8,100,000
− New salesperson's salary		75,000	75,000
− Lost cinema EBIT		500,000	500,000
EBITDA		$ 4,825,000	$ 4,825,000
− D&A		1,000,000	1,000,000
EBIT		$ 3,825,000	$ 3,825,000
× (1 − t)		0.70	0.70
NOPAT		$ 2,677,500	$ 2,677,500
+ D&A		1,000,000	1,000,000
CF Opns		$ 3,677,500	$ 3,677,500
− Cap Exp	$10,000,000	0	0
− Add WC	1,000,000	0	−1,000,000
= FCF	−$11,000,000	$ 3,677,500	$ 4,677,500
NPV @ 10%	$11,982,189		

5. The $75,000 annual salary for the new salesperson is an incremental cost that should be included in the analysis. Even though the marketing department is a corporate overhead department, in this case the salesperson must be hired specifically because of the new project.

The specific changes in the analysis from Exhibits 10.3 to 10.4 are as follows. Revenue and Op Ex after Year 0 have been reduced from $14,100,000 and $8,460,000, respectively, in Exhibit 10.3 to $13,500,000 and $8,100,000, respectively, in Exhibit 10.4. These changes reflect the $600,000 loss of revenues and the reduction in costs (60 percent of revenue) associated with the loss of the ability to host guest lectures. The $75,000 expense for the new salesperson's salary and the $500,000 reduction in the EBIT of the cinema are then subtracted from Revenue, along with Op Ex. These changes result in EBITDA of $4,825,000 in Exhibit 10.4, compared with EBITDA of $5,640,000 in Exhibit 10.3. The net result is a reduction in the project NPV from $15,487,664 (in Exhibit 10.3) to $11,982,189 (in Exhibit 10.4).

LEARNING
BY
DOING

NEED MORE HELP?

WileyPLUS

A P P L I C A T I O N   10.1

Using the General Rules for FCF Calculations

PROBLEM: You have owned and operated a pizza parlor for several years. The space that you lease for your pizza parlor is considerably larger than the space you need. To more efficiently utilize this space, you are considering subdividing it and opening a hamburger joint. You know that your analysis should consider the overall impact of the hamburger project on the total cash flows of your business, but beyond estimating revenues and costs from hamburger-related sales and the investment required to get the hamburger business started, you are unsure what else you should consider. Based on the five general rules for incremental after-tax cash flow calculations, what other factors should you consider?

APPROACH: Careful consideration of each of the five rules provides insights concerning the other factors that should be considered.

SOLUTION: Rule 1 suggests that you should only consider the incremental impact of the hamburger stand on actual overhead expenses, such as the cost of additional accounting support. Rule 2 indicates that you should consider the potential for the hamburger business to take sales away from (or cannibalize) the pizza business. Rule 3 suggests that you should carefully consider the opportunity cost associated with the excess space or any excess equipment that might be used for the hamburger business. If you could lease the extra space to someone else, for example, then the amount that you could receive by doing so is an opportunity cost and should be included in the analysis. Similarly, the price for which any excess equipment could be sold represents an opportunity cost. Rule 4 simply reminds you to consider cash flows from this point forward only. Forget sunk costs. Finally, Rule 5 tells you not to forget to account for the impact of taxes in your cash flow calculations.

Nominal versus Real Cash Flows

nominal dollars
dollar amounts that are not adjusted for inflation; the purchasing power of a nominal dollar amount depends on when that amount is received

real dollars
inflation-adjusted dollars; the actual purchasing power of dollars stated in "real" terms is the same regardless of when those dollars are received

In addition to following the five rules for incremental after-tax cash flow calculations, it is very important to make sure that all cash flows are stated in either nominal dollars or real dollars—not a mixture of the two. The concepts of nominal and real dollars are directly related to the discussion in Chapter 2 that distinguishes between (1) the nominal rate of interest and (2) the real rate of interest. **Nominal dollars** are the dollars that we typically think of. They represent the actual dollar amounts that we expect a project to generate in the future, without any adjustments. To the extent that there is inflation, the purchasing power of each nominal dollar will decline over time. When prices are going up, a given nominal dollar amount will buy less and less over time. **Real dollars** represent dollars stated in terms of constant purchasing power. When we forecast in real dollars, the purchasing power of the dollars in one period is equal to the purchasing power of the dollars in any other period.

To illustrate the difference between nominal and real dollars, let's consider an example. Suppose that the rate of inflation is expected to be 5 percent next year and that you just lent $100 to a friend for one year. If your friend is not paying any interest, the nominal dollar amount you expect to receive in one year is $100. At that time, though, the purchasing power of this $100 is expected to be only $95.24: $100/(1 + \Delta P_e) = $100/1.05 = 95.24, where ΔP_e is the expected rate of inflation as discussed in Chapter 2. In other words, if inflation is as expected, when your friend repays the $100, it will buy only what $95.24 would buy today. You will have earned a real return of $($95.24 - $100)/$100 = -0.0476$, or -4.76 percent, on this loan. Another way of thinking about this loan is that your friend is expected to repay you with dollars having a real value of only $95.24.

To understand the importance of making sure that all cash flows are stated in either nominal dollars or real dollars, it is useful to write the cost of capital (k) from Chapter 9 as:

$$1 + k = (1 + \Delta P_e) \times (1 + r) \tag{10.3}$$

In Equation 10.3, k is the nominal cost of capital that is normally used to discount cash flows and r is the real cost of capital.[2] This equation tells us that the nominal cost of capital equals the real cost of capital, adjusted for the expected rate of inflation. This means that whenever we discount a cash flow using the nominal cost of capital, the discount rate we are using reflects both the expected rate of inflation (ΔP_e) and a real return (r). If, on the one hand, we discounted a *real cash flow* using the *nominal cost of capital*, we would be overcompensating for expected inflation in the discounting process. On the other hand, if we discounted a *nominal cash flow* using the *real cost of capital* (r), we would be undercompensating for expected inflation.

In capital budgeting, we normally forecast cash flows in nominal dollars and discount them using the nominal cost of capital.[3] As an alternative, we can state the cash flows in real terms and discount them using the real cost of capital. This alternative calculation will give us exactly the same NPV. To see this, consider a project that will require an investment of $50,000 in Year 0 and will produce FCFs of $20,000 a year in Years 1 through 4. With a 15 percent nominal cost of capital, the NPV for this project is:

$$
\begin{aligned}
\text{NPV} &= \text{FCF}_0 + \frac{\text{FCF}_1}{1 + k} + \frac{\text{FCF}_2}{(1 + k)^2} + \frac{\text{FCF}_3}{(1 + k)^3} + \frac{\text{FCF}_4}{(1 + k)^4} \\
&= -\$50,000 + \frac{\$20,000}{1.15} + \frac{\$20,000}{(1.15)^2} + \frac{\$20,000}{(1.15)^3} + \frac{\$20,000}{(1.15)^4} \\
&= -\$50,000 + \$17,391 + \$15,123 + \$13,150 + \$11,435 \\
&= \$7,099
\end{aligned}
$$

Equation 10.3 can be used to calculate the real cost of capital if we recognize that it can be rearranged algebraically as:

$$r = \frac{1 + k}{1 + \Delta P_e} - 1$$

With a 5 percent expected rate of inflation, the real cost of capital is therefore:

$$r = \frac{1 + k}{1 + \Delta P_e} - 1 = \frac{1.15}{1.05} - 1 = 0.09524, \text{ or } 9.524\%$$

Discounting the nominal cash flows by the rate of inflation tells us that the real cash flows are:

Year 0	Year 1	Year 2	Year 3	Year 4
$-\$50,000$	$\dfrac{\$20,000}{1 + 0.05}$	$\dfrac{\$20,000}{(1 + 0.05)^2}$	$\dfrac{\$20,000}{(1 + 0.05)^3}$	$\dfrac{\$20,000}{(1 + 0.05)^4}$
$= -\$50,000$	$= \$19,048$	$= \$18,141$	$= \$17,277$	$= \$16,454$

---

[2] As discussed in Chapter 2, if we multiply the two terms on the right-hand side of Equation 10.3, we get $1 + k = 1 + \Delta P_e + r + \Delta P_e r$. Since the last term in this equation, $\Delta P_e r$, is the product of two fractions, it is a very small number and is often ignored in practice. Without this term, Equation 10.3 becomes $1 + k = 1 + \Delta P_e + r$ or $k = \Delta P_e + r$.

[3] Note that when we use the term *cost of capital* without distinguishing between the nominal or real cost of capital, we are referring to the *nominal* cost of capital. This is the convention that is used in practice. In this example, we use the terms *nominal* or *real* whenever we refer to the cost of capital for clarity. In the rest of this book, however, we follow convention by simply using the term *cost of capital* to refer to the nominal cost of capital.

Therefore, when we discount the real cash flows using the real cost of capital, we see that the NPV is:

$$NPV = -\$50,000 + \frac{\$19,048}{1.09524} + \frac{\$18,141}{(1.09524)^2} + \frac{\$17,277}{(1.09524)^3} + \frac{\$16,454}{(1.09524)^4}$$

$$= -\$50,000 + \$17,391 + \$15,123 + \$13,150 + \$11,435$$

$$= \$7,099$$

Notice that the present value of each of the annual cash flows is exactly the same when we use nominal cash flows and when we use real cash flows. This has to be the case because when we stated the NPV calculation in real dollars, we first divided the discount rate by 1.05. We then reduced the value of the future cash flows by discounting them by 5 percent. This is equivalent to reducing the numerator and the denominator in each present value calculation by the same fraction, which must result in the same answer.

LEARNING BY DOING

APPLICATION 10.2

NEED MORE HELP?

WileyPLUS

The Investment Decision and Nominal versus Real Dollars

PROBLEM: You are trying to decide how to invest $25,000, which you just inherited from a distant relative. You do not want to take any risks with this money because you want to use it as a down payment on a home when you graduate in three years. Therefore, you have decided to invest the money in securities that are guaranteed by the U.S. government. You are considering two alternatives: a three-year Treasury note and an inflation-indexed Treasury security. If you invest in the three-year Treasury note, you will be paid 3 percent per year in interest and will get your $25,000 back at the end of three years. If you invest in the inflation-indexed security, you will be paid 1 percent per year plus an amount that reflects actual inflation in each of the next three years. For example, if inflation equals 2 percent per year for each of the next three years, you will receive 3 percent each year in total interest. This interest on the inflation-indexed security will compound, and you will receive a single payment at the end of three years. If you expect inflation to average 2.5 percent per year over the next three years, should you invest in the three-year Treasury note or in the inflation-indexed Treasury security?

APPROACH: Compare the 3 percent return on the three-year Treasury note, which is a nominal rate of return, with the nominal rate of return that you can expect to receive from the inflation-indexed security and invest in the security with the highest rate. The nominal rate on the inflation-indexed security in each year equals the real rate of 1 percent plus the rate of inflation.

SOLUTION: Without doing any detailed calculations, it is apparent that you should invest in the inflation-indexed security. The reason is that if the rate of inflation turns out to be 2.5 percent, the inflation-indexed security will yield 3.5 percent (1 percent plus the 2.5 percent inflation adjustment) per year. With this investment, the real purchasing power of your money will increase by 1 percent per year. This will be true regardless of what inflation turns out to be during the three-year period. Assuming that you can reinvest the annual interest payments from the three-year Treasury note at 3 percent, if you buy this security, the real purchasing power of your money will increase by only 0.5 percent (3 percent interest rate less 2.5 percent inflation) per year.

Tax Rates and Depreciation

The United States has a very complicated corporate tax system. Corporations pay taxes at the federal, state, and local levels. Some governmental jurisdictions tax income, while others tax property or some other measure of value. Furthermore, a wide variety of deductions and adjustments are made to income or other measures of value when computing the actual taxes that a corporation owes. A detailed discussion of the different taxes that corporations pay and how they are computed is beyond the scope of this textbook. However, at this point, it is important for you to be familiar with the progressive tax system that we have in the United States and with the depreciation methods used for computing corporate tax obligations. These concepts are especially important in capital budgeting.

Marginal and Average Tax Rates

A **progressive tax system**, which we have in the United States, is one in which taxpayers pay a progressively larger share of their income in taxes as their income rises. This happens in a progressive tax system because the marginal tax rate at low levels of income is lower than the marginal tax rate at high levels of income. Recall from Chapter 3 that the marginal tax rate is the rate paid on the last dollar earned. The tax system in the United States is progressive for both individuals and corporations. For example, Exhibit 10.5 presents the 2012 federal tax rate schedule for single individuals. Notice that the percentage tax owed beyond the base amount in each row of Exhibit 10.5 increases as taxable income increases. In other words, the marginal tax rate, as well as the average tax rate, increases as an individual moves from one tax bracket to the next.

Exhibit 10.6 shows the 2012 tax rate schedule faced by a typical U.S. corporation (you may recall that a variation of this tax rate schedule is also presented in Exhibit 3.6). Notice that this schedule is also progressive. The U.S. corporate tax system in 2012 was structured so that the marginal rate exactly equaled the average tax rate for all levels of income above $18,333,333. If the corporation's taxable income is below $18,333,333, the marginal tax rate will not necessarily be the same as the average tax rate. These rates differ in all tax brackets below $18,333,333, except the $335,000 to $10 million bracket. Remember that since we use marginal tax rates in capital budgeting, you cannot simply divide the dollar taxes paid by the taxable income for a company to estimate the tax rate. This calculation gives you the average, not the marginal, tax rate.

Taxes and Depreciation

Corporations keep two sets of books. One set is kept for preparing financial statements in accordance with generally accepted accounting principles (GAAP). These are the financial statements that appear in the annual report and other documents filed with the Securities and Exchange Commission (SEC). The other set is kept for computing the taxes that the corporation actually pays. Corporations must keep two sets of books because the GAAP rules for computing income are different from the rules that the IRS uses.

One especially important difference from a capital budgeting perspective is that the depreciation methods allowed by GAAP differ from those allowed by the IRS. The straight-line depreciation method illustrated earlier in this chapter in the performing arts center example is allowed by GAAP and is often used for financial reporting. In contrast, an "accelerated"

progressive tax system
a tax system in which the marginal tax rate at low levels of income is lower than the marginal tax rate at high levels of income

---

EXHIBIT 10.5   **U.S. Tax Rate Schedule for a Single Individual in 2012**

The income tax system for individuals in the United States is progressive in that the tax rate increases with income. For very low income levels—say, $20,000 per year—individuals pay only 15 percent on each additional dollar they earn. For individuals who earn more than $388,350, this rate is 35 percent.

Taxable Income		Tax Owed
More Than	**But Not More Than**	
$0	$8,700	10% of amount beyond $0
$8,700	$35,350	$870.00 + 15% of amount beyond $8,700
$35,350	$85,650	$4,867.50 + 25% of amount beyond $35,350
$85,650	$178,650	$17,442.50 + 28% of amount beyond $85,650
$178,650	$388,350	$43,482.50 + 33% of amount beyond $178,650
$388,350	no limit	$112,683.50 + 35% of amount beyond $388,350

EXHIBIT 10.6 U.S. Corporate Tax Rate Schedule in 2012

Just like the tax system for individuals, the tax system for corporations in the United States is progressive, with marginal tax rates ranging from 15 percent to as high as 39 percent.

Taxable Income		
More Than	But Not More Than	Tax Owed
$0	$50,000	15% of amount beyond $0
$50,000	$75,000	$7,500 + 25% of amount beyond $50,000
$75,000	$100,000	$13,750 + 34% of amount beyond $75,000
$100,000	$335,000	$22,250 + 39% of amount beyond $100,000
$335,000	$10,000,000	$113,900 + 34% of amount beyond $335,000
$10,000,000	$15,000,000	$3,400,000 + 35% of amount beyond $10,000,000
$15,000,000	$18,333,333	$5,150,000 + 38% of amount beyond $15,000,000
$18,333,333	——————	35% on all income

LEARNING BY DOING

APPLICATION 10.3

Calculating Marginal and Average Tax Rates

PROBLEM: Assume that you are operating the pizza parlor and hamburger joint described in Learning by Doing Application 10.1. Because the business has become complicated, you have incorporated. From now on, earnings are subject to the corporate tax rates presented in Exhibit 10.6. If your corporation's total taxable income is $200,000 in 2012, how much does it owe in federal taxes? What are the corporation's marginal and average federal tax rates? If you were considering buying a new oven, which tax rate would you use when computing the free cash flows?

APPROACH: Use the rates presented in Exhibit 10.6 to calculate the total amount that you owe. The marginal federal tax rate is the rate in the "Tax Owed" column in Exhibit 10.6 that corresponds to the row in which the total taxable income earned by your restaurant is found. The ratio of the total amount that you owe divided by your total taxable income equals the average federal tax rate. You would use the tax rate that would be applied to the incremental after-tax free cash flows associated with the new oven.

SOLUTION: From Exhibit 10.6, you can see that with a taxable income of $200,000, your corporation will owe taxes of $22,250 + ($100,000 × 0.39) = $61,250. The marginal tax rate is 39 percent, and the average tax rate is $61,250/$200,000 = 0.306, or 30.6 percent. You will use the marginal rate of 39 percent when computing the free cash flows for the new oven.

Modified Accelerated Cost Recovery System (MACRS)
the accelerated depreciation method that has been in use for U.S. federal taxes since the Tax Reform Act of 1986 went into effect

method of depreciation, called the **Modified Accelerated Cost Recovery System (MACRS)**, has been in use for U.S. federal tax calculations since the Tax Reform Act of 1986 went into effect.[4] MACRS is an accelerated system in the sense that depreciation charges for all assets other than nonfarm real property (for example, buildings) are higher in the early years of an asset's life than with the straight-line method. MACRS thus enables a firm to deduct depreciation charges sooner, thereby realizing the tax savings sooner and increasing the present value of the tax savings. Since we want to estimate the actual incremental cash flows from a project in capital budgeting, we use the depreciation method allowed by the IRS in our calculations. This is the method that determines how much of a tax deduction a corporation actually receives for an investment.

Exhibit 10.7 lists the percentage of the cost of an asset that can be depreciated in each year for assets with 3-, 5-, 7-, 10-, 15-, and 20-year allowable recovery periods. The recovery periods

---

[4]Although some assets that were acquired before 1986 are still being depreciated using earlier methods, the vast majority of depreciation for existing assets and all depreciation for new assets are based on MACRS.

EXHIBIT 10.7 MACRS Depreciation Schedules by Allowable Recovery Period

The MACRS schedule lists the tax depreciation rates that firms use for assets placed into service after the Tax Reform Act of 1986 went into effect. The table indicates the percentage of the cost of the asset that can be depreciated in each year during the period that it is being used. Year 1 is the year in which the asset is first placed into service.

Year	3-Year	5-Year	7-Year	10-Year	15-Year	20-Year
1	33.33%	20.00%	14.29%	10.00%	5.00%	3.75%
2	44.45	32.00	24.49	18.00	9.50	7.22
3	14.81	19.20	17.49	14.40	8.55	6.68
4	7.41	11.52	12.49	11.52	7.70	6.18
5		11.52	8.93	9.22	6.93	5.71
6		5.76	8.92	7.37	6.23	5.29
7			8.93	6.55	5.90	4.89
8			4.46	6.55	5.90	4.52
9				6.56	5.91	4.46
10				6.55	5.90	4.46
11				3.28	5.91	4.46
12					5.90	4.46
13					5.91	4.46
14					5.90	4.46
15					5.91	4.46
16					2.95	4.46
17						4.46
18						4.46
19						4.46
20						4.46
21						2.24
Total	100.00%	100.00%	100.00%	100.00%	100.00%	100.00%

for specific types of assets are specified in the tax law that is passed by Congress and signed by the president. For instance, in 2012, the allowable recovery period was 5 years for computers and automobiles, 7 years for office furniture, 10 years for water transportation equipment such as barges, 15 years for gas stations, 20 years for farm buildings, 27.5 years for residential rental property, and 39.5 years for nonresidential real property (such as manufacturing buildings). Residential rental and nonresidential real property are depreciated using the straight-line method. Depreciation charges are intended to represent the cost of wear and tear on assets in the course of business. However, since they are set through a political process, they may be greater than or less than the actual cost of this wear and tear.

Note that the percentages in each column of Exhibit 10.7 add up to 100 percent. This is because the tax law allows firms to depreciate 100 percent of the cost of an asset regardless of the expected salvage value of that asset. Consequently, when we use the MACRS schedule to determine the tax depreciation, we do not have to worry about the expected salvage value for the asset.[5]

Let's consider an example to show how MACRS is applied. Suppose you are evaluating a project that will require the purchase of an automobile for $25,000. Since an automobile is a five-year asset under MACRS, you can use the percentages for a five-year asset in Exhibit 10.7 to calculate the annual depreciation deductions:

You can read more about tax rates and depreciation rules at the Internal Revenue Service Web site, http://www.irs.gov.

Year 1:	$25,000 × 0.2000 =	$5,000
Year 2:	$25,000 × 0.3200 =	$8,000
Year 3:	$25,000 × 0.1920 =	$4,800
Year 4:	$25,000 × 0.1152 =	$2,880
Year 5:	$25,000 × 0.1152 =	$2,880
Year 6:	$25,000 × 0.0576 =	$1,440
Total		$25,000

[5]Under GAAP accounting rules, if the salvage value can be estimated with reasonable certainty, it should be used in computing depreciation. However, in practice the expected salvage value of a new capital asset is often so uncertain that it is typically assumed to equal $0 even for financial reporting purposes.

Notice that even though the automobile is a five-year asset, there is a depreciation charge in the sixth year. This is because MACRS assumes that the asset is placed in service in the middle of the first year. As a result, the firm is allowed a deduction for half of a year in Year 1, a full year in Years 2 through 5, and half of a year in Year 6.

Recall that the FCF calculation, Equation 10.1, included incremental depreciation along with incremental amortization (D&A). We put depreciation and amortization together in the calculation because amortization is a noncash charge (deduction) like depreciation. It is beyond the scope of this book to discuss amortization in detail because the rules that govern it are complex. However, you should know that, as was discussed in Chapter 3, amortization, like depreciation, is a deduction that is allowed under the tax law to compensate for the decline in value of certain, mainly intangible, assets used by a business.

Computing the Terminal-Year FCF

The FCF in the last, or terminal, year of a project's life often includes cash flows that are not typically included in the calculations for other years. For instance, in the final year of a project, the assets acquired during the life of the project may be sold and the working capital that has been invested may be recovered. The cash flows that result from the sale of assets and recovery of working capital must be included in the calculation of the terminal-year FCF.

You can see this in the performing arts center example discussed earlier. Note that the Year 10, or terminal year, cash flows in this example are different from those in the other years. They include both CF Opns and investment cash flows that reflect recovery of net working capital investments. Net incremental additions to working capital (Add WC) that are due to the project are calculated as follows:

$$\text{Add WC} = \text{Change in cash and cash equivalents} + \text{Change in accounts receivable} \\ + \text{Change in inventories} - \text{Change in accounts payable} \qquad (10.4)$$

where the changes in cash and cash equivalents, accounts receivable, inventories, and accounts payable represent changes in the values of these accounts that result from the adoption of the project.

Looking at the components of Add WC, we can see that cash and cash equivalents, accounts receivable, and inventories require the investment of capital, while accounts payable represent capital provided by suppliers. When a project ends, the cash and cash equivalents are no longer needed, the accounts receivable are collected, the inventories are sold, and the accounts payable are paid. In other words, the firm recovers the net working capital that has been invested in the project. To reflect this in the FCF calculation, the cash flow in the last year of the project typically includes a *negative investment in working capital* that equals the cumulative investment in working capital over the life of the project. It is very important to make sure that the recovery of working capital is reflected in the cash flows in the last year of a project. In some businesses, working capital can account for 20 percent or more of revenue, and excluding working capital recovery from the calculations can cause you to substantially understate the NPV of a project.

In some projects, there will also be incremental capital expenditures (Cap Exp) in the terminal year. This is because, for example, the assets acquired for the project are being sold or there are disposal costs associated with them. In the performing arts center example, Cap Exp is $0 in year 10. This is because we were assuming that, other than the working capital, the investments at the beginning of the project would have no salvage value, there would be no disposal costs associated with the assets, and there would be no clean-up costs associated with the project in Year 10. When an asset is expected to have a salvage value, we must include the salvage value realized from the sale of the asset and the impact of the sale on the firm's taxes in the terminal-year FCF calculations. Any costs that must be incurred to dispose of assets should also be included. Finally, clean-up costs, such as those associated with restoring the environment after a strip-mining project, also must be included in the terminal-year FCF.

The salvage value realized from the sale of the assets used in a project includes both the cash that is actually realized when they are sold and, if the salvage value of any asset differs from its depreciated book value, the tax implications from the sale. To better understand how taxes affect the terminal-year cash flows for a project, let's make the performing arts center

EXHIBIT 10.8 MACRS Depreciation Calculations for the Performing Arts Center Project ($ thousands)

Using the percentages from the schedule in Exhibit 10.7, we can calculate the tax (MACRS) depreciation for each year during the life of the performing arts center project.

	Year 1	Year 2	Year 3	Year 4	Year 5	Year 6	Year 7	Year 8	Year 9	Year 10
Depreciation Calculations										
Beginning book value	$10,000	$9,000	$7,200	$5,760	$4,608	$3,686	$2,949	$2,294	$1,639	$983
MACRS percentage	10.00%	18.00%	14.40%	11.52%	9.22%	7.37%	6.55%	6.55%	6.56%	6.55%
MACRS depreciation	$1,000	$1,800	$1,440	$1,152	$922	$737	$655	$655	$656	$655
Ending book value	$9,000	$7,200	$5,760	$4,608	$3,686	$2,949	$2,294	$1,639	$983	$328

example more realistic. Recall that the initial Cap Exp in the performing arts center example was $10 million, that we used straight-line depreciation, and that we assumed that the salvage value would be $0 in Year 10. Now that we know about MACRS, let's more realistically assume that the allowable recovery period for this investment under MACRS is 10 years.

Exhibit 10.8 presents the depreciation calculations for this investment under MACRS. Note that since the amount of depreciation now changes over time, we can no longer present Years 1 through 9 together as we did in Exhibit 10.3. Also note that because MACRS allows only a half year of depreciation in Year 1, the book value of the investment is greater than $0 at the end of Year 10. In this case it is $328,000.

If we still assume a salvage value of $0 for this investment, the fact that the book value is positive means that the firm will have a tax loss when it writes off the remaining value of the investment at the end of the project. In other words, when the project ends, the firm will take a deduction when computing its taxes that equals the remaining $328,000 book value of the asset. With a 30 percent tax rate, this will result in a tax savings of $328,000 × 0.30 = $98,400. This tax savings must be reflected in the cash flow calculations in Year 10. Exhibit 10.9 illustrates the cash flow and NPV calculations for the performing arts center example with these changes. The $98,400 tax savings is included as a negative capital expenditure in Year 10 (as −98 since we are rounding to thousands).[6] Notice that the NPV has increased from $15,487,664 in Exhibit 10.3 to $15,610,135. The $122,471 difference reflects the present value of the tax savings from using MACRS depreciation instead of straight-line depreciation plus the tax savings from the disposal of the asset.

EXHIBIT 10.9 FCF Calculations and NPV for Performing Arts Center Project with MACRS Depreciation ($ thousands)

This exhibit shows the FCF calculations and the NPV for the performing arts center project when MACRS is used to compute depreciation. These calculations correspond to those in Exhibit 10.3, which reflect straight-line depreciation. Notice that the NPV is greater with the MACRS system because the tax shields from the depreciation are realized sooner.

	Year 0	Year 1	Year 2	Year 3	Year 4	Year 5	Year 6	Year 7	Year 8	Year 9	Year 10
Revenue		$14,100	$14,100	$14,100	$14,100	$14,100	$14,100	$14,100	$14,100	$14,100	$14,100
− Op Ex		8,460	8,460	8,460	8,460	8,460	8,460	8,460	8,460	8,460	8,460
EBITDA		$ 5,640	$ 5,640	$ 5,640	$ 5,640	$ 5,640	$ 5,640	$ 5,640	$ 5,640	$ 5,640	$ 5,640
− D&A		1,000	1,800	1,440	1,152	922	737	655	655	656	655
EBIT		$ 4,640	$ 3,840	$ 4,200	$ 4,488	$ 4,718	$ 4,903	$ 4,985	$ 4,985	$ 4,984	$ 4,985
× (1−t)		0.70	0.70	0.70	0.70	0.70	0.70	0.70	0.70	0.70	0.70
NOPAT		$ 3,248	$ 2,688	$ 2,940	$ 3,142	$ 3,303	$ 3,432	$ 3,490	$ 3,490	$ 3,489	$ 3,490
+ D&A		1,000	1,800	1,440	1,152	922	737	655	655	656	655
CF Opns		$ 4,248	$ 4,488	$ 4,380	$ 4,294	$ 4,225	$ 4,169	$ 4,145	$ 4,145	$ 4,145	$ 4,145
− Cap Exp	$10,000	0	0	0	0	0	0	0	0	0	−98
− Add WC	1,000	0	0	0	0	0	0	0	0	0	−1,000
= FCF	−$11,000	$ 4,248	$ 4,488	$ 4,380	$ 4,294	$ 4,225	$ 4,169	$ 4,145	$ 4,145	$ 4,145	$ 5,243
NPV @ 10%	$15,610										

---

[6]Including the tax savings as negative capital expenditure increases the FCF in Year 10 since we subtract all capital expenditures.

EXHIBIT 10.10 **FCF Calculations and NPV for the Performing Arts Center Project with a $1 Million Salvage Value in Year 10 ($ thousands)**

This exhibit shows the FCF calculations and NPV for the performing arts center project assuming that the salvage value of the $10 million capital investment is $1 million in Year 10. All other assumptions are the same as in Exhibit 10.9.

	Year 0	Year 1	Year 2	Year 3	Year 4	Year 5	Year 6	Year 7	Year 8	Year 9	Year 10
CF Opns		$4,248	$4,488	$4,380	$4,294	$4,225	$4,169	$4,145	$4,145	$4,145	$4,145
− Cap Exp	$10,000	0	0	0	0	0	0	0	0	0	−798
− Add WC	1,000	0	0	0	0	0	0	0	0	0	−1,000
FCF	−$11,000	$4,248	$4,488	$4,380	$4,294	$4,225	$4,169	$4,145	$4,145	$4,145	$5,943
NPV @ 10%	$15,880										

If the salvage value is greater than $0 but less than the book value of $328,000, the tax savings will be smaller than $98,400, and if the salvage value exceeds the book value, the firm will actually have a gain on the sale of the asset that will increase its tax liability. In either of these cases, you must include the proceeds from the sale of the assets and the tax effects in your cash flow calculations.

The general formula for calculating the tax on the salvage value for an asset is:

$$\text{Tax on sale of an asset} = (\text{Selling price of asset} - \text{Book value of asset}) \times t$$

where t is the firm's marginal tax rate.

To make sure we know how we use this equation, suppose that the salvage value (selling price) in Year 10 of the $10,000,000 investment in the performing arts center project is expected to be $1,000,000 and that the book value remains $328,000. In this case the firm will pay additional taxes of ($1,000,000 − $328,000) × 0.30 = $201,600 on the sale of the assets. Deducting this amount from the $1,000,000 that the firm receives from the sale of the assets yields after-tax proceeds of $798,400 and the cash flows illustrated in Exhibit 10.10.

LEARNING BY DOING

NEED MORE HELP?
WileyPLUS

APPLICATION 10.4

Accounting for Taxes When Assets Are Sold

PROBLEM: You have decided to replace an oven in your pizza parlor. The old oven originally cost $20,000. Depreciation charges of $15,000 have been taken since you acquired it, resulting in a current book value of $5,000. The owner of a restaurant down the street has offered you $3,000 for the old oven. If you accept this offer, how will the sale affect the cash flows from your business? Assume the marginal tax rate for your business is 39 percent.

APPROACH: First use the general formula presented above to calculate the tax on the salvage value. Then subtract (add) any tax obligation (savings) from (to) the amount that you will receive for the oven to obtain the total impact of the sale on the cash flows to your business.

SOLUTION: If you sell the old oven, you will receive a cash inflow of $3,000 from the purchaser in return for an asset with a book value of $5,000. With a 39 percent marginal tax rate, this will result in a tax of:

$$\text{Tax on sale of an asset} = (\text{Selling price of asset} - \text{Book value of asset}) \times t$$
$$= (\$3,000 - \$5,000) \times 0.39 = -\$780$$

Since you are selling the oven for less than its book value, you will realize a tax savings of $780. Therefore, the total impact of the sale on the cash flows from your business will be $3,000 + $780 = $3,780. Of course, the purchase price of the new oven will probably more than offset this amount.

Note that if the sale price exceeded the book value of the oven by $2,000, you would have a taxable gain and would have to pay $780. In this case, the cash flows received from the purchaser would be reduced, rather than increased, by $780.

Expected Cash Flows

It is very important to realize that in an NPV analysis we use the *expected* FCF for each year of the life of the project. Similar to the expected values calculated in Chapter 6, the expected FCF for a particular year equals the sum of the products of the possible outcomes (FCFs) and the probabilities that those outcomes will be realized.

To better illustrate this point, suppose that you have just invented a new board game and are trying to decide whether you should produce and sell it. If you decide to go ahead with this project, you estimate that it will cost you $100,000 for the equipment necessary to produce and distribute the game. Also suppose you think there are three possible outcomes if you make this investment—the game is very successful, game sales are acceptable but not exceptional, and game sales are poor—and that the probabilities associated with these outcomes are 25 percent, 50 percent, and 25 percent, respectively. If the FCFs under each of these three outcomes are as illustrated in Exhibit 10.11, then the expected values that you would discount in your NPV analysis are −$100.00, $48.75, $53.75, and $35.00 for years 0, 1, 2, and 3, respectively.[7] You should confirm that each of these values is correct to make sure that you understand how to calculate an expected FCF.

> **WE DISCOUNT *EXPECTED* CASH FLOWS IN AN NPV ANALYSIS**
>
> **BUILDING INTUITION**
>
> Not only are the FCFs that we discount forward looking, but they also reflect *expected* FCFs. Each FCF is a weighted average of the cash flows from each possible future outcome, where the cash flow from each outcome is weighted by the estimated probability that the outcome will be realized. The expected FCF represents the single best estimate of what the actual FCF will be.

With these FCF estimates, we can now calculate the NPV of the board game project. For instance, if your cost of capital is 10 percent, the NPV is:

$$
\begin{aligned}
NPV &= FCF_0 + \frac{FCF_1}{1 + k} + \frac{FCF_2}{(1 + k)^2} + \frac{FCF_3}{(1 + k)^3} \\
&= -\$100 + \frac{\$48.75}{1.10} + \frac{\$53.75}{(1.10)^2} + \frac{\$35.00}{(1.10)^3} \\
&= -\$100 + \$44.32 + \$44.42 + \$26.30 \\
&= \$15.04
\end{aligned}
$$

Since the project has a positive NPV, you should accept it.

We use *expected* FCFs in an NPV analysis because uncertainties regarding project cash flows that are unique to the project should be reflected in the cash flow forecasts. In Chapter 11 we will discuss why analysts who try to account for such uncertainties by adjusting the discount rate, rather than the cash flows, are wrong.

EXHIBIT 10.11 **Expected FCFs for New Board Game ($ thousands)**

The expected FCF for each year during the life of the board game project equals the weighted average of the possible FCFs in that year.

Outcome	Probability	Year 0	Year 1	Year 2	Year 3
Game is very successful	0.25	−$100	$70	$90	$60
Game sales are acceptable	0.50	−100	50	55	40
Game sales are poor	0.25	−100	25	15	0
Expected FCF		−$100.00	$48.75	$53.75	$35.00

---

[7]For simplicity, the dollar values in Exhibit 10.11 and the associated calculations on this page are reported in thousands.

> **BEFORE YOU GO ON**

1. What are the five general rules for calculating FCF?

2. What is the difference between nominal and real dollars? Why is it important not to mix them in an NPV analysis?

3. What is a progressive tax system? What is the difference between a firm's marginal and average tax rates?

4. How can FCF in the terminal year of a project's life differ from FCF in the other years?

5. Why is it important to understand that cash flow forecasts in an NPV analysis are expected values?

10.3 FORECASTING FREE CASH FLOWS

 LEARNING OBJECTIVE

Earlier, we discussed how to calculate the incremental free cash flows (FCFs) for a project. Of course, when we evaluate a project, we do not know exactly what the cash flows will be, and so we must forecast them. As the performing arts center example suggests, analysts do this for each line item in the FCF calculation for each year during the life of a project. We are now ready to discuss how these forecasts are prepared.

Cash Flows from Operations

To forecast the incremental cash flows from operations (CF Opns) for a project, we must forecast the incremental net revenue (Revenue), operating expenses (Op Ex), and depreciation and amortization (D&A) associated with the project, as well as the firm's marginal tax rate. To forecast Revenue, analysts typically estimate the number of units that will be sold and the per-unit sales price for each year during the life of the project. The product of the number of units sold and the per-unit sales price equals the Revenue (assuming that the project does not affect other product lines). Separating the Revenue forecast into incremental unit sales and price forces the analyst to think clearly about how well the project has to perform in terms of actual unit sales in order to achieve the forecasted Revenue.

variable costs
costs that vary directly with the number of units sold

fixed costs
costs that do not vary directly with the number of units sold

When forecasting Op Ex, analysts often distinguish between **variable costs**, which vary directly with unit sales, and **fixed costs**, which do not. To illustrate the difference, consider a situation in which the managers of a firm plan to introduce a video game player that uses virtual reality technology. An overseas design and manufacturing company will produce the components and ship them to the company, which will assemble, package, and ship the finished product. The main variable costs will be those associated with purchasing the components; the labor required for assembling the players; packaging materials; shipping; and perhaps sales and marketing. These variable costs will rise in direct proportion to the number of units produced. If the number of units doubles, for example, we would expect these costs to approximately double. Fixed costs, such as the costs associated with assembly space (assuming output can be increased by adding shifts rather than obtaining additional space) and administrative expenses, will not increase directly with the number of units sold.[8]

Distinguishing between variable and fixed costs simplifies the forecasting problem. If company analysts estimate Revenue for a project from unit sales and price forecasts, as described earlier, then the analysts can forecast variable costs by multiplying the variable cost per unit by the number of units expected to be sold each year. Fixed cost forecasts, in contrast, will not typically vary as closely with unit sales. They tend to be based on explicit estimations of the cost of manufacturing (assembly) space, salaries and number of people required for administration of the project, and so forth.

---

[8]In some instances, costs are "fixed" in the short run but variable in the long run. For example, if a firm leases manufacturing space under a long-term contract, it may not be possible to reduce the lease expense immediately if demand for the firm's products falls. However, it will be possible to do so at the expiration of the lease or by sub-leasing excess space.

Since D&A is determined by the amounts invested in depreciable assets and the lives over which these assets can be depreciated, this line item in the CF Opns calculation is computed based on the incremental capital expenditures (Cap Exp) associated with the project, the allowable recovery period, and the depreciation method used. Consequently, it is very important to carefully think through the size and timing of the Cap Exp and the nature of those assets to properly estimate the D&A deductions.

As discussed earlier, the tax rate that should be used when forecasting CF Opns is the marginal rate the firm expects to pay on the incremental cash flows generated by the project *in the future*. Past tax rates are relevant only to the extent that they tell us something about future tax rates. Federal, state, and local officials can change tax rates in the future, and to the extent that such changes can be predicted, they should be reflected in the cash flow forecasts. Unfortunately, such changes are difficult to predict. As a result, analysts normally use the firm's current marginal tax rate.

Cash Flows Associated with Capital Expenditures and Net Working Capital

As discussed earlier, we must consider two general classes of investments when calculating FCF: incremental capital expenditures (Cap Exp) and incremental additions to working capital (Add WC). Each presents its own special challenges in the preparation of forecasts. In this section, we consider several issues related to forecasting Cap Exp and Add WC.

Capital Expenditures

Cap Exp forecasts in an NPV analysis reflect the expected level of investment during each year of the project's life, including any inflows from salvage values and any tax costs or benefits associated with asset sales. As illustrated in the performing arts center example, capital expenditures are typically required at the beginning of a project. Many projects require an initial investment for the assets necessary to produce a product and then little or no investment until the end of the project, when the assets are sold for their salvage value.

Some projects, however, require substantial periodic investments to replace or refurbish assets or to shut down operations (clean-up costs) at the end of the project's life. For example, a chemical plant project might require a substantial investment every few years to refurbish worn equipment. In addition, environmental regulations are likely to require that the property on which a chemical plant is built be restored to its previous condition when it is dismantled. These are like the clean-up costs for the strip mine that we mentioned earlier. Investments such as these should be included in cash flow forecasts wherever appropriate.

 You can find a number of free Excel spreadsheets that can be used to forecast free cash flows and use these cash flows to value projects and entire firms at Matt Evans's Web site, http://www.exinfm .com/free_spreadsheets .html. Follow the links to the Web sites of the individual contributors, and you will find even more free cash flow models and related information.

Net Working Capital

As shown in Equation 10.4, cash flow forecasts in an NPV analysis include four working capital items: (1) cash and cash equivalents, (2) accounts receivable, (3) inventories, and (4) accounts payable.

Requirements for cash and cash equivalents and accounts receivable are typically forecast as constant percentages of revenue. The cash and cash-equivalent requirements represent the amount of cash needed to make timely payments to suppliers and employees, as well as for other ongoing expenses. This amount tends to vary with the nature of the project, but analysts can gain insights into the required level of cash, as a percentage of revenue, by examining the cash-to-revenue ratios for companies that operate comparable businesses. For example, if you are forecasting cash flows for a hotel project, you might look at the ratio of cash to revenue at public companies that are focused on the hotel business for an indication of how much cash is required per dollar of revenue.

Forecasting accounts receivable is relatively straightforward. If customers will be given 30 days to pay for purchases and, on average, are expected to take 30 days to pay, the average accounts receivable balance will equal 30 days' worth of revenue or 30 days/365 days per year = 0.0822, or 8.22 percent of annual revenue. This represents the amount of money that must be set aside to finance purchases by customers. For example, a company with $100 million in annual revenue can expect to have $8.22 million invested in accounts receivable at any point in time if its customers take an average of 30 days to pay for their purchases.

Inventories and accounts payable are generally forecast as a percentage of the cost of goods sold. Inventories are forecast this way because the cost of goods sold represents a measure of the amount of money actually invested in inventories. Accounts payable are forecast this way because the cost of goods sold is a measure of the amount of money actually owed to suppliers.

> **BEFORE YOU GO ON**

1. What is the difference between variable and fixed costs, and what are examples of each?

2. How are working capital items forecast? Why are accounts receivable typically forecast as a percentage of revenue and accounts payable and inventories as percentages of the cost of goods sold?

10.4 EVALUATING PROJECTS WITH DIFFERENT LIVES

LEARNING OBJECTIVE

One problem that arises quite often in capital budgeting involves choosing between two mutually exclusive investments. Recall from Chapter 9 that if investments are mutually exclusive, the manager can choose one investment or the other but not both. This choice is simple if the expected lives of the two investments are the same. We choose the investment with the larger NPV. This type of problem was illustrated in Chapter 9.

The analysis becomes more complicated, however, if the investments have different lives. For example, suppose that you run a lawn-mowing service and have to replace one of your mowers. Further suppose that you have two options: mower A, which costs $250 and is expected to last two years, and mower B, which costs $360 and is expected to last three years.

If the mowers are identical in every other way and you expect to be in the mowing business for a long time (in other words, you are going to continue to replace mowers as they wear out for the foreseeable future), then you cannot decide which mower to buy simply by comparing the $250 cost of mower A with the $360 cost of mower B. Mower A will provide two years of service, while mower B will provide three years of service.[9]

You might be tempted to choose the mower with the lowest initial investment per year of service. For example, you might choose mower B because the initial investment is $120 per year of service ($360 for three years) while mower A requires an initial investment of $125 per year of service ($250 for two years). As you will see, however, this reasoning can get you into trouble.

In this situation, we can effectively make the lives of the mowers the same by assuming repeated investments over some identical period and comparing the NPVs of their costs. In the mower example, we can do this by considering a six-year investment period. We determine the six-year period by multiplying the life of mower A by the life of mower B ($2 \times 3 = 6$). In six years you would buy mower A three times—in years 0, 2, and 4—or mower B twice—in years 0 and 3. If we assume that the cost of each mower will remain the same over the next six years, and if we use a 10 percent opportunity cost of capital, the NPVs of the *costs* of the two alternatives are:

$$NPV = FCF_0 + \frac{FCF_1}{1 + k} + \frac{FCF_2}{(1 + k)^2} + \cdots + \frac{FCF_n}{(1 + k)^n}$$

$$NPV_A = -\$250 + \frac{-\$0}{1.10} + \frac{-\$250}{(1.10)^2} + \frac{-\$0}{(1.10)^3} + \frac{-\$250}{(1.10)^4} + \frac{-\$0}{(1.10)^5} + \frac{-\$0}{(1.10)^6}$$
$$= -\$627.36$$

$$NPV_B = -\$360 + \frac{-\$0}{1.10} + \frac{-\$0}{(1.10)^2} + \frac{-\$360}{(1.10)^3} + \frac{-\$0}{(1.10)^4} + \frac{-\$0}{(1.10)^5} + \frac{-\$0}{(1.10)^6}$$
$$= -\$630.47$$

[9]If you don't expect to replace the machines as they wear out (for instance, if you plan to quit the mowing business in one year), then you can calculate the NPV of each mower, including the salvage values that you expect to realize for each at the end of the year, and choose the mower with the larger NPV.

Notice that mower A is actually cheaper over a six-year investment cycle. Over this period, it costs $627.36/6 = $104.56 per year in today's dollars, while mower B costs $630.47/6 = $105.08 per year.

Often, a much more efficient way of solving a problem of this nature is to compute the **equivalent annual cost (EAC)**. The EAC can be calculated as follows:

$$\text{EAC}_i = k\,\text{NPV}_i\left[\frac{(1+k)^t}{(1+k)^t - 1}\right] \qquad (10.5)$$

where k is the opportunity cost of capital, NPV_i is the NPV of the investment i, and t is the life of the investment.

Using Equation 10.5, we find that the EACs for mowers A and B are:

$$\text{EAC}_A = (0.1)(-\$250)\left[\frac{(1+0.1)^2}{(1+0.1)^2 - 1}\right] = -\$144.05$$

and

$$\text{EAC}_B = (0.1)(-\$360)\left[\frac{(1+0.1)^3}{(1+0.1)^3 - 1}\right] = -\$144.76$$

We can see that the EAC gives us the same answer as equating the lives of the investments and calculating the NPVs over a six-year investment cycle. This is to be expected, since the EAC simply reflects the annuity that has the same present value as the cost of an investment over the investment period we are considering. For instance, the NPV of the EAC for mower A over a six-year period is

$$\text{NPV}_A = \frac{-\$144.05}{1.1} + \frac{-\$144.05}{(1.1)^2} + \frac{-\$144.05}{(1.1)^3} + \frac{-\$144.05}{(1.1)^4} + \frac{-\$144.05}{(1.1)^5} + \frac{-\$144.05}{(1.1)^6}$$
$$= -\$627.38$$

This is the same NPV we obtained earlier (allowing for rounding differences).

The problem is similar but a bit more complicated if the revenues or operating costs associated with the two mowers differ. For simplicity, let's continue to assume that the mowers will generate the same revenue per year, but let's also assume that mower A will cost $50 per year to maintain and mower B will cost $55 per year to maintain. The NPVs of the two mowers in this case are:

$$\text{NPV}_A = -\$250 + \frac{-\$50}{1.10} + \frac{-\$50}{(1.10)^2} = -\$336.78$$

$$\text{NPV}_B = -\$360 + \frac{-\$55}{1.10} + \frac{-\$55}{(1.10)^2} + \frac{-\$55}{(1.10)^3} = -\$496.78$$

The EACs are:

$$\text{EAC}_A = (0.1)(-\$336.78)\left[\frac{(1+0.1)^2}{(1+0.1)^2 - 1}\right] = -\$194.05$$

and

$$\text{EAC}_B = (0.1)(-\$496.78)\left[\frac{(1+0.1)^3}{(1+0.1)^3 - 1}\right] = -\$199.76$$

Of course, we still want to choose mower A in this case since all that has really happened is that the EAC of mower A has gone up by $50 and the EAC of mower B has gone up by $55. In contrast, if the annual cost of maintaining mower A is $50 and the annual cost of maintaining mower B is $49, we would choose mower B. As confirmation, you should try the calculations for this example.

One other point should be made about the EAC concept. Despite its name, it does not apply only to costs. If we included revenues in the above analysis and both mowers had positive NPVs, we could still use the EAC formula to compare the two alternatives. The only difference in this case is that the decision criteria would be to choose the most positive EAC instead of the least negative.

equivalent annual cost (EAC) the annual dollar amount of an annuity that has a life equal to that of a project and that also has a present value equal to the present value of the cash flows from the project; the term comes from the fact that the EAC calculation is often used to calculate a constant annual cost associated with projects in order to make comparisons

LEARNING BY DOING

APPLICATION 10.5

Using EAC to Compare Projects with Different Lives

PROBLEM: You are looking at new ovens for your pizza parlor, and you see two models that would work equally well. Model A would cost $40,000 and last 10 years. Model B would cost $50,000 but would last 12 years and would require $500 less electricity per year than model A. Which model is less expensive? Assume a 10 percent opportunity cost of capital.

APPROACH: Use the EAC formula in Equation 10.5 to calculate the EAC of the initial investment for each model of oven. Add the annual electricity savings to the EAC of the initial investment for Model B. Choose the model with the smallest total EAC.

SOLUTION: The EACs for the initial investments in the two ovens are as follows:

$$EAC_A = (0.1)(-\$40,000)\left[\frac{(1 + 0.1)^{10}}{(1 + 0.1)^{10} - 1}\right] = -\$6,509.82$$

$$EAC_B = (0.1)(-\$50,000)\left[\frac{(1 + 0.1)^{12}}{(1 + 0.1)^{12} - 1}\right] = -\$7,338.17$$

Now since the electricity savings would be $500 per year in nominal dollars, we can simply add this amount to the EAC calculated for model B above to get the true $EAC_B = -\$7,338.16 + \$500 = -\$6,838.16.$[10] Since the EAC for model B is still more negative than that for model A, we would conclude that model A would be less expensive over its expected useful life.

SUMMARY OF Learning Objectives

1 **Explain why incremental after-tax free cash flows are relevant in evaluating a project and calculate them for a project.**

The incremental after-tax free cash flows, FCFs, for a project equal the expected change in the total after-tax cash flows of the firm if the project is adopted. The impact of a project on the firm's total cash flows is the appropriate measure of cash flows because these are the cash flows that reflect all of the costs and benefits from the project and only the costs and benefits from the project. The incremental after-tax free cash flows are calculated using Equation 10.2. This calculation is also illustrated in Exhibit 10.1.

2 **Discuss the five general rules for incremental after-tax free cash flow calculations and explain why cash flows stated in nominal (real) dollars should be discounted using a nominal (real) discount rate.**

The five general rules are as follows:

Rule 1: *Include cash flows and only cash flows in your calculations.* Stockholders care about only the impact of a project on the firm's cash flows.

Rule 2: *Include the impact of the project on cash flows from other product lines.* If a project affects the cash flows from other projects, we must take this fact into account in NPV analysis in order to fully capture the impact of the project on the firm's total cash flows.

Rule 3: *Include all opportunity costs.* If an asset is used for a project, the relevant cost for that asset is the value that could be realized from its most valuable alternative use. By including this cost in the NPV analysis, we capture the change in the firm's cash flows that is attributable to the use of this asset for the project.

Rule 4: *Forget sunk costs.* The only costs that matter are those to be incurred from this point on.

Rule 5: *Include only after-tax cash flows in the cash flow calculations.* Since stockholders receive cash flows after taxes have been paid, they are concerned only about after-tax cash flows.

Since a nominal discount rate reflects both the expected rate of inflation and a real return, we would be overadjusting for inflation if we discounted a real cash flow with a nominal rate. Similarly, if we discounted a nominal cash flow using a real discount rate, we would be undercompensating for expected inflation in the discounting process. This is why we discount nominal cash flows using only a nominal discount rate and we discount real cash flows using only a real discount rate.

3 **Describe how distinguishing between variable and fixed costs can be useful in forecasting operating expenses.**

Variable costs vary directly with the number of units sold, while fixed costs do not. When forecasting operating expenses, it is often useful to treat variable and fixed costs separately. We can forecast variable costs by multiplying unit variable costs by the number of units sold. Fixed costs are more accurately based on the specific characteristics of those costs, rather than as a function of sales.

---

[10]We could have also calculated the NPV for model B by discounting the $500 annual electricity savings by 10 percent and adding the present value of that savings stream to the $50,000 initial cost. Using this NPV in the EAC formula would also yield −$6,838.16.

Separating fixed costs from the variable also makes it easier to identify the factors that will cause them to change over time and therefore easier to forecast them.

 Explain the concept of equivalent annual cost and use it to compare projects with unequal lives.

The equivalent annual cost (EAC) is the annualized cost of an investment that is stated in nominal dollars. In other words, it is the annual payment from an annuity that has the same NPV and the same life as the project. Since it is a measure of the annual cost or cash inflow from a project, the EAC for one project can be compared directly with the EAC from another project, regardless of the lives of those two projects. Application of the EAC concept is illustrated in Section 10.4.

SUMMARY OF **Key Equations**

Equation	Description	Formula
10.1	Incremental free cash flow definition	$\text{FCF}_{\text{Project}} = \text{FCF}_{\text{Firm with project}} - \text{FCF}_{\text{Firm without project}}$
10.2	Incremental free cash flow calculation	$\text{FCF} = [(\text{Revenue} - \text{Op Ex} - \text{D\&A}) \times (1 - t)]$ $+ \text{D\&A} - \text{Cap Exp} - \text{Add WC}$
10.3	Inflation and real components of cost of capital	$1 + k = (1 + \Delta P_e) \times (1 + r)$
10.4	Incremental additions to working capital	$\text{Add WC} = \text{Change in cash and cash equivalents} + \text{Change in accounts receivable} + \text{Change in inventories} - \text{Change in accounts payable}$
10.5	Equivalent annual cost	$\text{EAC}_i = k\,\text{NPV}_i \left[\dfrac{(1 + k)^t}{(1 + k)^t - 1} \right]$

Self-Study Problems

10.1 Explain why the announcement of a new investment is usually accompanied by a change in the firm's stock price.

10.2 In calculating the NPV of a project, should we use all of the after-tax cash flows associated with the project or incremental after-tax free cash flows from the project? Why?

10.3 You are considering opening another restaurant in the TexasBurgers chain. The new restaurant will have annual revenue of $300,000 and operating expenses of $150,000. The annual depreciation and amortization for the assets used in the restaurant will equal $50,000. An annual capital expenditure of $10,000 will be required to offset wear and tear on the assets used in the restaurant, but no additions to working capital will be required. The marginal tax rate will be 40 percent. Calculate the incremental annual after-tax free cash flow for the project.

10.4 Sunglass Heaven, Inc., is launching a new store in a shopping mall in Houston. The annual revenue of the store depends on the weather conditions in the summer in Houston. The annual revenue will be $240,000 in a sizzling summer with a probability of 0.3, $80,000 in a cool summer with a probability of 0.2, and $150,000 in a normal summer with a probability of 0.5. What is the expected annual revenue for the store?

10.5 Sprigg Lane Manufacturing, Inc., needs to purchase a new central air-conditioning system for a plant. There are two choices. The first system costs $50,000 and is expected to last 10 years, and the second system costs $72,000 and is expected to last 15 years. Assume that the opportunity cost of capital is 10 percent. Which air-conditioning system should Sprigg Lane purchase?

Solutions to Self-Study Problems

10.1 A firm's investments cause changes in its future after-tax cash flows, and stockholders are the residual claimants (owners) of those cash flows. Therefore, the stock price should increase when stockholders expect an investment to have a positive NPV, and decrease when it is expected to have a negative NPV.

10.2 We should use incremental after-tax free cash flows from the project. Incremental after-tax free cash flows reflect the amount by which the firm's total cash flows will change if the project is adopted.

In other words, they represent the net difference in cash revenues, costs, taxes, and investment out-lays (for net working capital and capital expenditures) at the firm level with and without the project, which is precisely what the stockholders care about.

10.3 The incremental annual after-tax free cash flow is calculated as follows:

$$FCF = [(\$300,000 - \$150,000 - \$50,000) \times (1 - 0.4)] + \$50,000 - \$10,000 = \$100,000$$

10.4 The expected annual revenue is

$$(0.3 \times \$240,000) + (0.2 \times \$80,000) + (0.5 \times \$150,000) = \$163,000$$

10.5 The equivalent annual cost for each system is as follows:

$$EAC_1 = (0.1)(\$50,000)\left[\frac{(1.1)^{10}}{(1.1)^{10} - 1)}\right] = \$8,137.27$$

$$EAC_2 = (0.1)(\$72,000)\left[\frac{(1.1)^{15}}{(1.1)^{15} - 1)}\right] = \$9,466.11$$

Therefore, Sprigg Lane should purchase the first one.

Critical Thinking Questions

10.1 Do you agree or disagree with the following statement given the techniques discussed in this chapter? We can calculate future cash flows precisely and obtain an exact value for the NPV of an investment.

10.2 What are the differences between cash flows used in capital budgeting calculations and past accounting earnings?

10.3 Suppose that FRA Corporation already has divisions in both Dallas and Houston. FRA is now considering setting up a third division in Austin. This expansion will require that one senior manager from Dallas and one from Houston relocate to Austin. Ignore relocation expenses. Is their annual compensation relevant to the decision to expand?

10.4 MusicHeaven, Inc., is a producer of MP3 players, which currently have either 20 gigabytes or 30 gigabytes of storage. Now the company is considering launching a new production line making mini MP3 players with 5 gigabytes of storage. Analysts forecast that MusicHeaven will be able to sell 1 million such mini MP3 players if the investment is taken. In making the investment deci-sion, discuss what the company should consider other than the sales of the mini MP3 players.

10.5 QualityLiving Trust is a real estate investment company that builds and remodels apartment buildings in northern California. It is currently considering remodeling a few idle buildings that it owns in San Jose into luxury apartment buildings. The company bought those buildings eight months ago. How should the market value of the buildings be treated in evaluating this project?

10.6 High-End Fashions, Inc., bought a production line for ankle-length skirts last year at a cost of $500,000. This year, however, miniskirts are in and ankle-length skirts are completely out of fashion. High-End has the option to rebuild the production line and use it to produce miniskirts with an annual operating cost of $300,000 and expected revenue of $700,000. How should the company treat the $500,000 cost of the old production line in evaluating the rebuilding plan?

10.7 How is the MACRS depreciation method under IRS rules different from the straight-line depre-ciation allowed under GAAP rules? What is the implication on incremental after-tax free cash flows from firms' investments?

10.8 Explain the difference between marginal and average tax rates, and identify which of these rates is used in capital budgeting and why.

10.9 Under what circumstances will the sale of an asset result in a taxable gain? How do you estimate the taxes or tax benefit associated with the sale of an asset?

10.10 When two mutually exclusive projects have different lives, how can an analyst determine which is better? What is the underlying assumption in this method?

Questions and Problems

BASIC **>** **10.1** **Calculating project cash flows:** Why do we use forecasted incremental after-tax free cash flows instead of forecasted accounting earnings in estimating the NPV of a project?

10.2 **The FCF calculation:** How do we calculate incremental after-tax free cash flows from fore-casted earnings of a project? What are the common adjustment items?

10.3 The FCF calculation: How do we adjust for depreciation when we calculate incremental after-tax free cash flow from EBITDA? What is the intuition for the adjustment?

10.4 Nominal versus real cash flows: What is the difference between nominal and real cash flows? Which rate of return should we use to discount each type of cash flow?

10.5 Taxes and depreciation: What is the difference between average tax rate and marginal tax rate? Which one should we use in calculating incremental after-tax cash flows?

10.6 Computing terminal-year FCF: Healthy Potions, Inc., a pharmaceutical company, bought a machine at a cost of $2 million five years ago that produces pain-reliever medicine. The machine has been depreciated over the past five years, and the current book value is $800,000. The company decides to sell the machine now at its market price of $1 million. The marginal tax rate is 30 percent. What are the relevant cash flows? How do they change if the market price of the machine is $600,000 instead?

10.7 Cash flows from operations: What are variable costs and fixed costs? What are some examples of each? How are these costs estimated in forecasting operating expenses?

10.8 Cash flows from operations: When forecasting operating expenses, explain the difference between a fixed cost and a variable cost.

10.9 Investment cash flows: Zippy Corporation just purchased computing equipment for $20,000. The equipment will be depreciated using a five-year MACRS depreciation schedule. If the equipment is sold at the end of its fourth year for $12,000, what are the after-tax proceeds from the sale, assuming the marginal tax rate is 35 percent.

10.10 Investment cash flows: Six Twelve, Inc., is considering opening up a new convenience store in downtown New York City. The expected annual revenue at the new store is $800,000. To estimate the increase in working capital, analysts estimate the ratio of cash and cash-equivalents to revenue to be 0.03 and the ratios of receivables, inventories, and payables to revenue to be 0.05, 0.10, and 0.04, respectively, in the same industry. What is the expected incremental cash flow related to working capital when the store is opened?

10.11 Investment cash flows: Keswick Supply Company wants to set up a division that provides copy and fax services to businesses. Customers will be given 20 days to pay for such services. The annual revenue of the division is estimated to be $25,000. Assuming that the customers take the full 20 days to pay, what is the incremental cash flow associated with accounts receivable?

10.12 Expected cash flows: Define *expected cash flows,* and explain why this concept is important in evaluating projects.

10.13 Projects with different lives: Explain the concept of equivalent annual cost and how it is used to compare projects with different lives.

10.14 Projects with different lives: If you had to choose between one project with an expected life of five years and a second project with an expected life of six years, how could you do this without using the equivalent annual cost concept?

< INTERMEDIATE

10.15 Nominal versus real cash flows: You are buying a sofa. You will pay $200 today and make three consecutive annual payments of $300 in the future. The real rate of return is 10 percent, and the expected inflation rate is 4 percent. What is the actual price of the sofa?

10.16 Nominal versus real cash flows: You are graduating in two years. You want to invest your current savings of $5,000 in bonds and use the proceeds to purchase a new car when you graduate and start to work. You can invest the money in either Bond A, a two-year bond with a 3 percent annual interest rate, or Bond B, an inflation-indexed two-year bond paying 1 percent real interest above the inflation rate (assume this bond makes annual interest payments). The inflation rate over the next two years is expected to be 1.5 percent. Assume that both bonds are default free and have the same market price. Which bond should you invest in?

10.17 Marginal and average tax rates: Given the U.S. Corporate Tax Rate Schedule in Exhibit 10.6, what is the marginal tax rate and average tax rate of a corporation that generates a taxable income of $12 million in 2012?

10.18 Investment cash flows: Healthy Potions, Inc., is considering investing in a new production line for eye drops. Other than investing in the equipment, the company needs to increase its cash and cash equivalents by $10,000, increase the level of inventory by $30,000, increase accounts receivable by $25,000, and increase accounts payable by $5,000 at the beginning of the project. Healthy Potions will recover these changes in working capital at the end of the project 10 years later. Assume the appropriate discount rate is 12 percent. What are the present values of the relevant investment cash flows?

10.19 Cash flows from operations: Given the soaring price of gasoline, Ford is considering introducing a new production line of gas-electric hybrid sedans. The expected annual unit sales of the hybrid cars is 30,000; the price is $22,000 per car. Variable costs of production are $10,000 per car. The fixed overhead including salary of top executives is $80 million per year. However, the introduction of the hybrid sedan will decrease Ford's sales of regular sedans by 10,000 cars per year; the regular sedans have a unit price of $20,000, a unit variable cost of $12,000, and fixed costs of $250,000 per year. Depreciation costs of the production plant are $50,000 per year. The marginal tax rate is 40 percent. What is the incremental annual cash flow from operations?

10.20 FCF and NPV for a project: Archer Daniels Midland Company is considering buying a new farm that it plans to operate for 10 years. The farm will require an initial investment of $12 million. This investment will consist of $2 million for land and $10 million for trucks and other equipment. The land, all trucks, and all other equipment are expected to be sold at the end of 10 years for a price of $5 million, which is $2 million above book value. The farm is expected to produce revenue of $2 million each year, and annual cash flow from operations equals $1.8 million. The marginal tax rate is 35 percent, and the appropriate discount rate is 10 percent. Calculate the NPV of this investment.

10.21 Projects with different lives: You are trying to choose between purchasing one of two machines for a factory. Machine A costs $15,000 to purchase and has a three-year life. Machine B costs $17,700 to purchase but has a four-year life. Regardless of which machine you purchase, it will have to be replaced at the end of its operating life. Which machine should you choose? Assume a marginal tax rate of 35 percent and a discount rate of 15 percent.

10.22 Projects with different lives: You are starting a family pizza parlor and need to buy a motorcycle for delivery orders. You have two models in mind. Model A costs $9,000 and is expected to run for 6 years; Model B is more expensive, with a price of $14,000, and has an expected life of 10 years. The annual maintenance costs are $800 for Model A and $700 for Model B. Assume that the opportunity cost of capital is 10 percent. Which one should you buy?

ADVANCED ▷ **10.23** You are the CFO of SlimBody, Inc., a retailer of the exercise machine Slimbody and related accessories. Your firm is considering opening up a new store in Los Angeles. The store will have a life of 20 years. It will generate annual sales of 5,000 exercise machines, and the price of each machine is $2,500. The annual sales of accessories will be $600,000, and the operating expenses of running the store, including labor and rent, will amount to 50 percent of the revenues from the exercise machines. The initial investment in the store will equal $30 million and will be fully depreciated on a straight-line basis over the 20-year life of the store. Your firm will need to invest $2 million in additional working capital immediately, and recover it at the end of the investment. Your firm's marginal tax rate is 30 percent. The opportunity cost of opening up the store is 10 percent. What are the incremental free cash flows from this project at the beginning of the project as well as in years 1–19 and 20? Should you approve it?

10.24 Merton Shovel Corporation has decided to bid for a contract to supply shovels to the Honduran Army. The Honduran Army intends to buy 1,000 shovels per year for the next three years. To supply these shovels, Merton will have to acquire manufacturing equipment at a cost of $150,000. This equipment will be depreciated on a straight-line basis over its five-year lifetime. At the end of the third year, Merton can sell the equipment for exactly its book value ($60,000). Additional fixed costs will be $36,000 per year, and variable costs will be $3.00 per shovel. An additional investment of $25,000 in net working capital will be required when the project is initiated. This investment will be recovered at the end of the third year. Merton Shovel has a 35 percent marginal tax rate and a 17 percent required rate of return on the project. What is the lowest possible per shovel price that Merton can offer for the contract and still create value for its stockholders?

10.25 Rocky Mountain Lumber, Inc., is considering purchasing a new wood saw that costs $50,000. The saw will generate revenues of $100,000 per year for five years. The cost of materials and labor needed to generate these revenues will total $60,000 per year, and other cash expenses will be $10,000 per year. The machine is expected to sell for $1,000 at the end of its five-year life and will be depreciated on a straight-line basis over five years to zero. Rocky Mountain's tax rate is 34 percent, and its opportunity cost of capital is 10 percent. Should the company purchase the saw? Explain why or why not?

10.26 A beauty product company is developing a new fragrance named Happy Forever. There is a probability of 0.5 that consumers will love Happy Forever, and in this case, annual sales will be 1 million bottles; a probability of 0.4 that consumers will find the smell acceptable and annual sales will be 200,000 bottles; and a probability of 0.1 that consumers will find the smell unpleasant and annual sales will be only 50,000 bottles. The selling price is $38, and the variable cost is $8 per bottle. Fixed production costs will be $1 million per year, and depreciation will be $1.2 million. Assume that the marginal tax rate is 40 percent. What are the expected annual incremental cash flows from the new fragrance?

10.27 ACME Manufacturing is considering replacing an existing production line with a new line that has a greater output capacity and operates with less labor than the existing line. The new line would cost $1 million, have a five-year life, and be depreciated using MACRS over three years. At the end of five years, the new line could be sold as scrap for $200,000 (in Year 5 dollars). Because the new line is more automated, it would require fewer operators, resulting in a savings of $40,000 per year before tax and unadjusted for inflation (in today's dollars). Additional sales with the new machine are expected to result in additional net cash inflows, before tax, of $60,000 per year (in today's dollars). If ACME invests in the new line, a one-time investment of $10,000 in additional working capital will be required. The tax rate is 35 percent, the opportunity cost of capital is 10 percent, and the annual rate of inflation is 3 percent. What is the NPV of the new production line?

10.28 The alternative to investing in the new production line in Problem 10.27 is to overhaul the existing line, which currently has both a book value and a salvage value of $0. It would cost $300,000 to overhaul the existing line, but this expenditure would extend its useful life to five years. The line would have a $0 salvage value at the end of five years. The overhaul outlay would be capitalized and depreciated using MACRS over three years. Should ACME replace or renovate the existing line?

10.29 FITCO is considering the purchase of new equipment. The equipment costs $350,000, and an additional $110,000 is needed to install it. The equipment will be depreciated straight-line to zero over a five-year life. The equipment will generate additional annual revenues of $265,000, and it will have annual cash operating expenses of $83,000. The equipment will be sold for $85,000 after five years. An inventory investment of $73,000 is required during the life of the investment. FITCO is in the 40 percent tax bracket, and its cost of capital is 10 percent. What is the project NPV?

< **CFA PROBLEMS**

    a. $47,818.
    b. $63,658.
    c. $80,189.
    d. $97,449.

10.30 After estimating a project's NPV, the analyst is advised that the fixed capital outlay will be revised upward by $100,000. The fixed capital outlay is depreciated straight-line over an eight-year life. The tax rate is 40 percent, and the required rate of return is 10 percent. No changes in cash operating revenues, cash operating expenses, or salvage value are expected. What is the effect on the project NPV?
    a. $100,000 decrease.
    b. $73,325 decrease.
    c. $59,988 decrease.
    d. No change.

10.31 When assembling the cash flows to calculate an NPV or IRR, the project's after-tax interest expenses should be subtracted from the cash flows for:
    a. The NPV calculation, but not the IRR calculation.
    b. The IRR calculation, but not the NPV calculation.
    c. Both the NPV calculation and the IRR calculation.
    d. Neither the NPV calculation nor the IRR calculation.

Sample Test Problems

10.1 You purchased 100 shares of stock in an oil company, Texas Energy, Inc., at $50 per share. The company has 1 million shares outstanding. Ten days later, Texas Energy announced an investment in an oil field in east Texas. The probability that the investment will be successful and generate an NPV of $10 million is 0.2; the probability that the investment will be a failure and generate an NPV of negative $1 million is 0.8. How would you expect the stock price to change upon the company's announcement of the investment?

10.2 A chemical company is considering buying a heavy duty fan for its plant. The fan is expected to work forever and help cool the machines in the plant and, hence, reduce their maintenance costs by $4,000 per year. The cost of the fan is $30,000. The appropriate discount rate is 10 percent, and the marginal tax rate is 40 percent. Should the company buy the fan?

10.3 Hogvertz Elvin Catering (HEC) is considering switching from its old food maker to a new Wonder Food Maker. Both food makers will remain useful for the next 10 years, but the new food maker will generate a depreciation expense of $5,000 per year, while the old food maker will generate a depreciation expense of $4,000 per year. What is the after-tax free cash flow effect from depreciation of switching to the new food maker for HEC if the firm's marginal tax rate is 40 percent and the discount rate is 12 percent?

10.4 The Long-Term Financing Company has identified an alternative project that is similar to a project currently under consideration in all respects except one. That is, the new project will reduce the need for working capital by $10,000 during the 30-year life of the project. The cost of capital is 18 percent, and the marginal corporate tax rate for the firm is 34 percent. What is the after-tax present value of this new alternative project?

10.5 Choice Masters must choose between two projects of unequal lives. Project 1 has an NPV of $50,000 and will be viable for five years. Project 2 will be viable for seven years. The discount rate for both Project 1 and Project 2 is 10 percent. In order for Choice Master to be indifferent between the two projects, what must the NPV of Project 2 be?

Unilever's Sustainable Living Plan

Sustainability is all the buzz in business and is quickly becoming a mainstream topic. Governments as well as customers have been urging corporations to make themselves sustainable; but what does that mean?

What Is Sustainability?

Sustainability is acting to meet the needs of the present generation without compromising the ability of future generations to meet their own needs. For individuals it is a life style that attempts to reduce an individual's or society's use of Earth's natural resources. The European Union has adopted sustainability as an official policy, urging companies to follow sustainable practices as a means of achieving their corporate social responsibility goals to contribute to a better society and a cleaner environment.

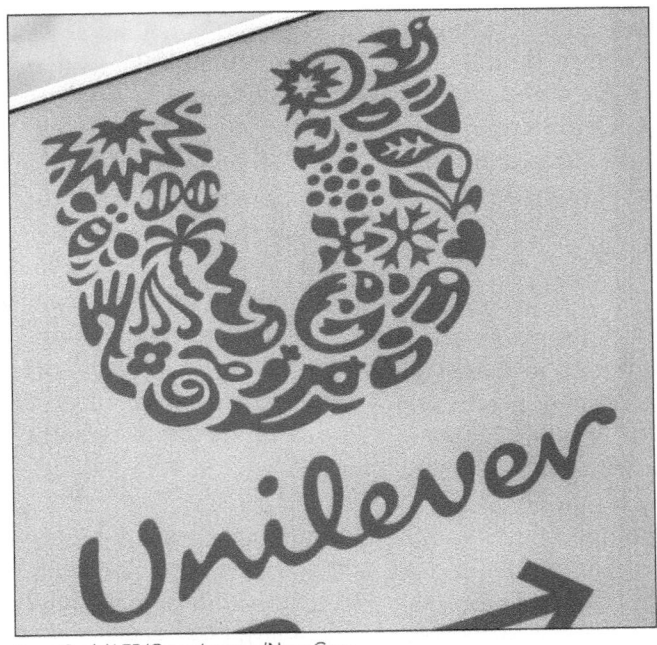

Koen Suyk/AFP/Getty Images/NewsCom

Unilever's Sustainability Plan

Talking about sustainability is one thing; doing it is another. In late 2010 one company, Unilever, took action by unveiling its global Sustainable Living Plan. Launched simultaneously in London, New York, Amsterdam, and New Delhi, the plan will affect all of Unilever's stakeholders worldwide—customers, suppliers, investors, employees, and the local communities where Unilever products are sold. It's not unusual for a company to try to reduce its CO_2 emissions or to reduce waste and water usage in its own manufacturing facilities. But Unilever's plan goes far beyond its plants. According to the company's management, more than two-thirds of greenhouse emissions and half the water in Unilever products' life cycles come from consumer use. Therefore, extending the plan to include consumers is a commitment on an unprecedented scale.

Accomplishing the Company's Sustainability Goals

How will Unilever accomplish its sustainability goals? Technological advances will enable the firm to achieve some. The company is developing products such as laundry detergents that work at lower temperatures and bath soaps that reduce the amount of hot water needed in showers and baths.

The company will accomplish other parts of its plan by requiring that suppliers meet sustainability goals.

Finally, Unilever will meet some goals by changing consumers' habits. For example, by 2015 Unilever aims to change the hygiene behavior of 1 billion consumers across Asia, Africa, and Latin America by promoting the benefits of hand washing with soap at key times. Though this may seem rudimentary by Western standards, every year more than 3.5 million children die before age five due to diarrhea and acute respiratory infections. Much of this is from poor hygiene habits.[1]

Overall, through its ambitious sustainability plan Unilever intends to (1) improve the health and well-being of more than 1 billion people: (2) purchase 100 percent of its agricultural raw material from sustainable businesses; and (3) reduce the environmental impact of everything it sells by one-half over the next 10 years while doubling its revenue. The major challenge the company faces is to increase sales without also increasing its environmental footprint. Dave Lewis, President of Unilever America, recognizes this dilemma: "We cannot choose between growth and sustainability. We have to do both."

Critics of the plan point out that much of its success depends on changing consumer behavior, which is largely beyond Unilever's control. Probably more

---

[1]Studies by Unilever have shown that hand washing at key hygienic occasions can reduce diarrheal disease by 25 percent, respiratory infection by 19 percent, and eye infections by 46 percent.

important, critics question whether the adoption of the plan will contribute to Unilever's bottom line. Being green and socially responsible are all well and good, but a public company needs to make money. A company that is not financially successful is not sustainable, good intentions notwithstanding.

Integrating Business Strategy and Sustainability Strategy

What makes Unilever's plan so intriguing to many is the way it integrates business strategy and sustainability strategy. Let's take one example: health and hygiene. Unilever claims it will use its Lifebuoy brand soap to encourage more hand washing in an effort to reduce diarrhea and respiratory diseases spread by germs. It will use its fluoride toothpaste and toothbrush brands to encourage brushing twice a day, which will reduce tooth decay in children by 50 percent compared to brushing once. It will make safe drinking water available to 500 million people through its affordable Pureit in-home water purifier. Through its Dove Social Mission, Unilever intends to use one of its best-known brands to enhance the self-esteem and thus improve the mental health of young women around the world.

Large companies are often criticized by nongovernmental organizations (NGOs). In the past, as a company headquartered in Europe where NGOs are particularly active, Unilever has been a target of such criticism. A common corporate strategy is to fight back. However, with its Sustainable Living Plan, Unilever has endorsed many NGO recommendations. For example, Unilever will use eggs from 100 percent cage-free chickens in all of its products—a common demand from animal rights NGOs. All Lipton tea will be purchased from Rainforest Alliance certified suppliers. Even Ben and Jerry's ice cream will be made from ingredients that are fair-trade certified.

In rural India, Unilever plans to link 500,000 small farmers into a unified supply network to improve their farming practices. The farmers will be required to adhere to Unilever's Sustainable Agriculture Code and for the first time will benefit from economies of scale that can improve their lives. What's in it for Unilever? It will gain a vastly expanded network of sustainable suppliers producing products at competitive prices. Building an adequate source of supplies is especially critical in a world where food shortages may become more common.

Critical Concerns and Responses

Is Unilever simply using the sustainability mantra as a device to increase its profits? To its critics, Unilever's motives are suspect. They claim it is pursuing sustainability, not because it is the right thing to do, but because it is good business. But are these two goals mutually exclusive? Can a firm's strategy seek to be profitable and sustainable? What's wrong with doing well by doing good? Nothing, according to Unilever management. They intend to lead the way in being a profitable, sustainable corporation.

DISCUSSION QUESTIONS

1. Should Unilever's stockholders endorse its sustainability plan? Why or why not?
2. Are there business advantages to using sustainable or green suppliers? If so, what are they? If not, do you think a traditional return on investment analysis captures all possible benefits of going green?
3. Are there any ethical criticisms of Unilever's sustainable living strategy? If so, what are they?

Sources: (1) http://www.sustainable-living.unilever.com/, (2) http://www.sustainable-living.unilever.com/the-plan/health-hygiene, (3) http://en.wikipedia.org/wiki/Sustainable_living, (4) http://www.epa.gov/sustainability.

The Cost of Capital

11

The Walt Disney Company announced in May 2010 that it would build a new hotel at Walt Disney World, its first new hotel at that theme park in seven years. The hotel, which is now being opened in several phases, has been named "Disney's Art of Animation Resort." It is being built on a 65-acre parcel of land across the lake from Disney's Pop Century Resort and will have 1,120 suites and 864 traditional hotel rooms when completed. Disney executives anticipate that the rooms in the Art of Animation Resort will be priced comparably to those at the Pop Century Resort, which begin at less than $100 per night.

As you can imagine, the cost of financing a project like this is substantial. Disney is a highly sophisticated and successful hotel and theme park developer and operator. Before the company announced the construction of the Art of Animation Resort, you can be sure that the managers at Disney carefully considered the financial aspects of the project. They evaluated the required investment, what revenues the new hotel was likely to generate, and how much it would cost to operate and maintain. They also estimated what it would cost to finance the project—how much they would pay for the debt and the returns equity investors would require for an investment with this level of risk. This "cost of capital" would be incorporated into their NPV analysis through the discounting process.

Accuately estimating the cost of capital is especially important for a capital-intensive project such as a hotel. The cost of financing a hotel like the one that Disney is building can easily total $50 or more per room rental. In other words, if an average room rents for $100, the cost of financing the project can consume 50 percent or more of the revenue the hotel receives from renting a room!

Learning Objectives

1 Explain what the weighted average cost of capital for a firm is and why it is often used as a discount rate to evaluate projects.

2 Calculate the cost of debt for a firm.

3 Calculate the cost of common stock and the cost of preferred stock for a firm.

4 Calculate the weighted average cost of capital for a firm, explain the limitations of using a firm's weighted average cost of capital as the discount rate when evaluating a project, and discuss the alternatives to the firm's weighted average cost of capital.

From this example, you can see how important it is to get the cost of capital right. If Disney managers had estimated the cost of capital to be 7 percent when it was really 9 percent, they might have ended up investing in a project with a large negative NPV. How did they approach this important task? In this chapter we discuss how managers estimate the cost of capital they use to evaluate projects.

CHAPTER PREVIEW

Chapter 6 discussed the general concept of risk and described what financial analysts mean when they talk about the risk associated with a project's cash flows. It also explained how this risk is related to expected returns. With this background, we are ready to discuss the methods that financial managers use to estimate discount rates, the reasons they use these methods, and the shortcomings of each method.

We begin this chapter by introducing the weighted average cost of capital and explaining how this concept is related to the discount rates that many financial managers use to evaluate projects. Then we describe various methods that

are used to estimate the costs of the three general types of financing that firms use to acquire assets—debt, common stock, and preferred stock—as well as the overall weighted average cost of capital for the firm.

We next discuss the circumstances under which it is appropriate to use the weighted average cost of capital for a firm as the discount rate for a project and outline the types of problems that can arise when the weighted average cost of capital is used inappropriately. Finally, we examine alternatives to using the weighted average cost of capital as a discount rate.

11.1 THE FIRM'S OVERALL COST OF CAPITAL

1 LEARNING OBJECTIVE

Our discussions of capital budgeting up to this point have focused on evaluating individual projects. We have assumed that the rate used to discount the cash flows for a project reflects the risks associated with the incremental after-tax free cash flows from that project. In Chapter 6, we saw that *unsystematic risk* can be eliminated by holding a diversified portfolio. Therefore, *systematic risk* is the only risk that investors require compensation for bearing. With this insight, we concluded that we can use Equation 6.10, to estimate the expected rate of return for a particular investment:

$$E(R_i) = R_{rf} + \beta_i[E(R_m) - R_{rf}]$$

where $E(R_i)$ is the expected return on project i, R_{rf} is the risk-free rate of return, β_i is the beta for project i, and $E(R_m)$ is the expected return on the market. Recall that the difference between the expected return on the market and the risk-free rate $[E(R_m) - R_{rf}]$ is known as the *market risk premium*.

Although these ideas help us better understand the discount rate on a conceptual level, they can be difficult to implement in practice. Firms do not issue publicly traded shares for individual projects. This means that analysts do not have the stock returns necessary to use a regression analysis like that illustrated in Exhibit 6.10 to estimate the beta (β) for an individual project. As a result, they have no way to directly estimate the discount rate that reflects the systematic risk of the incremental cash flows from a particular project.

In many firms, senior financial managers deal with this problem by estimating the cost of capital for the firm as a whole and then requiring analysts within the firm to use this cost of capital to discount the cash flows for all projects.[1] A problem with this approach is that it

---

[1]Surveys of capital budgeting practices at major public firms in the United States indicate that a large percentage (possibly as high as 80 percent) of firms use the cost of capital for a firm or a division in capital budgeting calculations. For a discussion of this evidence, see the article titled "Best Practices in Estimating the Cost of Capital: Survey and Synthesis," by R. F. Bruner, K. M. Eades, R. S. Harris, and R. C. Higgins, which was published in the Spring/Summer 1998 issue of *Financial Practice and Education*.

ignores the fact that a firm is really a collection of projects with different levels of risk. A firm's overall cost of capital is actually a weighted average of the costs of capital for these projects, where the weights reflect the relative values of the projects.

To see why a firm is a collection of projects, consider The Boeing Company. Boeing manufactures a number of different models of civilian and military aircraft. If you have ever flown on a commercial airline, chances are that you have been on a Boeing 737, 747, 757, 767, 777, or 787 aircraft. Boeing manufactures several versions of each of these aircraft models to meet the needs of its customers. These versions have different ranges, seat configurations, numbers of seats, and so on. Some are designed exclusively to haul freight for companies such as UPS and FedEx. Every version of every model of aircraft at Boeing was, at some point in time, a new project. The assets owned by Boeing today and its expected cash flows are just the sum of the assets and cash flows from all of these individual projects plus the other projects at the firm, such as those involving military aircraft.[2] This means that the overall systematic risk associated with Boeing's expected cash flows and the company's cost of capital are weighted averages of the systematic risks and the costs of capital for its individual projects.

If the risk of an individual project differs from the average risk of the firm, the firm's overall cost of capital is not the ideal discount rate to use when evaluating that project. Nevertheless, since this is the discount rate that is commonly used, we begin by discussing how a firm's overall cost of capital is estimated. We then discuss alternatives to using the firm's cost of capital as the discount rate in evaluating a project.

The Finance Balance Sheet

To understand how financial analysts estimate their firms' costs of capital, it is helpful to be familiar with a concept that we call the **finance balance sheet**. The finance balance sheet was referred to as the market-value balance sheet in Chapter 3. The main difference between the finance balance sheet and the accounting balance sheet is that the finance balance sheet is based on market values rather than book values. Recall that the total book value of the assets reported on an accounting balance sheet does not necessarily reflect the total market value of those assets. This is because the book value is largely based on historical costs, while the total market value of the assets equals the present value of the total cash flows that those assets are expected to generate in the future. The market value can be greater than or less than the book value but is rarely the same.

While the left-hand side of the accounting balance sheet reports the book values of a firm's assets, the right-hand side reports how those assets were financed. Firms finance the purchase of their assets using debt and equity.[3] Since the cost of the assets must equal the total value of the debt and equity that were used to purchase them, the book value of the assets must equal the book value of the liabilities plus the book value of the equity on the accounting balance sheet. In Chapter 3 we called this equality the *balance sheet identity*.

Just as the total book value of the assets at a firm does not generally equal the total market value of those assets, the book value of total liabilities plus stockholders' equity does not usually equal the market value of these claims. In fact, the total market value of the debt and equity claims differs from their total book value by exactly the same amount that the total market value of a firm's assets differs from its total book value. This is because the total market value of the debt and the equity at a firm equals the present value of the cash flows that the debt holders and the stockholders have the right to receive. These cash flows are the cash flows that the assets in the firm are expected to generate. In other words, the people who have lent money to a firm and the people who have purchased the firm's stock have the right to receive all of the cash flows that the firm is expected to generate in the future. The value of the claims they hold must equal the value of the cash flows that they have a right to receive.

The fact that the market value of the assets must equal the value of the cash flows that these assets are expected to generate, combined with the fact that the value of the expected cash

finance balance sheet
a balance sheet that is based on market values of expected cash flows

---

[2]The total expected cash flows at Boeing also include cash flows from projects that the firm is expected to undertake in the future, or what are often referred to as *growth opportunities*.

[3]We will discuss how firms finance their assets in more detail in Chapters 13 and 14. For the time being, we will simply assume that a firm uses some combination of debt and equity. Here we use the term *debt* in the broadest sense to refer to all liabilities, including liabilities on which the firm does not pay interest, such as accounts payable. As is common practice, we focus only on long-term interest-bearing debt, such as bank loans and bonds, in the cost of capital calculations. The reason for this is discussed in the next section.

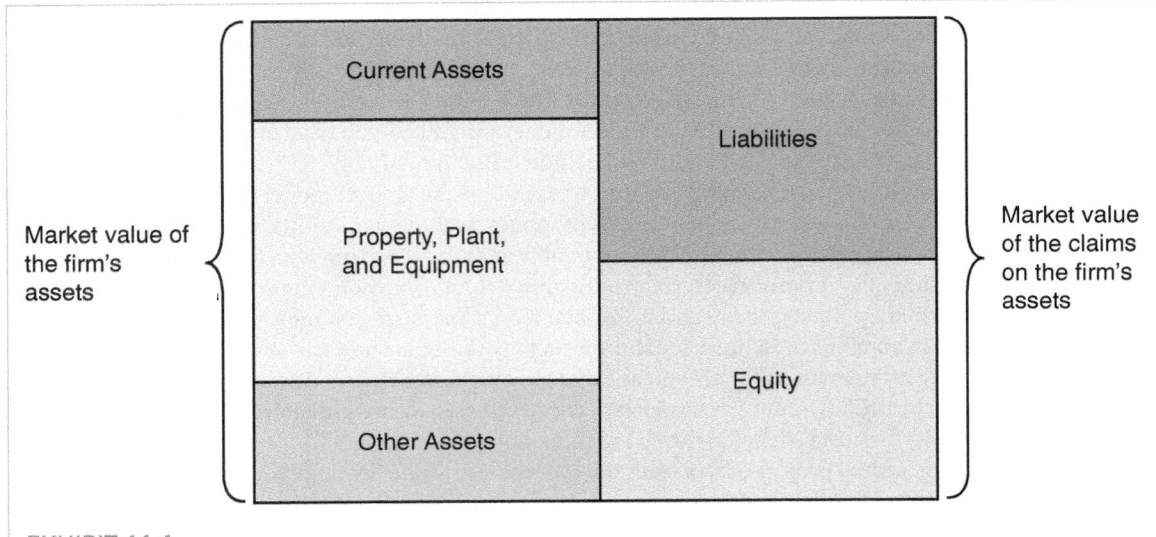

EXHIBIT 11.1
The Finance Balance Sheet

The market value of a firm's assets, which equals the present value of the cash flows those assets are expected to generate in the future, must equal the market value of the claims on those cash flows—the firm's liabilities and equity.

flows also equals the total market value of the firm's total liabilities and equity, means that we can write the market value (MV) of assets as follows:

$$\text{MV of assets} = \text{MV of liabilities} + \text{MV of equity} \tag{11.1}$$

Equation 11.1 is just like the accounting balance sheet identity. The only difference is that Equation 11.1 is based on market values. This relation is illustrated in Exhibit 11.1.

To better understand why the market value of the assets must equal the total market value of the liabilities and equity, consider a firm whose only business is to own and manage an apartment building that was purchased 20 years ago for $1,000,000. Suppose that there is currently a $300,000 mortgage on the building, the firm has no other liabilities, and the current market value of the building, based on the expected cash flows from future rents, is $4,000,000. What is the market value of all of the equity (stock) in this firm?

The fact that you paid $1,000,000 20 years ago is not relevant to this question. What matters in finance is the value of the expected cash flows from future rents, the $4,000,000. This is the market value of the firm's assets—the left-hand side of the balance sheet in Exhibit 11.1. Since we know that the firm owes $300,000, we can substitute into Equation 11.1 and solve for the market value of the equity:

$$\text{MV of assets} = \text{MV of liabilities} + \text{MV of equity}$$
$$\$4,000,000 = \$300,000 + \text{MV of equity}$$
$$\text{MV of equity} = \$4,000,000 - \$300,000 = \$3,700,000$$

If the cash flows that the apartment building is expected to produce are worth $4,000,000, then investors would be willing to pay $3,700,000 for the equity in the firm. This is the value of the cash flows that they would expect to receive after making the interest and principal payments on the mortgage. Furthermore, since, by definition, the mortgage is worth $300,000, the value of the debt plus the value of the equity is $300,000 + $3,700,000 = $4,000,000—which is exactly equal to the market value of the firm's assets.

As suggested at the beginning of this discussion, the idea of a balance sheet based on market values was discussed in Chapter 3. In that

BUILDING INTUITION

THE MARKET VALUE OF A FIRM'S ASSETS EQUALS THE MARKET VALUE OF THE CLAIMS ON THOSE ASSETS

The market value of the debt and equity claims against the cash flows of a firm must equal the present value of the cash flows that the firm's assets are expected to generate. This is because, between them, the debt holders and the stockholders have the legal right to receive all of those cash flows.

chapter we pointed out that a market-value balance sheet would be more useful to financial decision makers than would the ordinary accounting balance sheet. Financial managers are much more concerned about the future than the past when they make decisions. You might revisit the discussion of sunk costs in Chapter 10 to remind yourself of why this is true.

How Firms Estimate Their Cost of Capital

Now that we have discussed the basic idea of the finance balance sheet, consider the challenge that financial analysts face when they want to estimate the cost of capital for a firm. If analysts at a firm could estimate the betas for each of the firm's individual projects, they could estimate the beta for the entire firm as a weighted average of the betas for the individual projects. They could do this because, as we discussed earlier, the firm is simply a collection (portfolio) of projects. This calculation would just be an application of Equation 6.11:

$$\beta_{n \text{ Asset portfolio}} = \sum_{i=1}^{n} x_i \beta_i = x_1 \beta_1 + x_2 \beta_2 + x_3 \beta_3 + \cdots + x_n \beta_n$$

where β_i is the beta for project i and x_i is the fraction of the total firm value represented by project i.

The analysts could then use the beta for the firm in Equation 6.10:

$$E(R_i) = R_{rf} + \beta_i [E(R_m) - R_{rf}]$$

to estimate the expected return on the firm's assets, which is also the firm's cost of capital. Unfortunately, because analysts are not typically able to estimate betas for individual projects, they generally cannot use this approach.

Instead, analysts must use their knowledge of the finance balance sheet, along with the concept of market efficiency, which we discussed in Chapter 2, to estimate the cost of capital for the firm. Rather than using Equations 6.11 and 6.10 to perform the calculations for the *individual projects* represented on the left-hand side of the finance balance sheet, analysts perform a similar set of calculations for the *different types of financing* (debt and equity) on the right-hand side of the finance balance sheet. They can do this because, as we said earlier, the people who finance the firm have the right to receive all of the cash flows on the left-hand side. This means that the systematic risk associated with the total assets on the left-hand side is the same as the systematic risk associated with the total financing on the right-hand side. In other words, the weighted average of the betas for the different claims on the assets must equal a weighted average of the betas for the individual assets (projects).

Analysts do not need to estimate betas for each type of financing that the firm has. As long as they can estimate the cost of each type of financing—either directly, by observing that cost in the capital markets, or by using Equation 6.10—they can compute the cost of capital for the firm using the following equation:

$$k_{\text{Firm}} = \sum_{i=1}^{n} x_i k_i = x_1 k_1 + x_2 k_2 + x_3 k_3 + \cdots + x_n k_n \qquad (11.2)$$

In Equation 11.2, k_{Firm} is the cost of capital for the firm, k_i is the cost of financing type i, and x_i is the fraction of the total market value of the financing (or of the assets) of the firm represented by financing type i. This formula simply says that the overall cost of capital for the firm is a weighted average of the cost of each different type of financing used by the firm.[4] Note that since we are specifically talking about the cost of capital, we use the symbol k_i to represent this cost, rather than the more general notation $E(R_i)$ that we used in Chapter 6.

The similarity between Equation 11.2 and Equation 6.11 is not an accident. Both are applications of the basic idea that the systematic risk of a portfolio of assets is a weighted average of the systematic risks of the individual assets. Because R_{rf} and $E(R_m)$ in Equation 6.10 are the same for all assets, when we substitute Equation 6.10 into Equation 11.2 (remember that $E(R_i)$ in Equation 6.10 is the same as k_i in Equation 11.2) and cancel out R_{rf} and $E(R_m)$, we get Equation 6.11. We will not prove this here, but you might do so to convince yourself that what we are saying is true.

---

[4]As we will discuss in Section 11.2, if markets are efficient, the prices we observe in the markets will reflect the true costs of the different securities that the firm has outstanding.

To see how Equation 11.2 is applied, let's return to the example of the firm whose only business is to manage an apartment building. Recall that the total value of this firm is $4,000,000 and that it has $300,000 in debt. If the firm has only one loan and one type of stock, then the fractions of the total value represented by those two types of financing are as follows:

weighted average cost of capital (WACC)
the weighted average of the costs of the different types of capital (debt and equity) that have been used to finance a firm; the cost of each type of capital is weighted by the proportion of the total capital that it represents

$$x_{Debt} = \$300,000/\$4,000,000 = 0.075, \text{ or } 7.5\%$$
$$x_{Equity} = \$3,700,000/\$4,000,000 = 0.925, \text{ or } 92.5\%$$
$$\text{where } x_{Debt} + x_{Equity} = 0.075 + 0.925 = 1.000$$

This tells us that the value of the debt claims equals 7.5 percent of the value of the firm and that the value of the equity claims equals the remaining 92.5 percent of the value of the firm. If the cost of the debt for this business is 6 percent and the cost of the equity is 10 percent, the cost of capital for the firm can be calculated as a weighted average of the costs of the debt and equity:[5]

$$k_{Firm} = x_{Debt}k_{Debt} + x_{Equity}k_{Equity} = (0.075)(0.06) + (0.925)(0.10) = 0.097, \text{ or } 9.7\%$$

> ## BUILDING INTUITION
>
> ### A FIRM'S COST OF CAPITAL IS A WEIGHTED AVERAGE OF ALL OF ITS FINANCING COSTS
>
> The cost of capital for a firm is a weighted average of the costs of the different types of financing used by a firm. The weights are the proportions of the total firm value represented by the different types of financing. By weighting the costs of the individual financing types in this way, we obtain the overall average opportunity cost of each dollar invested in the firm.

Notice that we have used Equation 11.2 to calculate a **weighted average cost of capital (WACC)** for the firm in this example. In fact, this is what people typically call the firm's cost of capital, k_{Firm}. From this point on, we will use the abbreviation WACC to represent the firm's overall cost of capital.

LEARNING BY DOING

APPLICATION 11.1

NEED MORE HELP?
WileyPLUS

Calculating the Cost of Capital for a Firm

PROBLEM: You are considering purchasing a rug cleaning company that will cost $2,000,000. You plan to finance the purchase with a $1,500,000 loan from Bank of America (BofA) that has a 6.5 percent interest rate, a $300,000 loan from the seller of the company that has an 8 percent interest rate, and $200,000 of your own money. You will own all of the equity (stock) in the firm. You estimate that the opportunity cost of your $200,000 investment—that is, what you could earn on an investment of similar risk in the capital market—is 12 percent with that much debt. What is the cost of capital for this investment?

APPROACH: You can use Equation 11.2 to calculate the WACC for this firm. Since you are planning to finance the purchase using capital from three different sources—two loans and your own equity investment—the right-hand side of Equation 11.2 will have three terms.

SOLUTION:
We begin by calculating the weights for the different types of financing:

$$x_{BofA\ Loan} = \$1,500,000/\$2,000,000 = 0.75$$
$$x_{Seller\ loan} = \$300,000/\$2,000,000 = 0.15$$
$$x_{Equity} = \$200,000/\$2,000,000 = 0.10$$

where $x_{BofA\ loan} + x_{Seller\ loan} + x_{Equity} = 0.75 + 0.15 + 0.10 = 1.00$.
We can then calculate the WACC using Equation 11.2:

$$WACC = k_{Firm} = x_{BofA\ loan}k_{BofA\ loan} + x_{Seller\ loan}k_{Seller\ loan} + x_{Equity}k_{Equity}$$
$$= (0.75)(0.065) + (0.15)(0.08) + (0.10)(0.12)$$
$$= 0.728, \text{ or } 7.28\%$$

On average, you would be paying 7.3 percent per year on every dollar you invested in the firm. This is the opportunity cost of capital for the firm. It is the rate that you would use to discount the cash flows associated with the rug cleaning business in an NPV analysis.

---

[5]We are ignoring the effect of taxes on the cost of debt financing for the time being. This effect is discussed in detail in Section 11.2 and explicitly incorporated into subsequent calculations.

> **BEFORE YOU GO ON**

1. Why does the market value of the claims on the assets of a firm equal the market value of the assets?

2. How is the WACC for a firm calculated?

3. What does the WACC for a firm tell us?

11.2 THE COST OF DEBT

LEARNING OBJECTIVE

In our discussion of how the WACC for a firm is calculated, we assumed that the costs of the different types of financing were known. This assumption allowed us to simply plug those costs into Equation 11.2 once we had calculated the weight for each type of financing. Unfortunately, life is not that simple. In the real world, analysts have to estimate each of the individual costs. In other words, the discussion in the preceding section glossed over a number of concepts and issues that you should be familiar with. This section and Section 11.3 discuss those concepts and issues and show how the costs of the different types of financing can be estimated.

Before we move on to the specifics of how to estimate the costs of different types of financing, we must stress an important point: All of these calculations depend in some part on financial markets being efficient. We suggested this in the last section when we mentioned that analysts have to rely on the concept of market efficiency to estimate the WACC. The reason is that analysts often cannot directly observe the rate of return that investors require for a particular type of financing. Instead, analysts must rely on the security prices they can observe in the financial markets to estimate the required rate.

It makes sense to rely on security prices only if you believe that the financial markets are reasonably efficient at incorporating new information into these prices. If the markets were not efficient, estimates of expected returns that were based on market security prices would be unreliable. Of course, if the returns that are plugged into Equation 11.2 are bad, the resulting estimate for WACC will also be bad. With this caveat, we can now discuss how to estimate the costs of the various types of financing.

Key Concepts for Estimating the Cost of Debt

Virtually all firms use some form of debt financing. The financial managers at firms typically arrange for revolving lines of credit to finance working capital items such as inventories or accounts receivable. These lines of credit are very much like the lines of credit that come with your credit cards. Firms also obtain private fixed-term loans, such as bank loans, or sell bonds to the public to finance ongoing operations or the purchase of long-term assets—just as you would finance your living expenses while you are in school with a student loan or a car with a car loan. For example, an electric utility firm, such as FPL Group in Florida, will sell bonds to finance a new power plant, and a rapidly growing retailer, such as Target, will use debt to finance new stores and distribution centers. As mentioned earlier, we will discuss how firms finance themselves in more detail in Chapters 13 and 14, but for now it is sufficient to recognize that firms use these three general types of debt financing: lines of credit, private fixed-term loans, and bonds that are sold in the public markets.

There is a cost associated with each type of debt that a firm uses. However, when we estimate the cost of capital for a firm, we are particularly interested in the cost of the firm's long-term debt. Firms generally use long-term debt to finance their long-term assets, and it is the long-term assets that concern us when we think about the value of a firm's assets. By long-term debt, we usually mean the debt that, when it was borrowed, was set to mature in more than one year. This typically includes fixed-term bank loans used to finance ongoing operations or long-term assets, as well as the bonds that a firm sells in the public debt markets.

Although one year is not an especially long time, debt with a maturity of more than one year is typically viewed as permanent debt. This is because firms often borrow the money to pay off this debt when it matures.

We do not normally worry about revolving lines of credit when calculating the cost of debt because these lines tend to be temporary. Banks typically require that the outstanding balances be periodically paid down to $0 (just as we are sure you pay your entire credit card balance from time to time).

When analysts estimate the cost of a firm's long-term debt, they are estimating the cost on a particular date—the date on which they are doing the analysis. This is a very important point to keep in mind because the interest rate that the firm is paying on its outstanding debt does not necessarily reflect its current cost of debt. Interest rates change over time, and so does the cost of debt for a firm. The rate a firm was charged three years ago for a five-year loan is unlikely to be the same rate that it would be charged today for a new five-year loan. For example, suppose that FPL Group issued bonds five years ago for 7 percent. Since then, interest rates have fallen, so the same bonds could be sold at par value today for 6 percent. The cost of debt today is 6 percent, not 7 percent, and 6 percent is the cost of debt that management will use in WACC calculations. If you looked in the firm's financial statements, you would see that the firm is paying an interest rate of 7 percent. This is what the financial managers of the firm agreed to pay five years ago, not what it would cost to sell the same bonds today. The accounting statements reflect the cost of debt that was sold at some time in the past.

> **BUILDING INTUITION**
>
> **THE CURRENT COST OF LONG-TERM DEBT IS WHAT MATTERS WHEN CALCULATING WACC**
>
> The current cost of long-term debt is the appropriate cost of debt for WACC calculations. This is because the WACC we use in capital budgeting is the opportunity cost of capital for the firm's investors as of today. This means we must use today's costs of debt and equity when we calculate the WACC. Historical costs do not belong in WACC calculations.

Estimating the Current Cost of a Bond or an Outstanding Loan

We have now seen that we should not use historical costs of debt in WACC calculations. Let's discuss how we can estimate the current costs of bonds and other fixed-term loans by using market information.

The Current Cost of a Bond

You may not realize it, but we have already discussed how to estimate the current cost of debt for a publicly traded bond. This cost is estimated using the yield to maturity calculation. Recall that in Chapter 7 we defined the yield to maturity as the discount rate that makes the present value of the coupon and principal payments equal to the price of the bond.

For example, consider a 10-year bond with a $1,000 face value that was issued five years ago. This bond has five years remaining before it matures. If the bond has an annual coupon rate of 7 percent, pays coupon interest semiannually, and is currently selling for $1,042.65, we can calculate its yield to maturity by using Equation 7.1 and solving for i or by using a financial calculator. Let's use Equation 7.1 for this example.

To do this, as was discussed in the section on semiannual compounding in Chapter 7, we first convert the bond data to reflect semiannual compounding: (1) the total number of coupon payments is 10 (2 payments per year × 5 years = 10 payments), and (2) the semiannual coupon payment is $35 [($1,000 × 7 percent per year)/2 periods per year = $70/2 = $35]. We can now use Equation 7.1 and solve for i to find the yield to maturity:

$$P_B = \frac{C_1}{1+i} + \frac{C_2}{(1+i)^2} + \cdots + \frac{C_n + F_n}{(1+i)^n}$$

$$\$1,042.65 = \frac{\$35}{1+i} + \frac{\$35}{(1+i)^2} + \frac{\$35}{(1+i)^3} + \cdots + \frac{\$35}{(1+i)^9} + \frac{\$1,035}{(1+i)^{10}}$$

By trial and error or with a financial calculator, we solve for i and find:

$$i = k_{Bond} = 0.0300, \text{ or } 3.00\%$$

This semiannual rate would be quoted as an annual rate of 6 percent (2 periods per year × 0.03 per period = 0.06, or 6 percent) in financial markets. However, as explained in Chapter 7, this annual rate fails to account for the effects of compounding. We must therefore use

Equation 5.11 to calculate the effective annual interest rate (EAR) in order to obtain the actual current annual cost of this debt:

$$\text{EAR} = \left(1 + \frac{\text{Quoted interest rate}}{m}\right)^m - 1 = \left(1 + \frac{0.06}{2}\right)^2 - 1$$
$$= (1.03)^2 - 1 = 0.0609, \text{ or } 6.09\%$$

If this bond was sold at par value, it paid 7 percent when it was issued five years ago. Someone who buys it today will expect to earn only 6.09 percent per year. This is the annual rate of return required by the market on this bond, which is known as the effective annual yield.

Notice that the above calculation takes into account the interest payments, the face value of the debt (the amount that will be repaid in five years), and the current price at which the bond is selling. It is necessary to account for all of these characteristics of the bond. The return received by someone who buys the bond today will be determined by both the interest income and the capital appreciation (or capital depreciation in this case, since the price is higher than the face value).

We must account for one other factor when we calculate the current cost of bond financing to a company—the cost of issuing the bond. In the above example, we calculated the return that someone who buys the bond can expect to receive. Since a company must pay fees to investment bankers, lawyers, and accountants, along with various other costs, to actually issue a bond, the cost to the company is higher than 6.09 percent.[6] Therefore, in order to obtain an accurate estimate of the cost of a bond to the issuing firm, analysts must incorporate *issuance costs* into their calculations. Issuance costs are an example of *direct out-of-pocket costs*, the actual out-of-pocket costs that a firm incurs when it raises capital.

The way in which issuance costs are incorporated into the calculation of the cost of a bond is straightforward. Analysts use the *net proceeds* that the company receives from the bond, rather than the price that is paid by the investor, on the left-hand side of Equation 7.1. Suppose the company in our example sold five-year bonds with a 7 percent coupon today and paid issuance costs equal to 2 percent of the total value of the bonds. After paying the issuance costs, the company would receive only 98 percent of the price paid by the investors. Therefore, the company would actually receive only $1,042.65 \times (1 - 0.02) = \$1,021.80$ for each bond it sold and the semiannual cost to the company would be:

$$P_B = \frac{C_1}{1+i} + \frac{C_2}{(1+i)^2} + \cdots + \frac{C_n + F_n}{(1+i)^n}$$
$$\$1,021.80 = \frac{\$35}{1+i} + \frac{\$35}{(1+i)^2} + \frac{\$35}{(1+i)^3} + \cdots + \frac{\$35}{(1+i)^9} + \frac{\$1,035}{(1+i)^{10}}$$
$$i = k_{\text{Bond}} = 0.0324, \text{ or } 3.24\%$$

Converting the adjusted semiannual rate to an EAR, we see that the actual annual cost of this debt financing is:

$$\text{EAR} = (1.0324)^2 - 1 = 0.0658, \text{ or } 6.58\%$$

In this example the issuance costs increase the effective cost of the bonds from 6.09 percent to 6.58 percent per year.

The Current Cost of an Outstanding Loan

Conceptually, calculating the current cost of long-term bank or other private debt is not as straightforward as estimating the current cost of a public bond because financial analysts cannot observe the market price of private debt. Fortunately, analysts do not typically have to do this. Instead, they can simply call their banker and ask what rate the bank would charge if they decided to refinance the debt today. A rate quote from a banker provides a good estimate of the current cost of a private loan.

---

[6]These types of costs are incurred by firms whenever they raise capital. We only show how to include them in the cost of bond financing and, later, in estimating the cost of preferred stock, but they should also be included in calculations of the costs of capital from other sources, such as bank loans and common equity.

Taxes and the Cost of Debt

It is very important that you understand one additional concept concerning the cost of debt: In the United States, *firms can deduct interest payments for tax purposes.* In other words, every dollar a firm pays in interest reduces the firm's taxable income by one dollar. Thus, if the firm's marginal tax rate is 35 percent, the firm's total tax bill will be reduced by 35 cents for every dollar of interest it pays. A dollar of interest would actually cost this firm only 65 cents because the firm would save 35 cents on its taxes.

More generally, the after-tax cost of interest payments equals the pretax cost times 1 minus the tax rate. This means that the after-tax cost of debt is:

$$k_{\text{Debt after-tax}} = k_{\text{Debt pretax}} \times (1 - t) \qquad (11.3)$$

This after-tax cost of debt is the cost that firms actually use to calculate the WACC. The reason is that investors care only about the after-tax cost of capital—just as they care only about after-tax cash flows. Managers are concerned about what they actually have to pay for capital, and the actual cost is reduced if the government subsidizes debt by providing a tax break.

Taxes affect the cost of debt in much the same way that the interest tax deduction on a home mortgage affects the cost of financing a house. For example, assume that you borrow $200,000 at 6 percent to buy a house on January 1 and your interest payments total $12,000 in the first year. Under the tax law, you can deduct this $12,000 from your taxable income when you calculate your taxes for the year.[7]

Suppose that your taxable income before the interest deduction is $75,000 and, for simplicity, that both your average and marginal tax rates are 20 percent. Without the interest deduction, you would pay taxes totaling $15,000 ($75,000 × 0.20 = $15,000). However, because the interest payments reduce your taxable income, your taxes with the interest deduction will be only $12,600 [($75,000 − $12,000) × 0.20 = $12,600]. The ability to deduct the interest payments you made saved you $2,400 ($15,000 − $12,600 = $2,400)! This savings is exactly equal to the interest payment you make times your marginal tax rate: $12,000 × 0.20 = $2,400. Since you are saving $2,400, the after-tax cost of your interest payments is $9,600 ($12,000 − $2,400 = $9,600), which means that the after-tax cost of this debt is 4.80 percent ($9,600/$200,000 = 0.0480, or 4.80 percent). This is exactly what Equation 11.3 tells us. With $k_{\text{Debt pretax}}$ at 6 percent and t at 20 percent, Equation 11.3 gives us:

$$k_{\text{Debt after-tax}} = k_{\text{Debt pretax}} \times (1 - t) = 0.06 \times (1 - 0.2) = 0.0480, \text{ or } 4.80\%$$

Estimating the Cost of Debt for a Firm

Most firms have several different debt issues outstanding at any particular point in time. Just as you might have both a car loan and a school loan, a firm might have several bank loans and bond issues outstanding. To estimate the firm's overall cost of debt when it has several debt issues outstanding, we must first estimate the costs of the individual debt issues and then calculate a weighted average of these costs.

To see how this is done, let's consider an example. Suppose that your pizza parlor business has grown dramatically in the past three years from a single restaurant to 30 restaurants. To finance this growth, two years ago you sold $25 million of five-year bonds. These bonds pay interest annually and have a coupon rate of 8 percent. They are currently selling for $1,026.24 per $1,000 bond. Just today, you also borrowed $5 million from your local bank at an interest rate of 6 percent. Assume that this is all the long-term debt that you have and that there are no issuance costs. What is the overall average after-tax cost of your debt if your business's marginal tax rate is 35 percent?

The pretax cost of the bonds as of today is the effective annual yield on those bonds. Since the bonds were sold two years ago, they will mature three years from now. Using Equation 7.1,

---

[7]There is a limit on the total amount of home loan interest payments that you can deduct when you calculate your taxable income. For instance, in 2012 you could deduct interest payments on loans with a total face value of $1,100,000 ($1,000,000 mortgage plus $100,000 home equity loan).

we find that the effective annual yield (which equals the yield to maturity in this example) for these bonds is:

$$P_B = \frac{C_1}{1 + i} + \frac{C_2}{(1 + i)^2} + \cdots + \frac{C_n + F_n}{(1 + i)^n}$$

$$\$1,026.24 = \frac{\$80}{1 + i} + \frac{\$80}{(1 + i)^2} + \frac{\$1,080}{(1 + i)^3}$$

$$i = k_{\text{Bond pretax}} = 0.0700, \text{ or } 7.00\%$$

The pretax cost of the bank loan that you took out today is simply the 6 percent rate that the bank is charging you, assuming that the bank is charging you the market rate.

Now that we know the pretax costs of the two types of debt that your business has outstanding, we can calculate the overall average cost of your debt by calculating the weighted average of their two costs. Since the weights for the two types of debt are based on their current market values we must first determine these values. Because the bonds are currently selling above their par value, we know that their current market value is greater than their $25 million face value. In fact, it equals:

$$(\$1,026.24/\$1,000) \times \$25,000,000 = \$25,656,000$$

Since the bank loan was just made today, its value simply equals the amount borrowed or $5 million. The weights for the two types of debt are therefore:

$$x_{\text{Bonds}} = \$25,656,000/(\$25,656,000 + \$5,000,000) = 0.8369$$
$$x_{\text{Bank debt}} = \$5,000,000/(\$25,000,000 + \$5,000,000) = 0.1631$$

$$\text{where } x_{\text{Bonds}} + x_{\text{Bank debt}} = 0.8369 + 0.1631 = 1.000$$

The weighted average pretax cost of debt is:

$$k_{\text{Debt pretax}} = x_{\text{Bonds}}k_{\text{Bonds pretax}} + x_{\text{Bank debt}}k_{\text{Bank debt pretax}}$$
$$= (0.8369 \times 0.07) + (0.1631 \times 0.06) = 0.0586 + 0.0098$$
$$= 0.0684, \text{ or } 6.84\%$$

The after-tax cost of debt is therefore:

$$k_{\text{Debt after-tax}} = k_{\text{Debt pretax}} \times (1 - t) = 6.84\% \times (1 - 0.35) = 4.45\%$$

Calculating the After-Tax Cost of Debt for a Firm

PROBLEM: You have just successfully completed a leveraged buyout of the firm that you have been working for. To finance this $35 million transaction, you and three partners put up a total of $10 million in equity capital, and you borrowed $25 million from banks and other investors. The bank debt consists of $10 million of secured debt borrowed at a rate of 6 percent from Bank of America and $7 million of senior unsecured debt borrowed at a rate of 7 percent from JPMorgan Chase. The remaining $8 million was borrowed from an investment group managed by a private equity firm. The rate on this subordinated (junior) unsecured debt is 9.5 percent. What is the overall after-tax cost of the debt financing used to buy the firm if you expect the firm's average and marginal tax rates to both be 25 percent?

APPROACH: The overall after-tax cost of debt can be calculated using the following three-step process: (1) Calculate the fraction of the total debt (weight) for each individual debt issue. (2) Using these weights, calculate the weighted average pretax cost of debt. (3) Use Equation 11.3 to calculate the after-tax average cost of debt.

SOLUTION:

(1) The weights for the three types of debt are as follows:

$$x_{\text{Secured debt}} = \$10,000,000/\$25,000,000 = 0.40$$
$$x_{\text{Senior unsecured debt}} = \$7,000,000/\$25,000,000 = 0.28$$
$$x_{\text{Subordinated unsecured debt}} = \$8,000,000/\$25,000,000 = 0.32$$

(continued)

where $x_{\text{Secured debt}} + x_{\text{Senior unsecured debt}} + x_{\text{Subordinated unsecured debt}}$

$$= 0.40 + 0.28 + 0.32 = 1.00$$

(2) The weighted average pretax cost of debt is:

$$k_{\text{Debt pretax}} = x_{\text{Secured debt}} k_{\text{Secured debt pretax}} + x_{\text{Senior unsecured debt}} k_{\text{Senior unsecured debt pretax}}$$
$$+ x_{\text{Subordinated unsecured debt}} k_{\text{Subordinated unsecured debt pretax}}$$
$$= (0.40)(0.06) + (0.28)(0.07) + (0.32)(0.095)$$
$$= 0.0740, \text{ or } 7.40\%$$

(3) The after-tax cost of debt is therefore:

$$k_{\text{Debt after-tax}} = k_{\text{Debt pretax}} \times (1 - t) = 7.40\% \times (1 - 0.25) = 5.55\%$$

DECISION MAKING

EXAMPLE 11.1

Using the Cost of Debt in Decision Making

SITUATION: Your pizza parlor business has developed such a strong reputation that you have decided to take advantage of the restaurant's name recognition by selling frozen pizzas through grocery stores. In order to do this, you will have to build a manufacturing facility. You estimate that this will cost you $10 million. Since your business currently has only $2 million in the bank, you will have to borrow the remaining $8 million. You have spoken with two bankers about possible loan packages. The banker from Easy Money Financial Services offered you a loan for $6 million with a 6 percent rate and $2 million with a 7.5 percent rate. You calculate the pretax cost of debt for this package to be:

$$k_{\text{Loans pretax}} = (\$6,000,000/\$8,000,000)(0.06) + (\$2,000,000/\$8,000,000)(0.075)$$
$$= 0.0450 + 0.0188$$
$$= 0.0638, \text{ or } 6.38\%$$

Your local banker offered you a single $8 million loan for 6.35 percent. Which financing should you choose if all terms on all of the loans, other than the interest rates, are the same?

DECISION: This is an easy decision. You should choose the least expensive alternative—the loan from your local bank. In this example, you can directly compare the pretax costs of the two alternatives. You do not need to calculate the after-tax costs because multiplying each pretax cost by the same number, $1 - t$, will not change your decision.

> **BEFORE YOU GO ON**

1. Why do analysts care about the *current* cost of long-term debt when estimating a firm's cost of capital?

2. How do you estimate the cost of debt for a firm with more than one type of debt?

3. How do taxes affect the cost of debt?

11.3 THE COST OF EQUITY

 LEARNING OBJECTIVE

The cost of equity (stock) for a firm is a weighted average of the costs of the different types of stock that the firm has outstanding at a particular point in time. We saw in Chapter 8 that some firms have both preferred stock and common stock outstanding. In order to calculate the cost of equity for these firms, we have to know how to calculate the cost of both common stock and preferred stock. In this section, we discuss how financial analysts can estimate the costs associated with these two different types of stock.

Common Stock

Just as information about market rates of return is used to estimate the cost of debt, market information is also used to estimate the cost of equity. There are several ways to do this. The particular approach a financial analyst chooses will depend on what information is available and how reliable the analyst believes it is. Next we discuss three alternative methods for estimating the cost of common stock. It is important to remember throughout this discussion that the "cost" we are referring to is the rate of return that investors require for investing in the stock at a particular point in time, given its systematic risk.

Method 1: Using the Capital Asset Pricing Model (CAPM)

The first method for estimating the cost of common equity is one that we discussed in Chapter 6. This method uses Equation 6.10:

$$E(R_i) = R_{rf} + \beta_i[E(R_m) - R_{rf}]$$

In this equation, the expected return on an asset is a linear function of the systematic risk associated with that asset.

If we recognize that $E(R_i)$ in Equation 6.10 is the cost of the common stock (equity) used to finance the firm (k_{cs}) when we are calculating the cost of common equity and that $[E(R_m) - R_{rf}]$ is the market risk premium, we can rewrite Equation 6.10 as follows:

$$k_{cs} = R_{rf} + (\beta_{cs} \times \text{Market risk premium}) \tag{11.4}$$

Equation 11.4 is just another way of writing Equation 6.10. It tells us that the cost of common stock equals the risk-free rate of return plus compensation for the systematic risk associated with the common stock. You already saw some examples of how to use this equation to calculate the cost of equity in the discussion of the Capital Asset Pricing Model (CAPM) in Chapter 6. In those examples you were given the current risk-free rate, the beta for the stock, and the market risk premium and were asked to calculate k_{cs} using the equation. Now we turn our attention to some practical considerations that you must be concerned with when choosing the appropriate risk-free rate, beta, and market risk premium for this calculation.

The Risk-Free Rate. First, let's consider the risk-free rate. The current effective annual yield on a risk-free asset should always be used in Equation 11.4.[8] This is because the risk-free rate at a particular point in time reflects the rate of inflation that the market expects in the future. Since the expected rate of inflation changes over time, an old risk-free rate might not reflect current inflation expectations.

When analysts select a risk-free rate, they must choose between using a short-term rate, such as that for Treasury bills, or a longer-term rate, such as those for Treasury notes or bonds. Which of these choices is most appropriate? This question has been hotly debated by finance professionals for many years. We recommend that you use the risk-free rate on a long-term Treasury security when you estimate the cost of equity capital because the equity claim is a long-term claim on the firm's cash flows. As you saw in Chapter 8, the stockholders have a claim on the cash flows of the firm in perpetuity. By using a long-term Treasury security, you are matching a long-term risk-free rate with a long-term claim. A long-term risk-free rate better reflects long-term inflation expectations and the cost of getting investors to part with their money for a long period of time than does a short-term rate.

The Beta. If the common stock of a company is publicly traded, then you can estimate the beta for that stock using a regression analysis similar to that illustrated in Exhibit 6.10. However, identifying the appropriate beta is much more complicated if the common stock is not publicly traded. Since most companies in the United States are privately owned and do not

You can find current yields on Treasury bills, notes, and bonds at the Web site of the U.S. Federal Reserve Bank at http://www.federalreserve.gov/releases/H15/update.

---

[8]We use the term *risk-free* here to refer to assets that have no default risk. Investors in the assets can still face interest rate risk as described in Chapter 7.

Companies with publicly traded stock usually provide a lot of information about their businesses and financial performance on their Web sites. The Domino's Pizza Web site is a good example. Go to http://phx.corporate-ir .net/phoenix.zhtml?c= 135383&p=irol-irhome.

have publicly traded stock, this is a problem that arises quite often when someone wants to estimate the cost of common equity for a firm.

Financial analysts often overcome this problem by identifying a "comparable" company with publicly traded stock that is in the same business and that has a similar amount of debt. For example, suppose you are trying to estimate the beta for your pizza business. The company has now grown to include more than 2,000 restaurants throughout the world. The frozen-foods business, however, was never successful and had to be shut down. You know that Domino's Pizza, Inc., one of your major competitors, has publicly traded equity and that the proportion of debt to equity for Domino's is similar to the proportion for your firm. Since Domino's overall business is similar to yours, in that it is only in the pizza business and competes in similar geographic areas, it would be reasonable to consider Domino's a comparable company.

The systematic risk associated with the stock of a comparable company is likely to be similar to the systematic risk for the stock of the private firm because a stock's systematic risk is determined by the nature of the firm's business and the amount of debt that it uses. If you are able to identify a good comparable company, such as Domino's Pizza, you can use its beta in Equation 11.4 to estimate the cost of equity capital for your firm. Even when a good comparable company cannot be identified, it is sometimes possible to use an average of the betas for the public firms in the same industry.

The Market Risk Premium. It is not possible to directly observe the market risk premium. We just do not know what rate of return investors expect for the market portfolio, $E(R_m)$, at a particular point in time. Therefore, we cannot simply calculate the market risk premium as the difference between the expected return on the market and the risk-free rate, $[E(R_m) - R_{rf}]$. For this reason, financial analysts generally use a measure of the average risk premium investors have actually earned in the past as an indication of the risk premium they might require today.

For example, from 1926 through the end of 2011, actual returns on the U.S. stock market exceeded actual returns on long-term U.S. government bonds by an average of 5.63 percent per year. If, on average, investors earned the risk premium that they expected, this figure reflects the average market risk premium over the period from 1926 to 2011. If a financial analyst believes that the market risk premium in the past is a reasonable estimate of the risk premium today, then he or she might use 5.63 percent as the market risk premium in Equation 11.4.

With this background, let's work an example to illustrate how Equation 11.4 is used in practice to estimate the cost of common stock for a firm. Suppose that it is October 19, 2012, and we want to estimate the cost of the common stock for the oil company ConocoPhillips. Using yields reported in the *Wall Street Journal* on that day, we determine that 30-day Treasury bills have an effective annual yield of 0.10 percent and that 20-year Treasury bonds have an effective annual yield of 2.55 percent. From the MSN Money Web site (http://moneycentral. msn.com), we find that the beta for ConocoPhillips stock is 1.13. We know that the market risk premium averaged 5.63 percent from 1926 to 2011. What is the expected rate of return on ConocoPhillips common stock?

Since we are estimating the expected rate of return on common stock, and common stock is a long-term asset, we use the long-term Treasury bond yield of 2.55 percent in the calculation. Notice that the Treasury bill and Treasury bond rates differed by 2.45 percent (2.55 percent − 0.10 percent = 2.45 percent) on October 19, 2012. They often differ by this amount or more, so the choice of which rate to use can make quite a difference in the estimated cost of equity.

Once we have selected the appropriate risk-free rate, we can plug it, along with the beta and market risk premium values, into Equation 11.4 to calculate the cost of common equity for ConocoPhillips:

$$k_{cs} = R_{rf} + (\beta_{cs} \times \text{Market risk premium})$$
$$= 0.0255 + (1.13 \times 0.0563) = 0.0891, \text{ or } 8.91\%$$

This example illustrates how Equation 11.4 is used to estimate the cost of common stock for a company. How would the analysis differ for a private company? The only difference is that we would not be able to estimate the beta directly. We would have to estimate the beta using betas for similar public companies.

Calculating the Cost of Equity Using a Stock's Beta

PROBLEM: You have decided to estimate the cost of the common equity in your pizza business on October 19, 2012. As noted earlier, the risk-free rate and the market risk premium on that day were 2.55 percent and 5.63 percent, respectively. Since you have already decided that Domino's Pizza is a reasonably comparable company, you obtain Domino's beta from the Yahoo! finance Web site (http://finance.yahoo.com). This beta is 0.90. What do you estimate the cost of common equity in your pizza business to be?

APPROACH: Method 1 for calculating the cost of equity is to use the Capital Asset Pricing Model (CAPM). Therefore, in this example we will use Equation 11.4.

SOLUTION:

$k_{cs} = R_{rf} + (\beta_{cs} \times \text{Market risk premium}) = 0.0255 + (0.90 \times 0.0563) = 0.0762$, or 7.62%

Method 2: Using the Constant-Growth Dividend Model

In Chapter 8 we noted that if the dividends received by the owner of a share of common stock are expected to grow at a constant rate in perpetuity, then the value of that share today can be calculated using Equation 8.4:

$$P_0 = \frac{D_1}{R - g}$$

where D_1 is the dividend expected to be paid one period from today, R is the required rate of return, and g is the annual rate at which the dividends are expected to grow in perpetuity.

We can replace the R in Equation 8.4 with k_{cs} since we are specifically estimating the expected rate of return for investing in common stock (also the cost of equity if the firm has no other types of stock outstanding). We can then rearrange this equation to solve for k_{cs}:

$$k_{cs} = \frac{D_1}{P_0} + g \qquad (11.5)$$

While Equation 11.5 is just a variation of Equation 8.4, it is important enough to identify as a separate equation because it provides a direct way of estimating the cost of equity under certain circumstances. If we can estimate the dividend that stockholders will receive next period, D_1, and we can estimate the rate at which the market expects dividends to grow over the long run, g, then we can use today's market price, P_0, in Equation 11.5 to tell us what rate of return investors in the firm's common stock are expecting to earn.

Consider an example. Suppose that the current price for the common stock at Sprigg Lane Company is $20, that the firm is expected to pay a dividend of $2 per share to its common stockholders next year, and that the dividend is expected to grow at a rate of 3 percent in perpetuity after next year. Equation 11.5 tells us that the required rate of return for Sprigg Lane's stock is:

$$k_{cs} = \frac{D_1}{P_0} + g = \frac{\$2}{\$20} + 0.03 = 0.1300, \text{ or } 13.00\%$$

This approach can be useful for a firm that pays dividends when it is reasonable to assume dividends will grow at a constant rate and when the analyst has a good idea what that growth rate will be. An electric utility firm is an example of this type of firm. Some electric utility firms pay relatively high and predictable dividends that increase at a fairly consistent rate. In contrast, this approach would not be appropriate for use by a high-tech firm that pays no dividends or that pays a small dividend that is likely to increase at a high rate in the short run. Equation 11.5, like any other equation, should be used only if it is appropriate for the particular stock.

You might be asking yourself at this point where you would get P_0, D_1, and g in order to use Equation 11.5 for a particular stock. You can get the current price of a share of stock as well as the dividend that a firm is expected to pay next year quite easily from many different Web sites on the Internet—for example, MSN Money and Yahoo! Finance, which were both mentioned earlier. The financial information includes the dollar value of dividends paid in the past year and the dividend that the firm is expected to pay in the next year.

Estimating the long-term rate of growth in dividends is more difficult, but there are some guidelines that can help. As we discussed in Chapter 8, the first rule is that dividends cannot grow faster than the long-term growth rate of the economy in a perpetuity model such as Equation 8.4 or 11.5. Assuming dividends will grow faster than the economy is the same as assuming that dividends will eventually become larger than the economy itself! We know this is impossible.

You can obtain recent stock prices and financial information for a large number of firms from MSN Money at http://moneycentral.msn.com or from Yahoo! Finance at http://finance.yahoo.com/.

What is the long-term growth rate of the economy? Well, historically it has been the rate of inflation plus about 3 percent. This means that if inflation is expected to be 3 percent in the long run, then a reasonable estimate for the long-term growth rate in the economy is 6 percent (3 percent inflation plus 3 percent real growth). This tells us that g in Equation 11.5 will not be greater than 6 percent. What exactly it will be depends on the nature of the business and the industry it is in. If it is a declining industry, then g might be negative. If the industry is expected to grow with the economy and the particular firm you are evaluating is expected to retain its market share, then a reasonable estimate for g might be 5 or 6 percent.

Method 3: Using a Multistage-Growth Dividend Model

multistage-growth dividend model
a model that allows for varying dividend growth rates in the near term, followed by a constant long-term growth rate; another term used to describe the mixed (supernormal) dividend growth model discussed in Chapter 8

Using a **multistage-growth dividend model** to estimate the cost of equity for a firm is very similar to using a constant-growth dividend model. The difference is that a multistage-growth dividend model allows for faster dividend growth rates in the near term, followed by a constant long-term growth rate. If this concept sounds familiar, that is because it is the idea behind the *mixed (supernormal) growth dividend model* discussed in Chapter 8. In Equation 8.6 this model was written as:

$$P_0 = \frac{D_1}{1 + R} + \frac{D_2}{(1 + R)^2} + \cdots + \frac{D_t}{(1 + R)^t} + \frac{P_t}{(1 + R)^t}$$

where D_i is the dividend in period i, P_t is the value of constant-growth dividend payments in period t, and R is the required rate of return.

To refresh your memory of how this model works, let's consider a three-stage example. Suppose that a firm will pay a dividend one year from today (D_1) and that this dividend will increase at a rate of g_1 the following year, g_2 the year after that, and g_3 per year thereafter. The value of a share of this stock today thus equals:

$$P_0 = \frac{D_1}{1 + k_{cs}} + \frac{D_1(1 + g_1)}{(1 + k_{cs})^2} + \frac{D_1(1 + g_1)(1 + g_2)}{(1 + k_{cs})^3}$$
$$+ \left[\frac{D_1(1 + g_1)(1 + g_2)(1 + g_3)}{k_{cs} - g_3}\right]\left[\frac{1}{(1 + k_{cs})^3}\right]$$

In this equation, we have replaced the R in Equation 8.6 with k_{cs} since we are specifically estimating the expected rate of return for common stock. We have also written all of the dividends in terms of D_1 to illustrate how the different growth rates will affect the dividends in each year. Finally, we have written P_t in terms of the constant-growth model. If we substitute D_1, D_2, D_3, and D_4 where appropriate, you can see that this is really just Equation 8.6, where we have replaced R with k_{cs} and written P_t in terms of the constant-growth model:

$$P_0 = \frac{D_1}{1 + k_{cs}} + \frac{D_2}{(1 + k_{cs})^2} + \frac{D_3}{(1 + k_{cs})^3} + \left[\frac{D_4}{k_{cs} - g_3}\right]\left[\frac{1}{(1 + k_{cs})^3}\right]$$

All this equation does is add the present values of the dividends that are expected in each of the next three years and the present value of a growing perpetuity that begins in the fourth year. Exhibit 11.2 illustrates how cash flows relate to the four terms in the equation.

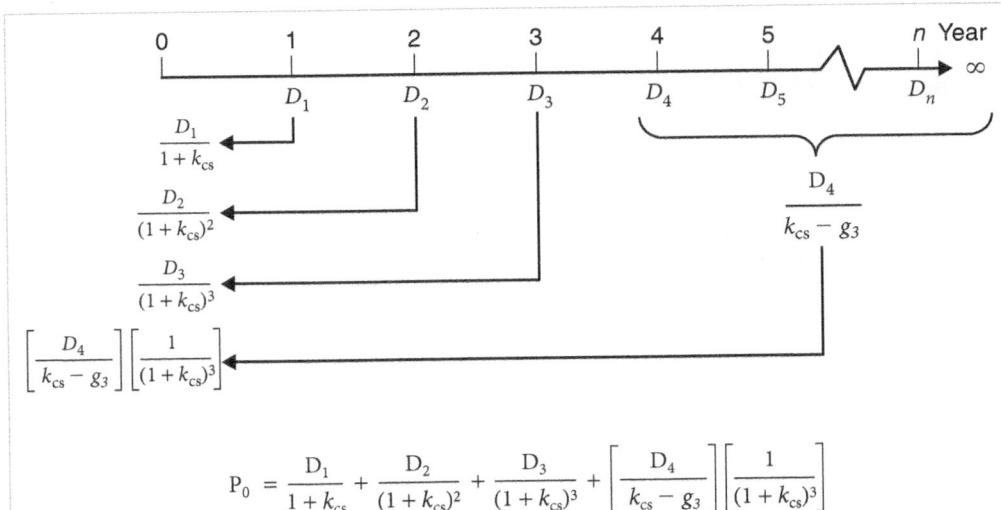

EXHIBIT 11.2
The Three-Stage Dividend Growth Equation

In the three-stage dividend growth model shown here, the price of a share of stock is equal to the present value of dividends expected to be received at the end of Years 1, 2, and 3, plus the present value of a growing perpetuity that begins in Year 4 and whose dividends are assumed to grow at a constant rate g_3 forever.

$$P_0 = \frac{D_1}{1 + k_{cs}} + \frac{D_2}{(1 + k_{cs})^2} + \frac{D_3}{(1 + k_{cs})^3} + \left[\frac{D_4}{k_{cs} - g_3}\right]\left[\frac{1}{(1 + k_{cs})^3}\right]$$

Note that the fourth term in Exhibit 11.2 is discounted only three years because, as we saw in Chapters 5 and 8, the constant-growth model gives you the present value of a growing perpetuity as of the year before the first cash flow. In this case since the first cash flow is D_4, the model gives you the value of the growing perpetuity as of Year 3.

A multistage-growth dividend model is much more flexible than the constant-growth dividend model because we do not have to assume that dividends grow at the same rate forever. We can use a model such as this to estimate the cost of common stock, k_{cs}, by plugging P_0, D_1, and the appropriate growth rates into the model and solving for k_{cs} using trial and error—just as we solved for the yield to maturity of bonds in Chapter 7 and earlier in this chapter. The major issues we have to be concerned about when we use a growth dividend model are (1) that we have chosen the right model, meaning that we have included enough stages or growth rates, and (2) that our estimates of the growth rates are reasonable.

Let's work an example to illustrate how this model is used to calculate the cost of common stock. Suppose that we want to estimate the cost of common stock for a firm that is expected to pay a dividend of $1.50 per share next year. This dividend is expected to increase 15 percent the following year, 10 percent the year after that, 7 percent the year after that, and 5 percent annually thereafter. If the firm's common stock is currently selling for $24 per share, what is the rate of return that investors require for investing in this stock?

Because there are four different growth rates in this example, we have to solve a formula with five terms:

$$P_0 = \frac{D_1}{1 + k_{cs}} + \frac{D_2}{(1 + k_{cs})^2} + \frac{D_3}{(1 + k_{cs})^3} + \frac{D_4}{(1 + k_{cs})^4} + \left[\frac{D_5}{k_{cs} - g_4}\right]\left[\frac{1}{(1 + k_{cs})^4}\right]$$

From the information given in the problem statement, we know the following:

$$D_1 = \$1.50$$
$$D_2 = D_1 \times (1 + g_1) = \$1.500 \times 1.15 = \$1.725$$
$$D_3 = D_2 \times (1 + g_2) = \$1.725 \times 1.10 = \$1.898$$
$$D_4 = D_3 \times (1 + g_3) = \$1.898 \times 1.07 = \$2.031$$
$$D_5 = D_4 \times (1 + g_4) = \$2.031 \times 1.05 = \$2.133$$

Substituting these values into the above equation gives us the following, which we solve for k_{cs}:

$$\$24 = \frac{\$1.50}{1 + k_{cs}} + \frac{\$1.73}{(1 + k_{cs})^2} + \frac{\$1.90}{(1 + k_{cs})^3} + \frac{\$2.03}{(1 + k_{cs})^4} + \left[\frac{\$2.13}{k_{cs} - g_4}\right]\left[\frac{1}{(1 + k_{cs})^4}\right]$$

As mentioned earlier, we can solve this equation for k_{cs} using trial and error. When we do this, we find that k_{cs} is 12.20 percent. This is the rate of return at which the present value of the cash flows equals $24. Therefore, it is the rate that investors currently require for investing in this stock.

USING EXCEL

SOLVING FOR k_{cs} USING A MULTISTAGE-GROWTH DIVIDEND MODEL

Because trial and error calculations can be somewhat tedious when you perform them by hand, you may find it helpful to use a spreadsheet program. If you would like to use a spreadsheet program to solve the preceding problem yourself, the output from the spreadsheet below shows you how to do it using trial and error.

Once you input the indicated numbers and formulas into cells B3 through B14, you can then vary the number in cell B2 until the number in cell B8 equals $24. Once you have built the model, you can also use the "goal seek" or "solver" functions in Excel to avoid having to manually solve the problem by trial and error. See the "Help" feature in Excel for information on how to use these functions.

◇	A	B	C	D
1				Comment
2	k_{cs} =	0.12205		Change this number until the P_0 equals $24.00
3	g_1 =	0.15		Growth rate in year 1
4	g_2 =	0.10		Growth rate in year 2
5	g_3 =	0.07		Growth rate in year 3
6	g_4 =	0.05		Growth rate for perpetuity
7				
8	P_0 =	$24.00		Formula: =NPV(B2,B11:B14) - This formula calculates the present value of the
9				future dividends in cells B11 to B14 using the discount rate in cell B2.
10	Year			
11	1	$1.500		D_1
12	2	$1.725		D_2 = B11*(1+B3)
13	3	$1.898		D_3 = B12*(1+B4)
14	4	$31.619		D_4 = [B13*(1+B5)] + [B13*(1+B5)*(1+B6)]/(B2-B6) - This formula calculates the
15				value of D_4 plus the present value of all the cash flows after year 4 in year 4 dollars.
16				

Which Method Should We Use?

We now have discussed three methods of estimating the cost of common equity for a firm. You might be asking yourself how you are supposed to know which method to use. The short answer is that, in practice, most people use the CAPM (Method 1) to estimate the cost of common equity if the result is going to be used in the discount rate for evaluating a project. One reason is that, assuming the theory is valid, CAPM tells managers what rate of return investors should require for equity having the same level of systematic risk that the firm's equity has. This is the appropriate opportunity cost of equity capital for an NPV analysis if the project has the same risk as the firm and will have similar leverage. Furthermore, CAPM does not require financial analysts to make assumptions about future growth rates in dividends, as Methods 2 and 3 do.

Used properly, Methods 2 and 3 provide an estimate of the rate of return that is implied by the current price of a firm's stock at a particular point in time. If the stock markets are efficient, then this should be the same as the number that we would estimate using CAPM. However, to the extent that the firm's stock is mispriced—for example, because investors are not informed or have misinterpreted the future prospects for the firm—deriving the cost of equity from the price at one point in time can yield a bad estimate of the true cost of equity.

Preferred Stock

As we discussed in Chapter 8, preferred stock is a form of equity that has a stated value and specified dividend rate. For example, a share of preferred stock might have a stated value of $100 and a 5 percent dividend rate. The owner of such a share would be entitled to receive a dividend of $5 ($100 × 0.05 = $5) each year. Another key feature of preferred stock is that it does not have an expiration date. In other words, preferred stock continues to pay the specified dividend in perpetuity, unless the firm repurchases it or goes out of business.

These characteristics of preferred stock allow us to use the perpetuity model, Equation 5.7, to estimate the cost of preferred equity. For example, suppose that investors would pay $85 for a share of the preferred stock mentioned above. We can rewrite Equation 5.7:

$$PVP = \frac{CF}{i}$$

as:

$$P_{ps} = \frac{D_{ps}}{k_{ps}}$$

where P_{ps} is the present value of the expected dividends (the current preferred stock price), D_{ps} is the annual preferred stock dividend, and k_{ps} is the cost of the preferred stock. Rearranging the formula to solve for k_{ps} yields:

$$k_{ps} = \frac{D_{ps}}{P_{ps}} \qquad (11.6)$$

Plugging the information from our example into Equation 11.6, we see that k_{ps} for the preferred stock in our example is:

$$k_{ps} = \frac{D_{ps}}{P_{ps}} = \frac{\$5}{\$85} = 0.0588, \text{ or } 5.88\%$$

This is the rate of return at which the present value of the annual $5 cash flows equals the market price of $85. Therefore, 5.88 percent is the rate that investors currently require for investing in this preferred stock.

It is easy to incorporate issuance costs into the above calculation to obtain the cost of the preferred stock to the firm that issues it. As in the earlier bond calculations, we use the net proceeds from the sale rather than the price that is paid by the investor in the calculation. For example, suppose that in order for a firm to sell the above preferred stock, it must pay an investment banker 5 percent of the amount of money raised. If there are no other issuance costs, the company would receive $85 \times (1 - 0.05) = \$80.75$ for each share sold, and the total cost of this financing to the firm would be:

$$k_{ps} = \frac{D_{ps}}{P_{ps}} = \frac{\$5}{\$80.75} = 0.0619, \text{ or } 6.19\%$$

Estimating the Cost of Preferred Stock

PROBLEM: You work in the treasury department at Wells Fargo & Company, and your manager has asked you to estimate the cost of each of the different types of stock that Wells Fargo has outstanding. One of these issues is an 8 percent noncumulative preferred stock that has a stated value of $1,000 and is currently selling for $927.90. Although this preferred stock is publicly traded, it does not trade very often. This means that you cannot use the CAPM to estimate k_{ps} because you cannot get a good estimate of the beta using regression analysis. How else can you estimate the cost of this preferred stock, and what is this cost?

APPROACH: You can also use Equation 11.6 to estimate the cost of preferred stock.

SOLUTION: First, you must find the annual dividend that someone who owns a share of this stock will receive. This preferred stock issue pays an annual dividend (for simplicity we are assuming one dividend payment per year) that equals 8 percent of $1,000 or $1,000 \times 0.8 = \$80$. Substituting the annual dividend and the market price into Equation 11.6 yields:

$$k_{ps} = \frac{D_{ps}}{P_{ps}} = \frac{\$80}{\$927.90} = 0.0862, \text{ or } 8.62\%$$

You may recall from the discussion in Chapter 8 that certain characteristics of preferred stock look a lot like those of debt. The equation $P_{ps} = D_{ps}/k_{ps}$ shows that the value of preferred stock also varies with market rates of return in the same way as debt. Because k_{ps} is in the denominator of the fraction on the right-hand side of the equation, whenever k_{ps} increases, P_{ps} decreases, and whenever k_{ps} decreases, P_{ps} increases. That is, the value of preferred stock is negatively related to market rates.

It is also important to recognize that the CAPM can be used to estimate the cost of preferred equity, just as it can be used to estimate the cost of common equity. A financial analyst can simply substitute k_{ps} for k_{cs} and β_{ps} for β_{cs} in Equation 11.4 and use it to estimate the cost of preferred stock. Remember from Chapter 6 that the CAPM does not apply only to common stock; rather, it applies to any asset. Therefore, we can use it to calculate the rate of return on any asset if we can estimate the beta for that asset.

> **BEFORE YOU GO ON**

1. What information is needed to use the CAPM to estimate k_{cs} or k_{ps}?

2. Under what circumstances can you use the constant-growth dividend formula to estimate k_{cs}?

3. What is the advantage of using a multistage-growth dividend model, rather than the constant-growth dividend model, to estimate k_{cs}?

11.4 USING THE WACC IN PRACTICE

4 LEARNING OBJECTIVE

We have now covered the basic concepts and computational tools that are used to estimate the WACC. At this point, we are ready to talk about some of the practical issues that arise when financial analysts calculate the WACC for their firms.

When financial analysts think about calculating the WACC, they usually think of it as a weighted average of the firm's after-tax cost of debt, cost of preferred stock, and cost of common equity. Equation 11.2 is usually written as:

$$\text{WACC} = x_{Debt}k_{Debt\ pretax}(1 - t) + x_{ps}k_{ps} + x_{cs}k_{cs} \tag{11.7}$$

where $x_{Debt} + x_{ps} + x_{cs} = 1$. If the firm has more than one type of debt outstanding or more than one type of preferred or common stock, analysts will calculate a weighted average for each of those types of securities and then plug those averages into Equation 11.7. Financial analysts will also use the *market values*, rather than the accounting book values, of the debt, preferred stock, and common stock to calculate the weights (the *x*'s) in Equation 11.7. This is because, as we have already seen, the theory underlying the discounting process requires that the costs of the different types of financing be weighted by their relative market values. Accounting book values have no place in these calculations unless they just happen to equal the market values.

Calculating WACC: An Example

An example provides a useful way of illustrating how the theories and tools that we have discussed are used in practice. Assume that you are a financial analyst at a manufacturing company that has used three types of debt, preferred stock, and common stock to finance its investments.

Debt: The debt includes a $4 million bank loan that is secured by machinery and equipment. This loan has an interest rate of 6 percent, and your firm could expect to pay the same rate if the loan were refinanced today. Your firm also has a second bank loan (a $3 million mortgage on your manufacturing plant) with an interest rate of 5.5 percent. The rate would also be 5.5 percent today if you refinanced this loan. The third type of debt is a bond issue that the firm sold two years ago for $11 million. The market value of these bonds today is $10 million. Using the approach we discussed earlier, you have estimated that the effective annual yield on the bonds is 7 percent.

Preferred Stock: The preferred stock pays an annual dividend of 4.5 percent on a stated value of $100. A share of this stock is currently selling for $60, and there are 100,000 shares outstanding.

Common Stock: There are 1 million shares of common stock outstanding, and they are currently selling for $21 each. Using a regression analysis, you have estimated that the beta of these shares is 1.1.

The 20-year Treasury bond rate is currently 2.55 percent, and you have estimated the market risk premium to be 5.63 percent using the returns on stocks and Treasury bonds from the 1926 to 2011 period. Your firm's marginal tax rate is 35 percent. What is the WACC for your firm?

The first step in computing the WACC is to calculate the pretax cost of debt. Since the market value of the firm's debt is $17 million ($4 million + $3 million + $10 million = $17 million), we can calculate the pretax cost of debt as follows:

$$k_{\text{Debt pretax}} = x_{\text{Bank loan 1}}k_{\text{Bank loan 1 pretax}} + x_{\text{Bank loan 2}}k_{\text{Bank loan 2 pretax}} + x_{\text{Bonds}}k_{\text{Bonds pretax}}$$
$$= (\$4/\$17)(0.06) + (\$3/\$17)(0.055) + (\$10/\$17)(0.07)$$
$$= 0.0650, \text{ or } 6.50\%$$

Note that because the $4 million and $3 million loans have rates that equal what it would cost to refinance them today, their market values equal the amount that is owed. Since the $10 million market value of the bond issue is below the $11 million face value, the rate that firm is actually paying must be lower than the 7 percent rate you estimated to reflect the current cost of this debt. Recall that as interest rates increase, the market value of a bond decreases. This is the negative relation that we referred to earlier in this chapter.

We next calculate the cost of the preferred stock using Equation 11.6, as follows:

$$k_{\text{ps}} = \frac{D_{\text{ps}}}{P_{\text{ps}}} = \frac{0.045 \times \$100}{\$60}$$
$$= \frac{\$4.5}{\$60} = 0.0750, \text{ or } 7.50\%$$

From Equation 11.4, we calculate the cost of the common equity to be:

$$k_{\text{cs}} = R_{\text{rf}} + (\beta_{\text{cs}} \times \text{Market risk premium}) = 0.0255 + (1.1 \times 0.0563)$$
$$= 0.0874, \text{ or } 8.74\%$$

We are now ready to use Equation 11.7 to calculate the firm's WACC. Since the firm has $17 million of debt, $6 million of preferred stock ($60 × 100,000 shares = $6 million), and $21 million of common equity ($21 × 1,000,000 shares = $21 million), the total market value of its capital is $44 million ($17 million + $6 million + $21 million = $44 million). The firm's WACC is therefore:

$$\text{WACC} = x_{\text{Debt}}k_{\text{Debt pretax}}(1 - t) + x_{\text{ps}}k_{\text{ps}} + x_{\text{cs}}k_{\text{cs}}$$
$$= (\$17/\$44)(0.0650)(1 - 0.35) + (\$6/\$44)(0.0750) + (\$21/\$44)(0.0874)$$
$$= 0.0683, \text{ or } 6.83\%$$

> You can see real-world WACC calculations at the New Zealand Web site for Pricewaterhouse-Coopers, the international accounting and consulting firm, at http://www.pwc.co.nz/appreciating-value/edition-three.

Calculating the WACC with Equation 11.7

PROBLEM: After calculating the cost of the common equity in your pizza business to be 7.62 percent (see Learning by Doing Application 11.3), you have decided to estimate the WACC. You recently hired a business appraiser to estimate the value of your stock, which includes all of the outstanding common equity. His report indicates that it is worth $500 million.

In order to finance the 2,000 restaurants that are now part of your company, you have sold three different bond issues. Based on the current prices of the bonds from these issues and the issue characteristics (face values and coupon rates), you have estimated the market values and effective annual yields to be:

Bond Issue	Value ($ millions)	Effective Annual Yield
1	$100	4.50%
2	187	4.90
3	154	5.40
Total	$441	

(continued)

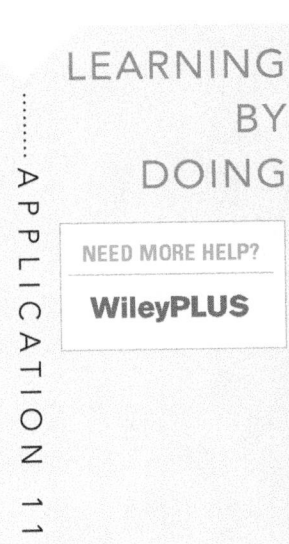

LEARNING BY DOING

APPLICATION 11.5

NEED MORE HELP?

WileyPLUS

Your company has no other long-term debt or any preferred stock outstanding. Both the marginal and average tax rates for your company are 20 percent. What is the WACC for your pizza business?

APPROACH: You can use Equation 11.7 to solve for the WACC for your pizza business. To do so, you must first calculate the weighted average cost of debt. You can then plug the weights and costs for the debt and common equity into Equation 11.7. Since your business has no preferred stock, the value for this term in Equation 11.7 will equal $0.

SOLUTION: The weighted average cost of the debt is:

$$k_{Debt\ pretax} = x_1 k_{1\ Debt\ pretax} + x_2 k_{2\ Debt\ pretax} + x_3 k_{3\ Debt\ pretax}$$
$$= (\$100/\$441)(0.0450) + (\$187/\$441)(0.0490) + (\$154/\$441)(0.0540)$$
$$= 0.0498,\ or\ 4.98\%$$

and the WACC is:

$$WACC = x_{Debt} k_{Debt\ pretax}(1 - t) + x_{ps} k_{ps} + x_{cs} k_{cs}$$
$$= (\$441/[\$441 + \$500])(0.0498)(1 - 0.20) + 0 + (\$500/[\$441 + \$500])(0.0762)$$
$$= 0.0592,\ or\ 5.92\%$$

DECISION MAKING

EXAMPLE 11.2

Interpreting the WACC

SITUATION: You are a financial analyst for the company whose WACC of 6.83 percent we just calculated in the main text. One day, your manager walks into your office and tells you that she is thinking about selling $23 million of common stock and using the proceeds from the sale to pay back both of the firm's loans and to repurchase all of the outstanding bonds and preferred stock. She tells you that this is a smart move because if she does this, the beta of the firm's common stock will decline to 0.90 and the overall k_{cs} will decline from 8.70 percent to 7.62 percent:

$$k_{cs} = R_{rf} + (\beta_{cs} \times Market\ risk\ premium) = 0.0255 + (0.90 \times 0.0563)$$
$$= 0.0762,\ or\ 7.62\%$$

What do you tell your manager?

DECISION: You should politely point out that she is making the wrong comparison. Since the refinancing will result in the firm being financed entirely with equity, k_{cs} will equal the firm's WACC. Therefore, the 7.62 percent should really be compared with the 6.83 percent WACC. If your manager goes through with the refinancing, she will be making a bad decision. The average after-tax cost of the capital that your firm uses will *increase* from 6.83 percent to 7.62 percent.

Limitations of WACC as a Discount Rate for Evaluating Projects

At the beginning of this chapter, we told you that financial managers often require analysts within the firm to use the firm's current cost of capital to discount the cash flows for individual projects. They do so because it is very difficult to directly estimate the discount rate for individual projects. You should recognize by now that the WACC is the discount rate that analysts are often required to use. Using the WACC to discount the cash flows for a project can make sense under certain circumstances. However, in other circumstances, it can be very dangerous. The rest of this section discusses when it makes sense to use the WACC as a discount rate and the problems that can occur when the WACC is used incorrectly.

Chapter 10 discussed how an analyst forecasting the cash flows for a project is forecasting the incremental after-tax free cash flows at the firm level. These cash flows represent the difference between the cash flows that the firm will generate if the project is adopted and the cash flows that the firm will generate if the project is not adopted.

Financial theory tells us that the rate that should be used to discount these incremental cash flows is the rate that reflects their systematic risk. This means that the WACC is going to be the appropriate discount rate for evaluating a project only when the project has cash flows with systematic risks that are exactly the same as those for the firm as a whole. Unfortunately, this is not true for most projects. The firm itself is a portfolio of projects with varying degrees of risk.

When a single rate, such as the WACC, is used to discount cash flows for projects with varying levels of risk, the discount rate will be too low in some cases and too high in others. When the discount rate is too low, the firm runs the risk of accepting a negative NPV project. To see how this might happen, assume that you work at a company that manufactures soft drinks and that the managers at your company are concerned about all the competition in the core soft drink business. They are thinking about expanding into the manufacture and sale of exotic tropical beverages. The managers believe that entering this market would allow the firm to better differentiate its products and earn higher profits. Suppose also that the appropriate beta for soft drink projects is 1.2, while the appropriate beta for tropical beverage projects is 1.5. Since your firm is only in the soft drink business right now, the beta for its overall cash flows is 1.2. Exhibit 11.3 illustrates the problem that could arise if your firm's WACC is used to evaluate a tropical beverage project.

In Exhibit 11.3, you can see that since the beta of the tropical beverage project is larger than the beta of the firm as a whole, the expected return (or discount rate) for the tropical beverage project should be higher than the firm's WACC. The Security Market Line indicates what this expected return should be. Now, if the firm's WACC is used to discount the expected cash flows for this project, and the expected return on the project is above the firm's WACC, then the estimated NPV will be positive. So far, so good. However, as illustrated in Exhibit 11.3, some projects may have an expected return that is above the WACC but below the SML. For projects such as those, using the WACC as the discount rate may actually cause the firm to accept a negative NPV project! The estimated NPV will be positive even though the true NPV is negative. The negative NPV projects that would be accepted in those situations have returns that fall in the red shaded area below the SML, above the WACC line, and to the right of the firm's beta.

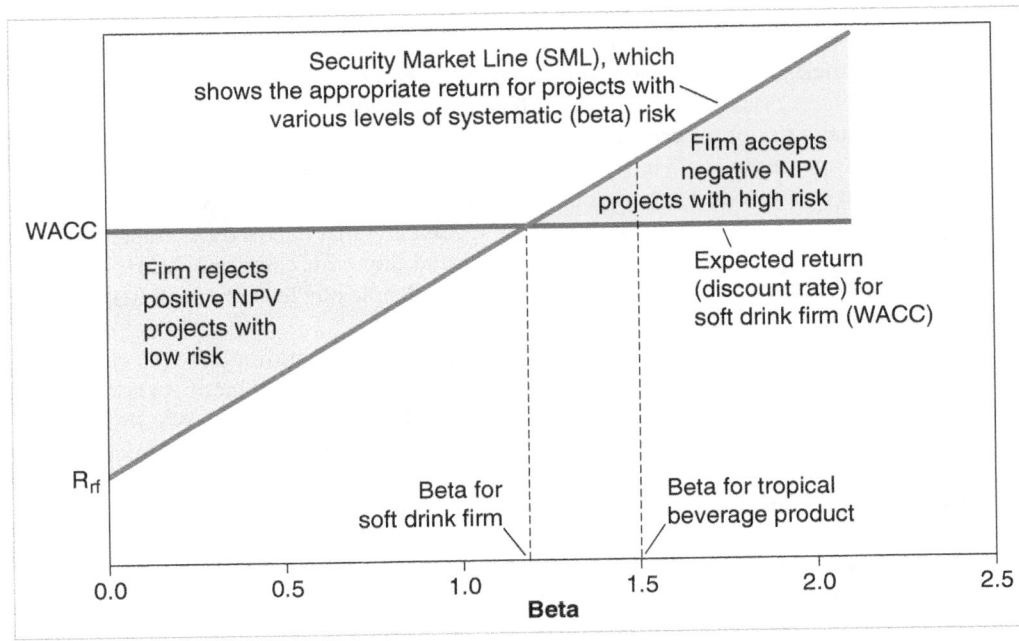

EXHIBIT 11.3
Potential Errors When Using the WACC to Evaluate Projects

Two types of problems can arise when the WACC for a firm is used to evaluate individual projects: a positive NPV project may be rejected or a negative NPV project may be accepted. For the tropical beverage example, if the expected return on that project was below the level indicated by the SML, but above the firm's WACC, the project might be accepted even though it would have a negative NPV.

In Exhibit 11.3 you can also see that using the WACC to discount expected cash flows for low-risk projects can result in managers at the firm rejecting projects that have positive NPVs. This problem is, in some sense, the mirror image of the case where the WACC is lower than the correct discount rate. Financial managers run the risk of turning down positive NPV projects whenever the WACC is higher than the correct discount rate. The positive NPV projects that would be rejected are those that fall into the green shaded area that is below the WACC but above the SML and to the left of the firm's beta.

To see how these types of problems arise, consider a project that requires an initial investment of $100 and that is expected to produce cash inflows of $40 per year for three years. If the correct discount rate for this project is 8 percent, its NPV will be:

$$\text{NPV} = \text{FCF}_0 + \frac{\text{FCF}_1}{1 + k} + \frac{\text{FCF}_2}{(1 + k)^2} + \frac{\text{FCF}_3}{(1 + k)^3}$$

$$= -\$100 + \frac{\$40}{1 + 0.08} + \frac{\$40}{(1 + 0.08)^2} + \frac{\$40}{(1 + 0.08)^3}$$

$$= \$3.08$$

This is an attractive project because it returns more than the investors' opportunity cost of capital.

Suppose, however, that the financial managers of the firm considering this project require that all projects be evaluated using the firm's WACC of 11 percent. When the cash flows are discounted using a rate of 11 percent, the NPV is:

$$\text{NPV} = -\$100 + \frac{\$40}{1 + 0.11} + \frac{\$40}{(1 + 0.11)^2} + \frac{\$40}{(1 + 0.11)^3} = -\$2.25$$

As you can see, when the WACC is used to discount the cash flows, the firm will end up rejecting a positive NPV project. The firm will be passing up an opportunity to create value for its stockholders. As an exercise, you might try constructing a numerical example in which a firm accepts a negative NPV project.

It is also important to recognize that when a firm uses a single rate to evaluate all of its projects, there will be a bias toward accepting more risky projects. The average risk of the firm's assets will tend to increase over time. Furthermore, because some positive NPV projects are likely to be rejected and some negative NPV projects are likely to be accepted, new projects on the whole will probably create less value for stockholders than if the appropriate discount rate had been used to evaluate all projects. This, in turn, can put the firm at a disadvantage when compared with its competitors and adversely affect the value of its existing projects.

The key point to take away from this discussion is that it is only correct to use a firm's WACC to discount the cash flows for a project if the expected cash flows from that project have the same systematic risk as the expected cash flows from the firm as a whole. You might be wondering how you can tell when this condition exists. The answer is that we never know for sure. Nevertheless, there are some guidelines that you can use when assessing whether the systematic risk for a particular project is similar to that for the firm as a whole.

The systematic risk of the cash flows from a project depend on the nature of the business. Revenues and expenses in some businesses are affected more by changes in general economic conditions than revenues and expenses in other businesses. For example, consider the differences between a company that makes bread and a company that makes recreational vehicles. The demand for bread will be relatively constant in good economic conditions and in bad. The demand for recreational vehicles will be more volatile. People buy fewer recreational vehicles during recessions than when the economy is doing well.

While total volatility is not the same as systematic volatility, businesses with more total volatility (uncertainty or risk) typically have more systematic volatility. Since beta is a measure of systematic risk, and systematic risk is a key factor in determining a firm's WACC, this suggests that the firm's WACC should be used only for projects with business risks similar to those for the firm as a whole. Since financial managers usually think of systematic risk when they think of underlying business risks, we can restate this condition as follows:

Condition 1: A firm's WACC should be used to evaluate the cash flows for a new project only if the level of systematic risk for the project is the same as that for the portfolio of projects that currently comprise the firm.

You have to consider one other factor when you decide whether it is appropriate to use a firm's WACC to discount the cash flows for a project. That is the way in which the project will be financed and how this financing compares with the way the firm's assets are financed. To better understand why this is important, consider Equation 11.7:

$$\text{WACC} = x_{\text{Debt}} k_{\text{Debt pretax}}(1 - t) + x_{\text{ps}} k_{\text{ps}} + x_{\text{cs}} k_{\text{cs}}$$

This equation provides a measure of the firm's cost of capital that reflects both how the firm's assets have been financed—that is, the mix of debt and preferred and common stock that was used to acquire those assets—and the current cost of each type of financing. In other words, the WACC reflects both the x's and the k's associated with the firm's financing. Why is this important? Because the costs of the different types of capital depend on the fraction of the total firm financing that each represents. If the firm uses more or less debt, the cost of debt will be higher or lower. In turn, the cost of both preferred stock and common stock will be affected. This means that even if the underlying business risk of the project is the same as that for the firm as a whole, if the project is financed differently than the firm as a whole the appropriate discount rate for the project analysis will be different from that for the firm as a whole.

> **Condition 2:** A firm's WACC should be used to evaluate a project only if that project uses the same financing mix—the same proportions of debt, preferred shares, and common shares—used to finance the firm as a whole.

In summary, WACC is a measure of the current cost of the capital that the firm is using to finance its projects. It is an appropriate discount rate for evaluating projects only if (1) the project's systematic risk is the same as that of the firm's current portfolio of projects and (2) the project will be financed with the same mix of debt and equity as the firm's current portfolio of projects. If either of these two conditions does not hold, then managers should be careful in using the firm's current WACC to evaluate a project.

Alternatives to Using WACC for Evaluating Projects

Financial managers understand the limitations of using a firm's WACC to evaluate projects, but they also know that there are no perfect alternatives. As we noted earlier in this chapter, there is no publicly traded common stock for most individual projects within a firm. It is, therefore, not possible to directly estimate the beta for the common stock used to finance an individual project.[9] Although it might be possible to obtain an estimate of the cost of debt from the firm's bankers, without an estimate of the common stock beta—and, therefore, the cost of common stock—it is not possible to obtain a direct estimate of the appropriate discount rate for a project using Equation 11.7.

If the discount rate for a project cannot be estimated directly, a financial analyst might try to find a public firm that is in a business that is similar to that of the project. For example, in our exotic tropical beverage example, an analyst at the soft drink company might look for a company that produces only exotic tropical beverages and that also has publicly traded stock. This public company would be what financial analysts call a **pure-play comparable** because it is exactly like the project. The returns on the pure-play company's stock could be used to estimate the expected return on the equity that is used to finance the project. Unfortunately, this approach is generally not feasible due to the difficulty of finding a public firm that is only in the business represented by the project. If the public firm is in other businesses as well, then we run into the same sorts of problems that we face when we use the firm's WACC.

pure-play comparable
a comparable company that is in exactly the same business as the project or business being analyzed

From a practical standpoint, financial managers, such as company treasurers and chief financial officers, do not like letting analysts estimate the discount rates for their projects. Different analysts tend to make different assumptions or use different approaches, which can lead to inconsistencies that make it difficult to compare projects. In addition, analysts may be tempted to manipulate discount rates in order to make pet projects look more attractive.

---

[9]Some firms have issued a type of stock that has an equity claim on only part of their business. If a project is similar to the part of the business for which "tracking stock" like this has been sold, the returns on the tracking stock can be used to estimate the beta for the common stock used to finance a project.

In an effort to use discount rates that reflect project risks better than the firm's WACC, while retaining control of the process through which discount rates are set, financial managers sometimes classify projects into categories based on their systematic risks. They then specify a discount rate that is to be used to discount the cash flows for all projects within each category. The idea is that each category of projects has a different level of systematic risk and therefore a different discount rate should be used for each. Exhibit 11.4 illustrates such a classification scheme.

The scheme illustrated in Exhibit 11.4 includes four project categories:

1. *Efficiency projects,* such as the implementation of a new production technology that reduces manufacturing costs for an existing product.

2. *Product extension projects,* such as those in which Boeing created variations of its aircraft, such as the Boeing 737, to help meet customer needs.

3. *Market extension projects,* in which existing products are sold in new markets, such as when Texas Instruments considers selling a new version of a computer chip that has been used in digital phones to digital camera manufacturers.

4. *New product projects,* in which entirely new products are being considered.

When using the scheme illustrated in Exhibit 11.4, the financial manager would assign a discount rate for each category that reflects the typical beta in the indicated range of betas. Such an approach is attractive because it is not generally difficult for analysts to figure out in which of the four categories particular projects belong, and it limits their discretion in choosing discount rates. Most important, it can reduce the possibility of accepting negative NPV projects or rejecting positive NPV projects. We can see the latter benefit by comparing the shaded areas in the figures in Exhibits 11.3 and 11.4. The total size of the shaded areas, which represents the possibility of making an error, is much smaller in Exhibit 11.4.

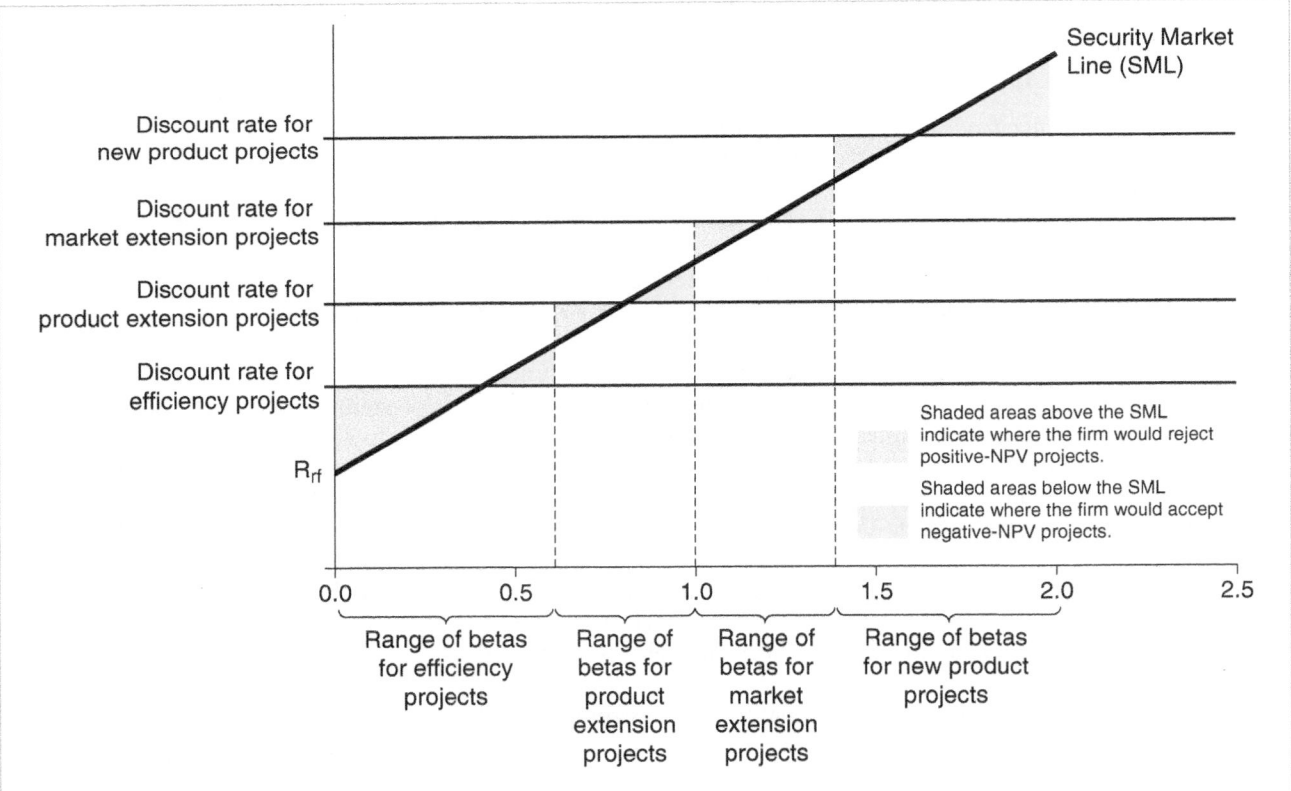

EXHIBIT 11.4

Potential Errors When Using Multiple Discount Rates to Evaluate Projects

The potential for errors—either rejecting a positive NPV project or accepting a negative NPV project—is smaller when discount rates better reflect the risk of the projects that they are used to evaluate. You can see this by noting that the total size of the shaded areas in this figure is smaller than the size of the shaded areas in Exhibit 11.3. In the ideal situation, where the correct discount rate is used for each project, there would be no shaded area at all in a figure like this.

> **BEFORE YOU GO ON**

1. Do analysts use book values or market values to calculate the weights when they use Equation 11.7? Why?

2. What kinds of errors can be made when the WACC for a firm is used as the discount rate for evaluating all projects in the firm?

3. Under what conditions is the WACC the appropriate discount rate for a project?

SUMMARY OF **Learning Objectives**

1 **Explain what the weighted average cost of capital for a firm is and why it is often used as a discount rate to evaluate projects.**

The weighted average cost of capital (WACC) for a firm is a weighted average of the current costs of the different types of financing that a firm has used to finance the purchase of its assets. When the WACC is calculated, the cost of each type of financing is weighted according to the fraction of the total firm value represented by that type of financing. The WACC is often used as a discount rate in evaluating projects because it is not possible to directly estimate the appropriate discount rate for many projects. As we also discuss in Section 11.4, having a single discount rate reduces inconsistencies that can arise when different analysts in the firm use different methods to estimate the discount rate and can also limit the ability of analysts to manipulate discount rates to favor pet projects.

2 **Calculate the cost of debt for a firm.**

The cost of debt can be calculated by solving for the yield to maturity of the debt using the bond pricing model (Equation 7.1), computing the effective annual yield, and adjusting for taxes using Equation 11.3.

3 **Calculate the cost of common stock and the cost of preferred stock for a firm.**

The cost of common stock can be estimated using the CAPM, the constant-growth dividend formula, or a multistage-growth dividend formula. The cost of preferred stock can be calculated using the perpetuity model for the present value of cash flows.

4 **Calculate the weighted average cost of capital for a firm, explain the limitations of using a firm's weighted average cost of capital as the discount rate when evaluating a project, and discuss the alternatives to the firm's weighted average cost of capital that are available.**

The weighted average cost of capital is estimated using either Equation 11.2 or Equation 11.7, with the cost of each individual type of financing estimated using the appropriate method.

When a firm uses a single rate to discount the cash flows for all of its projects, some project cash flows will be discounted using a rate that is too high and other project cash flows will be discounted using a rate that is too low. This can result in the firm rejecting some positive NPV projects and accepting some negative NPV projects. It will bias the firm toward accepting more risky projects and can cause the firm to create less value for stockholders than it would have if the appropriate discount rates had been used.

One alternative to using the WACC as a discount rate is to identify a firm that engages in business activities that are similar to those associated with the project under consideration and that has publicly traded stock. The returns from this pure-play firm's stock can then be used to estimate the common stock beta for the project. In instances where pure-play firms are not available, another alternative is for the financial manager to classify projects according to their systematic risks and use a different discount rate for each class of project. This is the type of classification scheme illustrated in Exhibit 11.4.

SUMMARY OF **Key Equations**

Equation	Description	Formula
11.1	Finance balance sheet identity	MV of assets = MV of liabilities + MV of equity
11.2	General formula for weighted average cost of capital (WACC) for a firm	$k_{Firm} = \sum_{i=1}^{n} x_i k_i = x_1 k_1 + x_2 k_2 + x_3 k_3 + \cdots + x_n k_n$
11.3	After-tax cost of debt	$k_{Debt\ after\text{-}tax} = k_{Debt\ pretax} \times (1 - t)$
11.4	CAPM formula for the cost of common stock	$k_{cs} = R_{rf} + (\beta_{cs} \times \text{Market risk premium})$
11.5	Constant-growth dividend formula for the cost of common stock	$k_{cs} = \dfrac{D_1}{P_0} + g$
11.6	Perpetuity formula for the cost of preferred stock	$k_{ps} = \dfrac{D_{ps}}{P_{ps}}$
11.7	Traditional WACC formula	$WACC = x_{Debt} k_{Debt\ pretax}(1 - t) + x_{ps} k_{ps} + x_{cs} k_{cs}$

Self-Study Problems

11.1 The market value of a firm's assets is $3 billion. If the market value of the firm's liabilities is $2 billion, what is the market value of the stockholders' investment and why?

11.2 Berron Comics, Inc., has borrowed $100 million and is required to pay its lenders $8 million in interest this year. If Berron is in the 35 percent marginal tax bracket, then what is the after-tax cost of debt (in dollars as well as in annual interest) to Berron.

11.3 Explain why the after-tax cost of equity (common or preferred) does not have to be adjusted by the marginal income tax rate for the firm.

11.4 Mike's T-Shirts, Inc., has debt claims of $400 (market value) and equity claims of $600 (market value). If the after-tax cost of debt financing is 11 percent and the cost of equity is 17 percent, what is Mike's weighted average cost of capital?

11.5 You are analyzing a firm that is financed with 60 percent debt and 40 percent equity. The current cost of debt financing is 10 percent, but due to a recent downgrade by the rating agencies, the firm's cost of debt is expected to increase to 12 percent immediately. How will this change the firm's weighted average cost of capital if you ignore taxes?

Solutions to Self-Study Problems

11.1 Since the identity that Assets = Liabilities + Equity holds for market values as well as book values, we know that the market value of the firm's equity is $3 billion − $2 billion, or $1 billion.

11.2 Because Berron enjoys a tax deduction for its interest charges, the after-tax interest expense for Berron is $8 million × (1 − 0.35) = $5.2 million, which translates into an annual after-tax interest expense of $5.2/$100 = 0.052, or 5.2 percent.

11.3 The U.S. tax code allows a deduction for interest expense incurred on borrowing. Preferred and common shares are not considered debt and, thus, do not benefit from an interest deduction. As a result, there is no distinction between the before-tax and after-tax cost of equity capital.

11.4 Mike's T-Shirts's total firm value = $400 + $600 = $1,000. Therefore,

Debt = 40% of financing
Equity = 60% of financing
$\text{WACC} = x_{Debt}k_{Debt}(1 - t) + x_{ps}k_{ps} + x_{cs}k_{cs}$
$\text{WACC} = (0.4 \times 0.11) + (0.6 \times 0.17) = 0.146$, or 14.6%

11.5 The pretax debt contribution to the cost of capital is $x_{Debt} \times k_{Debt}$, and since the firm's pretax cost of debt is expected to increase by 2 percent, we know that the effect on WACC (pretax) will be 0.6 × 0.02 = 0.012, or 1.2 percent. Incidentally, if we assume that the firm is subject to the 40 percent marginal tax rate, then the after-tax increase in the cost of capital for the firm would be 0.012 × (1 − 0.4) = 0.0072, or 0.72 percent.

Critical Thinking Questions

11.1 Explain why the required rate of return on a firm's assets must be equal to the weighted average cost of capital associated with its liabilities and equity.

11.2 Which is easier to calculate directly, the expected rate of return on the assets of a firm or the expected rate of return on the firm's debt and equity? Assume that you are an outsider to the firm.

11.3 With respect to the level of risk and the required return for a firm's portfolio of projects, discuss how the market and a firm's management can have inconsistent information and expectations.

11.4 Your friend has recently told you that the federal government effectively subsidizes the use of debt financing (vs. equity financing) for corporations. Do you agree with that statement? Explain.

11.5 Your firm will have a fixed interest expense for the next 10 years. You recently found out that the marginal income tax rate for the firm will change from 30 percent to 40 percent next year. Describe how the change will affect the cash flow available to investors.

11.6 Describe why it is not usually appropriate to use the coupon rate on a firm's bonds to estimate the pretax cost of debt for the firm.

11.7 Maltese Falcone, Inc., has not checked its weighted average cost of capital for four years. Firm management claims that since Maltese has not had to raise capital for new projects in four years, they should not have to worry about their current weighted average cost of capital. They argue that they have essentially locked in their cost of capital. Critique management's statements.

11.8   Ten years ago, the Edson Water Company issued preferred stock at a price equal to the par value of $100. If the dividend yield on that issue was 12 percent, explain why the firm's current cost of preferred capital is not likely to equal 12 percent.

11.9   Discuss under what circumstances you might be able to use a model that assumes constant growth in dividends to calculate the current cost of equity capital for a firm.

11.10   Your boss just finished computing your firm's weighted average cost of capital. He is relieved because he says that he can now use that cost of capital to evaluate all projects that the firm is considering for the next four years. Evaluate that statement.

Questions and Problems

11.1   Finance balance sheet: KneeMan Markup Company has total debt obligations with book and market values equal to $30 million and $28 million, respectively. It also has total equity with book and market values equal to $20 million and $70 million, respectively. If you were going to buy all of the assets of KneeMan Markup today, how much should you be willing to pay?   **< BASIC**

EXCEL®
More interactive Excel® exercises available in
WileyPLUS

11.2   WACC: What is the weighted average cost of capital?

11.3   Taxes and the cost of debt: How are taxes accounted for when we calculate the cost of debt?

11.4   Cost of common stock: List and describe each of the three methods used to calculate the cost of common stock.

11.5   Cost of common stock: Whitewall Tire Co. just paid an annual dividend of $1.60 on its common shares. If Whitewall is expected to increase its annual dividend by 2 percent per year into the foreseeable future and the current price of Whitewall's common shares is $11.66, what is the cost of common stock for Whitewall?

11.6   Cost of common stock: Seerex Wok Co. is expected to pay a dividend of $1.10 one year from today on its common shares. That dividend is expected to increase by 5 percent every year thereafter. If the price of Seerex common stock is $13.75, what is the cost of its common equity capital?

11.7   Cost of common stock: Two-Stage Rocket paid an annual dividend of $1.25 yesterday, and it is commonly known that the firm's management expects to increase its dividend by 8 percent for the next two years and by 2 percent thereafter. If the current price of Two-Stage's common stock is $17.80, what is the cost of common equity capital for the firm?

11.8   Cost of preferred stock: Fjord Luxury Liners has preferred shares outstanding that pay an annual dividend equal to $15 per year. If the current price of Fjord preferred shares is $107.14, what is the after-tax cost of preferred stock for Fjord?

11.9   Cost of preferred stock: Kresler Autos has preferred shares outstanding that pay annual dividends of $12, and the current price of the shares is $80. What is the after-tax cost of new preferred shares for Kresler if the flotation (issuance) costs for preferred are 5 percent?

11.10   WACC: Describe the alternatives to using a firm's WACC as a discount rate when evaluating a project.

11.11   WACC for a firm: Capital Co. has a capital structure, based on current market values, that consists of 50 percent debt, 10 percent preferred stock, and 40 percent common stock. If the returns required by investors are 8 percent, 10 percent, and 15 percent for the debt, preferred stock, and common stock, respectively, what is Capital's after-tax WACC? Assume that the firm's marginal tax rate is 40 percent.

11.12   WACC: What are direct out-of-pocket costs?

11.13   Finance balance sheet: Explain why the total value of all of the securities used to finance a firm must be equal to the value of the firm.   **< INTERMEDIATE**

11.14   Finance balance sheet: Explain why the cost of capital for a firm is equal to the expected rate of return to the investors in the firm.

11.15   Current cost of a bond: You know that the after-tax cost of debt capital for Bubbles Champagne is 7 percent. If the firm has only one issue of five-year bonds outstanding, what is the current price of the bonds if the coupon rate on those bonds is 10 percent? Assume the bonds make semiannual coupon payments and the marginal tax rate is 30 percent.

11.16 Current cost of a bond: Perpetual Ltd. has issued bonds that never require the principal amount to be repaid to investors. Correspondingly, Perpetual must make interest payments into the infinite future. If the bondholders receive annual payments of $75 and the current price of the bonds is $882.35, what is the after-tax cost of this debt for Perpetual if the firm is in the 40 percent marginal tax rate?

11.17 Current cost of a bond: You are analyzing the cost of debt for a firm. You know that the firm's 14-year maturity, 8.5 percent coupon bonds are selling at a price of $823.48. The bonds pay interest semiannually. If these bonds are the only debt outstanding, what is the after-tax cost of debt for this firm if it has a 30 percent marginal and average tax rate?

11.18 Taxes and the cost of debt: Holding all other things constant, does a decrease in the marginal tax rate for a firm provide incentive for the firm to increase or decrease its use of debt?

11.19 Cost of debt for a firm: You are analyzing the after-tax cost of debt for a firm. You know that the firm's 12-year maturity, 9.5 percent semiannual coupon bonds are selling at a price of $1,200. If these bonds are the only debt outstanding for the firm, what is the after-tax cost of debt for this firm if it has a marginal tax rate of 34 percent? What if the bonds are selling at par?

11.20 Cost of common stock: Underestimated Inc.'s common shares currently sell for $36 each. The firm's management believes that its shares should really sell for $54 each. If the firm just paid an annual dividend of $2 per share and management expects those dividends to increase by 8 percent per year forever (and this is common knowledge to the market), what is the current cost of common equity for the firm and what does management believe is the correct cost of common equity for the firm?

11.21 Cost of common stock: Write out the general equation for the price of the stock for a firm that will grow dividends very rapidly at a constant rate for the four years after the next dividend is paid and will grow dividends thereafter at a constant, but lower rate. Discuss the problems in estimating the cost of equity capital for such a stock.

11.22 Cost of common stock: You have calculated the cost of common stock using all three methods described in this chapter. Unfortunately, all three methods have yielded different answers. Describe which answer (if any) is most appropriate.

11.23 WACC for a firm: The managers of a firm financed entirely with common stock are evaluating two distinct projects. The first project has a large amount of unsystematic risk and a small amount of systematic risk. The second project has a small amount of unsystematic risk and a large amount of systematic risk. Which project, if taken, is more likely to increase the firm's cost of capital?

11.24 WACC for a firm: The Imaginary Products Co. currently has debt with a market value of $300 million outstanding. The debt consists of 9 percent coupon bonds (semiannual coupon payments) which have a maturity of 15 years and are currently priced at $1,440.03 per bond. The firm also has an issue of 2 million preferred shares outstanding with a market price of $12.00. The preferred shares pay an annual dividend of $1.20. Imaginary also has 14 million shares of common stock outstanding with a price of $20.00 per share. The firm is expected to pay a $2.20 common dividend one year from today, and that dividend is expected to increase by 5 percent per year forever. If Imaginary is subject to a 40 percent marginal tax rate, then what is the firm's weighted average cost of capital?

11.25 Choosing a discount rate: For the Imaginary Products firm in Problem 11.24, calculate the appropriate cost of capital for a new project that is financed with the same proportion of debt, preferred shares, and common shares as the firm's current capital structure. Also assume that the project has the same degree of systematic risk as the average project that the firm is currently undertaking (the project is also in the same general industry as the firm's current line of business).

11.26 Choosing a discount rate: If a firm's management anticipates financing a project with a capital mix that is different from its current capital structure, describe how the firm is subjecting itself to a calculation error if its historical WACC is used to evaluate the project.

ADVANCED > **11.27** You are analyzing the cost of capital for MacroSwift Corporation, which develops software operating systems for computers. The firm's dividend growth rate has been a very constant 3 percent per year for the past 15 years. Competition for the firm's current products is expected to develop in the next year, and MacroSwift is currently expanding its revenue stream into the multimedia industry. Evaluate the appropriateness of continuing to use a 3 percent growth rate in dividends for MacroSwift in your cost of capital model.

11.28 You are an external financial analyst evaluating the merits of a stock. Since you are using a dividend discount model approach to evaluate a cost of equity capital, you need to estimate the dividend growth rate for the firm in the future. Describe how you might go about doing this.

11.29 You know that the return of Momentum Cyclicals common shares is 1.6 times as sensitive to macroeconomic information as the return of the market. If the risk-free rate of return is 2.55 percent and market risk premium is 5.63 percent, what is Momentum Cyclicals' cost of common equity capital?

11.30 In your analysis of the cost of capital for a common stock, you calculate a cost of capital using a dividend discount model that is much lower than the calculation for the cost of capital using the CAPM model. Explain a possible source for the discrepancy.

11.31 RetRyder Hand Trucks has a preferred share issue outstanding that pays a dividend of $1.30 per year. The current cost of preferred equity for RetRyder is 9 percent. If RetRyder issues additional preferred shares that pay exactly the same dividend and the investment banker retains 8 percent of the sale price, what is the cost of the new preferred shares for RetRyder?

11.32 Enigma Corporation's management believes that the firm's cost of capital (WACC) is too high because the firm has been too secretive with the market concerning its operations. Evaluate that statement.

11.33 Discuss what valuable information would be lost if you decided to use book values in order to calculate the cost of each of the capital components within a firm's capital structure.

11.34 Hurricane Corporation is financed with debt, preferred equity, and common equity with market values of $20 million, $10 million, and $30 million, respectively. The betas for the debt, preferred stock, and common stock are 0.2, 0.5, and 1.1, respectively. If the risk-free rate is 2.55 percent, the market risk premium is 5.63 percent, and Hurricane's average and marginal tax rates are both 30 percent, what is the company's weighted average cost of capital?

11.35 You are working as an intern at Coral Gables Products, a privately owned manufacturing company. Shortly after you read Chapter 11 in this book, you got into a discussion with the Chief Financial Officer (CFO) at Coral Gables about weighted average cost of capital calculations. She pointed out that, just as the beta of the assets of a firm equals a weighted average of the betas for the individual assets, as shown in Equation 6.11:

$$\beta_{n\text{ Asset portfolio}} = \sum_{i=1}^{n} x_i\beta_i = x_1\beta_1 + x_2\beta_2 + x_3\beta_3 + \cdots + x_n\beta_n$$

the beta of the assets of a firm also equals a weighted average of the betas for the debt, preferred stock, and common stock of a firm:

$$\beta_{n\text{ Asset portfolio}} = \sum_{i=1}^{n} x_i\beta_i = x_{\text{Debt}}\beta_{\text{Debt}} + x_{\text{ps}}\beta_{\text{ps}} + x_{\text{cs}}\beta_{\text{cs}}$$

Why must this be true?

11.36 The CFO described in Problem 11.35 asks you to estimate the beta for Coral Gables's common stock. Since the common stock is not publicly traded, you do not have the data necessary to estimate the beta using regression analysis. However, you have found a company with publicly traded stock that has operations exactly like those at Coral Gables. Using stock returns for this pure-play comparable firm, you estimate the beta for the comparable company's stock to be 1.06. The market value of that company's common equity is $45 million, and it has one debt issue outstanding with a market value of $15 million and an annual pretax cost of 4.85 percent. The comparable company has no preferred stock.

a. If the risk-free rate is 2.55 percent and the market risk premium is 5.63 percent, what is the beta of the assets of the comparable company?

b. If the total market value of Coral Gables's financing consists of 35 percent debt and 65 percent equity (this is what the CFO estimates the market values to be) and the pretax cost of its debt is 5.45 percent, what is the beta for Coral Gables's common stock?

11.37 Estimate the weighted average cost of capital for Coral Gables using your estimated beta and the information in the problem statement in Problem 11.36. Assume that the average and marginal tax rates for Coral Gables are both 25 percent.

CFA PROBLEMS [>] **11.38** The cost of equity is equal to the:

    a. Expected market return.

    b. Rate of return required by stockholders.

    c. Cost of retained earnings plus dividends.

    d. Risk the company incurs when financing.

11.39 Dot.Com has determined that it could issue $1,000 face value bonds with an 8 percent coupon paid semiannually and a five-year maturity at $900 per bond. If Dot.Com's marginal tax rate is 38 percent, its after-tax cost of debt is closest to:

    a. 6.2 percent.

    b. 6.4 percent.

    c. 6.6 percent.

    d. 6.8 percent.

11.40 Morgan Insurance Ltd. issued a fixed-rate perpetual preferred stock three years ago and placed it privately with institutional investors. The stock was issued at $25.00 per share with a $1.75 dividend. If the company were to issue preferred stock today, the yield would be 6.5 percent. The stock's current value is:

    a. $25.00.

    b. $26.92.

    c. $37.31.

    d. $40.18.

11.41 The Gearing Company has an after-tax cost of debt capital of 4 percent, a cost of preferred stock of 8 percent, a cost of equity capital of 10 percent, and a weighted average cost of capital of 7 percent. Gearing intends to maintain its current capital structure as it raises additional capital. In making its capital-budgeting decisions for the average-risk project, the relevant cost of capital is:

    a. 4 percent.

    b. 7 percent.

    c. 8 percent.

    d. 10 percent.

11.42 Suppose the cost of capital of the Gadget Company is 10 percent. If Gadget has a capital structure that is 50 percent debt and 50 percent equity, its before-tax cost of debt is 5 percent, and its marginal tax rate is 20 percent, then its cost of equity capital is closest to:

    a. 10 percent.

    b. 12 percent.

    c. 14 percent.

    d. 16 percent.

Sample Test Problems

11.1 The Balanced, Inc., has three different product lines. Its least risky product line has a beta of 1.7, while its middle-risk product line has a beta of 1.8, and its most risky product line has a beta of 2.1. The market value of the assets invested in these lines is $1 billion for the least risky line, $3 billion for the middle-risk line, and $7 billion for the riskiest product line. What is the beta of the assets of The Balanced, Inc.? (Hint: see Problem 11.35)

11.2 Ellwood Corp. has a five-year bond issue outstanding with a coupon rate of 10 percent and a price of $1,039.56. If the bonds pay coupons semiannually, what is the pretax cost of the debt and what is the after-tax cost of the debt? Assume the marginal tax rate for the firm is 40 percent.

11.3 Miron's Copper Corp. management expects its common stock dividends to grow 1.5 percent per year for the indefinite future. The firm's shares are currently selling for $18.45, and the firm just paid a dividend of $3.00 yesterday. What is the cost of common stock for this firm?

11.4 Micah's Time Portals has a preferred stock issue outstanding that pays an annual dividend of $2.50 per year and is currently selling for $27.78 a share. What is the cost of preferred stock for this firm?

11.5 The New Age Co. has a portfolio of projects with a beta of 1.25. The firm is currently evaluating a new project that involves a new product in a new competitive market. Briefly discuss what adjustment New Age might make to its 1.25 beta in order to evaluate this new project.

Financial Planning and Managing Growth

CHAPTER SIXTEEN

Learning Objectives

1. Explain what a financial plan is and why financial planning is so important.

2. Discuss how management uses financial planning models in the planning process, and explain the importance of sales forecasts in the construction of financial planning models.

3. Discuss how the relation between projected sales and balance sheet accounts can be determined, and analyze a strategic investment decision using a percent of sales model.

4. Describe the conditions under which fixed assets vary directly with sales, and discuss the impact of so-called lumpy assets on this relation.

5. Explain what factors determine a firm's sustainable growth rate, discuss why it is of interest to management, and compute the sustainable growth rate for a firm.

In January 2008 the decline in performance of the Starbucks Corporation had come to a head. Former CEO Howard Schultz once again took over the day-to-day operations of the coffee giant in an effort to restructure the company. The growth of Starbucks had been meteoric: from six stores in 1987 to more than 17,000 stores and outlets in over 40 countries. Fast growth for Starbucks had come at a price. Management was concerned that the company had lost its focus on product quality and the customer experience in Starbucks stores. These issues hindered the company's ability to attract customers who were willing to pay for its premium-priced products. Increased competition for coffee consumers from brands such as McDonald's and Dunkin' Donuts, combined with the global economic downturn, also hurt Starbucks's bottom line and the firm's investors took notice. Fourth quarter net income in 2008 was down 97 percent from 2007, and the company's stock price had declined over 50 percent during the previous year.

In a letter to his employees, Schultz summarized the problems that rapid growth had brought the firm: "If we take an honest look at Starbucks today, then we know that we are emerging from a period in which we invested in infrastructure ahead of the growth curve. Although necessary, it led to bureaucracy. We will now shift our emphasis back onto customer-facing initiatives, better aligning our back-end costs with our business model."

Starbucks management focused its restructuring efforts on slowing growth. Starting in 2008, Starbucks canceled the opening of more than 100 stores, closed approximately 900 poorly performing outlets (most of which were in the United States), and cut nearly $600 million in costs.

At the same time, Starbucks shifted its new store investment to more profitable foreign markets. Additional efforts were dedicated to improving product quality and customer experience. For example, warm breakfast sandwiches were eliminated because they competed with the coffee aroma in stores. The company also required that all employees take a three-hour training session on making espresso. Finally, Starbucks management made an effort to compete with value-based rivals by introducing a lower-cost brand called Pike Place.

Starbucks's restructuring has been a success for its investors. Between 2009 and 2012, the firm's net income increased 254 percent, with 142 percent of this increase occurring between 2009 and 2010 alone. The company's stock price rose from a low of $9.00 per share in 2008 to $53.63 per share on December 31, 2012. Despite its turnaround, Starbucks's rapid expansion and severe decline in operating performance serves as a stark reminder of the need for thoughtful corporate growth, combined with feasible operating and financial strategies. This chapter discusses how firms plan for the future and manage growth to create value.

CHAPTER PREVIEW

It is often said that a company that fails to plan for the future may have no future. In the short run, a firm may do well being opportunistic—reacting quickly to events as they unfold. To succeed over the long term, however, a firm must be innovative and must plan and employ a strategy that generates sustainable profits. Top executives spend a lot of time thinking about the types of investments the firm needs to make and how to finance them. The process that executives go through is called financial planning, and the result is called a financial plan.

This chapter focuses on long-term financial planning. We begin with a discussion of the firm's strategic plan and its components. We then discuss the preparation of a financial plan. Next, we turn our attention to financial planning models used in the preparation of financial plans. These models generate projected financial statements that estimate the amount of external funding needed and identify other financial consequences of proposed strategic investments. We end the chapter by examining the relation between a firm's growth and its need for external funding. Managing growth is an important topic, because growth without sufficient profits can lead to cash flow shortages and bankruptcy.

16.1 FINANCIAL PLANNING

 LEARNING OBJECTIVE

financial planning
the process by which management decides what types of investments the firm needs to make and how to finance those investments

financial plan
a plan outlining the investments a firm intends to make and how it will finance them

Top management engages in long-term **financial planning** because experience has shown that having a well-articulated **financial plan** helps them create value for stockholders. Planning is important for established businesses because it forces management to systematically think through the firm's strategies, much like preparing a business plan helps an entreprenuer. Not surprisingly, the lack of planning is a common reason for poor performance and bankruptcy. For example, the bankruptcy filing by Ronco Corporation in June 2007 was attributed to a failure to plan and recognize the importance of the firm's traditional distribution channels. Ronco was the manufacturer of the Veg-O-Matic vegetable slicer and other novelty gadgets, such as Mr. Microphone and a device that mixes eggs inside the shells.[1]

The Planning Documents

When top management begins to prepare a company's financial plan, it must answer four basic questions. First, where is the company headed? Second, what assets does it need to get there?

---

[1]Ronco's founder, Ron Popeil, became a minor household celebrity hawking the firm's products on late-night television.

Third, how is the firm going to pay for these assets? And finally, does the firm have enough cash to pay its day-to-day bills as they come due?

These questions are answered in four important planning documents: (1) the *strategic plan*, which describes where the firm is headed and articulates the strategies that will be used to get it there; (2) the *investment plan*, which identifies the capital assets needed to execute the strategies; (3) the *financing plan*, which explains how the firm will raise the money to buy the assets; and (4) the *cash budget*, which determines whether the firm will have sufficient cash to pay its bills. These four planning documents provide the foundation for the firm's *financial plan*, which consolidates the documents into a single scheme. Thus, the financial plan is a blueprint for the firm's future.

Exhibit 16.1 shows the relations among the various plans and budgets. Notice that information from the strategic plan flows down to the financial plan and information from the other plans and the cash budget flows up to the financial plan.

The Strategic Plan

Strategic planning is the most crucial planning step. The strategic plan sets out the vision for the firm—what management wants the firm to become—and establishes the strategies that management will use to achieve their vision. Overall, the strategic plan provides high-level direction to management for making business decisions and guidance about what the firm will and will not do.

Preparing the strategic plan is the responsibility of top management, with the financial manager as a key participant and the board of directors as approver of the plan. The strategic plan covers all areas in the firm, such as operations, marketing, finance, information systems, and human resource management. The plan determines the lines of business in which the firm will compete and the relative emphasis placed on each business activity. It also identifies

strategic planning
the process by which management establishes the firm's long-term goals, the strategies that will be used to achieve those goals, and the capabilities that are needed to sustain the firm's competitive position

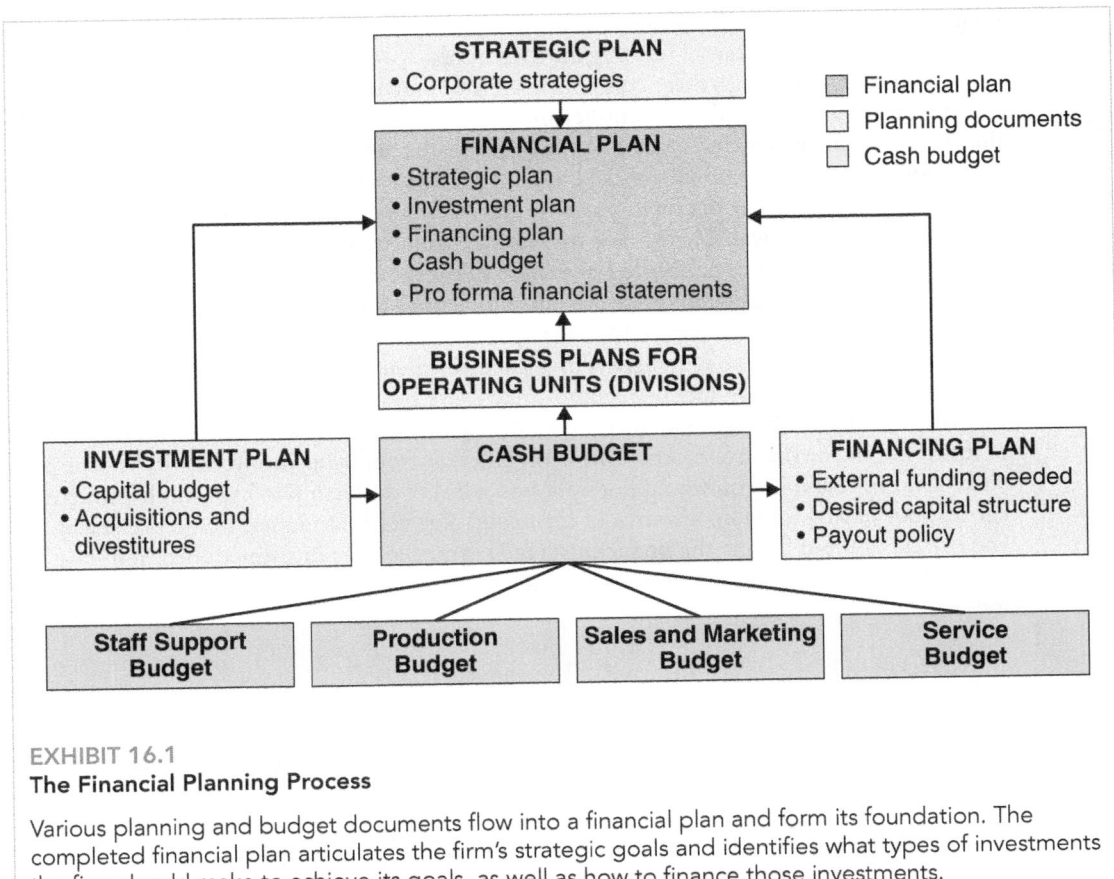

EXHIBIT 16.1
The Financial Planning Process

Various planning and budget documents flow into a financial plan and form its foundation. The completed financial plan articulates the firm's strategic goals and identifies what types of investments the firm should make to achieve its goals, as well as how to finance those investments.

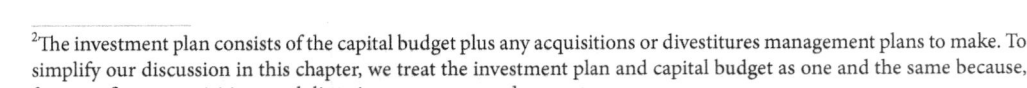

BUILDING INTUITION

A FIRM'S STRATEGY DRIVES ITS BUSINESS DECISIONS

The firm's business strategy drives all of its decisions. It determines the firm's lines of business, the products it will sell, its method of producing them, and the geographic markets in which it will compete. Thus, a company's strategy defines its competitive position within its industry. To be successful, a firm must formulate the right strategy and have a management team that can implement it. Management is always searching for a strategy that gives the firm a sustainable competitive edge.

major areas for investments in productive assets: capital expenditures, the acquisition of a firm, or the launch of a new line of business. When deemed necessary, the plan also identifies mergers, alliances, and divestitures that management may seek to strengthen the firm's business portfolio.

The Investment Plan

The investment plan, also known as the capital budget, lays out the firm's proposed spending on capital assets for the year.[2] The capital expenditures support the firm's business strategy. Some capital expenditures pay for significant new additions, such as a new building, a new plant, or a new production line. Other capital expenditures are for more routine items, such as the replacement of old equipment and machinery. Once made, capital expenditures define a firm's line of business for years to come. For example, Ford Motor Company could not suddenly start making tennis shoes instead of cars because Ford's long-term assets hardly lend themselves to manufacturing shoes and the cost of conversion would be prohibitive. The preparation of the capital budget and the decision criteria for selecting capital projects are discussed in Chapters 9 through 11.

The Financing Plan

Once the capital budget is set, management must decide how to finance the assets. The simplest financing environment is one in which all capital projects are financed using *internally* generated funds. This means that the firm's earnings, less cash used to pay dividends or repurchase stock, provide the necessary capital. However, only rarely does a firm finance all its projects in this way, as most firms have more capital projects than they can fund internally. Thus, management must seek *external* funding from a variety of sources, such as bank borrowing, selling of long-term debt, and issuance of additional equity. Overall, the goal of the financing plan is to determine how much external funding the firm needs.

The financing plan has three components. First, a financing plan states the dollar amount of *external funding needed* and identifies the sources of funds available to the firm. Second, the plan states management's *desired capital structure* for the firm. This is important because it determines the relative amounts of debt and equity funds to be raised externally. Finally, the financing plan establishes the firm's *payout policy*, which is relevant because it directly affects the amount of funds available for new investment projects. That is, the more funds the firm pays out as cash dividends or uses to repurchase stock, the more external capital the firm must raise if its internally generated funds are not sufficient to fund its investments. Capital structure policy is discussed in Chapter 14, and payout policy in Chapter 15.

An important point to note here is that the investment (capital budgeting) and financing decisions *cannot* be made independently—they must be considered together. The reason is that when management makes an investment decision, it must already have identified a source of funds to pay for the investment. This is no different from what you would do in your personal life. For example, you would not walk into a BMW dealership to buy a high-priced new car without having lined up a source of financing. Nor, for that matter, would the dealer sell you the car without having the financing already arranged. The investment decision (buy the car) and the financing decision (get an auto loan) are made simultaneously and hence are not independent.

Operating Unit (Divisional) Business Plans

Another component of the financial plan is made up of the *business plans* prepared by the various operating units or divisions within the firm. Each operating unit business plan describes

> A source for sample business plans, including financial plans, is the Center for Business Planning at http://www.businessplans.org/tabplan.html.

---

[2]The investment plan consists of the capital budget plus any acquisitions or divestitures management plans to make. To simplify our discussion in this chapter, we treat the investment plan and capital budget as one and the same because, for most firms, acquisitions and divestitures are not regular events.

what the unit will do to achieve the firm's strategic goals. It also identifies the resources the unit needs and includes a detailed budget. It is here at the operating unit level that much of the firm's budget work is done.

For example, assume that one of Ford Motor Company's strategic goals is to manufacture and sell jet-skis through its marine division. The division has some idle capacity in one of its manufacturing plants. Thus, as part of the division's business plan, it submits a capital budgeting request to enter the jet-ski market. (Of course, to be included in Ford's capital budget, the jet-ski project must have an NPV greater than $0.)

Cash Budget

The cash budget for the firm is the aggregation (adding up) of the cash budgets from all of the operating units plus the cash budget for the corporate offices. The cash budget focuses exclusively on when the firm actually receives and pays out cash. The firm's cash needs may vary weekly, monthly, and seasonally, as well as with predictable events such as payroll payments, payment of cash dividends, and debt retirements. If a shortfall of cash develops, the cash budget indicates the amount of money the firm needs to borrow and the anticipated borrowing cost.

As Exhibit 16.1 shows, the planning process drills down deep into the firm and gathers cash budget information on the myriad of activities that take place. If cash budgets are not well managed and monitored, serious cash shortages can occur. Tools used in cash management are discussed in Chapter 12.

Concluding Comments

The principal benefit of financial planning is that it establishes financial and operating goals for the firm and communicates them throughout the organization. The financial plan also helps to align the actions of managers and their operating units with the firm's strategic goals. Thus, the plan acts as a catalyst to get everyone in the firm moving in the same direction. To build support for the financial plan and energize people's actions, top management should involve managers and other leaders in the firm at all levels in the planning process. An old axiom in management says that people support plans when they have had meaningful involvement in the plans' preparation.

> **BEFORE YOU GO ON**

1. What are the four planning documents on which the financial plan is based?

2. What is the strategic plan?

3. How are the investment decision and financing decision related?

16.2 FINANCIAL PLANNING MODELS

LEARNING OBJECTIVE

Financial planning models are used to analyze how proposed investments and financing alternatives affect a firm's financial statements. The models are usually run on computer spreadsheets, which reduce the drudgery of tracing investment, financing, and operating decisions through a company's accounting system. While commercial planning models have an aura of sophistication about them, most are built around the same basic concepts presented in this chapter.

In this section, we build a simple financial planning model to show how such models are constructed, how they work, and how their output is generated. Once you understand this model, you can easily step up to more advanced models.

The Sales Forecast

The sales forecast is the most important input for developing a financial planning model. Most firms generate their own sales forecasts. However, forecasting techniques vary widely, ranging from "seat-of-the-pants" forecasts—wherein the sales manager and key sales staff members talk it over and give their best estimate—to forecasts generated by complex statistical models. In addition, because the performance of the national and international economies have an effect on a company's sales volume, most companies use economic forecasts as part of their sales forecasting process. Large companies often hire consulting firms that specialize in forecasting to help prepare sales forecasts under different scenarios. As you would expect, their services are quite expensive; economic forecasts can also be obtained from many regional banks at modest prices.

Building a Financial Planning Model

A financial planning model is no more than a series of equations that are used to generate projected financial statements for a company, such as an income statement or a balance sheet. The three basic components of a financial planning model, shown in Exhibit 16.2, are (1) inputs to the model, (2) the model itself, and (3) outputs from the model—the projected financial statements. Let's discuss each component in turn.

Inputs to the Model

As shown in the exhibit, important inputs to the financial planning model include current financial statements, sales forecasts, and investment and financial policy decisions.

Hoovers provides financial statements for publicly held firms online at http://www.hoovers.com. Another source for financial statements is the EDGAR database of the Securities and Exchange Commission: http://www.sec.gov.

Current Financial Statements. The starting point for constructing a financial planning model is the firm's current income statement and balance sheet. These statements serve as a baseline.

Sales Forecasts. For most financial planning models, the principal input variable is a forecast of the firm's sales or sales growth rate. The sales forecast is the key driver in financial models because so many items on the income statement and balance sheet vary with changes in the level of sales. For example, if sales increase, it stands to reason that the firm will use more labor and raw materials. Higher sales may also require additional investments in capital assets.

Sales forecasts are given for some time period, such as a quarter or a year, and are often expressed as percent change in sales:

$$\%\Delta S = \frac{(S_{t+1} - S_t)}{S_t} \tag{16.1}$$

where:

$\%\Delta S$ = percent change in net sales
S_t = level of net sales in period t
S_{t+1} = level of net sales in period $t+1$

Sales are calculated as the number of units sold times the price at which they are sold. For an example of how Equation 16.1 is used, if the current year's sales (S_t) are \$100 million and the

Inputs to the Model	The Financial Planning Model	Outputs from the Model
• Current financial statements • Sales forecasts • Investment and financial policy decisions	• Equations generating financial statements • Key economic assumptions	• Projected financial statements • Financial ratios • Cash budget

EXHIBIT 16.2
The Components of a Financial Planning Model

We can categorize the parts of a financial planning model as inputs, the model itself, and outputs. Models allow management to generate projected financial statements which enable them to see the financial impact of strategic initiatives.

forecasted sales for next year (S_{t+1}) are $120 million, applying Equation 16.1 yields the percent growth in sales over the coming year:

$$\% \Delta S = \frac{(S_{t+1} - S_t)}{S_t} = \frac{(\$120 - \$100)}{\$100} = 0.20, \text{ or } 20\%$$

Investment and Financial Policy Decisions. Preparing a financial planning model requires top management to make a number of investment and financial policy decisions. These decisions impose constraints on the financial model's outputs that must be recognized during its preparation. Some important investment and financial policy decisions are:

- *Investment policy decisions:* Identify the investment decisions to be evaluated as part of the financial planning process. Typically, these are large capital expenditures such as building a new manufacturing facility, entering a new line of business, or acquiring another firm.
- *Financial policy decisions:*
  - *Capital structure decision:* Determines management's targeted capital structure—its willingness to use financial leverage.
  - *Financing decision:* Determines the acceptable type of financing—retained earnings, equity, preferred stock, and/or long-term debt.
  - *Payout decision:* Identifies the firm's dividend and stock repurchase policies for the sales period.

The Financial Planning Model

A financial planning model is a set of equations that generate projected financial statements. Along with the sales forecast and the investment and financial policy decisions, management must specify key assumptions regarding how the income statement and the balance sheet accounts vary with sales. For example, suppose that, based on historical data, a company finds that cost of goods sold is 80 percent of sales and inventory and accounts receivables are each 15 percent of sales. In such a case, it might be reasonable to assume that these relations will hold for the projected income statement and balance sheet. Thus, if sales are projected to be $100 million next year, the projected cost of goods sold will be $80 million ($100 million × 0.80 = $80 million) and inventory and accounts receivable will both be $15 million ($100 million × 0.15 = $15 million).

Financial Statement Items Often Vary with Sales

PROBLEM: You have the following information: (1) sales this year are $50 million; (2) sales are expected to grow by 20 percent next year; and (3) for the current year, accounts receivable are 7 percent of sales and inventory is 10 percent of sales. Your boss has asked you to estimate next year's sales, accounts receivable, and inventory.

APPROACH: You can rearrange Equation 16.1 to find next year's sales level (S_{t+1}). Then, assuming accounts receivable and inventory grow proportionately with sales, you can use the result to calculate the expected levels of accounts receivable and inventory for next year.

SOLUTION:

$$\% \Delta S = \frac{(S_{t+1} - S_t)}{S_t}$$

$$0.2 = \frac{(S_{t+1} - \$50,000,000)}{\$50,000,000}$$

$$S_{t+1} = (0.2 \times \$50,000,000) + \$50,000,000$$
$$= \$60,000,000$$

$$\text{Accounts receivable} = \$60,000,000 \times 0.07 = \$4,200,000$$

$$\text{Inventory} = \$60,000,000 \times 0.10 = \$6,000,000$$

Outputs from the Model: Projected Financial Statements

The outputs from the financial planning model are projected financial statements called **pro forma financial statements**. In finance and accounting, the term *pro forma* means forecasted or projected.[3] The statements produced by a financial planning model are forecasted based on the inputs and assumptions entered into the model. In addition to pro forma financial statements, computer-based planning models usually generate a set of financial ratios similar to those discussed in Chapter 4 and include features that enable management to prepare a cash budget.

pro forma financial statements
projected financial statements that reflect a set of assumptions concerning investment, financing, and operating decisions

A Simple Planning Model

Let's work through a simple example to see how a financial planning model generates pro forma financial statements and is used to analyze a strategic investment.[4] This simple model, along with the other planning models presented in this chapter, is a **percent of sales model**, in which most of the variables in the model vary directly with the level of sales. Keep in mind that more sophisticated planning models are built around the same basic concepts—there are just more assumptions to deal with. The important point here is to make sure you understand how the model is built on a set of assumptions and how it generates the pro forma financial statements.

percent of sales model
a simple financial planning model that assumes that most income statement and balance sheet accounts vary proportionally with sales

Generating Pro Forma Statements

Sleepy Hollow Corporation's financial statements for the year that just ended are shown in simplified form in the following table:

Sleepy Hollow Corporation
Current Financial Statements ($ millions)

Income Statement		Balance Sheet			
Net sales	$1,000	Assets	$600	Debt	$400
Costs	700			Equity	200
Net income	$ 300	Total	$600	Total	$600

Sleepy Hollow's management expects sales to increase by 15 percent for the coming year. Assume that the financial statement accounts vary directly with changes in sales and that management has no financing plan at this time. Given this information, we can make the following calculations:

$$\text{Projected sales} = \$1,000 \text{ million} \times 1.15 = \$1,150 \text{ million}$$
$$\text{Projected costs} = \$700 \text{ million} \times 1.15 = \$805 \text{ million}$$

We now have the sales and cost figures for the firm's pro forma income statement:

Sleepy Hollow Corporation
Pro Forma Income Statement ($ millions)

Net sales	$1,150
Costs	805
Net income	$ 345

Thus, the firm's projected net income is $345 million.

Turning to the balance sheet, since we are assuming that all financial statement items vary with the change in sales, the projected values for the balance sheet accounts are:

$$\text{Projected assets} = \$600 \text{ million} \times 1.15 = \$690 \text{ million}$$
$$\text{Projected debt} = \$400 \text{ million} \times 1.15 = \$460 \text{ million}$$
$$\text{Projected equity} = \$200 \text{ million} \times 1.15 = \$230 \text{ million}$$

---

[3]The phrase *pro forma* is a Latin term that literally means "as a matter of form." In its modern context in finance and accounting, *pro forma* refers to data that are hypothetical.

[4]Note that to simplify the analysis, some of the income statement and balance sheet accounts used in the planning model are aggregated. For example, in our initial planning model, the balance sheet lists only total assets, debt, and equity.

and the resulting pro forma balance sheet is:

Sleepy Hollow Corporation Pro Forma Balance Sheet ($ millions)			
Assets	$690 ($90)	Debt	$460 ($60)
		Equity	230 (30)
Total	$690 ($90)	Total	$690 ($90)

The numbers in parentheses are the changes between the current and projected dollar amounts. Notice that all the balance sheet figures have increased by 15 percent and that the balance sheet balances. This is because both the sources and use of funds have increased by 15 percent. The $90 million in new assets is being financed by $30 million from retained earnings (internal financing) and $60 million from new long-term debt (external funding).

The balance sheet balances, but if you look back at the income statement, you may notice that the equity account does not look right. Recall that Sleepy Hollow's projected net income was $345 million. Adding this amount to the initial equity account balance of $200 million yields a final equity balance of $545 million ($345 million + $200 million = $545 million). As you can see, the equity balance in the pro forma balance sheet is $230 million. Why the apparent conflict?

As a general rule, whenever account balances differ or there is some confusion about an account, the easiest way to determine what is going on is to reconcile the account. For the equity account, if the firm is not expected to sell or repurchase stock, there are two basic transactions that could take place during the year: (1) the firm could generate income that is added to retained earnings and (2) management could pay a cash dividend or repurchase stock, which is subtracted from retained earnings (dividends) or reflected in the treasury share account (repurchased stock). Since the pro forma equity balance is lower than the sum of the initial equity account balance plus Sleepy Hollow's net income, the forecasts assume the firm will pay a dividend or repurchase stock. We can calculate how large this dividend or repurchase is as follows:

Beginning equity balance	=	$200 million
+ Net income	=	345 million
− Dividend or repurchase	=	X
Ending equity balance	=	$230 million

Solving for X, we find that:

Dividend or repurchase = ($200 million + $345 million) − $230 million = $315 million

The reconciliation makes the dividend or repurchase transaction transparent. It is clear that with a net income of $345 million and the constraint that the ending equity balance is $230 million, the firm must pay a $315 million cash dividend or repurchase $315 million of shares.

Evaluating an Investment Opportunity

Now let's suppose that Sleepy Hollow is considering building a new manufacturing plant. The project is estimated to cost $200 million and is to be financed entirely with debt. As in the prior example, sales are expected to increase by 15 percent for the year, and the plant will be placed in service the following year. Finally, assume that all financial statement accounts vary directly with changes in sales and that the current payout policy is to pay a $315 million cash dividend.

To determine whether the project is feasible as planned, management needs to prepare a set of pro forma financial statements that include the cost of the new facility. Sleepy Hollow's pro forma income statement will not change because of the building project. Thus, we can use Sleepy Hollow's income statement shown earlier. The preliminary pro forma balance sheet for the project, which excludes external funding, is as follows:

Sleepy Hollow's Building Project Preliminary Pro Forma Balance Sheet ($ millions)			
Asset	$690 ($90)	Debt	$400
New facility	200 ($200)	Equity	230 ($30)
Total	$890	Total	$630

We can see that total assets are $890 million, composed of the $690 million ($600 million ×
1.15 = $690 million) we calculated earlier plus $200 million for the new facility. The value of
the equity account remains unchanged at $230 million ($200 million × 1.15 = $230 million),
because it is subject to the 15 percent growth limit, and management must pay the $315 mil-
lion cash dividend. Since we do not know the amount of debt needed, we enter debt at the
current balance sheet amount of $400 million.

Now, comparing the totals, we see that the balance sheet does not balance: total assets
are $890 million, while total debt and equity equals $630 million. The difference between
the two numbers is $260 million ($890 million − $630 million = $260 million). This "plug
value" is the amount of **external funding needed (EFN)** by the firm. EFN is the additional
debt or equity a firm needs to issue so that it can meet its total funding requirements. In this
analysis, we refer to EFN as the plug value because it is the number we have to plug into the
balance sheet to get it to balance. In our example, the firm must issue $260 million of debt
because, as you recall, management made a decision to finance the new project entirely
with debt.

The final balance sheet, which includes the building project, is shown in the following
table. Overall, the firm is financing $290 million of new assets: $200 million for the new facility
and $90 million for new assets to support the increase in sales expected next year. The funding
is a combination of internal and external funding, which totals $290 million: $260 million in
debt (external) and $30 million in additions to retained earnings (internal). The firm is also
able to pay the required $315 million of cash dividends. If the firm can borrow the $260 million at a reasonable rate, it will be able to generate sufficient funds to finance the $200 million
capital project and pay the required cash dividend of $315 million.

**external funding needed
(EFN)**
the additional debt or equity
a firm must raise from external
sources to meet its total
funding requirements

Sleepy Hollow's Building Project
Final Pro Forma Balance Sheet ($ millions)

Asset	$690	($90)	Debt	$660	($260)
New facility	200	(200)	Equity	230	(30)
Total	$890	($290)	Total	$890	($290)

DECISION MAKING

EXAMPLE 16.1

Informed Judgment about Risk

SITUATION: You are given some additional information about Sleepy Hollow Corporation's use of financial leverage, as shown:

Debt to total assets before capital project   = $400/$600 = 66.7%
Debt to total assets after capital project   = $660/$890 = 74.2%
Industry average debt to total assets   = 40.0%

What should management do in light of this information?

DECISION: Sleepy Hollow's current leverage ratio of 66.7 percent is already high
compared with the industry average of 40 percent. If the firm goes ahead with the project, the leverage ratio will increase to 74.2 percent, which is even higher. The high debt
ratio makes the firm more risky and could negatively affect its stock price, its borrowing
cost, and even its ability to borrow money. A more prudent alternative would be to fund
at least part of the $290 million of new assets ($90 million + $200 million = $290 million)
with internally generated funds by reducing dividends or with externally raised equity by
selling new stock, or both.

The important point here is that financial planning models do not think for management. Even though the balance sheet balances and results are consistent with the firm's
financing plan, management must apply informed judgment.

16.3 A BETTER FINANCIAL PLANNING MODEL

The preceding section presented a simple financial planning model that assumes *all* income and balance sheet accounts vary directly with sales. Although that assumption is helpful to simplify calculations, it does not reflect what happens in the real world. We now relax our assumptions so that our model is more realistic and generates more accurate forecasts. We assume that all working capital accounts—current assets and liabilities—vary directly with sales. For other accounts in the financial statements, independent forecasts may be required, or values may be set by management based on other criteria. To illustrate the process, we will work through an example.

LEARNING OBJECTIVE 3

The Blackwell Sales Company

The Blackwell Sales Company is a small, privately owned company located in College Station, Texas. The firm serves the oil and gas exploration industry in Texas and the adjoining states. It sells and does light manufacturing of rigging equipment for oil and gas exploration. The firm's management owns 75 percent of the stock, with the balance owned by friends and outside investors. Blackwell's management is projecting a banner year, as sales are expected to increase 30 percent. The reason for the large increase is an oil and gas shortage caused by political instability in the Middle East. Because of the high-risk nature of their business, management is very conservative with respect to any action that might materially increase the firm's risk. Some of the management team is concerned about the risk associated with increasing sales by 30 percent in a one-year period.

The financial manager looks at the firm's financial statements and provides the following information:

- Net sales during the fiscal year that just ended were $2 million.
- Historical financial data indicate that the total cost of producing the firm's services and products averages 85 percent of sales.
- The firm's average tax rate is 34.1 percent and is not expected to change.
- The firm's payout policy is to pay 33.5 percent of earnings as cash dividends.

The Income Statement

Exhibit 16.3 shows the firm's current (most recent) and pro forma income statements. Let's look at the calculations used to arrive at the pro forma income statement. Management expects sales to increase by 30 percent next year, and so projected sales are $2 million × 1.30 = $2.6 million. Since total costs have averaged 85 percent of sales, projected total costs are $2.6 million × 0.85 = $2.21 million. Projected taxes, which are 34.1 percent of taxable income, are 0.341 × $390,000 = $132,990, which we will round to $133,000 for simplicity. Subtracting taxes from taxable income, we arrive at the firm's projected net income of $257,000.

Blackwell's cash dividend is $86,000 (0.335 × $257,000 = $86,095, which we will round to $86,000), and the remaining $171,000 of net income (0.665 × $257,000 = $170,905) is retained in the firm as an addition to retained earnings.

EXHIBIT 16.3	Blackwell Sales: Current and Pro Forma Income Statements ($ thousands)

The pro forma income statement for Blackwell Sales assumes that the income statement items vary directly with sales.

	Current	Pro Forma	Assumptions
Net sales	$2,000	$2,600	Sales increase: 30%
Costs	1,700	2,210	Total costs = 85% of sales
Taxable income	$ 300	$ 390	
Taxes (34.1%)	102	133	
Net income	$ 198	$ 257	
Dividends	$ 66	$ 86	Dividend policy: 33.5% of net income
Addition to retained earnings	$ 132	$ 171	

dividend payout ratio
the proportion of net income paid out (distributed) as dividends

retention (plowback) ratio
the proportion of net income retained in the firm

These amounts relate to two ratios we will use in this chapter: the **dividend payout ratio** and the **retention ratio, or plowback ratio**. The formulas and calculations for Blackwell are as follows:

$$\text{Dividend payout ratio} = \frac{\text{Cash dividends}}{\text{Net income}} \tag{16.2}$$

$$= \frac{\$86,000}{\$257.000} = 0.335, \text{ or } 33.5\%$$

$$\text{Retention (plowback) ratio} = \frac{\text{Addition to retained earnings}}{\text{Net income}} \tag{16.3}$$

$$= \frac{\$171,000}{\$257.000} = 0.665, \text{ or } 66.5\%$$

The dividend payout ratio shows the percentage of the firm's earnings paid out as cash dividends to stockholders. Similarly, the retention ratio tells what percentage of the firm's earnings is retained in the firm. Generally speaking, smaller, fast-growing companies plow back all or most of their earnings into the business, whereas more established firms with slower growth rates and larger cash flows distribute more of their profits to stockholders. Notice that the sum of the retention ratio and the dividend payout ratio equals 1.000 (0.335 + 0.665 = 1.000). This is because every dollar of net income is either paid out as a cash dividend or retained in the firm.

The Balance Sheet

To generate a pro forma balance sheet, we start with the current balance sheet, as shown in Exhibit 16.4. For each account that varies directly with sales, the exhibit gives the relation as a percent of sales for the current year. Notice that these percentages differ among the accounts. How do we determine which accounts vary with sales, and how do we know the relevant percentages? Fortunately, the process is straightforward.

Historical Trends

We begin by looking at balance sheet accounts that might vary with sales. To do this we gather four or five years of historical accounting data and express those data as a percent of sales. A trend may be self-evident, or some simple trend lines can be fit to the data to identify trends. In either case, this process allows the financial manager to decide which financial accounts can safely be estimated as a percent of sales and which must be forecast using other information.

The following table shows several years of historical data from Blackwell's balance sheet accounts, and the far-right column contains the final forecast values for 2014. We now discuss

EXHIBIT 16.4   Blackwell Sales: Current Balance Sheet ($ thousands)

In this balance sheet for Blackwell Sales, many accounts vary directly with sales. The projected percent of sales is shown for each of these accounts. The accounts labeled "n/a" do not change proportionately with sales.

Assets	Current	Projected % of sales	Liabilities and Stockholders' Equity	Current	Projected % of sales
Current assets			Current liabilities		
Cash	$ 100	5%	Accounts payable	$ 60	4%
Accounts receivable	120	6	Notes payable	140	n/a
Inventory	140	7	Total	$ 200	n/a
Total	$ 360	18%	Long-term debt	$ 200	n/a
			Owner's equity		
			Common stock	$ 10	n/a
			Retained earnings	590	n/a
			Total equity	$ 600	n/a
Net fixed assets	640	32	Total liabilities and		
Total assets	$1,000	50%	stockholders' equity	$1,000	50%

the rationale for assigning a percent of sales figure to each balance sheet account. We look first at the working capital accounts: cash, accounts receivable, inventory, and accounts payable.

	Percent of Sales				
					Forecast
	2010	2011	2012	2013	2014
Cash	5%	5%	4%	5%	5%
Accounts receivable	10	9	9	9	6
Inventory	7	8	7	6	7
Accounts payable	4	4	4	3	4
Net fixed assets	30	32	34	32	32

Working Capital Accounts

The key working capital accounts tend to vary directly with sales. Take inventory as an example. As sales increase, the firm needs to increase the level of inventory proportionately to support the higher sales level. The historical data in the table support this view. Inventory levels have been a relatively constant percentage of sales, varying from 6 to 8 percent. In selecting the appropriate percentage for the planning process, management must consider what the firm's optimal inventory ratio is. On the one hand, as discussed in Chapter 12, management would like to minimize inventory levels, because inventory is expensive to finance. On the other, if inventory levels become too low, the firm may lose sales because of stockouts, which occur when an order comes in and there is no product to sell. Let's assume that Blackwell's management determines that 7 percent of projected sales is the right inventory-to-sales ratio for the firm.

The ratio of accounts receivable to sales has been 9 percent for the last several years. However, firms with similar credit policies operate with a receivables-to-sales ratio of 6 percent. As sales have increased, Blackwell has provided proportionately more credit to its customers. To improve the firm's performance to industry standards, management decides to collect receivables more aggressively and targets a ratio of 6 percent. Management has also targeted cash accounts totaling 5 percent of sales. Management believes that a 5 percent cash ratio provides adequate liquidity to fund ongoing operations and pay for unexpected emergencies, yet does not tie up an excessive amount of cash in low-yielding assets.

On the liability side, the firm's historical data show that accounts payable vary with sales. This seems reasonable, since the greater a firm's sales, the more orders the firm will have to place with its suppliers. Management is satisfied with the firm's vendor relationships and the payment schedule for vendors. Hence, accounts payable are forecast to be 4 percent of sales.

Fixed Assets

We assume that the company's net fixed assets vary with the level of sales. An examination of historical data confirms that this is a reasonable assumption. Blackwell's management decides to use the firm's four-year historical average—32 percent—for the projected ratio of fixed assets to sales. Thus, for every $100 in sales, the firm needs $32 of fixed assets to support the sales.

We should note that such a relation between fixed assets and sales may not always hold. The reason is that fixed assets may vary directly with sales only when a firm is operating at full capacity and fixed assets can be added in small increments. For example, if a firm has a large amount of unused capacity, its sales could increase by 20 percent without adding any new fixed assets. We will come back to this issue in more detail later in the chapter. For Blackwell, the data support the proportional fixed assets-to-sales ratio, so we can proceed on that basis.

As a final comment, notice in Exhibit 16.4 on the asset side of the balance sheet that the total percent of sales for asset items adds up to 50 percent. This means that total assets are 50 percent of sales. The ratio of total assets to sales is called the *capital intensity ratio* and is calculated for Blackwell Sales as follows:

$$\text{Capital intensity ratio} = \frac{\text{Total assets}}{\text{Net sales}} \tag{16.4}$$

$$= \frac{\$1 \text{ million}}{\$2 \text{ million}} = 0.5, \text{ or } 50\%$$

The capital intensity ratio, which is the inverse of the total asset turnover ratio discussed in Chapter 4 (Equation 4.7), tells us something about the amount of assets the firm needs to generate $1 in sales. The higher the ratio, the more capital the firm needs to generate sales—that is, the more *capital intensive* the firm. Firms that are highly capital intensive tend to be more risky than similar firms that use less fixed assets. If there is a downturn in sales, profits decrease sharply for firms with high fixed costs because fixed costs cannot be reduced in the short term. High capital intensities are generally associated with high fixed assets and correspondingly high fixed costs. With a 50 percent capital intensity ratio, Blackwell Sales is not a highly capital-intensive firm. Examples of capital-intensive industries are the airline and the automobile industries; for example, both United Airlines and Ford Motor Company have capital intensity ratios greater than 100 percent.

Liabilities and Equity

For most firms, the remaining liability accounts on the balance sheet do not vary with sales. Their values typically change because of management decisions, such as the decision to pay off a loan or issue debt. Thus, each liability and equity account must be evaluated separately.

Turning to individual accounts, notes payable typically represent short-term borrowing. This account value will only change with some decision by Blackwell's management, such as making a payment on a note or borrowing more money from a bank. Thus, the account's value does not vary with sales, as indicated by the "n/a," or "not applicable," in Exhibit 16.4. Similarly, the account value for long-term debt changes only when management decides to issue or retire debt. The same argument holds for the common stock account, which changes only when management decides to sell or repurchase common shares. The last account is retained earnings. Retained earnings may or may not vary directly with sales. The reason for the ambiguity is that the amount of funds in retained earnings depends not only on the firm's earnings, but also on the firm's dividend policy, which is set by management. Thus, for now, both the common stock and the retained earnings accounts are entered as n/a in Exhibit 16.4.

The Preliminary Pro Forma Balance Sheet

We are now in a position to construct a preliminary pro forma balance sheet, as shown in Exhibit 16.5. The preliminary pro forma balance sheet is a first approximation in deciding how the firm should fund the assets it needs to support an increase in sales of 30 percent. Once it is constructed, management can develop a suitable financing plan.

EXHIBIT 16.5 Blackwell Sales: Preliminary Pro Forma Balance Sheet ($ thousands)

This preliminary pro forma balance sheet for Blackwell Sales is a first approximation in deciding how to fund anticipated growth. At this stage of the analysis, the balance sheet will not balance (Total Assets will not equal Liabilities and Stockholders' Equity), and the difference will be the plug value, which is usually the amount of external funding the firm will need in order to fund investments and operations.

Assets			Liabilities and Stockholders' Equity		
	Projected	Change		Projected	Change
Current assets			Current liabilities		
Cash	$ 130	$ 30	Accounts payable	$ 104	$ 44
Accounts receivable	156	36	Notes payable	140	0
Inventory	182	42	Total	$ 244	$ 44
Total	$ 468	$108	Long-term debt	$ 200	$ 0
			Owner's equity		
			Common stock	$ 10	$ 0
			Retained earnings	761	171
			Total equity	$ 771	$171
Net fixed assets	832	192	Total liabilities and		
Total assets	$1,300	$300	stockholders' equity	$1,215	$215
			External funding needed (EFN)	$ 85	$215

To construct the preliminary pro forma balance sheet, we follow these steps:

1. We first calculate the projected values for all the accounts that vary with sales, and we enter these values into the preliminary pro forma balance sheet.

2. We then compute and enter the projected value of any other balance sheet accounts for which an end-of-period value can be forecast or otherwise determined.

3. For all the accounts for which end-of-period values could not be forecast or otherwise determined (the n/a accounts), we enter the current year's value.

4. Typically, the balance sheet will not balance at this point. We thus compute the plug value, which balances the balance sheet. The plug value will involve the accounts marked "n/a" in the initial balance sheet (Exhibit 16.4). We must analyze these accounts in light of the firm's capital structure and dividend policies. The plug value is usually the amount of external funding needed (EFN), because we are usually adding new assets to the balance sheet to support growth; thus, total assets exceed total liabilities plus equity.

Let's work through each step using numbers from the Blackwell case.

Step One. We calculate the projected balance sheet values for the accounts that vary with sales as follows (projected sales are $2.6 million):

- Cash is projected to be 5 percent of sales: $2.6 million × 0.05 = $130,000.
- Accounts receivable is projected to be 6 percent of sales: $2.6 million × 0.06 = $156,000.
- Inventory is projected to be 7 percent of sales: $2.6 million × 0.07 = $182,000.
- Net fixed assets are projected to be 32 percent of sales: $2.6 million × 0.32 = $832,000.
- Accounts payable are projected to be 4 percent of sales: $2.6 million × 0.04 = $104,000.

These values, along with the differences between the current and forecast amounts, are shown in Exhibit 16.5.

Step Two. We now consider the balance sheet accounts that do not vary with sales. We can determine the value of retained earnings, since the firm has a dividend policy of paying out one-third of earnings as dividends. Recall from our earlier discussion that projected net income is $257,000 and the proportion of that amount going to retained earnings is $171,000 (0.665 × $257,000 = $171,000). Thus, the end-of-year account balance is $761,000 ($590,000 + $171,000 = $761,000), where $590,000 is the current retained earnings balance.

Step Three. The remaining accounts that do not vary with sales represent sources of financing for the firm: notes payable, long-term debt, and common stock. These accounts are entered into the preliminary pro forma balance sheet at their current values, as shown in Exhibit 16.5.

Step Four. As predicted, the preliminary pro forma balance sheet does not balance at this point: projected assets total $1.3 million, and projected sources of funding (debt and equity) total $1.215 million. The difference between these two values is our plug value. The plug value represents EFN, which is $85,000 ($1.3 million − $1.215 million = $85,000). Since we are dealing with a financing decision, all accounts with the n/a designation represent possible financing options. Management must use its judgment and its knowledge of Blackwell Sales to select the appropriate financing for the firm.

What the Findings Mean

What does all the information in Exhibit 16.5 tell management? First, if sales increase as projected, the firm's total assets will expand by $300,000. Of that $300,000 increase, $108,000 will go to increase current assets and $192,000 will go to increase the firm's fixed assets.

Second, the $300,000 in additional assets could be financed as follows: $171,000 from internally generated funds (the addition to retained earnings), $44,000 from expanded trade credit (the increase in accounts payable), and $85,000 of external funding from the sale of debt or equity or both.

Management's Decision

How should Blackwell Sales fund the $300,000 to support the 30 percent increase in sales? The firm could issue debt, equity, or reduce dividends. Alternatively, the firm could rethink its strategy and scale back the 30 percent targeted growth figure. Suppose Blackwell's management team meets to discuss the findings from Exhibit 16.5. After much discussion, they reach a consensus on the following points:

1. The firm has a unique opportunity to ride a strong market for oil and gas development and wants to pursue the 30 percent sales growth targeted.

2. Management is concerned about issuing more debt because of the volatility of the oil and gas exploration business.

3. Management prefers not to issue more common stock for fear of diluting earnings.

4. Management would like to pay an annual dividend but only when justified.

What does management do? In the end, management decides to pay no cash dividend to stockholders for the coming year. Thus, the $300,000 increase in assets is funded entirely from earnings. This decision is made to avoid the risks associated with additional debt and the dilution of earnings that would result from issuing additional common stock.

The Final Pro Forma Balance Sheet

Exhibit 16.6 shows the final pro forma balance sheet reflecting the decision to temporarily suspend dividends and fund the expansion with internal funds (retained earnings). As you recall, Blackwell's net income is $257,000; and thus, the retained earnings account is increased by $257,000, making the final balance $847,000 ($590,000 + $257,000 = $847,000). Since the proposed dividend of $86,000 now goes entirely into retained earnings, a source of funds, and the firm's additional financing needs are $85,000, there is $1,000 ($86,000 − $85,000 = $1,000) available to reduce debt. The most likely course of action is to reduce notes payable by $1,000, making notes payable $139,000 rather than $140,000.[5]

---

[5]Alternatively, we could have redone the preliminary pro forma balance sheet and found: Total Assets = $1.3 million and Total Liabilities and Stockholders' Equity = $1.301 million ($244,000 + $200,000 + $857,000 = $1,301,000). Since Liabilities and Stockholders' Equity is greater than Total Assets, we have more funds than we need. To make the balance sheet balance, we elect to reduce the notes payable by $1,000.

EXHIBIT 16.6 Blackwell Sales: Final Pro Forma Balance Sheet ($ thousands)

The final pro forma balance sheet reflects Blackwell management's decision to temporarily suspend dividends and fund its growth with internal funds (retained earnings). Although financial models can determine the amount of EFN needed, management must make the final decision about how to fund the firm's capital requirements.

Assets			Liabilities and Stockholders' Equity		
	Projected	Change		Projected	Change
Current assets			Current liabilities		
Cash	$ 130	$ 30	Accounts payable	$ 104	$ 44
Accounts receivable	156	36	Notes payable	139	−1
Inventory	182	42	Total	$ 243	43
Total	$ 468	$ 108	Long-term debt	$ 200	0
			Owner's equity		
			Common stock	$ 10	0
			Retained earnings	847	257
			Total equity	$ 857	257
Net fixed assets	832	192	Total liabilities and		
Total assets	$ 1,300	$ 300	stockholders' equity	$ 1,300	$ 300
			External funding needed (EFN)	$ 0	$ 300

Finally, it is important to note that financial models do not make decisions; only the firm's management can do that. Financial models can only generate numbers given the inputs and assumption made when constructing the model. Once constructed, financial models can help management evaluate strategic alternatives, assess their financial impact on the firm, and determine whether they are consistent with the firm's financial policies. In the Blackwell case, management suspended its dividend policy.

Blackwell's Alternative Plan

PROBLEM: Let's continue the Blackwell Sales example. Suppose that Blackwell's management now decides to pay a cash dividend but to reduce the payout to 10 percent of net income. Reconcile Blackwell's retained earnings account.

APPROACH: First, we must calculate the new dividend payout and the amount of funds going into retained earnings. Since net income remains unchanged at $257,000, we calculate the dividends and addition to retained earnings by multiplying the net income by the payout and the retention percentages. Second, we must calculate the impact of the new dividend policy on the retained earnings account. An easy way to do this is to reconcile the retained earnings account.

SOLUTION: The calculations for the new dividend payout and the addition to retained earnings are:

(1) Cash dividends = 0.10 × $257,000 = $25,700.
(2) Addition to retained earnings = 0.90 × $257,000 = $231,300.

The calculations to reconcile the retained earnings account are:

Beginning retained earnings balance	$590,000
+ Net income	257,000
− Dividends	25,700
Ending retained earnings balance	$821,300

Thus, the new retained earnings balance is $821,300.

LEARNING BY DOING

APPLICATION 16.2

536   CHAPTER 16 | Financial Planning and Managing Growth

> ## BEFORE YOU GO ON

1. How are historical financial data used to determine the forecast values of balance sheet accounts?

2. Why might you expect accounts receivable to vary with sales?

16.4 BEYOND THE BASIC PLANNING MODELS

 LEARNING OBJECTIVE

In this section, we tie up some important loose ends concerning financial planning models. We first consider some shortcomings of the simple models we have been discussing and describe how more sophisticated models address those shortcomings. We then discuss additional benefits of financial planning.

Improving Financial Planning Models

Much of the discussion concerning the planning models developed in this chapter focuses on the underlying process for generating pro forma statements. We readily admit that our models lack sophistication. However, our goal is to have you understand how planning models work so that when you move to more elegant computer-based models, you will be an informed user capable of understanding the models' limitations and strengths. We now discuss some of the improvements you should expect to find incorporated in most computer-based models.

Interest Expense

One omission from the models presented in this chapter is that they fail to account for interest expense in the financial statements. A problem we face in modeling is that interest expense cannot be estimated accurately until the cost and amount of borrowing have been determined, and the cost of borrowing depends in part on the amount of borrowing. Thus, we cannot accurately estimate one without the other. More sophisticated financial models estimate interest payments and borrowings simultaneously.

Working Capital Accounts

Another weakness in our percent of sales model is the assumption that working capital increases proportionally with sales. Seasoned financial managers know that increases in some working capital accounts are not proportional to sales; this is particularly true for cash balances and inventory. Exhibit 16.7, for example, shows the inventory-to-sales ratios for two situations: one where inventory varies directly with sales and one where it does not. The black line illustrates the assumption that changes in inventory vary in proportion to changes in sales. Notice that inventory gets very small as sales approach zero. When inventory varies in proportion to sales, the inventory/sales ratio is 50 percent, regardless of the level of sales. The red line illustrates a different relation. Here, at sales of $300,000, the inventory/sales ratio is 70 percent ($210,000/$300,000 = 0.70, or 70 percent), and at sales of $500,000 it declines to 50 percent ($250,000/$500,000 = 0.50, or 50 percent). The important point here is not the ratio calculations but the fact that working capital does not increase directly with sales. Instead, it increases at a decreasing rate as sales increase. This is a common relation between inventory and sales and between cash and sales.

Fixed Assets

lumpy assets
fixed assets added as large, discrete units; these assets may not be used to full capacity for some time, leaving the company with excess capacity

Another issue concerns the way we handled fixed assets. Specifically, we assumed that when sales increase, fixed assets are added in small increments and that production facilities are always operating near or at full capacity. This is not typically the case. In most instances, fixed assets are added as large discrete units, and much of a firm's capacity may not be utilized for some period of time. These types of assets are often called **lumpy assets**. Let's look at an example.

Suppose you and a group of investors decide to enter the market for frozen Mexican snack foods, which you believe is a growing market. You buy a small food-manufacturing facility that

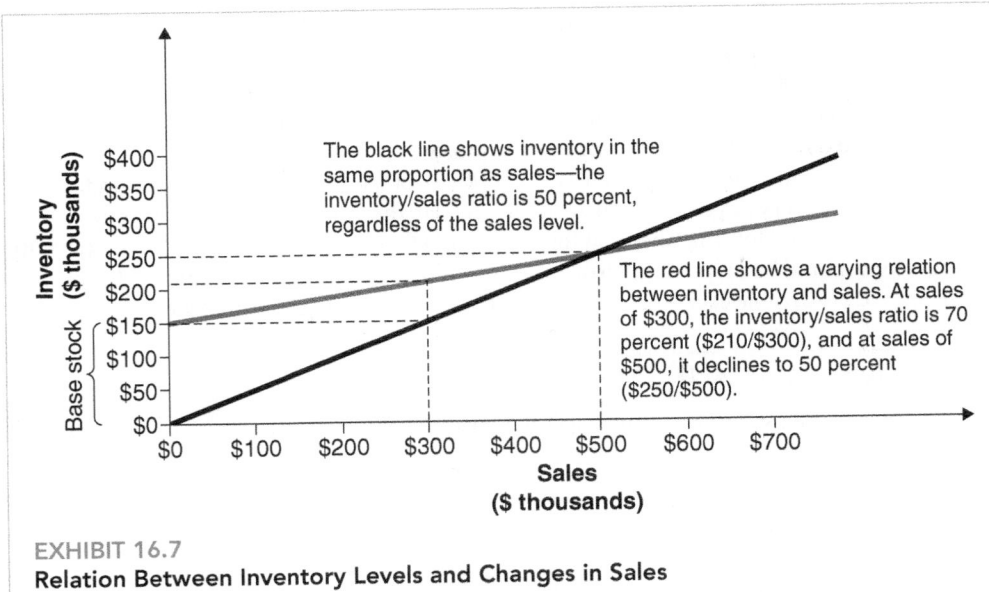

EXHIBIT 16.7
Relation Between Inventory Levels and Changes in Sales

This graph shows inventory-to-sales ratios for two situations: one in which inventory varies directly with sales (black line) and one in which it does not (red line). Financial managers know from experience that most working capital accounts, such as inventory, do not increase directly with sales. Instead, they increase at a decreasing rate as sales increase.

can easily be converted to manufacture Mexican snack foods. Exhibit 16.8 illustrates your initial situation. After you make the purchase, your sales are zero, and you have $100,000 in fixed assets, which will support sales of up to $150,000. Thus, the facility has $150,000 in excess capacity.

Over time, sales expand to $75,000. At this level, no additional assets are needed (Point A in the exhibit) because the firm still has excess capacity of $75,000 ($150,000 − $75,000 = $75,000). When the firm's sales expand to $150,000 (Point B), however, the firm no longer

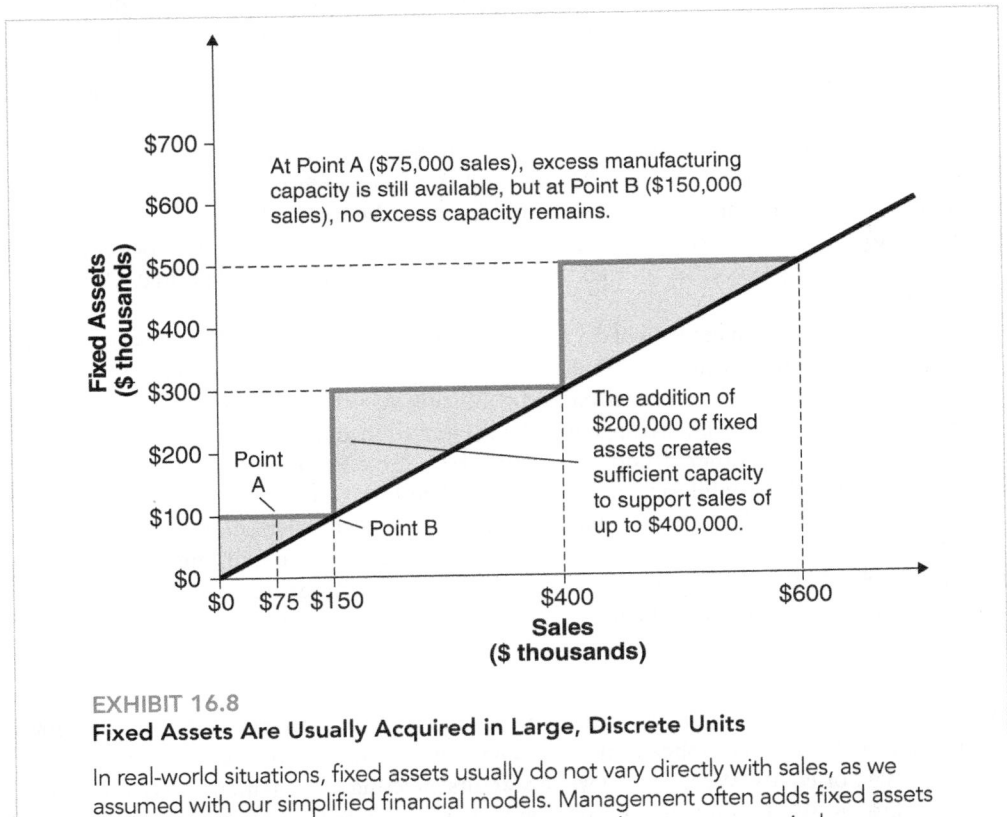

EXHIBIT 16.8
Fixed Assets Are Usually Acquired in Large, Discrete Units

In real-world situations, fixed assets usually do not vary directly with sales, as we assumed with our simplified financial models. Management often adds fixed assets in very large increments in order to add capacity in the most economical way.

has idle capacity. You determine that a $200,000 addition to fixed assets is the most economical way to gain additional capacity. If you make this investment, the firm will have $300,000 ($100,000 + $200,000 = $300,000) in fixed assets, which will support sales up to $400,000. Notice that when your firm is at Point B, the threshold point, even a small increase in sales results in more than doubling the firm's fixed assets.

In financial planning, management must account for the fact that investments in fixed assets often come in very large increments, or "lumps." Furthermore, a significant amount of lead time is often required to bring them on line. Thus, as a firm nears full manufacturing capacity, management should begin planning to acquire additional fixed assets in the future. In contrast, if a firm has considerable excess capacity, sales growth will not require additions to fixed assets.

> **BEFORE YOU GO ON**

1. Why is it that some working capital accounts may not vary proportionately with sales?

2. What are lumpy assets, and how do these assets vary with sales?

16.5 MANAGING AND FINANCING GROWTH

 LEARNING OBJECTIVE

We close the chapter with a discussion of how a business can grow and the need to manage growth. When companies add assets through acquisition or the capital budgeting process, they grow in size. If the rate of growth is rapid, much of the asset expansion will likely require external funding. Rapid growth is often a goal of management because it helps a company gain market share quickly and strengthen its competitive position in the marketplace. In addition, managers of companies with high growth rates often receive accolades and recognition from investors and their peers for their business acumen. Overall, rapid growth is considered a desirable achievement.

Rapid growth can have a dark side, however. As a firm grows rapidly, management might finance the growth with long-term debt in a way that increases the firm's overall financial leverage. Higher financial leverage increases the probability that a firm will face financial distress if business conditions deteriorate. If management is using a lot of debt financing and sales then unexpectedly plunge, causing cash flows to decline, the firm may not have enough cash to pay long-term debt holders and other creditors.

An example of a firm that used too much debt to finance growth is Boston Chicken, Inc., the former operator and franchiser of Boston Market, a chain of fast-food restaurants offering reasonably priced home-style meals. The firm burst onto the national scene in 1993 as one of the hottest initial public offerings (IPOs) of the year. The first day of trading, its stock price shot up 143 percent! Early successes allowed the firm to expand rapidly from an initial 33 stores to over 1,200.

Beginning in 1996, management decided to go head-to-head with McDonald's and Burger King in the highly competitive fast-food lunch market. Boston Chicken used a lot of debt to finance this effort, but the market proved to be difficult. As sales began to slow, management began to tinker with the menu. Management teams moved in and out, menus grew more complex, service and quality suffered, and sales continued to drop. By October 1998, poor sales and a debt load of over $900 million forced Boston Chicken into bankruptcy. In December 1999, McDonald's bought the firm for a bargain-basement price of $173.5 million.

How does rapid growth cause businesses like Boston Chicken to fail? The classic formula for business failure is rapid expansion, a lack of solid long-term planning, and an insufficient equity base or, put another way, the use of too much financial leverage.

External Funding Needed

When a firm expands rapidly, its operations might not be able to generate sufficient cash flows to meet all of its financial obligations. If this happens, management must look for outside funding—debt or equity. We now explore the factors affecting management's decision to seek external funding. We do so by developing some relations between a firm's growth rate and the amount of external funding needed (EFN).

Growth and External Funding

The best way to understand the relation between growth and external funding is in the context of a rapidly growing firm and its financial statements. The firm we use is called Empire Enterprises, which is a hypothetical real estate investment firm located in New York City that engages in real estate development and property management. Empire is a public company whose stock is listed on the NYSE.

Exhibit 16.9 shows the current income statement and balance sheet for Empire Enterprises. Last year Empire had total assets of $50 million, book equity of $30 million, and generated $10 million of earnings on $100 million in sales. Empire's management team believes the firm can increase sales by 20 percent for the coming year. All costs and assets are assumed to grow at the same rate as sales, 60 percent of earnings are paid as cash dividends, and the board of directors is reluctant to issue additional common stock.

Given this information, we can prepare the pro forma income statement and balance sheet for Empire Enterprises, which appear in Exhibit 16.10. The income statement shows both sales and costs increasing by 20 percent for the year: projected sales are $120 million ($100 million × 1.20 = $120 million), projected costs are $108 million ($90 million × 1.20 = $108 million), and thus, the firm's projected net income is $12 million ($120 million − $108 million = $12 million).

Turning to the pro forma balance sheet, we see that the total assets for the firm are $60 million ($50 million × 1.20 = $60 million). For the moment, we hold total debt constant at $20 million so that we can compute the EFN needed to support the 20 percent increase in sales. The firm's payout policy calls for 40 percent of earnings to be retained in the firm, since 60 percent will be paid to stockholders as a dividend. Thus, given net income of $12 million, the addition to retained earnings is $4.8 million (0.40 × $12 million = $4.8 million). The equity account is increased to $34.8 million ($30.0 million + $4.8 million = $34.8 million).

After these changes have been made, the pro forma balance sheet does not balance. Total assets equal $60.0 million, and total liabilities and equity equal $54.8 million. The difference, $5.2 million ($60.0 million − $54.8 million = $5.2 million), is the EFN. The $10 million ($4.8 million + $5.2 million = $10 million) investment is being financed from two sources: $4.8 million from the addition to retained earnings and $5.2 million from external funding. The EFN could be either debt or equity, but in Empire's case it will be long-term debt, since Empire's board is reluctant to issue equity.

So far, we have calculated EFN exactly as we did in the previous sections. However, we are now going to build a mathematical model to calculate EFN. The model will allow us to better understand the relation between a firm's growth ambitions and the amount of EFN.

EXHIBIT 16.9 **Empire Enterprises: Income Statement and Balance Sheet ($ millions)**

The exhibit shows the current income statement and balance sheet for Empire Enterprises. Management believes that the firm can increase sales by 20 percent for the coming year. All costs and assets are assumed to grow at the same rate as sales, 60 percent of earnings are paid out as dividends, and the directors do not want to issue additional common stock.

Income Statement

Net sales	$100.0
Costs	90.0
Net income	$ 10.0
Dividends	$ 6.0
Addition to retained earnings	$ 4.0

Balance Sheet

Assets		Percentage of Sales	Liabilities and Stockholders' Equity		Percentage of Sales
Assets	$50.0	20.0%	Total debt	$20.0	n/a
			Equity	30.0	n/a
Total assets	$50.0		Total liabilities and stockholders' equity	$50.0	

EXHIBIT 16.10   **Empire Enterprises: Pro Forma Income Statement and Balance Sheet ($ millions)**

The pro forma balance sheet for Empire Enterprises does not balance, and the difference is the amount of EFN. Because the company's board does not wish to issue common stock, the funding will have to take the form of long-term debt.

Income Statement (Pro Forma)

Net sales	$120.0
Costs	108.0
Net income	$ 12.0
Dividends	$ 7.2
Addition to retained earnings	$ 4.8

Balance Sheet (Pro Forma)

Assets			Liabilities and Stockholders' Equity		
	Projected	Change		Projected	Change
Assets	$60.0	$10.0	Total debt	$20.0	$0.0
			Equity	34.8	4.8
Total assets	$60.0	$10.0	Total liabilities and stockholders' equity	$54.8	$4.8
			External funding needed (EFN)	$ 5.2	$5.2

A Mathematical Model

Looking at the pro forma balance sheet calculations for Empire Enterprises (Exhibit 16.10), we can see that new investments are determined by the firm's total assets and projected growth in sales:

$$\text{New investments} = \text{Growth rate} \times \text{Initial total assets}$$

For Empire, the calculation is $10 million = 0.20 × $50 million. Note that to calculate new investments, we multiply the firm's initial total assets by the expected growth rate in sales forecasted by management. The new investments are the capital expenditures and the increase in working capital necessary to sustain the increase in sales.

Conceptually, the new investments are funded first by internally generated funds, which come from earnings retained in the firm. Once those funds are exhausted, the remainder of new investments must be financed externally by the sale of debt or equity, or some combination of both. Thus, the amount of EFN can be expressed as:

$$\text{EFN} = \text{New investments} - \text{Addition to retained earnings} \qquad (16.5)$$

Substituting Growth rate × Initial total assets for New investments in Equation 16.5 yields the following:

$$\text{EFN} = (\text{Growth rate} \times \text{Initial total assets}) - \text{Addition to retained earnings} \quad (16.6)$$

Applying Equation 16.6 to our Empire Enterprise situation, we get the following results:

$$\text{EFN} = (0.20 \times \$50 \text{ million}) - \$4.8 \text{ million} = \$10 \text{ million} - \$4.8 \text{ million}$$
$$= \$5.2 \text{ million}$$

The result, $5.2 million, agrees with the financial planning model calculation for Empire Enterprises presented earlier.

Equation 16.6 highlights two important points. First, holding dividend policy constant, the amount of EFN depends on the firm's projected growth rate. The faster management expects the firm to grow, the more the firm needs to invest in new assets, and the more capital it has to raise. The potential sources of external capital are the sale of new stock and the sale of long-term debt. Second, the firm's payout policy also affects EFN. Holding the growth rate constant, the higher the firm's dividend payout ratio, the larger the amount of external debt or equity financing needed. Also, since EFN is the net amount of external funding needed, the more stock a firm repurchases, the more new capital it must raise to satisfy its EFN requirements if EFN is positive.

EXHIBIT 16.11
External Funding Needed (EFN) and Growth for Empire Enterprises

The exhibit graphically illustrates Equation 16.6, showing the connection between growth rate in sales and EFN. The horizontal axis plots the firm's projected growth rate, and the vertical axis plots EFN. The upward slope of the line illustrates how external funding increases with the growth rate, assuming that the dividend policy is held constant.

A Graphical View of Growth

Exhibit 16.11 illustrates Equation 16.6—the relation between sales growth rate and EFN—for Empire Enterprises. The horizontal axis plots the firm's projected growth rate, and the vertical axis plots EFN. The slope of the line illustrates how EFN increases with the growth rate, assuming that dividend policy is held constant. As you can see, the line is upward sloping. This means that as the growth rate increases, the amount of EFN increases.

As a reference point in the exhibit, we plotted Empire's EFN value of $5.2 million when the firm's sales are growing at a 20 percent rate. If you want to generate the line yourself, all you need to do is make another calculation of EFN at a different growth rate, plot the points, and connect them with a straight line. However, the important point here is not the mechanics of generating the graph in Exhibit 16.11 but the interpretation of the line.

Turning to the exhibit, you can see that at low growth rates Empire Enterprises will generate more funds from earnings than it will spend on new investments. In these situations, the calculated value for EFN is negative (EFN < 0), and the firm has a surplus of funds. In other words, the internally generated funds exceed the firm's planned investments. With the surplus funds, management may elect to retire some debt or repurchase some common stock. For example, at a 0 percent rate of growth, no funds are needed for expansion, and all the retained earnings are surplus, as we can see by using Equation 16.6:

$$\text{EFN} = (\text{Growth rate} \times \text{Initial total assets}) - \text{Addition to retained earnings}$$
$$= (0.0 \times \$50 \text{ million}) - \$4.8 \text{ million}$$
$$= -\$4.8 \text{ million}$$

With a higher growth rate, the surplus becomes smaller and smaller as more and more funds are used to finance the new investments. At a growth rate of 9.6 percent, the surplus equals zero, as does the calculated value of EFN. Next we explain how to calculate the growth rate at which the surplus equals zero. The key point here is that the higher the rate at which a firm grows, the more external funding it requires.

The Internal Growth Rate

Management often has an interest in knowing the rate at which the firm can grow using just internally generated funds. This rate is called the **internal growth rate (IGR)**. The IGR is the maximum growth rate that a firm can achieve without external funding. To determine this rate, we set Equation 16.6 equal to zero (EFN = 0) and solve for the growth rate. Thus,

$$\text{EFN} = (\text{Growth rate} \times \text{Initial total assets}) - \text{Addition to retained earnings} = 0$$

internal growth rate (IGR)
the maximum growth rate that a firm can achieve without external funding

Rearranging terms yields the internal growth rate:

$$IGR = \frac{\text{Addition to retained earnings}}{\text{Initial total assets}} \qquad (16.7)$$

The managerial implications of the formula are straightforward. Firms that can generate a higher volume of retained earnings and/or use fewer assets can sustain a higher growth rate without raising more capital. For the Empire Enterprises example, the internal growth rate is calculated as:

$$IGR = \frac{\text{Addition to retained earnings}}{\text{Initial total assets}}$$
$$= \frac{\$4.8 \text{ million}}{\$50 \text{ million}} = 0.096, \text{ or } 9.6\%$$

To gain more insight into what factors determine a firm's internal growth rate, we can manipulate Equation 16.7 by multiplying both the numerator and the denominator by net income and total equity, as follows:

$$IGR = \frac{\text{Addition to retained earnings}}{\text{Total assets}} \times \frac{\text{Net income}}{\text{Net income}} \times \frac{\text{Total equity}}{\text{Total equity}}$$

If we then rearrange terms, we arrive at the following expression:

$$IGR = \frac{\text{Addition to retained earnings}}{\text{Net Income}} \times \frac{\text{Net income}}{\text{Total equity}} \times \frac{\text{Total equity}}{\text{Total assets}}$$

From the discussions in Chapter 4 and in this chapter, we know the following: (1) plowback ratio = addition to retained earnings/net income; (2) return on equity = net income/total equity; and (3) equity multiplier = total assets/total equity.[6] This means that we can write the above equation as:

$$IGR = \text{Plowback ratio} \times \text{Return on equity} \times \text{Measure of leverage} \qquad (16.8)$$

Equation 16.8 tells us that firms that achieve higher growth rates without seeking external funding tend to have one or more of the following characteristics:

- They have dividend policies that retain a high proportion of earnings inside the firm—that is, they have a high plowback ratio.
- They are able to generate a high net income with a smaller amount of equity than other firms and hence have a high return on equity (ROE).
- They use low amounts of leverage; thus, their debt-to-equity ratios are low.

The Sustainable Growth Rate

sustainable growth rate (SGR)
the rate of growth that a firm can sustain without selling additional equity while maintaining the same capital structure

Another growth rate helpful in long-term planning is the **sustainable growth rate (SGR)**, which is the rate of growth that the firm can sustain without selling additional equity while maintaining the same capital structure. You may wonder why management is interested in the sustainable growth rate. The sustainable growth rate is important to managers of firms that are likely to generate excess funds internally and who want to determine the payout ratio that enables them to fund their firms' growth while maintaining their current capital structures.

The sustainable growth rate is the rate at which a firm can grow using only (1) internally generated funds from earnings and (2) external funds from the sale of new debt while maintaining a constant debt-equity ratio. As it turns out, SGR is a function of the firm's plowback ratio and the return on equity (ROE). SRG can be expressed as follows:

$$SGR = \text{Plowback ratio} \times \text{ROE} \qquad (16.9)$$

For Empire Enterprises, the sustainable growth rate is:

$$SGR = 0.4 \times \frac{\$10 \text{ million}}{\$30 \text{ million}}$$
$$= 0.4 \times 0.333$$
$$= 0.133, \text{ or } 13.3\%$$

---

[6]Note that the measure of leverage in Equation 16.8, total equity/total assets, is the inverse of the equity multiplier, Equation 4.11.

The 13.3 percent rate is a fairly high SGR that is driven by the company's rather hefty 33.3 percent return on equity.

An analysis of a company's SGR relative to the company's actual growth rate can provide management with some insights into problems the firm may face in the future. For example, if a firm's actual growth rate consistently exceeds its SGR, management knows that unless they sell new equity, the firm will have a cash shortage problem in the future because of the need to purchase new assets to generate the growth. The SGR model does not, however, tell management how fast the firm should grow. That decision requires informed judgment about the attractiveness of the investment opportunities available to the firm.

Empire's Ambitious Growth Plan

DECISION MAKING

EXAMPLE 16.2

SITUATION: You are part of the Empire Enterprises finance team. The firm's strategic plan calls for revenues to grow at 20 percent next year. As mentioned, the board of directors is not interested in using any external equity funding. Some members of the team question whether these goals are realistic.

You have just been asked to comment on the proposed growth plan at a meeting. You have a little over an hour to prepare. During the time available, you completed the following calculations using data from the most recent and the pro forma income statements and balance sheets (Exhibits 16.9 and 16.10):

- EFN = (Growth rate × Initial total assets) − Addition to retained earnings = (0.20 × $50 million) − $4.8 million = $5.2 million
- IGR = Addition to retained earnings/initial assets = $4.8 million/$50 million = 0.96, or 9.6%
- SGR = Plowback ratio × ROE = 0.40 × 0.333 = 13.3%

Given the above information, what can you say about this ambitious growth plan?

DECISION: You begin by applauding the visionary nature of the strategic plan. Clearly, you want to keep your job. You point out, however, that the firm is facing some challenges. First, Empire's IGR is 9.6 percent, which is the maximum growth rate the firm can achieve without any kind of external funding. This amount is substantially below the desired growth rate of 20 percent. Second, you note that Empire's EFN is $5.2 million. This means that $5.2 million of external capital will have to be raised by selling equity, debt, or some combination of the two. Finally, Empire's SGR is 13.3 percent—also below the 20 percent growth target. Empire cannot grow more than 13.3 percent without selling equity if management wants to keep the firm's capital structure at its current level.

Sustainable Growth and Financial Statements

LEARNING BY DOING

APPLICATION 16.3

PROBLEM: Because of your presentation (see Decision-Making Example 16.2), Empire's top management team has had second thoughts about their goal of growing the firm 20 percent during the next year. As a result, they have asked that you prepare pro forma financial statements at a sales growth rate equal to the firm's SGR of 13.3 percent.

APPROACH: For the income statement, all costs grow at the same rate as revenues. Thus, you can multiply the current period's net sales and costs by 1.133 to calculate the projected values of sales and costs. To construct the balance sheet, you must first compute the values of accounts that vary with net sales. Since you have no information about how much of Empire's total debt is long-term debt, you should enter its total debt value of $20 million, along with all the information you have on the balance sheet accounts. Finally, to make the balance sheet balance, you should calculate the amount of EFN.

(continued)

SOLUTION:

$$\text{Net sales} = \$100 \text{ million} \times 1.133 = \$113.30 \text{ million}$$
$$\text{Costs} = \$90 \text{ million} \times 1.133 = \$101.97 \text{ million}$$

The income statement is:

Empire Enterprises
Pro Forma Income Statement ($ millions)

Net sales	$113.30
Costs	101.97
Net income	$ 11.33

Dividend = Net income × Payout ratio = $11.33 million × 0.60 = $6.80 million

Addition to retained earnings = Net income × Plowback ratio = $11.33 million × 0.4 = $4.53 million

Forecast value of the assets: $50 million × 1.133 = $56.65 million

Value of the equity: $30 million + $4.53 million = $34.53 million, where $30 million is the initial value and $4.53 million is the addition to retained earnings

Value of debt plus equity: $20 million + 34.53 million = $54.53 million

The balance sheet does not balance ($56.65 million assets > $54.53 million debt plus equity), and the difference ($2.12 million) is the plug number, which is the EFN. Thus, to achieve the 13.3 percent rate of growth, Empire will need to issue $2.12 million in long-term debt, which will bring the debt account to $20 million + $2.12 million = $22.12 million. The resulting balance sheet is as follows:

Empire Enterprises
Pro Forma Balance Sheet ($ millions)

Assets		Liabilities and Stockholders' Equity	
Assets	$56.65	Total debt	$22.12
		Equity	34.53
Total assets	$56.65	Total liabilities and stockholders' equity	$56.65

Growth Rates and Profits

So far, we have focused on a firm's rate of growth. In the final analysis, however, the critical question in business is not how fast the firm can grow, but whether the firm can sustain rapid growth and maintain a satisfactory level of profits. In reality, it is very difficult to achieve and sustain rapid growth in a competitive market and remain profitable. The business arena is littered with failed growth firms like Boston Chicken.

To provide a reality check, only 7 percent of publicly traded U.S. companies increase both revenues and operating profits by an average of 10 percent a year. Experts generally agree that growth rates at or above 10 percent are very difficult to sustain for established companies.

Growth as a Planning Goal

The final question we address is whether growth by itself is an acceptable strategic goal. We pose this question because it is common for top management to set growth rates as goals for the firm or operating divisions. In fact, there is nothing a CEO likes to do better at the annual meeting than point out that "last year, under my leadership, Sleepy Hollow exceeded its goal of 10 percent growth," and have it followed by a hearty round of applause. Growth rate goals are popular because they are easy to communicate and understand. But are they appropriate goals for financial planning? The short answer is "no." Let's consider why this is the case.

As we discussed in Chapter 1, an appropriate goal for management is maximizing the market value of stockholders' equity. If management invests in productive assets with positive NPVs, finances them at the lowest possible cost, and skillfully manages these assets, the company should be profitable and grow in size. This growth results from making sound business decisions and executing strategies that create sustainable competitive advantages over the long term. Thus, growth is an acceptable goal as long as it is anchored to a sound business strategy that will generate an increase in stockholder value.

> **BEFORE YOU GO ON**

1. What two factors determine the amount of EFN?
2. What is IGR, and why is it of interest to management?
3. If a firm continually exceeds its SGR, what problems may it face in the future?

SUMMARY OF **Learning Objectives**

1 **Explain what a financial plan is and why financial planning is so important.**

A financial plan is a set of actionable goals derived from the firm's strategic plan and other planning documents, such as the investment and financing plans. The financial plan focuses on selecting the best investment opportunities and determining how they will be financed. The financial plan is a blueprint for the firm's future. Financial planning is important to management because the plan communicates the firm's strategic goals throughout the organization, builds support for the firm's strategies, and helps align operating unit goals with the firm's strategic goals.

2 **Discuss how management uses financial planning models in the planning process, and explain the importance of sales forecasts in the construction of financial planning models.**

Financial models are the analytical part of the financial planning process. A planning model is simply a series of equations that model a firm's financial statements, such as the income statement and balance sheet. Once the model is constructed, management can generate projected (pro forma) financial statements to determine the financial impact of proposed strategic initiatives on the firm.

For most financial planning models, a forecast of the firm's sales is the most important input variable. The sales forecast is the key driver in financial planning models because many items on the income statement and balance sheet vary directly with sales. Thus, once sales are forecasted, it is easy to generate projected financial statements using the historical relation between a particular account and sales.

3 **Discuss how the relation between projected sales and balance sheet accounts can be determined, and analyze a strategic investment decision using a percent of sales model.**

Historical financial data can be examined to determine whether and how a variable changes with sales. One way to do this is to prepare a table that shows four or five years of historical financial statement account data as a percent of sales. Then fit trend lines to the data to see what type of relation exists between that variable and sales. Many income statement and balance sheet items vary directly with sales, but others may vary in a nonlinear manner. The analysis in the Blackwell Sales Company example illustrates how to analyze a strategic investment decision.

4 **Describe the conditions under which fixed assets vary directly with sales, and discuss the impact of so-called lumpy assets on this relation.**

Fixed assets vary directly with sales only when assets can be added in small increments and production facilities are operating near full capacity. This is typically not the case. In most situations, fixed assets are added in large, discrete units, and as a result, much of the new capacity may go unused for a period of time. These types of assets are often called lumpy assets. After lumpy assets are added, sales can increase for a period of time with no corresponding change in the level of fixed assets.

5 **Explain what factors determine a firm's sustainable growth rate, discuss why it is of interest to management, and compute the sustainable growth rate for a firm.**

A firm's sustainable growth rate (SGR) is the maximum rate at which the firm can grow without external equity funding and with leverage held constant. The determinants of a firm's SGR are (1) profit margins (the greater a firm's profit margin, the greater the firm's SGR); (2) asset utilization (the more efficiently a firm uses its assets, the higher its SGR); (3) financial leverage (as a firm increases its use of leverage, its SGR increases); (4) payout policy (as a firm decreases its payout ratio, its SGR increases); and (5) economic conditions (the more favorable the economic environment, the higher the firm's SGR). Management may be interested in knowing the SGR for two reasons. First, the SGR is the rate of growth at which a firm's capital structure (debt to equity) will remain constant without the firm selling or repurchasing stock. Second, if a firm's actual growth rate exceeds its SGR, the firm could face cash shortage problems in the future unless it can sell new equity. Learning by Doing Application 16.3 uses the SGR formula.

SUMMARY OF Key Equations

Equation	Description	Formula
16.1	Percent change in sales	$\%\Delta S = \dfrac{(S_{t+1} - S_t)}{S_t}$
16.2	Percent of net income paid out as dividends	$\text{Dividend payout ratio} = \dfrac{\text{Cash dividends}}{\text{Net income}}$
16.3	Percent of net income retained (plowed back into the firm)	$\text{Retention (plowback) ratio} = \dfrac{\text{Addition to retained earnings}}{\text{Net income}}$
16.4	Level of assets needed to generate $1 of sales	$\text{Capital intensity ratio} = \dfrac{\text{Total assets}}{\text{Net sales}}$
16.5 & 16.6	External funding needed to support growth in sales	$\text{EFN} = \text{New investments} - \text{Addition to retained earnings}$ $= (\text{Growth rate} \times \text{Initial total assets}) - \text{Addition to retained earnings}$
16.7 & 16.8	Internal growth rate (level of growth that can be supported without raising external funds)	$\text{IGR} = \dfrac{\text{Addition to retained earnings}}{\text{Initial total assets}}$ $= \text{Plowback ratio} \times \text{Return on equity} \times \text{Measure of leverage}$
16.9	Sustainable growth rate (level of growth that can be supported without raising external equity or increasing current leverage)	$\text{SGR} = \text{Plowback ratio} \times \text{ROE}$

Self-Study Problems

16.1 The Starlight, Inc., financial statements for the fiscal year ended June 30, 2013, are presented below. The firm's sales are projected to grow at a rate of 20 percent next year, and all financial statement accounts will vary directly with sales. Based on that projection, develop a pro forma balance sheet and income statement for the fiscal year ending June 30, 2014.

Starlight, Inc., Balance Sheet as of June 30, 2013

Assets:		Liabilities and Stockholders' Equity:	
Cash	$ 25,135	Accounts payable	$ 67,855
Accounts receivable	43,758	Notes payable	36,454
Inventories	167,112		
Total current assets	$236,005	Total current liabilities	$104,309
Net fixed assets	325,422	Long-term debt	223,125
Other assets	13,125	Common stock	150,000
		Retained earnings	97,118
Total assets	$574,552	Total liabilities and equity	$574,552

Starlight, Inc. Income Statement for the Fiscal Year Ended June 30, 2013

Net sales	$1,450,000
Costs	812,500
EBITDA	$ 637,500
Depreciation	175,000
EBIT	$ 462,500
Interest	89,575
EBT	$ 372,925
Taxes (35%)	130,524
Net income	$ 242,401

16.2 Use the financial information for Starlight from Self-Study Problem 16.1. Assume now that equity accounts do not vary directly with sales, but change when retained earnings change or new equity is issued. The company pays 45 percent of its income as dividends every year. In addition, the company plans to expand production capacity by building a new facility that will cost $225,000. The firm has no plans to issue new equity this year and any funds that need to be raised will be raised through the sale of long-term debt. Prepare a pro forma balance sheet using this information.

16.3 Use the financial statements from Self-Study Problem 16.1 and the information from Self-Study Problem 16.2 to calculate the company's retention (plowback) ratio, external funds needed (EFN), internal growth rate (IGR), and sustainable growth rate (SGR).

16.4 Northwood Corp. has a dividend payout ratio of 60 percent, return on equity of 14.5 percent, total assets of $11,500,450, and equity of $4,652,125. Calculate the firm's internal rate of growth (IGR).

16.5 Renewal Company has net income of $1.25 million and a dividend payout ratio of 35 percent. It currently has equity of $2,875,223. What is the firm's sustainable growth rate?

Solutions to Self-Study Problems

16.1 The pro forma statements for Starlight are as follows:

Starlight, Inc. Balance Sheet as of June 30, 2014

Assets:		Liabilities and Stockholders' Equity:	
Cash	$ 30,162	Accounts payable	$ 81,426
Accounts receivable	52,510	Notes payable	43,745
Inventories	200,534		
Total current assets	$283,206	Total current liabilities	$125,171
Net fixed assets	390,506	Long-term debt	267,750
Other assets	15,750	Common stock	180,000
		Retained earnings	116,542
Total assets	$689,462	Total liabilities and equity	$689,462

Starlight, Inc. Income Statement for the Fiscal Year Ended June 30, 2014

Net sales	$1,740,000
Costs	975,000
EBITDA	$ 765,000
Depreciation	210,000
EBIT	$ 555,000
Interest	107,490
EBT	$ 447,510
Taxes (35%)	156,629
Net income	$ 290,882

16.2 The pro forma income statement is the same as that shown in the solution to Self-Study Problem 16.1. We now have to account for the payment of dividends. Since the company pays 45 percent of its net income as dividends, the retained earnings for 2014 is calculated as follows:

Retained earnings from 2014 income = $290,882 × (1 − 0.45) = $159,985.
- This is the amount by which retained earnings will increase in 2014, from $97,118 to $257,103.
- No new equity is added.
- The increase in assets is financed externally through the sale of long-term debt.

The pro forma balance sheet is as follows:

Starlight, Inc. Balance Sheet as of June 30, 2014

Assets:		Liabilities and Stockholders' Equity:	
Cash	$ 30,162	Accounts payable	$ 81,426
Accounts receivable	52,510	Notes payable	43,745
Inventories	200,534		
Total current assets	$283,206	Total current liabilities	$125,171
Net fixed assets	390,506	Long-term debt	382,188
Addition to fixed assets	225,000	Common stock	150,000
Other assets	15,750	Retained earnings	257,103
Total assets	$914,462	Total liabilities and equity	$914,462

16.3 The retention (plowback) ratio, external funds needed, internal growth rate, and sustainable growth rate are calculated as follows:

$$\text{Retention (plowback) ratio} = \frac{\text{Addition to retained earnings}}{\text{Net income}}$$
$$= \frac{\$159,985}{\$290,882}$$
$$= 0.55, \text{ or } 55\%$$

$$\text{EFN} = (\text{Growth rate} \times \text{Initial total assets}) - \text{Addition to retained earnings}$$
$$= (0.20 \times \$574,552) - \$159,985$$
$$= -\$45,075$$

Thus, without considering the investment of $225,000 for the new facility, the firm will not need any external funding. However, if you add the investment, then,

$$\text{EFN} = \text{New investments} - \text{Addition to retained earnings}$$
$$= (0.20 \times \$574,552) + \$225,000 - \$159,985$$
$$= \$179,925$$

$$\text{IGR} = \frac{\text{Addition to retained earnings}}{\text{Initial total assets}}$$
$$= \frac{\$159,985}{\$574,552}$$
$$= 0.278, \text{ or } 27.8\%$$

$$\text{SGR} = \text{Plowback ratio} \times \text{ROE}$$
$$= \frac{\text{Addition to retained earnings}}{\text{Net income}} \times \frac{\text{Net income}}{\text{Total equity}}$$
$$= 0.55 \times 0.715$$
$$= 0.393, \text{ or } 39.3\%$$

16.4 We calculate Northwood's internal growth rate as follows:

$$\text{IGR} = \text{Plowback ratio} \times \text{ROE} \times \text{Measure of leverage}$$
$$= 0.40 \times 0.145 \times \frac{\$4,652,125}{\$11,500,450}$$
$$= 0.0235, \text{ or } 2.35\%$$

16.5 Renewal's sustainable growth rate is:

$$\text{SGR} = \text{Plowback ratio} \times \text{ROE}$$
$$= 0.65 \times \frac{\$1,250,000}{\$2,875,223}$$
$$= 0.283 = 28.3\%$$

Critical Thinking Questions

16.1 What is financial planning? What four types of plans/budgets are involved in financial planning?

16.2 Why is the capital budget an important part of a firm's financial planning?

16.3 Why do financing and investment decisions have to be made concurrently?

16.4 Explain how sales can be used to develop pro forma financial statements.

16.5 Why is sales not always a good measure to use in forecasting fixed assets?

16.6 List all the accounts that can be affected by the "plug" value. How does this value help managers?

16.7 Explain why the fixed asset account may or may not vary with sales.

16.8 How does the dividend payout ratio affect the amount of funds needed to finance growth?

16.9 Define internal growth rate (IGR). Identify the characteristics of a high-growth firm that has no external funds needed.

16.10 What is the sustainable growth rate? Why is it important?

Questions and Problems

16.1 Strategic plan: Explain the importance of the strategic plan.

16.2 Capital budget: What are the various steps in preparing a capital budget?

16.3 Financing plan: What are the elements of a financing plan?

16.4 Financial planning: Identify the steps in the financial planning process.

16.5 Financial modeling: List the various elements of financial modeling.

16.6 Payout ratio: Define the retention (plowback) ratio and the dividend payout ratio.

16.7 Addition to retained earnings: Northwood, Inc., has revenue of $455,316, costs of $316,487, and a tax rate of 31 percent. If the firm pays out 45 percent of its earnings as dividends every year, how much earnings are retained and what is the firm's retention ratio?

16.8 Payout and retention ratio: Goodwin Corp. has revenues of $12,112,659, costs of $9,080,545, interest payments of $412,375, and a tax rate of 34 percent. It paid dividends of $1,025,000 to its stockholders. What are the firm's dividend payout ratio and retention ratio?

16.9 Percent of sales: Cattail Corporation's financial statements for the fiscal year just ended are shown below:

Cattail Corporation
Financial Statements for Fiscal Year Just Ended ($ thousands)

Income Statement		Balance Sheet			
Net sales	$1,500	Assets	$700	Debt	$600
Costs	350			Equity	100
Net income	$1,150	Total	$700	Total	$700

Cattail management expects sales to increase by 14 percent next year. Assume that the financial statement accounts vary directly with changes in sales and that management has no financing plan at this time. Given this information, develop a pro forma income statement for Cattail for the next fiscal year.

16.10 Percent of sales: Given the data for Cattail Corporation in Problem 16.9, if you assume that all balance sheet items also vary with the change in sales, develop a pro forma balance sheet for Cattail for the next fiscal year. Assuming that the firm did not sell or repurchase stock, what is the cash dividend implied by the pro forma income statement and balance sheet?

16.11 Capital intensity ratio: Define capital intensity ratio, and explain its significance.

16.12 Capital intensity ratio: Tantrix Confectioners has total assets of $3,257,845 and net sales of $5,123,951. What is the firm's capital intensity ratio?

16.13 Capital intensity ratio: McDonald Metal Works has been able to generate net sales of $13,445,196 on assets of $9,145,633. What is the firm's capital intensity ratio?

16.14 Capital intensity ratio: For McDonald Metal Works in Problem 16.13, how much must net sales grow if the capital intensity ratio has to drop to 60 percent? State your answer as both a percent of sales and a dollar sales increase.

16.15 Internal growth rate: Swan Supply Company has net income of $1,212,335, assets of $12,522,788, and retains 70 percent of its income every year. What is the company's internal growth rate?

16.16 Sustainable growth rate: If Newell Corp. has a ROE of 13.7 percent and a dividend payout ratio of 32 percent, what is its sustainable growth rate?

16.17 EFN and growth: Refer to Exhibits 16.10 and 16.11 in the text. The EFNs for several growth rates for Empire Enterprises are as follows:

Growth Rate (%)	EFN ($ millions)
0%	−$4.8
5	−2.3
9.6	0.0
10	0.2
15	2.7
20	5.2

Check the calculations and plot the line to replicate the graph in Exhibit 16.11.

INTERMEDIATE > **16.18 Retention ratio:** Refer to Problem 16.7. Northwood expects to increase its sales by 15 percent next year. All costs vary directly with sales. If Northwood wants to retain $65,000 of earnings next year, will it have to change its dividend payout ratio? If so, what will be the new dividend payout and retention ratios for the firm?

16.19 Capital intensity: Identify two industries (other than airlines) that are capital intensive. Using online or other data sources, compute the capital intensity ratio for the largest firm in each of the chosen industries.

16.20 Percent of sales: Tomey Supply Company's financial statements for the most recent fiscal year are shown below. The company management projects that sales will increase by 20 percent next year. Assume that all costs and assets increase directly with sales. The company has a constant 33 percent dividend payout ratio and has no plans to issue new equity. Any financing needed will be raised through the sale of long-term debt. Prepare pro forma financial statements for the coming year based on this information, and calculate the EFN for Tomey.

Tomey Supply Company Income Statement and Balance Sheet

Income Statement		Balance Sheet	
Net sales	$1,768,121	Assets:	
Costs	1,116,487	Current assets	$280,754
EBT	$ 651,634	Net fixed assets	713,655
Taxes (35%)	228,072	Total assets	$994,409
Net income	$ 423,562		
		Liabilities and Equity:	
		Currrent liabilities	$167,326
		Long-term debt	319,456
		Common stock	200,000
		Retained earnings	307,627
		Total liabilities and equity	$994,409

16.21 Internal growth rate: Using the pro forma financial statements for Tomey Supply Company developed in Problem 16.20, find the internal growth rate for Tomey.

16.22 Sustainable growth rate: Use the following pro forma information for Tomey Supply Company for next year: net income = $508,275; addition to retained earnings = $340,544; common equity = $848,171; net sales = $2,121,745. Assume that management does not want the ratio of long-term debt to equity to exceed the current long-term debt-to-equity ratio of 63 percent and also does not want to issue new equity. What level of sales growth can Tomey Supply Company sustain? Calculate the new sales level.

16.23 Sustainable growth rate: Rowan Company has a net profit margin of 8.3 percent, debt ratio of 45 percent, total assets of $4,157,550, and sales of $6,852,654. If the company has a dividend payout ratio of 67 percent, what is its sustainable growth rate?

16.24 Sustainable growth rate: Refer to the information for Rowan Company in Problem 16.23. The firm's management desires a sustainable growth rate (SGR) of 10 percent but does not wish to change the company's level of debt or its payout ratio. What will the firm's new net profit margin have to be in order to achieve the desired growth rate?

16.25 Sustainable growth rate: Rocky Sales, Inc., has current sales of $1,215,326 and net income of $211,253. It also has a debt ratio of 25 percent and a dividend payout ratio of 75 percent. The company's total assets are $712,455. What is its sustainable growth rate?

16.26 Sustainable growth rate: Ellicott Textile Mills management has reported the following financial information for the year ended September 30, 2013. The company generated a net income of $915,366 on a net profit margin of 6.4 percent. It has a dividend payout ratio of 50 percent, a capital intensity ratio of 62 percent, and a debt ratio of 45 percent. What is the company's sustainable growth rate?

16.27 Internal growth rate: Given the information in Problem 16.26, what is the internal growth rate of Ellicott Textile Mills?

16.28 Internal growth rate: Fantasy Travel Company has a return on equity of 17.5 percent, a total equity/total assets ratio of 65 percent, and a dividend payout ratio of 75 percent. What is the company's internal growth rate?

16.29 EFN: Maryland Micro Brewers generated revenues of $12,125,800 with a 72 percent capital intensity ratio during the year ended September 30, 2013. Its net income was $873,058. With the introduction of a half dozen new specialty beers, management expects to grow sales by

15 percent next year. Assume that all costs vary directly with sales and that the firm maintains a dividend payout ratio of 70 percent. What will be the EFN needed by this firm? If the company wants to raise no more than $750,000 externally and is not averse to adjusting its payout policy, what will be the new dividend payout ratio?

16.30 EFN: Ritchie Marble Company has total assets of $12,899,450, sales of $18,174,652, and net income of $4,589,774. Management expects sales to grow by 25 percent next year. All assets and costs (including taxes) vary directly with sales, and management expects to maintain a payout ratio of 65 percent. Calculate Ritchie's EFN.

16.31 EFN: Norton Group, Inc., expects to add $1,213,777 to retained earnings and currently has total assets of $23,159,852. If the company has the ability to borrow up to $1 million, how much growth can the firm support if it is willing to borrow to its maximum capacity?

16.32 EFN: Capstone Marketing Group has total assets of $5,568,000, sales of $3,008,725, and net income of $822,000. The company expects its sales to grow by 12 percent next year. All assets and costs (including taxes) vary directly with sales, and the firm expects to maintain a payout ratio of 55 percent. Calculate Capstone's EFN.

16.33 Maximum sales growth: Given the data for Capstone Marketing Group in Problem 16.32, what would Capstone's payout ratio have to be for the firm's EFN to be zero?

16.34 Maximum sales growth: Rockville Consulting Group expects to add $271,898 to retained earnings this year. The company has total assets of $3,425,693 and wishes to add no new external funds for the coming year. If assets and costs vary directly with sales, how much sales growth can the company support while retaining an EFN of zero? What is the firm's internal growth rate?

16.35 The financial statements for the year ended June 30, 2013, are given below for Morgan Construc- ◁ **ADVANCED**
tion Company. The firm's sales are projected to grow at a rate of 25 percent next year, and all financial statement accounts will vary directly with sales. Based on that projection, develop a pro forma balance sheet and an income statement for the 2014 fiscal year.

Morgan Construction Company Balance Sheet as of June 30, 2013

Assets:		Liabilities and Stockholders' Equity:	
Cash	$ 3,349,239	Accounts payable	$ 9,041,679
Accounts receivable	5,830,754	Notes payable	4,857,496
Inventories	22,267,674	Total current liabilities	$13,899,175
Total current assets	$31,447,667	Long-term debt	29,731,406
Net fixed assets	43,362,482	Common stock	19,987,500
Other assets	1,748,906	Retained earnings	12,940,974
Total assets	$76,559,055	Total liabilities and equity	$76,559,055

Morgan Construction Company Income Statement for the Fiscal Year Ended June 30, 2013

Net sales	$193,212,500
Costs	45,265,625
EBITDA	$ 47,946,875
Depreciation	23,318,750
EBIT	$ 24,628,125
Interest	11,935,869
EBT	$ 12,692,256
Taxes (35%)	4,442,290
Net income	$ 8,249,966

16.36 Use the financial information for Morgan Construction Company from Problem 16.35. Assume now that equity accounts do not vary directly with sales but change when retained earnings change or new equity is issued. The company pays 75 percent of its income as dividends every year. In addition, the company plans to expand production capacity by expanding the current facility and acquiring additional equipment. This will cost the firm $10 million. The firm has no plans to issue new equity this year. Prepare a pro forma balance sheet using this information. Any funds that need to be raised (in addition to changes in current liabilities) will be in the form of long-term debt. What is the external funding needed in this case?

16.37 Using the information for Morgan Construction Company in the preceding problem, calculate the firm's internal growth rate and sustainable growth rate.

16.38 Use the information for Morgan Construction Company from Problems 16.35 and 16.36. Assume that equity accounts do not vary directly with sales, but change when retained earnings change or new equity is issued. The company's long-term debt-to-equity ratio is approximately 90 percent, and its equity-to-total assets ratio is about 43 percent. The company management wishes to increase its equity-to-total assets ratio to at least 50 percent. Management is willing to reduce the company's payout ratio, but will retain no more than 40 percent of earnings. The company will raise any additional funds needed, including funds for expansion, by selling new equity. No new long-term debt will be issued. Prepare pro forma statements to reflect this new scenario.

  a. What is the external funding needed to accommodate the expected growth?
  b. What is the firm's internal growth rate?
  c. What is the firm's sustainable growth rate?
  d. How much new equity will the firm have to issue?
  e. What is the firm's new equity ratio and debt-to-equity ratio?

16.39 Munson Communications Company has just reported earnings for the year ended June 30, 2013. Below are the firm's income statement and balance sheet. The company had a 55 percent dividend payout ratio for the last 10 years and does not plan to change this policy. Based on internal forecasts, the company expects the demand for its products to grow at a rate of 20 percent for the next year and has projected the sales growth for 2014 to be 20 percent. Assume that equity accounts and long-term debt do not vary directly with sales, but change when retained earnings change or additional capital is issued.

Munson Communications Company Balance Sheet as of June 30, 2013

Assets:		Liabilities and Stockholders' Equity:	
Cash	$ 1,728,639	Accounts payable	$ 4,666,673
Accounts receivable	3,009,421	Notes payable	2,507,094
Inventories	11,492,993	Total current liabilities	$ 7,173,767
Total current assets	$16,231,054	Long-term debt	13,345,242
Net fixed assets	22,380,636	Common stock	10,165,235
Other assets	1,748,906	Retained earnings	9,676,351
Total assets	$40,360,595	Total liabilities and equity	$40,360,595

Munson Communications Company Income Statement for the Fiscal Year Ended June 30, 2013

Net sales	$79,722,581
Costs	59,358,499
EBITDA	$20,364,082
Depreciation	7,318,750
EBIT	$13,045,332
Interest	3,658,477
EBT	$ 9,386,855
Taxes (35%)	3,285,399
Net income	$ 6,101,456

  a. What is the firm's internal growth rate (IGR)?
  b. What is the firm's sustainable growth rate (SGR)?
  c. What is the external funding needed (EFN) to accommodate the expected growth?
  d. Construct the firm's 2014 pro forma financial statements under the assumption that long-term debt will provide all external funding.

Sample Test Problems

16.1   Mercury Corp. has annual sales of $2,512,654, costs of $1,080,227, interest payments of $132,375, and a tax rate of 34 percent. It pays annual dividends of $525,000 to its stockholders. Calculate the firm's dividend payout ratio and retention ratio.

16.2   Assume that Rex Corp. is operating at a capital intensity ratio of 63.5 percent and is able to generate net sales of $3,123,443. What is the book value of the firm's assets?

16.3   Centennial Beverages currently has sales of $1,415,326, net income of $411,253, a debt ratio of 25 percent, and a dividend payout ratio of 70 percent. The company also has total assets of $1,850,325. What is its sustainable growth rate?

16.4   Given the information in Sample Test Problem 16.3, what is the internal growth rate of Centennial Beverages?

16.5   Mirabelle Company has total assets of $3,267,450, sales of $5,174,652, and net income of $1,789,774. The company's management expects sales to grow by 20 percent next year. All assets and costs (including taxes) vary directly with sales, and management expects to maintain a payout ratio of 75 percent. Calculate the external funding needed (EFN).

Future Value and Present Value Tables

Appendix Tables

A-1 Future Value Factors for $1 Compounded at *i* Percent Per Period for *N* Periods

A-2 Present Value Factors for $1 Received at the End of *N* Periods, Discounted at *i* Percent Per Period

A-3 Future Value of Annuity Factors for $1 Received Per Period for Each of *N* Periods, Compounded at *i* Percent Per Period

A-4 Present Value of Annuity Factors for $1 Received Per Period for Each of *N* Periods, Discounted at *i* Percent Per Period

APPENDIX

TABLE A-1 · Future Value Factors for $1 Compounded at *i* Percent Per Period for *N* Periods

i

N	1%	2%	3%	4%	5%	6%	7%	8%	9%	10%
1	1.010	1.020	1.030	1.040	1.050	1.060	1.070	1.080	1.090	1.100
2	1.020	1.040	1.061	1.082	1.103	1.124	1.145	1.166	1.188	1.210
3	1.030	1.061	1.093	1.125	1.158	1.191	1.225	1.260	1.295	1.331
4	1.041	1.082	1.126	1.170	1.216	1.262	1.311	1.360	1.412	1.464
5	1.051	1.104	1.159	1.217	1.276	1.338	1.403	1.469	1.539	1.611
6	1.062	1.126	1.194	1.265	1.340	1.419	1.501	1.587	1.677	1.772
7	1.072	1.149	1.230	1.316	1.407	1.504	1.606	1.714	1.828	1.949
8	1.083	1.172	1.267	1.369	1.477	1.594	1.718	1.851	1.993	2.144
9	1.094	1.195	1.305	1.423	1.551	1.689	1.838	1.999	2.172	2.358
10	1.105	1.219	1.344	1.480	1.629	1.791	1.967	2.159	2.367	2.594
11	1.116	1.243	1.384	1.539	1.710	1.898	2.105	2.332	2.580	2.853
12	1.127	1.268	1.426	1.601	1.796	2.012	2.252	2.518	2.813	3.138
13	1.138	1.294	1.469	1.665	1.886	2.133	2.410	2.720	3.066	3.452
14	1.149	1.319	1.513	1.732	1.980	2.261	2.579	2.937	3.342	3.797
15	1.161	1.346	1.558	1.801	2.079	2.397	2.759	3.172	3.642	4.177
16	1.173	1.373	1.605	1.873	2.183	2.540	2.952	3.426	3.970	4.595
17	1.184	1.400	1.653	1.948	2.292	2.693	3.159	3.700	4.328	5.054
18	1.196	1.428	1.702	2.026	2.407	2.854	3.380	3.996	4.717	5.560
19	1.208	1.457	1.754	2.107	2.527	3.026	3.617	4.316	5.142	6.116
20	1.220	1.486	1.806	2.191	2.653	3.207	3.870	4.661	5.604	6.727
21	1.232	1.516	1.860	2.279	2.786	3.400	4.141	5.034	6.109	7.400
22	1.245	1.546	1.916	2.370	2.925	3.604	4.430	5.437	6.659	8.140
23	1.257	1.577	1.974	2.465	3.072	3.820	4.741	5.871	7.258	8.954
24	1.270	1.608	2.033	2.563	3.225	4.049	5.072	6.341	7.911	9.850
25	1.282	1.641	2.094	2.666	3.386	4.292	5.427	6.848	8.623	10.835
30	1.348	1.811	2.427	3.243	4.322	5.743	7.612	10.063	13.268	17.449
35	1.417	2.000	2.814	3.946	5.516	7.686	10.677	14.785	20.414	28.102
40	1.489	2.208	3.262	4.801	7.040	10.286	14.974	21.725	31.409	45.259
45	1.565	2.438	3.782	5.841	8.985	13.765	21.002	31.920	48.327	72.890
50	1.645	2.692	4.384	7.107	11.467	18.420	29.457	46.902	74.358	117.390

i

11%	12%	13%	14%	15%	20%	25%	30%	35%	40%
1.110	1.120	1.130	1.140	1.150	1.200	1.250	1.300	1.350	1.400
1.232	1.254	1.277	1.300	1.323	1.440	1.563	1.690	1.823	1.960
1.368	1.405	1.443	1.482	1.521	1.728	1.953	2.197	2.460	2.744
1.518	1.574	1.530	1.689	1.749	2.074	2.441	2.856	3.322	3.842
1.685	1.762	1.842	1.925	2.011	2.488	3.052	3.713	4.484	5.378
1.870	1.974	2.082	2.195	2.313	2.986	3.815	4.827	6.053	7.530
2.076	2.211	2.353	2.502	2.660	3.583	4.768	6.275	8.172	10.541
2.305	2.476	2.658	2.853	3.059	4.300	5.960	8.157	11.032	14.758
2.558	2.773	3.004	3.252	3.518	5.160	7.451	10.604	14.894	20.661
2.839	3.106	3.395	3.707	4.046	6.192	9.313	13.786	20.107	28.925
3.152	3.479	3.836	4.226	4.652	7.430	11.642	17.922	27.144	40.496
3.498	3.896	4.335	4.818	5.350	8.916	14.552	23.298	36.644	56.694
3.883	4.363	4.898	5.492	6.153	10.699	18.190	30.288	49.470	79.371
4.310	4.887	5.535	6.261	7.076	12.839	22.737	39.374	66.784	111.120
4.785	5.474	6.254	7.138	8.137	15.407	28.422	51.186	90.158	155.560
5.311	6.130	7.067	8.137	9.358	18.488	35.527	66.542	121.710	217.790
5.895	6.866	7.986	9.276	10.761	22.186	44.409	86.504	164.310	304.910
6.544	7.690	9.024	10.575	12.375	26.623	55.511	112.450	221.820	426.870
7.263	8.613	10.197	12.056	14.232	31.948	69.389	146.190	299.460	597.630
8.062	9.646	11.523	13.743	16.367	38.338	86.736	190.050	404.270	836.680
8.949	10.804	13.021	15.668	18.822	46.005	108.420	247.060	545.760	1171.300
9.934	12.100	14.714	17.861	21.645	55.206	135.520	321.180	716.780	1639.800
10.026	13.552	16.627	20.362	24.891	66.247	169.400	417.530	994.660	2297.800
12.239	15.179	18.788	23.212	28.625	79.497	211.750	542.800	1342.700	3214.200
13.585	17.000	21.231	26.462	32.919	95.396	264.690	705.640	1812.700	4499.800
22.892	29.960	39.116	50.950	66.212	237.370	807.790	2619.900	8128.500	24201.000
38.575	52.800	72.069	98.100	133.170	590.660	2465.100	9727.800	36448.000	130161.000
65.001	93.051	132.782	188.880	267.860	1469.700	7523.100	36118.000	163437.000	700037.000
109.530	163.980	244.641	363.670	538.760	3657.200	22958.000	134106.000	732857.000	
184.560	289.000	450.735	700.230	1083.600	9100.400	70064.000	497929.000		

TABLE A-2 Present Value Factors for $1 Received at the End of N Periods, Discounted at i Percent Per Period

i

N	1%	2%	3%	4%	5%	6%	7%	8%	9%	10%
1	.990	.980	.971	.962	.952	.943	.935	.926	.917	.909
2	.980	.961	.943	.925	.907	.890	.873	.857	.842	.826
3	.971	.942	.915	.889	.864	.840	.816	.794	.772	.751
4	.961	.924	.888	.855	.823	.792	.763	.735	.708	.683
5	.951	.906	.863	.822	.784	.747	.713	.681	.650	.621
6	.942	.888	.837	.790	.746	.705	.666	.630	.596	.564
7	.932	.871	.813	.760	.711	.665	.623	.583	.547	.513
8	.923	.853	.789	.731	.677	.627	.582	.540	.502	.467
9	.914	.837	.766	.703	.645	.592	.544	.500	.460	.424
10	.905	.820	.744	.676	.614	.558	.508	.463	.422	.386
11	.896	.804	.722	.650	.585	.527	.475	.429	.388	.350
12	.887	.788	.701	.625	.557	.497	.444	.397	.356	.319
13	.879	.773	.681	.601	.530	.469	.415	.368	.326	.290
14	.870	.758	.661	.577	.505	.442	.388	.340	.299	.263
15	.861	.743	.642	.555	.481	.417	.362	.315	.275	.239
16	.853	.728	.623	.534	.458	.394	.339	.292	.252	.218
17	.844	.714	.605	.513	.436	.371	.317	.270	.231	.198
18	.836	.700	.587	.494	.416	.350	.296	.250	.212	.180
19	.828	.686	.570	.475	.396	.331	.277	.232	.194	.164
20	.820	.673	.554	.456	.377	.312	.258	.215	.178	.149
21	.811	.660	.538	.439	.359	.294	.242	.199	.164	.135
22	.803	.647	.522	.422	.342	.278	.226	.184	.150	.123
23	.795	.634	.507	.406	.326	.262	.211	.170	.133	.112
24	.788	.622	.492	.390	.310	.247	.197	.158	.126	.102
25	.780	.610	.478	.375	.295	.233	.184	.146	.116	.092
30	.742	.552	.412	.308	.231	.174	.131	.099	.075	.057
35	.706	.500	.355	.253	.181	.130	.094	.068	.049	.036
40	.672	.453	.307	.208	.142	.097	.067	.046	.032	.022
45	.639	.410	.264	.171	.111	.073	.048	.031	.021	.014
50	.608	.372	.228	.141	.087	.054	.034	.021	.013	.009

11%	12%	13%	14%	15%	20%	25%	30%	35%	40%
.901	.893	.885	.877	.870	.833	.800	.769	.741	.714
.812	.797	.783	.769	.756	.694	.640	.592	.449	.510
.731	.712	.693	.675	.658	.579	.512	.455	.406	.364
.659	.636	.613	.592	.572	.482	.410	.350	.301	.260
.593	.567	.543	.519	.497	.402	.328	.269	.223	.186
.535	.507	.480	.456	.432	.335	.262	.207	.165	.133
.482	.452	.425	.400	.376	.279	.210	.159	.122	.095
.434	.404	.376	.351	.327	.233	.168	.123	.091	.068
.391	.361	.333	.308	.284	.194	.134	.094	.067	.048
.352	.322	.295	.270	.247	.162	.107	.073	.050	.035
.317	.287	.261	.237	.215	.135	.086	.056	.037	.025
.286	.257	.231	.208	.187	.112	.069	.043	.027	.018
.258	.229	.204	.182	.163	.093	.055	.033	.020	.013
.232	.205	.181	.160	.141	.078	.044	.025	.015	.009
.209	.183	.160	.140	.123	.065	.035	.020	.011	.006
.188	.163	.141	.123	.107	.054	.028	.015	.008	.005
.170	.146	.125	.108	.093	.045	.023	.012	.006	.003
.153	.130	.111	.095	.081	.038	.018	.009	.005	.002
.138	.116	.098	.083	.070	.031	.014	.007	.003	.002
.124	.104	.087	.073	.061	.026	.012	.005	.002	.001
.112	.093	.077	.064	.053	.022	.009	.004	.002	.001
.101	.083	.068	.056	.046	.018	.007	.003	.001	.001
.091	.074	.060	.049	.040	.015	.006	.002	.001	
.082	.066	.053	.043	.035	.013	.005	.002	.001	
.074	.059	.047	.038	.030	.010	.004	.001	.001	
.044	.033	.026	.020	.015	.004	.001			
.026	.019	.014	.010	.008	.002				
.015	.011	.008	.005	.004	.001				
.009	.006	.004	.003	.002					
.005	.003	.002	.001	.001					

N	1%	2%	3%	4%	5%	6%	7%	8%	9%	10%
1	1.000	1.000	1.000	1.000	1.000	1.000	1.000	1.000	1.000	1.000
2	2.010	2.020	2.030	2.040	2.050	2.060	2.070	2.080	2.090	2.100
3	3.030	3.060	3.091	3.122	3.152	3.184	3.215	3.246	3.278	3.310
4	4.060	4.122	4.184	4.246	4.310	4.375	4.440	4.506	4.573	4.641
5	5.101	5.204	5.309	5.416	5.526	5.637	5.751	5.867	5.985	6.105
6	6.152	6.308	6.468	6.633	6.802	6.975	7.153	7.336	7.523	7.716
7	7.214	7.434	7.662	7.898	8.142	8.394	8.654	8.923	9.200	9.487
8	8.286	8.583	8.892	9.214	9.549	10.897	10.260	10.637	11.028	11.436
9	9.369	9.755	10.159	10.583	11.027	11.491	11.978	12.488	13.021	13.579
10	10.462	10.950	11.464	12.006	12.578	13.181	13.816	14.487	15.193	15.937
11	11.567	12.169	12.808	13.486	14.207	14.972	15.784	16.645	17.560	18.531
12	12.683	13.412	14.192	15.026	15.917	16.870	17.888	18.977	20.141	21.384
13	13.809	14.680	15.618	16.627	17.713	18.882	20.141	21.495	22.953	24.523
14	14.947	15.971	17.086	18.292	19.599	21.015	22.550	24.215	26.019	27.975
15	16.097	17.291	18.599	20.024	21.579	23.276	25.129	27.152	29.361	31.722
16	17.258	18.639	20.157	21.825	23.657	25.673	27.888	30.324	33.003	35.950
17	18.430	20.012	21.762	23.698	25.840	28.213	30.840	33.750	36.974	40.545
18	19.615	21.412	23.414	25.645	28.132	30.906	33.999	37.450	41.301	45.599
19	20.811	22.841	25.117	27.671	30.539	33.760	37.379	41.446	46.018	51.159
20	22.019	24.297	26.870	29.778	33.066	36.786	40.995	45.762	51.160	57.275
21	23.239	25.783	28.676	31.969	35.719	39.993	44.865	50.423	56.765	64.002
22	24.472	27.299	30.537	34.248	38.505	43.392	49.006	55.457	62.873	71.403
23	25.716	28.845	32.453	36.618	41.430	46.996	53.436	60.893	69.532	79.543
24	26.973	30.422	34.426	39.083	44.502	50.816	58.177	66.765	76.790	88.497
25	28.243	32.030	36.459	41.646	47.727	54.865	63.249	73.106	84.701	98.347
30	34.785	40.568	47.575	56.085	66.439	79.058	94.461	113.280	136.300	164.490
35	41.660	49.994	60.462	73.652	90.320	111.430	138.230	172.310	215.710	271.020
40	48.886	60.402	75.401	95.026	120.800	154.760	199.630	259.050	337.880	442.590
45	56.481	71.893	92.720	121.020	159.700	212.740	285.740	386.500	525.850	718.900
50	64.463	84.579	112.790	152.660	209.340	290.330	406.520	573.770	815.080	1163.900

11%	12%	13%	14%	15%	20%	25%	30%	35%	40%
1.000	1.000	1.000	1.000	1.000	1.000	1.000	1.000	1.000	1.000
2.110	2.120	2.130	2.140	2.150	2.200	2.250	2.300	2.350	2.400
3.342	3.374	3.407	3.440	3.472	3.640	3.813	3.990	4.172	4.360
4.710	4.779	4.850	4.921	4.993	5.368	5.766	6.187	6.633	7.104
6.228	6.353	6.480	6.610	6.742	7.442	8.207	9.043	9.954	10.196
7.913	8.115	8.232	8.536	8.754	9.930	11.259	12.756	14.438	16.324
9.783	10.089	10.405	10.730	11.067	12.916	15.073	17.583	20.492	23.853
11.859	12.300	12.757	13.233	13.727	16.499	19.842	23.858	28.664	34.395
14.164	14.776	15.416	16.085	16.786	20.799	25.802	32.015	39.696	49.153
16.722	17.549	18.420	19.337	20.304	25.959	33.253	42.619	54.590	69.814
19.561	20.655	21.814	23.045	24.349	32.150	42.566	56.405	74.697	98.739
22.713	24.133	25.650	27.271	29.002	39.581	54.208	74.327	101.840	139.230
26.212	28.029	29.985	32.089	34.352	48.497	68.760	97.625	138.480	195.920
30.095	32.393	34.883	37.581	40.505	59.196	86.949	127.910	187.950	275.300
34.405	37.280	40.417	43.842	47.580	72.035	109.680	167.280	254.730	386.420
39.190	42.753	46.672	50.980	55.717	87.442	138.100	218.470	344.890	541.980
44.501	48.884	53.739	59.118	65.075	105.930	173.630	285.010	466.610	759.780
50.396	55.750	61.725	68.394	75.836	128.110	218.040	371.510	630.920	1064.600
56.939	63.440	70.749	78.969	88.212	154.740	273.550	483.970	852.740	1491.500
64.203	72.052	80.947	91.025	102.440	186.680	342.940	630.160	1152.200	2089.200
72.265	81.699	92.470	104.760	118.810	225.020	429.680	820.210	1556.400	2925.800
81.214	92.503	105.491	120.430	137.630	271.030	538.100	1067.200	2102.200	4097.200
91.148	104.600	120.205	138.290	159.270	326.230	673.620	1388.400	2839.000	5737.100
102.170	118.150	136.831	158.650	184.160	392.480	843.030	1806.000	3833.700	8032.900
114.410	133.330	155.620	181.870	212.790	471.980	1054.700	2348.800	5176.500	11247.000
199.020	241.330	293.199	356.780	434.740	1181.800	3227.100	8729.900	23221.000	60501.000
341.590	431.660	546.681	693.570	881.170	2948.300	9856.700	32422.000	104136.000	325400.000
581.820	767.090	1013.704	1342.000	1779.000	7343.800	30088.000	120392.000	466960.000	
986.630	1358.200	1874.165	2490.500	3585.100	18281.000	91831.000	447019.000		
1668.700	2400.000	3459.507	4994.500	7217.700	45497.000	280255.000			

Present Value of Annuity Factors for $1 Received Per Period for Each of *N* Periods, Discounted at *i* Percent Per Period

i

N	1%	2%	3%	4%	5%	6%	7%	8%	9%	10%
1	0.990	0.980	0.971	0.962	0.952	0.943	0.935	0.926	0.917	0.909
2	1.970	1.942	1.913	1.886	1.859	1.833	1.808	1.783	1.759	1.736
3	2.941	2.884	2.829	2.775	2.723	2.673	2.624	2.577	2.531	2.487
4	3.902	3.808	3.717	3.630	3.546	3.465	3.387	3.312	3.240	3.170
5	4.853	4.713	4.580	4.452	4.329	4.212	4.100	3.993	3.890	3.791
6	5.795	5.601	5.417	5.242	5.076	4.917	4.767	4.623	4.486	4.355
7	6.728	6.472	6.230	6.002	5.786	5.582	5.389	5.206	5.033	4.868
8	7.652	7.325	7.020	6.733	6.463	6.210	5.971	5.747	5.535	5.335
9	8.566	8.162	7.786	7.435	7.108	6.802	6.515	6.247	5.995	5.759
10	9.471	8.983	8.530	8.111	7.722	7.360	7.024	6.710	6.418	6.145
11	10.368	9.787	9.253	8.760	8.306	7.887	7.499	7.139	6.805	6.495
12	11.255	10.575	9.954	9.385	8.863	8.384	7.943	7.536	7.161	6.814
13	12.134	11.348	10.635	9.986	9.394	8.853	8.358	7.904	7.487	7.103
14	13.004	12.106	11.296	10.563	9.899	9.295	8.745	8.244	7.786	7.367
15	13.865	12.849	11.938	11.118	10.380	9.712	9.108	8.559	8.061	7.606
16	14.718	13.578	12.561	11.652	10.838	10.106	9.447	8.851	8.313	7.824
17	15.562	14.292	13.166	12.166	11.274	10.477	9.763	9.122	8.544	8.022
18	16.398	14.992	13.754	12.659	11.690	10.828	10.059	9.372	8.756	8.201
19	17.226	15.678	14.324	13.134	12.085	11.158	10.336	9.604	8.950	8.365
20	18.046	16.351	14.877	13.590	12.462	11.470	10.594	9.818	9.129	8.514
21	18.857	17.011	15.415	14.029	12.821	11.764	10.836	10.017	9.292	8.649
22	19.660	17.658	15.937	14.451	13.163	12.042	11.061	10.201	9.442	8.772
23	20.456	18.292	16.444	14.857	13.489	12.303	11.272	10.371	9.580	8.883
24	21.243	18.914	16.936	15.247	13.799	12.550	11.469	10.529	9.707	8.985
25	22.023	19.523	17.413	15.622	14.094	12.783	11.654	10.675	9.823	9.077
30	25.808	22.396	19.600	17.292	15.372	13.765	12.409	11.258	10.274	9.427
35	29.409	24.999	21.487	18.665	16.374	14.498	12.948	11.655	10.567	9.644
40	32.835	27.355	23.115	19.793	17.159	15.046	13.332	11.925	10.757	9.779
45	36.095	29.490	24.519	20.720	17.774	15.456	13.606	12.108	10.881	9.863
50	39.196	31.424	25.730	21.482	18.256	15.762	13.801	12.233	10.962	9.915

11%	12%	13%	14%	15%	20%	25%	30%	35%	40%
0.901	0.893	0.885	0.877	0.870	0.833	0.800	0.769	0.741	0.714
1.713	1.690	1.668	1.647	1.626	1.528	1.440	1.361	1.289	1.224
2.444	2.402	2.361	2.322	2.283	2.106	1.952	1.816	1.696	1.589
3.102	3.037	2.974	2.914	2.855	2.589	2.362	2.166	1.997	1.849
3.696	3.605	3.517	3.433	3.352	2.991	2.689	2.436	2.220	2.035
4.231	4.111	3.998	3.889	3.784	3.326	2.951	2.643	2.385	2.168
4.712	4.564	4.423	4.288	4.160	3.605	3.161	2.802	2.508	2.263
5.146	4.968	4.799	4.639	4.487	3.837	3.329	2.925	2.598	2.331
5.537	5.328	5.132	4.946	4.772	4.031	3.463	3.019	2.665	2.379
5.889	5.650	5.426	5.216	5.019	4.192	3.571	3.092	2.715	2.414
6.207	5.938	5.687	5.453	5.234	4.327	3.656	3.147	2.752	2.438
6.492	6.194	5.918	5.660	5.421	4.439	3.725	3.190	2.779	2.456
6.750	6.424	6.122	5.842	5.583	4.533	3.780	3.223	2.799	2.469
6.982	6.628	6.302	6.002	5.724	4.611	3.824	3.249	2.814	2.478
7.191	6.811	6.462	6.142	5.847	4.675	3.859	3.268	2.825	2.484
7.379	6.974	6.604	6.265	5.954	4.730	3.887	3.283	2.834	2.489
7.549	7.120	6.729	6.373	6.047	4.775	3.910	3.295	2.840	2.492
7.702	7.250	6.840	6.467	6.128	4.812	3.928	3.304	2.844	2.494
7.839	7.366	6.938	6.550	6.198	4.843	3.942	3.311	2.848	2.496
7.963	7.469	7.025	6.623	6.259	4.870	3.954	3.316	2.850	2.497
8.075	7.562	7.102	6.687	6.312	4.891	3.963	3.320	2.852	2.498
8.176	7.654	7.170	6.743	6.359	4.909	3.970	3.323	2.853	2.498
8.266	7.718	7.230	6.792	6.399	4.925	3.976	3.325	2.854	2.499
8.348	7.784	7.283	6.835	6.434	4.937	3.981	3.327	2.855	2.499
8.422	7.843	7.330	6.873	6.464	4.948	3.985	3.329	2.856	2.499
8.694	8.055	7.496	7.003	6.566	4.979	3.995	3.332	2.857	2.500
8.855	8.176	7.586	7.070	6.617	4.992	3.998	3.333	2.857	2.500
8.951	8.244	7.634	7.105	6.642	4.997	3.999	3.333	2.857	2.500
9.008	8.283	7.661	7.123	6.654	4.999	4.000	3.333	2.857	2.500
9.042	8.304	7.675	7.133	6.661	4.999	4.000	3.333	2.857	2.500

Solutions to Selected Questions and Problems

B

CHAPTER 1

1.1 The two basic sources of funds for all businesses are debt and equity.

1.3 A profitable firm is able to generate enough cash flows from productive assets to cover its operating expenses, taxes, and payments to creditors. Unprofitable firms fail to do this, and therefore they may be forced to declare bankruptcy.

1.5 A firm should undertake a capital project only if the value of its future cash flows exceeds the cost of the project.

1.7 The financial manager must make working capital decisions regarding the level of inventory to hold, the terms of granting credit (account receivables), and the firm's policy on paying accounts payable.

1.9 *Advantages*: easiest business type to start; least regulated; owners have full control; all income is taxed as personal income. *Disadvantages*: unlimited liability of proprietor; initial capital limited to proprietor's wealth; difficult to transfer ownership.

1.11 The owners of a corporation are its stockholders, and the evidence of their ownership is represented by shares of common stock.

1.13 Double taxation occurs when earnings are taxed twice. The owners of a C-corporation are subject to double taxation—first at the corporate level when the firm's earnings are taxed and then again at a personal level when the dividends they receive are taxed.

1.15 The board of directors of a corporation is responsible for serving the interests of stockholders in managing the corporation. It is possible that the interests of managers may deviate from those of their stockholders. The board's objective is to hire and monitor managers to ensure that they are acting in the best interests of the stockholders. Board duties include hiring and firing the CEO, setting CEO pay, and monitoring the investment decisions of managers.

1.17 Problems include: It is difficult to determine what is meant by profits; it does not address the size and timing of cash flows (it does not account for the time value of money); and it ignores the uncertainty (risk) of cash flows.

1.19 Factors that affect the stock price include: The characteristics of the firm, the economy, economic shocks, the business environment, expected cash flows, and current market conditions.

1.21 If a firm's stock price falls sustainably below its maximum potential price, it might attract corporate raiders. These persons look for firms that are fundamentally sound but poorly managed, so that they can buy the firm, turn it around, and sell it for a profit.

1.23 A lack of business ethics can lead to corruption, which, in turn, creates inefficiencies in an economy, inhibits the growth of capital markets, and slows the rate of overall economic growth. For example, the Russian economy has had a relatively difficult time attracting foreign investment since the fall of the Soviet Union due, in part, to corruption in the business community and local and national governments. Lower foreign investment has led to slower overall economic growth than the country might otherwise have enjoyed.

1.25 An information asymmetry exists when one party to a business transaction possesses information that is not available to the other parties in the transaction. If the parties with less information understand their relative disadvantage, they are likely to pay lower prices for the goods or services they purchase, or charge higher prices for the goods and services that they sell.

CHAPTER 2

2.1 The role of the financial system is to gather money from businesses and individuals who have surplus funds and channel funds to those who need them. The financial system consists of financial markets and financial institutions.

2.3 Saver-lenders are those who have more money than they need right now. The principal saver-lenders in the economy are households. Borrower-spenders are those who need the money saver-lenders are offering. The main borrower-spenders in the economy are businesses and the federal government.

2.5 Your security seems to be marketable, but not liquid. Liquidity implies that when a security is sold, its value will be preserved; marketability does not.

2.7 Trader, Inc., is more likely to go public because of its larger size. Though the cost of SEC registration and compliance is very high, larger firms can offset these costs by the lower funding cost in public markets. Smaller companies find the cost prohibitive for the dollar amount of securities they sell.

2.9 **a.** secondary; **b.** primary; **c.** primary

2.11 **a.** $300,000; **b.** 3.05%; **c.** $9,850,000

2.13 Financial intermediaries allow smaller companies to access the financial markets. They do this by converting securities with one set of characteristics into securities with another set of characteristics that meets the needs of smaller companies. By repackaging securities, they are able to meet the needs of different clients.

2.15 Money markets are markets where short-term debt instruments with maturities of less than one year are bought and sold. Capital markets are markets where equity securities and debt instruments with maturities of more than one year are sold.

2.17 Treasury bills, bank negotiable CDs, and commercial paper

2.19 The strong-form of market efficiency states that all information is reflected in the security's price. In other words, there is no private or inside information that, if released, would potentially change the price. The semistrong-form of market efficiency holds that all public information available to investors is reflected in the security's price. Therefore, insiders with access to private information could potentially profit from trading on this information before it becomes public. Finally, the weak form of market efficiency holds that there is both public and private information that is not reflected in the security's price and having access to it can enable an investor to earn abnormal profits.

2.21 Yes. The last sentence in the Problem 2.20 problem statement suggests why this might happen. If, on the same day of the announcement, some very bad news about the future prospects for Zippy became public or if the market went down substantially, Zippy's stock price might also have gone down despite the positive sales and earnings announcement.

2.23 Public markets are organized financial markets where the public buys and sells securities through their stockbrokers. The SEC regulates public securities markets in the United States. In contrast, private markets involve direct transactions between two parties. These transactions lack SEC regulation.

2.25 The real rate of interest measures the return earned on savings, and it represents the cost of borrowing to finance capital goods. The real rate of interest is determined by the interaction between firms that invest in capital projects and the rate of return they expect to earn on those investments, and individuals' time preference for consumption. The rate of interest is determined when the desired level of savings equals the desired level of investments in the economy.

2.27 The Fisher equation is an equation that shows how the expected annualized change in commodity prices (ΔP_e) is related to the nominal and real rates of interest. It is used to determine the nominal rate that protects the buying power of a lender's money from changes in inflation. It is also used to determine the interest rate, by subtracting ΔP_e from the nominal interest rate, that would exist in the absence of inflation.

2.29 Yes. The CD will be worth $1,067.50 at the end of the year, and the price of the trip will be $1,066.

CHAPTER 3

3.1 $97,118

3.3 FIFO makes sense during times of rising prices because it allows the firm to eliminate the lower-priced inventory first, which results in higher profit margins.

3.5 $6,655,610

3.7 $242,401.25

3.9 −$132.085

3.11 Noncash expenses are expenses identified on income statement that did not result in cash flows. Depreciation and amortization are examples of such expenses.

3.13 $284,061

3.15 The **average tax rate** is the total taxes paid divided by taxable income. The **marginal tax rate** is the tax rate that is paid on the last dollar of income earned, or the rate that will be paid on the next dollar earned.

3.17 $502,838

3.19 $153,470

3.21 $137,263

3.23 $1,804,546

3.25 $620,878

3.27 $218,364.32; 34%; 34%

3.29 $715,720

3.31 $198,152

3.33 CFNWC = −$16,467
CFLTA = $291,401

CHAPTER 4

4.1 The quick ratio provides a better measure of liquidity because it includes only the most liquid of the current assets.

4.3 $1,627,579

4.5 2.87 times; 127.1 days

4.7 2.65; 0.623; 29.9%

4.9 29.93%

4.11 **a.** Trademark is not doing as well as its competitors. The total asset and inventory turnover ratios indicate that the firm either needs to increase its sales relative to its level of total assets and inventory or reduce its total assets and inventory relative to its level of sales. In addition, the lower quick ratio indicates that Trademark has less liquidity. The higher DSO indicates that accounts receivable are relatively high.
b. Average industry ratios serve as benchmarks that management can use to assess a firm's performance. While no two firms are identical in any industry, the average ratios across an industry are generally good target ratios for a firm.

4.13 1.34

4.15 $3,825,000

4.17 $843,863

4.19 2.27; 1.27

4.21 51.2%; 19.1%; 12.6%

4.23 0.41; 36.02%; 18.32%; 25.92%

4.25 34.4 times; 22.04 times

4.27 $6,473,600; 5.7%

4.29 $10,226,559; $88,236,056; 0.82

4.31 Current ratio = 0.77; quick ratio = 0.57; gross margin = 51.2%; profit margin = 12.6%; debt ratio = 0.70; long-term debt to equity = 0.73; interest coverage = 20.6; ROA = 11.4%; ROE = 37.5%

4.33 Profit margin = 12.61%; total asset turnover = 0.90; equity multiplier = 3.30; return on equity = 12.61% × 0.90 × 3.30 = 37.5%

4.35 $292,756.63

4.37 Current ratio = 1.81; quick ratio = 1.19; inventory turnover = 3.50; accounts receivable turnover = 5.16; DSO = 70.76; total asset turnover = 1.23; fixed asset turnover = 7.15; total debt ratio = 0.63; debt to equity ratio = 1.72; equity multiplier = 2.72; times interest earned = 17.56; cash coverage = 25.94, gross profit margin = 0.36; net profit margin = 0.08; ROA = 0.10; ROE = 0.27

CHAPTER 5

5.1 $10,036.69

5.3 $1,108.86

5.5 $661.24

5.7 The loan from your uncle would cost 7.42%; You should borrow from the bank.

5.9 $17,498.75

5.11 $38,652.76

5.13 $75,423.49

5.15 $1,361,642.36

5.17 **a.** $15,000; **b.** $6,000; **c.** $10,000

5.19 5%

5.21 $1,490,348.16

5.23 **a.** $5,232.09; **b.** $3,934.48; **c.** $6,067.86;
d. $3,374.51; **e.** $2,933.78

5.25 **a.** $4,848.92; **b.** $4,749.54; **c.** $4,710.31;
d. $4,697.22; Samantha should invest in choice D.

5.27 $34,231.57

5.29 $610.27

5.31 $63,760.19

5.33 $2,633,199

5.35 13.96%

5.37 3.69 years $\Rightarrow$ Year 4; $2,752,671.62

5.39 Current: $12,847,215.41; Team's Offer: $11,374,540.65;
Counteroffer $14,519,339.52. The counteroffer has the best value for the player.

5.41 The 25 equal payments are worth $54,199,920; You should choose the lump sum option.

5.43 **a.** $86,124.36; **b.** $14,156.64; **c.** $71,967.72; **d.** $6,627.21

5.45 $2,103.89

CHAPTER 6

6.1 A holding period return is the total return over some investment or "holding" period. It consists of a capital appreciation component and an income component. A holding period return reflects past performance. An expected return is the probability-weighted average of the possible returns from an investment. It describes a possible return (or even a return that may not be possible) for a yet-to-occur investment period.

6.3 $78,000

6.5 Stock B

6.7 Risk that cannot be diversified away is *systematic risk*. It is the only type of risk that exists in a diversified portfolio, and it is the only type of risk that is rewarded in asset markets.

6.9 Since a U.S. Treasury bill has no systematic risk, its beta should equal 0.

6.11 The CAPM describes the relation between systematic risk and the expected return that investors require for bearing that risk.

6.13 $1,250

6.15 0.145; 0.162

6.17 0.125; 0.168

6.19 $\sigma_{12} = 0.12, 0.1225$; $\sigma_{12} = 0, 0.0625$; $\sigma_{12} = -0.12, 0.0025$

6.21 Your portfolio contains no unsystematic risk, but it does contain systematic risk. Therefore, the market should compensate the holder of this portfolio for the systematic risk that the investor bears. A risk-free security has no risk, and therefore requires no compensation for risk bearing. The expected return of your portfolio should therefore be greater than the return from the risk-free security.

6.23 The statement is false. A portfolio of all assets would only eliminate unsystematic risk. The systematic risk would remain. If you could eliminate both systematic and unsystematic risk, the expected rate of return on the market portfolio would be equal to the risk-free rate of return, and we know that this is not true.

6.25 0.124

6.27 0.185; 0.165

6.29 0.19

6.31 If all investors require returns that compensate them for the level of risk that they bear, then undiversified investors will require a greater return for a given investment than diversified investors. In other words, diversified investors will be willing to pay a higher price for an asset than will undiversified investors. Therefore, a diversified investor is the marginal investor whose purchase will determine the price, and therefore the expected return for an asset.

6.33 The first security is underpriced, and the second is overpriced.

6.35 $\sigma_{RA} = 0.06$; $\beta_B = 2.25$; $\rho_{RC,M} = 1.00$; $\rho_{RM,M} = 1.00$; $\beta_M = 1.00$;
$\rho_{RT\text{-}bill,M} = 0$; $\beta_{T\text{-}bill} = 0$
$E(R_A) = 0.125$; $E(R_B) = 0.1625$; $E(R_C) = 0.075$

A comparison of the expected returns that are given in the problem statement, with the returns that CAPM predicts (which are presented above), indicates that you should buy stocks A and C and avoid stock B.

CHAPTER 7

7.1 $1,147.20

7.3 $1,008.15

7.5 $975.91

7.7 $359.38

7.9 6.58%; 6.69%

7.11 9.52%

7.13 $1,000

7.15 $912.61; 1,370 contracts

7.17 $1,079.22

7.19 12.45%

7.21 7.23%; 7.36%

7.23 11.49% (EAY = 11.82%)

7.25 8.65% (EAY = 8.84%)

7.27 **a.** $924.75; **b.** 9.67% (EAY = 9.90%)

7.29 **a.** $904.76; **b.** $1,086.46, $832.53
c. Bond prices decrease when interest rates go up and increase when interest rates go down.
d. $1,063.42, $866.65

7.31 **a.** $25
b. The stock price would have to increase by two standard deviations ($2 \times \$5 = \$10$) for the price to increase to $25 and for conversion to become attractive to the investors. From Chapter 6 we know that 95% of possible outcomes fall within 1.96 standard deviations of the mean (average) value in a normal distribution. This means that there is approximately a 5 percent chance that the stock price will move up or down by $10 or more. Since the normal distribution is symmetric, this means that there is only a 2.5 percent chance that Zippy's stock price will increase enough for it to become attractive for the investors to exercise the conversion option in the next year.

CHAPTER 8

8.1 A stock market index is an index used to measure the performance of a stock market. These indexes reflect the value of the stocks in a particular market, such as the NYSE or the NASDAQ, or across markets, and they increase and decrease as the values of the stocks go up and down. Examples of stock market indexes include the Dow Jones Industrial Average, the New York Stock Exchange Index, the Standard & Poor's 500 Index, and the NASDAQ Composite Index.

8.3 National Association of Securities Dealers Automatic Quotation system. NASDAQ is one of the world's largest electronic markets, listing over three thousand companies.

8.5 $14.24

8.7 $27.39

8.9 $8.50

8.11 $31.12

8.13 12.15%

8.15 $56.90

8.17 $2.46

8.19 $21.07

8.21 $5.15

8.23 $23.35

8.25 $32.34

8.27 $25.95

8.29 $2.15

8.31 $73.94

8.33 **a.** $34.45

    b. No, she should not buy more shares. This stock is overpriced with the stock selling at a higher price than what it is worth. She should sell her shares.

8.35 **a.** $6.37; **b.** $62.03; **c.** $48.24

8.37 **a.** $2.41; **b.** $37.86; **c.** $20.67

    d. No, the length of the holding period has no bearing on today's stock price.

CHAPTER 9

9.1 $62,337

9.3 Yes; NPV = $134,986.

9.5 Blanda should invest in System 2. The NPV of System 1 is $22,969.42, and the NPV of System 2 is $36,001.43.

9.7 2.87 years

9.9 3.45 years

9.11 33.8%

9.13 The profitability index is computed as the ratio of NPV plus initial investment to initial investment. In the capital rationing process, we can calculate the profitability index for each potential investment and choose the projects with the largest indexes until we run out of capital. This follows the basic principle that we need to choose the set of projects that creates the greatest value given the limited capital available.

9.15 −$351,223

9.17 System 200 will be chosen. NPV = $75,758 for System 200 and NPV = −$56,667 for System 100.

9.19 Project A = 4+ years; Project B = 3+ years. Since the firm's acceptance criteria is three years, neither project will be accepted.

9.21 4.19 years

9.23 17.4%

9.25 System 1 IRR = 83.93%; System 2 IRR 50.07%. System 1 NPV = $22,969.42; System 2 NPV = $36,001.43. System 1 delivers a higher IRR because it requires a lower initial investment and the cost is recovered the first year. Thus, even with lower cash inflows in the years after startup, System 1 is able to deliver a higher return on the initial investment. System 2 has a higher initial investment but delivers a higher net cash flow for the firm.

9.27 **a.** 6.97%; **b.** 13.3%; **c.** 14.2%

9.29 Compute the profitability index for each of the projects. PI_A = 1.50; PI_B = 1.64; PI_C = 1.56; PI_D = 1.57. With $30,000, you should invest in B, D, and C. The total cost is $27,000, and the total NPV is $16,000.

9.31 NPV of Project 1 = −$668,283 (reject); NPV of Project 2 = $375,375 (accept)

9.33 At 14.8%, only Project 2 will be accepted. At 13.6%, Projects 2 and 3 will be accepted.

9.35 Project 1 should be accepted. Its NPV = $186,683 and its IRR = 20.1%. Project 2 has NPV = −$76,796 and IRR = 12.4%.

9.37 Project 1 = 16.1%; Project 2 = 13.7%; Project 3 = 10.9%

9.39 **a.** 5.45 years; **b.** 4.1%; **c.** −$2,043,927; **d.** 3.1%

9.41 **a.** A = $147,891, B = $166,553; **b.** A = 27.2%, B = 26.1%; **c.** Both should be accepted under the NPV and IRR decision criteria; **d.** Both projects will be accepted. They are independent and both have a positive NPV.

9.43 NPV_x = $2,650.78; NPV_y = $2,189.06; PI_x = 1.1325; PI_y = 1.1095 Both methods rank Project X over Project Y. However, both projects should be accepted under the NPV criteria. Therefore, both should be accepted if they are independent and sufficient resources are available. If the projects are mutually exclusive, the project with the higher NPV or PI, which in this case is Project X, should be chosen.

9.45 Discounted payback period is 1.01 years longer than the payback period.

9.47 IRR = 28.79%

CHAPTER 10

10.1 The main reason is that accounting earnings generally differ from free cash flows, and free cash flows are what stockholders care about.

10.3 Subtract depreciation from EBITDA, multiply by (1 − tax rate), and add back depreciation. This enables us to account for the fact that depreciation reduces the taxes that must be paid.

10.5 The average tax rate is the total amount of tax divided by total amount of money earned, while the marginal tax rate is the rate paid on the last dollar earned. Use the marginal tax rate when calculating incremental after-tax free cash flows.

10.7 Variable costs vary directly with the number of units sold. Fixed costs do not vary with the number of units sold.

10.9 $9,009.60

10.11 $1,370

10.13 The Equivalent Annual Cost (EAC) is the annual payment from an annuity that has a life equal to that of a project and that has the same NPV as the project.

10.15 $891.84

10.17 marginal = 35%; average = 34.2%

10.19 $168,020,000

10.21 EAC_A = −$6,569.55; EAC_B = −$6,199.69; You should choose machine B because it has the lowest equivalent annual cost.

10.23 NPV = $12,950,929; you should approve the project.

10.25 Yes; the NPV = $38,356.

10.27 −$363,814

CHAPTER 11

11.1 $98 million

11.3 When we calculate the cost of debt for a U.S. firm, we must take into account the tax subsidy given in the United States for interest payments on debt. For every dollar the firm pays in interest, the firm's tax bill will decline by ($1 × t), where t is the firm's marginal tax rate. We adjust for this tax benefit by multiplying the pretax cost of debt by (1 − t). This calculation gives us the after-tax cost of debt. We use the after-tax cost of debt for cost of capital calculations such as when we calculate the WACC.

11.5 16%

11.7 10%

11.9   15.8%

11.11   9.4%

11.13   The owners of all of the securities that have been sold to finance a firm, collectively, own all of the cash flows that the assets of the firm generate. The value of these securities must equal the value of these cash flows and, therefore, the value of the firm.

11.15 $1,000

11.17   7.7%

11.19   4.63%, 6.27%

11.21 $$P_{cs} = \frac{D_1}{1 + k_{cs}} + \frac{D_1(1 + g_1)}{(1 + k_{cs})^2} + \frac{D_1(1 + g_1)^2}{(1 + k_{cs})^3} + \frac{D_1(1 + g_1)^3}{(1 + k_{cs})^4}$$
$$+ \frac{D_1(1 + g_1)^4}{(1 + k_{cs})^5} + \frac{D_1(1 + g_1)^4(1 + g_2)}{(k_{cs} - g_2)(1 + k_{cs})^6}$$

It is easy to see that in order to solve for a cost of capital, k_{cs}, you must have a good idea of what g_1 and g_2 are. If those growth rates are poor estimates, then the calculation for k_{cs}, will also be a poor estimate.

11.23   Markets adjust the cost of capital according to the level of systematic risk in a project. Therefore, the project with the greatest level of systematic risk will have the greatest positive impact on the cost of capital for the firm, even if it has the lowest level of unsystematic risk.

11.25   Since Imaginary will be financing the project with the same mix of capital that the firm is currently utilizing for its projects, we will have met the first restriction concerning financing mix. In addition, the new project will have the same degree of systematic risk (in addition to being in the same general line of business). Therefore, Imaginary can use the 9.26 percent cost of capital to evaluate its project.

11.27   While the growth in dividends has been extremely constant for MacroSwift over the last 15 years, it is appropriate to assume a constant-growth rate only if that same rate is expected to continue in the future. Two factors will act to alter that growth in the future. MacroSwift will have competition for its current products in the near future, and that could alter the firm's growth rate. In addition, the firm is expanding its product line into an area that will probably not yield the same level of growth. It is, therefore, unlikely that MacroSwift's dividend growth rate will continue at a 3 percent annual rate. This suggests that you should consider something other than constant growth in your modeling.

11.29   11.56%

11.31   9.78%

11.33   Market returns are impounded in market prices. If those prices are ignored, then the efficiency of the market's information process is also essentially ignored. Since the market adjusts securities prices according to the expected return for investing in a security, then ignoring that information is the same as ignoring what the market deems to be an appropriate cost of capital for the firm.

11.35   Since, collectively, the debt and equity holders are entitled to receive all of the cash flows that the assets of the firm are expected to produce, the systematic risk of the cash flows that they are entitled to receive must be the same as the systematic risk of the cash flows the assets are expected to produce.

11.37   7.11%

CHAPTER 12

12.1   Wolfgang's cash conversion cycle is 69 days. Since this is less than the industry average of 75 days, the firm is more efficient than the average firm in the industry in managing its working capital.

12.3   −3 days; the amount of time Devon takes to turn over its inventory and to collect its receivables is three days shorter than the amount of time Devon takes to pay its suppliers.

12.5   73 days

12.7   44.59%

12.9 $4,908.80

12.11   7.61%

12.13   21.42%

12.15   75.9 days. It takes nearly 76 days from the time the firm pays for its raw materials to the time it realizes cash from its credit sales.

12.17 $1,511,918

12.19   36.5 days

12.21   129.7 days

12.23   16 orders

12.25   8.775%

12.27   5.54%

12.29 $9,324

12.31   28.2 days

12.33 $7,500; 37.1%

12.35   **a.** Increase, Increase; **b.** Increase, Increase; **c.** No change, Decrease; **d.** Increase, Increase; **e.** Increase, No change.

12.37   **a.** 67.9 days; **b.** 80.6 days; **c.** 105.7 days; **d.** 148.5 days; **e.** 42.8 days.

12.39   **a.** $10,000; **b.** 63.2%; **c.** 85.06%

CHAPTER 13

13.1   As explained in this chapter, in general terms the business plan describes (1) what you want the business to become, (2) why consumers will find your product(s) attractive (the value proposition), (3) how you are going to accomplish your objectives, and (4) what resources you will need.

13.3   Sell the business, take it public, or remain a private company.

13.5   Examine comparable companies and see what prices their shares are trading for; a discounted cash flow analysis.

13.7   Debt issues that are complex in nature or that are issued in uncertain times often are sold through negotiated sales. This allows the underwriter to better control the conditions of the sale and to better explain the firm to potential investors, thereby keeping issue costs relatively low.

13.9 $24,308,528

13.11   The steps in a general cash offering are (1) decide what to issue, (2) approvals, (3) registration statement, (4) final price, and (5) closing.

13.13   As the size of a securities issue increases, the total flotation costs per security decline.

13.15   Nalco is probably better off choosing to sell debt in the public market, given its size.

13.17   The borrowing cost will increase to 9.43%

13.19   You can fund the project in stages. This will allow you to review the project's profitability before you commit to further financing. You can also require the entrepreneurs to invest some of their own capital, which will tie them to the project by making it more costly for them to abandon it.

13.21 $1,220,000

13.23 $68,700,000; $15,300,000

13.25   **a.** $130 million; **b.** $121 million; **c.** $9 million

13.27   6.52%; If the economy is supposed to improve (deteriorate), interest rates are likely to go up (down) in the near future. This could make the cost of borrowing more (less) expensive.

CHAPTER 14

14.1 The assumption that there are no information or transaction costs.

14.3 The value of the firm is independent of the proportion of debt and equity utilized by the firm under Modigliani and Miller's Proposition 1.

14.5 20%

14.7 18%

14.9 $150,000,000

14.11 10.5%

14.13 42%

14.15 Information or transaction costs would reduce the total value that is available for the debt holders and the stockholders and, therefore, the value of the firm.

14.17 $530,000,000

14.19 Lower productivity due to lower morale and job hunting and higher recruiting costs are among the costs of financial distress that the firm will incur.

14.21 The managers expect to lose their jobs in one year whether they take on the project and work hard or not. They have no incentive to take on the project. Declining it makes the shortage to the debt holders greater, and any possible return to the stockholders smaller than it would be if the firm followed the rule of always accepting positive NPV projects.

14.23 Given the information in the question, we would expect that an increase in the marginal tax rate will increase the value of the tax shield and increase the amount of debt in the optimal capital structure.

14.25 That internally generated equity is utilized first as a source of financing does not mean that the internally generated funds are cheaper than debt. Internally generated funds belong to stockholders and are therefore really equity financing, which we know to be more expensive than debt.

14.27 Under these conditions, the value of the firm will increase with the amount of debt financing that is used due to the interest tax shields. The conservative approach will not maximize firm value.

14.29 $810,000,000

14.31 If enough debt is used to finance this firm, then the challenges of ensuring that the firm produces enough cash to make interest and principal payments would provide managers of the firm with incentives to work on new positive NPV projects rather than spend their Fridays in Cancun.

CHAPTER 15

15.1 This reduction could indicate that management expects a lower level of profitability in the future (negative signal). It could also indicate that Poseidon requires additional money to invest in positive NPV projects that were not previously available (positive signal).

15.3 The proper cronological order is (1) Declaration date, (2) Ex-dividend date, (3) Record date, (4) Payment date.

15.5 Any cash paid to stockholders through a dividend reduces the value of the assets that remain in the firm to secure the creditors' claims.

15.7 $9.75

15.9 With a stock repurchase, stockholders can decide whether to participate. If they choose to participate, there are tax advantages for the stockholders, relative to a dividend.

15.11 Relaxing the no transaction cost assumption increases the cost of producing a homemade dividend (or the cost of undoing unwanted dividends). This makes a firm's dividend policy a relevant factor when valuing its shares.

15.13 The value of dividend-paying stocks should decrease relative to the value of nondividend-paying stocks.

15.15 Reducing a dividend may indicate that a firm does not have sufficient cash, which would be a negative signal. On the other hand, when a high-growth firm increases its dividend, the increase may be interpreted as indicating that the firm has fewer positive NPV projects and that its growth rate will decline, which is also a negative signal.

15.17 You would probably prefer that the firm initiate a stock repurchase. You can opt not to sell your shares to the firm but still participate in the increased value of the firm's shares since your pro-rata share of the expected future cash flows generated by the firm will increase. You would probably not prefer a dividend payment since you would then be required to receive the cash if you were the registered owner of the shares on the record date.

15.19 Assuming that managers are acting to maximize firm value, any time they are repurchasing shares they must be doing so because they believe that the firm's shares are undervalued and that repurchasing shares is a positive NPV project. In repurchasing the shares, management is utilizing inside information to take advantage of the sellers of those shares in a way that benefits the remaining stockholders of the firm. Consequently, management is not doing something in the interest of all stockholders. Stockholders who sell will be selling at a lower price than they could have realized had they held their shares until the inside information became public.

15.21 (1) Open-market purchase—the firm simply purchases the shares in the market, (2) Tender offer—the firm makes an offer through a general announcement, offering to buy up to a certain number of shares from anyone who wishes to sell, (3) Targeted stock repurchase—the firm directly negotiates with an individual stockholder to buy shares from that individual. Exhibit 15.3 presents data on stock price reactions.

15.23 The purpose of setting the ex-dividend date before the record date is to allow time for a sale of securities to be completed and recorded before the record date. Since the settlement period was reduced from five days to two days, we should also have seen the number of days between the ex-dividend date and the record date reduced, which we did.

15.25 Paying a dividend reduces the value of equity and thereby increases the debt-to-total-capital ratio in a levered firm.

15.27 $15

15.29 $72,500

15.31 $150,000

15.33 Ultimately, the best decision will depend on a comparison of the advantages and disadvantages of a special dividend and a share repurchase, in view of the characteristics of your company and your objectives. If speed is a primary concern, a special dividend is likely to be your only choice. On the other hand, if speed is not a primary concern, a share repurchase might be more appropriate.

CHAPTER 16

16.1 The strategic plan drives all decision making within the firm and covers all areas of a firm's operations.

16.3 The financing plan identifies EFN, sources of funding, target capital structure, and dividend policy.

16.5 The important elements of financial modeling are sales and cost forecasts, investment decisions, financing requirements and decisions, and pro-forma statements.

16.7 55%

16.9 Net sales $1,710; Costs $399; Net income $1,311

16.11 The capital intensity ratio measures the amount of assets needed to generate $1 in sales.

16.13 68.02%

16.15 6.8%

16.17 Exhibit 16.11 gives you the plot.

16.19 The electric utilities industry and the aluminum processing industry are capital intensive.

16.21 8%

16.23 8.2%

16.25 9.9%

16.27 5.2%

16.29 35.9%

16.31 9.6%

16.33 27.4%

16.35

Morgan Construction Company—Pro Forma Balance Sheet for June 30, 2014

	2013		2014		2013		2014
Cash	$ 3,349,239	1.25	$ 4,186,548	Accounts payable	$ 9,041,679	1.25	$11,302,098
Accounts receivable	5,830,754	1.25	7,288,442	Notes payable	4,857,496	1.25	6,071,869
Inventories	22,267,674	1.25	27,834,593	Total current liabilities	$13,899,174		$17,373,968
Total current assets	$31,447,666		$39,309,583				
				Long-term debt	29,371,406		37,164,258
Net fixed assets	43,362,482	1.25	54,203,102	Common stock	19,987,500	1.25	24,984,375
Other assets	1,748,482	1.25	2,186,133	Retained earnings	12,940,974	1.25	16,176,217
Total assets	$76,559,054		$95,698,818	Total liabilities & equity	$76,559,054		$95,698,818

Morgan Construction Company
Pro Forma Income Statement for the Fiscal Year Ended
June 30, 2014

	2013		2014
Net sales	$193,212,500	1.25	$241,515,625
Costs	145,265,625	1.25	181,582,031
EBITDA	$ 47,946,875		$ 59,933,594
Depreciation	23,318,750	1.25	29,148,438
EBIT	$ 24,628,125		$ 30,785,156
Interest	11,935,869	1.25	14,919,836
EBT	$ 12,692,256		$ 15,865,320
Taxes (35%)	4,442,290	1.25	5,552,862
Net income	$ 8,249,967		$ 10,312,458

16.37 3.37%; 6.26%

16.39 **a.** 4.31%; **b.** 13.86%; **c.** $4,777,333;
    d. See the following financial statements

Munson Communications Company—Pro Forma Balance Sheet for June 30, 2014

	2013		2014		2013		2014
Cash	$ 1,728,639	1.20	$ 2,074,367	Accounts payable	4,666,673	1.20	$ 5,600,007
Accounts receivable	3,009,421	1.20	3,611,305	Notes payable	2,507,094	1.20	3,008,513
Inventories	11,492,993	1.20	13,791,592	Total current liabilities	$ 7,173,767		$ 8,608,521
Total current assets	$16,231,054		$19,477,264				
				Long-term debt	13,345,242		16,687,821
Net fixed assets	22,380,635	1.20	26,856,763	Common stock	10,165,235		10,165,235
Other assets	1,748,906	1.20	2,098,688	Retained earnings	9,676,351		12,971,137
Total assets	$40,360,595		$48,432,714	Total liabilities & equity	$40,360,595		$48,432,714

Munson Communications Company
Pro Forma Income Statement for the Fiscal Year Ended
June 30, 2014

	2013		2014
Net sales	$79,722,581	1.20	$95,667,097
Costs	59,358,499	1.20	71,230,199
EBITDA	$20,364,082		$24,436,898
Depreciation	7,318,750	1.20	8,782,500
EBIT	$13,045,332		$15,654,398
Interest	3,658,477	1.20	4,390,172
EBT	$ 9,386,855		$11,264,226
Taxes (35%)	3,285,399	1.20	3,942,479
Net income	$ 6,101,456		$ 7,321,747

CHAPTER 17

17.1 $183.77

17.3 **a.** MP11.8483/$; **b.** €1.1747/£; **c.** C$0.0316/Rs

17.5 Same cost in both cities based on the spot rate!

17.7 $9,400

17.9 $3,753,295

17.11 **(i)** The forward premium (discount) = (SF1.045/$ − SF1.0434/$)/ SF1.0434/$ = 0.15%, so there is a forward premium on the Swiss franc.

(ii) The forward premium (discount) = (¥82.40/$ − ¥82.56/$)/ ¥82.56/$ = −0.19%, so there is a forward discount on the Japanese yen.

(iii) Given the data on forward rates in (i) and (ii) we can expect the Swiss franc to appreciate relative to the U.S. dollar and the Japanese yen can be expected to depreciate relative to the U.S. dollar.

17.13 5.73%

17.15 €1.1952/£

17.17 SK6.8761/SF

17.19 Transaction exposure is related to foreign exchange risk faced by firms that are expecting revenues in foreign currency or have expenses in foreign currency that relate to transactions they have already entered into. As the exchange rate changes, the home currency value of these revenues or expenses changes. If exchange rate changes are more permanent in nature and modify the way a firm does its business, then we say that a firm is facing operating exposure.

17.21 5.44%

17.23 €0.007368/¥

17.25 Rs43.43/$

17.27 $3,250,307

17.29 $5,286.50

17.31 $7,807.35

17.33 4,426.87 million won; yes, the project should be accepted.

17.35 2.92%; 2.95%; The domestic bond issue will have the lowest cost to the firm.

17.37 $64,062.50; $61,875; Daiwa's offer has the lower interest cost.

Glossary

A

accounting rate of return (ARR) a rate of return on a capital project based on average net income divided by average book value over the project's life; also called the *book value rate of return*

agency conflicts conflicts of interest between a principal and an agent

agency costs the costs arising from conflicts of interest between a principal and an agent—for example, between a firm's owners and its management

amortization schedule a table that shows the loan balance at the beginning and end of each period, the payment made during that period, and how much of that payment represents interest and how much represents repayment of principal

amortizing loan a loan for which each loan payment contains repayment of some principal and a payment of interest that is based on the remaining principal to be repaid

angels (angel investors) wealthy individuals who invest their own money in new ventures

annual percentage rate (APR) the simple interest rate charged per period multiplied by the number of periods per year

annuity a series of equally spaced and level cash flows extending over a finite number of periods

annuity due an annuity in which payments are made at the beginning of each period

asset substitution problem the incentive that stockholders in a financially leveraged firm have to substitute more risky assets for less risky assets

average tax rate total taxes paid divided by taxable income

B

balance sheet financial statement that shows a firm's financial position (assets, liabilities, and equity) at a point in time

bankruptcy legally declared inability of an individual or a company to pay its creditors

bankruptcy costs, or costs of financial distress costs associated with financial difficulties a firm might experience because it uses debt financing

benchmark a standard against which performance is measured

best-effort underwriting underwriting agreement in which the underwriter does not agree to purchase the securities at a particular price but promises only to make its "best effort" to sell as much of the issue as possible above a certain price

beta (β) a measure of nondiversifiable, systematic, or market risk

bid price the price a securities dealer will pay for a given stock

book value the net value of an asset or liability recorded on the financial statements—normally reflects historical cost

bootstrapping the process by which many entrepreneurs raise seed money and obtain other resources necessary to start their businesses

brokers market specialists who bring buyers and sellers together, usually for a commission

business risk the risk in the cash flows to stockholders that is associated with uncertainty due to the characteristics of the firm's assets

C

Capital Asset Pricing Model (CAPM) a model that describes the relation between risk and expected return

capital budgeting the process of choosing the productive assets in which the firm will invest

capital lease a lease that has the characteristics of a sale

capital markets financial markets where equity and debt instruments with maturities greater than one year are traded

capital rationing a situation where a firm does not have enough capital to invest in all attractive projects and must therefore ration capital

capital structure the mix of debt and equity that is used to finance a firm

cash conversion cycle the length of time from the point at which a company pays for raw materials until the point at which it receives cash from the sale of finished goods made from those materials

cash flow to investors the cash flow that a firm generates for its investors in a given period, excluding cash inflows from the sale of securities to investors

chief financial officer (CFO) the most senior financial manager in a company

coefficient of variation (CV) a measure of the risk associated with an investment for each 1 percent of expected return

collection time (float) the time between when a customer makes a payment and when the cash becomes available to the firm

commercial paper short-term debt in the form of promissory notes issued by large, financially secure firms with high credit ratings

common-size financial statement a financial statement in which each number is expressed as a percentage of a base number, such as total assets or net revenues (net sales)

common stock an equity share that represents the basic ownership claim in a corporation; the most common type of equity security

603

compensating balances bank balances that firms must maintain to at least partially compensate banks for loans or services rendered

compounding the process by which interest earned on an investment is reinvested, so in future periods interest is earned on the interest as well as the principal

compound interest interest earned both on the original principal amount and on interest previously earned

consumer credit credit extended by a business to consumers

contingent projects projects whose acceptance depends on the acceptance of other projects

conventional cash flow a cash flow pattern consisting of an initial cash outflow that is followed by one or more cash inflows

corporation a legal entity formed and authorized under a state charter; in a legal sense, a corporation is a "person" distinct from its owners

cost of capital the required rate of return for a capital investment

country risk the political uncertainty associated with a particular country

coupon payments the interest payments made to bondholders

coupon rate the annual coupon payment of a bond divided by the bond's face value

covariance of returns a measure of how the returns on two assets covary, or move together

crossover point the discount rate at which the NPV profiles of two projects cross and, thus, at which the NPVs of the projects are equal

current assets assets, such as accounts receivable and inventories, that are expected to be liquidated (collected or sold) within one year

D

dealers market specialists who make markets for securities by buying and selling from their own inventories

declaration date the date on which a dividend is publicly announced

default risk the risk that a firm will not be able to pay its debt obligations as they come due

depreciation allocation of the cost of an asset over its estimated useful life to reflect the wear and tear on the asset as it is used to produce the firm's goods and services

direct bankruptcy costs out-of-pocket costs that a firm incurs when it gets into financial distress

discount bonds bonds that sell at prices below par (face) value

discounted payback period the length of time required to recover a project's initial cost, accounting for the time value of money

discounting the process by which the present value of future cash flows is obtained

discount rate the interest rate used in the discounting process to find the present value of future cash flows

diversification reducing risk by investing in two or more assets whose values do not always move in the same direction at the same time

dividend something of value distributed to a firm's stockholders on a pro-rata basis—that is, in proportion to the percentage of the firm's shares that they own

dividend payout ratio the proportion of net income paid out (distributed) as dividends

dividend reinvestment program (DRIP) a program in which a company sells new shares, commission free, to dividend recipients who elect to automatically reinvest their dividends in the company's stock

dividend yield a stock's annual dividend divided by its current price

E

earnings per share (EPS) net income divided by the number of common shares outstanding

economic order quantity (EOQ) order quantity that minimizes the total costs incurred to order and hold inventory

effective annual interest rate (EAR) the annual interest rate that reflects compounding within a year

effective annual yield (EAY) the annual yield that takes compounding into account; another name for the effective annual interest rate (EAR)

efficient market hypothesis a theory concerning the extent to which information is reflected in security prices and how information gets incorporated into security prices

efficient market market where prices reflect the knowledge and expectations of all investors

equivalent annual cost (EAC) the annual dollar amount of an annuity that has a life equal to that of a project and that also has a present value equal to the present value of the cash flows from the project; the term comes from the fact that the EAC calculation is often used to calculate a constant annual cost associated with projects in order to make comparisons

Eurocredits short- to medium-term loans of a Eurocurrency to multinational corporations and governments of medium to high credit quality

Eurocurrency a time deposit that is in a bank located in a country different from the country that issued the currency

Eurodollar a U.S. dollar deposited in a bank outside the United States

ex-dividend date the first day on which a stock trades without the rights to a dividend

expected return an average of the possible returns from an investment, where each return is weighted by the probability that it will occur

external funding needed (EFN) the additional debt or equity a firm must raise from external sources to meet its total funding requirements

extra dividend a dividend that is generally paid at the same time as a regular cash dividend to distribute additional value

F

face value, or par value the amount on which interest is calculated and that is owed to the bondholder when a bond reaches maturity

factor an individual or a financial institution, such as a bank or a business finance company, that buys accounts receivable without recourse

finance balance sheet a balance sheet that is based on market values of expected cash flows

financial assets assets that are claims on the cash flows from other assets; business loans, stocks, and bonds are financial assets

financial intermediation conversion of securities with one set of characteristics into securities with another set of characteristics

financial leverage the use of debt in a firm's capital structure; the more debt, the higher the financial leverage

financial planning the process by which management decides what types of investments the firm needs to make and how to finance those investments

financial plan a plan outlining the investments a firm intends to make and how it will finance them

financial ratio A number from a financial statement that has been scaled by dividing by another financial number

financial restructuring a combination of financial transactions that changes the capital structure of the firm without affecting its real assets

financial risk the risk in the cash flows to stockholders that is due to the way in which the firm has financed its assets

financial statement analysis the use of financial statements to evaluate a company's overall performance and assess its strengths and shortcomings

firm-commitment underwriting underwriting agreement in which the underwriter purchases securities for a specified price and resells them

firm's marginal tax rate (t) the tax rate that is applied to each additional dollar of earnings at a firm

firm value, or enterprise value the total value of the firm's assets; it equals the value of the equity financing plus the value of the debt financing used by the firm

fixed costs costs that do not vary directly with the number of units sold

fixed-income securities debt instruments that pay interest in amounts that are fixed for the life of the contract

flexible current asset management strategy current asset management strategy that involves keeping high balances of current assets on hand

foreign exchange market international markets where currencies are bought and sold in wholesale amounts

foreign exchange rate risk, or exchange rate risk the uncertainty associated with future currency exchange rate movements

formal line of credit a contractual agreement between a bank and a firm under which the bank has a legal obligation to lend funds to the firm up to a preset limit; also known as revolving credit

forward rate a rate agreed on today for an exchange to take place on a specified date in the future

future value (FV) the value of an investment after it earns interest for one or more periods

future value of an annuity (FVA) the value of an annuity at some point in the future

G

general cash offer a sale of debt or equity, open to all investors, by a company that has previously sold stock to the public

generally accepted accounting principles (GAAP) a set of rules that defines how companies are to prepare financial statements

globalization the removal of barriers to free trade and the integration of national economies

growing annuity an annuity in which the cash flows increase at a constant rate

growing perpetuity a cash flow stream that grows at a constant rate forever

H

hedge a financial transaction intended to reduce risk

I

income statement a financial statement that reports a firm's revenues, expenses, and profits or losses over a period of time

incremental additions to working capital (Add WC) the investments in working capital items, such as accounts receivable, inventory, and accounts payable, that must be made if the project is pursued

incremental after-tax free cash flows the difference between the total after-tax free cash flows at a firm with a project and the total after-tax free cash flows at the same firm without that project; a measure of a project's total impact on the free cash flows at a firm

incremental capital expenditures (Cap Exp) the investments in property, plant, and equipment and other long-term assets that must be made if a project is pursued

incremental cash flow from operations (CF Opns) the cash flow that a project generates after all operating expenses and taxes have been paid but before any cash outflows for investments

incremental depreciation and amortization (D&A) the depreciation and amortization charges that are associated with a project

incremental net operating profits after tax (NOPAT) a measure of the impact of a project on the firm's cash net income, excluding the effects of any interest expenses associated with financing the project

independent projects projects whose cash flows are unrelated

indirect bankruptcy costs costs associated with changes in the behavior of people who deal with a firm when the firm gets into financial distress

informal line of credit a verbal agreement between a bank and a firm under which the firm can borrow an amount of money up to an agreed-on limit

information asymmetry the situation in which one party in a business transaction has information that is unavailable to the other parties in the transaction

initial public offering (IPO) the first offering of a corporation's stock to the public

insolvency the inability to pay debts when they are due

intangible assets nonphysical assets such as patents, mailing lists, or brand names

interest on interest interest earned on interest that was earned in previous periods

interest rate risk uncertainty about future bond values that is caused by the unpredictability of interest rates

internal growth rate (IGR) the maximum growth rate that a firm can achieve without external financing

internal rate of return (IRR) the discount rate at which the present value of a project's expected cash inflows equals the present value of the project's outflows; it is the discount rate at which the project's NPV equals zero

inventory carrying costs expenses associated with maintaining inventory, including interest forgone on money invested in inventory, storage costs, taxes, and insurance

investment banks firms that underwrite new security issues

investment-grade bonds bonds with low risk of default that are rated Baa (BBB) or above

L

lease (rental agreement) a financial arrangement in which the user of an asset pays the owner of the asset to use it for a period of time

lessee the user of a leased asset

lessor the owner of a leased asset

limited liability the legal liability of an investor is limited to the amount of capital invested in the business

limited liability partnerships and companies (LLPs and LLCs) hybrid business organizations that combine some of the advantages of corporations and partnerships; in general, income to the partners is taxed only as personal income, but the partners have limited liability

liquidating dividend the final dividend that is paid to stockholders when a firm is liquidated

liquidity the ability to convert an asset into cash quickly without loss of value

lockbox A system that allows geographically dispersed customers to send their payments to a post office box near them

London Interbank Offer Rate (LIBOR) the interest rate British-based banks charge each other for short-term loans; also, commonly used as the base rate for Eurodollar loans that are not between two banks

long-term funding strategy financing strategy that relies on long-term debt and equity to finance both fixed assets and working capital

lumpy assets fixed assets added as large, discrete units; these assets may not be used to full capacity for some time, leaving the company with excess capacity

M

marginal tax rate the tax rate paid on the last dollar of income earned

marketability the ease with which a security can be sold and converted into cash

market informational efficiency the degree to which current market prices reflect relevant information and, therefore, the true value of the security

market operational efficiency the degree to which the transaction costs of bringing buyers and sellers together are minimized

market portfolio the portfolio of all assets

market risk a term commonly used to refer to nondiversifiable, or systematic, risk

market value the price at which an item can be sold

maturity matching strategy financing strategy that matches the maturities of liabilities and assets

Modified Accelerated Cost Recovery System (MACRS) the accelerated depreciation method that has been in use for U.S. federal taxes since the Tax Reform Act of 1986 went into effect

modified internal rate of return (MIRR) an internal rate of return (IRR) measure that assumes cash inflows are reinvested at the opportunity cost of capital until the end of the project

money center banks large commercial banks that provide both traditional and investment banking services throughout the world

money markets markets where short-term debt instruments are traded

multinational corporation a business firm that operates in more than one country

multistage-growth dividend model a model that allows for varying dividend growth rates in the near term, followed by a constant long-term growth rate; another term used to describe the mixed (supernormal) dividend growth model discussed in Chapter 8

mutually exclusive projects projects for which acceptance of one precludes acceptance of the other

N

net present value (NPV) method a method of evaluating a capital investment project that measures the difference between its cost and the present value of its expected cash flows

net working capital the dollar difference between current assets and current liabilities

nominal dollars dollar amounts that are not adjusted for inflation; the purchasing power of a nominal dollar amount depends on when that amount is received

nominal rate of interest the rate of interest that is unadjusted for inflation

noninvestment-grade bonds bonds rated below Baa (or BBB) by rating agencies; often called *speculative-grade bonds, high-yield bonds,* or *junk bonds*

normal distribution a symmetric frequency distribution that is completely described by its mean and standard deviation; also known as a bell curve due to its shape

North American Industry Classification System (NAICS) a classification system for businesses introduced to refine and replace the older SIC system

NPV profile a graph showing NPV as a function of the discount rate

O

offer (ask) price the price at which a securities dealer seeks to sell a given stock

open-market repurchase the repurchase of shares by a company in the open market

operating cycle the average time between receipt of raw materials and receipt of cash for the sale of finished goods made from those materials

operating lease a lease that does not have the characteristics of a sale

opportunity cost the return from the best alternative investment with similar risk that an investor gives up when he or she makes a certain investment

opportunity cost of capital the return an investor gives up when his or her money is invested in one asset rather than the best alternative asset

optimal capital structure the capital structure that minimizes the cost of financing a firm's activities

ordinary annuity an annuity in which payments are made at the ends of the periods

P

partnership two or more owners who have joined together legally to manage a business and share in its profits

par-value bonds bonds that sell at par value, or face value; whenever a bond's coupon rate is equal to the market rate of interest on similar bonds, the bond will sell at par (face) value

payable date the date on which a company pays a dividend

payback period the length of time required to recover a project's initial cost

payout policy the overall policy concerning the distribution of value from a firm to its stockholders

pecking order theory the theory that in financing projects, managers first use retained earnings, which they view as the least expensive form of capital, then debt, and finally externally raised equity, which they view as the most expensive

percent of sales model a simple financial planning model that assumes that most income statement and balance sheet accounts vary proportionally with sales

permanent working capital the minimum level of working capital that a firm will always have on its books

perpetuity a series of level cash flows that continue forever

portfolio the collection of assets an investor owns

post a specific location on the floor of a stock exchange at which auctions for a particular security take place

postaudit review an audit to compare actual project results with the results projected in the capital budgeting proposal

preferred stock an equity share in a corporation that entitles the owner to preferred treatment over owners of common stock with respect to dividend payments and claims against the firm's assets in the event of bankruptcy or liquidation, but that typically has no voting rights

preliminary prospectus the initial registration statement filed with the SEC by a company preparing to issue securities in the public market; it contains detailed information about the issuer and the proposed issue

premium bonds bonds that sell at prices above par (face) value

present value (PV) the current value of future cash flows discounted at the appropriate discount rate

present value of an annuity (PVA) the present value of the cash flows from an annuity, discounted at the appropriate discount rate

primary market a financial market in which new security issues are sold by companies directly to investors

principal the amount of money on which interest is paid

private information information that is not available to all investors

privately held (closely held) corporations corporations whose stock is not traded in public markets

private placement the sale of an unregistered security directly to an investor, such as an insurance company or a wealthy individual

productive assets the tangible and intangible assets a firm uses to generate cash flows

profitability index (PI) a measure of the value a project generates for each dollar invested in that project

pro forma financial statements projected financial statements that reflect a set of assumptions concerning investment, financing, and operating decisions

progressive tax system a tax system in which the marginal tax rate at low levels of income is lower than the marginal tax rate at high levels of income

public information information that is available to all investors

public markets markets regulated by the Securities and Exchange Commission in which securities such as stocks and bonds are publicly traded

pure-play comparable a comparable company that is in exactly the same business as the project or business being analyzed

Q

quoted interest rate a simple annual interest rate, such as the APR

R

real assets nonfinancial assets such as plant and equipment; productive assets are real assets; many financial assets are claims on cash flows from real assets

real dollars inflation-adjusted dollars; the actual purchasing power of dollars stated in "real" terms is the same regardless of when those dollars are received

real investment policy the policy relating to the criteria the firm uses in deciding which real assets (projects) to invest in

realized yield for a bond, the interest rate at which the present value of the actual cash flows from a bond equals the bond's price

real rate of interest the interest rate that would exist in the absence of inflation

record date the date by which an investor must be a stockholder of record in order to receive a dividend

regular cash dividend a cash dividend that is paid on a regular basis, typically quarterly

repatriation of earnings restrictions restrictions placed by a foreign government on the amount of cash that can be repatriated, or returned to a parent company by a subsidiary doing business in the foreign country

residual cash flows the cash remaining after a firm has paid operating expenses and what it owes creditors and in taxes; can be paid to the owners as a cash dividend or reinvested in the business

restrictive current asset management strategy current asset management strategy that involves keeping the level of current assets at a minimum

retention (plowback) ratio the proportion of net income retained in the firm

S

seasoned public offering (SEO) the sale of securities to the public by a firm that already has publicly traded securities outstanding

secondary market a financial market in which the owners of outstanding securities can sell them to other investors

Security Market Line (SML) a plot of the relation between expected return and systematic risk

semistrong-form of the efficient market hypothesis the theory that security prices reflect all public information but not all private information

Sharpe Ratio A measure of the return per unit of risk for an investment

shelf registration a type of SEC registration that allows firms to register to sell securities over a two-year period and, during that time, take the securities "off the shelf" and sell them as needed

shortage costs costs incurred because of lost production and sales or illiquidity

short-term funding strategy financing strategy that relies on short-term debt to finance all seasonal working capital and a portion of permanent working capital and fixed assets

simple interest interest earned on the original principal amount only

sole proprietorship a business owned by a single individual

special dividend a one-time payment to stockholders that is normally used to distribute a large amount of value

specialist the trader designated by an exchange to represent orders placed by public customers at auctions of securities; specialists handle a small set of securities and are also allowed to act as dealers

spot rate the exchange rate for immediate delivery

stakeholder anyone other than an owner (stockholder) with a claim on the cash flows of a firm, including employees, suppliers, creditors, and the government

stand-alone principle the principle that allows us to treat each project as a stand-alone firm when we perform an NPV analysis

standard deviation (σ) the square root of the variance

Standard Industrial Classification (SIC) System a numerical system developed by the U.S. government to classify businesses according to the type of activity they perform

statement of cash flows a financial statement that shows a firm's cash receipts and cash payments and investments for a period of time

stock dividend a distribution of new shares to existing stockholders in proportion to the percentage of shares that they own (pro rata); the value of the assets in a company does not change with a stock dividend

stock repurchase the purchase of stock by a company from its stockholders; an alternative way for the company to distribute value to the stockholders

stock split a pro-rata distribution of new shares to existing stockholders that is not associated with any change in the assets held by the firm; stock splits involve larger increases in the number of shares than stock dividends

strategic planning the process by which management establishes the firm's long-term goals, the strategies that will be used to achieve those goals, and the capabilities that are needed to sustain the firm's competitive position

strong-form of the efficient market hypothesis the theory that security prices reflect all information

sustainable growth rate (SGR) the rate of growth that a firm can sustain without selling additional equity while maintaining the same capital structure

systematic or nondiversifiable risk risk that cannot be eliminated through diversification

T

tangible assets physical assets such as property, plant, and equipment

targeted stock repurchase a stock repurchase that targets a specific stockholder

tender offer an open offer by a company to purchase shares

term loan a business loan with a maturity greater than one year

term structure of interest rates the relation between yield to maturity and term to maturity

time value of money the difference in value between a dollar in hand today and a dollar promised in the future; a dollar today is worth more than a dollar in the future

time zero the beginning of a transaction; often the current point in time

total holding period return the total return on an asset over a specific period of time or holding period

trade credit credit extended by one business to another

trade-off theory the theory that managers trade off the benefits against the costs of using debt to identify the optimal capital structure for a firm

transnational corporation a multinational firm that has widely dispersed ownership and that is managed from a global perspective

treasury stock stock that the firm has repurchased from investors

trend analysis analysis of trends in financial data

true (intrinsic) value for a security, the value of the cash flows an investor who owns that security can expect to receive in the future

Truth-in-Lending Act a federal law requiring lenders to fully inform borrowers of important information related to loans, including the annual percentage rate charged

Truth-in-Savings Act a federal law requiring institutions offering consumer savings vehicles, such as certificates of deposit (CDs), to fully inform consumers of important information about the savings vehicles, including the annual percentage rate paid

U

underinvestment problem the incentive that stockholders in a financially leveraged firm have to turn down positive NPV projects when the firm is in financial distress

underpricing offering new securities for sale at a price below their true value

underwriting syndicate a group of underwriters that joins forces to reduce underwriting risk

unsystematic or diversifiable risk risk that can be eliminated through diversification

V

variable costs costs that vary directly with the number of units sold

variance (σ^2) a measure of the uncertainty associated with an outcome

venture capitalists individuals or firms that invest by purchasing equity in new businesses and often provide entrepreneurs with business advice

W

weak-form of the efficient market hypothesis the theory that security prices reflect all information in past prices but do not reflect all private or all public information

wealth the economic value of the assets someone possesses

weighted average cost of capital (WACC) the weighted average of the costs of the different types of capital (debt and equity) that have been used to finance a firm; the cost of each type of capital is weighted by the proportion of the total capital that it represents

Y

yield curve a graph representing the term structure of interest rates, with the term to maturity on the horizontal axis and the yield on the vertical axis

yield to maturity for a bond, the discount rate that makes the present value of the coupon and principal payments equal to the price of the bond

Subject Index

Company Index

BUILDING INTUITION

Throughout the book important finance principles and concepts are identified and emphasized in *Building Intuition* boxes. These boxes restate an important finance concept that has been discussed in the main text, such as the importance of cash flows, and provide an intuitive example or explanation of the concept. The *Building Intuition* boxes and the pages on which they appear are as follows:

Notes

Notes

Notes

Notes